KU-779-917

TIME'S ANVIL

ENGLAND, ARCHAEOLOGY
AND THE IMAGINATION

RICHARD MORRIS

H2
2/15

PHOENIX

A PHOENIX PAPERBACK

First published in Great Britain in 2012
by Weidenfeld & Nicolson
This paperback edition published in 2013
by Phoenix,
an imprint of Orion Books Ltd,
Orion House, 5 Upper St Martin's Lane,
London WC2H 9EA

An Hachette UK company

1 3 5 7 9 10 8 6 4 2

© Richard Morris 2012

The right of Richard Morris to be identified as the author of
this work has been asserted by him in accordance with the
Copyright, Designs and Patents Act 1988.

All rights reserved. No part of this publication may be
reproduced, stored in a retrieval system, or transmitted,
in any form or by any means, electronic, mechanical,
photocopying, recording or otherwise, without the prior
permission of the copyright owner.

A CIP catalogue record for this book
is available from the British Library.

ISBN 978-1-7802-2244-8

Typeset by Input Data Services Ltd,
Bridgwater, Somerset

Printed and bound by CPI Group (UK) Ltd,
Croydon CR0 4YY

The Orion Publishing Group's policy is to use papers that
are natural, renewable and recyclable products and
made from wood grown in sustainable forests. The logging
and manufacturing processes are expected to conform to
the environmental regulations of the country of origin.

www.orionbooks.co.uk

Man, being the servant and interpreter of Nature, can do and understand so much and so much only as he has observed in fact or in thought of the course of nature: beyond that he neither knows anything nor can do anything.

Francis Bacon, *Novum Organum*

Now, now look how the holy pilgrims ride,
Clouds are their chariots, angels are their guide:
Who would not here for him all hazards run
That thus provides for him when this world's done.

John Bunyan, *The Pilgrim's Progress*

For Alan and Griselda

CONTENTS

CONTENTS

ILLUSTRATIONS

PROLOGUE

Nikolaus – from 1969, Sir Nikolaus – Pevsner gave the Reith Lectures in 1955; his subject, 'The Englishness of English Art'. Pevsner had been born into a Russian-Jewish family in Leipzig in 1902. Towards the end of the first lecture he reflected on his credentials for talking about Englishness. 'Why should I, with a never fully conquered foreign intonation, I who am not too certain of the difference between a centre forward and a leg volley, stand here to talk to you about the Englishness of English art? My defence is that in order to see clearly what is what in national character it is perhaps a good thing at one stage to have come in from outside and then to have settled down to become part of it.'[1]

Pevsner had been exploring the history of art and architecture since his teens, influenced by teaching which emphasized the influence 'of both national character and the "spirit of the age"'.[2] After studies at Munich, Berlin and Frankfurt, he embarked on a doctoral thesis that surveyed the seventeenth- and eighteenth-century town houses of his home city.[3] In 1924 he joined the Gemäldegalerie in Dresden to work on Italian baroque painting, moving to the University of Göttingen in 1929.[4] Then he visited England. 'It was a discovery,' he said twenty-five years later. 'Few people on the Continent knew about English art then or had studied it. I was able to travel a good deal and started teaching the history of English art. In connection with that I began collecting material on this problem of Englishness.'[5]

After Hitler came to power the scope for assembling such material increased. As a Jew Pevsner was debarred from his university post, and '"encouraged to resign" from all professional bodies and associations in Germany'.[6] October 1933 found him on Cologne railway station, writing to his wife while on his way to England. From London he wrote: 'This is a very modest country, satisfied with very little. All morning one can see one's breath indoors ... To look at it positively, I suppose people are closer to nature ...'[7] Funds from the Academic Assistance Council and the support of friends enabled the award of a two-year fellowship at the University of Birmingham.[8] Pevsner found digs in the household of Francesca Wilson, a Quaker teacher, author and campaigner whom he had earlier met in Germany. Wilson owned a roomy brick-built Victorian house in Duchess Road, Edgbaston, where between relief work in European trouble spots she cared for a succession of Russian émigré children and shared the house with boarders and refugees.[9] In 1934 Pevsner did not like Birmingham. 'The town is awful,' he wrote. 'The moment you come off the four or five main streets, you are amidst two-storey houses in grubby brick, indescribably dreary and sooty.'[10] Yet despite the upheaval and intermittent low spirits this was a productive time: 1936 saw the publication of an influential book on the Modern Movement which with other works extended to England the growing reputation he had already begun to enjoy in Germany.[11]

Nine years and five books later, Pevsner and the Penguin paperback pioneer Allen Lane were walking in Lane's rose garden at Silverbeck, beside the River Colne in Middlesex.

> … Lane asked casually what kind of books Pevsner would publish, given a free hand. Taking the 'free hand' at face value, Pevsner took the opportunity to point out two striking gaps in English art-histori-cal literature. There was, he remarked, no detailed survey of European art as a whole … Nor, he continued, further possessed by the spirit of enterprise, was there any English equivalent to Dehio's catalogue of significant German buildings – something that might locate English architecture in the European context and at the same time demon-strate its uniqueness.[12]

Before they left the garden Allen had agreed to both, and the first vol-umes of the Buildings of England series, Cornwall and Nottinghamshire, appeared in 1951. Some doubted that such a laborious enterprise would ever be finished; others sneered, or could not see how the project differed from other existing guidebook series.[13] But Pevsner was industrious and organized, sifting written sources with the help of a research assistant and his wife, then 'criss-crossing England in a succession of unreliable old cars'[14] for a few weeks each year during university vacations to view the buildings, writing up entries in the evenings.[15] Ten years on, sixteen volumes were in print. By the last, Staffordshire (1974), second editions were appearing. Parallel series have since been published for Scotland, Wales and Ireland.

To maintain pace and deepen coverage, from the early 1960s Pevsner enlisted the help of co-workers. However, while along the way 'Pevsner' became a multi-author institution it had begun as a survey of buildings in one country viewed through the eyes of one brought up in another. At the end of his final lecture on 'The Englishness of English Art' Pevsner told his listeners of the 'national art and architecture which is all your own', adding 'or, will you give me leave to say, our own?'[16]

Pevsner's England, like the past, was a foreign country;[17] one of those he recruited to help carry forward its exploration was the architectural historian David Verey, who wrote the two volumes on Gloucestershire (1970). By this stage 'a Pevsner' typically opened with a portrait of the geology, topography and historical geography of a county. Here is how the volumes on Gloucestershire originally began:

> When the Romans left Britain, the Saxon invaders began to settle in the plains. These areas had been deliberately avoided by the earlier Neolithic and Iron Age tribes because they had no tools capable of working the heavy clay soil. They therefore kept to districts like the Cotswolds, which had much lighter soils, and where the forest cover was thinner. The Saxons of course had better ploughing implements, and so were able to work the heavy Lias clays of the plains.[18]

Tribes, invaders, technological asymmetry, primordial forest, tillage and nationhood – Verey's list of then-current suppositions belongs to that catalogue of things about history that 'everyone knows'. The catalogue is constantly being updated, but it is intriguing how loath we are to let go of the clichés. Stone Age hunters, for instance, are still widely perceived to have been dimmer than you or me (for if they had been as smart as us, the reasoning seems to run, then surely they would not have been living in a Stone Age). Romans civilized Britons, but you are reading this in English rather than Italian or Celtic because when the Romans left the Britons were confined to Cumbria, Wales and the south-west by ethnic-cleansing Anglo-Saxons. Belief that ancient woodland survived on a large scale until the later Middle Ages itself survived until recently.[19] 'Medieval' is used as a synonym for functional hopelessness ('My dear, the plumbing was simply *medieval*'),[20] just as sports journalists use 'Neanderthal' to call up clumsiness, grunting and mud. In many minds the past was a time when almost everyone died young, agriculture was inefficient, and entire villages were forsaken because of plague. Above all, the past was excruciatingly slow – it appears to have taken three-quarters of a million years to invent the wheel, centuries to build a cathedral, and most people never travelled more than a few miles from the places where they grew up. Or so people say. Like Robin Hood,[21] such ideas have a consoling constancy.

Most people know in their bones, if not in their heads, that history is enquiry, and that enquiry is prompted by scepticism. If it were otherwise then the past would be no more than a rhyme or a story, something to memorize, whereas its natural condition is to set us puzzles and be argued over. The opening of the 2002 edition of Gloucestershire, for example, is wholly different from the 1970 introduction above.[22] In twenty years' time it will be posing new questions, just as the explanation of the British Empire that was given to me fifty years ago is not one I recognize today. Even something as recent as the Cold War is subject to perpetual reassessment. Since 1991 entire institutions have come into being to try to figure out the essence of the 'open yet restricted' confrontation that lasted forty years and apparently cost eight trillion dollars. Their effort is not for want of evidence. In contrast to earlier periods for which sources are sparse, inconsistent or just absent, the records of the Cold War are abundant. Historians will study them for years not because anyone – yet – doubts that there was a Cold War, but to fathom its effects on our lives and beliefs, and its consequences.[23]

History's subject is change, its causes and means. Why was change slow or tentative at some times yet energizing in others? Insight into the past must modify understanding of the present, in which case the reverse applies – 'now' must shape understanding of 'then'. Either way, the past involves us as well as L. P. Hartley's 'they' who do things differently. In doing so it harnesses the imaginative power and curiosity that characterizes our species. The thrust of a question will alter according to who asks it, when, or why, and within what framework of thought or knowledge. Moreover, different kinds of source call for different skills in interrogation. Text, object, landscape, residue, symbol – each calls for its own kind of examination before one can be put into conversation with the others or woven into narrative.

This book is about the archaeological strands in that weave. It examines commonly held ideas about England's past and asks what light archaeology sheds on them. Like Pevsner's Buildings of England, the subjects reach from prehistory to the end of the twentieth century. Among them are human ancestries, Man's relationship with Nature, the making of the landscape, settlement, Tudor drama, a battle, twentieth-century conflict, industrialization and a saint. As well as being spread across three-quarters of a million years, each topic sits at a different point along the continuum between epoch and the fleeting moment.

In some places this becomes a history of archaeology. In others it is my history in archaeology. But mainly it is about how the past is read, and about what we ourselves bring to the reading as well as what we find.

All historians 'work within limits of contemporary knowledge' which they enlarge 'as they may by their own imagination'.[24] But if imagination is the anvil on which readings of the past are formed, whose imaginations do we trust? Fifty years ago this would have seemed an odd question, for archaeology was then in the hands of respected people – university academics, extra-mural lecturers, keepers of museum collections, government officials – most of whom believed in realist history and in whose views about 'what happened' the public had trust. Today the views are contradictory, and trust has faltered. Aside from an increase of cynicism towards expert opinion generally, the emergence of historical sciences in the context of Western nationalism and empire-building has left their practice tainted and finds reflection in as many different identities as there are groups to express them. However, while there may no longer be one 'us' to dictate whose perspectives should be adopted and whose not, what follows will argue that everyone can – and should – choose those to whom they wish to listen. An infinitely subdivided past is permeable not only to conscientious searchers but also to cranks, falsifiers and obsessives, not to mention faiths and political parties who assert entire alternative histories. In the world of multi-vocal history, this book will ask, how does an everyday reader tell these apart?

The result, on one level, is an anthology. On another, it is an expedition. On yet another it will find that apparently unconnected subjects are bound by threads that run across millennia. I have tried to write without assuming special knowledge. The references are simply for those who want to go further, or to see, so to speak, where I have been. The book centres on England, because England is where I am most at home. But the world is made up of neighbourhoods, and to belong to a neighbourhood is to be a citizen of the world.

INTRODUCTION

ON TIME AND ARCHAEOLOGY

> Jumbled in one common box
> Of their dark stupidity,
> Orchid, swan, and Caesar lie;
> Time that tires of everyone
> Has corroded all the locks,
> Thrown away the key for fun.
>
> W. H. Auden, 'Domesday Song',
> 1941, *Collected Poems* (1994)

Look to the right of Pieter Bruegel's engraving *The Triumph of Time* (1574): there is a human landscape in summer – people, crops, farmsteads, all under a placid sky in which soar summer birds. To the left, smoke blows from a wasted town. A procession trudges past leafless trees; in its midst, a cart drawn by skinny horses. Upon the cart, a model of the world, new-mapped, its oceans busy with ships, encircled by figures of the zodiac. The scene is interlined with ticking clocks and scales, running sand and tolling bells. In this future-past, the processional sun is an unsmiling horse brass. Behind the cart rides a hooded skeleton with a scythe, followed by Fame, trumpet ablast, borne on an elephant. The procession trudges from west to east (we can work this out by looking at the orientation of the church) – the toy sun is going backwards. In Bruegelland, the present does not leave the past behind; time engulfs the future. The cortège crunches through the debris of human life – a crown, a flagon of wine, a hat. Purse, books, music: Time consumes one and all.[1]

What or who is this gobbler? Different ages find different answers. Some say that time is a property of the universe, others that it is an illusion. Judaeo-Christian thought awards it a beginning and anticipates an

*1. Time is drawn forward by the horses of the sun and moon in Pieter
Bruegel's* The Triumph of Time, *engraved by Philip Galle, 1574*

end, and so implies that outside this envelope it does not exist. Newton
turned this inside out, considering our universe to be embraced by
an absolute time, its bodies and forces integrated in a great whirring
apparatus: 'Absolute, true and mathematical time, of itself and from its
own nature, flows equably without relation to anything external.'[2] The
philosopher-writer Lewis Mumford, writing in the 1930s, reflected that
the mechanical clock, an invention that appeared in Europe during the
thirteenth century, 'dissociated time from human events and helped
create the belief in an independent world of mathematically measurable
sequences: the special world of science'.[3] Within this 'special world',
however, Einstein's theory of special relativity (1905) did away with the
idea that distance, time and mass are absolute, showing instead that
they change depending on the relative speeds of the observer and the
observed. So, if you travel close to the speed of light with respect to
a fixed observer, time slows almost to a standstill. In this condition,
a hundred years in the life of an observer might appear as seconds to
you.

    Such a relative flow annuls any idea of absolute time or simultaneity.

That is, events that are concurrent for two observers may not be so for a third observer in a different frame of reference. Although these effects are most pronounced at extreme relative speeds, they are also locally measurable – for example, from satellites or even with atomic clocks that travel on aeroplanes. General relativity takes the effect further, by combining space and time into space-time. Space-time is affected (warped) by heavy masses, such as stars or black holes that curve space-time around themselves, giving rise to what Newton led us to think of as gravity. In result, time flows more slowly when you are close to a heavy object like our planet, and faster as you move away from it. This can be measured by taking an atomic clock up a mountain. The effect becomes yet more pronounced when you approach a black hole, since, in principle, as you come near to the event-horizon of a black hole, time will draw to a standstill, and you will look out to see the rest of the universe ageing rapidly around you.

The next step comes from the theory of black holes and gravitational collapse which shows that in principle it is likely that a black hole has a corresponding 'other side', joined to the first black hole by a worm hole. Theory suggests that this 'other side' need not be in the same place, or even the same time. It might, indeed, be at another time, in another universe. Currently, there are no physical laws to prevent this. Taking an extreme view, there is nothing in the laws of physics to prevent time travel – a condition which would make archaeology redundant. Or would it?

According to the eighth-century Northumbrian monk Bede, popularizer of Dionysius Exiguus' system of situating historical events in a continuous run of years from the birth of Christ, there are different kinds of time, and three ways of reckoning them: according to Nature, by custom or by authority.[4] Thus the Sabbath is kept every seven days by divine authority, whereas market day or a month of thirty days is decided by human custom. For natural measurement of time, we look to the sky. Our days are defined by the time that the world takes to turn upon its axis; our lives are numbered by the Earth's journeys around the sun. Another pulse derives from the phases of the moon. Latin *mensura* ('measure'), whence 'menstrual', Greek *mēn* ('month'), Old English *mōna* – these words and the ideas behind them belong to one family: counting moons has been a way of reckoning time as far back as history runs. Lunar months, however, are not integers of a solar year. The search for a proportional relationship between the cross-rhythms of sun and moon has absorbed people for millennia. As Bede explained:

> Those who probe with subtlety into these matters confirm that, in fact, the Moon has – setting aside the calculation of the 'leap of the Moon' – 12 hours less [than 30 days], and the Sun has 10½ hours more. Thus with nature as our guide we discover that the solar year is made up of 365¼ days but the lunar year is finished in 354 days if it is common . . .[5]

The Jewish calendar is lunar in its basis, the later Roman calendar solar. In medieval Europe, the tricky task of integrating the two fell to the Church. And while the moon ran its complete course in a cycle of nineteen years, 'each of the planets as well is borne around the zodiac at its own rate'.

> This Nature was created by the one true God when He commanded that the stars which He had set in the heavens should be the signs of the seasons, days and years; it is not, as the folly of the pagans asserts, a creating goddess, one amongst many.[6]

For Bede and his contemporaries there were different kinds of natural year: 'a lunar year and a solar year, a separate year for [each of] the wandering stars, and one for all the planets, which is particularly called "the great year"'.[7]

Astronomical rhythms – 'starry time' – may seem to be universal, but on an interplanetary scale they are relative and local. Elsewhere in the solar system time would seem to be something other than here. Against Earth reckoning, a Pluto day lasts 153 hours, and for every year that elapses on Jupiter over eleven pass on Earth. Here on Earth, too, time becomes a counterpoint of pulses if we use other recurrent rhythms to measure it. The tempo of organic reproduction, for instance, varies according to the size of species: generally, the smaller, the faster. A sequoia that has stood on the Sierra Nevada for twenty centuries may take a hundred years to reproduce, whereas some kinds of bacteria will multiply in the time it takes you to read this paragraph.

Time, space and environment go together. It is hard to think of time without space; the French word for time is the same as for weather: *temps*.[8] Time helps to locate place, and interest in time's measurement comes to the fore in epochs when explorers thrive. The realization in the sixteenth century that longitude could be ascertained by comparing local time with an absolute world time was one of the factors which stimulated the desire for ever more accurate clocks. In our own day, the demands of space travel have had a similar effect.

Most of us today think of time as a flow from past to future. As perspectives go, however, this is new. Many in history have regarded time as cyclical. Aristotle considered time to be unreal, for the past was gone, the future had yet to be, 'and the present is a point without dimensions'. Time, he thought, was more like colour, a property which resides in other things rather than existing independently. In Aristotle's view, time was dependent on motion, for 'the measurement of motion involves primarily the measurement of the space traversed', which can only be done with reference to time. Aristotle's God is consequently aloof, beyond time, neither originating nor intervening in a universe which 'contains motion, but not fundamental change'.[9]

Jewish tradition, in contrast, visualizes a creative God who sets new things in motion. 'Part of this emphasis on history rather than recurrence can be seen in the biblical historicization of the festivals; instead of being merely seasonal, they have become commemorations of the Exodus and the Sinai revelation, events unique in the history of the world.'[10]

Linear time supposes a start to count from, and runs towards an end. At the close of the fourth century, Augustine of Hippo was puzzling over eternity. If God made time itself, were there periods of time that He did not make?[11] Augustine wondered if a sliver of time present, divided so minutely as to be observationally stable, might give an inkling of eternity. Reflecting that the mind conflates information from the past and thought about the future in its efforts to make sense of things in the present, he proposed three kinds of time in human consciousness. 'The time present of things past is *memoria*; the time present of things present is *contuitus*; the time present of things future is *expectatio*.'[12] For Bede, the smallest unit of time was indivisible, denoted by the Greek word *atomos*, 'that which cannot be cut'. Bede reflected on the moment of the Resurrection, when 'We shall all rise … in the twinkling of an eye'. Many writers, he said, had unguardedly supposed an atom to equate with the tiny interval of time when our eyelids blink in reaction to an anticipated blow.[13]

History-as-enterprise is our ever evolving struggle to make sense of the route and distance we have covered, and thus to take bearings on the directions in which we move. Archaeology is the part of that venture which looks for meaning in the materials discarded by time's procession – the junk on the ground in Bruegelland. In Augustinian terms these bits and pieces are intriguing. Made long ago, they still exist now. Straight away, however, we hit a snag: there is no agreement on what the fragments mean, or how they might be read. By the early twentieth century history was assumed to be well mapped by historians who could tell us 'what happened'. Time's relics were fitted into an existing framework, or ordered in such a way as to make one. More recently, that kind of canonical reading has been challenged. Some now say there never was a particular story, that the past is trackless, existing only in our minds or as an entanglement of as many different paths as there are people to imagine them. In the twenty-first-century West, where days are planned to the instant and 'historic' in the mouths of sports commentators has come to mean 'unprecedented', many historians have abandoned grand narrative for the micro-particulars of ordinary lives: a morning in the life of a fourteenth-century peasant becomes as interesting as the reign of a king.

To these random intimacies archaeology is oddly suited, for the ground is often a bit like photographic film, registering certain things regardless of their importance. In the study of these images, and through the sifting of things made, built, abandoned, broken, forgotten, lost, hidden, eaten, buried, grown, killed, worshipped, or just marks – like the footprints of a group of people who walked across mudflats in the Severn estuary some six or seven thousand years ago, one child running – moments can be made out. On the wall of a cave in southern France is the stencil of a hand held against the rock maybe as long ago as thirty thousand years. If you plot the position and angle of every flake struck from a nodule of flint in the course of making a tool, the work of ten minutes half a million years ago can be reconstructed. In the side of a quarry at the foot of the Sussex Downs, sands and pebbles are infused with the swirl of waves that lapped at the base of sea cliffs tens of millennia before the last ice age. At Hambledon Hill in Dorset excavation glimpses the aftermath of a fight among some of England's first farmers: the remains of a man and woman are being gnawed and dragged about by dogs or wolves.[14] In a church on the edge of the North York Moors, tiny stalactite-like columns of lime plaster dangle from the vault of the crypt, the last drips still poised where they congealed nine centuries ago. In the archaeological finds store of the Goode Shippe *Mary Rose*, Henry VIII's warship that sank in July 1545, ropes from her rigging still smell of tar.

Organic deposits at the Roman fort of Vindolanda near Hadrian's Wall have preserved wooden leaf tablets bearing memoranda, letters, military records and accounts from the end of the first century AD. We sift them like the contents of a wastepaper basket tipped on to a table. Part of one note describes the javelin-handling skills of 'Brittunculi' – a new word, the slang diminutive of Britons, its modern sense maybe something like 'little Brits' (or is this understated soldiers' irony?). Another tablet records the strength of a cohort of Tungrians – how many are fit for duty, how many unfit, how many away. Octavius writes to Candidus about some animal hides which are currently paused at Catterick (the roads are bad and he doesn't want to risk the draught animals), and asks for cash to cover a grain purchase. A notebook itemizes commodities like wine, local beer and pork dripping. Claudia Severa, the wife of Aelius Brocchus, invites her friend Lepidina, *karissima*, to visit on her birthday. On 7 March we glimpse a working party of thirty men burning stone to make lime.[15]

'I who am dead a thousand years ... Send you my words for messengers':[16] at first sight the Vindolanda tablets seem like postcards from the past. Yet they also tantalize, for the postcards were not addressed to us, and there is little in them that connects with anything else of which we know. What was morale like in the First Cohort of Tungrians? What was one of the absent soldiers doing in London? In the list of commodities, do the entries cluster round 24 June because this was the midsummer festival, or just because this was the fragment to survive? And who was Lepidina – what happened to her? We shall never know, just as Claudia Severa was not to know that nearly two millennia later her letter would be the earliest known example of writing in Latin by a woman.

Archaeology's eye for the fractional and intimate is matched by another for history's long flows. 'We deal in time wholesale,' said the field archaeologist O. G. S. Crawford. Increasingly, we can measure past economies, track technological change, follow fashion, watch the evolution of religion, observe the unfolding of childhood play, tell where people were born, chart humanity's relationship with the environment. Such insights run into the present, for while archaeology's independence of text is an asset in text's absence it can bring even greater virtues in its presence. As we shall see, some of archaeology's most creative adventures involve recent subjects and colloquy with documents.

The oldest documents in the world date from around 3000 BC. Archaeology reaches more than five hundred times as far, and with the help of science enjoys an ever improving ability to say how old things are. History without sequence is nullity, and new knowledge about sequence has a value which extends beyond detail for its own sake. The fact that Stonehenge turns out to have been begun a millennium sooner than was once believed has ramifications in Arizona as well as

Wiltshire. The lithe horse – or is it a wolfhound?[17] – etched into chalk at Uffington in Berkshire, for long credited to people who lived two or three generations before Julius Caesar, is now understood to be up to a thousand years older. The strange oaken circle surrounding an inverted tree bole found on the north Norfolk coast was begun in 2049 BC, in the spring. When we contemplate the paintings of animals in the cave of Chauvet-Pont-d'Arc in the Ardèche, the worth of accurate dating becomes clear. What are said to be the oldest known cave paintings in the world are startlingly accomplished. From analysis of torch smudges and charcoal we can see that the cave was used not once (and not only by humans – bears wallowed in its darkness) but in a series of episodes several thousand years apart. The first paintings may have been made up to 350 centuries ago.[18] They show different animals in ways which catch not only their likeness but also their essence: lions – intentness; bison – power; horses – grace. The animal paintings are a source of wonder. The genius with which they were depicted preceded the invention of some of the weapons used to kill them.

Have you found anything interesting? Anyone who has worked on an excavation will tell you that this is the question that they most often hear from members of the public. It is a testing question, for by the umpteenth time of its asking a fresh reply is difficult. To the asker, on the other hand, it is obvious. If you come across people privileged to be looking through a gateway into another world, to ask *What can you see?* is irresistible.

There might be another question: *Have you found anything new?* I've never been asked this, which is odd, because something new – 'new' whether in the sense of 'better understood', 'hitherto unseen' or 'result of a new kind of observation' – is what archaeology is about. Otherwise, why do it? But there again, curiously, much popular interest in the past seems to be driven less by a desire for new knowledge than by yearning for reassurance, or latent desire for thrill. For some, history is a comfort blanket. No matter how many battle-damaged skulls we find, the fact that swords kill people remains headline news, whereas the rewriting of narratives that explain why the battles were fought is not. This may be because an entire generation has grown up unaware of what the narratives were, its expectations shaped by a curriculum in which for practical purposes most of the human past is sidelined.[19] It might also be because somewhere deep inside ourselves we have not yet quite outgrown the pre-Renaissance view that the past has little to tell us beyond that which we have forgotten.

The rating of finding above interpretation is also influenced by the extent to which spectacular discoveries are made by history's laity. The Dead Sea Scrolls were found by a shepherd. The terracotta army of China's first emperor was found by a farmer. Lascaux's painted caves were discovered by chance. Lindow Man was hoiked out of peat on a conveyor belt heading towards grow-bags. Hikers found the man who had lain refrigerated for 5,300 years in an Alpine glacier. A farmer pinpointed 60,000-year-old deposits containing traces of hunting Neanderthals at Lynford. The Hoxne hoard was turned up by a gentleman searching for a lost hammer. The Staffordshire hoard of Anglo-Saxon gold was found by an unemployed gentleman with a metal detector. Treasure in the British Museum seems all the more appealing when it is ordinary folk rather than academics who find it.

More typically, however, new understanding arises not from bombshell discoveries but from a fluctuating interplay between different patterns of knowledge and question. Seen alone, the individual records that make up such patterns may look trifling, even pointless, and gathering them is time-consuming and sometimes expensive. It is their cumulative impact which is large. Science adds to their reach. Ever-improving techniques such as multispectral or neutron imaging, stable isotope analysis and molecular biology (these are examples) enable the posing of new questions. Another influence, just mentioned, is the controversial hobby of metal detecting, which is revealing patterns so strange that we hardly yet know what to make of them. Moreover, while science is popularly credited with a knock-down ability to scotch fallacies and make breakthroughs, its innovations often increase uncertainty, by multiplying questions and reshuffling the range of possibilities from which to choose. Science can also confuse the picture when good scholars in their own disciplines turn archaeologist manqué, and use obsolete or over-simplified historical models as the starting points for their interventions. The continuing controversy over the dating of human arrival in Australia or America, the two radiocarbon revolutions or doubts about the dauntingly early dates for paintings in the Chauvet caves[20] are examples from a flow of revisionism which makes it risky to rely on any individual scientific announcement until it has been well corroborated, and its context explored.

Archaeology is sometimes charged with an inability to engage with the individual other than as a box of bones or an anonymous grain swept along by impersonal environmental and economic processes. It is true that the bones of a fourteenth-century peasant will not disclose

whether he had a sense of humour, whether he was a yardlander cultivating twenty-five acres or an elite peasant holding land for several families. Excavation of his house will not reveal his nickname, or whether
his aunt hated him. Did he like to watch sunsets, sing in a fine tenor
voice, or weep when his favourite dog died? These are questions we can
never answer. Archaeology cannot directly enter human consciousness,
and there are other realms from which we are cut off. Yet to concede
that 'Men's evil manners live in brass; their virtues / We write in water'[21]
is not to agree that archaeology is materialism leached of humanity. No
conceivable written source would tell us about our peasant's sensibility
either. The challenge is to frame questions which material evidence can
answer, rather than to grieve for the silences where it cannot.

Like a satellite in asymmetric orbit, now distant, now swinging in
close, archaeology takes us both far and close to lived lives.[22] Building
layouts offer insights into security and privacy. Residues point to specialist processes, ink to writing, inscriptions to peasant literacy. Tools
attest tasks, crafts and special talent; instruments, the modes and pitches
of lost melodies. Contours of worn floors reflect flows of daily movement around the house. Outside, fields and the bones of animals used
for dairying, wool or traction together tell us about animal demography
and the farming economy. Food remains and utensils show what was
eaten, in what quantities, how it was cooked, occasionally (from the
condition of fruit stones, comminuted bone or pips in fossil turds) even
whether a morsel was gulped or savoured. From sources of manufac-
tured goods we can map market networks or distances travelled, while
the ease with which they were covered will be mirrored in the geography
and quality of bridges and roads, and the social co-operation required
to maintain them. Objects give glimpses of the wider world in which
our peasant lived, even his sense of what was far or near – where friends
and locals ended and strangers began. In the churchyard, his bones may
show whether he went hungry as a child or suffered an accident in his
early teens, whether gallstones tormented him or parasites gnawed his
gut, how long he lived and maybe how he died.

While archaeology's currency is material, it can take us beyond materialism. Weather's changefulness is discernible in environmental remains
which register ancient frosts, droughts and rains. Or again, archaeology
brushes aspects of spirituality's avowal, if not belief. In the sludge of the
peasant's well may lie a badge of his pilgrimage; in the cavity of a cathedral wall, the hidden relic of a holy man, now nameless yet polished by
the touch of his among a million hands; in his grave, a white stone.

In some quarters an idea has taken hold that physical remains have a dispassionate authority which enables them to compensate for biases and gaps in written records, or to compensate for the obsessions of past historians. In result there are those who look to archaeology to offset Carlyle's view of history as the biography of great men, or to give witness that is independent of the specialized networks who have 'acted as gate-keepers to our historical knowledge' through control of what was written down or published.[23] While it is the case that archaeology gives us autonomous facts on the ground, the material record is itself slanted by what was made or has survived, by the things which earlier generations of antiquaries chose to study or ignore, and by the ways in which the meanings of objects change in concert with our own changing interests. If archaeological remains do not lie, it is only because they are dumb,[24] conveying nothing (nothing of much interest, anyway) of their own accord. Insofar as meaning comes from a dialogue between what we find and what we bring to what we find, the production of narrative is a kind of ventriloquism. It is not only logic or science that we bring, but also our imaginations.

If it is moot whether archaeology can give voice to the oppressed, it can at least help to restore their powers of decision. Whether the white stone was placed in our peasant's hand by his priest or his lover, whether it denotes Revelation's last things, whether it was something invested with immemorial meaning or emptied of it, the stone reflects intent, a thing done or imagined which puts us in the presence of what was mortal. Something rather than nothing, it is part of the flow from then to now, a place to start.

One thing we bring to time is a compulsion to split it up. We may do this more or less arbitrarily (the Bronze Age), for the organization of material, as if imposing co-ordinates on a map, or critically (Tudor England), investing different eras with personalities. We like to think that such period identities are inherent, although in our hearts we know that one age is defined by contrast with another: Roman is opposed to Saxon, the Commonwealth to the Restoration, the Roaring Twenties to the Hungry Thirties. Periods are defined as much by what they are not as by what they are.[25]

The hankering after framework is fairly recent, although – and here is a luscious paradox – it is not quite clear when it began, different aspects having stirred at different times. Early Christian chronographers like Eusebius of Caesarea, Augustine, Isidore and Bede variously divided world history into ages which had both actual and spiritual significance.

Eusebius attempted a synchronization of biblical and secular time.[26] Augustine visualized a parallel between Six Ages and the six days of creation, and a further analogy with the six stages of human life.[27] In his *The Reckoning of Time*, Bede wrote that the Sixth Age would be divided from a Seventh (a time of rest in another life, which 'holy souls, released from their bodies, will possess in Christ')[28] by the Judgement. In the future will come the Seventh Age, paralleling the seventh day of creation, when God rested from his labours. Then comes the Eighth, the 'blessed repose of paradise'. Like the eighth day after creation ('which will not have other days following it' but 'will abide, one and unending'), the Eighth Age will be the end of time.[29]

For as long as the Bible *was* history, the need to investigate it was limited by assumptions about what was already known. Classical authors looked back to a golden age, although some did show awareness of technological progress. Seneca, for instance, realized that there had been a time when the human race had lived closer to Nature. In that age, he thought, land had been untilled and undivided, houses were primitive rustic shelters, and the arch, weaving, wheel-thrown pottery and metal were unknown. The question of how such discoveries had been achieved interested him greatly.[30] Advances in technology and art during the Middle Ages were apparently unaccompanied by a general theory of progress. Until the sixteenth century an 'inventor' was, as its Latin root *invenio* reminds us, a person 'who found something which had been lost, not one who devised a new solution unknown to previous generations'.[31] This is odd, as fashions and technologies changed as much between, say, 1200 and 1500 as during the three centuries that followed. Medieval records often speak of 'new work', but consciousness of change in style and historical documents seems to find an extended vocabulary only from around 1500.[32] The sixteenth century is abuzz with time-aware terms like 'epoch', 'anachronism', 'new-fangled' and 'out of date'. 'Monument', in its sense of something that commemorates a past action or period, is also met around this time. Keith Thomas suggested that printing may have helped to shift perceptions, for every book carried a date which drew attention to the difference between the ideas it contained and those of the time in which they were read.[33] It is around this time, too, that date-stones begin to appear over the doors of some buildings, while scholars across Europe began to appreciate that customs and law could not be considered apart from the ages and societies to which they had belonged.

Medieval time had been irregular, some days and tides being more propitious than others. Bell time, the time of agricultural seasons, the academic year and the calendar of holy days were each associated with their own ideas and myths.[34] Growing analytical awareness began to undermine these cycles, to contradict prophecies and unsettle tradition. Time in an economy based on land is cyclical, whereas in a world of coin and markets time is money. One result of that change was a need for new myths to replace those that had been displaced. Another was the dethroning of the Ancients. Until the sixteenth century, there was an idea that most of what could be known already was known, and that history recurred through cycles. Behind this lay the Great Year – a term of centuries whereafter all moving bodies in the heavens were believed to return to their original places.[35] While this prevailed, the pursuit of knowledge was less a quest for the new than a project to rediscover what had been forgotten. 'If there be nothing new, but that which is / Hath been before ...' begins Shakespeare's fifty-ninth sonnet. During the sixteenth and seventeenth centuries, as interest in the past shifted from ancient wisdom to change,[36] greater emphasis was given to differences between the present and the past, and to the possibility of unfolding knowledge. One thing that epitomized that was gunpowder, and the transformation of military technology from medieval to modern. This in turn re-raises Seneca's question: how does technological change happen? Many today assume a simplified linear narrative in which progress follows an inevitable logic. But perhaps this is because technological history is written by its winners, emphasizing functional determinism at the expense of things that may once have seemed promising yet turned out to be dead ends.

Archaeology's criteria for dividing time are crude. French Annales historians warned us years ago against the risks of compartmentalization, yet even now many suppose concepts like 'the Iron Age' or 'early Anglo-Saxon' to be cultural realities. We have tended to assume that material evidence will embody and reflect social, political or ethnic entities which are mostly of our own invention (we speak of 'Celtic metalwork', 'Norman churches' and 'Georgian houses'), and tend to map them against units of historical geography, like nations or counties. This book will point out that when different kinds of material are looked at together, not only do their patterns seldom coincide with conventional periods or administrative regions, but they are often not even in accord with each other. Just as most colours lie beyond the range of the human eye, so do different kinds of material pattern exist outside history's conventional frameworks, suggesting other paths – if we can find them – along which to retrace our human passage.

André Burguière draws attention to two coexisting conceptions of history.

> The first ... seeks to achieve a psychological or political identification with the past by precisely reconstituting what happened. In that view, the past is *magister vitae*, a precedent to be imitated or avoided. That conception fosters the political uses of history. It is now experiencing a revival with the attention to the effects and imperatives of memory. The other manner of apprehending history is to consider the past a field of observation for learning the general characteristics of humankind and of societies along with the geographical diversity of cultures and societies, but with an added dimension: our genealogical relationship into the past.[37]

Readers will recognize the influence of the first in today's Britain. This book belongs to the second.

PART ONE
LEARNING TO LOOK

2. (Previous page) *Cover of booklet produced in 1919 to stir interest in the potential of aerial photography*

1

HEARTLAND

'Parochialism is universal; it deals with the fundamentals.'

Patrick Kavanagh

Jack Morris, born 1897, son of a Southwark builder, survives fighting on the western front in the Great War. On the first day of October 1922 he marries Bessie Mitchell, daughter of a Fulham fireman, some-time Nippy at a Lyons Corner House and his elder by a year. They are my grandparents.

Bright and chatty, Jack works as a tennis-racket stringer. As piano tuners are to concert pianists, so is Jack to tennis stars. He tunes their instruments, and progresses to managing a shop which sells sports equipment. Shuttlecocks, punchballs and swimming caps take him and Bessie to Bristol, then back to London, where until 1941 they live in a terraced house near Finsbury Park. February 1941, to be more precise. Jack is out fire-watching and Bess is crouching under the stairs when the Heinkel passes. When Jack comes back the house is gone. Bess has gone too, and for a few minutes, glass and slates crunching underfoot, he is at the world's end. Then a neighbour tells him that Bess is down at the rest centre. He finds her drinking a cup of tea.

They move to another house. The Luftwaffe find that, too.

Relatives in west London take them in, which is a squeeze, until yet another bomb cuts the tenement in half.

Jack's employers send him to run their shop in Birmingham. The shop is opposite the cathedral in the city centre, above which wheel noisy, immeasurable flocks of starlings on winter evenings. Jack and Bess rent a bungalow in Great Barr while looking for somewhere permanent. In 1945 they find it: a nice 1930s semi in Northfield, a once-upon-a-time Worcestershire village which was overrun by Birmingham's spread earlier in the century. The house is in Great Stone Road. It has coloured panes to either side of the front door, and a bay-windowed front room where the fire is lit only on Christmas Day. It is here that you put your best glass, framed photographs of your children, a *Pears Cyclopaedia* (which has a vivid section on fatal diseases), a couple of Reader's Digest condensed books, and – when bananas and oranges reappear – a bowl of fruit. To the side stands a lean-to where coal is stored and Jack keeps his paint, putty and a step-ladder. Behind runs a garden with space for vegetables, roses, gooseberries and raspberries, a patch of lawn. At the far end, beyond a young mountain ash, the garden is bounded by a fence of creosoted boards.

If you look out of the front-room bay window at about twenty past six on a weekday evening you will see Jack, fresh off a tram from the city centre, sauntering downhill, brown mackintosh open, belt swinging, the *Evening Despatch* a white tube rising from a pocket. Behind him at the top of the hill stands a pub, the Black Horse, which looks like a half-timbered manor house. Years later I find that before the war there was a vogue for building pubs like this, when breweries hoped that bygone styles would attract a more discerning clientele. This appeal to nostalgia is lost on Jack, although he reads the *Daily Express* and worships Churchill. Bess frowns on pubs, preferring tea and Adam's ale. On Christmas Day Jack and his son

3. Jack Morris, October 1920

4. Bessie Mitchell, Christmas 1917

will go into the Black Horse, for an hour or so, after church.

Jack and Bess never go to church, but their son does. He is a vicar. John was born back in 1923. He grew into a spirited lad who liked to immobilize London Underground escalators by jamming the tip of an umbrella in the crack between their moving stairs. He was also a romantic who read widely, and an artist, perhaps even a talented artist, but as soon as he was sixteen Jack bundled him out of school and told him to look for a job. Finding one around then wasn't difficult, as the United Kingdom had just declared war on Germany and there were plenty of opportunities. As soon as John was old enough he volunteered to fly.

The RAF sent him to train in Canada, where he fell in love with a drama teacher. In May 1944 the war separates them – he is sent back to Britain, then to Italy, whence during the war's last months he flies reconnaissance missions over the shrinking Reich. Along the way he meets people who set him thinking and change his direction. When the Air Force release 164121 Flying Officer J. R. Morris at the end of 1945 he marries the drama teacher (this is when Jack and Bess planted the mountain ash) and goes to Oxford to study theology. In 1947, I am born.

In summer 1950 we move to Hockley, a poor district of inner Birmingham where my father begins work as a curate. As Pevsner saw in 1934 we are 'amidst two-storey houses in grubby brick, indescribably dreary and sooty' (p. 2). No trees, nor grass, nor even weeds grow around our house – a vast, cold and mostly unfurnished nineteenth-century clergy residence wedged between a church hall, a pen-nib works and a cardboard-box factory. The houses hereabouts are tight packed, gapped by bombing. Not all the city is so hard featured. Thursday is my father's day off, so on Thursdays we usually board a number 70 tram which takes us out to Northfield. From the top of the tram you can look into Edgbaston's gardens, and the woody grounds of Selly Oak's training colleges seem almost rural.

The trams are primrose and blue, bow-ended, with a single headlight that gives them a one-eyed, Cyclopean stare, and flanks which advertise Bovril, the *Evening Despatch*, Invicta Underwear, Chunky Marmalade and the New Weekly Wash Sensation, Tide. Trams also carry notices which forbid spitting (a prohibition I do not yet connect with the TB sanatorium at West Heath where my mother will soon go to teach English to refugees) and the city's coat of arms. The crest fascinates me. Below it a man and a woman stand either side of a shield. Over the shield is a helmet, and above that a turret, whence rises a flexed arm with a hand that grips a forging hammer.

Occasionally I am left to stay at Northfield, where Jack entertains me by putting his glasses on the cat, and himself by teaching me to do things he knows will shock my mother when she comes back – like pretending to extract his teeth with a pair of pliers. In summer, long after bedtime I lie looking out of the open window, smelling the roses and creosote, watching the moon take shape beyond shrieking swifts, listening to the distant gamelan of shunted coal trucks.[1] And I am terrified. If I fall asleep I shall be unconscious, and might remain so for anything up to eight hours. *Eight hours.* I try to count up to a minute, extrapolate from that to an hour, then from one hour to eight. Such time is unimaginable, making sleep an oblivion that gives me a frantic feeling. I want it to be tomorrow, *now.* And usually, the next thing I know, it is. Unless a nightmare intervenes. In that case, the arm in the crest slowly straightens, then slams down the forging hammer with a crash.

Birmingham, wrote the French aristocrat Alexis de Tocqueville after his visit to the city in 1835, 'is an immense workshop, a huge forge, a vast shop. One sees only busy people and faces brown with smoke.'[2] Birmingham specializes in many things – cocoa, chocolate, glass and rubber – but its soul is in metal. One hundred and fifty years ago, Birmingham's citizens were coming to think of metal as we now look upon plastic – an all-purpose material out of which virtually anything might be made. One of the exhibits at the Great Exhibition of 1851 (displayed in a Crystal Palace which, naturally, had been prefabricated in Birmingham) was a brass bedstead in the style of the French Renaissance. In the 1890s even Birmingham's street lavatories were made of iron.

Brummies wind, beat, melt, forge or cast different metals into a myriad things: nails, bolts, screws, pins, staples, needles, thimbles, wire, springs, buckets, pails, tea pots, buttons, badges, buckles, cartridges, pistols, rifles, jacks, plaques, knacks, tacks, knobs, fobs, hinges, machine tools, dynamos, girders, lamp-posts, jewellery, tins, pens, nibs, toys, bicycles, motor bikes, coffin plates and – since Herbert Austin put a factory on two acres of land near the edge of the city in 1905 – cars.

Austin was not the first on the spot. In 1893, the copperplate printers White & Pike Ltd went there to produce decorated tin boxes. The site was well served by road, the Birmingham–Gloucester railway runs right through, and the rural site gave room for expansion. Their venture failed, but Austin bought the vacant works and began to design and build cars. Nearby Birmingham contained people with the skills he needed to do so. Within four years the workforce had risen to a thousand. During the Great War Austin's were diverted to the making of shells, jerrycans, trucks and aircraft. In 1919 car-making resumed. But post-war demand was initially small, most of the workforce was dismissed and the company was on the brink of closure. Nineteen-twenty-two saw a change in fortune. Herbert Austin hit on a new kind of car: small, affordable, a vehicle for the masses – the Austin Seven. By the late 1920s Austin's was turning out 25,000 cars a year, and employing 8,000 workers to build them.

Half a century on, over twenty thousand people work at the Austin (this is how the factory is locally known) and the works has spread across a hundred acres. Twenty thousand is three Roman legions, the population of a town. Yet because Longbridge is new-sprung ('a self-explanatory name of recent origin', as the *Oxford Dictionary of English Place-Names* condescendingly puts it) it is not yet a parish. In 1952, the Rev. John Morris is asked to establish one. To begin, he buys a map. I am looking at it now: Ordnance Survey Sheet SP 07, beige and blue cover, *About 2½ Inches to One Mile*, revised price 5/6d net.

I am also looking at my mother's Boots scribbling diary for that year – *56th year of publication, British Manufacture Throughout, three days on a page*. It records the day on which we moved. At the garden's end is a climbable tree – a copper beech. Dots against certain dates presumably denote my mother's menstrual cycle, and hope for the sister or brother I never had. The diary brushes against memory: I remember the weather next day, and rapture at finding a garden behind the house. Longbridge in the mid-1950s consists of two different landscapes which seem to have been randomly edited together. Work is about to start on a tower block on the site of a medieval timber-framed moated farm. In the stillness of the moat's warm brown water, huge tadpoles wriggle. Roads are being ruled across meadows. Housing estates stand in pasture, as if fallen from the sky. Almost every field contains a pond, or a spring, or a damp place where newts thrive. Waste ground is coloured by butterflies and ox-eye daisies. Across the road is a hedgebank where you can dig for pig-nuts. The shadows which seem to have been pencilled under leaves of rosebay willowherb, abundant on cindery ground beside the railway, are Elephant Hawk Moth caterpillars.

It is not just nature and industry that are entangled here, but culture too. Beyond the moated farm is a bit of the American Midwest: an estate of two hundred wooden houses supplied by the Aladdin Company of Bay City, Michigan, in 1917. They came as kits, to house Austin workers recruited from across Britain. For their day, the houses were well appointed: each had central heating, an indoor lavatory, a bathroom, a gas washing boiler and a large garden. They line roads with grassy margins called 'Avenues' and 'Drives' that are shaded by rows of trees.

There is an indefinable enchantment about this place, at this time. It might have something to do with boundaries, or transformation. For some, the age of gold is always just past, just behind, over the last hill.[3] For me, then, it was always just ahead, and to the west, where the hilly skyline is crowned by a clump of beeches. Beyond it some magic surely lies.

The Birmingham–Gloucester railway is a timeline along which the Devonian or Pines Express pump white steam as they hurry to a south-west where they will be when I am having my tea. The old county boundary is so close that in five minutes you can walk out of Worcestershire into Warwickshire and back again. And if you set off in any direction but north, Longbridge is closer to quiet field corners 'where the flies gather and old horses shake their sides'[4] than it is to the city. In Longbridge, in the 1950s, you always feel as if you are on the edge of something, something vital – a continuous sensation of about-to-be.

Running through these scenes is the A38, the Bristol Road, on its way to Worcester (and eventually, I suppose, to Bristol). For much of its line the Bristol Road is a boulevard, one of a number in Birmingham which reflect progressive planning in the 1920s, with a chestnut-shaded central reservation that the trams have all to themselves. The trams turn at Rednal, a mile or so south, where the terminus is a stately loop fringed by elaborate iron shelters and overlooked by a wavy ridge of pointed hills. These are the Lickeys.

'In all the Green Border-land of the Black Country,' wrote Elihu Burritt in 1868, 'there are no hills more grateful and delightful for airing one's body and soul than the Lickey cluster, overlooking Bromsgrove.' Burritt had been born into a poor, devout family in New Britain, Connecticut, in 1810. An avid reader in childhood, he became a linguist and campaigner for causes that included the abolition of slavery and universal brotherhood. He was partly self-taught, having in his teens apprenticed himself in the local forge after the death of his father. Swinging a hammer on the anvil was combined with continuing studies in mathematics, Latin, French and Greek.[5] When in 1865 Abraham Lincoln appointed him Consular Agent for the United States in Birmingham, the 'learned blacksmith' (as Longfellow called him) found himself in a realm of forges, which he toured on foot and about which he wrote in his report to the US government at the end of his consular term. Around 'the smoky district' was a 'green border-land' that included the Lickey Hills. Burritt was struck by the Lickeys' resemblance to the Highlands – hills clad in 'genuine Scotch firs and larches' and carpeted with springy heather. On any summer day when the sun shines, he said, the Lickeys 'are set to the music of merry voices of boys and girls, and older children who feel young on the purple heather at fifty'.[6] In 1888 Birmingham's Society for the Preservation of Open Spaces bought Rednal Hill and presented it to the city for public recreation. Other hills and adjoining areas were acquired through gifts and purchases. The coming of trams made them easily accessible to Brummy day trippers who could frequent wood-built tearooms evocative of Tyrolean mountain lodges. By mid-morning on Easter Monday 1924 around ten thousand people were queuing in Navigation Street for Lickey trams. When the trams are scrapped in 1952 some of them have covered more miles back and forth to Rednal than the distances to be travelled by Apollo spacecraft on their moon journeys in the next decade.

From the top of Bilberry Hill it is said that on the clearest days and with the keenest eyes you can see the glint of the Severn estuary. I never see this myself, but reason while out walking the dog that if it is true then it means that we are, in a way, sort of, within sight of the sea, and therefore, in a sense, at the seaside. Casuistical this may be, but the idea is faintly comforting during the fifty weeks of the year when the sweet-and-sour tang of scorching paint and welded metal and the thumps, clangs and plumes of steam make it obvious that we are next to the Austin. In any case, while Longbridge cannot really be claimed as seaside, there is no doubt about the nearness of the Malvern Hills. Their purple humps are easily seen from Lickey, and a Midland Red bus will take you to them. From there, after a long steep scramble through rocks, rowan trees and gorse, you can look into Wales.

We go to Wales in 1955, staying in a borrowed caravan on the Gower Peninsula, overlooking Rhossili Bay. I have never been anywhere like this before. Rhossili has a huge sweep of beach, a tidal island, sand dunes from which to jump and pretend you can fly, a stream to dam, the story of Catherine of Braganza's lost treasure ship, and a hill.

Rhossili Down rises abruptly behind the caravan. You scramble over a drystone wall silvered by snails with stripy shells, and there it is – a scarp of red sandstone clad in turf and bracken, whirring with grasshoppers and smelling of sheep. On the first evening my father and I climb it. At the top, circled by a buzzard, we sit to watch the sun set. Near by are bumps and oddly placed stones. As usual, my father has a map.

The stones, he says, looking at it, are known locally as Swine Houses. I think of pigs, but in a series of steps which I do not entirely understand he explains that the swine began as 'sweyne', and the houses aren't really houses but 'howes'. So the mounds are Sweyne's Howes, whoever Sweyne was and whatever a howe might be. My father thinks they are burial chambers, and that they might be several thousand years old.

I take this in with a shiver. At the far end of Rhossili Down we have seen some overgrown concrete hut bases which date from the war, before I was born, and are therefore Very Old. Time before birth, indeed, is another kind of unconsciousness which has lately begun to keep me awake. But several thousand years? Aside from that, was Sweyne buried here? *Is he still buried here?* The sun sinks, becoming an orange blister on the horizon. In its last seconds the bleb is visibly shrinking, witness to a turning world.

It is cooler now, and I am a little scared. We stand, and set off down the hill. Now and then I look over my shoulder. Back in the caravan it is safe and warm. The Calor gas lamps have been lit and give off a comforting smell.

Swine Houses are the least of it. A couple of days later my father reads aloud from a book. Somewhere hereabouts is a cave, Goat's Hole Cave at Paviland, where in 1823 a geologist called William Buckland discovered the bones of extinct animals together with a human skeleton, ceremonially buried with ivory ornaments and perforated sea shells, and caked in red ochre. Buckland believed the bones to be those of a woman, so the find became known as the Red Lady.[7] *The Red Lady of Paviland.* I repeat this to myself, because it sounds thrilling, although the book says that the lady turned out to be a man. On the last day of the holiday we set out to look for the cave. It isn't easy. Even to see the entrance you must approach over rocks from seaward, and you can do this only at low tide. We fail to find it, and are likewise thwarted the following year.

In my tenth year there is a break from holidays in Wales. Instead there is to be a fortnight in Guernsey, and we are to travel by air. The news brings on a kind of fever. What is it like to fly? Seeking a hint of the sensation I repeatedly jump off the garage roof, pester my father and pore over flying maps he brought back from the war. Eventually the day arrives. We are being driven to Elmdon Airport, through Hall Green and Acocks Green, along roads lined with mountain ash trees afire with berries. Elmdon (I later realize) is the place evoked by J. B. Priestley in the opening of his wartime aircraft factory novel *Daylight on Saturday*.[8] It has a white art deco terminal with a curved façade suggesting an ocean liner and cantilevered canopies outspread at the sides. Parked close by is the aircraft in which we are to fly. It is a Dakota, and like Priestley's novel it dates from 1943. I did not know this at the time, of course, but such is the fineness of aviation's written record that one can trace the machine's history. After so much anticipation the flight itself seems straightforward, perhaps because for much of it we are in cloud and there is little to see. But the Dakota is wonderfully noisy, and towards the end the friendly stewardess offers each passenger a boiled sweet. Sucking it, she explains, will help equalize pressures as the aeroplane descends. We break cloud, and through wriggles of moisture on the window we glimpse waves breaking on rocks and rows of glasshouses.

We stay in St Peter Port, not far from Victor Hugo's house in Rue Hautville. There are fine beaches, with exotic shells and pebbles. The water is warmer than it is around Wales. At intervals around the coast stand concrete cylindrical observation towers built during the recent German occupation. They have tiers of horizontal slits, like multiple mouths with fixed grins. Tall, tapered, flat topped, they might be cousins of Easter Island statues.

One afternoon we walk to the north-east of the island to look at a prehistoric site about which my father has read. It is called Le Déhus.[9] Outside there is not much to see – a grassy mound about sixty feet across that turns out to be mainly restoration not much older than the German-built towers.[10] Within, a different story: entrance is through a passage formed of edge-set rocks covered by massive flat slabs. Nowadays it is all very tidy and internally lit, but my memory is of a hot, silent afternoon, collecting the key from a nearby farm to unlock an iron grille, a hand-held lamp and going in bent double. At first the passageway is narrow, with side openings to small chambers; further on the roof lifts and the passage broadens into more generous space. The book my father has been reading tells of things found here during excavations begun in 1837: masses of limpet shells, pottery vessels, a polished green serpentine axe, and the remains of perhaps eleven people.[11] Crouching there in the dark it is not difficult to imagine them, or indeed to imagine what would happen should a capstone suddenly fall. My father holds the lamp up at an angle. There looking back at me from the underside of a capstone is a face. It is looking at me. It has been staring down for six thousand years.[12]

Back in Birmingham, I begin excavations in the garden, soon abandoned, and open a museum in the front room. The museum has two exhibits: a fossil from Whitby, contributed by an aunt, and a prehistoric flint tool from Arkansas presented by an elderly schoolteacher with silvery hair who still wears starched wing collars. The fossil (an ammonite) is for the moment off the scale. I can just about cope with the flint. It is, the gentleman tells me, about ten thousand years old. My mother reads the label, smiles indulgently and says that I misheard. It can't be that old. But I did not, and it is.

Time, I am beginning to see, is a big place. Yet whatever time is, it does not seem to be uniformly calibrated. There is infant's time, child's time, time that flashes past and time that drags, lifetime, family time, remembered time, recorded time, geological time, cyclical time, once upon a time, deep time. And some of these times are, so to speak, telescopic, one nested in the next. This is brought home soon after Jack and Bess retire. In 1962 they return to Sussex, to a village just along the coast from Brighton where their marriage began all those years before. At first Jack goes for long walks on Bost Hill, and devotes himself to his new garden. But within three years he is dead. Gas and shrapnel back in 1917, or more probably the twenty Players he has smoked every day since, have taken their toll. My father takes his father's ashes up on to the Downs near Chanctonbury Ring, where now they mingle with others a hundred lifetimes older.

That was the summer when the Ministry of Works sent a young archaeology graduate and some workmen to examine part of a Roman fort near my school. On spare afternoons I went to help – or, more strictly, to hang around. The dig provided an indestructible alibi for absence from compulsory games. But sometimes there were real jobs to do. There were instructive moments, as when an eminent academic came to give opinion on the coarse pottery (most Roman sites yield this by the bucketful), found it unedifying and ordered most of it to be thrown away.

Intrigued, I wrote off for the Council for British Archaeology's Calendar of Excavations. Back came some duplicated pages looking a bit like a parish magazine, containing a list of forthcoming excavations which needed volunteers. I pored over it for days. It was full of magical names. Which one to choose, where to go? The Iron Age hillfort at Pilsden Pen? The Roman fort at Cripplegate? The world of medieval peasants at Wharram Percy? An Anglo-Saxon settlement at Mucking? One name I knew well: Burry Holmes, the tidal island at the end of Rhossili Bay. Here were said to be traces of an Iron Age settlement, and a medieval hermitage. I wrote to the director, who replied in a scrawly letter in reddish-brown ink. The handwriting was illegible. Hoping for the best, I assumed he meant 'come', and when the summer term ended, I went.

No Land Rover met the bus, and the insistence of my mother that I would need all that my wardrobe contained meant that together with the heavy canvas tent I was over-laden for the two-mile trek across the sand dunes. When I arrived, the tide was in, the island cut off, and it was raining. After two hours watching fit young people in shorts moving about purposefully on the far side of the tidal channel, I was able to cross, feeling a complete fool as I picked my way between rock pools to introduce myself to a supervisor who was not expecting me. Too tired for explanations, I pitched my tent, crawled in and fell asleep. Some time later I was awake again. It was still light. The tent had collapsed, its canvas moulded to my body like a shroud. Shadows across the canvas indicated several people standing outside. At length, a resigned voice said: 'It's that new young man from Birmingham.'

At the end of the first fortnight came a rest day. Another newcomer, a student teacher, had the day off too, and on that bright Sunday morning we set out to walk the five-odd miles to the Paviland Cave. The tide was down, and we went straight to it.

Inside looking out, you see the Bristol Channel. As human time goes, this is a new picture. If you had stood here about ten thousand years ago, the climate would have been warming, the sea level rising, and a little to the north land bulged upwards by the weight of the recent ice sheet still formed a causeway to Ireland. A couple of thousand years earlier there was more land – from Paviland you could have walked to France – and a spasm of cold was asserting itself after an interlude of warmth. At 18,000 years back the glacial ice front lay just to the north and the view was of polar desert, on land exposed by a sea much lower than today's. At 29,000 the scene was different again: grassland, with groups of mammoth, horse, bison and woolly rhinoceros moving about upon the plain. On some days then, at some times of year, in some years, you might even have seen people, or a curl of smoke. But not many people. There may then have been no more than a few hundred people in all of Britain, and in arctic 22,000 BC, none. If something like a speed camera had been fitted in the cave's entrance during the years between, its cumulative record might have registered fewer people than drink in the Black Horse on a single evening.

Such swings of climate are common. In the past 650,000 years there have been eight large glacial pulsations, within which at least eleven lesser and more small-time cycles were interspersed. The norm for the greater part of that time has been cold tundra – something like modern Siberia north of the forested taiga. The present temperate episode in which we live is fleeting. The land is changing, too. Ten thousand years ago Britain was not 'the British Isles' but the edge of a European peninsula. Where the North Sea now lies there was land stretching to Scandinavia: a region several times larger than Britain today, with hills, lakes and rivers, a landscape where the Thames joined the Rhine, and where people lived. Around seven to eight thousand years ago most of the plain had gone, although there seems to have been an island nearly as big as Denmark just sixty miles or so off what we now know as the Lincolnshire coast.[13] Land loss continued, so that in a few centuries more the North Sea was not so very different in extent from what it is now. Global sea level has been rising and falling for the last two and a half million years, rhythmically transforming Britain from island to peninsula and back again.[14] Change is what climate and sea-level do. Nature is change. An ecosystem's destiny is always to be in the process of becoming something else.[15]

Humanity's achievement is to be the one animal species out of upwards of one and a half million currently named on the planet to have discovered this story; its weakness, to suppose itself to be the story's subject. Such self-consciousness is nevertheless part of the story, for mankind is the product of an evolutionary trend in which cultural adaptations have been persistently selected. As Bernard Campbell has put it, 'Animals adapt to their environment by changing their genes; humans have come to change their environment to preserve their genes.'[16] Except, of course, that our ability to contemplate genes does not acquit us from membership of a natural world governed by laws, one of which is that sooner or later all species become extinct. Indeed, for a creature which has made a career out of altering environments to further its own interests, mankind is oddly unwilling to engage with environmental realities, from the Book of Genesis onwards imagining Nature as its object, rather than itself as Nature's subject.[17] Nowhere is this presumption more evident than in relation to ecology and climate change, where notions of 'restoration ecology' and 'nature conservation' – in themselves warranted reactions to global despoliation – reinforce an idea that we know what Nature *ought* to be doing. Assumptions about global warming focus on carbon at the expense of other issues and the amplitude of longer trends. Green radicalism's militant assumption of a once perfect planet with which mankind has broken faith[18] is no less hubristic.

Humility would be wiser. But perhaps it is too soon, and maybe too late, for that. The knowledge that Earth's life has been developing for over three billion years has been acquired in less than three lifetimes, and on the day in 1965 when I stood looking out of the Paviland Cave at 3.20 in the afternoon (by a quirk, as I was writing this my long-forgotten post-card describing the day turned up), the climatic oscillations outlined above were themselves only just then being discovered.

Prehistory itself is a fairly new idea. When William Buckland stepped into the cave in 1823 the word did not exist.* There was no need for it, although some already had their suspicions that the world was older than hitherto supposed. The eighteenth-century antiquary John Frere, for instance, was tempted to refer what we now think of as Palaeolithic tools (Palaeolithic – the Stone Age: the earliest and longest stage in human development) 'to a very remote period indeed; even beyond that of the present world'.[19] Another scholar had argued that the age of the world was 75,000 years. The word 'scientist' itself had only been coined a few decades before.

If scientific understanding of the past was to grow it required a framework. One of those who provided it was James Hutton, who in 1788 had presented evidence not only that the Earth was many millions of years old, but also that the rocks at its surface were in a state of constant renewal. Hutton's theory – strengthened by William Smith's map which classified geological strata, published in 1815, and by Charles Lyell's *Principles of Geology* (1831–3) – left no place for a biblical Creation. The Earth could not have been made at one stroke, Hutton argued, but was being perpetually re-formed through a cycle of erosion, eruption, sedimentation and uplift.

While Lyell was a late convert to the antiquity of Man, he and Hutton provided Charles Darwin with the deep time in which biological evolution could be entertained.[20] Even so, despite mounting evidence from different sources for the immense antiquity of the universe, human history remained trapped inside a Creationist bubble which would not be convincingly popped until the 1850s.[21] In 1823, it was still widely considered that the Old Testament did provide the early world with a continuous story, and that by reading the story backwards you could calculate when the Creation occurred. Scholars had worked on this for centuries. The resulting date, several authorities agreed, was 4004 BC. In

* The word *préhistoire* seems to have been coined in 1833, but came into general use after the publication in 1865 of John Lubbock's *Prehistoric Times*.

1819, therefore, the year in which Buckland was appointed Reader in Geology at the University of Oxford, the world was 5,823 years old, and still in its Sixth Age.

Ebullient and enquiring, accustomed to ride about on a black mare bedangled with bags of fossils, Buckland was also a clerk in holy orders, to whom it seemed logical that scripturally attested events such as the Great Flood should be witnessed in the geological record.[22] In 1819 his fieldwork took him to the Lickey Hills (the wavy ridge that overlooks Longbridge) where he found water-borne deposits of 'such exact resemblance' to others he had seen in Warwickshire and Oxfordshire that it was 'impossible' not to refer them all 'to one and the same common cause, viz. a recent deluge acting universally and at the same period over the whole globe'.[23]

Another who thought along these lines was Baron Georges Leopold Cuvier,[24] anatomist and Chancellor of the University of Paris, of whose *Essay on the Theory of the Earth* (1822) Buckland approved.[25] 'If there be any one fact thoroughly established by geological investigation,' Cuvier wrote, 'it is the certainty of the low antiquity of the human race.' Cuvier was one of a number of academics who believed that there had been a series of extinctions as a result of periodic 'transient deluges' after which new forms of life appeared. Since humans were present only on the last occasion, there were no witnesses to the earlier inundations. Catastrophism, itself a house of many rooms, was adumbrated by two of Cuvier's pupils, who proposed a 'remarkable system of twenty-seven successive and separate acts of creation and catastrophes'.[26]

The year before he went to Paviland, Buckland visited Kirkdale, in Yorkshire, drawn by reports of a cave that contained hyena bones.[27] The reports were true. At Kirkdale the Hodge Beck cuts through a limestone hillside, exposing a system of caves rich in ancient bones. The hyenas, he first surmised, had been trapped there by the universal flood. The cave also contained bones belonging to lion, tiger, hippopotamus, elephant and other exotic animals, some now extinct. Such remains were familiar from 'diluvial' gravels in various other parts of the country, where their presence had hitherto been explained as the debris of drowned creatures whose carcasses had drifted hither and yon around the planet before the universal ocean receded.[28] Yet at Kirkdale this argument wouldn't work, for if the hyenas had retreated into the cave in the face of rising water, they must have been locally resident when the deluge began. Likewise, if the other bones were the refuse of hyena scavenging, then the same held good for them. Had lions really prowled pre-Flood Yorkshire? Perhaps the climate then had been warmer. Or maybe beasts now local to Africa had once ranged more widely? It was with such thoughts in mind that Buckland went to Paviland in the following year. Here too there were bones of extinct animals, but many of them belonged to *cold*-climate creatures like reindeer, and mammoth. Buckland side-stepped this by declaring his Red Lady to have been a Romano-Briton, and the mammoth to have been dug up by the Romans and placed with the burial.

Doubts about Old Testament chronology grew. The observation of more and more remains of departed creatures, sometimes intercalated between man-made objects, made it increasingly a question how so many geological events and climatic swings of the supposed pre-Flood epoch could be accommodated in the first six chapters of Genesis. Geologists were also beginning to have second thoughts about the 'diluvial' sands and gravels. Fourteen years after Buckland visited Paviland, a new theory was advanced to explain them: the action of ice.

As geological knowledge expanded, geologists began to notice that some rocks occur far from the places where they outcrop. Various ideas were put forward to explain these foreign pieces (the geological term for them is 'erratics'), one being that they had travelled in icebergs set adrift by the Flood and came to rest when the icebergs thawed.[29] It was noticed that glaciers, too, carried deposits scoured from the land across which they travelled, and released them when they melted. Glacial erosion, moreover, leaves distinctive landforms and marks: U-shaped valleys, rocks smoothed at one end and roughened at the other, striated surfaces, and dumps of drift where ice retreats. Such effects could be studied in the Alps, Norway or Canada where glaciers were still active, but by the late 1820s it was coming to be recognized that ice-modified landscapes could also be seen in areas where historically no ice had lain.[30] Louis Agassiz, a proponent of this theory, invited Buckland to Switzerland to study the effects of glaciation at first hand. Buckland inferred that at some time in the past there had been an ice age.

Conclusive evidence for the ancientness of humanity was meanwhile accumulating. In central France, Auguste Aymard, an enthusiast for archives and fossils, and the mayor of Vals-près-le-Puy, published evidence for the presence of human fossils embedded in volcanic breccia. In northern France, Marcel-Jérôme Rigollot, a physician based in Amiens, found flint tools associated with the bones of elephants deep in undisturbed gravel. And not far away at Abbeville Jacques Boucher de Perthes was making similar discoveries. Although at the time it was questioned by some whether such flints had really been 'worked' at all, and it was suggested by others (paradoxically) that they were modern fakes that had been planted,[31] Boucher de Perthes saw that bones of extinct mammals were mingled with stone tools in geologically stratified deposits at depths of many feet. The clarity of the geostratigraphy enabled deductions which put the pre-biblical making of the artefacts beyond doubt, and Boucher de Perthes said so in a succession of publications.[32] However (and not for the last time in this book), whether or not something is accepted depends not only on the evidence on which it rests but on the perspectives behind its reception. Members of the Cuvier school saw no reason to attend to Boucher de Perthes' findings, partly because his field observations were accompanied by all kinds of baroque speculations that could easily be dismissed, but also because they were held to be conceptually impossible. But late in the 1850s there came a 'sudden change of opinion'.[33]

The standard explanation for this 'sudden and complete revolution' runs something like this: for a quarter of a century geologists had been aware of claims from various parts of Europe for the occurrence of bones of man, or man-made things, in collocation with remains of extinct animals like bear, elephant or rhinoceros. However, many of these finds had been made in caves, and since caves could have been occupied at different times, things found within them could have been mixed up by flowing water and other processes; there was consequent reluctance to accept such evidence as conclusive. But in 1858–9 came the discovery and excavation of a 'virgin cave' containing animal bones and stone implements in a sealed deposit.

The cave was found in January 1858 in the course of quarrying at Windmill Hill, Brixham in Devon. With funds from the Royal Society and oversight by members of Britain's geological elite,[34] a controlled excavation was begun in July under the on-the-spot charge of William Pengelly, a Cornish-born mathematics tutor and geologist based in Torquay. Pengelly was self-taught, having been put to work on his father's coastal vessel at the age of twelve. A voracious reader, he used his spare time to study mathematics, later moving to Torquay where he opened a school and fostered all kinds of beneficial enterprises – a Mechanics' Institute, reading clubs, local societies. He became interested in geology, immersed himself in the new science, lectured widely, and by 1858 was ready both by reputation and in skill to grasp the opportunity that arose when Dr Hugh Falconer of the Geological Society of London invited him to oversee the fieldwork in Brixham cave.[35] Pengelly applied his mathematical expertise to the invention of a system of recording which would enable every piece of bone or artefact to be provenanced to that part of the cave deposit from which it came.[36] The result, as Pengelly afterwards recalled, was the recovery of 'flint implements commingled with remains of the mammoth and his companions ... in such a way as to render it impossible to doubt that man occupied Devonshire before the extinction of the cave mammals'.[37]

Sir Charles Lyell summed up what this meant in a lecture to the British Association in September 1859. 'No subject', he began, 'has excited more curiosity and general interest among geologists and the public than the question of the antiquity of the human race.' The Brixham finds corroborated the evidence that had been accumulating at the hands of Boucher de Perthes and Rigollot in France, and which Lyell had been to see for himself earlier in the summer. In result there was no longer room for doubt that a 'vast lapse of ages' lay between the era in which the fossil implements were framed and the Roman invasion of Gaul.[38]

The Brixham excavation – and with it Pengelly's foresight – thus became a moment of 'scientific awakening'.[39] Pengelly went on to undertake important excavations in the much larger 'ossiferous cave' at Torquay now known as Kent's Cavern. But there is a twist in the tale. The stratigraphic security of the Brixham deposits, the clinching evidence cited by Lyell and Falconer, has since been questioned. It appears that the deposits were not, after all, protected from the kinds of intermingling that had aroused scepticism at other sites, and that the excavators were probably aware of this – or at least they had the experience to work it out if they had been so minded. Instead, what seems to have happened is that an elite group of scientists, aware of an idea whose time had come, aware too of their collective credibility, selected the Brixham opportunity as the occasion to state the case.[40] However this may be, Lyell was aware that the pre-biblical existence of Man rested in a larger theoretical context. As he put it towards the end of his lecture to the British Association in 1859: 'On this difficult and mysterious subject, a work will shortly appear by Mr Charles Darwin, the result of twenty years observation and experiment ... by which he has been led to the conclusion that those powers of nature which give rise to races and permanent varieties in animals and plants, are the same as those which, in much longer periods, produce species, and, in a still longer series of ages, give rise to differences of generic rank.'[41]

The Origin of Species was published two months later. For anyone living through those days the conceptual implications were shattering.[42]

Imagine early-nineteenth-century antiquaries and historians to have
occupied a corridor six yards long – the six yards being proportional to
biblical time. In 1859 the room's far wall (already weakened by Hutton,
Rigollot and the rest) gives way. In that instant the view down the
passage lengthens from yards to miles. Modern science measures the
length. In Britain, the corridor runs for more than 280 miles. In Africa,
it is over two thousand.

Returning to school for the autumn term, I decide to read archaeology at university. In the level tones that friends use when they are telling
you something for your own good, my housemaster warns against this.
Archaeology is a pseudo-science, a rag-bag for dilettantes. And in any
case, there are no jobs. I should study a proper subject like English or
history, and then turn to archaeology if I must (although the implication is that by then the fever will have subsided). But being eighteen and
immersed in Eric Wood's *Field Guide to Archaeology*, I go ahead anyway.

Wood's book is beguiling, but not problem-free. When explaining
a crinkle-crankle or telling you what a bee-bole is, his *Field Guide* is a
delight, but its commentaries on prehistory leave me baffled: 'here was
found a sequence of occupation, divided by layers of slabs fallen from
the cave roof in the glacial phases of the last (Würm) glaciation, from
Mousterian to the Gravettian which became the native Creswellian
culture of Britain, and from then to the Mesolithic'.[43] What does this
mean? About Würm I know a little – that was the last of the four great
Alpine cold epochs proposed by Albrecht Penck and Eduard Bruckner
about which we are currently hearing in geography classes,[44] and which
work just then in progress in Cambridge and Chicago will soon drasti-
cally modify. But what is Mousterian, or Gravettian? And how, exactly,
did Gravettian become Creswellian? Prehistory seems more like an
incantation than a science.

From visits to the library I find that many of these names derive from
a classification of human cultural development by the French anthropologist Gabriel de Mortillet, who realized that different types of stone
tool and the remains of particular groupings of prehistoric animals
sometimes occur together, and that in places it is possible to put these
assemblages into relative sequence. The names come from the sites where
this was done. Thus 'Mousterian' derives from a cave at Le Moustier
in the Dordogne. Mortillet's culture-period theory supposed Man's
evolution to have followed a line from primitivism to intellectual pre-
eminence. Hence, crudely wrought objects should be older than things
finely wrought. So far, so clear, yet Wood's conversational informality

– 'The earlier men did not disappear at once, for the Chatelperronians absorbed a few Mousterian ideas' – is unsettling. What does he mean by 'a few Mousterian ideas', and how were they absorbed? According to Wood's time-chart, the third phase of 'Mousterian' lasted nearly 25,000 years. Whoever the Chatelperronians were, they seem not to have been very quick on the uptake.

In July 1966 I am all set to read history and archaeology at a provincial university. However, a freak set of A-level results takes me instead to Oxford in the following year, and since Oxford does not then teach archaeology I settle for English. On my first evening an old hand takes me to the Gardener's Arms in an area of condemned housing near Paradise Square. My first terms, he tells me, will be devoted to Old English and Latin, the better to read epics like *Beowulf* and the *Aeneid* in their original languages. Lying awake that night the soft chiming of railway trucks carried on the west wind makes me think of Northfield and my grandparents. The changeability of wind also recalls Jude on the Berkshire downs at dusk, looking at the 'halo or glow-fog' formed by the distant lights of Christminster and imagining himself joined to the city by the arrival of a breeze which had been in the city 'between one and two hours ago, floating along the streets, pulling round the weather cocks'.[45]

Down in Sussex Bess lives through her seventies, caring for two older sisters, sustained by Adam's ale and gentle stoicism. My father has moved to a parish in Surrey, where six-thousand-year-old flint tools lie in the upcast from newly dug graves. Every Tuesday, his day off, he drives down to see her. In vacations I go too, and it is during one of these visits that Bess starts to talk about the Battle of Waterloo. Her grandfather had been there. He had told his son – Bess's father, my great-grandfather – about things he saw. Bess's father told her, and now she is telling me. Nearly two centuries have been jumped in three conversations involving four individuals.

Roughly the same interval lay between the detachment of the provinces of Britain from the Roman Empire early in the fifth century and the arrival of Augustine and his mission at the end of the sixth. Events in those two centuries apparently had greater long-term consequences for Britain than during any other corresponding period (not the least of them being the arrival of the Anglo-Saxons, with whose irregular verbs I am wrestling at Oxford), although what those events were is a matter about which historians argue. Yet it appears that such a gap could be bridged by conversations between three or four well-placed people. If we extend that idea, the number of people theoretically needed to relay some impression of the last ceremony held at Stonehenge, and so shed light on the question of what one of the world's oldest buildings was actually *for*, might be as few as fifty – less than a busload.

And yet, of course, this can't be right. For transmission to occur there would have to be consciousness of something to transmit – a message, which even if it existed would not behave like an imperishable artefact passing from hand to hand. Rather, it would subsist in Chinese whispering, continuously transforming in reaction to questions asked, contexts changing and influences absorbed. Nor could it be a simple linear descent, increasingly smudged but maybe ultimately recognizable, for as time passed the process of transmission would become ever more diffuse and eventually dissolve.

Similar cautions apply to recent events. Whatever it was that Bess's grandfather said he saw at Waterloo cannot now be credited with an exact historicity. About 185,000 men took part in that battle. Each saw it differently, and all – Wellington, Blücher and Napoleon unexcepted – selectively. The influence of context on historical sources is widely understood. Not so well accepted is the tendency of eyewitness accounts to factual inaccuracy. In any case, it is a question whether Bess's memories of memories will add much to what was written in letters, diaries or dispatches on the evening of 18 June 1815. Even those original sources cannot necessarily be read as straightforward narrative: continuity of text does not guarantee continuity of meaning.[46]

These are things to think about at Oxford, where the English syllabus introduces me not only to Old English, but to Middle English, to the history of language and linguistics, to Gawain, to myth and to stories. If excavation is one avenue into the past, words and language form another. I wonder, in a vague way, taking text and oral tradition together, if we might characterize the voices of the last two or three hundred years as variably audible – medieval utterance as breaking up, the silences growing longer with distance – and prehistory as soundless.

Unless, that is, we are hoping for easy answers or listening for the wrong things. If we are less literalistic, a present past might be murmuring all around us – in names, in place names, in language itself, in the print-through of legend and mythology. This might be mere aleatoric jabber, but there seems to be a point where public and private memory meet, whereafter a body of ideas, sayings, ideas, stories, tunes – some ancient, some new, a collection part random, part culturally selected, part trivial, part seminal – is borne along as a more or less undifferenti-ated mass.

Like some feature of oceanic circulation, a conflux of deep and shal-low, warm and cool, drawing from both but behaving as neither, might memories of between fifty and several thousand years ago become con-temporaneous? If so, in result, do some names resonate with ideas, and archaeology with stories? For instance, what is it about a journey that pierces us? Odysseus, Maelduin – Shackleton? Is it that beneath our surface there is the anamnesis of millennia of travel from one hunting territory to another?

A story written down in the twelfth century tells that the wizard Merlin brought the stones of Stonehenge from Ireland. Is it coinci-dence that many of the stones *were* fetched from afar, and from the west? A substantial part of the monument is built of rocks brought from the Preseli Hills in Wales. Stuart Piggott's suggestion that the legend embodied a folk memory has attracted little support from folk-lore scholars, who point out that gods, giants and wizards were routinely credited with the construction of megaliths. Yet it is not clear why a general pattern of alleged truth should invalidate the possibility of an individual truth. Maybe the busload of messengers is not such a wild idea after all.

This kind of speculation does not go down well with my tutors, who are frustrated by my lack of interest in palatal diphthongization or Dryden, and unwilling to listen to wild ideas about folklore. In any case, May 1970 finds me revising in a feverish effort to compensate for having devoted my time to other things during the three years that have passed in a flash. Yet even during the longueurs of revising Chaucer and Tudor lyrics, the possible connotations of Arthurian legend or of the head which speaks in George Peele's *Voice from the Well* will not go away. 'The sword in the stone is a perfect image of the mystery of smelting metals.'[47]

Examinations near, the weather grows hotter. Stuck indoors, revis-ing the history of English, my thoughts drift to the midlands where there are mounds bearing mysterious names like Baslow – 'Bassa's *hlaw*', *hlaw* being an Old English word for hill or burial mound. Wolferlow is 'Wulfhere's mound', Offlow 'Offa's mound', and so on. Most barrows were raised in prehistory, but Wulfhere, Andhere and Offa are Anglo-Saxon names. Is it possible that some of these tumuli remember the very individuals they cover? Easily kindled, such speculation is just as easily doused. Think back, for instance, to those shivery Swine Houses on Rhossili Down. The name looks Scandinavian. Svein was a Danish and Norse name, and 'howe' comes from the Old Scandinavian *haugr*, a hillock or burial mound. This much is tolerably certain. But what does it denote? Did a Norse venturer called Sweyne die hereabouts? For a Northman this would be a good place to finish. Or perhaps Sweyne had settled here, and lent his name to existing mounds on his land? Or there again, he might have come from England, where Nordic names like Gunnhildr, Tostig and Swegn were fashionable in the eleventh century, and much of England was ruled by men of Scandinavian descent. During the reign of Cnut (1016–35), indeed, England and Denmark had been governed together, with cultural ramifications that lasted so long that an English Sweyne would be just as plausible in the twelfth century, when Henry I made inroads into southern Wales. (Prehistoric burial places could be repeatedly renamed: years later I read that quite a few prehistoric barrows in East Anglia bear the names of Norman and later medieval landowners.)[48] Plausibility, however, is just guess-work which is not in conflict with the facts at our disposal. In any case, whoever Sweyne was (and we don't have to believe in him at all – the name might be a mishearing, or derive from myth), the mounds originally had nothing to do with the period which awarded the name. They are prehistoric, heaped up longer before Sweyne's day than we live after. All of which shows that place names change (the 'Longbridge Estate' in 1920 is now the 'Austin Village'), and since new names (in Britain, 'new' generally means 'up to a thousand years old') often supplant older ones, the chronology of place names seldom converts straightforwardly into a chronology for the places themselves.

Revision for the history of English further reminds me that Britain's landscape has been named in successive languages. Like layers of wind-blown sand, each coating has sometimes masked and sometimes merged with earlier toponymy, one layer smoothing into another. Of the earliest names there seem to be not many. But prominent among them are names of rivers and hills.[49] There are names on my Longbridge horizon in this class: Malvern; Arden; I wonder about the River Rea that washes past the Austin; even Barr, where Jack and Bess rented the bungalow in 1943. Rivers like Severn and Avon flow through time as well as landscape. There are sounds in Derwent, Humber, Thames and Trent that go back at least to the first millennium BC, and probably – like the Granta of Rupert Brooke's Grantchester – further.[50]

How much further? The burial found at Paviland was of a young man who is now thought to have died between 33,000 and 34,000 years ago.

This dating is the result of recent reanalysis using high-precision methods that were unavailable even a few years ago.[51] Until recently other objects and bones were held to indicate that the cave was intermittently visited by people, bears and hyenas in following millennia. One of the latest was a piece of whittled ivory, for which a radiocarbon determination suggested a date between 18,600 and 19,700 BC.[52] The date has since been questioned;[53] if it were in the right area the ivory's owner's presence would have coincided with a period of glacial advance, when iced winds blew, glaciers returned and the hunters retreated south. Jacquetta Hawkes wrote that we cannot have inherited a single syllable of one name from the epoch of the 'Red Man'. She was probably right, for when the ice melted about 12,500 years ago and the hunters came back, names, language and the land itself had changed. We know nothing of their speech. I wish I had paid more attention to the classes on linguistics, and the study of tongues that no longer exist by working backwards from those that do. But it is too late: on a bright morning in June 1970 I am walking into town for my first exam, and time has run out.

Arriving at the Examination Schools, uncharacteristically tidy in subfusc, fountain pen poised, I have no right to feel composed. Off we go: fourteen three-hour papers, morning and afternoon, one after the other. Between papers I keep revising, in the porters' lodge, in the bath, on the lavatory, anywhere, the champion of Chaucer or Crabbe until that paper is done and on to the next. I settle into a rhythm and it becomes a bit like a job. At the end, on Tuesday 16 June, we step out into Merton Street, on the threshold of the rest of our lives.

Results are announced a few weeks later. I have a second. The news pleases Bess. It pleases me, too, for after so much backsliding I know how lucky I am to emerge with any degree at all. For the same reason, the result seems ill deserved, almost illusory. As for being on a threshold – threshold to what?

For reasons that are not part of the story, finding an answer to this question does not become pressing until the following autumn, by when I am married and penniless, and it has become very pressing indeed. We are living in a remote, thin-walled cottage in the Vale of York where winds gusting under the door make the carpet undulate. My wife teaches, is pregnant and will have to give up work at Christmas. I need a job.

Advertisements in local newspapers call for experience that I do not have. Looking at them, indeed, I fear that I am unqualified for anything.

Then a friend calls. For several years York Minster has been under emergency repair: there are fears for its stability, and great holes are being dug to enable the reinforcement of its foundations. Archaeologists are digging ahead of the engineers and contractors, but do so under pressure. They are short-handed. Would I be available to help for a few days?

On the following Monday morning I go over to York to introduce myself to the director. I am told that he is called Derek. At ten minutes to nine I arrive at the west end of York Minster and ask for directions. One of the contractor's men says that the archaeologists are based among the Portakabins beside the chapter house. He guides me. Inside, the nave is afforested with scaffolding, scented with cement and new-sawn wood, clamorous with banging and drills, dusty shadows pierced by spouts of welders' sparks. As we walk along a scaffolded catwalk, the plywood boards boom under our feet. Beneath, the cathedral floor is cut open, revealing outlines of buildings lying aslant three or four yards below. Sticking out of the excavation sides are what look like cream-coloured twigs and dowels. They are human bones.

We cross the north transept and pass into the north choir aisle. Derek emerges from a side passage. He is on his way to the dark room. Derek's expression is polite yet bears the impatience of one who lacks time for triviality. He cross-examines. Where have I dug? Have I done much surveying? Can I use a level? The answers I hear myself give do not sound convincing, and it is clear that I shall be on trial. He asks a colleague to escort me to an area being dug at the base of the north-west tower. Two people are already working here, and for the rest of the day we shovel earth, pick our way through cobbles, and clean and draw traces of a structure that adjoined a medieval gate into the precinct. Beneath run Roman walls. The contractors are keen to move in, the tempo brisk. Even so, at eleven we break for coffee round the corner at the Lite Bite, and in the afternoon when Great Peter sounds four, the din of drilling, hammering and banging subsides and yields to the first harmonies of choral evensong.

At the day's end, Derek reappears. Can I come back tomorrow?

At tomorrow's end I am again invited back. This continues until the end of the week, when we are paid – £20.00. 'Can you come back next week?' At the end of next week: 'Can you work through the weekend?' The contractors will take over this area next Monday whether we've finished or not.

We work through Saturday night. A last act on the chilly Sunday morning is to remove some tiles lining a Roman doorway. We do it as an afterthought, really, for hereabouts Roman tile occurs by the ton. However, tiles were sometimes stamped by the legion that made them, and complete specimens always invite a close look. So off they come.

As the first tile is eased away, the mason's trowel-marks are revealed in the mortar behind it. *Swish, swash, swosh*: the three splodges from his trowel might have been slapped on half a minute ago. The tile bears a stamp: LEG IX HISP – *Legio IX Hispana*, the Ninth (Spanish) Legion. Near the stamp is the paw-mark of a dog that wandered across the tile stack before the tiles were fired. The mason and the dog lived around 1,780 years ago. In these plain traces they are so close. I remember a poem by D. H. Lawrence.

> Things men have made with wakened hands, and put soft life into
> are awake through years with transferred touch, and go on glowing
> for long years.
> And for this reason, some old things are lovely
> warm still with the life of forgotten men who made them.[54]

The next week becomes a month, the month turns into another month. In the event I stay for three years. This is my real university.

My colleagues include students who join us in vacations, one or two locals, ne'er-do-wells, a couple of shipyard workers from Tyneside, novices and a few diggers from 'The Circuit' – a fluid network of lusty, roving figures who live by moving from one Ministry of Works-funded dig to another. Off duty in pubs or the Lite Bite, we talk about what we are finding, and what we think it means. Such talk, like all talk, is conditioned by things that 'everybody knows'. Topical in this connection (since we're working inside a former Roman fortress) is how the Anglo-Saxons took over southern Britain after the Romans left, which of course they must have done because we talk in English and England is full of places with Old English names. Other things we take for granted include migration and invasion as causes of cultural change, the Celtic west and the English east, central southern England as the mother country of classic sites in British prehistory,[55] and human development along a line from grunting savagery to enlightenment. Not all of us are convinced by the notion that archaeology's usefulness fades after the later Middle Ages, but this was evidently the prevailing view four years before when most of the upper deposits in the middle of the cathedral had been summarily shovelled away.

For middle-class children like me, many of these ideas had been formed from reading 1950s encyclopaedias, improving comics like the

Eagle or articles in the annuals given at Christmas that contained stories about bright children catching spies, advice on how to make a crystal set and cutaway diagrams of the Bristol Britannia. Only ten years before, the Ladybird Book *Stone Age Man in Britain* had advised young readers that if they could see the first hunter-gatherers who colonized Britain after the last ice age they 'should probably think that they were not human beings at all, because they were covered with hair and had fierce animal-like faces'. The account continued: 'These men of thousands of years ago were able to talk and think, but only in a very simple way.'[56] The Ladybird Book about William the Conqueror said that the Norman Conquest was a kind of destiny required for England's fulfilment, for after 'more than six hundred years of fear and uncertainty' England needed a strong king and William brought order and fair government.[57] In the chapters that follow a recurring theme will be how one generation's certainty becomes the fallacy of the next.

History's community of sources and methods might be likened to different senses or kinds of consciousness. Oral report could be history's ears, documents and science its thought, mythology the subconscious, archaeology the eyes and touch. While each supplies information in its own specialized way – synaesthesia apart, we do not listen with our eyes or smell with our ears – the senses are mutually reinforcing, disclosing more together than when used alone. Each new perception, moreover, modifies its predecessors, while evidence provided by one may enable new enquiry by another. Looking at how archaeology looks is thus our next step.

And Birmingham? Thomas Carlyle wrote of it to his brother on 10 August 1824: 'the whole is not without its attractions, as well as repulsions, of which when we meet, I will preach to you at large'.[58]

2

'THAT SECRET AND RESERVED FEELING'

'Is there anybody there?' said the Traveller,
  Knocking on the moonlit door;
And his horse in the silence champed the grasses
  Of the forest's ferny floor:
And a bird flew up out of the turret,
  Above the Traveller's head:
And he smote upon the door again a second time;
  'Is there anybody there?' he said.
But no one descended to the Traveller;
  No head from the leaf-fringed sill
Leaned over and looked into his grey eyes,
  Where he stood perplexed and still.

Walter de la Mare, 'The Listeners',
The Complete Poems of Walter de la Mare, 1969

In 1948 a ploughman working in north Norfolk turned up a lump of yellow metal. A friend told him that it was a bit of a brass bedstead. Someone else was not so sure; the ploughman took it to the keeper of Norwich Museum. Not a bedstead, said the keeper, but a torc – a prehistoric neck-ring. It was made of gold, and about two thousand years old. The find was made at Ken Hill in Snettisham, close to the Wash.

Excavations at the spot found three shallow pits in which more objects had been placed. In 1950 new cultivation brought up a fabulous neck-ring formed from intertwined filaments of electrum. More than a kilogram of gold and silver had gone into its making around 75 BC.[1] The British Museum described it as one of the most elaborate things ever made in the ancient world.

Ploughing produced more neck-rings, also coins and ingots. Then

finds dwindled. As if to compensate, in 1985 another field in the parish
yielded the stock of a Roman jeweller: scrap silver, ingots, a little gold,
a quartz burnishing tool, carnelian gems. It dated to about AD 155, about
two centuries after the Iron Age hoards.[2] Rumours of more finds circulated. Inevitably, the question was asked: why were so many valuable
things being found in one neighbourhood?

In 1989 a metal-detector user began to re-examine the field at Ken
Hill where the original find had been made twenty-one years before. At
first he found little, but on the August Bank Holiday weekend of 1990
he pinpointed another Iron Age hoard.[3] British Museum archaeologists
were called. They reasoned that if one hoard could lie below the bite of
the plough then there might be more, and so launched a fresh campaign
of excavation. Working across a quarter of an acre they found another
five hoards. Three of them had been configured with upper and lower
pits, the upper apparently acting as a decoy to divert attention from
more valuable material beneath. Just as the work was ending, a sixth
hoard came to light. Richest of all, it included twelve torcs of gold and
silver.

What was this place? Scene of a deposit made in panic? Of offerings?
A treasury?

There was no sign that the objects had been buried in fright, or for

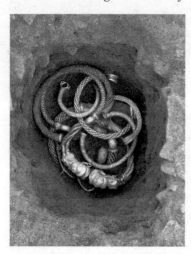

5. Gold and silver neck-rings buried
at Snettisham, Norfolk, in the first
century BC

safekeeping. In any case, there was
no known nearby community that
was likely to have had such riches
to deposit. The deposits lay within
a large, twenty-acre ditched enclosure, and this encouraged speculation about a temple precinct. But
there was no temple, and the date
of the enclosures was uncertain.[4]

Whatever the explanation, the
discoveries proved the power of
the metal detector. Such machines
had been on the commercial
market since the 1960s. Using
them, it has been said, is a bit like
angling – solitary, you do it outdoors, in all weathers, it calls for
special skills, and long periods
of inactivity are punctuated by

momentary tremors of thrill. Detectors also bring finds of poignancy: a lost keepsake, small change dropped by Victorian children conkering round a horse-chestnut tree, or a Tommy's cap badge. Bullets fired during a Civil War skirmish. Crossbow bolts. A Viking-age stirrup mount. Or even, if you are dead lucky, a box containing 14,780 late Roman coins, precious metal jewellery and tableware – the Hoxne hoard, found in 1992.[5]

Like the splodges of mortar described in Chapter 1, such finds are widely said to tap a kind of force – the power to shrink time, and to connect the human community across millennia. This power goes largely unnoticed by the Department for Education, for which history's purpose is to help young people 'to ask and answer questions of the present' and 'to develop their own identities'.

> History prepares pupils for the future, equipping them with knowledge and skills that are prized in adult life, enhancing employability and developing an ability to take part in a democratic society. It encourages mutual understanding of the historic origins of our ethnic and cultural diversity, and helps pupils become confident and questioning individuals.[6]

Fair enough. And to fire 'pupils' curiosity and imagination, moving and inspiring them with the dilemmas, choices and beliefs of people in the past' seems an honourable aim. But one consequence of seeking to justify history by stressing its contemporary relevance is that it gives succour to the notion that while transfers of thought and feeling run between adjoining generations they do not for any distance run across them.[7] On this view, history is a kind of social reagent whose usefulness lessens as time passes, until a point is reached at which it has no effect at all. Despite rhetoric about the value of history 'to make connections within and across different periods and societies', in teaching about Britain neither the English school curriculum nor the UK's test for citizenship looks back further than the Romans.[8]

Individuals press the opposite: the older or stranger something is, the stronger the reaction. A 350-year-old child's shoe in the palm of your hand may make you want to cry. A silver-gilt boar from Bosworth battlefield connects you to the last minutes of one of Richard III's companions. An Iron Age coin bearing some of the earliest syllables to reach us – a name, say, like TINCOMARUS – can raise the hairs on the back of your neck. In the presence of a Lower Palaeolithic hand axe, half a million years crushes to an instant.

Such experiences suggest that as well as being a humanity-science, archaeology is also a branch of Gothic romance. The popular success of this genre, said Sir Walter Scott, comes from its art of 'exciting surprise and horror' – the release of 'that secret and reserved feeling of love for the marvellous and supernatural which occupies a hidden corner in almost everyone's bosom'.[9] Such feeling can be evoked by what is 'Waste, desolate, where Ruin dreary dwells',[10] or by a

> dismal cirque
> Of Druid stones, upon a forlorn moor,
> When the chill rain begins at shut of eve,
> In dull November ...[11]

The lines from Keats's *Hyperion* illustrate a further characteristic of Gothic fiction, that half-seen things stir powerful feelings. The marvellous, said Scott, 'loses its effect by being brought much into view'.[12]

Archaeology is cousin to Gothic romance because it brings moments of exciting surprise and evokes uncertainties: we are still unsure what dismal cirques on forlorn moors were for, how Lower Palaeolithic hand axes were used, or why shoes were put into the roofs of houses. The state of *not* knowing is akin to reading a novel or poem that arouses the imagination without allowing it to be gratified. Druids and Druidism loomed large in the eighteenth and early nineteenth centuries because archaeology and Romanticism 'walked hand in hand'.[13] With the 'white-haired Druid bard sublime' ran an exquisite sense of uncertainty about what it was that Druids did, and a corresponding morbid pleasure in contact with the monuments, graves and skeletons imagined to have been connected with them.[14]

While for archaeologists, then, the past is just a job, for many others it has been, and remains, a realm of feelings and dreams. The dreaming is ancient; only the metaphors change. Stone axes were once 'thunderstones'. Griffins, satyrs and wyverns may have been conjured from the sight of fossils of extinct animals.[15] And just as Gothic fiction was 'fundamentally linked to colonial settings, characters, and realities as frequent embodiments of the forbidding and frightening',[16] so the past becomes a colony ruled by Mother Present. Like the exotic monkey's paw in W. W. Jacobs's short story, an object arriving from time afar is charged with strange powers.

The medieval world had a word for the force which emanates from special things: *virtus*, potency. Under the metal detector *virtus* burst out anew. And as it did so archaeologists looked on with fascination and alarm. Fascination, because metal detectors are very efficient at pin-pointing metal objects missed by eye, and so can bring forth bodies of new data. Alarm, because most of the finds were going unreported, sites were being rifled, and tabloid publicity was putting the accent on cash rather than knowledge. Rattled by signs that study of the past was reverting to plunder, many archaeologists called for metal detecting to be curbed.[17]

Detectorists replied by accusing their accusers of hypocrisy. If knowledge was important, why did so many excavated sites lie unpublished? Come to that, if it was wrong for metal-detector users to scan topsoil, by what logic did archaeologists prepare a site for excavation by machining off the overburden? Metal detectors seldom located objects more than a few inches deep, so where was the harm in searching land which had been disturbed by the plough? The real objection, they said, came from prejudice. Treasure hunters made magnificent finds at no cost to the state. Archaeologists were just preachy and jealous.

Other tensions simmered. Whereas archaeologists were mostly university-educated, many detectorists came from working-class back-grounds and lacked formal historical training. Some began to portray themselves as people's historians, and their hobby as a counter-culture to academia. Others stressed individual liberty, caricaturing calls for the overhaul of ancient-monument laws as Marxist propaganda. In reply, the archaeological community compared treasure hunters to the *tombaroli* who robbed Etruscan tombs, or the *huaqueros* who have devastated archaeological sites of Central America to supply Western markets. Unsurprisingly, detectorists from Doncaster and Sunderland do not take kindly to being likened to those who currently plunder Chinese tombs or who ransacked the ancient sites of countries like Montenegro after the collapse of Yugoslavia.[18] Such oversimplified portrayals, each side trying to paint the other into a single corner, became causes of resentment in themselves.

Some of the detectorists' complaints had justice: treasure hunting is not necessarily the same thing as metal detecting. The metal detector is just a machine, and holding one no more makes you a looter than holding a knife makes you a murderer. What counts is the intention behind the machine's use. Some treasure hunters, like archaeologists, claimed to be acting in history's interests. A few antiquity dealers downplayed Britain's wealth in the more distant past, suggesting that there was never much here in the first place. It is true that, if you want to make a fast buck, metal detecting over the croft of a fourteenth-century peasant is not the place to start. But the protestation that Britain was an also-ran in the treasure league is disingenuous. A succession of finds like the Mildenhall treasure, the Water Newton silver or the Staffordshire hoard – 'the largest archaeological Anglo-Saxon find ever unearthed' – shows that extraordinary concentrations of portable wealth did exist in early Britain.[19] The blankly serene stare of the Roman face-mask and helmet found at Crosby Garrett reminds us that more are there for the finding.

As dispute rumbled on, metal-detecting finds began to crystallize into patterns that historians did not expect and could not ignore. While media reports gave an impression that it was big, glittery discoveries that shone new light into history's dark corners, the cumulative picture being built up from small, often individually insignificant finds was starting to suggest remarkable things. Assessment of the early medieval economy, for instance, had hitherto made assumptions on the basis of the evidence of small numbers and restricted distributions of later-seventh- and eighth-century silver coins. One assumption said that economic activity in the seventh century was small. Another stated that commerce in the period was closely regulated by kings and magnates. The coins in question are often wonderfully intricate, but very small – so small, indeed, that when they are on or in the ground they are near invisible. Economic historians had accordingly drawn their conclusions mainly from coins derived from hoards and excavations, neither of which turn out to typify the kinds of circumstance in which coins had been carried or used. The metal detector, by contrast, is good at pinpointing single coins that were accidentally lost. Such losses are a better guide to economic activity than hoards, and by the early twenty-first century detectorists were finding them in such numbers as to demand rethinking both of the scale of the early medieval economy and of the ways in which it worked.[20] More on this later: the point here is that archaeology's underlying aversion to unbridled treasure hunting stemmed not from jealousy, but from frustration: if new-found objects pass unrecorded into private hands or go into the market unprovenanced such rethinking can never take place.

No one knows how many finds go unrecorded, or where historical understanding would be if they were recorded.[21] In any case, it is not just reporting that is needed but a system of reception to record provenance and make the results accessible.[22] This raises further questions. Most fields in England contain enough junk to fill a skip: what should be provenanced? Surely there is no point in reporting every speck of debris or lump of corroded iron? And who is to say what a record-worthy object should be? The answer to that question will in turn be influenced by the scale on which recording takes place. A single potsherd from one field may be neither here nor there, whereas larger patterns of things that are individually trivial can enable and illuminate questions we would never otherwise ask.

The self-belief of archaeologists in telling the public that they should report archaeological finds because it is in the national interest to do so was prefigured over two centuries ago when antiquaries reflected on the relationship between their work and public life. Antiquaries who studied past societies considered themselves to be 'uniquely well-placed to comprehend their development and to apply these lessons to the conduct of public life'.[23] In the view of the antiquary Richard Gough, writing in 1770, the antiquary's task was to furnish facts to enable a fuller, truer reading of written sources, and so serve the public and honour his country: 'The arrangement and proper use of facts is HISTORY; – not a mere narrative taken up at random and embellished with poetic diction, but regular and elaborate inquiry into every ancient record and proof, that can elucidate or establish them.'[24]

Home ground was important. Part of the antiquary's role was to advance study of the British home.[25] In the country house of Sir Walter Vivian, summoned up by Tennyson in *The Princess* (1847), there is a private museum with contents that both reflect Britain's imperial span and memorialize the place and those who have lived there.

> Carved stones of the Abbey-ruin in the park,
> Huge Ammonites, and the first bones of Time;
> And on the tables every clime and age
> Jumbled together; celts and calumets,
> Claymore and snowshoe, toys in lava, fans
> Of sandal, amber, ancient rosaries,
> Laborious orient ivory sphere in sphere,
> The cursed Malayan crease, and battle-clubs
> From the isles of palm: and higher on the walls,
> Betwixt the monstrous horns of elk and deer,
> His own forefathers' arms and armour hung.[26]

For Gough and others, antiquarianism was a kind of patriotism, wherein 'all antiquities merited attention because they were all an essential part in the continuum of British history. One area should not be given priority over another simply on the grounds of taste, but all should be evaluated for their contribution to the recovery of the nation's past.'[27] Above all, the antiquary must publish: knowledge unshared is no knowledge at all.

This helps to contextualize why it was that by the late twentieth century archaeologists believed that their discipline's methods, painstakingly evolved from antiquarianism and geo-sciences over several centuries, were the only dependable way to address the material past,[28] and that treasure hunting was a kind of relapse. Moreover, there was something surreal in the combination of the metal detector with fieldwork methods of the days of George III. A similar juxtaposition in medicine would combine, say, stem-cell research with leeches. Was it really going to be necessary to learn how to look all over again, to re-explain and rejustify all the original lessons?

The underlying issue, we have seen, had less to do with methods than with aims. The destructiveness of eighteenth- and early nineteenth-century excavators derived not from incompetence but from efficiency. For antiquaries interested in specimens rather than context, the most economical way to retrieve things like cremation urns or weapons was to sink a narrow shaft at points where they were expected.[29] Antiquarianism's limitation was thus not its field methods but the narrowness of its questions, to which the methods were simply a response. By going back to those earlier questions, treasure hunting showed that its ultimate threat lay in its power to trivialize.

Since it is ideas that determine what we wish to look at,[30] we may ask what casts of thought were abroad in the later eighteenth and early nineteenth centuries – the age of revolutions, inventions and romantic turmoil – when so many familiar things were seen in new ways. Among them were clouds, hitherto regarded as random shapes. In 1803 a pharmacist and sky-watcher called Luke Howard published an *Essay on the Modification of Clouds* which argued that clouds could be categorized according to their visible characteristics. He suggested a nomenclature – cirrus, cumulus, stratus, nimbus – and drew attention to the relationships between different types of cloud and different kinds of weather.[31] It followed that weather itself could be foreseen. The same applied to ground. Only two years before, a thirty-two-year-old surveyor, William Smith, had produced the draft of a geological map of England. Years of exploration along exposures made by digging canals, and the seminal work of James Hutton in ascertaining that rocks are arranged in superimposed layers, had taught him that rocks of different kinds did not occur randomly. On the contrary, they had order and relative position. Like Luke Howard, Smith gave names to the newly recognized formations. His map was published in 1815. It had mind-boggling implications. Minerals, for instance, did not occur haphazardly or where God had mislaid them. Just as clouds could be read as signs of 'vast atmospheric processes'[32] and inform the forecasting of weather, so knowledge of strata could be used to predict the whereabouts of coal and minerals. For a nation with an expanding empire and an industrial revolution in full swing, this opened the way to wealth and international dominance.

Another who denoted things and concepts which up to then had not intellectually existed was Thomas Rickman, who in the year that Smith published his geological map was nearing the end of a decade's study of old buildings. Until then, medieval architecture, like clouds before Howard, had been a kind of chaos. This was not for want of effort. As far back as the 1670s the antiquary John Aubrey had attempted the chronological study of buildings.[33] 'England after the death of Cromwell was more concerned than ever with better understanding its medieval [and] historical past.'[34] Curiosity about things Gothic had been growing since the 1650s, and by the early 1800s medieval buildings were much illustrated and discussed.[35] However, attempts to produce an accurate account of the development of Gothic architecture in England had been confounded by the mingling of fact with fancy, and the running together of surmise and observation. When Jane Austen finished *Northanger Abbey* in 1803 in most cases no one knew how old such buildings were.

Thomas Rickman had not set out to crack the Gothic code. His first plan was to be a doctor. But curiosity about architecture drew him aside. For ten years he toured, looking at nearly three thousand buildings, and in 1817 he published findings which rested on direct enquiry. Self-effacingly entitled *An Attempt to Discriminate the Styles of Architecture in England*, the book was a landmark in exploration of the past. Over the next six decades it ran to seven editions.[36]

Rickman noticed that most buildings are the result of more than one episode of construction. By applying the principle of stratification borrowed from the new geology it was possible to sort different phases of fabric into relative sequence. For example, if one stage of a tower stands upon another, the lower part has to precede the upper, and hence must be older if only by a few days. Likewise, if a wall is pierced by an under-built arch or window, the interrupted fabric must be older than the work which disturbs it, even if it is physically higher. Rickman found that where fabric contained stylistic features, the styles consistently fell into a sequence which corresponded with the succession that had been independently established by stratification. Thus, round-headed arches preceded pointed ones, and windows containing tracery always occurred later in a building sequence than those without it.

Finally came dates. Although most medieval buildings lacked direct indications of age, Rickman found a few cases in which contemporary written records could be shown beyond doubt to refer to particular pieces of fabric. By comparing these date-anchored buildings with fabrics of similar style it was possible to form criteria which were generally applicable to structures of otherwise unknown age.[37] Rickman coined names for the styles: Norman, Early English, Decorated and Perpendicular. Like cirrus and cumulus, and despite those who considered the system to be 'a gross violation of history and fact',[38] they have entered the language.

Rickman lived towards the end of an age which had exulted in categorization. History was now subdivided into antiquity, the Middle Ages and modern times – a scheme which had been visualized by Italian scholars in the fifteenth century and since popularized by Christoph Cellarius' *Universal History* (1683). During the eighteenth century anything which lived or breathed had been classified, and the urge to order things according to systems had since been extended to rocks, minerals and microscopic organisms.[39] In 1818 – one year after the first edition of Rickman's book – Jöns Jakob Berzelius ascertained atomic weights for all but four of the forty-nine customary chemical elements. Geologists had begun to formulate a timescale involving periods, epochs and eras. The same idea was being extended to architectural style – an organizing of culture prompted by the observation of Nature. Rickman went further, for his system introduced the idea that artistic creativity can be paragraphed into spans of time with different moods.

As Rickman's *Attempt to Discriminate the Styles of Architecture* went to press, the thought that human time itself might be expressively classified was turning in the mind of the director of the Danish National Museum in Copenhagen, Christian Jurgensen Thomsen. Thomsen was testing a recent suggestion that people in Scandinavia's early past had worked first exclusively in stone and wood, then added copper, and only latterly had discovered iron. By comparing groups of objects and their provenances (a task made possible by the emergence of public museums as places where such things could be studied together and compared), Thomsen found that it was indeed the case that certain types of artefact occurred together but not in the company of others. By 1820 he had arrived at a tentative division of antiquity into three ages – an age which had used stone, a second age which had discovered bronze, and a third that used iron. Thus began a paradigm which Europe still uses; it was soon realized that different systems would be needed for other continents where technology had evolved differently.

Some of Thomsen's and Rickman's co-workers believed in the possibility of value-free observation. Sir Richard Colt Hoare's *Ancient Wiltshire* appeared between 1810 and 1821,[40] its confident epigraph – 'We speak from facts, not theory' – proclaiming Hoare's belief in the possibility of presenting evidence recorded in the field with complete detachment.[41] James Douglas took a similar position in his *Nenia Britannica* (1793).[42] Douglas (a military engineer, surveyor and geologist, afterwards ordained) and Hoare (the leisured master of Stourhead) epitomized aspects of the social and intellectual context in which objectivism has arisen.

Division of the past into episodes defined by material remains rather than language or social development called for a new kind of historical criticism. The systems made by Thomsen and Rickman were based on looking in a way governed by a theoretical standpoint. Rickman's theory combined the law of stratification and a hypothesis about the conformity of style; Thomsen's drew conclusions from association, provenance and sequence. However, both were imagined constructs, and while each has had enduring value as a way of ordering thought and observation, neither has any claim to an independent or absolute existence. Both, moreover, were influenced by contemporary perceptions in ways that remind us – again – that what we see is influenced by what we think. Just as one twelfth-century writer had seen Stonehenge not as a structure but as a heap of natural boulders, only fifteen decades have passed since antiquaries explained the metal straps of sixth-century buckets as 'crowns', or saw the bosses of Anglo-Saxon shields as Roman helmets. Scientists in early Georgian England found nothing odd in the idea that a stone might take the shape of a sea urchin: 'if a perfectly symmetrical crystal could grow out of apparently nothing … then why should not the same kind of inexplicable and enigmatic natural force make a stone that looked like a shell…?'[43] Eighty years after Rickman, another architectural historian pointed out that how you periodize great medieval churches will depend on which aspects of them you select: if it is the plan, then there are not four periods but two; if vaulting, then five. He described Rickman's phases as 'figments of the imagination', which of course they were.[44] But that is rather the point: the ordering of observation, the recognition of things which belong together or apart, is not once for all but a continuing process governed by where, when and how we look.

Comparative observation is helped by consistency in the record of what is observed. This was not obvious at the beginning of the nineteenth century, when in addition to the discrepancies which could arise when field drawings and engravings for publication were made by different people, it was not uncommon for errors to be compounded by illustrators who worked from earlier depictions rather than directly from the original subject. Another habit of the time was to combine a field record with a speculative completion, making no distinction to enable the viewer to tell where one began and the other ended.[45]

Visual conventions evolved. In the eighteenth and earlier nineteenth centuries, some artists liked to place buildings in more respectable surroundings than they actually enjoyed. The trim lawns peopled by promenading gentry which surround great churches depicted in watercolours were sometimes faked to conceal disorder or slum housing. Photography, far from ushering in a new age of realism, did not eliminate such manipulation but added to its possibilities, as photographers mingled the skies and weathers of one subject with the features of another. Illustration for archaeological purposes became a subject of debate. Should surfaces be rendered by likeness, or with conventions? Should the artist's purpose be idealized completion or as-found depiction? Was the aim to catch the essence of something, or to provide a dispassionate record of particular properties? And what does 'dispassionate' mean?

If finding a grammar of observation was one step in forming this new mental climate, exploration of Nature's order was another. Until James Hutton demonstrated in 1785 that the principles behind geological processes like the silting of rivers or erosion were constant, this was not self-evident. After publication of Hutton's *The Theory of the Earth* and Charles Lyell's *Principles of Geology*, the corollary for history was that the present could be used as a key to understanding the past.[46] For archaeology this meant that the further human past was not irretrievable, but a realm about which rational questions could be asked.[47] More recently, however, this realization has been modified by the recognition that we cannot necessarily explain past human behaviour simply by extrapolation from our own experience, and by the disintegration of any stable definition of who 'we' are. Later on we shall see that features in the material record for which explanations may look obvious (for instance, that something was done in a particular way for reasons of economy or defence, or because it was better than an earlier way of doing it) may have been the result of quite different influences. The act of looking itself undergoes change.[48] Alongside the constancy of

6. *How things are seen: engraving of crypt of St Mary, Lastingham, North Yorkshire, from John Britton's* Architectural Antiquities of Great Britain *(1819). Posed tools provide a rough scale. The depiction of some features that are no longer there and misrepresentation of others makes it hard to define the border between true and conjectural record.*

Nature's principles, therefore, runs a potential for symbolic discontinuity. As for 'we', the displacement of master narrative by many histories – determined by gender, religion, ancestry and any number of other identities – multiplies the ways in which we look. In one way this is exhilarating; in another, if the past is infinitely divided nothing is shared and history begins to gnaw at its own roots. We shall come to this. Meanwhile, still the most radical perspective of all, launched in 1859, was Charles Darwin's *On the Origin of Species* – 'the preservation of favoured races in the struggle for life'.[49] Twelve years later came *The Descent of Man*, in which humanity was located neither outside nor above Nature, but within it. Reflecting on this during the Second World War, the prehistorian Grahame Clark wrote:

> It is a fact, which may explain many of the ills from which the world has suffered, that science turned her attention last upon human kind – the sun, the moon and the stars, the structure of the earth, the rocks,

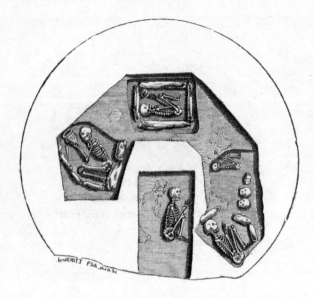

L JEWITT FSA DIR SC

7. *How things are seen: plan of burials in barrow at Hay Top, Monsal Dale, Derbyshire, excavated by Thomas Bateman in 1851. The record is schematic, bears no scale or north point, and its pattern of trenches (and hence of burials) may reflect Bateman's excavating strategy rather than the structure of the barrow itself.*

plants, insects, fishes and beasts of the field, all were subjected to the scrutiny of men of science, while Man, perhaps because made in the image of God, was accepted like a sacrament and set apart.[50]

Darwin's triumph, said Clark, 'was to bring man down to earth, to draw him within the field of scientific observation and so to make possible his own emancipation'.

With these four steps taken – classification, the ability to ascertain sequence, time-depth, and evolution by natural selection – modern archaeology's heart was set beating.

3

LET US SEE

Enough of Science and of Art;
  Close up those barren leaves;
Come forth, and bring with you a heart
  That watches and receives.

William Wordsworth,
'The Tables Turned', *Lyrical Ballads*, 1798

On the Origin of Species invited new questions about looking. Might history, like Nature, be an uninterrupted system obeying essential laws, revealing constant progress and dominance of the strong?[1] If so, history's work (and archaeology's with it) must surely be to uncover the system.

Did things evolve?[2] Comparison of artefacts suggested that in some sense they did – that objects and structures undergo changes of style and form which epitomize progress. We have noted that by the 1830s the principle of style criticism was being applied to great buildings like cathedrals, which were coming to be seen not as homogeneous monuments but as continuous records of structural change which could be sorted into different stages of development – an idea which in due course was extended to the sites on which they stood, and thence to the very ground itself. The same principle could in turn be applied to objects found *in* the ground – things like brooches or spearheads, eventually the forms and fabrics of ceramics. Another auxiliary speciality thus loomed: the classification of things according to selected characteristics – cultural typology. By categorizing and sorting things into sequence, the past – and, from that, the future – might be knowable.

A further body of thought was educed by Darwin's work: social evolution, with its proposition that humanity passes through recognizable cultural phases. Much of the running here was made in America, where anthropologists had been able to study the continent's pre-European populations at close quarters. They arrived at a scheme which ascended from a primal state of savagery (the hunter-gatherer-fisher), to barbarism (the first farmers) to civilization. The 1870s saw a volley of publications that linked Darwin's work with the study of early human development.[3] By the century's end we find historians like Lord Acton crediting history with two derivations from science, 'both based upon a belief in fact: a theory of classification and a theory of evolution'.[4]

Alongside this perception of history and archaeology as prongs of scientific enquiry another dimension of archaeology was taking shape: conservation. Publication of *The Descent of Man* in 1871 coincided with a growing concern for the protection of land, archaeological sites and buildings. Like a shifting breeze, ideas aback of conservation arrived from different directions. One of them was wilderness – Nature. In his *Guide to the Lakes* (1810, expanded 1820–35) William Wordsworth differentiated between 'the country as formed by nature', and the country 'as affected by its inhabitants' – some of whom were tourists, 'new settlers' or purveyors of 'false tastes'[5] (ideas which invite thought about the significance of 'old settlers' and 'true tastes'). In the eyes of Romantic philosophers and artists, places hitherto looked upon as dangerous, harsh or uncivil might instead be reimagined as restorative and comely. 'Every man', said Ralph Waldo Emerson, 'is so far a poet as to be susceptible of these enchantments of nature.'[6] As the industrial revolution quickened so did the idea of delimiting areas of land to keep nature in a pristine state. Wild and semi-wild areas had been set aside before, of course, but whereas something like a medieval hunting forest was for the benefit of an elite, Wordsworth advanced the idea of a region like the Lake District as 'a sort of national property, in which every man has a right and an interest who has an eye to perceive and a heart to enjoy'. In 1832 the North American painter George Catlin wondered about the possibility of 'some great protecting policy of government' to secure a park 'containing man and beast, in all the wild freshness of their nature's beauty'. In wilderness Henry Thoreau saw 'the preservation of the world'.[7] Thoreau reflected that while the United States had already acquired a worldwide reputation, the country itself was still largely unexplored: in the 1840s even New York State still had unsettled land within its borders.[8] A decade later Thoreau noted in his journal that every town should have a park, 'or rather a primitive forest, of five hundred or a thousand acres, where a stick should never be cut for fuel, a common possession for ever, for instruction and recreation.' Or again:

> The kings of England formerly had their forests 'to hold the king's
> game', for sport or food, sometimes destroying villages to create or
> extend them; and I think they were impelled by a true instinct. Why
> should not we, who have renounced the king's authority, have our
> national preserves, where no villages need be destroyed, in which the
> bear and panther, and some even of the hunter race, may still exist,
> and not be 'civilized off the face of the earth,' – our forests, not to hold
> the king's game merely, but to hold and preserve the king himself also,
> the lord of creation, – not for idle sport or food, but for inspiration
> and our own true recreation?[9]

'Recreation' is the key word: put a hyphen into it (as Thoreau sometimes
did) and it means not leisure activity but self-renewal. Wilderness was
the realm that enabled re-creation. In nineteenth-century Europe, real
wilderness – the land of hope, rebirth and long life – had gone centuries before. In America it was still there. Industry and development
destroyed wilderness, and by doing so not only impoverished the human
spirit but denied the means of its renewal. If we must live with the consequences of civilization, then at least let them be balanced by 'national
preserves'. Primal areas where no stick need be cut would be places of
memory as well as regeneration – and they should be for all.

Conservation thus drew on a body of thought that was counter-
industrial and fired by social concern. Archaeological sites fitted into
this because they were a subset of the environment, and because in
Europe some of them evidenced past ways of life that mirrored the
still-living 'hunter race' that Thoreau and Catlin hoped would live on
in America. By being instructive, historic places further extended the
idea of self-renewal. Deeper than this, though, was a perception of the
pre-industrial past as a place in time that paralleled wilderness in geographical space – a slower-paced realm of pure life-giving existence, as
it was, before everything became sullied or began to fail. What was old
was more ennobling than what was new, because it had its own organic,
creatively true and coherent network – the result of deep-rooted tradition which set it beyond fashion or unthinking utilitarianism.

With amenity and duty to posterity, then, ran a desire to remain in
touch with the past through the protection of ancient sites and buildings which were its remaining symbols. In Britain this wish found official expression in 1841, through the setting up of a Select Committee on
National Monuments and Works of Art.[10] This was over half a century

before the founding of the National Trust 'for the protection of the public interests in the open spaces of the country'. Between the two came William Morris and John Ruskin, who in 1877 pressed the case for protecting land and buildings for public favour by forming the Society for the Protection of Ancient Buildings. At its heart was the idea that buildings and monuments of earlier ages evoke melancholy, an emotion then held to be purer and deeper than joy and to be a stimulant to imaginative consciousness. This emotional dimension – the higher end of the coincident horror and pleasure of Gothic romance – accordingly predisposed archaeology and architectural history to study older, more monumental structures at the expense of the recent, the mean or the commonplace. Medieval churches were being closely studied a full century before the homes of the peasants who worshipped in them. Great medieval buildings had a political as well as an aesthetic significance. Morris saw them as heralds of socialism – the results of a freedom of hand and mind which had willingly, even eagerly, subordinated itself to co-operative harmony.[11] With that ran sympathies for organicism, crafts and localism.

These threads and more were gathered in the work and influence of Alfred Russel Wallace. One of the stars of the conservation movement, in earlier life he had been an adventurer, a surveyor, a student of the migration of birds, an entomologist and a bio-geographer (the idea of bio-regions was his). Later, with Darwin, Wallace was the co-originator of evolutionary theory and the author of *Darwinism* (1889). Wallace was further a social theorist, and a socialist, who argued that the state should buy out existing landowners and then lease land back to citizens on a basis that reflected both its intrinsic value and worth that had been added to it. Wallace saw that value could inhere in aspects such as amenity and history as well as economic productivity, and accordingly suggested ways of applying land nationalization to public benefit that included ancient monuments, greenbelts, parks and public access to open space.[12]

Allied with Wallace was the banker John Lubbock, a self-made man whose wide interests (among which were social insects, the registration of schoolteachers and governance of the British Museum) do not make it easy to see how his seventy-nine years could have accommodated them.[13] Lubbock was a neighbour of Darwin, and his book *Prehistoric Times* (1865) was already widely read. Lubbock bought Avebury, Silbury Hill and the West Kennet long barrow out of concern for their care. 'A wise system of education', he said, 'will at least teach us how little man yet knows.'

From 1872 Lubbock campaigned for legislation which would provide for a National Monuments Commission, a list of sites which could not be altered without permission, and an inspectorate with the duty of reporting on the condition of national monuments and advising on the best means for their care. The Tories parried the Bill year after year, gradually enfeebling its provisions and calling it 'burglary by daylight', but after they lost the 1880 election, a bill was enacted. The first Chief Inspector of Ancient Monuments was a retired soldier and husband of Lubbock's daughter: Lieutenant-General Augustus Lane-Fox Pitt Rivers.[14]

Pitt Rivers combined the landowning and military backgrounds of Richard Colt Hoare and James Douglas. Like Hoare, he used an inherited estate (all 27,000 acres of it) for archaeological research; like Douglas he was an expert surveyor and methodical excavator. His excavation methods drew from the example of William Pengelly, of whose three-dimensional grids and datum levels in excavations at Brixham and Kent's Cavern he was aware (see pp. 38–9).[15] A devout believer in systematic classification of types for the illumination of human evolution, Pitt Rivers was also a public communicator, believing that 'the facts of evolution … can be taught by museums, provided they are arranged in such a manner that those who run may read', this being because 'the working class have but little time for study'.[16]

Pitt Rivers had his work cut out. Although Lubbock had already drawn up a list of monuments to be taken into state care, the Act provided few powers, no budget and no staff. Repair was often unaffordable, and even basics like fencing and noticeboards had to be struggled for. Pitt Rivers paid for some work and all travel out of his own pocket. In 1890 he declined his salary on the grounds that his post was a sinecure. He wrote to a friend: 'Neither government nor parliament care a button for ancient monuments.'[17]

Pitt Rivers did what he could. His work in the field was everything that that of some antiquaries had not been – systematic, orderly, scrupulous in recording of objects and features, and conscientious in publishing records of what he found. When Mortimer Wheeler returned from the Great War and first saw Pitt Rivers's volumes on *Excavations in Cranborne Chase*, published privately between 1887 and 1898, he was amazed. Pitt Rivers's work epitomized the ideal of controlled discovery, yet by the early 1920s his methods had been all but forgotten. Wheeler was puzzled. 'Nobody paid the slightest attention to the old man. One of his assistants had even proceeded to dig up a lake-village much as Schliemann had dug up Troy or St John Hope Silchester: like potatoes.

Not only had the clock not gone on, but it had been set back.'[18]

Wheeler studied Pitt Rivers's precepts. The director of an excavation should train a disciplined team. The team should work under the director's eye (this was new – hitherto, directors had usually left manual work to workmen). The purpose of excavation demanded 'the most careful observation and recording of the stratification of deposits and buried structures so that their relative ages could be established and their nature understood'. This meant that everything should be recorded in three dimensions, so that any object, structure or deposit could be accurately reinstated in relation to all the others.

8. *Excavation of henge ditch at Avebury, Wiltshire, under direction of Harold St George Gray, 1911*

Next: 'A discovery dates only from the time of the record of it, and not from the time of its being found in the soil.' Here was 'the ultimate moral and scientific duty of the field archaeologist'.[19] To Wheeler, an unrecorded discovery was not just an unfind, but an annihilation of knowledge. (In Goethe's aphorism, 'Only everybody can know the truth.') And third:

> excavators, as a rule, record only those things which appear to them important at the time, but fresh problems in Archaeology and Anthropology are constantly arising, and it can hardly fail to have escaped the notice of anthropologists that, on turning back to old accounts in search of evidence, the points which would have been most valuable have been passed over from being thought uninteresting at the time. Every detail should, therefore, be recorded in the manner most conducive to facility of reference, and it ought at all times to be the chief object of an excavator to reduce his own personal equation to a minimum.[20]

Publications should be structured accordingly: facts first, meaning later.[21]

Here was the crux. Did archaeology find facts? If it did, could it find them in such a way as to enable others to reinterpret them – or even find and record them regardless of whether the excavator recognized them for what they would become? And if it is possible for an excavator to reduce personal equation to a minimum, what is the effect of that remaining part of a personal connection that cannot be eliminated? Can there be such things as degrees of objectivity?

Archaeology's adaptation of geology's law of superposition did, usually, confer sureness about sequence. Experience also showed that for analytical purposes it was fair to divide the residues and traces of material lives and surroundings into discrete units. A carpet must be laid down after the fixing of the floorboards upon which it lies, even if only by a few minutes, and a tack driven through the carpet into a floorboard must be successor to them both. Since deposits have boundaries which are, within tolerances, measurable, their horizontal and vertical limits can be planned, recorded and co-located. Separate units can then be sequenced, and cultural material within them can be studied in relation to questions of use, or date, or symbolism, or whatever aspect of interpretation is being pursued. (A lot of cultural material in a given deposit is left over from earlier periods: have a look in your garden.) Subtleties can be explored: for instance, the distance between the find-spots of

conjoining fragments of pottery or bone can show how material has
been deposited, spread or redeposited. And while sequence supplies relative date, an expanding battery of scientific chronometric methods can
show actual date. From these we might find that our carpet was woven a
century before the making of the floor upon which it was finally placed,
or that timbers of the floor were reused and so older than the building.

So far, so good. But there is a limit to how far observation, classification or analysis will translate into historical understanding.
Archaeology's apprehension is filtered through the senses of looking,
touching and analysing, governed by consideration and imagination,
advised by experience. We know from experience that meaning is not
always self-evident, that things we see or feel can be mediated by symbolism and context as well as by some notional reality. A corollary of
the idea that archaeology finds facts would be that the more facts we
find, the fuller our understanding will be. Yet this is not so: for all the
effort that has been put into the study of Stonehenge, for instance, by
the twentieth century's end we were not much closer to understanding
what it was for than we were at the beginning.[22] W. H. Auden made a
similar point in his poem 'Archaeology':

> From murals and statues
> we get a glimpse of what
> the Old Ones bowed down to,
>
> but cannot conceit
> in what situations they blushed
> or shrugged their shoulders.[23]

Darwin warned about the fallacy of value-free science. Looking back at
geology in the 1830s he recalled a school of thought which said that the
geologist's job was to observe and not theorize.

> I well remember someone saying that at this rate a man might as well
> go into a gravel-pit and count the pebbles and describe the colours.
> How odd it is that anyone should not see that all observation must be
> for or against some view if it is to be of any service.[24]

Pitt Rivers was among the first excavators to collect mundane material
like potsherds that earlier antiquaries had ignored. Whereas antiquaries
had previously limited their collecting to things they found interesting, Pitt Rivers reasoned that anything, however humdrum, might have
something to say if you asked it the right questions. It followed that

everything should be systematically collected and recorded. In that lay both enlightenment and fancy, for the idea that *everything* is recordable can be put into effect only through human decision on what is recorded, and how. The systematic collection of archaeological data thus calls for choices. Or as Einstein said to Werner Heisenberg in 1926: 'Whether you can observe a thing or not depends on the theory which you use. It is the theory which decides what can be observed.'[25]

Science regularly escorts new kinds of evidence on to history's stage. Once they are there, new kinds of theory and observation become possible. Until the Swedish naturalist-geologist Lennart von Post realized that pollen grains could provide information about the stratification of peat, environment and climatic history, pollen was ignored; once he had demonstrated it in 1916, excavators sampled for pollen.[26]

In Britain, it was not until the 1930s that archaeologists began to view domestic animal bones and plant remains as evidentially valuable. Curiosity about them arose among a group of young prehistorians who were keen to know about everyday life in prehistory. Among the first sites chosen to light up this subject was an Iron Age farm at Little Woodbury, near Salisbury. The site had been discovered from the air,[27] and the man invited to excavate it was Gerhard Bersu, an archaeologist from Silesia who like Pevsner had been forced out of his academic post by the Nazis and came to Britain. Woodbury changed the way in which prehistoric life in Britain was visualized. Hitherto it had been generally assumed that early people lived in holes in the ground.[28] Bersu showed that in fact they had lived in generously proportioned timber-built round-houses.[29] The 'pit dwellings' turned out to be storage pits, yet again demonstrating that what you see is governed by how you look. Bersu the outsider, like Pevsner, enabled insiders to see what was already under their noses.

Bersu's looking extended to environment as well as culture. He introduced British archaeologists to the systematic collection of animal bones and seeds because they offered insights into the dynamics of past economies, stockmanship, diet and environments. Until then such things had usually either not been looked for or thrown away, while the bones of some creatures (like fish) are so small that they cannot be efficiently retrieved by eye and call for fine sieving – a process that requires effort and equipment that hitherto no one had thought to provide. Further, the identification of fish remains is specialized and can be time-consuming – sorting eel vertebrae, for instance, ranks high in the list of seemingly thankless tasks. Yet such remains can tell about more than nutrition and diet. Traces of deep-sea fish, for instance, have implications for the kinds of craft needed to catch them.[30] In such ways might fish-bones found far inland tell of early seafaring.

In 1940, after the fall of France, along with about 75,000 others of German background, Bersu was interned. Five years later the Attlee government in Britain set about the introduction of National Parks, Sites of Special Scientific Interest, the Green Belt and the Nature Conservancy. Looking back, those steps look like life-affirming actions in reaction to the war just fought, but in fact they were taken on the basis of preparatory work that had been going on for some decades; indeed, it was the wartime coalition government that appointed a National Parks Committee, one of its last acts before the result of the 1945 general election was declared.[31] Perhaps as a subset of the renewed focus on Nature interest in past interactions between people and environment grew broader. In August 1945 the recently formed Wild Life Conservation Special Committee noted that analysis of pieces of charcoal found at different levels could throw light on what had been growing in a neighbourhood at different times. The Committee further noticed that the coupling of archaeological and botanical evidence with what could be derived from the sub-fossil remains of snails and other animals would 'contribute to the elucidation of human, biological and climatic prehistory'.[32] Charcoal, snail shells and the bones of small creatures like voles duly joined the list of things that archaeologists collected.[33]

In York in the early 1970s we sometimes asked each other why we were retrieving and bagging all the bird bones that were strewn through the deposits in Roman barrack blocks. Most of them were fowl, but from the systematic study of York's avian remains we now know that birds like egret, stork and white-tailed eagle were in the vicinity a thousand years ago;[34] it was not climate change that drove them out but loss of habitat caused by human encroachment. By the 1970s, too, it was coming to be realized that remains of beetles and insects offer insights into past habitats and environments. Many such creatures are habitat-specific, and their hard exoskeletons of chitin, a naturally occurring polymer, survive for millennia. In conjunction with other kinds of evidence, beetle elytra give clues to the state of woodland, drainage, pasture and hygiene. And so it goes on: pubic lice, intestinal parasites, mud from mires, turds – the list of things at which archaeology can look is infinitely extensible.[35] Intellectually exhilarating, this is also a sorcerer's apprentice, unleashing a rising flood of information that becomes increasingly difficult to marshal or sift for use.

Looking must have a standpoint, which may be physical or intellectual. What you see on your hands and knees differs from what is visible from two thousand feet up, or in scuba gear inside the hull of a sixteenth-century carrack five fathoms down. Only in the mid-twentieth century did historians begin to take real account of this. V. H. Galbraith said that archaeology's way was opened once enquirers began 'to use their eyes as well as their heads'.[36] His remark could just as well have been put the other way round: what you see depends on where you are, and what you think determines what you see. Either way, as the French historian-geographer Lucien Febvre liked to say, there is no history other than that of the present. In 1936 the archaeologist-philosopher R. G. Collingwood reflected: 'Prehistoric flints or Roman pottery acquire the posthumous character of historical evidence not because the men who made them thought of them as historical evidence, but because *we* think of them as historical evidence.'[37] The corollary, Collingwood argued, is that the past has no valid existence outside present thought; efforts to interpret it must involve a search for the problems and viewpoints to which past actions were intended as responses. Inevitably, that search will be influenced by memory.[38]

Such a search raises the challenge of how, or indeed if, in a given moment a searcher can transcend his or her cultural standpoint – for it is culture that determines our suppositions and influences the things at which we wish to look or from which we turn away. History's highway is paved with examples. During the earlier eighteenth century, for instance, interest in the Vikings was negligible, until Romanticism redefined the sublime as the violation of convention, whereupon Viking culture became attractive to composers, artists and historians.[39] Europeans still talk of a New World, even though it was there all along, and continue to suppose that the Americas were 'discovered' in the fifteenth century even though people had been living there for perhaps fifteen thousand years. If it is true that there has never been a period 'at which human beings have been more aware of the extent to which the past is their own creation',[40] we might ask if we have ever been more unaware of what it is we have created.

A declared standpoint is sometimes scorned as being the dull alternative to intuition or imagination. But theory's models are no more than shuttering for ideas, and it is through imagination that such ideas are invented, renovated or discarded.[41] One scheme of thought often triggers an upside-down opposite. In the 1920s, for instance, the Darwinian–Marxist view of inevitable progress was answered by a

quirky counter-theory of regress, from a degraded present to a noble
pre-industrial past. One of its instigators was the ruralist writer H. J.
Massingham, who drew extensively on archaeology and in 1926 published a book called *Downland Man* which was unscientific to the point
of being lunatic fringe, yet was intermittently penetrating in ways that
outflanked conventional approaches. 'Modern archaeology is in bond to
the fixed mechanical, evolutionary dogma that progress is an operative
force among men by its own volition and that the sapling comes before
the tree, the hut before the castle, the lower before the higher development, simply because it does.'[42] Massingham believed that Avebury was
the earliest of megalithic centres – a holy city, 'Neolithic London and
Jerusalem in one', the product of a sophisticated civilization which had
been born at its high point and then declined. This defied the then conventional notion of prehistoric people as dullard savages, and rejected
the nostrum that the further back in prehistory you go, the dimmer
people would have been. Instead, he argued, 'we are witness of an organ-
ised whole of civilised minds with definite aims'.[43]

Massingham was at most peripheral to mid twentieth-century
archaeology, but his challenge to technological determinism and the
patronizing of older cultures resonates today, just as it contested the
earlier twentieth-century consensus that ideas and social practices travel
from higher to lower centres of culture. The nineteenth-century socio-
anthropological model of a progress from savagery through barbarism
to civilization had been elaborated by a model of mounting complexity:[44] smallest and simplest, the *band* (hunter-gatherer-fisher); larger, but
not yet much elaborated, but with early signs of division of labour, the
segmentary society; the appearance of an aristocracy, with sharpening
contrasts of wealth and widening systems of exchange, the *chiefdom*;[45]
largest in area and most complex, the *state*, with its more multifaceted
divisions of labour and class, social surplus concentrated through deity
or king, and the attraction of power away from families and people
towards institutions.[46] Each was deemed to have left material correlates – of technology, settlement form, land-use, type and elaboration
of structures, relationships between places – which if properly recorded
and analysed would be specific to a particular stage.

But again, we ask, what do we mean by 'properly recorded and analysed'? Pitt Rivers had believed that the systematic classification of
objects, structures and traditions would disclose a variety of types current over a restricted area, their totality amounting to a 'culture' which
can be equated with a past people or racial group. By recording and

mapping them, archaeology could reconstruct past societies and plot the trajectory of social development.

One who took thinking about 'material culture' to a new level was Vere Gordon Childe, who in 1927 (the year after publication of *Downland Man*) was appointed to the newly created chair of prehistoric archaeology at the University of Edinburgh. Only five years before he had been unemployed. Following an upbringing in Australia, education in classics and philosophy, and study of prehistoric Greece at Oxford, he returned to an academic post in Australia from which he was soon driven out because of his strongly held socialist and pacifist views. Other rejections followed. When a political career with the New South Wales Labor Party came to naught, Childe refocused. He returned to Europe, toured north Mediterranean countries and central Europe to study sites and archaeological collections, and began work on a book which went off like a bomb when it was published in 1925. *The Dawn of European Civilization* was one in a stream of more than 600 publications which Childe produced before he fell – apparently intendedly – from a cliff in the Blue Mountains in 1957. Remembered variously as 'ugly, awkward and shy',[47] an outsider who at once begrudged yet savoured his peculiarity,[48] 'austere' yet also someone with a sense of humour and liking for food and wine – make your choice – Childe is celebrated above all as 'the man who made order out of archaeological chaos'.[49]

Childe's gift was lucidly to organize and combine masses of hitherto disparate facts and observations and put them in service of new explanatory theories.[50] His themes were big-boned – the change from seeking wild food to farming, the rise of social complexity, urbanism. He posed vital questions and explained how they could be tackled.[51] 'No book quite like this has ever been written,' said O. G. S. Crawford, reacting to *Man Makes Himself* in the opening of a wholehearted review.[52] *What Happened in History* (1942) has been claimed as 'the most widely read book ever written by an archaeologist'.[53]

Childe saw that certain cultural changes had occurred independently in different parts of the world. He wanted to know why. His thinking about material culture proposed that a complex of regularly associated traits could be taken as representing the way of life of a particular people.[54] He peered into the processes of change, suggesting that long-persisting traits would reflect peoples or ethnic groups, whereas functionally efficient advances would pass swiftly between peoples because of the advantages of adopting them. Diffusion, then, would be the motor driving change in human history.[55] Or as Crawford paraphrased it, 'human history is seen as the interaction between man and his environment, which includes of course other groups of men'.[56] In this there was a twist. Childe argued that human beings do not adapt to their surroundings as they really are but rather as they imagine them. 'Each individual carries about in her or his mind a "cultural map" incorporating knowledge acquired through learning and experience, from which that individual selects the data required to adapt to the social and natural environment.'[57] Usually there is enough correspondence between the real world and its imaginary counterpart for individuals and communities to make running adaptations in response to external change, or to rationalize incongruities. From this interplay come further stimuli for change.

On the basis that types are determined by convention rather than by function, and hence must correspond with the social group that hallows the convention, 'material culture' for a time became archaeology's reality, being read across not only into (and out of) cultural but also anatomical groupings. By the 1930s such groupings were becoming the subject of ever more elaborate classification. In 1940, state-of-the-art prehistory could discuss the amalgamation of bold, 'tall long-headed Battle-axe folk' with equally adventurous but round-headed Beaker folk,* to produce 'a mixed race with a mixed culture'.[58] The idea of 'mixed race' presupposes 'pure race'. As a fierce opponent of Nazi 'Aryan' nonsense[59] and champion of human amity it was not Childe's fault that one branch from this line of thought led to the gas chambers.

> Remember me when I am dead
> and simplify me when I'm dead.

wrote Keith Douglas, three years before his own death in 1944.

> As the processes of earth
> strip off the colour and the skin
> take the brown hair and the blue eye
>
> and leave me simpler than at birth
> when hairless I came howling in
> as the moon entered the cold sky.
>
> Of my skeleton perhaps
> so stripped, a learned man will say
> 'He was of such a type and intelligence,' no more.

---

* So called because a particular type of drinking cup was usually buried with them.

Such a type and intelligence . . . Today, those elaborately classified peoples, each with its own head-shape, stature and racial identity tag, have
dissolved not only under self-reproach or the human genome,[60] but in
the face of yet newer mappings of newer kinds of data which show
no correspondence with conventional political or cultural territories,
or peoples. Such culture groups, we now see, were projections at least
as much of our own assumptions as of the supposedly objective criteria by which we imagined them to be determined. Yet only fifty years
ago, they appeared to fit with recent national experience. Archaeology's
early years had coincided with an age of colonial expansion and the
elaboration of nation states. It is not surprising, then, that archaeology
should have been harnessed to the imperialist cause (a comparison of
the images on Georgian British coins and Roman currency is instructive),[61] or that archaeology's subsequent explorations of earlier periods
should have been interpreted in the light of colonial experience. The
settlement of Britain itself was visualized in terms of a succession of
increasingly well-organized peoples who periodically arrived from other
parts of Europe to move things on. With this went ideas of cultural
hybridity, like 'the Romano-Briton', akin to the Anglo-Indian.

History through a colonial lens was mirrored by excavation method,
which in Britain down to the 1950s placed reliance on vertical control
whereby events in the life of a place, each chapter with its own layers,
each layer a stage in a story, were read off serially from sections as if from
a railway timetable. The method is vividly demonstrated in Wheeler's
work at Maiden Castle, where the box grid and deep ditch sections
excavated between 1934 and 1937 reflect a kind of certitude about archaeology's capacity to reveal narrative of its own accord.

British emphasis on sections was in contrast with the method tried at
Gunderup in Denmark by the Danish archaeologist and human geographer Gudmund Hatt. Hatt reasoned that horizontal patterning and
subtle differences in the use of space between and around structures
could not be detected simply by sinking trenches within or across them.
This was especially true in the elucidation of settlements where timber
buildings rest on the ground rather than being dug into it. Moreover,
a deposit that is thin in one place may be several feet thick or discontinuous near by, so what a section reveals will depend on where it is
put, not on what the deposit is actually like. In the 1930s, excavators in
the Netherlands , Germany and Denmark accordingly developed a new
way of excavating, working across a large area and recording deposits
three-dimensionally, in plan. This approach was first used on a medieval

9. *Box grid excavation at Maiden Castle, Dorset, led by Mortimer Wheeler, 1936*

site in Denmark by Axel Steensberg at Store Valby from 1945 to 1953. Methodologically it was a tour de force, working from what was known from written records to what was unknown revealed by excavation. At one point, the relationship between the two even allowed Steensberg's team to detect the former positions of furniture.[62]

Danish interest in daily life and local economy was fostered by the fact that, unlike Britain, Denmark was a country 'dominated by small farmers who had a great interest in settlement and environmental history, in contrast to the imperial and colonial aspirations of Britain which emphasised progress and change through conquest and colonisation'.[63] Steensberg's methods involved the exposure of substantial areas to reveal the inherent complexity of everyday existence. As we shall see in later chapters, the gradual adoption of area methods in post-war Britain similarly coincided with a shift of emphasis, from monumental buildings and grand narratives to ordinary settlements and interactions between people, land, climate and environment.[64]

Chronology, it has been said, is the eye of history, and since the middle of the twentieth century there has been a search for scientific ways to assign date regardless of typology or cultural assumptions. Such methods have given history new eyes. The radioactive clocks of potassium-argon and fission-track dating tick back for five million years. For more recent times, two techniques in particular, radiocarbon and tree-ring dating, have revolutionized history. Both were pioneered in the United States.

Radiocarbon dating originated during the later 1940s out of wartime research.[65] It has become archaeology's main tool for dating organic remains such as seeds, bone, leather or cloth from the last five hundred centuries. The method's basis is that carbon in Nature exists in three main forms, the isotopes carbon-12, carbon-13 and carbon-14. In a given sample of carbon the bulk of atoms will be of carbon-12. Atoms of the isotope carbon-14 are much scarcer, and also unstable. William Libby, the American chemist who devised the method, ascertained that C14 in the environment is replenished at a constant level by the production of new atoms formed from the bombardment of nitrogen-14 in the upper atmosphere by cosmic radiation. Living things mirror this ambient level by taking up carbon from Nature, chiefly through plants. But when organisms die, uptake stops. Since C14 decays steadily, measurement of the degree of decay enables calculation of the time that has elapsed since the source of the sample died.

A radiocarbon date reported from the laboratory is expressed in radiocarbon (not solar) years before the present (BP). Since 'present' is always changing, for radiocarbon purposes it is set at 1950 when the method first came into use. The method does not yield specific dates, but with a given degree of probability indicates a span of time from which the sample comes. This is not yet a calendric span. The amount of radiocarbon in the atmosphere has varied as time has passed, and to find the true age of the sample we need to know how that atmospheric concentration has changed. One way of doing this is to cross-check radiocarbon dates against ages ascertained in other ways – for instance, by counting tree-rings (see below), by making determinations on organic residues in the laminations of silt that settle annually in lakes, or through analysis of atmospheric composition at different times in the past from pockets of gas that have been entombed by annual layers of ice. The result is an adjusted date span which for published purposes is then converted to years BC or AD, the abbreviation 'cal' being inserted to confirm that the calibrated adjustment has been made.[66]

In the later 1970s improvements in the analytical process overcame an early drawback, which was the method's large appetite for sample material. Hitherto, things that were delicate, small or precious – say, an illuminated manuscript, or the fragment of an early fossil human – were not readily open to dating because too much of the original would have to be sacrificed for the sample. Today, the requirement for the normal process has fallen to a few grams, while yet more sensitive Accelerator Mass Spectrometry (which counts all the atoms) calls for no more than one or two milligrams and in certain circumstances can work with less. The result is that dates can now be provided for important or disputed things that were hitherto off limits – like the illuminated Gospels kept in the Ethiopian monastery of Abuna Garima. Tradition links these manuscripts with the Byzantine missionary Garima who is said to have arrived in Ethiopia's northern highlands at the end of the fifth century AD. Expert opinion put the making of the Gospels some six hundred years later – until radiocarbon dating by the University of Oxford placed their making in the period 330–650. Whether or not the saint himself had a hand in them, the Garima Gospels now appear to be a 'unique survival of an early Christian text in sub-Saharan Africa – pre-dating all others by more than 500 years'.[67]

Radiocarbon dating has enabled independent comparison of the dates of social changes, monuments and settlements in different places. Traditionally, prehistoric things like pottery or ritual monuments that looked alike in different places were assigned to the same period on the strength of their similarity. In the 1960s radiocarbon dating began to show that for Europe many of these assumptions were false – for instance, that monuments (like Stonehenge) previously imagined to have been 'influenced' by Mediterranean exemplars were in fact older than the presumed prototypes. In the face of these altered sequences diffusion lost its status as the motor for culture change in European prehistory, and with it lapsed 'the chess game of migrations, which pre-historians used to play with such enthusiasm, moving "cultures" and "peoples" from place to place'.[68] From radiocarbon and other physical dating methods that have since been developed, a new prehistoric chronology has emerged, and with it new narratives (pp. 171–2).[69]

An important influence on the radiocarbon revolution has come from the mathematical work of an eighteenth-century Nonconformist minister, Thomas Bayes. Bayes's fame rests on a theorem concerning probability that was published two years after his death.[70] Born probably in 1701, Bayes came from a family which some decades back had made a fortune in the cutlery trade in Sheffield and had since moved into professional life in London. Little is known about him. As a dissenter, Bayes was excluded from Oxford and Cambridge, attending instead the University of Edinburgh where alongside divinity he studied Latin, Greek and mathematics. After Edinburgh Bayes returned to London, where he worked until 1733 or early 1734, when he moved to be minister of the Mount Sion meeting house in Tunbridge Wells. In parallel with his devotional and pastoral work, Bayes was active as a mathematician. In 1742 he was elected a Fellow of the Royal Society. One of his proposers was Philip Stanhope, the second Earl Stanhope, a man with keen mathematical interests and a neighbour at Tunbridge Wells; at least two others were friends of Isaac Newton. Bayes 'was a strong Newtonian in his scientific outlook' and had already attracted interest through his work on infinite series, and on calculus.[71]

We do not know when Bayes became interested in probability theory, but in the mid-1750s he responded to a recent publication by Thomas Simpson which argued that the mean of a set of observations gives 'a better estimate of a location parameter than a single observation'. Writing to a friend, Bayes pointed out that this might not be the case in the presence of what today we would call measurement bias.

> Now that the errors arising from the imperfection of the instruments & the organs of sense shou'd be reduced to nothing or next to nothing only by multiplying the number of observations seems to me extremely incredible. On the contrary the more observations you make with an imperfect instrument the more certain it seems to be that the error in your conclusion will be proportional to the imperfection of the instrument made use of. For were it otherwise there would be little or no advantage in making your observations with a very accurate instrument rather than with a more ordinary one, in those cases where the observation cou'd be very often repeated: & yet this I think is what no one will pretend to say.[72]

Pursuing his theme, Bayes went on to produce his theorem, which is a way to infer the degree of likelihood to which a hypothesis may be correct. Bayesian inference has come to be much used in medicine, economics and artificial intelligence; in the last quarter-century it has revolutionized later prehistory.

The value of Bayesian inference for archaeological chronometry relates to the fact that the true date for a radiocarbon sample may apparently lie anywhere within a bracket several hundred years wide.[73] As others have noted, this can give us false impressions – for instance, that events in prehistory always moved slowly: a sense increased when determinations are viewed side by side and their combined differences add up to hundreds of years.[74] An impression of gradualness is especially likely if the material being sampled is older or more recent than the structure or event that we are trying to date. A radiocarbon determination refers to the sample, not necessarily to the event or episode that the archaeologist may be trying to date. For instance, a piece of animal bone may lie in the ground for hundreds of years before it is incorporated into (say) the upcast of a ditch. To find the date of the ditch we must show a clear and near-contemporary relationship between the sample and the ditch's digging. Illustrations of this are all around us: if you walk across a field or look at objects in garden soil, most of the things you see – like shards of pottery, bits of glass, lumps of coal – will have been lying there for decades and some for centuries. Equally, it is not unusual for objects or environmental remains from the present to find their way into older deposits. In a drought, for instance, deep cracks may open, allowing the introduction of modern objects into older strata, while the actions of earthworms, burrowing creatures and root systems can redistribute material between deposits. It follows that radiocarbon determinations have varying degrees of relevance, and that there is a relationship between their evidential usefulness, risk of contamination and stratigraphic status to which Bayesian methods can assign degrees of sureness.

The results can be startling. Look, for instance, at the revised date for a fragment of human bone from Kent's Cavern, Devon, which was announced a few days before the completion of this book. As we saw in Chapter 1, Kent's Cavern has long been recognized as one of Europe's important and motivating sites for the study of environmental history over the last three-quarters of a million years. In 1927 a fragment of maxilla – upper jawbone – was excavated and initially identified as having belonged to a modern human of Upper Palaeolithic age. In 1989 the bone was directly radiocarbon dated, giving an age between 36.4 and 34.7 thousand years cal BP. In 2004 a team brought together by Chris Stringer began a reassessment. Further dating tests on the maxilla itself failed, but Bayesian analysis of new ultrafiltered bone collagen dates from animal bones by which the maxilla was stratigraphically bracketed put its date back to 44.2–41.5 thousand years cal BP. The maxilla from Kent's Cavern thus becomes the oldest modern human fossil yet known in north-western Europe. More significantly, it 'demonstrates the wide and rapid dispersal of early modern humans across Europe' more than forty thousand years ago.[75]

For nearer times, tree-ring dating has become the single most powerful chronometric tool since the emergence of archaeology itself. This is because of its precision. As a tree grows, new wood is added each year. Each annual growth layer varies in width according to environmental influences: chiefly, but not exclusively, annual fluctuation in weather. For a given tree there will be local influences, such as the character of its site or the effects of things like insect attack, but in general trees of one species growing in the soil of one area will show similar variations in annual growth. By charting and overlapping signatures from trees of different ages, it is possible to compile continuous sequences which run for centuries. When signatures from timbers found during excavation or from the study of buildings are compared with a reference chronology it may be possible to locate the sample within a particular term of years. If the sample still bears bark, the outermost ring will have grown in the last year before the tree was felled. In temperate regions, the rings of trees provide dates that can pinpoint the ages of timber structures as far back as ten thousand years.[76]

The first known instance of the use of tree-rings to date an ancient site was in Tennessee, in 1820, just three years after Rickman published his treatise on architectural styles, and within a few months of Christian Thomsen's proposal of a three-age system for the prehistory of the Old World. The method was refined in the 1920s by an American astronomer, Andrew Elliot Douglass, who was interested in the possibilities of tree-rings as surrogate indicators of climate.[77] Tree-rings have in their turn since been used to adjust and calibrate the radiocarbon timescale.

Tree-ring dating's ability to provide exact dates for things like church roofs, doors, harbours and boats acts to refocus assumptions not only about the things themselves but also about narratives of settlement, buildings, journeys, trade and art. To illustrate, while a felling date of 1222 for oak timbers used to roof the east end of Salisbury Cathedral is no surprise (it agrees with what was already known), it confirms that the trees concerned had grown in Ireland, their import to Salisbury reflecting some dispute or pressure on local supply.[78] Similarly, for as long as the timbers were imagined to be more recent, the significance of Arabic numerals among the assembly marks was overlooked. The widened use of such numerals (which originated in India) would in due course have enormous implications for computation and accounting. Jacqueline Stedall points out that the real advance was not in the arrival of the Hindu–Arabic symbols themselves 'but in the system of place-value introduced with them … with its unprecedented computational power and flexibility'. This is so – using individual alphabetic characters to identify timbers was in itself no breakthrough. Nonetheless, it is notable to see such use occurring almost exactly alongside their earliest occurrences in England in the work of scholars. Robert Grosseteste, for instance, *Magister scholarum* in Oxford (1213–31), later Bishop of Lincoln, appears to have been using them by 1215.[79]

Another case: a quarter of a century of excavation along the banks of the River Thames in London has uncovered a succession of timber waterfronts, set one in front of another and alternating with dumps of refuse. The sequence runs from the Roman period to the end of the Middle Ages. Since tree-ring dating enables most of its stages to be sharply dated, the thousands of artefacts which lie in the intervening refuse deposits are tightly bracketed by structures of known age. This has had a revolutionary effect on the calibration of other things as varied as medieval dress fashions, international trade and economic cycles. The implications for pottery have been transforming: locally made and imported ceramics that could once at best be dated to one or two centuries may now be dated to within thirty years. Since some wares circulated afar, these results affect knowledge of economies, buildings and processes in distant places.[80]

A third example touches politics and the way written records are read. Thirty years ago historians credited the early ninth-century Danish king Godred with far-sightedness for his initiation of the Danevirke – a system of ditches and ramparts which runs across the base of the Jutland Peninsula between the Baltic and the North Sea. By this stroke, 'goods and ships could avoid the long and inhospitable west coast of Jutland and the waters of the Skagerrak in favour of an eight-mile portage and quick access to the Belts and the Baltic – and all on Danish territory'.[81] The Danevirke was ascribed to Godred on the strength of an entry in later Frankish annals. We now know that much of the system was nearly three-quarters of a century older. Tree-rings supply an exact date – 737 – for the felling of trees used in part of its construction. Other parts are older still. So, the annals described not the beginning of the Danevirke but a new phase within an existing system that had undergone successive changes. This puts Godred's far-sightedness, and commercial expansion in north-west Europe, in a new light.[82]

The idea of world prehistory has been with us for nearly half a century, yet while for European purposes the idea of successive waves of migrant people as the main cause of cultural change was undermined by radiocarbon dating (that discrediting coming on the heels of decolonization, which in turn gives a context for diffusionism's notoriety, as if others' pasts had earlier been violated), its legacy lives on. Invaders and Settlers continue to thrive in the earlier stages of England's National History Curriculum, and as names like English Heritage remind us archaeology is still largely organized and funded within the confines of politics and institutional remits which bear no relation to the patterns of what is actually being studied. There is no such thing as Scottish or Serbian prehistory, only the study of prehistory within what is now Scotland or Serbia. As Europe's history shows well enough, modern states hardly signify as organizing units for the study of the deeper human past, although the past signifies very strongly as an organizing principle for the modern state. As you read this, somewhere in the world ardent nationalists will be on the lookout for historical things that underwrite present identities, or making plans to destroy someone else's. Israel, Macedonia and Kashmir provide examples, but the condition is near-universal. A *Times* leader writer reflected in May 1994 that while the discovery of half-million-year-old hominin remains at Boxgrove, Sussex, was 'not a moment for chauvinism', 'every Englishman may walk a little taller in the recognition that he is descended from such a striking creature'. We address the past using terms taken straight from contemporary identities as if helpless to think in any other way.[83]

Or again, periodization. For four centuries we have boxed our ancestors in ages which we ourselves have defined for reasons ranging from the practical to the whimsical. The 'Iron Age', for instance, was originally conceived simply as a way of organizing certain kinds of archaeological material in the absence of written records. This is why in those parts of Europe like Sweden where writing arrived late, the Iron Age continues well into the Middle Ages, whereas for working purposes in southern Britain (but not in Ireland) it ends with the arrival of the Romans. Similarly, 'the Celts' or 'the early Anglo-Saxon period' are not historical givens but results of our decisions about what belongs with or is divided from what. Framework is useful (as Pevsner said, 'Fixed terms for styles of ages are there to keep a host of data in reasonable order'),[84] but there are many different ways of paragraphing the past. Archaeology's early enthusiasm for dividing time (as if mirroring geological strata) inevitably brought difference, change and contrast to the fore, for it was these things which gave periods their edges. In so doing we may well have created, or at least exaggerated, a history of 'pivotal moments' and 'watersheds' between epochs of our own making. More recent approaches to material culture give more weight to endurance and continuity, and (on the broader view) to gradually changing systems wherein different elements co-evolve at different speeds, in different ways.

Standpoint reflects nurture. A social or class history of archaeology has yet to be written; when it is, it will be seamed with insights. Stuart Piggott believed that an underrated factor in the emergence of local archaeological societies in the 1840s was 'the sheer intolerable boredom of the winter in country house or rectory, parsonage or gentleman's place'. The early archaeological societies also contained women, 'and so just slightly loosened the constructing bonds of contemporary convention', while in their bringing together of people of common interests and different ages the societies' lectures and excursions had a power to break, 'however partially, through the strict divisions of the rigidly stratified social structure of the day'.[85]

In other parts of nineteenth- and earlier twentieth-century British society there was a suspicion that field archaeology was not entirely respectable. This derived partly from what archaeology studied, and partly from the people who studied it. Prehistory had been unpleasantly toilsome. 'I could not bear to plunge myself into the very depths of that noisome cavern, and to toil through centuries of dirt and darkness,' shuddered Thomas Arnold, a Regius Professor of History, in 1841.[86] Field archaeology was practical, dirty-fingernailed and hence a little tradesmanlike, in contrast to the gentler calling of the antiquary. Excavations were social microcosms, divided on class lines. Labourers did heavy work while gentlemen, occasionally ladies, presided. There were class-based skirmishes to determine archaeology's place in the system of knowledge. For J. H. Parker in 1870, the adoption of archaeology by the University of Oxford could not come soon enough. A time would arrive, he said, when 'any educated man will feel it a disgrace to be ignorant of it'.[87] Some felt that a greater disgrace lay the other way about. When Lord Dacre (formerly Hugh Trevor-Roper, Oxford's Professor of Modern History) was appointed Master of a Cambridge college in 1980, one of his new colleagues went to see him about the creation of an archaeological teaching fellowship. Dacre was aghast. 'He listened to me with ill-disguised surprise and disfavour and said: "Is archaeology really an honours subject here in Cambridge? It is not in Oxford, you know."'[88] Trevor-Roper was not the only don who had been educated in days when public schools had derided sciences, mathematics and modern languages, and in later life bridled at subjects like archaeology. Between the wars, M. R. James evoked similar feelings at the start of a ghost story. James introduces 'Professor Parkin', an academic who, when asked to take a look at the remains of a Templars' preceptory in the course of a golfing holiday, 'rather sniffed at the idea that planning out a preceptory could be described as useful'.[89]

How would Professor Parkin have taken to Mortimer Wheeler? Wheeler was well educated but not public school, a graduate but not of Oxbridge, clear officer material (he fought in both world wars, commanding an anti-aircraft regiment in the second) yet not in every way convincing as a gentleman. Behind his impact on archaeology lay a middle-class upbringing in late nineteenth-century Bradford. Bradford was stubbornly Yorkshire yet cosmopolitan, grubby yet proud and lively, trade-linked with the world's corners.[90] Wheeler's childhood was a rich world of home-made magazines, artistic curiosity, walks across antiquity-studded moors, natural history and cultural contact with German Jewry, the Labour movement and music. Like his Bradford near-contemporary J. B. Priestley, he had flair as a communicator. He spoke, wrote and drew well. He turned archaeology into news, thrust its stories into tabloid newspapers, and when television arrived he put them there too. Yet for all that, or because of it, or because of his energy and flair in seduction, he was an arriviste. A man of 'strategy, order and wide views', Rik to friends, Sir Mortimer to the public, behind his back some called him Flash Alf.

Figures like Wheeler enjoyed digging and liked to get their hands dirty, but the tradition of part-time directors who turned up intermittently to make interpretative pronouncements continued at least until the 1960s. And just as players often made better cricketers than gentlemen, so did jobbing diggers often outshine their masters. Some became archaeological Bunters and Jeeveses, supremely capable but never emerging in their own right. Others, like Basil Brown, became bellwethers for the famous. It was Brown who in 1938, amid east Suffolk's sandy heaths and pine trees, by invitation of the landowner began to explore some mounds at a place called at Sutton Hoo.[91] A contemporary remembers him.

> [Brown's] pointed features gave him the, not inappropriate, appearance of a ferret and were invariably topped with a rather disreputable trilby hat, while a somewhat moist and bubbling pipe protruded dead ahead from his mouth. He had ... gravitated to archaeology without any real training thanks to a quite remarkable flair for smelling out antiquities ... The sad thing is that with training he might have been a brilliant archaeologist ...[92]

Digging into a mound in the summer of 1939, Brown found the apparition of a seventh-century ship. Within it were the funeral goods of a great man. Brown's exploration of the vessel 'amounted to excavation of genius',[93] but when its importance became clear, the Office of Works and the British Museum took control.

The Sutton Hoo ship burial was one of those rare discoveries which divide a subject into before and after, changing utterly the way in which history is written and literature is read. For many, the simultaneously blank yet sullen countenance of his helmet is the defining icon of early medieval England. It is the world of *Beowulf* made real. Yet in the form we see it the helmet is no older than the Beatles. It was no image at all until its finding, along with 263 other objects of gold, garnet, bronze, enamel, iron, silver, maple wood, burrwood, glass, bone, textile, beeswax, horn, feathers, beaver-skin and otter fur, and the ship which cradled them – and no image, either, until after the war, when the hundred and more corroded pieces into which it had flaked were recomposed.[94]

This illustrates another principle of standpoint and seeing, that what we look at transforms as time passes. One of the main influences, in some respects *the* main influence, that governs what archaeology can see is the way in which things change or decay in the ground – taphonomy. The uncoverers of the ship in Mound One at Sutton Hoo, like their successors in the burial room of the Prittlewell Prince,[95] did not find objects identical to those which had been put there in the early seventh century, or in the same positional relationships. Each item had made its own way through time, the whole constellation of things transforming in result. A few pieces, like the great gold buckle, arrived as new. More typically, objects were in different stages of decay. The ship was rosily delineated by its rusting rivets. Some of the organics, like bags and cloths, were turned to tinted sand. An unknown number did not arrive at all. The hero's bones were absent, save perhaps as a chemical signature for which the searchers in July 1939 did not look. The objects had been piled in heaps, which had subsided, just as the wooden chamber in which they were placed had eventually rotted and burst inwards. And it was not just the physicality of the ship and its funerary cargo which had changed. Time also diffracts meaning.[96]

Whatever its destiny, each evidential particle of the material past fades or resurrects in its own way, and at its own pace. The silvery, electroplated tea pot bought by my mother in 1950 might survive for several hundred years in a dry cupboard, where corrosion will nevertheless one day eat all but its Bakelite handle. Cardboard cocoa packaging from Bournville would last only a fraction of that time, while a cabbage leaf will decompose in weeks. But change the conditions, and endurance changes too. If the cupboard were damp the tea pot and cardboard

10. *Sutton Hoo, 1939: the ship*

11. *Sutton Hoo, July 1939: Mrs Pretty (landowner, seated foreground, holding opera glasses) and lady companion (far side of trench, prone) watch as O. G. S. Crawford (left), Charles Phillips (standing in front of planning frame) and Sir John Forsdyke (sitting right) are among those surrounding W. F. Grimes (on ground) as he exposes an artefact.*

would both be gone sooner, whereas the breakdown time of the leaf would remain about the same. In a peat bog, by contrast, acidity, tannin and dearth of oxygen would stifle decay so that even the cabbage leaf might last for several thousand years. Despite the creosote, the wooden fence which stood at the bottom of Jack and Bess's garden fifty years ago has decayed, although outlines of the holes which held its earthfast uprights will still be ghosted in the ground. So, too, may be some of the bolts and screws which fastened the fence's frame, and the nearby skeleton of Bess's cat.[97] Bone in favourable conditions will last for thousands of years – much longer than iron. On the other hand, scavenging animals do not chew bolts, but will crunch bone. The survival of bone is thus more than a matter of chemistry.

The idea that cultural evolution should be susceptible to exploration through interactions between cultural behaviour and environmental change was taken further in the late 1950s. It took its cue from structural anthropology, which 'reduces the diversity of cultures to a range of combinations (in the construction of myths, kinship systems, forms of language and so on), which are both governed and limited by the structures of the human mind and perhaps, in the last instance, by the organization of the brain'.[98] In this premise that 'evacuates the historical density of societies',[99] human actions and behaviours would be disassembled into subsystems operating within and between societies, the material correlates of each being opened to study as a separate variable. This done, the recurrence of material patterns and forms of social organization would attest to the existence of underlying and consistent structures. Originating in the United States, this 'New Archaeology' borrowed analytical tools from the sciences, put a premium on hypothesis testing and highlighted the virtues of quantification and pattern in matching questions to data.[100]

At the time this was heady stuff, and some of the tools that it developed remain in use. Taking Ernest Gellner's model anatomization of a 'characteristic agro-literate polity', for instance, we could devise archaeological ways to test his proposition that the ruling class will consist of a horizontal stratum made up of highly differentiated and specialized layers – the military, administrators, clerics and so on – beneath which there is 'another world' of laterally separated peasant communities living 'inward-turned lives', among whom almost no one 'has an interest in promoting cultural homogeneity'.[101] Such a model is worth testing for the implications of Gellner's further observations about the way in which a nation remembers itself.

The whole system favours horizontal lines of cultural cleavage, and it may invent and reinforce them when they are absent. Genetic and cultural differences are attributed to what were in fact merely strata differentiated by function, so as to fortify the differentiation, and endow it with authority and permanence. For instance, in early nineteenth-century Tunisia, the ruling stratum considered itself to be Turkish, though quite unable to speak that language, and in fact of very mixed ancestry and reinforced by recruits from below.

Substitute early England for Tunisia and an interesting line of enquiry results to which we shall return.*

By the 1980s attempts to investigate social subsystems, each supposedly whirring with its own clockwork, were coming to seem artlessly optimistic; there was a reaction to the never-quite-attained explanations and skirting of cultural complexities. Moreover, champions of hypothesis-testing did not always differentiate between deduction and true inductive argument, for while deductive and inductive reasoning work differently, neither comes closer than the other to certitude about its premises.

The New Archaeology has left its mark. However, while most archaeologists would agree that archaeology's goal is 'to explain what happened in the past as well as to describe it'[102] they seem unable to resign themselves 'to the idea of a human nature given once and for all'.[103] With that reluctance has emerged a claim that man-made things are not simply sources of information about the past but have an innate import. Things we use, the buildings that house us and landscapes through which we move are more than the mere results of human action: they are socio-cultural influences in themselves, and hence part of the process, as well as the result, of change. This view has been widely embraced by archaeological theorists since the 1980s. Its attraction is that it releases archaeology from the narrow role of providing historical data, launches it into grand enquiry and challenges the imagination to frame the questions. Its drawback is the scale of the challenge, and the consequent difficulty of reducing any enquiry to manageable proportions, or of bringing it within workable boundaries – and the lack of any overt line of attack.[104] The upshot of both is provisionality in everything, a kind of pessimism in the presence of piles of fascinating cross-cutting observation and interpretation that lead to no sure conclusion.

* See Chapter 8.

Thus far discussion has mostly turned on what is buried and hidden, and hence mainly on excavation. This reflects our tendency to regard the past as lying beyond a boundary, another world to be investigated, as distinct from the present, which is experienced. But the greater part of time's legacy is all around us. It is the world in which we live – fields, trees, houses, the bend in the road, the oddly terraced hillside, entire town plans – experienced, often subconsciously, every day. During the last fifty years, and building on older traditions, an increasingly large part of archaeology's effort has gone into the reading of landscape.[105] This involves both the survey and study of landscape's surface, and increasingly sophisticated ways of seeing into the ground without disturbing it. While such work may have less immediate entertainment value than excavation, we shall see in following chapters how it is reshaping our outlook on the past. We shall also find that the 'how' of looking involves more than technology, being substantially conditioned by social memory.[106]

So many standpoints – yet despite them, how can we hope to glean meaning from remains which are not representative of what, historically, there was, or what we would like to examine, where all parts are in co-varying states of transformation, and our own questions are always on the move?

Perhaps we should think of archaeology as embracing three axes, each characterized by its own methods and degree of definitude. One axis is that of field technique, with which goes sequence and dating. A second links taphonomy and the ever changing condition of material from the past with our changing ability to extract meaning from it. A third is the evolution of the theoretical frameworks which govern the first two. The three axes together are less like intersecting lines than a network of surfaces, each crumpled into the other, unpredictable in their relations yet deterministic.[107]

We might add a fourth axis: flow. Back in the days of Pitt Rivers, or Wheeler, or Clark, archaeologists were few, and the capacity of county societies was restricted. The number of projects in progress at any one time was accordingly small, and their selection and geography were narrowly governed. Since the 1970s this has changed: as we shall see in Chapter 6, professional archaeology has burgeoned, while more recently it has become mandatory for developers of land to ensure that the archaeological consequences of development are properly provided for. In result, 'Many of the established type-sites that featured prominently in textbooks written only twenty years ago now seem to be exceptional, commonplace, or even irrelevant.'[108] In this success there is also a risk, for so great has been the inflow of information that it threatens to outrun our ability to make sense of what it means. The coincidence of the microprocessor with the data flood is timely, but remembering Darwin's axiom ('all observation must be for or against some view if it is to be of any service') the computer's analytical power can be released only through human imagination. The challenge is to bring the four axes – chronometry, theory, range of observation, volume of observations – into some mutually reinforcing relationship.

With our first axis and looking goes a dimension thus far unmentioned – the sky. For a discipline which has its stock in trade in the ground, it is curious that one of the strongest influences on its development has been what can be seen from the air. This is not only because the aerial view shows familiar things in unusual ways, or that it is an efficient way of scanning large areas, or even that under certain conditions it reveals things that cannot be seen on the ground at all. All these things are so, but a further power of aerial reconnaissance is to enable us to study together subjects that are usually considered apart.

The idea of looking down from the sky, like a god, was an ancient dream. Volundr (Wayland), the flying smith of Germanic folklore, was depicted on tenth-century carvings in a feathered machine with the head of a bird. In the sixteenth century Tudor and Flemish map-makers visualized cities seen from the sky. At the beginning of the nineteenth century the architect Sir John Soane set his students the exercise of drawing Stonehenge as a thermalling buzzard might have seen it. The idea of flying stirred imagination: painters and writers launched air fleets across the Channel long before technology enabled warring nations actually to do so.

Most agree that powered flight in fixed-wing machines began on a December morning in 1903, when Orville Wright flew 120 feet along a beach in North Carolina. He was by no means the first person to fly. Ascent in baskets lifted by balloons went back to the days of Mozart, and others since had often flown in gliders, gas balloons, powered dirigibles, even slung under kites. Some of them had covered long distances or ascended to considerable heights.[109] By the mid-nineteenth century observation from tethered balloons had for some nations become a routine part of battle, and by the century's end balloons were being used to obtain aerial views of historic places. In 1906 photographs of Stonehenge, the first of the monument, possibly of any archaeological monument anywhere, were taken from a 'war balloon', by an officer of

the Royal Engineers.[110] Balloons, however, were less than ideal for targeted reconnaissance, since in the absence of power or directional control they went where the wind took them. What was new about the
Wrights' machine were the control surfaces which he and his brother
Wilbur had devised to guide it in different axes, and the presence of
an engine-driven propeller to push it forward. Powered flight would
revolutionize human relations, not always for the best. 'Thank God,
men cannot as yet fly,' Thoreau had written in his journal on 3 January
1861, 'and lay waste the sky as well as the earth!' Only one lifetime later,
Robert de Marolles asked, 'Is not to fly to achieve a synthesis whose
exact parallel is not provided by any other human activity?'[111]

Until the mid-twentieth century, when it became routine, powered
flight was widely conceived as a source of exceptional cultural stimu-
lus.[112] Flying bestowed this, so the theory went, by lifting the hearts of
those who did it above the mediocre and restoring them to a finer state
of consciousness. For the traveller, its ever increasing speeds dissolved
old boundaries and barriers, distorting the sense of passage from place
to place and altering the state of mind in which one departed or arrived.
In flight, Jules Roy said, beauty, danger and freedom combined in a
kind of purified world. As whirled colours become white 'the aviator
sees clearly the essential'. Flight also meant rapid innovation: for millennia technology had crept and crawled, whereas in the giddy world of
aviation 'everything is scrapped in a year'. Beyond this, aeroplanes stood
apart from the degradation of industry and mechanization; they flew
from wide green spaces, their realm was the sky. And as the architect and
modernist seer Le Corbusier put it, they 'add a new feature to our senses
... A new basis for sensitivity.'[113] Le Corbusier considered the aerial view
to confer a kind of intensified lucidity: 'When the eyes see clearly, the
mind can decide clearly.'[114] The aerial standpoint was 'indifferent to our
thousand-year old ideas'. Old cities viewed from above could be understood for what they were: 'unforgiving ... decadent, amazing, mad'. The
aerial view was thus a kind of truth, and the aircraft which afforded it
a figure of modernity. Everything before the aircraft was 'finished'.[115]

The 'new lucidity', its technology honed by the Great War, offered
archaeologists a new way to study the past. It also promised new efficiency: the aerial camera covers more in an hour than survey on the
ground can register in years. This would lead historical narrative in new
directions. It would also help to reposition archaeology intellectually,
away from nostalgia, taste and romanticism, towards modernity.

4

ALBION FROM ABOVE

Consider this and in our time
As the hawk sees it or the helmeted airman:
The clouds rift suddenly – look there
At cigarette-end smouldering on a border
At the first garden party of the year.
Pass on, admire the view of the massif
Through plate-glass windows of the Sport Hotel ...

W. H. Auden, 'Consider', 1930,
Collected Poems, 1994

Nineteen-forty, a Sunday in late autumn. Major George William Graham Allen is riding his motorbike between Oxford and Dorchester-on-Thames. The bike uses less fuel than a car; petrol is rationed; Allen is thrifty. Nonetheless, he is going some. A bystander near Nuneham Courtney estimates his speed at between 60 and 70 miles per hour.

Allen approaches a blind summit. Not far beyond its crest Flying Officer William Ebbutt is in a car approaching from the other direction. Ebbutt slows, preparing to turn across the southbound lane to enter a field. Allen breasts the brow of the hill. Unsighted until the last seconds, neither he nor Ebbutt have time in which to avoid each other. A dent in the rear of Ebbutt's car shows where Allen's motorcycle struck it. Allen slides for thirty yards in a shower of sparks, receiving neck and head injuries from which he immediately dies. He was forty-nine. At the inquest, a verdict of accidental death is recorded. Ebbutt is exonerated.

Around Oxford the tragedy is news. Obituaries look back on achievements that include brave service in the Great War, the giving of advice to the government about road transport, and the governing directorship

of John Allen & Sons (Oxford) Ltd, a firm that makes, repairs and operates agricultural machinery and road rollers.[1] Allen's are well regarded
both by their employees and by their customers. The firm is progressive
and considerate, operates a generous superannuation scheme and provides for the welfare of its workforce.

Allen was unmarried, which perhaps was just as well, for friends credit
him with so many interests that it is difficult to imagine how marriage
could have been combined with them. He adored old cars, which he
rebuilt with his own hands. He was chairman of the National Traction
Engine Owners' Association. He collected penny black stamps, not so
much because of their value as because he was fascinated by the plating
and inks with which they had been printed. Not long before his death
he had become absorbed by astronomy. A keen cricketer, he played for
the works team. A few obituaries mention his contribution to archaeology through aerial photography. A long run of coincidences prepared
him for that.

George Allen's father grew up on a farm in Northern Ireland, two
miles from Comber, three and a half from Dundonald, in County
Down. His name was John, and the farm was called Unicarval. Unicarval
had been the family home for a generation. John Allen's father was
another George Allen, and he owned Unicarval because *his* father, Dr
John Allen of Larne, County Antrim, had cared for two brothers into
their old age, in gratitude for which they bequeathed their property to
him.[2]

Grandfather George bred shorthorn cattle that were admired around
the world. Well respected, George was a JP in Downpatrick. And near
by, between the railway line and the main Belfast road, there was a
blacksmith's shop.[3] John loved this place. As a boy he spent days here,
making gear wheels before he was in his teens. As a schoolboy in Belfast
he disappeared during teaching hours for an entire term. The school
imagined him to be ill; he was in the shipyards.

When John was seventeen the steam-plough manufacturer John
Fowler of Leeds sent one of its units over to Ireland, hoping for business in the northern counties. The ploughing set had two engines and
a reversible, double-ended plough that was pulled across the field by
a wire cable rolling on a drum under the engine. Such ploughs could
carve six or eight furrows each time they crossed a field. This was against
what could be accomplished by a pair of horses, which might manage
an acre in a day. Here is the first coincidence: most of the fields in the
north of Ireland were too small for a steam ploughing set to operate

effectively. George Allen's farm at Unicarval was the only one in the area with fields large enough to demonstrate the system. Young John Allen watched, was smitten, applied to Fowler's for training, was accepted, and after apprenticeship went to North America where there were really large fields to plough in Dakota and Minnesota.

Returning to England he went to Dorset as manager for Frank Eddison, who owned the Dorchester Steam Plough Works. A linked concern was that of Eddison and Nodding in Oxford. The owner, Walter Eddison, was absent, so John Allen transferred to Oxford to run the business, which became the Oxfordshire Steam Ploughing Company. John had both business and engineering acumen. The company prospered. And by now he was married.

In 1884 or thereabouts he was travelling on a train to Dorchester. Into the railway carriage stepped Elizabeth Sampson, who was escorting her younger brother home from school. As with the steam plough, it was love at first sight – but unlike the steam plough, etiquette prevented John from speaking to the young lady. Resourceful as ever, he got off where she got off and asked a member of the station staff who she was. A year passed until he found a mutual friend who could introduce them. They married on 26 November 1885, in the chapel of ease at Brympton.

John and Elizabeth rented a house in Iffley called Wootton. Here two of their three children were born. The eldest was George, born in 1891, our subject. Three years later came Phebe. When Cullimore was born in 1897 they bought another Iffley house, The Elms. The Elms had an acre of ground in which the children could play, views of the Thames and of Oxford's spires.

The name Cullimore marks another bit of fortune. John Allen had been given the opportunity to buy the Oxfordshire Steam Ploughing Company but lacked the capital with which to do so. John's uncle, Daniel Cullimore, stepped in with a loan, and some years later converted the loan to a gift. Cullimore and his wife had no children; John Allen gave the name Cullimore to his youngest son as a way of keeping the memory of his benefactor alive. In years ahead, co-ownership of the thriving company would provide George Allen with the time and resources to enable him to fly.

Like their father, George, Phebe and Cullimore were mechanically minded, scientifically curious, good with their hands, beneficially active. Until they were eleven, Phebe and Cullimore were educated at home by a governess, then at boarding school. At home, Phebe went with her father to the works and accompanied him to visit machinery in the field.

John Allen invented products – a scarifier, a new kind of roller. As motor cars appeared he produced rollers and tarring machines to produce road surfaces upon which they could run. John Allen also bought cars and encouraged his sons and daughter to drive them. George often drove with Phebe, who by the age of twelve could handle a heavy Napier 6. There were no nearby garages, so they maintained the cars themselves, learning to service the vehicles, take down carburettors and magnetos, and set the brakes. If spare parts were needed, John Allen had them copied in the works.

Such resourcefulness and unconventionality allow us to gauge the temper of life in a happy, united family. In 1970, Phebe wrote: 'My parents always trusted us and we were allowed far more scope than other children because my father was very go ahead. As a result we did not have to do things behind their backs. They only insisted we told the truth.'

Phebe gives us other glimpses, like mummers in the hallway at Christmas, the Christmas ham from Unicarval, the mulberry tree in the rectory garden, or the gardener who died and whose six children were all started in jobs at the works. Although John Allen was by now a leading Oxford citizen, his heart was still in Unicarval. Each August the family returned to spend a month with Granny Allen in the family home.

George, meanwhile, attended a boarding preparatory school in Iffley, then Boxgrove School, Guildford, then Clifton College. From there he joined the army, going to Woolwich in the hope of becoming a military engineer. But the Royal Engineers rejected him. He returned to civilian life and went to Africa for a year as the pupil of a friend of his father who was building a bridge in the Orange Free State.

Which brings us to 1914. Here there are parallel stories to be told, of the firm, and of the adventures of Cullimore and George. First, the firm. As U-boats tried to starve Britain, John Allen was hired by the government to organize the ploughing of land to grow food. In autumn and winter their plough sets – each of two engines, a water cart and an accommodation caravan for the crew of six men – journeyed across England to accelerate ploughing and extend the area under cultivation. They worked seven days a week. By now, John Allen had a workforce of about a hundred, and a fleet of six cars, four of which were used to keep contact with the mobile ploughing sets. For this effort John Allen was awarded the OBE at the war's end.

In tandem with the ploughing and rolling roads on behalf of

surrounding county councils, Allen was making common cause with a neighbouring manufacturer up the road in Cowley – William Richard Morris, later Lord Nuffield. Allen and Morris collaborated on the manufacture of weapons and ordnance. Along the way, in 1915 Morris provided a car for Phebe which was built from spare parts. When George and Cullimore returned from the war, the Oxford Steam Plough Company became John Allen & Sons. After four years of full order books, the company had a strong base upon which to build.

The war in which both sons had fought and been injured – George by gas, Cullimore by a sniper – extended George Allen's preparation for his contribution to archaeology. In 1914, the twenty-three-year-old George was at first unsuccessful in finding a place in the army. The Oxfordshire Light Infantry had more volunteers than they needed and the Royal Engineers again turned him down. However, he did find a niche in a motor battalion of the Army Service Corps. So did Cullimore, who though underage earned an immediate commission by coaxing the engine of a broken-down bus into life, thereby winning the instant admiration of the mechanically illiterate officer whose task it was to transport troops in the bus.

For the first years of the war, George oversaw the taking of supplies and ammunition up to the line. This was dangerous work, and on one trip at night his convoy of trucks advanced so far along a road that they found themselves behind German lines. With the introduction of the tank in 1916 George was a natural candidate for the Tank Corps, in which he became workshop officer, responsible for the tanks' engines. At Cambrai in 1917 he was responsible for the successful manoeuvring of 150 tanks to their start line, at night. He was awarded the Military Cross, and by the end of the war was a staff officer with the rank of major.[4] His experiences and participation for the entire war caused him to retain this title. For the rest of his life, he was known as 'the major'.

John Allen now stepped back and returned with his wife and Phebe to Unicarval, leaving George and Cullimore to run the works. Cullimore married, and bought Wootton. George continued to live at The Elms. The business prospered. In addition to agricultural machinery, the expertise they had gained in transport, road-rolling and road-making paid further dividends. As their friendly neighbour Morris was demonstrating, the age of the mass-produced car was at hand.

A decade later, well off, the business running smoothly and with a little time on his hands, George Allen engaged with a new hobby that combined movement and mechanics: flying. His first flight was from the grass aerodrome at Woodley, near Reading, on 4 April 1929. His log book records the take-off just after noon. The aeroplane was a de Havilland Moth – a DH 60 – and the instructor at the controls was R. T. Shepherd. Like the Morris Minor and Austin 7 on the ground, the Moth was democratizing transport. It was economical to run, mechanically dependable and – as aeroplanes went – affordable. The flight lasted fifty minutes. Later in the afternoon there was a second trip. Allen was enthusiastic. During the rest of April he put in nine hours under instruction. On the 25th he made his first solo flight – one circuit, of five minutes.[5]

The Moth, the instruction and use of the field at Woodley were provided by the firm of Phillips & Powis. The firm had been formed only a few weeks before, and the airfield itself had only just opened. Allen was one of its first pupils. In ten years' time, Woodley would be an important centre of aircraft design and manufacture. In April 1929 it had one small shed, one pilot and one engineer.

In June 1929 Allen bought his own Moth, and with Phillips he flew it up to Woodley from the de Havilland works at Stag Lane. Stag Lane was then a rural concatenation of huts and sheds on London's northern outskirts near the Edgware Road. London was then coming to be ringed by airfields used for commercial and recreational purposes. Some of them were associated with particular manufacturers – like Hawker at Kingston upon Thames and Langley near Slough; Fairey at Hayes; Napier at Acton Vale; and Handley Page at Cricklewood. Further out were Vickers (with Hawker again) at Brooklands and Weybridge, Percival at Luton (previously at Gravesend), and Miles at Woodley. Some of these locations were the result of business histories going back to the Great War or before, but they also reflected outer London as a realm of light engineering, progressive technology and electrical manufacture, echoed to this day in the art deco factories and business units that line main roads west and north out of the city. Most of these airfields have since been engulfed by development, or were too small to remain viable beyond the 1940s. Together with the specialized industries that supported them they formed a stage in London's social and cultural development that went with Odeons, estates of semis, the first dual carriageways – features of inter-war life that have since become the subject of archaeological study in themselves.

During July, Allen's log shows that he flew on average one day in two. As experience grew, he began to take the Moth on cross-country flights – north to Oxford, south to Hamble, to Heston on London's western edge, to Brooklands. He was also becoming interested in the Oxfordshire village of Clifton Hampden. One day in late July he flew there from Reading, and on three subsequent cross-countries he used the village as a turning point. He was sizing it up. On 21 August 1929 he landed in a field at Clifton Hampden, and from this date the Moth was based there. In September, his log book shows, he began to take up passengers. Among the first were Phebe, and the works manager.

In spring the following year, 1930, Allen made longer sorties: to Hull, to Bristol, to Coventry. In July he flew up to Blackpool and across the Irish Sea to visit the family at Unicarval. In August he became yet more adventurous, taking the Moth to Brussels, and on to Antwerp, and Amsterdam.

Allen's skill in making these journeys is not to be underestimated. The Moth had an open cockpit. There was no radio. Meteorological information was limited, forecasting winds was difficult. On several occasions, sudden deteriorations in weather caused him to force-land. The only navigational aids were a compass and map. And the Moth was not fast. Its cruising speed was 85 miles per hour; against a strong headwind speed over the ground might be no more than that of a motorbike.

Periodically Allen flew the Moth down to Stag Lane for maintenance. While there he had the opportunity to study other de Havilland products. Among them was the new Puss Moth, a cabin monoplane with a high wing. In this machine, you did not need to be wrapped or helmeted against the elements, and the view was better. Whereas forward and downward vision from the DH 60 was restricted by the in-line cylinders of the Cirrus engine and the biplane format, the cylinders of the Puss Moth's Gypsy engine were inverted, offering a much better view. Here is another coincidence – the right aircraft at the right time. Major Allen sold his DH 60 to the London Aeroplane Club, and on 28 March 1931 became the owner of G-ABKD, a new Puss Moth.

That summer Allen ventured ever further afield. Alongside his local flying he made sorties to Norfolk, Yorkshire and Nottingham. Possibly he was training himself in long-distance navigation. At any rate, come September he went to Berlin. He flew via Lympne in Kent, which was the departure point for many of the long-distance record attempts which were being made around this time by flyers like Amy Johnson and Bert Hinkler, both of whom used Puss Moths for some of their flights. Allen flew to Brussels. From there, Cologne, on to Hanover, and finally to the futuristic airport being laid out at Tempelhof. After a day

12. Major Allen and his Puss Moth, 'Maid of the Mist'

in Berlin he returned via Amsterdam, making this leg in a single flight that lasted three and a half hours.

Thus far, Allen's flying looks recreational: as his skills improved and confidence increased, so he tested himself with new challenges. The field at Clifton Hampden was his own airstrip. An entry in the 1932 issue of the AA *Register of Landing Grounds* advised incoming pilots to take care of the new haystacks that had arisen just over the boundary. In more coincidences, there were other things just over the boundary. Clifton Hampden was amid one of the densest concentrations of air-visible prehistoric sites in England, and every time Allen took off or returned to land, he overflew them.

As well as being a gifted engineer Allen had the curiosity of an historical geographer. He was intrigued by mysterious names of ancient monuments which appeared on maps, and tramped fields and downs in search of them. Since taking up flying he had begun to notice circles and patterns outlined in crops and on the earth. Such marks were striking in summer, and particularly so in the early summer of 1932. 'At first', he wrote, 'I did not realise that these marks were the same sites as those which had long interested me on the ground, and that now I was merely seeing them more clearly than had been possible before.' Allen soon understood not only that was he looking at sites that were already known, but that he was also finding new ones.[6] He had recently read a book about archaeology and flying. It was called *Wessex from the Air*, and he wrote to one of its authors to introduce himself. The author wrote back. His name was Osbert Guy Stanhope Crawford.

'O. G. S. Crawford' in bylines on academic articles, 'Ogs' to friends, Crawford was Britain's leading aerial archaeologist and archaeological officer for the Ordnance Survey. Restless, active, he was also founder-editor of the periodical *Antiquity* which he had launched four years before.

Crawford had been born in 1886, in Bombay, where his father was a judge of the Indian high court. Both his parents died before he was eight, his mother when he was but a few days old, and from the age of twelve weeks he was placed in the care of relatives in England. That tragedy might have been worse had it not been for the relatives. Dora, whom he called Auntie Do, and Gertrude, who became known as Pogga, were affectionate and encouraging. A third aunt, Edith, was the family intellectual – the one who could write Greek and Hebrew. But Edith was also vigorous, a source of life and fun. She made up stories and rhymes, and it was said that before she joined the Order of the Sisters of Mercy she had once laid out a London pickpocket with a straight left.

The aunts went back a long way – Do to 1836, Pogga to 1846. Their outlook was devout but unstuffy, 'Georgian rather than Victorian', with unfamiliar speech patterns that said untwentieth-century things like *fiff*pence and *Suth*ampton. When the aunts began to teach Osbert to write, they made him write a double 's' in the eighteenth-century fashion, making the first 's' like an 'f' without the cross-stroke. At first they lived in London, where Osbert remembered 'muffin-men and crossing-sweepers, hansom-cabs and four-wheelers, horse-buses, horse trams to Hampstead, the smell of horse-dung and of the gardens in Park Place'.[7] In the mid-1890s the aunts moved to a house near Newbury, where the garden adjoined a meadow at the foot of the Downs, astride the boundary between Hampshire and Berkshire.

Osbert was red-haired, by turns enthusiastic and downright, given to a prickly independence and moments of uncontrolled frustration when he hurled his cap to the ground. In him there was also misanthropy and the trace of a loner. He was sent to Marlborough College, where bullying, compulsory games and the impersonality of the place caused him to take refuge in the solitude of cross-country running and cycling. From this he grew to love maps, like Allen relishing their textures, conventions and colours, strange names and monuments. He ranged far into surrounding downland, visiting churches, Avebury and Stonehenge.

Harold Peake, then working on the *Victoria County History of Berkshire*, lived near by and encouraged the teenager's interest in topography. Harold and his wife Charlotte 'spurned organized religion, wore sandals and went in for vegetarianism, Japanese art, the resuscitation of folk ritual and the re-organization of mass society'.[8] The Peakes were well off, patrons of outdoor plays, masques and dancing, their household thronged by up-and-coming talents. The teenage Crawford became a protégé, encouraged to approach the past through visual and material evidence. 'What Crawford picked up from Peake was that the best guide to Britain's misty past was not books but the landscape itself.'[9]

Osbert went to Oxford to study geography, afterwards obtaining a junior post in the university's newly founded School of Geography. But all along he had been engaging in archaeological fieldwork.[10] August 1914 found him digging a Berkshire long barrow with a friend. In September Crawford enlisted in the London Scottish Regiment, and over the winter of 1914–15 served as an infantryman in France. Later in 1915 he transferred to what became the Field Survey Company of the Third Army: a unit that made detailed maps of the area around the River Somme that the Third Army now held. As the dispositions of weapons and trenches changed so the maps had to be updated. Much of the new detail came from aerial photography.

The war had hastened aircraft development. By a quirk, Stonehenge had briefly been at the hub of pre-war British aviation. Early flyers liked the area because of its openness and lack of obstruction. In 1909 the army erected two sheds at Larkhill for the support of experimental aviation. More followed, some put up by individual owners, others by Sir George White's British and Colonial Aeroplane Company, and yet more by the newly formed Royal Flying Corps. As the row of sheds lengthened, a gap was left to maintain the view of midsummer sunrise from the Stones. Larkhill's public flying demonstrations were rather like race meetings, attracting thousands in an atmosphere of good-humoured festivity. Then in 1914 civilian flying was suspended, the site was requisitioned, and the frail machines with names like Coanda, Challenger and Boxkite were gone.[11] In 1914 aeroplanes were feeble and unreliable. Only two years later they were fast, robust and dependable, and the British alone had used them to take several million aerial photographs of the western front.[12]

Early in 1917 Crawford himself applied to join the Royal Flying Corps. This was the second time he had done so, and on this occasion he was accepted. He became an air observer – the crew member who served as lookout, navigator, gunner and photographer. After training he was posted back to France, and almost immediately shot down. Injured by a bullet through his right foot, he was returned to England to convalesce. While doing so he began to write a book. He called it *Man and his Past*.

In the autumn of 1917 Crawford was again sent out to France, now with 48 Squadron, which flew Bristol Fighters. Crawford's geographical and archaeological background stood him in good stead for the many reconnaissance operations that followed, when his awareness of historical features in the landscape enabled him to sketch-plot enemy positions with such accuracy that for a time one of his superiors suspected him of making them up. Near the end of his tour Crawford was sent on a difficult mission deep into enemy territory. This called for navigation by dead reckoning, and it ended in a forced landing well behind enemy lines. Taken prisoner, in due course Crawford escaped, swimming a river in spate to do so. Recaptured, he was sent to the prisoner-of-war camp at Holzminden, where a mass breakout was being organized.[13] Unable to take part because his late arrival did not qualify him for a place in the tunnel, he 'traded food for maps copied from a dictionary'. Released at the war's end, Crawford completed *Man and his Past* and took the manuscript to the Oxford University Press, which published it.

He joined the Ordnance Survey, which in 1920 was still publishing maps bearing things with unscholarly names like 'giants' graves' while omitting monuments about which facts existed.[14] Crawford's brief was to correct these weaknesses, and to compile period maps, the first of which, the *Map of Roman Britain*, appeared in 1924. In some ways this was a dream job, combining so many things that Crawford loved – archaeology, topography, bicycling across Britain, and maps. In others it was oppressive. The Ordnance Survey was under-funded, and although it now lay in the domain of the Board of Agriculture, its military origins were still reflected in a senior staff of elderly army officers who resented civilians in general and Crawford in particular. These gentlemen were accustomed to work at a stately pace in the Survey's Southampton office while NCOs and other ranks went out to do the practical surveying. Crawford's insistence on doing his own fieldwork baffled them, although his absences came to be accepted because the office was quieter when he was away.

Crawford preferred cycling to motoring, partly because he disliked cars, but also because a bicycle enabled him to look over hedges into fields and so relish the nuances of landscape. Crawford kitted out for an expedition was a breathtaking sight:

a sort of modern White Knight, his handlebars loaded with two large shopping bags full of rolls of maps, another slung inside the frame, and sundry other objects attached at random. As his work progressed he would send the completed maps back to Southampton by post, so his burden became progressively diminished, but it was a dangerous and unwieldy arrangement under the best of conditions.[15]

There was, of course, another way to appreciate the gradations of landscape. Even before the Great War, Crawford had realized that aerial reconnaissance offered a way not only to find ancient sites, but also to study and comprehend the past through spatial logic. While excavation probed the accumulations of time, aerial archaeology could explore area. In 1923 he addressed a meeting of the Royal Geographical Society about this,[16] and by writing about it in newspapers he made it topical.

The 1923 lecture led to a meeting with Alexander Keiller, heir to a successful marmalade business in Dundee and a fervent amateur archaeologist. Keiller, then in his thirties, had further devotions: women, skiing, speeding down country lanes in his Bugatti, and flying.[17] In the summer of 1924 Keiller rented an aircraft, Crawford found a cavalryman's map-board to plot the path of each sortie, and together they set forth on a series of flights across Wiltshire, Hampshire and Dorset.

One result of this project was an improving understanding of why and how things seen from above strike the eye. Earthworks were seen best not under bright overhead sun, which tended to flatten them, but under light which modelled their detail, so that even features invisible on the ground could be recovered. Hence, for earthwork photography the hour, season, weather and atmospheric conditions were important. Ploughsoil registered through contrasts of colour, as between, say, the reflective white chalk of a barrow mound and the black silt of its surrounding ditch. Vegetation reacted to the depth, moistness and compaction of soil to give clues to the presence of buried features. Antiquaries had been aware of marks in crops and grass since the sixteenth century, but had seldom seen them from the points of vantage needed to display their meaning.[18] Since all these things were co-varying, and some of them were evanescent, the timing of reconnaissance was critical. Beyond that, the presence and strength of marks in crops depended not only on weather, soil or species of plant, but also on climatic and agricultural influences in the past. Crawford gathered some of these lessons in an Ordnance Survey technical paper, and in a landmark book,

Wessex from the Air, published in 1928, which incorporated fifty of their best photographs.[19]

Wessex from the Air revealed the power of reconnaissance, how more could be captured in one photograph than could sometimes be gained

13. Hod Hill, Dorset, photographed by O. G. S. Crawford, 1924. The site controls a 'natural gateway' between the south coast and Bristol Channel along the valley of the River Stour. Hod Hill was fortified in late prehistory, then by the Romans who put their characteristically formal camp in its corner. Outlines of circular buildings are visible inside the hillfort.

in years on the ground. It also brought hitherto unknown kinds of settlement into view and so into mind. In the 1920s the idea of a Neolithic period, the age of first farmers, was still quite recent, and knowledge of its characteristic places and artefacts was tentative. Alongside the flying, Keiller was beginning to explore a curious enclosure at a place called Windmill Hill in Wiltshire. Formed of concentric but interrupted ditches and banks, the ditches laden with pottery, organic debris, animal remains, human bone and worked flint, Windmill Hill subsequently came to define the material countenance of the early Neolithic in southern Britain.[20] In the next seven decades, over sixty more places like this would be discovered, most of them from the air.

For all its newness, a temporary effect of *Wessex from the Air* was the reinforcement of assumptions about the historical significance of the kinds of light-soiled, semi-open landscapes in which Crawford himself had grown up. Although he had since roamed in Russia (by the late 1920s he was a devotee of Marxist analysis and the Soviet Union), Poland and Syria, travelled in Africa and bought a house in Cyprus, the chalkland retained special meaning. Wessex was chosen for study partly because Crawford lived there, but also because it seemed to him that few other parts of Britain were so rich in earthworks or freer from masking vegetation. This seemed to buttress the idea that ran back through Pitt Rivers at least to Colt Hoare, that Wessex was of pre-eminent significance for prehistory, a core which made everywhere else peripheral.

While Crawford led the way in aerial reconnaissance for archaeology, he was not the only one taking aerial photographs. The extension of the Great War's fighting had brought archaeologically rich territories like rural north Africa, Syria and Iraq under the aerial lens, revealing possibilities for research across large areas where little or no previous work had taken place. Some of the earliest archaeological reconnaissance anywhere had been undertaken in Palestine by flyers of the German Air Force operating with Ottoman forces.[21] Crawford himself went to Iraq and Palestine, realizing that air survey was ideal for the primary exploration of lost settlements in desert terrain: an aircraft could cover wide spaces in a short time, and at a fraction of a land expedition's cost.[22] At home, meanwhile, crews of the recently formed Royal Air Force regularly took such images during exercises and cross-countries, and since Crawford worked for the same government it seemed sensible for him to have access to the pictures they were taking. His requests were at first refused, but eventually the Air Ministry yielded to his badgering. When he toured RAF stations to see what they held his effort was rewarded by a spectacular photograph revealing an extension to the Avenue that leads to Stonehenge.[23]

One of the pilots who responded to Crawford's enquiries was Squadron Leader Gilbert Insall, a survivor of the Great War (in which he had been awarded the Victoria Cross) who afterwards elected to make his career in the RAF.[24] Flying near Amesbury in December 1925 Insall noticed a ploughed field spotted with chalky marks enclosed by a circle. He kept watch on the site until the following summer, when colour contrasts in ripening wheat resolved into concentric rings of pits enclosed by a curving ditch. Excavation later that year revealed the pits to have been settings for timber posts, the largest pits apparently having held imposing oak trunks. With its concentric settings, axis aligned on the summer solstice, and entrance causeway, the new find was inevitably christened Woodhenge.[25] In 1929, following Insall's return from a tour in Iraq, he and Crawford found another timber henge, at Arminghall near Norwich. Also pictured around this time was the astonishing plan of the Roman town at Caistor-by-Norwich, where streets, walls, squares, even individual buildings were branded into the pasture by summer drought.

Such images stirred the thought that aerial survey could illuminate settlement history across entire regions.[26] How was that to be undertaken? Like the Christian missionaries of the first century who had preached their way from city to city around Asia Minor, the air photographers of the 1920s were a tiny group whose evangelism was limited not by what they said but to where they went. Until 1930, when Insall and Crawford separately made reconnaissance trips to northern England and Scotland, the potential of north Britain was unknown.[27] Like Tudor chorographers, archaeologists between the wars were looking at Britain with new eyes. There was talk of a survey of 'all archaeological England'.[28] It is said that Keiller even toyed with hiring the *Graf Zeppelin*, telling Stuart Piggott that its designer, Hugo Eckener, had advised that the airship was so low and roomy that 'you could plot sites straight on to six-inch maps – and it's even got a bar!'[29] For the public, the possibilities of aerial survey sharpened the distinction between the work of archaeologists and that of historians. Both dealt with the past, but from different perspectives: whereas historians sought to reconstruct in words a passive past that was no longer there, aerial photography actively revealed history in modern surroundings, wherein crops and soil registered things from far-back times that had otherwise disappeared.[30] This helped to align archaeology with modernity, a discipline that went with science, speed and evidence visible in the here and now, distinct from the nostalgia and tradition that went with Deep England. (As if to emphasize this, in 1935 Allen bought a Miles Hawk – a state-of-the-art low-wing cantilever monoplane. As a racehorse is usually ridden by a professional jockey rather than its owner, Allen never flew the Hawk, which was regularly piloted by Owen Cathcart-Jones, a professional competitor airman who in 1934 had obtained the round-trip record in the MacRobertson Trophy Air Race from London to Melbourne.)

This immediacy of air archaeology was borne in from the late 1920s when RAF pictures of the silt fens of Cambridgeshire and Lincolnshire came into Crawford's hands. In theory there should have been little archaeology to see on them; the accepted view said that aside from renegades like Hereward the Wake the Fenland had been more or less devoid of residents until the early seventeenth century. The Fenland's early desolation, indeed, seemed all the greater when contrasted with the achievements of eighteenth- and nineteenth-century agricultural improvers. Very well, a few folk had lived on certain islands, or entered the area at intervals to pursue fish or fowl, or to harvest reeds. But that was it. Or was it? The eighteenth-century antiquary William Stukeley had grown up in Holbeach and recorded many Roman finds there-abouts. Later collectors had been puzzled by the frequency with which such finds derived from unpromising areas. To what did they point? The RAF pictures suggested that there was indeed a limit to how much could be attributed to the carelessness of fishers and fowlers.

> [When] we were given our first look at the air-photographic cover of the Fenland … we were startled to find that almost all of the Fenland, except the Isle of Ely and much of the skirtlands near higher ground at the edges, were covered by an irregular network of settlements, farms, watercourses and droveways amounting to a map of an earlier period and way of life on which the modern scene had been superimposed.[31]

At Crawford's instigation, new photographs were taken of the silt fen between Crowland and Holbeach. They confirmed that Roman occupation of the Fens had been widespread, with large areas under cultivation and settlements laid out in relation to a system of creeks, rivers, causeways and canals that predated the eighteenth-century drainage. Roman Fenland, they began to realize, had been rather drier and more habitable than it became in following centuries, when the level of water rose. And behind that landscape lay another: an earlier system of fields, probably referable to the Bronze Age, and many prehistoric barrows in situations which were waterlogged before AD 1650.[32] All of which meant that the history of Fenland had not been a story of desolation tamed by modern engineers, but a cycle of recurrent reconfiguration. Recent study indicates that the great meres of Fenland – Soham Mere, Ramsey Mere, Whittlesey Mere and so on – took shape in the early Middle Ages.[33] Peat growth had been intermittent, with phases of shrinkage and subsidence as well as accumulation. Its organic matter apart, peat consists mostly of water. Hence, when the water table falls, peat shrinks and ground level falls, leaving the silty beds of former rivers and meres as low, firm ridges available for habitation. Some of the earliest settlement was found on what were thought to be sandhill outliers of the Breck country which had been slowly engulfed by peat growth, and then re-exposed as peat shrank.

Findings in the Fens caused Crawford's colleague C. W. Phillips to reflect that this part of England was after all only a department of the history of the formation of the North Sea. If anyone had then flown to look, the same principle could have been applied elsewhere – around the Isles of Scilly,[34] for instance, or eastern Yorkshire, where an old coastline wanders far inland, its forgotten course ghosted in where settlements are or are not, and in otherwise perplexing finds of seagoing boats on

14. Ancient fields and watercourses at Upwell Fen, Norfolk

East Riding farms.[35] Nature's boundaries are always in flux. Knowing where they ran at different times helps understanding of human choices.

Marks of prehistoric farming in the Fenland reminded Phillips of some traces he had seen in the upper Thames valley: a comparison which incidentally illustrated the precept that just as the study of one artefact in isolation from the rest of its kind would be meaningless, so things seen from the air needed to be methodically mapped, because forms and distributions reinforce or qualify one another. This was where things stood when out of the blue Crawford received a letter from George Allen. Crawford replied by encouraging Allen to investigate Oxford's surroundings, especially the gravels of the upper Thames and their tributary valleys. And as Allen's great endeavour began, yet another coincidence strikes us: that summer, the summer of 1933, was one of the twentieth century's hottest.

> The whole of the Thames valley and its tributaries have come out in a violent rash, circles and marks everywhere. I have taken a very large number of photos, many most excellent, and even now have only about half what shows, and I fear rain has destroyed many. However, if I get no more this year I will be satisfied ... The weather breaking is a nuisance and has had an almost instantaneous effect on the marks. Most of them vanished or became faint in a night.[36]

The marks were traces of the homes, fields, rituals and graves of people who had lived in the upper Thames valley for the past six thousand years.

Allen generally flew alone, and the commercially available cameras he had tried were either too bulky for use while flying solo in a small machine or else had other drawbacks. That winter he accordingly retired to his workshop to make his own camera. He gave it careful thought. In calm weather the Puss Moth was docile, and when properly trimmed would fly 'hands off' for long enough to take a picture. However, the clear well-lit days that are best suited for air photography can also be bumpy, and it was not always easy to hold a camera while managing the aircraft in the kind of tight turn that is often needed to get a good downward view. The camera body thus needed to be simple and robust enough to be picked up or put down in the transition from controls to photography. Allen provided two grips, one on each side, to assist a firm grasp and to guard against judder caused by the slipstream. With the camera held in both hands, a simple cross-hair sight atop the body would enable him to frame the shot, which would be taken through a 4.5 lens of 8½ inches focal length.

Squinting through the home-made viewfinder, what did he see? On the Downs of Berkshire and Wiltshire there were earthwork camps and great extents of early fields and lynchets. These were already known, although the aerial perspective enabled new and better appreciation of their extent and relationships. Elsewhere, however, Allen photographed things hitherto unseen: at Drayton near Abingdon, a henge; at Church Down, great rings; at Dorchester, Benson and Drayton, extraordinary parallel lines that ran across country for hundreds, even thousands of yards. According to E. Thurlow Leeds, Keeper of the Ashmolean Museum in Oxford, Allen revolutionized knowledge of early settlement in the upper Thames valley.

> For the fumbling searches and hypotheses of the past he substituted rapidity and certainty by furnishing archaeological workers with a brilliantly documented survey, not only of sites already partially known, but of many others whose existence was previously entirely unsuspected, though many of them are of the highest importance.[37]

Henges, settlements, farms, field systems, villas – here was a new province of the past.

Some of Allen's discoveries set the archaeological world back on its heels. The only parallel-sided avenues hitherto known were at Stonehenge and in Cranborne Chase. The antiquary William Stukeley had called them cursūs on account of the part-resemblance to a Roman race course. Allen had now found six or seven more, and his method of discovery – tracing contrasts of colour in growing crops – would soon lead to the recognition of dozens. A colleague in 1949 reflected that Allen had 'virtually created' the cursūs as a class of site. Some of them ran for miles. Their scale implied a significant social context. Such discoveries '*made* one think, and think on new lines'.[38]

As early as 1933 Crawford was urging Allen to write a book.[39] Even before Allen began it, his photographs were beginning to unsettle the presumption that river valleys had been inaccessible to early settlement.[40] Their significance lay not just in the revelation of new kinds of monument or of past settlement in unexpected places. Rather, they changed the very basis upon which prehistory had hitherto been entertained. Conventional opinion then held that early Britain had been blanketed by impenetrable forest or swamp,[41] and that the Anglo-Saxons had opened out southern Britain by converting wildwood to farmland. In Chapters 6 and 7 it will be argued that this national foundation story was willingly received; yet if an area like the valley of the upper Thames

15. Enclosures for the dead, settings for timber ring and parallel-sided avenue near Dorchester, Oxfordshire, 1938

16. Dorchester henge, Oxfordshire, July 1938

was so thoroughly settled and farmed by the first millennium BC, and if vast avenues were being ruled across it two and a half thousand years before that, how could it be said that Anglo-Saxon colonists had arrived in an untamed land?

The powerful effect of Allen's photographs resulted from the coming together of otherwise unconnected things. Already mentioned have been his family background, his interests in agriculture and land, access to time and money, practical experience of mechnical things, the emergence of private flying, the configuration of the Puss Moth and the location of his airstrip. But even these do not exhaust the list. A further influence was the geology of the area over which he flew. Crops that grow on free-draining gravel soils are more responsive to the aerial camera than those that grow, say, on clay. If Allen had begun flying, say, from Longbridge, his results would have been different, and his subsequent engagement perhaps less.

A second key factor was his agricultural engineer's habit of visiting sites on the ground, the better to understand why he had found them. By doing this he learned that the long roots of lucerne give good results above deeply buried features, and that fungus rings are distinct from round barrows or the turning circles of horses. He knew, too, that rabbits like to work in loosened ground, and found that ground temperatures differ according to the extent of past disturbance, so that frost above a refilled pit may melt sooner than over the subsoil into which the pit was cut. George Allen worked out the grammar of ground. Crawford and Keiller had described *Wessex from the Air* as 'an expedition', with all the implications of news brought back from a new-found land. Allen's knowledge of agriculture and crops caused him to calculate that different things are visible at different times. He accordingly pioneered iterative reconnaissance, returning in successive years to gather cumulative insights from responses that vary according to climate, agricultural regime and local weather. This tenacity, said E. T. Leeds, led him 'to secure the fullest details or to elucidate any obscure or doubtful point'.

Allen pondered why some crops were responsive and others not, or why a field devoid of interest for years should suddenly burst forth in marks like some rarely flowering desert cactus. It was also a question why some areas never showed anything. Did this mean they had always been empty? Part of the answer, we now know, was that ancient landscapes hitherto presumed destroyed (or until the 1930s simply unimagined) were sometimes coated by layers of alluvium or hill-wash, or lay beneath vegetation which translates nothing to the aerial camera, or had been ploughed down. In a later chapter we shall see how the kind of work pioneered by Allen can now be complemented by other, newer forms of remote sensing.

For future conservation, as a record of what not long afterwards was destroyed, and as tokens of two hot, rainless Junes, George Allen's photographs are evocative, providential and unsurpassed. Among them, too, are pictures which show Allen's delight in the surroundings in which he lived. He adored patterns – the swirl of streets in a new housing estate, the texture of orchards, fields on the Welsh border. His fascination for transport led him to trace the building of new roads in a countryside not yet cluttered with distribution sheds and random development.

Allen's aerial visits to excavations capture the ethos, methods and society of inter-war archaeology. His year-by-year record of Wheeler's excavation at Maiden Castle traces the work's progress and discipline, the regimented camp site, London visitors' cars and the daring minimalism of Wheeler's strategy. He took special interest in the excavation of a Roman villa that he had photographed in Ditchley Park, Oxfordshire, in 1934. The villa's existence had been known for years, but Allen's photographs revealed it with unprecedented clarity – the entire layout was ghosted in a crop that grew above the mansion's remains. The pictures excited calls for an excavation. An excavation committee was formed which R. G. Collingwood agreed to chair. The committee launched an appeal (to which Ditchley Park's owner, the Anglo-American Ronald Tree, gave £25) and invited C. A. Ralegh Radford to direct the work.[42]

Radford was thirty-four years old when he received the invitation in January 1935. He was widely travelled, had access to private means, and since 1933 had led an annual excavation on Tintagel Island recording traces of what he believed – incorrectly, as it eventually turned out – to have been a Celtic monastery.[43] His excavation strategy for Ditchley assumed that the villa's plan ('except for small details') was already known from Allen's photographs, so it would only be necessary to 'uncover an area sufficient for accurate measurement', to 'establish the sequence' of any features so revealed, and to recover enough objects 'to fix the date of the different building periods'.[44] The villa's plan seemed so clear that Crawford questioned the need for any digging at all. However, there were questions which only excavation could answer. Was the villa on a virgin site or had there been an earlier farm? What kind of agricultural economy had been practised? And how had the villa met its end?[45] Radford and Collingwood considered that narrow trenches laid out to intersect walls or run through rooms would ascertain the answers.[46]

17. Excavation at Maiden castle, 1935. Thomas Hardy had likened Maiden Castle to an 'enormous many-limbed organism of an antediluvian time ... lying lifeless, and covered with a thin green cloth, which hides its substance, while revealing its contour': A Tryst at an Ancient Earthwork *(1885).*

Excavation began in August 1935 and ran through the autumn. The narrative derived by Radford from the results now looks unduly simple: a first villa standing by the late first century, a damaging fire around AD 200, an interlude of abandonment followed by rebuilding on a larger scale. At the end there was no sign of upheaval or misfortune. Rather, the economic life of the estate appeared to have continued into the fifth century while the house ran down – a state of affairs which led Radford to wonder if there had been an absentee landlord.

Radford's inferences from the capacity of the granary and other agricultural evidence led him to suggest that the villa estate had covered some thousand acres. This was about one-third of the area that belonged to Ditchley House, the early-Georgian mansion designed by James Gibbs which had been occupied since 1933 by the Conservative M.P. Ronald Tree and his glamorous Virginia-born wife Nancy.[47] Among finds from the villa were continental tablewares, glass from Egypt, and fragments of painted plaster from scenes that had adorned the walls. No one then (or, apparently, since) saw an analogy between the life of the villa and of the house. Nancy Tree is better remembered under her later married name of Nancy Lancaster, the designer who by re-imagining the furnishing, décor and gardens of English country houses influenced Anglo-American taste in the later twentieth century.[48] In the early 1930s Deborah Mitford was a teenager living ten miles away. She remembered the house before the Trees' arrival: 'empty and desolate, the park full of rabbits and sad white grass in the time of the agricultural depression of the early 1930s.' When Nancy and Ronald arrived 'it came to life, and there they created perfection'.[49] Among the visitors who enjoyed this 'perfection' were David Niven, Noël Coward and Anthony Eden. Possibly only Major Allen, the lone bachelor circling overhead in his Puss Moth, thought about both households at once.

Allen photographed other pre-war excavations at Verulamium, West Kennet, Silchester and Woodbury. His 1938 Woodbury photographs show three parallel rectangular areas under excavation. When these had been completed Bersu turned to the intervening areas, the resulting composite plan giving the impression of a single exposure.[50] On a flight to the Roman city at Wroxeter in August 1938 Allen skimmed round the summit of the Wrekin, taking a succession of photographs; he might have imagined himself a swift. For students of heritage management, his record of Stonehenge captures the onset of popular tourism by motor car, the first car park, the shifting axes of roads. For devotees of industrial history and the inter-war economy, his archive is a cornucopia: gasworks, cement production, brick kilns, railways – they are all there. The record of Oxford's industrial suburb at Cowley is especially full. He photographed the motor works of his father's friend Morris and the rise of the Pressed Steel Company, and traced new patterns of housing being built to accommodate those who worked in them. In contrast is the sunlit peace of the Radcliffe Camera and Oxford High Street on a summer's morning.

And Crawford? O. G. S Crawford's apparently disparate activities cohered around a vision of science-led progress towards world civilization: 'Evolution held the key to the future development of the planet, and it was imperative that the findings of its scholars were conveyed to the citizens of the world so that they would know the truth, and be prepared.'[51] What could be described could also be understood: by collecting, recording and assembling facts, the patterns of human development would be made clear. Air photography was thus an instrument of progress – about the future as well as the past.[52] In March 1938 some of Allen's photographs featured in an exhibition in London of recent archaeological discoveries,[53] and Crawford went to lecture on the subject in Berlin.

The Berlin visit was partly prompted by his friend Gerhard Bersu, the German archaeologist whom the Nazis had dismissed from the Frankfurt Institute.* Until then, air-archaeology had been largely ignored in Germany. 'It is not often one can teach the Germans a new technique, particularly in photography,' recalled Crawford, 'and I felt rather proud to be asked to do so.' A number of the photographs he selected were Allen's. In choosing them Crawford realized how far the subject had developed since publication of *Wessex from the Air*. The Ordnance Survey ignored his suggestion that they should publish the pictures in a semi-popular book. In Berlin, on the other hand, Crawford was fêted. First there was an informal seminar and then a lecture at the Air Ministry. The lecture was given in German by a reader (Bersu had translated it) while Crawford stood on the platform, pointing to details on a huge screen. The audience of four hundred included Luftwaffe and Wehrmacht officers, although not the British ambassador, who pleaded a prior engagement at a football match. Afterwards, Crawford was introduced to a director of Lufthansa, who asked permission to publish the lecture. Crawford agreed, with the caveat that he did not have the authority to agree.[54] This was wise, as both the Ordnance Survey and HM Treasury objected, and then relented on condition that the Germans should pay a copyright fee of half a crown for each photograph reproduced. Crawford exploded, and eventually the absurdity was dropped. The monograph appeared under the title *Luftbild und Vorgeschichte* ('Aerial pictures and prehistory'). It was the best general account of air-archaeology yet, and was pregnant with ironies – a subject which had been institutionally ignored by the nation in which it had been pioneered, being celebrated by the government which had ousted Gerhard Bersu from his academic post.

Summer 1939 found Crawford bustling about, as photographer at Sutton Hoo in the last days of July, then back in Germany at the International Archaeological Congress in Berlin. At August's end, as the last hours of peace ran out and colleagues back in Suffolk at Sutton Hoo were making their last survey drawings of the ship of an unknown hero, Crawford was talking with German, Russian and Italian academics about the common history of a shared continent, and several thousand copies of *Luftbild und Vorgeschichte* were circulating in Germany.

* See p. 71.

On Sunday 27 August 1939 Allen took off in mid-afternoon and flew to circle nearby Wittenham Clumps, twin hills crowned with beech trees that overlook the upper Thames and the Vale of the White Horse. He was in the air for about an hour and a half, landing just after five. He never flew again. On the following Sunday the world went to war for the second time in the twentieth century, and civilian flying was suspended. Allen gave his Puss Moth to the government. In 1942 it was recycled for spares.

The war drew many of Britain's academic archaeologists into air-photograph interpretation.[55] Wheeler called this 'women's work', but it was a natural transfer of skills.[56] To photographic intelligence were recruited academics like Arnold Taylor, a future Chief Inspector of Ancient Monuments, and the archaeologist Glyn Daniel. It was partly on Daniel's instigation that other colleagues were drawn in, until more Cambridge archaeologists were working on Allied reconnaissance than in Cambridge. Charles Phillips, Crawford's comrade and the excava-tor of Sutton Hoo, went to work on air-photograph interpretation at RAF Medmenham, where in 1944 he met a twenty-year-old artist and amateur archaeologist from Surrey called Brian Hope-Taylor. Hope-Taylor made models of special targets to be attacked by the Allies – a task fraught with security risks (because the models were made well in advance of the attacks) which it was Phillips's job to contain.

After the war Hope-Taylor used the techniques of area excavation evolved in Denmark to excavate Yeavering, a seventh-century centre of Northumbrian royal power, which was discovered from the air in 1947 by another of Crawford's protégés, a young Cambridge don called Kenneth St Joseph who had worked for Bomber Command during the war, and whose obsession with the doings of the Roman army in Scotland led him to make periodic flights to north Britain. On the way there and back he took photographs of things he saw. At first St Joseph used aircraft occasionally loaned by the RAF, later a hired aeroplane, and from 1962 a machine owned by the university. Some five thousand hours of reconnaissance were flown from Cambridge between 1945 and 1980. The effects were reminiscent of *Wessex from the Air* – new knowl-edge, changed perceptions.

When military-trained pilots returned to civilian life after the war, some of them turned to private flying, and archaeology. This new gener-ation of archaeological flyers was larger than the company of air workers in the 1930s. It was also more widely spread, which meant that more of Britain was routinely accessible to photographers who became attuned to regional variations of soil, cropping, weather and past settlement.[57] One of them was Derrick Riley, an executive in Sheffield's steel industry and former bomber pilot. In 1943 Riley had been posted to an aerodrome in the country of the upper Thames. When off duty he sometimes took the bus into Oxford to look at Allen's photographs in the Ashmolean Museum. Riley was fascinated not only by what he saw as he flew over the area but also by the factors which caused him to see it.[58] Nearly forty years later he published a book which got to grips with the mysteries of crop marks – why, for instance, fields of beet which are blank in one year may display a colossal Iron Age field system in the next. During the years between, Riley systematically quartered southern Yorkshire and north Nottinghamshire in different seasons and weathers. Among his discoveries was a type of field system which seemed to recur over a wide area. He seldom saw much of it at any one time, but as different portions were glimpsed, photographed and mapped in different years, an accumulated picture was fitted together. Like giant brickwork, the apparition ran for mile after mile.[59]

The consequence of the expanding picture was a realization that aerial survey was not simply a way of finding sites, and that excavation was not necessarily the best way to understand them. The very idea of 'site'

18. *Field system at Rossington, South Yorkshire, photographed by Derrick Riley, 1975. Riley tracked parts of such systems from season to season until it became clear that they extended for long distances.*

began to dissolve in the face of the sheer extensiveness of what the aerial camera revealed. At best, 'site' was an artificial construct, an area delineated for present convenience rather than denoting any past reality. 'Site' was also deceiving, for it invited you to look inwards rather than out to the surrounding area and horizons that gave it meaning. Crawford said that alongside frameworks of period and typology archaeology also needed a grammar of space and time. But for the war, the circulation of *Luftbild und Vorgeschichte* might have spread his call through Europe. In the event, the war and the descent of the Iron Curtain that followed delayed this for another half-century.

The end of the Cold War allowed air-archaeologists into skies from which they had been excluded for forty years, or had never entered. The moment was akin to the slow swinging open of a pair of great bronze doors. In Italy, early twentieth-century paranoia about aerial spying caused a ban on aerial photography that was not repealed until the early twenty-first century. In former Warsaw Pact countries like Romania and Bulgaria even consciousness of landscape had been restrained, for public access to larger-scale maps – and hence knowledge about the bones of landscape – had been restricted.[60] The dormancy of air-archaeology behind the Iron Curtain had given rise to modern legends – for instance, that central European soils and crops were not conducive to the kinds of marks seen by Allen or Crawford. First results discovered Roman legions campaigning far from where anyone expected them, and eastern extensions of monument forms hitherto presumed to belong to Atlantic Europe. The Cold War had conditioned prehistory into seeing an image of itself.[61]

Crawford did not live to see aerial archaeology put on to the international footing for which he had striven. Striving epitomized him; his life appears as a kind of beneficial restlessness, a stream of activity that leaves anyone who thinks of it feeling short-winded. Writing books and essays, always on the move, on foot or by bicycle, working across so wide a range – topography, place names, flying, photography, buildings, prehistory – cajoling, mapping, editing *Antiquity*, flinging his cap to the ground when frustrated, pursuing intellectual kinships with figures like Collingwood, gripped by a publicist's desire to push archaeology out to the world, mapping the path to a global future 'free from superstition, religion and nationalism':[62] where did he find the time? Crawford's first editorial for *Antiquity* caught history's purpose before politicians and educational consultants lost confidence in the joy of human curiosity: 'The universal interest in the past is perfectly natural. It is the interest in life itself.'

The Second World War was not the kind of development that Crawford had expected to see. His faith in science and human progress was shaken, and by the late 1940s he realized that his confidence in the Soviet Union had been betrayed. For 'the man who had rejected the millenarianism of his upbringing, putting his faith in another kind of deliverance for the world ... it now looked as though that deliverance was not to be. Beliefs, like buildings, can become ruins, and when they crumble they surely take part of their human hosts with them.'[63] And scarcely had the great aerial discoveries begun to percolate into historical consciousness than it was recognized that intensified agriculture, forestry and construction were destroying them.[64] In retirement Crawford began to write general books, for which he was admonished by younger archaeologists who thought him out of touch.[65]

Lover of cats, disliker of telephones, television, typewriters and gadgets generally, disappointed Marxist, eventually discarded by some of those whose careers he had fostered, Crawford died in his sleep in the night of 28/29 November 1957. That Thursday – or had it turned to Friday? – was just four days past the anniversary of Allen's death, and one day short of the anniversary of the air raid that had destroyed many of his papers.[66]

Each generation supposes its predecessors to have been somehow nobler, more hard-working and instrumental than the leaders of its own. In the cases of Osbert Crawford and George Allen, this might actually be so.

PART TWO
SWAN MUSIC

19. (Previous page) *Flute made from mammoth ivory, Geissenklösterle, SW Germany, c.40,000–45,000 BC*

5

THE OLD ONES

Sessile, unseeing,
the Plant is wholly content
with the Adjacent.

Mobilised, sighted,
the Beast can tell Here from There
and Now from Not-Yet.

Talkative, anxious,
Man can picture the Absent
and Non-Existent.

W. H. Auden, 'Progress?', 1972,
Collected Poems, 1994

Old Ones lived on Earth before and alongside us. In many ways we resemble them, and some of them we knew. But they were not exactly us, nor are we more complete versions of them. From what we know they were simply others, with other histories.

Old Ones occupied parts of Africa and Asia for several million years before they began to probe the Mediterranean; they never entered the Americas. No sure date can yet be put on their arrival in Europe, but there are signs that they were here upwards of 0.78 million years ago.[1] If imagining 0.78 million is difficult, an analogy may help. If we think of time as distance, and 0.78 million years as the length of a cricket pitch, then proportional to this the beginning of the national history curriculum is about the length of a matchbox from the pitch's near end. The period back to the end of the last glaciation occupies maybe a foot. Another foot will take us to the animal paintings in the caves of the Dordogne and southern France, a further six inches to the horses and

lions of Chauvet. The rest, the remaining sixty-four or so feet, is the
time of the Old Ones.

Let us look at their surroundings. In Chapter 1 we saw how nineteenth-century geomorphologists came to understand that parts of the
world have repeatedly been scoured by ice. By the early 1900s it was
reckoned that four great episodes of cold had descended on Europe
within the last two million years. This view lasted until the 1960s, when
analysis of oxygen isotopes drawn from sea-floor sediments enabled the
production of a finer record of climatic fluctuation. What this showed
was that warm–cold cycles had been more numerous than previously
believed. In place of the stately fourfold schema being taught for O
Level geography in the 1960s the new reading looked more like the
trace of an electro-cardiograph: a flicker of pulsating shifts from warm
to cold and back again, each main cycle lasting about a hundred thousand years, and itself subject to further internal wavering.

Such climatic swings bring changes in sea level, vegetation and
animal life. The extent of ice affects the relative level of land and sea in
two main ways. One, called *eustasy*, derives from influences upon global
sea level. There is only so much water on the planet and at times of
extreme cold much of the water that would normally be returned to the
oceans through rain or snow is withheld in ice, so that sea level falls. The
sea can go very low. Sixteen thousand years ago, when ice covered north
Britain and most of Wales, sea level was about 300 feet lower than today.
At such times continental shore lines move outward, land areas grow
and islands fuse with the mainland. A recent project has mapped the
realm of former rivers, valleys, plains and low hills that lie beneath the
North Sea.[2] When climate warms the process goes into reverse: water is
returned to circulation and sea level rises.

Eustasy works in tandem with another process, *isostasy*, which concerns the equilibrium of the Earth's crust. Rather as treacle behaves if a
spoon is gently pressed upon its surface, land beneath an ice sheet will
sink under its weight, while land in the ice sheet's vicinity is bulged
upwards. When the pressure is removed, the unburdened land rebounds,
and the forebulge subsides. Isostatic uplift can outpace sea-level rise,
leaving bygone coastlines stranded inland or hoisting beaches above
later sea level.

One result of these processes is that for most of the last million years
'our island story' has been nothing of the kind – Britain has been part
of the continental land mass. Sometimes called a 'land bridge' (perhaps
the idea of a 'bridge' is soothing to those for whom British separateness

is important?), it was usually something more than that. Less than nine thousand years ago Britain was a peninsula of northern Europe. Six hundred thousand years ago England and France were joined by chalk downland. The English Channel was then not open but a great inlet that ended to the east in a bay rimmed by white cliffs. The chalk was breached in the aftermath of a glacial period that began around 450,000 years ago, when advancing ice across what is now the North Sea dammed the outflow of rivers to create a lake that extended from what is now Suffolk to northern Germany. The lake grew to the size of modern Lake Superior; eventually the water overtopped the chalk ridge, becoming a deluge that carved open the Straits of Dover. An even greater flood from a yet greater glacial lake has been postulated about 160,000 years ago.[3] Thereafter, like a gate swinging in the wind, the Channel and North Sea have sometimes been open or, when the sea is low, closed.

These are but two episodes among many. These relative changes affect rivers – their routes, whether they are cutting down or backing up, whether they are fast-flowing or sluggish, whether they fit the valleys along which they flow, sometimes whether they exist at all. Around twenty thousand years ago there was a Channel River that flowed westwards from the Kent–Calais area for about 300 miles until its waters met the Atlantic west of Cornwall and Brittany. Fed by ancestors to the Rhine, the Thames, the Seine and the Meuse, this mighty waterway was larger than any in Europe today. Eight hundred thousand years back the greatest waterway of southern Britain was not the Thames or the Severn, but a now vanished river known to quaternary scientists as the Bytham, a river greater than the Rhine, which rose in the west midlands and flowed eastwards until the Anglian ice sheets scrubbed it away. Ancestors of the Thames were fickle, at some times flowing out through an estuary that today lies drowned in the bed of the North Sea, at others merging with a proto-Medway to form a river that flowed north-east across what are now the Essex marshes towards a European north coast. After the successive meltings and retreats of ice sheets, the valleys of such great rivers offered lines of access along which animals and people could return. Their journeys are ghosted in stone tools, fossils and bones scattered among the gravels and terraces of ancestor waterways like the Solent River, the Thames and the Bytham.[4]

As land-forms changed, so did biota. If a satellite-borne camera had stared down at Britain for the last three-quarter of a million years, its record would show pulsations from ice desert to tundra, from tundra to sub-arctic species like birch, juniper and Scots pine, thence to more abundant woodlands and grasslands, and back again as the cycle repeated. Animals arrive and depart, at each stage learning migration instinct anew. When the sea is low they move to places which at other times are inaccessible. Contrariwise, if climatic change is swift, the time needed for adjustment may not always be there. One sudden alteration occurred a little after 13,000 years ago, when the world's emergence from the last ice age went into reverse, and Britain's mean annual temperature dropped by c.15°C in about a decade.[5] The resulting freeze lasted for a thousand years, when ice returned to Scotland and the Lake District. Eurasia's animal and plant species have dwindled during the last million years; if cold returned so quickly, it has been suggested, the lie of mountain chains may have meant that populations of some species of plant and insect lacked the time to retreat across the Alps or Pyrenees.[6]

Workers in gravel quarries sometimes find the remains of departed creatures – woolly mammoth, woolly rhinoceros, reindeer, musk ox and bison. These were cold-climate animals, denizens of the steppe. In warmer epochs, herds of aurochs grazed. With them were mammals like beaver, wolf, bear, boar and deer, and creatures we now associate with sub-tropical regions – like lion, elephant (several kinds, one of spectacular size), rhino, many kinds of deer, antelope, even hippopotamus.

It would be natural to see such creatures as pointers to times when Britain was warmer than now, and in some periods (as evidenced by the hippo), it was. Overall, however, the climatic evidence says that past warm-interlude temperatures were not vastly out of line with those of today, and that the average for the greater part of the last half-million years was cooler. The salutary explanation is that lion, straight-tusked elephant and the rest prospered in the rich environment of temperate Europe, from which they were eventually evicted by loss of habitat. We New Ones are forever adapting the environment, intruding on other species' habitats to suit ourselves and as our numbers increase we expel them. The African savannah with its droughts and scarcities is not the heartland of antelope and rhino, but their last retreat.

A striking feature of the departed creatures is how large they often were. By today's standards some species of now extinct horse, deer and bovids were colossal. Again, the increase in hominin activity is likely to have been a factor in their disappearance. Large animals yield more food than small ones, and while they will have been challenging to hunt and kill, for Old Ones the warm interglacials with their grand beasts were times of plenitude.

If we sieve the sands and silts which were trodden by great mammals, a more delicate picture emerges. Remains of creatures like the hazel dormouse and birch mouse, rodents like the red-backed vole, water vole and pine vole, different species of bat, insect and bird, are proxy indicators for local environments. Some of these animals have hardly changed during the last two million years. Others show alteration at particular times. A number became extinct. Not all are present at every stage. The permutations in which they occur, their times of occupancy and absence, all help us to discern and date different episodes.

One creature we seldom see is Man. On the strength of skeletal remains alone, indeed, until about forty thousand years ago we would suppose Old Ones in Britain to have been about as infrequent as walkers on the moon. So far, all their known bones from Britain together would scarcely fill a shoe-box. But large numbers of stone tools and the debris from making them attest their presence. The tools occur in the vicinity of old river channels, caves and marine platforms. Near by are sometimes found the bones of other animals bearing marks showing that Old Ones slew and butchered them. Excavations in front of an ancient sea cliff at Boxgrove in Sussex have identified a place where Old Ones gathered five hundred thousand years ago to break the carcasses

of the animals they had hunted, and made the tools to do so. Boxgrove has yielded bones of horse, red deer and rhinoceros which under magnification display the grooves that result from tools used in skinning, dismemberment and marrow extraction. In one bone a sliver of flint was found embedded within the cut stroke where it had snapped off.[7]

Boxgrove is the kind of place at which to hearken to 'the echo of a lost sound'.[8] Why do we know so few places like it? Part of the answer is that each subsequent glaciation rasped the land, sculpted and re-sculpted what was there before, and then sluiced away much of the debris when it melted. Only rarely are we

20. *Boxgrove biface*   likely to find original deposits that

have escaped the mayhem caused by successive glaciations. By contrast, Old Ones' stone tools survive like other bits of stone – but not only or even mainly in the places where they were made or used. Like pebbles and cobbles, stone tools were bowled along by torrents and rivers until they came to rest in the terraces of rivers, beds of lakes and estuarine outwash. In other words, objects that Old Ones made from stone were typically redistributed where glacial run-off and rivers later took them. More than this, the tendency for Old Ones to make the same kinds of tools for millennia means that stylistically identical artefacts may have been fashioned hundreds of thousands of years apart. In result, the places and numbers in which we find tools do not necessarily reflect the whereabouts or numbers of the people who made them. All we can say is that the populations appear to have been small – maybe as small as a few hundred in all of southern Britain at any given time. Intact locales that might be archaeologically recognizable were thus sparse even before ice sheets disturbed them. Boxgrove, we have seen, is one of them. Lynford, in Norfolk, where animal remains from molluscs to mammoths came to rest in gravels and silts in an area where a river wandered between lagoons, is another.[9] Pakefield in Suffolk has produced evidence for human presence around 0.7 million years ago,[10] Happisburgh, now on the Norfolk coast, once beside the mouth of an Ur-Thames, is a fourth.[11] The rarity of such open locations is one reason why caves have figured so often in the Old Ones' record, not necessarily because Old Ones were cavemen, but because that stereotype arises from the fact that it is often caves that have sheltered evidence from outside events.

As in a symbolist poem, Palaeolithic Britain resembles a house containing signs that someone has been living in it, yet is unnervingly still. This may be because, for tens of millennia at a stretch, no one was here. There is next to no sign of them, for instance, between 180,000 and 60,000 years ago. There may be environmental reasons for that – for example, because climatic fluctuations and sea-level changes were so rapid that Old Ones were unable to recolonize after glacial episodes. Or it may be that the paucity of undisturbed deposits bearing evidence of human life gives an impression of absence when in reality there were Old Ones here all along. A further possibility, suggested by recent research, is that there was a gradual decline in hominin population over the preceding three hundred thousand years, and that the 'age of absence' was accordingly the culmination of a trend. If so, what caused it?

Other things are unnerving. In the making of stone tools, why did so little change between 800,000 and 300,000–200,000 years ago, when

a new way of making tools appeared? Fifty years ago when the human
story was seen as progress from stooped to upright, dim to clever, grunting to blank verse, the answer seemed obvious – variations in the style
and workmanship of tools were assumed to reflect a gradual extension
of skills and abilities, perhaps even the work of different species. A re-
reading of the evidence finds that different styles and forms coexisted,
and that some tool types were little altered from one end of the period
to the other. Moreover, types of tool once credited to specific species of
Old One may have been made by several. Even the identity of the species is controversial: are we looking at one or two types of Old One, or
many?

The shape and size of the human evolutionary tree is provisional.
It is not yet clear whether we have drawn it too starkly or made it too
bushy, whether on the basis of fragmentary remains we have under- or
over-classified species, or even whether some of the twigs and branches
have been correctly connected. In the mid-twentieth century, following a period when almost every new-found fossil had been accorded
the status of a new species, opinion swung towards the view that species had been over-classified. What human evolution needed, said the
gradualists, was a spring clean, and one of its effects was a cull in the
number of accepted hominid species represented in the fossil record.
The geneticist Theodosius Dobzhansky declared that all human evolution within the last million years had taken place inside the borders of
one species, *Homo sapiens*.[12] Writing in the 1970s, Ernst Mayr believed
that the story was contained in no more than three, none of which had
coexisted.[13] Since then, however, the main body of opinion has swung
back towards the plural reading. Some of the species crossed off in the
1940s and 1950s have been reinstated, and more have been added. Even
while this chapter was being written, discoveries of two new hominin
types were announced.[14]

While debate about the shape of the species tree will continue, it is
safe to say that the traditional view of human emergence as a journey
towards perfection has missed something. Many now perceive the process as episodic, not gradual, and the notion of 'emergence', implying as
it does a progress, and therefore a destiny, should arguably be set aside.
The past two million years have seen the appearance and disappearance of a number of hominin species, some of which coexisted and all
of which, apart from ourselves, are now extinct. Hence our uniqueness
derives not from being at the summit of evolutionary progress, nor from
having crossed some threshold to a place outside Nature, but from the

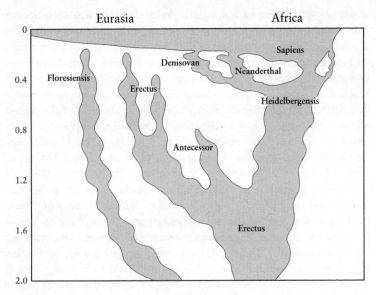

21. *Phylogeny of the human family (after Chris Stringer, 2011)*

fact that while there has been more than one human history, ours happens to embrace the others because we are the only ones left to look back at them.

What do we see? There were different kinds of Old Ones. From the evidence of fossils it seems that the human tree germinated in Africa five million or more years ago. The first known *Homo* species branch off at around 2,300,000 years, evolving through further forms, at least one of which, *Homo erectus*, begins to spread into central and eastern Asia. Thus far (about two million years back) Europe seems to have been unpeopled. From a million years ago more people begin to journey out of Africa into the world beyond. Some time before 780,000 years ago, a few are glimpsed on Europe's margins, as at Gran Dolina in Spain and Happisburgh in Suffolk.[15] It may be that such finds reflect ephemeral episodes of occupancy, and it is not yet clear whether those involved belonged to one human species or several.[16] However this may be, from around 500,000 years ago the European fossil and archaeological records reveal what looks like a distinct species – *Homo heidelbergensis*.[17]

The species was named after a jawbone found in a sandpit at Mauer, near Heidelberg, in 1907. Recorded in at least eleven European sites, Heidelbergs seem to occur widely, with finds claimed as far apart as

Ethiopia, central Africa and China. Very possibly it was a Heidelberg we saw at Boxgrove. However, while finds of their objects and activity sites are well documented, fossils of the people themselves remain fugitive. Hence, in assigning particular traits to Heidelbergs it may be that we are attributing things to one species that actually belong to several. Having registered the risk we can say that – earlier sporadic visits apart – hominids of the Heidelberg era (in Europe, roughly 800,000 to 250,000 years ago) were Europe's original Old Ones. When evidence from different sources is conflated, they emerge as tall and strongly built, with brain volumes not far from the average of our own, and faces that jutted forward of the brain case rather than descending sheer as in ourselves. Heidelbergs made weapons and tools not only out of stone but also from wood and bone. Their technology was 'layered', some items being made to assist in the making of others, and since the survival of organic materials is poor, their craft attainments may have been greater than those we now see. Heidelbergs were once regarded as scavengers, but it seems from Boxgrove's animal remains that they were skilled hunters who took priority over other carnivores at kills. More recent sites at Terra Amata in southern France and Germany give hints that they built shelters and had control of fire. Whether they possessed language in any familiar sense is unknown. The consensus is that they did not, but there is a school of thought which attributes some capacity for speech to the very origin of *Homo*. The verdict of Boxgrove's excavator gives pause: 'Elements of planning depth, cooperation, and technology, often assumed to be restricted to modern humans, are already within the behavioural repertoire of these hominids. Combining these elements with their large physique ... the Boxgrove hominids would have cut formidable figures in the landscape.'[18]

Heidelberg Old Ones or a close relative may have been our own ancestors. They may also have been the forebears of the Neanderthals, a regional variant of striking appearance which from DNA evidence is thought to have begun to branch off from our lineage maybe 500,000 years ago. The Neanderthals' heyday seems to have been during the last interglacial, when their province reached from the Atlantic to Uzbekistan.[19] Some time before four hundred centuries ago their numbers begin to dwindle, their occupancy fragmenting into increasingly separated and shrinking enclaves, until they disappear around 30,000 years ago.[20]

The public remains fascinated by Neanderthals, perhaps because almost everything about them seems equivocal. In Britain we find their tools but hardly ever glimpse the people themselves. They evoke the Gothic responses explored in Chapter 2: fascination tinged by alarm, a pang of horror, even pity. Modern research looks past this, finding them to have been versatile, pioneers in varied habitats under hard weathers, makers of sophisticated hafted tools and composite weapons, wearers of simple ornaments, revisitors of favourite sites, builders of shelters, capable hunters, mutually supportive and users of fire. Occasionally, at least, they buried their dead, although whether for practical or transcendental reasons we cannot tell. Nor do we know if, or how much, they spoke. Like the Heidelbergs, Neanderthals did possess the evolved vocal tract that is needed to support speech, but their material lives do not show enough symbolic complexity to convince all scholars that we are in the presence of elaborated language, just as the range of their accomplishments is difficult to entertain in language's absence.

If Neanderthal Old Ones did speak, did they converse with New Ones? New Ones – us – arrived in the Middle East maybe sixty thousand years ago, having apparently differentiated as a new species in Africa some time in the previous hundred thousand years.[21] The New Ones' earliest sites in the Middle East yield tools which resemble those associated with Neanderthals. Like the pause as a newborn child gathers breath for its first yell, some thousands of years pass before New Ones become obviously innovative. Yet even in that first stage, they were doing new things. Their patterns of movement look different, and they disposed of their dead in ways that suggest concern. Whereas Neanderthal groups seem to have been small, and tended to source stone for their tools from the near vicinity, New Ones collected materials from far away – either because they journeyed to do so, or because they were able to develop relationships with other groups that enabled exchange.[22]

New Ones, it seems, were characterized by a powerful curiosity, an ability to think outside themselves, to imagine places or people they could not see. Their inquisitiveness extended beyond distances of trade and travel to the boundary of life itself, and so into time. It has been asked if later Neanderthal burials were made in imitation of New Ones' graves. In some areas, New Ones and Neanderthals did coexist. New Ones reached south-east Europe around 45,000 years ago. At several European sites there is evidence to suggest that the occupation of Neanderthals and New Ones alternated, while objects attributed to New Ones have been found at several places with Neanderthal remains. Another question: did some of the apparent behavioural differences between Old and New Ones have anything to do with childhood – the time when new sounds and words are improvised, symbols are created in play, and the absorption of language and concepts is effortless? Childhood among Old Ones was very short. Its extension even by a year or two may have had cultural consequences that are yet invisible in the physical record.

Whether or not Old Ones talked, did they sing? Music circumvents speech, and pitch and rhythm go with the rites of task – pounding, striking, stretching, tapping, tugging. Different kinds of stone, wood and bone are as much or more recognizable by sound as by sight. And in echoes across valleys, lakes and woodlands, there were ways in which certain places could become special. Music unites work and ceremony; labour can be dance. Some have wondered if – and, if so, why – the human vocal tract evolved faster than those centres of the brain concerned with language. Chant or vocalizing might explain. Even today, a few languages recorded by anthropologists are based on clicking rather than the phonetically graduated sounds with which we are familiar. That is, rhythm may have preceded or run alongside tonality.

Whether or not Old Ones sang, few things from prehistory are more charged with possibility than the flute found at Geissenklösterle, in the region of the upper Danube in southern Germany. Carved nearly 37,000 years ago from a swan's wing bone, it is the oldest musical instrument yet found in Europe.[23] Its player has been assumed as a New One;[24] similar instruments, not quite as old but of the period, and whistles made from the toe bones of other animals, have been found elsewhere.[25] Did a Neanderthal hear any of them? If so, how did he hear? As noise, with perplexity? Or as beauty, with tears? The flutes are exploratory, of no obvious economic use (unless, like Papageno's, they were for luring birds), yet they are expressive in ways which carry across time and space. In time far ahead, the swan will be the bird said to sing at the approach of its own death.

Species. How do we differentiate between human species? As a rule of thumb, 'species' is a unit of classification which is characterized by some biological actuality; however, it has no single meaning, and definitions vary according to context and life form involved. Among sexually reproducing life forms, 'species' is widely held to describe a group of organisms with reproductive cohesion – a set of beings who will breed successfully among themselves, but not with members of other species.[26] There is argument about this, and there are other definitions, but the concept is more readily applicable to vertebrate animals and insects than it is to plants (many of which hybridize readily, and some of which self-pollinate) or to asexual life forms for which the definition does not work at all.

The working definition used by Chris Stringer rests on the fossil record – the features of a skeleton which when taken together form a distinct morphological group that can be compared with and told apart from other such groups.[27] 'Species' thus becomes a pragmatic category, its boundaries decided by ourselves with results 'which may or may not always work when compared with the reality of nature'.[28] On this definition, some human species need not have been reproductively isolated from each other. In the same way as species with very recent genetic divergence can interbreed (examples are wolf, coyote, dingo), so there may have been reproductive interaction between New and Old Ones. In the case of Neanderthals and us this now looks very likely: in 2010 the Neanderthal Genome Analysis Consortium found that New Ones in Europe and Asia do carry some Neanderthal genes.[29] In comparison with the genomes of people today it was found that those from Europe, China and New Guinea lie a little closer to the Neanderthal sequence than do those from Africa. The inference is that if you are from Europe, Asia or New Guinea 'you probably have a bit of Neanderthal in your make up'.[30]

How that transfer occurred is a question which illustrates the extent to which variables governing human dispersal may have interacted. One prospect raised by Stringer is that some sixty thousand years ago New Ones bred with Neanderthals as they left Africa. No more than a few thousand people may have been involved in that exodus, so it would have needed no more than the absorption of a handful of Neanderthals into the migrating group 'for the genetic effect – greatly magnified as modern human numbers exploded – to be felt tens of thousands of years later'.[31] Another possibility is a pulse of moderns moving out of Africa that interbred with members of another group of New Ones who had themselves interbred with Neanderthals at an earlier stage. There are candidates for such a population.[32] 'If a thousand of those early moderns mixed with just fifty Neanderthals and then survived somewhere in Arabia or North Africa, could they have subsequently interbred with the Out of Africa emigrants 60,000 years later, and passed on their hidden component of Neanderthal genes?'[33]

Species are populations, and evolution's motor is that no two members of one population are exactly alike. Members of a species share the same genetic constitution – a genotype. Members or groups of members also display varying characteristics of appearance which result from the interplay of their genotype with its environment – a phenotype.[34] Since each member is unique (the opposite of the racist expectation of correspondence to an idealized type), and since each differs from all the others, mostly in fractional ways, and since such differences are usually inherited, individuals living long enough to breed will generally do so because they are the ones whose traits are best fitted to their environment. For as long as that environment remains steady, beneficial traits will grow in prevalence as generations pass. If conditions change, evolution will select other differences and take a new path.

For about a century, the palaeontological view of speciation was one of 'phyletic gradualism', which held that 'new species arise from the slow and steady transformation of entire populations'.[35] However, in the eyes of some this is not what the fossil record appears to show. At species level some of the transitional forms we would expect to see are missing. Moreover, there are fossil sequences in which species arrive unheralded and vanish abruptly, to be supplanted by others that are not always their closest relatives. Such irregularity could reflect a number of things. It might be – as Darwin thought – because the fossils available for study are a haphazard selection: the fossil record itself is imperfect, and is never going to provide more than 'an approximate reflection of real-world complexities'.[36] Gaps might also be because some transitional stages pass too quickly to register as individualized fossils, or because some key changes have been behavioural or intellectual rather than anatomical, and so have left no fossil trace. Or it could be because the concept of phyletic gradualism is itself flawed.

It remains a question how speciation actually occurs, and how we observe it. If the definition of biospecies is reproductive affiliation within a population and incompatibility between different populations, it is not clear how such units would emerge within a continuum of fractional changes. If species are evolutionary units with continuity in space and time,[37] they are not static genealogical entities.[38] However, while species must be distinct at any given moment, in a longitudinal across-time view 'the boundaries between forms must blur ... a continuous lineage cannot be broken into objective segments'.[39] On this view life-forms collectively are like a river, and insofar as species exist within its flow, it is we who delimit them, so to speak, by stopping the river and dividing it at arbitrary points, like frames from a film. Faced with a fossil of intermediate form, the convention of classification obliges a palaeontologist to assign it either to one side of a divide or to another, or to create a new divide.[40] On the other hand, to know to which species an

individual fossil belongs, says Ian Tattershall, 'is the single most important question you can ask of it; and it is a biological question, not the
luck of the geological draw'.[41]

While the number of known fossils has risen since Darwin's day, the
gaps and discontinuities noted above have stayed much the same.[42] It
might therefore be asked whether irregularity in the fossil record could
reflect some underlying reality rather than a problem with the sources.
In the early 1960s the zoologist Ernst Mayr suggested that new species
come into being when populations of an existing species become separated. Unable to interbreed, such populations will begin to drift apart
genetically. Small populations are more genetically unstable than large
ones, so speciation is more likely to occur within peripheral rather than
parent populations. Once extant, a new species may expand from its
marginal source into the range of the unchanged parent.[43]

The fragmentation of populations could be the result of a variety of
factors, some of which we have already met – like migration in the face
of climate change or the formation of seas. Different kinds of barrier
take shape at different speeds. Tens of millions of years may pass during
the upthrusting of a mountain chain. Seas have been created in tens of
thousands of years and less. A glacial episode, we have seen, may begin
in as little as a decade.

Taking up an idea of Ernst Mayr about the relationship of genetic
environment to speciation, in 1972 the palaeontologists Niles Eldredge
and Stephen Jay Gould put forward a theory they called 'punctuated
equilibrium', in which long spells of stability are spasmodically interrupted by the appearance of new species and the disappearance of
existing ones.[44] We have already seen things like this: tools that stay
unchanged for hundreds of thousands of years, or the appearance of
New Ones – modern *Homo sapiens*, us – about 150,000 years ago.[45]
The idea also squares with discoveries in human biology that challenge wide-held assumptions. The Neanderthal Genome Analysis
Consortium has found not only that European and Asian moderns
carry some Neanderthal genes, but also that human remains discovered
in a southern Siberian cave – 'Denisovans' – shared a common ancestor with New Ones and Neanderthals, but differed from other known
human types.[46] The Siberian Old Ones lived between thirty thousand
and fifty thousand years ago; the extent of differences between mitochondrial DNA from a Denisovan bone sample and mtDNA from
New Ones and Neanderthals suggests an origin for the Denisovans well
back in time, perhaps over half a million years.[47] While their genes seem

not to have passed into the human stock of modern Europe, they did contribute to those of people in Melanesia – what today are the Pacific islands bounded by New Caledonia, the Norfolk Islands and Papua New Guinea. The emerging pattern – which reverses older assumptions – is thus of some interbreeding between Old and New Ones, the Old Ones in Europe being Neanderthals and those in Melanesia from northern Asia.

Despite abundant evidence that earlier humans were adapted to their environments, the legend which paints them as inferior versions of us lives on. We are, we continue to be told, 'at the apex of evolution', and there has been 'an ascent of Man'. In most minds the Old Ones are still regarded as subhuman trial pieces on the way to becoming 'fully human'. Even then we set further tests. The earliest New Ones are sometimes called 'anatomically modern humans', as if minds and bodies were evolving differentially. The archaeologist Sir Leonard Woolley demanded evidence of progress, as if its absence was a defect: 'we let experience shape our views and actions: this is so much the case that when tradition is absent or crystallises into unreasoned convention, as it has done with the Australian Bushmen, progress stops.' E. H. Carr argued that 'only those peoples which have succeeded in organising their society in some degree cease to be primitive savages and enter into history'. On this view, it is history that defines our genes rather than the other way round.

'Once we have a language, we soon want narratives,'[48] and once we have a narrative we are loath to part with it. The staying power of the idea of evolution as an ascent towards our own fulfilment recalls a child's grip on a comfort blanket. The notion flourishes almost by default. Closely linked with it is the idea of apartness: if we are not actually outside Nature, we are its pinnacle, busy looking for new ways to harness or subjugate its forces – rivers are there to be straightened or dammed,[49] earth to be tilled, forests to be managed – or feeling guilt for the consequences of doing so.

'That man stands outside of nature', wrote the theologian Reinhold Niebuhr, 'in some sense is admitted even by naturalists who are intent upon keeping him as close to nature as possible. They must at least admit that he is *homo faber*, a tool-making animal.' Which he is – save that we now know that tool-making is not a uniquely human, nor even a hominid, attribute. Other creatures select and use tools, and we have seen that functionally sophisticated tools were being made by Old Ones long before the appearance of ourselves.

For Rousseau, the definition of humanity lay in freedom. Animals lacked it, he thought, because their behaviour is automatic, governed by instinct, whereas Man is intellectually self-governing. However, when Rousseau wrote his *Discourse on the Origin and Foundations of Inequality among Men* he did not know that there has been more than one kind of man. If Rousseau was right to differentiate between man and animals, where would we now draw that line? Between ourselves and the other hominids, or around hominins as a group? We have already seen signs of self-transcendence among Neanderthals: they cared for each other, and may have known a world of the spirit.

Extinction comes into it. It is a concept from which we shy, perhaps because it seems to be the reverse of progress, or because it evokes guilt – as in the case of the Neanderthals, or the numberless species of animal and plant which have been eradicated by New Ones' ever accelerating intrusion on their habitat. Yet in evolution, extinction is normal. Sooner or later, it seems, most species become extinct. Hence, the idea that Old Ones disappeared because they were in some way bungling or less efficient than ourselves rests on no logical basis. On the contrary, Heidelbergs and Neanderthals were very well adapted to the lives they lived, and flourished on the planet for periods far longer than our own tenancy has yet run. For sheer recklessness, indeed, it is only us New Ones who have so far evolved the capacity to destroy ourselves in a high-voltage flash, like some unsupervised child playing with dodgy wiring.

Despite this, we sustain a stubborn belief that our 'culture' is distinct from 'Nature'. Our freedom to choose unreason – to embrace pain, discomfort, even death – is held to make Man the 'anti-natural being'. When a lapwing feigns injury to decoy a predator, it is unlikely that the bird plans this through a process of imagination, whereas it is the presence of creative volition which is claimed to characterize our human ability to make ourselves our own subject.[50] From there, it is but a step to the idea that our capacity for self-transcendence demonstrates that while we live in Nature, we are also spirits existing outside it: that the very effort to estimate the significance of our rational faculties implies a degree of transcendence over ourselves 'which is not fully defined or explained in what is usually connoted by "reason"'.[51] Hence we are, many continue to insist, in some way exceptional. We are not simply more versatile than slugs, border collies or sloths, but uniquely gifted. A divine spark glows within us. If we are demi-animal, then surely we must also be demi-god. To which we could reply: despite our hubris, we are just another species (whatever that is), our rapid increase in population akin to a vast algal bloom.

What was it in the genome New Ones which enabled them to ascertain the thread of life? Their appearance in Europe around 45,000 years ago opened with 15,000 years or so of coexistence with Neanderthal people in which the Neanderthals declined, perhaps for one reason, perhaps for many.[52] (By this time, it seems from their mtDNA, there may have been as few as 3,500 breeding Neanderthal females across Europe and western Asia: 'we can see how they could have been a threatened species even without the destabilizing impact of the arrival of modern humans in their home territories'.)[53] Among New Ones, the later stages of this transition begin to glow with innovation – not just new tools, modernistic weapons of increased range or self-adornment, but things which as far as we know were entirely novel, like the sculpting and painting of animals from the surroundings in which they lived. The joyful horses of Chauvet may have been painted several thousand years before the earliest known spear-thrower.[54] Some New Ones lived longer than the Old, who seldom survived beyond their twenties. There were ceremonies. Journeys were made to look over hills and far away – in due course, as far as the moon. Things were given or taken across increasing distances. Music was made from the bones of swans, whistles from the knuckles of deer. Burgeoning language, a medium for myth and a barn for knowledge and experience, enriched social life and deepened community memory. And linked to all of these things was the increasing use of symbolism.

Was it language alone that made this difference? Old as well as New Ones may have spoken, and while New Ones transmit experience and feeling beyond the confines of circumstance, store emotion in stories and songs which outlast your life or mine, it is a modern assumption that this ability was unique. What, for instance, if New Ones had myths, or if Old Ones made finer flutes? We recall Childe's proposition that human beings do not adapt to their surroundings as they really are but rather as they imagine them (p. 76). That would accord with the school

22. *Engraving of horse from Robin Hood cave, Derbyshire, c.12,500 BC*

of psychology which says that we do not read the world by systematically sifting all possible facts and observations on every occasion, but
rather by anticipating our physical and social surroundings in the light
of collectively held suppositions.[55] A distinction between New and Old
Ones might thus be looked for less in the sequences of task behind
the shapes of particular tools, or signatures of settlement, and more in
evidence for how such supposals take shape. For instance, not only may
New Ones' templates have differed from those held by their cousins, but
there may also have been more readiness to revise them. Imagination
comes to the fore, and with it the possibility that different schemas have
correspondences in the material record that enable us, however tentatively or provisionally, to recognize them.

We have seen that one of British archaeology's first encounters with
a New One was in the cave at Paviland, on the Gower Peninsula – the
red-ochre-stained skeleton of a man who was interred with perforated
periwinkles and a mammoth ivory circlet over thirty thousand years
ago.[56] Older still was the New One whose jaw was found in Kent's
Cavern, now put at more than forty thousand years (p. 82), at the outer
limit of New Ones' dispersal into Europe. At that point another glacial
period lay ahead, and human time still had three hundred centuries to
run even to the age of north European hunter-gatherers who would
return to thrive when the ice departed. When it did, the hunter-
gatherers moved into a plenitude of local environments which ripened
as climate warmed. There was room to spare. Their foraging regions
were defined as much by time as by space, for since animals and birds
travelled seasonally the New Ones who hunted them did so too. At
this point, eight or nine thousand years ago, there are signs that some
areas were still empty, that others overlapped, and that yet others did
not touch. But maybe there were moments to come together: occasions
to exchange – things, memories, genes. Maybe also tunes, and stories.
Meetings called for times, and special places. No one knows how many
lived in Mesolithic Britain. Brave estimates have suggested c.12,000 and
c.6,500 as upper and lower plausible limits for England, perhaps 27,000
for the British Isles as a whole. That is, the equivalent to a couple of
commuter villages. Where did they come from?

Archaeology is not always good at seeing the difference between
ideas borne by migrating people and the effects of ideas passing
between people who stay where they are. Genes, on the other hand,
flow between generations according to autonomous principles, and pal-
aeogenetics has accordingly been hailed as the branch of science that

will settle all arguments about ethnic origins. Sooner or later perhaps it will. But in the meantime we are returned to the axiom that what you think determines what you see: the data of molecular biology carry meaning only in relation to questions or hypotheses; if questions or hypotheses change, so will answers. In the case of Britain, palaeogenetic studies were for some time influenced by historical assumptions that put Neolithic farmers, Anglo-Saxon migrants and Vikings in the foreground, and assumed that Britain's first post-glacial population would have been overwhelmed by later immigration. Moreover, the initial studies were looking at palimpsests of gene flows, with blurry chronology and with insufficient knowledge of population sizes.[57] As the picture clarifies, it becomes possible to differentiate between those who immediately returned after the ice, and those who followed.[58] What this indicates is an initial repopulation of Britain from two directions: from the east, from Moldavia and the Ukraine through central Europe, and from the south, from what is now Spain. Many of the subsequent smaller pulses were of course themselves drawn from pools that had been filled from the same earlier springs. What is striking about them is how modest are the contributions of those, like the Anglo-Saxons, or the first farmers, who later dominate history's record.[59]

Prehistory thus redeems us from ethnic divisions, exposing them as masks which await those with the courage to strip them back. Identity is no longer a biological bondage, nor a number tattooed on the wrist. The races by which we were once accustomed to define ourselves turn out to have been dictated not by blood, but by ourselves. We are who we choose to be. Moreover, far from condemning us to personal insignificance, this solidarity relocates us in relation to speech, myth and place. Poets knew this all along, just as there is a kind of beauty in the lopsided snowflakes of geneticists' network diagrams.

'Snow' is one of the things for which Old European languages generally have a common word. Around 9,500 years ago icebergs floated as far south as Portugal. The possibility that 'snow' recollects an epoch, rather than a kind of weather or a homeland with cold winters, invites thought. With it runs a possible explanation for the recurrence of certain river names – like Don – right across Europe. There are for instance five rivers called Stour in England, five rivers Stura in northern Italy, a Sturh in Lower Saxony and two occurrences of Styr in the Ukraine. Some such recurrent river names appear in classical writings, and it has long been agreed that a number of them go back at least to late prehistory.[60] But 'we might now prefer, following the more subtle linguistic history promoted by Krahe (1964), Nicolaisen (1982) and Kitson (1996),[61] to speculate that the name was "Old European", i.e. pre- or non-Celtic Indo-European, mainly because there are no rivers with a name from this root in the modern Celtic lands, nor any words of a relevant form in the modern Celtic languages'.[62] Could it then be that some of them belong to the period 10,000–7,500 years ago, when northern Europe was reoccupied – that some of the New Ones' syllables have after all come down to us? Or does the horizon of river names like Thames and Don belong with the first farmers c.6,000 years ago?

None of this is exclusive, the treacherous trappings of some romanticized Upper Palaeolithic *Urheimat*. Newcomers to Europe around forty thousand years ago came from somewhere else, and a far-far time there was when their ancestors were newcomers too. When Henry Thoreau said that 'Mythology is the crop which the Old World bore before its soil was exhausted,' he was possibly wrong, for the spores of some myths may have entered his continent from the same source as they entered ours. The true solidarity is global.

For all the wonder of science's gaze into distant time, there is a stab of recognition around six or seven thousand years ago. As parts of the north European plain drowned under a rising sea and Britain-as-island took shape, some compression of population followed. Not long afterwards, the balance that New Ones seem for a time to have kept with their surroundings began to alter. Pollen records show changes in vegetation. People had begun to cut down trees. The idea of *a* past, a past with 'remembered or imagined beginnings', as distinct from my yesterday or your last year, may have originated then.[63] And with a past comes a future.

6

NOTES FROM A DARK WOOD

A Saturday afternoon in November was approaching the time
of twilight, and the vast tract of unenclosed wild known as
Egdon Heath embrowned itself moment by moment . . . It was
at present a place perfectly accordant with man's nature – neither
ghastly, hateful, nor ugly; neither commonplace, unmeaning,
nor tame; but, like man, slighted and enduring; and withal singularly colossal and mysterious in its swarthy monotony.

Thomas Hardy, *The Return of the Native*, 1878

My first visit to what was then Czechoslovakia, that part which
remembered itself as Bohemia, was in the time of glasnost. It
was a hot day. We'd driven across Germany, past Bayreuth and up to a
border post staffed by Czech military police. Immaculately turned out
but not yet schooled in customer relations, they peremptorily waved us
away. This crossing was restricted – commercial vehicles only. To leave
Germany, we had to go south to another border post. We turned, and for
an hour drove between tall trees. Here, surely, was not a wood, nor any
wood. Was not this part of *the* wood, *Wald*: Germany's romantic heart,
realm of folk-wandering, remnant of an imagined age when wood was
everywhere and wood was home? A wood that once, not so long ago,
was a place to meet a wolf, be startled by a boar; in winter, be shocked
by a frost-spirit blooming out of an oak; in summer, to chance upon a
tree where a god dwells?[1]

We reached the second border post. My passport was out of date.
I fidgeted as the young Czech guard turned its pages. If he spotted
the fault I would be home sooner than planned. Memories of the *Wald*
linger in England too. The word lies behind our 'wold', although come
to think of it neither the Wolds of Yorkshire or Lincolnshire, nor the

Cots*wolds*, nor even Newton Broms*wold* now seem decidedly woody. Rather the opposite. But they are hilly. Did the difficult-to-cultivate flanks of wolds once carry trees?[2] Or is it upland that is *Wald*'s underlying meaning – as in Stow-*on*-the-Wold – whence perhaps also the idea of a divide between one region and another? That would make sense. Over the hills and far away. However that may be, although the Weald (that word again), the *miclan wudu* ('great wood') claimed by the *Anglo-Saxon Chronicle* to have been 120 miles from east to west and 30 miles broad, is now dissected by lanes and domesticated by hamlets, pubs, greens, Volvo dealers, stations for commuters and paddocks for their daughters' ponies, there is still a lot of green on the Ordnance Survey maps for this part of England. Was it vastly woodier nine hundred years ago? Whatever the Anglo-Saxon chronicler said, much of the England recorded by the Conqueror's surveyors in 1086 was not thronged with trees. In Britain, for illimitable, disorientating, closed-canopy, pathless dark *Urwald*, we must go back at least six thousand years.[3] Here in south-west Germany this was not *the* wood, nor anything like it. For anything that resembles Europe's primeval woodland you must go to the Belovezhskaya Pushcha/Białowieża Forest on the border between Belarus and Poland.

The guard returned the passport. We passed through. On the other side, evening light lit buildings with peeling paint and gilded insects drifted above quiet side streets where children played. It was as if we had stepped back half a century.

Although the reality of the Old Wood lies more than sixty centuries

back, its images live. One of the letters in the Old English alphabet was called 'thorn'. *The Dream of the Rood*, the oldest English poem, is the song of a tree.[4] The vocabulary of Anglo-Saxon building attests a world where 'to build' was *timbrian*, 'buildings' were *getimbro*, and *beam* meant 'tree' or 'post'. And when churches were later made of stone, masons turned them back into woodland again by chiselling beech twigs, haws, ivy and woodbine upon their walls, and carving

23. Vaulting boss, Rochester Cathedral

stony thickets through which peered startled wildmen, spewing foliage from wide-open mouths.[5] Woodlands were also the habitat of war gods: their steady supplies of coppice wood were turned into charcoal, which was used to make iron.

Greenwood is the realm of renewal, liberty, longevity. The world's oldest living things are trees. Some of the bristlecone pines which grow in the cool, dry air on the slopes of the White-Inyo Mountains in California are more than four thousand years old. Britain's oldest yews are older than any European document. In legend, greenwood had to be large enough to enable giants to wield uprooted trees like clubs, outlaws to vanish in them and children to become irretrievably lost. In the romance of Arthur's court, the king himself was a man of the forest, and forest-wilderness was a region of trial, penitence, holiness and validity.[6] Romantic novelists put forests into their plots and wolves into their forests. Symbolist imagination conjured woodland stillness. For younger readers there was a genre of adventure story depicting resourceful children who escaped from enemies, hard-hearted stepmothers or cruel public schools into woodland freedom. Even today, when over 90 per cent of Britain's people live in towns and most of her trees live in plantations, a tragic nostalgia abides: the wildwood in *The Wind in the Willows*, the Ashdown Forest, where Christopher Robin's childhood friends were abandoned as he outgrew them, or the Forest of Dean recollected in Dennis Potter's *The Singing Detective*. Legends abide, too: despite the fact that deciduous trees will resurrect if they are cut, the fallacy is repeated that Tudor builders switched from timber to brick because timber had become scarce. The reality was more subtle: while woodlands were indeed cut back, brick formed part of a new visual culture, in which different building materials projected social and political messages.

However the Old Wood was imagined, there was an assumed reality behind it. Until the 1960s it was widely believed that most of pre-Iron Age Britain had been blanketed by the natural vegetation of prehistory, and that swathes of this primordial woodland were still standing until the Middle Ages.[7] This was warranted by the Ordnance Survey, which in 1935 showed remnants of the Old Wood on its map of Dark Age Britain – areas like the Chiltern forest that hemmed London from the north; Andredsweald sprawling from Hampshire to Kent; Selwood across Dorset; Bruneswald reaching from the Fens into Huntingdonshire; Wyre, Morfe and Tolkien's childhood Kinver clumped in the western midlands. Stretches of these were supposed to have been standing until the thirteenth century. In one or two places they probably were, for waterlogged structural timbers found in London show that tall, columnar oaks were still available until AD 1300, whereafter they disappear. These trees were typically two to three hundred years old, and their narrow growth-rings show that they had grown steadily in tall dark woodland – conceivably the last vestiges of native wildwood, more probably from areas that had reverted to such woodland following earlier clearance.[8] By this date, however, tall oaks with pillar-like trunks were rare, and for big projects like cathedrals they were often sourced from far away.

A decade or so before the Ordnance Survey mapped Dark Age Britain, a map published in George Macaulay Trevelyan's *History of England* (1926) had simplified things by not showing woodland at all. Trevelyan assumed that impassable forest or swamp lay virtually everywhere, so for practical purposes prehistoric England and the Old Wood were one and the same.[9] The supposition of impassability nevertheless raised questions. How, for instance, did prehistoric people travel? They obviously did travel, because as early as the later fourth millennium BC axes fashioned from Cornish stone were being taken to what is now Essex and Yorkshire, and from Lake District outcrops to the Fens. Meanwhile, Yorkshire jet went to Wessex, while tools of stone from Northern Ireland arrived in Kent; amber was prized everywhere. Whether such items and materials were passed from hand to hand like relay batons or systematically transported in ceremonies of exchange, cross-country movement evidently took place. As we saw in the previous chapter, exchange over distance is both a characteristic of New Ones and a potential source of power.

The means, most agreed, was the use of river corridors, and a network of long-distance trackways. Especially trackways. Historians fantasized about them. Ancient trackways, said Trevelyan, ran 'along bare downs and ridges, linked up the various centres of civilisation which were otherwise separated by wide morasses and long leagues of forest'.[10] Downland ridges were also imagined as highways for great cattle drives. The historical geographer Professor H. C. Darby ventured that the Icknield Way and the Pilgrims' Way might already have been old when the Romans arrived.[11] Trevelyan was sure that they were, proclaiming the Icknield Way to have existed 'ages before the arrival of the Celt', and its purpose to have been to connect East Anglia's agricultural civilization with the great Wessex culture centred on the circles of Avebury and Stonehenge. Already we detect a pattern: long-term stability punctuated by the arrival of newcomers who initiate change, and the importance of Wessex.

The idea that Wessex was an early-settled cultural core rested on a belief that its free-draining soils and semi-open chalkland were attractive to ill-equipped early farmers. To a degree it also reflected the whereabouts of the archaeologists themselves. In the nineteenth century antiquarianism and estate ownership had coincided in several chalky areas, like Dorset and Wiltshire, while in the earlier twentieth century many of the active amateurs – figures like the two doctors who practised in Hove, Dr Eliot Curwen and his son Dr Eliot Cecil Curwen – worked on chalk landscapes such as the South Downs. Despite their archaeological activism, the Curwens believed that the world had been created in 4004 BC and 'had no great use for palaeolithic man'.[12]

So it was that the idea of chalkland as Earlyland came to pervade twentieth-century perception. We recall the inter-war ruralists who believed that Britain's golden age lay in its pre-industrial past, when 'skywedded' chalk uplands were 'for twenty centuries the principal home' of people who had been peace-loving, egalitarian and culturally advanced.[13] Elsewhere, wildwood and marsh, 'still impenetrable save by a few daring hunters', lay deep to either side of the Icknield Way. For Trevelyan, as for Angela Carter, the forest was a region in which it was not wise to get lost, a wilderness wherein wayfarers listened anxiously 'to distinguish the howl of wolves, the roar of bears or the yet more dreaded voice of hostile tribesmen'.[14] Others dreamed about ancient networks of green lanes, mystical alignments and latent powers.[15] They still do. Some of today's Druids tell of a countrywide network of ancient tracks linking sacred sites, the routes contoured to avoid forested and boggy areas.

Popular historians took their information from reputable authorities, some of whom, like Professor V. Gordon Childe, Director of the Institute of Archaeology in the University of London (1946–56), we have already met. Childe stated that the first farmers encountered a universal forest which alternated with bog, and that neither they nor their Bronze Age successors had the tools or social solidarity to do much about it.[16] As an order of magnitude, in the mid-twentieth century it was reckoned that when the Romans arrived about four-fifths of southern Britain were empty, and that when they left, around 360 years later, woodland regenerated, reclaiming much of what land had been cleared. This meant that the first large, sustained and permanent clearances were credited to the Anglo-Saxons.

All these suppositions coalesced in one grand explanatory model for Britain's settlement from the end of the ice age to the days of the Plantagenets. It was a story of slow, intermittent expansion, where settlements were created in waves of colonization. The model stated that the legacy of prehistoric population and Romanization had been so small as to leave ample room for Anglo-Saxon settlers in the fifth century. It assumed that plenty of spare land was still available in the ninth century, when Danes turned from fighting to farming and Scandinavian settlement on a large scale was reflected in place-name elements like -*by* and -*thorp*.[17] The 'mass of place-name evidence' showed how the 'attack on wooded countryside was prosecuted with vigour between the fifth and the eleventh century'.[18] When William I conquered England, her villages, hamlets and farms were still 'islands in a sea of waste', and millions of acres still remained 'to be rescued from their natural state'.[19] Along with this ran a popular idea that villages could continue to grow 'as long as a narrowing belt of forest remained from which acres could be taken for tillage'.[20] Even on easily worked soils, so the story went, only during the thirteenth century did the millennia-long process of tree clearance approach completion, when pressure on rural resources intensified to a point which demanded the ploughing up of remaining marginal land to feed a rapidly rising population. Pressure was then released in the demographic crash of the fourteenth century, and a period of contraction ensued.

So things stood until the early 1970s, when BBC television still gave this out as the national narrative. By then, however, a rethink was in progress. In 1966 the Ordnance Survey had deleted 'natural woodland' from the second edition of its *Map of Britain in the Dark Ages*. Within ten years, the waves of invaders had mostly subsided, and in less than twenty it was uncontroversial to say that far from there being impenetrable forests throughout prehistoric times, the great attack on woodland had begun about six thousand years ago, and that by 1000 BC 'there was probably less woodland in England than there is now'.[21] What had happened?

The new reading came from concurrent revolutions. Domesday studies and place names, archaeology, aerial reconnaissance and the radiocarbon revolution showed the landscape to have been more extensively settled from an earlier date than anyone had supposed. Pollen analysis and the study of fossil insects and soils confirmed that inroads into the Old Wood began at least seven thousand years back, and that by c.2000 BC clearance was well advanced.

Environmental science found little sign of wholesale regeneration of woodland in the period of socio-economic collapse that was held to have followed the withdrawal of Roman military power at the beginning of the fifth century. A new generation of historians argued that the Anglo-Saxons, far from laboriously hewing their way into a tree-clad solitude, had settled a land where resources were 'as fully exploited in the seventh and eighth centuries as they were in the eleventh'.[22] Domesday Book, for long held to depict a thinly populated landscape with much Old Wood survival, was on reassessment found to say something more interesting and complicated. Even the philologists who had taught that place names echoed the stages by which England had been settled began to revise their inferences. Their esoteric insurrection got under way about 1960.[23] And so the stage was set.

Archaeology's contributions rolled in from at least five directions. First was the already outlined contribution of airborne survey, now being undertaken annually over most parts of the country. Second was a rising population of archaeologists, some now stationed in local government where the creation of databases of existing knowledge enabled hitherto dispersed records and new observations to be brought together and methodically summed.

Third, there was a lot of opportunity for observation. When the UK's agricultural and construction cycles are in upswing they expose new evidence for past settlement while simultaneously destroying it. This was notable during the 1970s and 1980s, when more archaeological sites were recognized than had been catalogued during the subject's entire history down to 1945. Equally staggering was the fact that most of this new picture was destroyed by the same processes which found it. Agriculture and forestry were the main obliterators, but since their processes did not require notification through the planning system, it was the making of new towns, factories, motorways, and the extraction of aggregates, to which later twentieth-century archaeology mostly hitched its wagon. The extent of past land use had been hugely underestimated.[24] New roads and towns demanded aggregates, and alongside the snaky motorways which peeled back long strips of countryside there ran a number of intensive explorations of floodplain being dug up to supply sand and gravel. Some of these areas had been identified as important since the 1930s, when pioneers like Crawford and Allen had photographed spaghetti-like tangles of settlement traces, burial mounds, ceremonial sites and land divisions. When unravelled by excavation in the last quarter of the twentieth century, sometimes in projects which covered scores of acres, such areas were typically found to have evolved from a mosaic

of clearances in the fourth millennium BC to intensified land use during
the Bronze Age.[25]

Fourth were the fieldworkers, at first often amateurs, who as members of evening classes, Workers' Educational Association groups and
local societies were inspired to go out and study their own surroundings.
They found evidence for substantial prehistoric and Roman settlements
under woodlands like Wychwood in Oxfordshire,[26] in the Weald,[27] on
heavy soils or in inhospitable areas where the doctrine of slow growth
said they had no business to be. The woodlands were time-out-of-mind
ancient, yes, but it was becoming clear that they had usually grown back
across areas that had once been farmed. It was also becoming clear that
such switches of use could have occurred more than once.[28]

And last, the later 1960s and 1970s was a time of projects which
shifted away from the study of disembodied sites towards the evolution
of the landscape itself.[29]

As the new area-based studies began to report and compare their
findings, England's map became a kind of Advent calendar upon
which one door after another sprang open to reveal sequences running
back to the Bronze Age or Neolithic. Densities increased. In eastern
Northamptonshire the number of known Roman settlements trebled
between 1956 and 1976. By 1930 about thirty-six Romano-British settlements had been identified in the valley of the River Nene; by 1972, over
four hundred.[30]

A more complicated case was Dartmoor. Bigger than Rutland,
Dartmoor was long known to be thronged with ancient enclosures,
houses, alignments and cairns.[31] More perplexing was why the moor's
111,000 bare, high acres should have bustled with activity between four
and three thousand years ago. Across the moor run low but distinct
overgrown walls known locally as reaves. Early in the nineteenth century the reaves had been proposed as pre-Roman, but this idea faded
until by the 1900s reaves were widely regarded as more recent.[32] During
the 1960s and 1970s fieldworkers looked again.[33] What they found was
a number of parallel-sided lands running across the moor, regardless
of terrain. Relationships with other features pointed to a date in the
second millennium BC, although in some places there were indications
that reaves were selectively reinscribing something older.[34] Whenever
the reaves had been made, however, much effort had gone into them: in
total they ran for at least twenty-five miles.

Results of recent pollen study suggest that between ten thousand and
eight thousand years ago most of Dartmoor apart from the rocky tors

came to be clad by trees.[35] In following millennia there was an opening out of the woodland accompanied by a spread of heathland, the development of peat and a descent of the tree line. Reasons for the changes are indistinct, but may have involved a combination of clearance by people and natural responses to changing conditions.[36] By c.1400 BC most of the moor was open and embossed by reaves, which when mapped resolved into a system of estate-like territories, varying between eight and twenty-seven square miles in size. Each territory contained a spectrum of valley land, hill-slope and high ground,[37] which suggested a division between common grazing and areas reserved for specialized purposes. This implied a number of 'territorial groups, clustered round an extensive, probably common resource'.[38] The fact that such large systems had been laid out seemed to imply either group co-operation or a supreme authority to which all deferred – unless, of course, the boundaries were older or reflected long-standing agreement.[39] Reassessment has emphasized the influence of older alignments (like trackways or areas of clearance) and veered away from the influence of central planning towards an always evolving 'landscape of transition'.[40]

Dartmoor's alignments were not unique. Elsewhere, fieldwork, aerial reconnaissance and in due course excavation tripped off by the planning system showed that 'in many parts of prehistoric Britain land was divided as comprehensively and intricately as in any later period'.[41] It now looks as though parallel-sided field systems were laid out at different times during the Bronze Age across much of southern Britain, from Cornwall to the Wash.[42] In some areas ghostly boundaries run across country for miles, under housing estates and out again.

Archaeologists began to rethink assumptions about why traces of early habitation and land use survived so well, in relief, in upland areas like moors, downs and heaths. The answer, they realized, was not that such regions had been more heavily occupied in the past, or that other areas had been less settled, but because they were on the whole less intensively cultivated later on. When timber ran out in the uplands stone was plentiful, and while dry-built walls may tumble, the stones themselves do not decay. Signs of early land use thus tend to be more readily legible in upland and marginal areas than in regions where incessant ploughing has smudged the traces of softer or ephemeral materials like earth and timber. From the 1960s it began to dawn on observers that this had skewed not only the meaning of what archaeologists and historians had been seeing, but also the way in which they had gone about looking for it. Knowledge about past settlement is conditioned not just by what was

24. Stone rows at Merrivale, Dartmoor. The purpose of such rows remains uncertain. A recently found row of stones buried in peat has been dated to 3,500 BC.

originally there, but by what has happened to it since.[43] Areas containing conspicuous field monuments had naturally attracted attention, so increasing knowledge about areas where settlement was already known, while diverting attention from those where it was not.[44] The idea of a near-empty prehistoric Britain had been a self-reinforcing illusion.

I recall a day in the late 1980s when I was taken to visit a remote (as I thought) prehistoric settlement under excavation in Snowdonia. To reach it we had to walk for a mile across moorland, among rocks and boulders which protruded from the grasses, sedges and boggy pools. On arrival, we looked at a sizeable area from which the turf had been peeled back. Here too lay boulders, but now came the shock: the removal of vegetation showed the stones not to be the random bestowal of some departed glacier, but the result of human purpose: they marked field edges, gates, trackways, even parts of buildings. With a prickly sensation we saw that the entire landscape in which we stood was not wild but derelict. It had been configured by people, who had gone.

Their going was part of a wider process of fluctuating coming and going from areas we would now consider marginal or wild. Most of Britain's moors and heaths owe their modern face to interaction between people and Nature in later prehistory. Norfolk's Breckland, now sparsely settled, was once more densely populated. By c.800 BC, human exploitation had turned the New Forest into acid heathland.[45] The North York Moors, England's largest surviving upland heath, were once clad in brown earths that were eroded and leached following the destruction of woodland.[46] Thomas Hardy's Egdon Heath, the strange furze-covered landscape that was home to coppery butterflies in *The Return of the Native*, was based on the district between Wool and Bere Regis in Dorset. Along with other Dorset lowlands, 'haggard Egdon' passed into marginality after Bronze Age farmers had soured its soils. A proposition emerges: in European imagination, the idea of wilderness as being on culture's edge takes shape about three thousand years ago, and the boundary moves back and forth.

Hence, some pieces of wilderness were once civilized, desertion was seldom final and the boundary was never absolute. In the uplands, optimists returned at intervals to augment their holdings with land nibbled from moorland edges, or to plant new homesteads in places which the lie of the land and weather patterns dictated would coincide with old ones. More enduring, and later expanding, was seasonal usage as summer pasture and the mining of minerals as a digression from farming. In the long run, however, all was transitory, leaving tumbled houses, burial cairns, stone circles, lead rakes, smelters, hushes, flues, leats, tracks, cattle-trails and lime-kilns strewn across moors and hills. If these areas feel less wild than haunted, it is because they are.

In thinking about the interplay between people and their surroundings, perhaps we should not aggrandize the people. Interference with woodland can be what ecologists call a 'proximal trigger' – the immediate impetus for ecological change which is ultimately governed by something else, such as fluctuation in sea-level, seasonal temperature or rainfall. Britain is a land of diverse, subtly contrasting environments, and the Old Wood itself was never in permanent equilibrium. Hence, the fact that moors and heaths were once wooded does not certify that they would all still be so if people had not intervened. In some areas, prehistoric people may simply have hastened changes that would have happened anyway.[47]

Something of this is illustrated by Thorne and Hatfield Moors, two raised mires in the Humberhead Levels, a wetland in south Yorkshire and north-west Lincolnshire which enjoys the twin distinction of being depicted on one of Britain's earliest surviving maps[48] and until recently of being destroyed by peat mining. The mires lie close, yet differ. Thorne is underlain by the clayey silts of a pro-glacial lake, whereas the Hatfield peats overlie gravels and low dunes of wind-blown sand.[49] By about 7000 BP these surfaces were covered by damp mixed oak woodland dominated by tall trees.

The mires, surrounding fields and nearby Isle of Axholme overlie such trees where they fell. In 1701, a local cleric noted the remains of 'infinite millions of the Roots and Bodies of Trees of all bignesses great and little'. One columnar oak trunk measured 120 feet before branching, suggesting that it grew in closed-canopy woodland. Other witnesses spoke of 'firr trees above thirty yards long', discounting 'many yards at the small end'. These were Scots pines. One of them dug up in the 1840s had stood ninety-three feet tall, with a girth in its middle register greater than five feet. These lordly trees were prehistoric. Peat extraction in 1993 exposed thousands more, giving a glimpse of change, decay and regeneration within a few square miles of the Old Wood.

The story of that Wood had begun millennia sooner, when the ice had departed and trees slowly reclaimed Britain's tundra. The first arrivals were arctic pioneers – juniper, birch, sallow, willow and pine. After them came hazel and elm, followed by oak and alder, then lime. Later still holly, ash, beech, hornbeam and maple.[50] These advances were made not one by one, but in a counterpoint of varying speeds, directions and climacterics.[51] Which takes us to about eight thousand years ago. For two millennia more, the trees competed with each other to form a series of co-evolving woodland types which covered most of Britain save for small specialized areas like mountain summits, Dartmoor tors and coastal marshes.[52]

One of the losers in these slow-motion contests was the Scots pines. From about 5,700 years ago the native pines were 'out-competed on fertile soils by trees such as oak, and on wetter soils by alder',[53] and thus exiled to more acidic and less fertile terrain. Their chief kingdom became the eastern Scottish highlands. As millennia passed, the Old Wood sorted itself into a number of slowly fluctuating zones. In lowland England and Wales there were extensive tracts of lime-dominated woodland, with oak in the north and west, giving way to birch and pine in northern Scotland.[54] The provinces were not exclusive. 'Within them were different communities of trees, punctured by rock outcrops, rivers, lakes and fens, which increased in complexity from north to south, and from west to east.'[55]

These old growth forests were structurally complex and rich eco-
systems, characterised by significant numbers of huge, long-lived
trees. The canopy was multi-layered, composed of crowns of trees of
different types and ages. Dead wood was abundant as both standing
and fallen trunks. Every component of the forest, from the crowns to
the roots buried in the soil, would support, and was supported by, a
great web of organisms.[56]

Here it is: the Old Wood, on the eve of the Neolithic. And note that
a lot of it was dead or senescent: in any given decade insects and fungi
feasted on huge fallen trees, some of which had been saplings three
or four centuries before. Hence, not all of the Old Wood was closed-
canopy woodland: evidence points to it as having been discontinuous,
in places akin to pasture woodland, in other areas closed-canopy dark
woodland, a mosaic of semi-open, evolving habitats where spaces created by wind-blow, fire, insect attack, disease and contrasts in soil and
water table gave opportunities for browsing animals and the people who
hunted them.[57] More general clearances could also occur naturally, as
they did across Thorne and Hatfield Moors after c.3000 BC, when peat
began to form. Oaks dislike oozy ground, and in time the peat overwhelmed them, burying dead trees and stifling new ones.

What turned the woodland to mire? By analogy with events elsewhere it is tempting to blame people. Certainly, people were not far
away. The mires have produced prehistoric tools, a pollen record which
points to developing agriculture near by, bog bodies and (later) a wooden
trackway which enabled people to cross the waterlogged remains of the
decaying forest.[58] The track is one of many well-crafted wooden structures which have been recognized across prehistoric wetlands, reminding us that bogs and marshes, far from being the outlaw-haunted wastes
depicted in early twentieth-century histories, were rich and special places
into and across which people regularly moved.[59] The fact that they did
so here, however, does not account for the altering environment which
instituted the mire, for which a possible explanation is the rising level
of the North Sea, which caused the backing up of freshwater drainage
and a consequential uplift of the water table in the Humberhead Levels.
If people played any part it may have been indirectly, and from afar.
The replacement of woodland by grassland elsewhere raised groundwater levels, and so increased both surface run-off and the flow of
streams. In contrast with what was going on around the upper Thames
basin, where land clearance enlarged the volume of water in rivers, made

their flows uneven and increased the likelihood of flooding,[60] Thorne and Hatfield may have been influenced by farming on the Pennine flank to the west.

The drowning of the oaks did not see an end to the Old Wood, which merely changed. Its new incumbents were Scots pines, which for half a millennium flourished on the Hatfield peats at some times and moiled during others. Tree-ring dates suggest that the pines' heyday was during the first half of the third millennium BC.[61] Locally, however, they survived longer, persisting until the Middle Ages as pine heath on the sandy crowns of the peat-lapped ancient dunes, and as solitary trees possibly to this day. Scots pines also grew on Thorne, where their success in recolonizing the peat during drier episodes for another thousand years invites review of their supposed more general decline.[62]

In one respect Scots pines were at a disadvantage: whereas most broad-leaves will regrow if you cut them down, Scots pines are killed by coppicing or pollarding. *Pinus silvestris* was thus vulnerable to human attack, and it has been wondered if people contributed to its decline by removing it to make room for other species which could be managed for timber and wood in perpetual succession.[63] The Humberhead peat moors thus take on extra interest, for their Bronze Age pine woods were repeatedly consumed by fires. The blazes scorched trees which had already died of other causes and were lying on the woodland floor, and burned others alive, flaring up into the woodland canopy. In all probability the fires were kindled by lightning – which invites thought about the extent to which Neolithic clearances and natural fires went together.[64] In evolutionary terms it also reminds us that *Pinus* is, so to speak, programmed to self-immolate – the flammability of its oils assisting periodic conflagrations which consume undergrowth, debris and competitors, thereby clearing the field for new trees.[65]

Among the trees pickled in the basal peats of Thorne and Hatfield Moors were the remains of beetles and insects which had fed or lived upon them. Beetles are fastidious in diet and lifestyle. Many of the species found here were partial to wood or bark in different stages of decay – something which is in turn characteristic of ancient undisturbed woodland, where moribund and fallen trees mingle with others in their prime. Quite a number of these decay-loving species are now rare or locally extinct. Their decline during later prehistory reflected the fragmentation of the Old Wood, and the increasing difficulty that beetles experienced in crossing ever wider tracts of open land to find geriatric trees.[66] At Thorne and Hatfield, and places like them, the underlying reasons for the beetles' restriction seem to have been elemental – the slowly altering mutual influences of earth, fire, air and water. Elsewhere, however, by the later Bronze Age there is every sign that mature trees were being felled before they became rotten or fell over.

The realization that prehistoric living had not been confined to now marginal areas or downland raised a question: what had been going on elsewhere? Until the 1960s the reply had ranged between 'not much' and 'very little', because the idea of an all-pervasive, impassable Old Wood assumed the inability of anyone before the doughty Anglo-Saxons to confront it. But with mounting evidence that the Old Wood had been thinned early and largely destroyed before the early Middle Ages, the first supposition collapsed, and thereby raised a question about the second.

Of course, in contemplating evidence for the extensiveness of later prehistoric land use we need to take care: prehistory's oceanic enormity means that things which are closely grouped in space may lie far apart in time, and vice versa. The reverse – as we are about to see – must also be reckoned with: events that we may imagine were long spread out may have bunched together. When all is assessed, however, there is an unmistakable trend, from clearances which by 2500 BC had in many areas created an open park-like countryside, towards more intensive clearance and methodical division of land which is evident in the Iron Age.[67] This does not necessarily signify economic progress: trees were rich and potentially lasting resources from which, if carefully managed, people could obtain a perpetual supply of timber and roundwood for buildings, fences, hurdling, tools, weapons, containers, boats, fire and more.[68] The incentive not to over-deplete woodland was accordingly strong. Signs of excessive clearance are correspondingly telling, and may reflect stress as much as progress.

Thus far we have followed the story forward. But we began from two directions, the second being an assumption that clearance of the Old Wood was still incomplete in the Middle Ages. In the 1960s a number of scholars began to think about this. One of them was a young fieldworker called Christopher Taylor, who embarked on a study of Whiteparish, in Wiltshire, because he lived there.

Whiteparish today is a small village amid six thousand acres of varied soils. Whiteparish apparently escaped notice in surviving written records until the late thirteenth century. Its scatter of farms thus looked like a typical case of forest-edge settlement which in all probability began no sooner than the days of Henry II.

Digging no holes and working with no special equipment, Taylor looked at the area in its entirety, measured faint earthworks, plotted the scatters left by different episodes of inhabitancy and re-examined the documents. The resulting picture differed from the conventional story. Farms attributed to thirteenth- and fourteenth-century expansion turned out to be older. Re-readings of documents produced evidence for the existence of one farm as early as the tenth century, and showed that twelfth-century clearances had been less drastic than once supposed.[69] Some farms were discovered to be the attenuated remnants of entire settlements which had arrived and faded without ever entering the written record. Far from being a typical case of late settlement, Whiteparish's occupation began before the Romans. Significantly, Iron Age fields visible over the northern part of the parish lay beyond the furthest extent of medieval cultivation, implying that elsewhere the latter had obliterated the former. Taylor also identified a phenomenon of drift in which settlements edge sideways through progressive renewal on slightly different sites.

Taylor challenged four time-honoured suppositions: that places had generally come into existence in 'waves of colonisation' or grown outwards from stable centres;[70] that the earliest recorded reference to a place was likely to approximate to the time when the place was first settled; that a place omitted from Domesday Book did not exist in 1086; and that continuity of habitation presupposed continuity of site, or indeed the reverse. The new reading visualized extensive earlier settlement, and fluidity as well as fixity of habitation within an older framework of fields, estates and lanes.

What of Domesday? Uncritical use of Domesday Book had long been a problem. Historians, however, had already realized that its use for the reconstruction of eleventh-century conditions required better understanding of what the survey was for and how it had been made.

The Norman Conquest led to rapid upheaval within England's elite, with land and assets changing hands on a grand scale. The king accordingly needed a baseline for what was due to the Crown. Domesday's purpose was to ascertain the resources of estates and their extents, and so discover what they were worth to their landlords, and what was owed to the king. It was not intended to provide incidental detail for all individual settlements. As the survey had proceeded, moreover, there were running modifications to what information was recorded and how it was presented, which meant that data gathered in one county might not be available for another, or might be given in a different way.[71] So comparisons called for care. The extent of Domesday Book's unreliability as a guide to the extent of rural settlement in eleventh-century England is notably seen in Kent, where independent near-contemporary lists revealed 159 places which were not mentioned in Domesday Book at all. Such omissions were particularly numerous in the Weald.[72]

Domesday did not always say much about marsh, fen, heath or moor. This was not because such areas were useless but because rights to their resources were spread through communities so that, in effect, nobody owned them. Wastes – from Latin *vastum*, 'wilderness' – produced reeds for thatching, eels, fish, fowl, furze, peat for fuel, cranberries, horse mushrooms, heather for foraging bees, pasture for intermittent grazing, and turf for fires and kilns. In prehistory they also yielded exotic things, like the feathers of crane and pelican, used for special regalia. Wastes, like woods, were places where specialized crafts and smallholdings went well together.[73]

Other things could go with wet wastes, such as seasonal clouds of biting midges, recollected in place names like Midgehall and Midgley. In places these were so vicious as to make their neighbourhoods seasonally uninhabitable. Malaria-bearing mosquitoes bred in parts of England at least from Tudor times until the mid-nineteenth century, whereafter the disease declined to the last known indigenous case in the 1950s.[74] We do not know if malaria was endemic around southern Britain's wetlands in prehistory, or whether, if it was, it was a factor that restricted settlement. What we do know is that later malaria was not confined to saltwater marshes and fens. Its range extended from the south coast up to Yorkshire, where Thorne Moors had a Midgehall Bridge, and visitors described a marshland where people were stupefied by laudanum shipped over from Hull as a defence against the ague.

Thorne's mosquitoes raise a wider point: there were areas which were more trouble than they were worth. In prehistory some neighbourhoods may have been looked upon as spiritually hostile. A view has grown that hunter-gatherers were in complete balance with their environment, in effect that wilderness before farming did not exist because there would have been nothing from which to differentiate it.[75] However, it may equally be (as in later Arthurian literature) that some parts of the Old Wood were conceived as 'good' and others as risky, and that *Urwald* pathways and clearings had imagined meanings.[76] With this in mind it comes as no surprise that wet wastes in later prehistory were sometimes scenes of ceremony and ritual drownings.

Early modern exploitation of the wastes at Thorne and Hatfield is instructive. At least from the seventeenth century these 'wastes' were sources for recycling on an epic scale. Local people 'tried' the peat with iron rods to locate fallen trees. Neolithic and Bronze Age pines were then dug up for fuel (which when burned gave 'a ranke sweet savour'), to make keels and masts for ships, fence palings, ceiling laths, rafters, fencing, gateposts and boarding for cattle sheds, and to extract turpentine. Bog oaks were turned into houses, furniture, ornaments, and their entwined roots were used 'for a kind of rustic fencing'. This was quite a lot for a waste.

If the assets of miscellaneous wastes could be understated in Domesday, its surveyors took a close interest in woodland. This was partly because of its value, and partly, in some areas, because of its scarcity. Lincolnshire's Domesday woodland, for instance, accounted for only 3.5 per cent of the county area. Wood pasture, Domesday's *silva pastilis*, was used for grazing. *Silva minuta*, coppice wood, was managed as a renewing source of timber and wood. Little of a tree went to waste. Oak bark was used in tanning, underwood and brushwood fired kilns and furnaces, a lime's bark went for bast fibre and its leaves for fodder.[77]

Domesday's figures suggest that no more than 15 per cent of late eleventh-century England was under woodland.[78] For reasons given, little if any of that is likely to have had a continuous existence since the age of the Old Wood. Yet some of it was still old. We have seen that three-hundred-year-old oaks grew within carrying distance of London as late as the thirteenth century.[79] Henry III was born as close to the end of Roman Britain as we live after him; much of the woodland that stood in his day was still there in the nineteenth century, and by the same logic some of what was growing in the thirteenth century could have germinated in the fifth.

Destroyers of woodland in the early twenty-first century use machines which can eradicate a thousand years of life in a couple of days. How much greater was the achievement of the first clearance of millions of acres of Old Wood by a tiny population initially using stone tools. How this was done is one of prehistory's conundrums: as we have seen, most trees are not killed by being cut down. Unless stumps are dug out, or new shoots are suppressed by perpetual browsing, trees regrow. Grazing can extinguish woodland – sheep and cattle are partial to leaves and bark, and the ground-furrowing snouts and trampling of pigs will mash ground and destroy seedlings – but the permanent, managed presence of a lot of animals is needed to do it. The presence of pigs and cattle in enhanced numbers is certainly likely to have been one factor. But, like ring-barking, the killing of trees does not clear them. Fire would have destroyed pines, but hardwoods will not burn readily unless they are cut up. There are signs that some trees were first checked by the setting of fires at their feet, to burn off bark and weaken them, and then left to blow over in gales.[80] If so, early farmers adopted strategies with horizons far beyond individual lifetimes. And perhaps they did. Silbury Hill, one of the world's largest prehistoric mounds, was once imagined to have been heaped up within one or two generations. Refined scientific dating now indicates that the Hill's evolution was more like that of a cathedral, an elaboration over centuries, beyond the life of any one person.[81]

There are signs, too, that early woodland clearance involved more than slog and functionalism.[82] At Sutton Hoo several thousand years before Anglo-Saxon settlers reached it 'the people of Neolithic Suffolk may have been aware of the special asset that they were destroying, even then':

> small pits have been found containing whole pots of characteristic thick-walled flint-tempered earthenware. The pits are often sited around or near large untidy hollows with half-dark, half-bright coloured fill. These hollows were recognised for what they are following the great storm of 1987, which created a host of new examples of the genre: they are 'tree pits', formed when a tree is pushed over and uprooted and the root mantle left to rot.[83]

The link between tree-pits and pot-pits was uncertain, but both kinds of pit contained domestic debris. Whether this reflected land clearance, abandonment or ceremony connected with one, or both, are questions to which we shall return.

Clearance of the Old Wood was technically remarkable. England's area is about 50,350 square miles. Arbitrarily assuming 70 per cent of that area to have been substantially wooded six thousand years ago, and clearance to have reduced 75 per cent of the forest by 500 BC, a steady rate of clearance would average slightly less than four square miles per year: that is, 2,560 acres. This may not sound much. But if, say, it took a year for two people to rid an acre of trees, then clearance would require a workforce of more than five thousand, devoted to nothing else, each year, every year, for four thousand years. That notional estimate makes no allowance for the effort needed to reclear areas where regeneration occurred, let alone the practice of agriculture, or the making of monuments which begin to appear during the fourth millennium BC.[84]

Clearance, moreover, was not undertaken steadily. There was local variation, exception and reversal.

Some woodland clearance took place *before* the advent of farming. The evidence of pollen, insects and snails suggests that thereafter it was sometimes transient, and far from complete by the late Neolithic (say, around 4,500 years ago), when insect fauna still signal the presence of old forest habitats. Some thinning could have occurred naturally. A decline in elm pollen after c.4000 BC might reflect disease rather than the axe or pigs.[85] Hence, to see the opening phase of deforestation (a phase which on the scale of recent history would have lasted from Roman days to now) simply as a side-effect of advancing agriculture and rising population is perhaps too simple.[86] But, by the later Bronze Age (say, around three thousand years ago), *Urwald* habitats were becoming rare. Somewhere between c.2500 and 1000 BC, the tempo quickened.

The Neolithic was once seen as the work of outsiders: a revolution which began with a kind of agronomic D-Day, when continental farmers and herdsmen sprang ashore and set about felling forests, tilling fields and building homesteads. Until the later twentieth century it was normal to attribute significant change to change-bringers who came from elsewhere, just as colonial powers had recently brought it to large parts of Africa and Asia. However it happened it was agriculture which enabled specialization and so paved the way for broadening culture, science and the modern world. Inevitably, therefore, the arrival of cultivated cereals, domesticated animals and settlement was seen as a break with the past, the first step on the road to the world in which we live. Just as inevitably the preceding hunter-gatherer age was depicted as non-progress – a problem awaiting solution. But there is another way of looking at the Mesolithic: that five thousand years of equilibrium might be counted some kind of success.

New readings refocus assumptions. Everyone accepts that European agriculture originated in the Middle East, whence the domestication of animals and seeds, technology, and some people, spread westward. Discussion continues as to how or why this happened. Debate about the extent and character of population movement is especially vigorous. Was it the idea of farming that moved, or the farmers? And if it was the farmers who moved, were pre-existing hunters displaced, or did dispute arise within existing hunter-gatherer communities about what the future should be?[87]

Alongside the traditional hypotheses there arose others, of which until recently the most influential was the idea of a slow spreading out of new agricultural settlements. First put forward in 1971 by A. J. Ammerman and L. L. Cavalli-Sforza and elaborated since, in effect this was a slowly moving cultural ripple travelling at a rate of a few miles for each generation. With it would go an increase in population that should be reflected in the genetic composition of resulting populations, while its 'why?' was taken care of by a mathematical argument which said that, once started, the wave of population expansion would gain its own momentum and spread 'at a constant radial rate'.[88]

For reasons just given, in the 1970s and 1980s the idea of migration without colonialism was politically as well as intellectually attractive. 'Here', wrote Colin Renfrew, 'is a process which results in an increase of population on an absolutely revolutionary scale, spreading across the lands in question, yet without any suggestion of advance planning, and without any individuals having to move very far.'[89] The 'wave of advance' theory was subsequently developed to embrace the genetic composition of its expected resulting populations[90] and the dispersal of language.[91]

However, if this was part of the story, the rest is still uncertain. The population growth that the model predicts is not everywhere reflected archaeologically, while molecular data have been used contradictorily, by some to downplay the contribution of Neolithic lineages and by others to stress them.[92] Perhaps it is unnecessary to seek an explanation for the Neolithic in any single process, or its beginning in one transition.[93] In parts of Britain there are indications that indigenous hunter-gatherers had long kept open some woodland clearings, to encourage game, and it has been suggested that they began a gradual adjustment to agricultural living, not by abandoning the itinerancy of hunting, gathering and fishing but by adding animal husbandry and intermittent cultivation to it.[94] In southern England and central Scotland, however, a systematic survey of radiocarbon evidence has found an abrupt increase in population density at just the time that cultigens first appear, around 4000 BC. These results 'are best explained by groups of farmers from the Continent independently colonizing England and Scotland'.[95] Utterly remarkable is the chronology of their coming. In 2011, a consortium of archaeologists and archaeological scientists announced findings from the application of the methods of Thomas Bayes – the Presbyterian mathematician met in Chapter 3 – to over 2,000 calibrated radiocarbon dates. The results show that Neolithic innovations arrived in south-east England about 4050 cal BC and spread into central southern England in the space of just two or three lifetimes. Extension to western Britain, Scotland and Ireland occurred within five or six more.[96]

Deciduous woodland was still extensive when the innovators arrived in the Thames gateway a generation or so before 4000 BC. In some areas woodland was well interspersed with clearings, in others hardly at all. In a land near empty, the innovators could settle at will. Communities were small, widely separated and intermittently itinerant, moving to take in new land while old clearances recuperated or reverted to woodland. The emphasis was on animals augmented by cereals, rather than the other way round. Such a gentle transition could help to explain the episodic, possibly cyclical character of early woodland clearance, and give a context for what followed.[97] Like clothes awaiting children to grow into them, over much of the country the space available for one fellowship might have exceeded its needs, the land not yet requiring a detailed charting of where one community's interests ran out or another's began. Indeed, where farming communities are small and precarious it is in their strong interests that there should be opportunities for them to meet and mingle, to exchange breeding animals, seeds, partners and perhaps the pottery which at this time occurs across much larger distances than we can surmise for the communities themselves. Socializing and farming are thus things that go together. Equally, we may have underestimated the extent to which hunter-gatherers were well settled within particular localities (eight thousand years ago, what did 'local' mean?) or ecological niches – that is, that the contrast between itinerancy and 'settling down' may have been over-sharpened. But of course, as populations rose (higher birth rate follows residence in one place) a time would come when one community's expansion would rub against that of another. This would bring the risk of friction, and the need for boundaries and new rules by which to live. That time was still some two thousand years in the future, but there is tension even here at the outset: 'Grazing farm animals, wild animals, arable fields, managed woodland and somewhere to live safely and comfortably were all conflicting and incompatible requirements within this restricted landscape range, and the phenomenon of enclosure was created as a result of this conflict.'[98]

Towards the end of the thirty-eighth century cal BC people began to construct substantial enclosures in parts of southern Britain. The enclosures draw on features already found on the near continent, and the practice of making them grew sharply in the thirty-seventh century cal BC, thereafter slackening and coming to a halt by 3,500 cal BC. We call them causewayed enclosures.[99] As with the onset of agricultural innovation, Bayesian chronology shows them to have been the work of just a few generations.[100] Such enclosures were not the earliest visible things

25. *Causewayed enclosure at Knap Hill, Wiltshire, overlooking the Vale of Pewsey. The discontinuous earthwork and tilt are characteristic of such enclosures, many of which were created in the thirty-seventh century cal BC.*

to do with farming: houses (so far, in Britain, not many), places for the dead (long burial mounds for early dynasties of founding farmers) and innovative technology like pottery arose sooner. But the enclosures fascinate scholars, perhaps because despite several centuries' study we still have no sure idea what they were for. Typically, we have labelled them according to an idiosyncrasy of construction (the 'causeways' being short stretches of undug ground left between discontinuous enclosing ditches) rather than an apprehension of function, although earlier generations of archaeologists did call them 'camps', which now seems misleading.[101] At any rate, they were not places of permanent mass residence, and the traces of use at one do not always correspond with those at another. Intriguing, too, are their distribution, micro-topography and rarity. Causewayed enclosures were first detected by antiquaries on the higher ground of southern England at places like Windmill Hill[102] and Hambledon. Aerial reconnaissance extended their range to river gravels of the midlands. Very likely more await discovery, though given air-archaeology's intensity since the 1960s, perhaps not that many more. When all possible candidates are put together the current total for the entire British Isles does not exceed 140,* and the majority of certain cases – just sixty-six of them – fall east of a line between the Humber and Devon. On the other hand, the present distribution is one of earth-dug enclosures, and it is possible that there were analogous places formed in different ways that are currently invisible.

Attempts to fit causewayed enclosures into modern ways of thought soon founder in the face of contradictions. Although not permanently lived in, some do contain buildings; although not built just as forts, some were attacked; although usually unsuited for the long-term keeping of cattle, animals were often corralled in them. Neither purely ceremonial nor economic nor domestic, at different times some seem to have been all three, while others were none.[103]

These apparent variations and ambiguities are surely signs of a world which joined things that we now think of as separate, and of diversity in an era when communities were small and widespread and pressures for consensus were correspondingly low. Today we make distinction between places where we join to celebrate, mourn, worship, eat or die. At some enclosures, on the other hand, we glimpse all these things together. There is also a contemporary tendency to see the past in terms of static functions, what a place was 'for', as distinct from *processes*, the perpetuity of what went on.[104]

The communal character of the first monuments is reflected in the scale of effort needed to make them, and the things which went with cyclical gatherings – feasts, the exchange of goods, finding sexual part- ners, handling or deposition of the dead. This suggests that their sites originated in intermittent earlier episodes of coming together. Routes of seasonal journeys, the names of hills, valleys, rivers, open spaces, springs and pools, perhaps even memories of eventful happenings, or places where lightning had branded clearings in the Old Wood, were inwrought in the surroundings in which the monuments appeared.[105] In looking behind rather than at the monuments, therefore, at surrounding landscapes or vistas rather than simply at sites, we can ask if some of them stood in places of longer-standing significance, to which struc- tures in the fourth millennium BC gave a new kind of embodiment. Causewayed enclosures, once imagined to have been the focal points of territories, might just as well have been liminal, located where the interests of some recently arrived innovators brushed against others,[106] or in places which were significant for reasons that have no modern

---

* For comparison, the total number of Iron Age hillforts currently known is about 1,500.

analogy. Here and there are hints that monumentality was not necessarily new, so much as new expressed. Several sites have yielded evidence for the earlier existence of large timber uprights,[107] and we can speculate about spaces framed by natural features – woodland clearings which prefigured later layouts, for instance.[108] The tendency for some Neolithic monuments to occur in lines, as if in cross-country procession, has caused several archaeologists to ask whether this reflected the way in which the earliest farmed landscape was formed, or the presence of processional routes or corridors. Perhaps significantly in this context, just as the making of causewayed enclosures came to an end in the thirty-sixth century cal BC, so did the making of cursūs – those inscrutable parallel-sided features discovered by Major Allen in the 1930s – begin.[109] If primeval woodlands were opened along seasonal migration routes rather than by the expansion of isolated clearings, then 'it might be more accurate to think of narrow passages becoming broad corridors growing into self-contained landscapes'.[110] Perhaps clearance itself was a kind of ceremony? In later imagination both timber and quarries belonged to that part of Nature which answered the world of culture, with rituals attendant on the selection of quarries, stones and trees.

Alongside monuments in woodland there is a matter of woodland in monuments. Something like ten thousand tree trunks were used to palisade one of the enclosures at West Kennet Farm, for instance, and hundreds of mature trees were required for the later concentric circles or rotunda at Durrington Walls. The palisaded enclosure built about 4,110 years ago within the henge at Mount Pleasant called for the felling of nearly one and a half square miles of oak forest. And these were not the largest sites of their kind.[111]

Pollen, insect and plant remains from the ground surfaces that underlie Neolithic monuments often show them to have been built on grassland, sometimes on ploughsoil, although often with woodland in the vicinity.[112] By the thirtieth century BC, in areas where monuments occur (which was not everywhere) it seems that clearance was well advanced. Just as evidently, monument builders still had access to generous timber supplies – although whether these were close to hand or brought from afar, taken from managed or unmanaged woodland, we seldom know. One wonders if the construction of certain kinds of monument was itself a ceremony of clearance. Beyond that is symbolism suggested by the monuments themselves. The concentric rings of timber uprights at Durrington, for instance, could almost be seen as stylized woodland. Was this another aspect of the long transformation of human relationships with landscapes, animals, vegetation, from a condition of coalescence with Nature to one of imagined control?[113]

The opening of the Old Wood was linked with a changing conception of space and time. Literally, horizons changed. Areas once masked became open. Vistas and skylines were new seen. Faraway features acquired unexpected presence. New openness must also have been balanced by intimacy – areas which retained woodland and therefore complexity. Important in the Middle Ages and today, the 'open' and 'closed' landscapes we shall meet in Chapter 7 may have been prefigured this far back.

Just as the first enclosures seem to have linked life and death, so too do they seem to have embraced different perceptions of time. Radiocarbon dates from cattle bones found in monuments of this time show that some of them were appreciably *older* than the structures in which they were found. Were they therefore being carried around, or placed at certain points for intermittent retrieval and display?

Consciousness of time is prefigured in monuments where early farmers were buried. Frameworks created from large numbers of high-precision radiocarbon dates within a Bayesian framework have enhanced our grasp of the sequences behind early Neolithic burial places in southern Britain.[114] If cases recently examined are typical, then the making of ostentatious mausolea (long cairns, long barrows, chambered tombs – the forms varied) got under way in the thirty-eighth century BC and flourished through the thirty-seventh. Underneath them are sometimes found traces of action a few generations before – a midden of the fortieth century cal BC at Ascott-under-Wychwood (Oxfordshire),[115] burials in a wooden compartment at Wayland's Smithy (now Oxfordshire, once Berkshire).[116] What the sequences suggest is agricultural communities establishing themselves for several generations, then memorializing their founding dynasties. Bayesian valuations suggest primary interments over a few generations – two or three at Hazleton (Gloucestershire),[117] up to five at Ascott, just a lifetime at West Kennet.[118] Sometimes there was a pause with a resumption of burial a generation or two later. But the overall impression is of brief, flaring intensity – a commemoration of families and groups who began to change the world. Six thousand years later we are still thinking about them.[119]

To begin to sum up: we have seen the main sources for the idea of plodding expansion, and dealt with four of them: the fallacy that landscape clearance did not fully get into its stride until the Middle Ages; an impression from pre-Bayesian radiocarbon that the onset of farming was protracted; over-literal or uncritical use of Domesday; and an assumption that the conversion of heath, fen, moor and woodland to arable to feed a growing population in the twelfth and thirteenth centuries involved areas that either had previously been ignored or had not seen settlement before. Since almost all landscape can be used for something, the underlying issue was one not of agriculture (= civilization) versus Old Wood (= cultural inferiority) but of what balance was to be struck between different resources and uses. This balance was continually shifting. Excessive woodland clearance was not a sign of cultural attainment – 'Man's Conquest of Nature', as Childe put it in the first sentence of his *Prehistoric Communities of the British Isles* – so much as a symptom of its crisis.

We have also seen that woodland shrinkage was not steady paced; there were times and places when clearance paused and trees came back. In the long run, however, it was inexorable, and in later prehistory the development of metallurgy speeded it up. The decline of woodland habitats can be followed by proxy in the rising pollens of clearance herbs, changes in alluviation and the flow of rivers, the spread of domesticated stock and local extinctions. Deprived of its habitat, the aurochs – the large, wild and far from placid ancestor of European domestic cattle – disappears from the archaeological record some time around 1300 BC. The formidable brown bear lingered longer, lynx longer still, in the high Pennines into the early Middle Ages.[120] But in the field systems of late prehistory, stencilled in barley and wheat across miles of eastern counties, in the moorland reaves and East Anglian linearities, is written the death of the Old Wood.

Mysteries often have a concluding twist – that moment when someone turns to the detective and says: 'There's just one thing I don't understand ...' In this story there are several loose ends. One concerns those long-distance trackways to which pre-war historians were so attached (as indeed was a certain kind of aunt, who upon your arrival would ask, with breathless intensity, 'Did you come by the *ridge* route?'). The other was the idea that place names record survival of the Old Wood long into the Middle Ages.

In one sense the trackways are a non-issue, as whether or not they existed now has no bearing on the reality of the obstacles that were once imagined to call them into being. Obviously, there *were* tracks and packways for the haulage across country of salt, timber, slaves and other kinds of goods, and for the driving of animals. However, the demise of the Old Wood annuls the notion that ridgeways were for its avoidance, just as the survival of sophisticated wooden causeways through wetlands disposes of the idea that fen and marsh were inaccessible. Ridgeways seem prominent today not because they were the backbone of early communications but because their predominantly pastoral surroundings have preserved them. Across lower, arable landscapes, by contrast, signs of prehistoric traffic have been fogged by ploughing and development.

While evidence for prehistoric travel across all kinds of terrain has grown, confidence in the necessary antiquity of ridgeways has faltered. A number of them plainly are not new – several are mentioned in pre-Conquest sources, and the 'Icknield' of the Icknield Way was so strange that even the Anglo-Saxons were not sure what it meant.[121] However, the idea that ridgeways *typically* go back to the Neolithic is supposition. Old roads are difficult to date, because each renewal tends to over-write what was there before, but there are places where ridgeways are now fitted into a relative chronology which puts them into later prehistory. For at least some of its length, for instance, the famous Oxfordshire–Wiltshire Ridgeway must be younger than the Bronze Age boundaries across which it runs.[122] But that, arguably, is less interesting than the realization that prehistory's greatest trunk routes were not trackways at all. They were rivers.

In 1996 the archaeologist Andrew Sherratt published a short meditation on rivers called Avon. *Abona*, whence today's Welsh *Afon*, was a British word for 'river'. Sherratt argued that several of the rivers which bear this name once formed parts of a single trade route – in effect, that 'Avon' meant not 'a river' but '*the* river', even though different rivers were involved. This answers an earlier-posed question: why it was that Wessex, a region not rich in natural resources, was at certain times so affluent and politically pre-eminent. Sherratt's reply was that Wessex lay at the heart of a network of wealth-bringing connections: between northern France and Brittany in the south, Wales and southern Ireland in the west, and the Irish Sea and Western Isles to the north. Prehistoric Britain oscillated between different, sometimes competing axes: 'via Wessex to France and the Atlantic, or via the Thames to the North Sea and the Rhineland'.[123] Not just prehistoric Britain, either: similar swings help to explain why Winchester was England's capital in the tenth century yet in eclipse only two hundred years later, or why Anglo-Saxon England's greatest cities, situated close to the tidal limits of anciently named rivers, looked east or south.

And the other argument – the place names? In 1849 the historian

John Mitchell Kemble suggested that settlements of the first English-speaking immigrants were typified by particular kinds of place name.[124] These included names which were held to reflect the clearance of woodland in later colonization.[125] This doctrine went virtually unchallenged until the 1960s, when it was realized that place names of the supposedly oldest kind hardly ever coincided with contemporary archaeological evidence for the Anglo-Saxons themselves.[126] It was also realized that inferences about some supposedly 'later' place names might have to be revised. Names referring to woodland clearings, for instance, did not have to denote clearances which had just taken place – they might reflect interspersed woods and open country.[127]

A related argument turned on the Scandinavian names with which many of England's northern and eastern counties are richly flavoured – names held to have originated when Viking soldiers turned to farming in the later ninth century. If it was true that the dwellings of Anglo-Saxons and Viking arrivistes alike 'were so many pioneer settlements battling to reduce the wood'[128] then large tracts of land must still have remained unsettled. Debate about this began in the 1950s, when one historian questioned the density of Scandinavian colonization, and another – a young man called Peter Sawyer – reassessed sources for the size of Viking armies.[129] Sawyer concluded that membership of the largest armies was to be reckoned in hundreds rather than thousands, and that the scale of the following settlement might likewise have been exaggerated. The Danes as settlers, in other words, were initially an elite who exercised influence through power and control of estates and tribute rather than weight of numbers. In the 1970s Sawyer opened a second front, arguing that rural resources in seventh- and eighth-century England were already fully used, and hence that there was little vacant land available when the Scandinavians arrived.

Not everyone agreed. 'It seems likely', said the place-name scholar Margaret Gelling in 1978, apparently through clenched teeth, 'that there will always be historians who do not believe that the appearance of a large number of place-names in a new language is evidence of a large-scale settlement by the speakers of the new language.'[130] But this is not the point. Archaeology now reveals many thousands of places to have been settled before the dates of the names by which we now know them. Place names change, and the language of a name need no more signify the origin of the place than the Scandinavian word *lundr*, 'wood' (as in place names like Lound or Rockland), must denote trees planted by Vikings. Some 'Anglo-Saxon' or 'Scandinavian' names were adaptations or translations of older names;[131] yet others were formed in later centuries, and hence are a guide less to the initial scale of settlement than to the continuing influence of English and Scandinavian speech upon local dialects.

The age of the hunter-gatherers was possibly the most dangerous in which anyone could have lived, so it is not sentimentality which lies behind an idea that the epoch of the Old Wood was the last, perhaps only, age of oneness between the worlds of the spirit, of knowledge and of life – three realms of meaning which the tree continues to symbolize.[132] Shakespeare catches that in *The Tempest*. Caliban, hunter-gatherer-monster, covenants himself to the dodgy pair of Trinculo and Stephano, promising to pluck them berries, catch fish, fetch their wood, dig pig-nuts with his long fingernails, show them where crab-apples grow and lead them to a jay's nest.[133] Trinculo and Stephano are from the new world of ocean-going ships, astrolabes, great houses, metaphysical literature, high fashion and alcohol. They talk in prose. Caliban comes from the Mesolithic. He speaks in verse.

PART THREE

HOME FROM HOME

26. (Previous page) *Tenth-century grave-marker from church at Middleton-by-Pickering, North Yorkshire. The man commemorated may have been a founder-leader of the planned community and fields.*

7

TALL NETTLES

No traveller comes easily to a lost village ...You must be friend to mud, to green lanes and unused footpaths, to rotting foot-bridges and broken stiles, to brambles and to barbed wire. It is a landscape which has forgotten that human beings may want access, and it may be pardoned for its forgetfulness. It is so long since anyone wanted to come this way.[1]

Maurice Beresford, *The Lost Villages of England*, 1954

Maurice Beresford never owned nor drove a car. His journeys into the field were by bus or train, then on foot, map in hand, dog at heel. Beresford bore out R. H. Tawney's remark that what historians needed 'was not more documents but stouter boots'. Years later he liked to joke that the main thing with which the lost villages on his distribution maps connected was the geography of public transport.

This chapter and the next explore a mystery and contemplate a revelation. The mystery is why the human landscape of southern Britain is so varied. The revelation: a picture of ordinary life from later prehistory to the Norman Conquest in a few square miles. The story begins in muddy lanes and the world of redbrick dons after the Second World War and takes us into environmental and economic history, and human relationships. Other subjects are met as we go. Among them are the rise of local history, the impacts (again) of metal detecting, historical ecology and deeper orderings of the human landscape. These last, shadowy leviathans live under the threshold of historical consciousness, many fathoms down. They will break surface near the book's end.

Until the publication of *Lost Villages* such places had not much fea-tured in historical thought. One reason for that was the belatedness of archaeological interest in the Middle Ages generally. Until the late 1930s 'medieval archaeology' barely existed,[2] and insofar as it did its subject was monuments of the privileged such as castles and manors. Curiously, during the 1840s, the decade that saw the *floruit* of railway building and founding of county archaeological societies,[3] there had been a stir of interest in ordinary things and local surroundings, but enquiry soon reverted to institutions and the people who ran them – the nobility, the Church, the gentry.[4] This appeared to give archaeology little to do, for if ordinary people were regulated by an elite then presumably anything one might wish to know about them could be found in the elite's records.

By the end of the 1930s a few deserted villages had found their way into the record. Hadrian Allcroft, author of a long-celebrated book called *Earthwork of England* (1908), had identified a number of them. In 1925 O. G. S. Crawford published an RAF photograph of a once-upon-a-time village at Gainsthorpe, in Lincolnshire.[5] Coincidentally, around that same time editors of the Lincoln Record Society were preparing the text of the Lincolnshire Domesday for publication. In doing so they realized that a number of the vills named in the survey had since disappeared, and added a list of them.[6] Between 1937 and 1939 traces of a medieval peasant settlement were examined at Beere in Devon.[7] In 1939 trial excavations were made on the site of a deserted village at Seacourt just outside Oxford.[8] Seacourt was dated by written records, and it was accordingly hoped that the site would provide a framework for the chronology of medieval pottery and small objects more generally. Moreover, as this was the first medieval village known to have been excavated, it was hoped that the excavations would stimulate 'a fresh archaeological approach to the problems of mediaeval economic history' and the changing status of England's peasantry in the later Middle Ages.[9]

From 1945, just as Clement Attlee's government put new emphasis on the welfare of ordinary people, so did historians and archaeologists increasingly bring everyday existence to the fore. Among them was the art historian and archaeologist Rupert Bruce Mitford, the man who had trenched Seacourt. Back from the war, Bruce Mitford called again for the study of low-status places to balance preoccupation with the monumental and aristocratic. Another with similar interests was William George Hoskins, a Devonshire man who in the 1930s had taught economics at University College Leicester. After war service as a statistician Hoskins returned to Leicester, now in the department of history. Hoskins believed in fieldwork, and had used his wartime exile

27. *Gainsthorpe, Lincolnshire, the first deserted medieval settlement to be rediscovered from the air. Statutory protection of the former village contrasts with unrestricted ploughing round about.*

in London to identify classes of document that could be used to throw light on rural society.

A third influence was John Hurst. At the age of twenty-one, just out of the army, Hurst went to Trinity College Cambridge to study archaeology. Over the next three years, frustrated by Cambridge's fixation with prehistory and the fewness of its opportunities for training in the field, Hurst joined the excavation of a moated manor near London which was producing a lot of medieval pottery. At that time few attempts had been made to classify such material, study its regional variations or date the products of different kilns. Hurst accordingly embarked on analysis of medieval ceramics, and when he finished his degree in 1951 he took his growing knowledge into the Ministry of Works as an Assistant Inspector of Ancient Monuments. This was also the year in which he joined forces with Maurice Beresford to study a forgotten medieval settlement that

Beresford had found the year before while walking on the Yorkshire Wolds. It lay in a secluded valley, and its name was Wharram Percy.

At twenty-eight Beresford was a little older than Hurst, and further on in his career. But like Hoskins he believed in fieldwork, and like Hurst he was attracted to things around the edges of conventional subjects. Beresford had grown up in Sutton Coldfield, on the northern edge of Birmingham. In his teens he had developed keen and contrasting enthusiasms that included maps, history, opera and social justice. Eloquent and sharp-witted, in 1938 he went to study economic history at Cambridge, where one of his teachers was John Saltmarsh, the librarian of King's College who the year before had been appointed a lecturer in economic history. Unusually for an economic historian of that period, Saltmarsh took students outdoors to look at buildings and the land itself. Land, after all, had been the basis of the economy for the greater part of history. Until his co-option into the ranks of wartime academic code-breakers at Bletchley Park, Saltmarsh helped to put Beresford on the path he subsequently travelled.

After graduation Beresford worked from 1942 to 1948 as warden of an adult education centre in Rugby. From here he tramped the surrounding Warwickshire countryside. Applying the Saltmarsh approach – visual evidence coupled with study of primary written records – Beresford began to document the traces of villages that had failed to survive.[10] Among the records was a list of Warwickshire abandonments which had been compiled in the fifteenth century by John Rous, a priest and antiquary with wide connections who had an eye for historical change.[11] From what Rous said, one possible cause was the expulsion of villagers from certain places to turn arable over to pasture and make way for sheep.[12]

In 1948 Hoskins published a list of deserted villages in Leicestershire which complemented Beresford's work across the border in Warwickshire.[13] In this year, too, Beresford was appointed to a lectureship in economic history at the University of Leeds, whence he extended his fieldwork into the Vale of York and on to the Yorkshire Wolds. Late medieval abandonments on the Wolds had been extensive, providing Beresford with new examples and insights that could be compared with those he had already examined in Warwickshire.

The emptiness of lost villages stirs 'secret and reserved feelings'.* Their grassy undulations prompt visitors to imagine what it was that stilled

* See p. 52.

these places, and the experience of their villagers.[14] In 1948 Beresford accordingly introduced the subject to a general readership through an article in *Country Life*. One of those who read it was an editor at the Lutterworth Press, who invited Beresford to write a book: the genesis of *The Lost Villages of England*. And it was also in 1948 that the historian of medieval trade and rural society M. M. Postan, sensing something new in the air, organized a seminal meeting in Cambridge to consider how field and archive research could be taken forward together. Hoskins and Beresford were there. So was Axel Steensberg, pioneer of area excavation (see p. 78) – a technique that John Hurst realized was needed to make sense of the remains of Wharram Percy.[15]

If one reason for the previous disregard of lost villages was a focus on other things, another was the belief among some economic historians that they did not exist. Of course, no one denied that *some* settlements had been abandoned. The issue was one of scale, and a wish to read Tudor history in a particular way. Abandonment, so the sceptics said, had been occasional, not something widespread that accordingly required general explanation. Indeed, the more emphatic the sources, the less some historians were inclined to believe them. E. F. Gay, for instance, dismissed Tudor accounts of depopulation as 'hysterical and rhetorical complaint'. Their 'very exaggeration', he said, condemned them as wrong.[16] Such doubts found their way into mainstream narrative. Here is our old friend George Macaulay Trevelyan:

> we hear much of rural depopulation in Tudor times, because it was
> then regarded as a grave evil … There were some such cases, and there
> would have been more but for the agitation and the consequent action
> by government to restrain such enclosure. But the 'rural depopulation'
> in Tudor times was only sporadic and local, and was more than made
> up elsewhere.[17]

'Sporadic and local' put it cautiously. Five years before the publication of *Lost Villages*, the economic historian Sir John Clapham had pronounced them 'singularly rare'.[18] As the geographer W. G. East mused during the discussion that followed a lecture given by Beresford to the Geographical Society on 2 April 1950, Beresford was a 'bold man to come here and challenge Sir John Clapham and Professor Tawney on matters of economic history'. And it was not only Clapham and Tawney whom Beresford was contradicting. Another unbeliever was the referee hired by the Lutterworth Press to peer-review the manuscript of Beresford's book. Lutterworth went ahead anyway, and after the publication of *Lost*

Villages it became difficult (though, for a few diehards, not impossible) to dispute that there were indeed a lot of lost villages for historians to explain.[19] Beresford had listed over a thousand of them.

Around lost villages lay lost fields, which often were not lost if you knew what you were looking for. Travellers crossing England from, say, Bristol to Durham by rail will know those long, round-backed undulations which roll like ocean swell across the surface of pasture. During train journeys north from Birmingham in the early 1950s, or south, below the Lickey Bank and on towards Cheltenham, their rhythms mesmerized me, especially in early June when buttercups striped the ridges gold. I often wondered what they were. Beresford's book explained them as the remains of medieval ploughlands. Blocks of strips with the same trend had been gathered into furlongs,* and a group of furlongs formed a larger land which was cropped in rotation with one or two others. Lacking permanent subdivisions, tenurially subdivided, communally organized, these were the remains of open-field agriculture.

It had long been understood that ridges bore the stamp of old ploughing, and in 1938 an account of the medieval system had been published which many historians had accepted.[20] However, not everyone accepted that there was a general identity between medieval strips and still-visible ridges.[21] One tendency asserted that extensive medieval survival was not to be expected because the English landscape had been almost wholly reshaped by enclosure after 1700. Another challenged the general coincidence of ridges with medieval strips on the grounds that different kinds of ridge had been made at later times (which is true) and hence that no continuity from medieval ridges could be expected (which is not). One academic went so far as to claim that most ridge and furrow still to be seen dated from the nineteenth century. Beresford answered the disbelievers. There were, he agreed, 'always dangers in urging a general identity, such as that of ridges and strips'.[22] However, the suggestion that recent ploughing had produced furlong patterns seemed 'to overestimate the ability or the knowledge of the ploughmen of the last two centuries to etch an open-field pattern between and through the modern hedges'.[23]

How far back could such patterns be traced? Surviving Tudor maps are uncommon, but Beresford found enough of them to show a close, often precise match between the physique of strips and furlongs as they

---

* Whence our furlong – an eighth of a mile – although a 'furrow-long' was originally a unit of cultivation rather than a measure of distance.

28. Medieval open fields overlain by enclosure, Edgehill, Warwickshire, photographed 1947

existed in the later sixteenth century and the patterns to be seen in the same localities on modern air photographs. If this did not certify the fields to be older than Elizabeth I, it did at least show them to be no younger. And the air photographs indicated their extent. In the open-field heartlands, areas like Buckinghamshire north of the Chilterns, south-east Warwickshire, parts of Bedfordshire and Northamptonshire, routinely 75 per cent and sometimes as much as 90 per cent of the surface of a given township was engraved with ridge and furrow.[24]

A third approach went further. On almost every air photograph of a lost village over which Beresford pored, the ridge and furrow began where the village crofts and garths ended.[25] Settlements and fields fitted together. If the townships were medieval, the townfields were medieval too. Moreover, while farming writers did sometimes refer to the throwing up of ridges at later dates, the likelihood that a village abandoned at the end of the Middle Ages would have 'seen much of any

plough between its depopulation and the ploughing-up campaign of
1940' seemed small. In fact, as the relative rewards of wool and cereals
swung to and fro, there were occasions when some furlongs went back
to the plough, and out again. But on the whole Beresford had a point.

Rumours about the modernity of medieval ridge and furrow nevertheless lingered. One of them even claimed that ridges belonged to the
Dig for Victory campaign in the Second World War. Ridging was indeed
practised at that time, but the telling of modern from ancient ridging is
normally straightforward if you go to look. The corollary is that anyone
who does not look may be misled. And since until the earlier twentieth
century agrarian history had been a mainly indoor business, it is not difficult to see how the challenging of its settled assumptions by patches
of rumpled ground or clumps of nettles might call for a special kind of
open-mindedness. What was really new was the placing of documents
and landscape in dialogue, and the study of localities rather than sites.

Local history had been gaining ground since the 1920s. It had ante-
cedents in earlier genres, such as the work of monastic historians to
document the continuous histories of their houses, Tudor chorography,
seventeenth- and eighteenth-century accounts of counties and towns,

29. *Work for an open landscape: harrowing, from the Luttrell Psalter, f.171r
(c.1325 × 1350). Elsewhere the page bears verses from Psalm 95 about land
and husbandry, and the Luttrell arms proclaim the manorial family's status
'as God's local regents, guarantors of a good harvest, and of souls for the lord'*
(The Luttrell Psalter. A facsimile, *Michelle P. Brown (Commentary)*,
British Library, 2006, 46).

and parish histories which related the descent of manors and the pedigrees of landed families. The usefulness and continuity in these endeavours have sometimes been under-emphasized.[26] However, while in important respects the new local history built on them, it also differed.[27] Antiquarianism had tended to amass and classify information rather than ask questions, and in its earlier stages had been indiscriminate in mixing legend, received statements and verifiable fact. In the nineteenth century historians began to examine local themes more critically, by direct enquiry. Even then there was a tendency to expect local history to be national history in microcosm,[28] while curiosity about the diversity of places was offset by theories which assumed the alikeness of feudal village communities and set them in a uniform countryside.[29]

The *Victoria History of the Counties of England* was begun in 1899 to make a 'record of England's places and people from earliest times to the present day'. The project boosted interest in local history and gave it a new platform, while the creation in 1908 of a research fellowship in the subject by the University of Reading gave it further standing. The appointee was a young man called Frank Stenton, who went on to write the twentieth century's leading account of Anglo-Saxon England. Stenton's selection helps to explain why so much of local history's back-country should have been in the east midlands, for he was a Nottinghamshire man who retained a home in the county and links with historians at Nottingham University. One of them was Professor J. V. D. Owen, a former Stenton pupil. Another was David Chambers, the son of a farmer near Eastwood (D. H. Lawrence's birthplace), who in the mid-1920s studied under Owen's supervision, and then joined the university's newly opened adult education department, where local history was popular. Chambers's book *Nottinghamshire* (1932) inspired Beresford, and several of his pupils – like W. E. Tate, author of *The Parish Chest* (1946) – became influential figures in the field.

Interest spread. Supported by grants from the Carnegie Trust, local history committees were set up to co-ordinate village classes. A committee for Lindsey (a district of Lincolnshire) started in 1927, and a Lindsey Local History Society followed. One of its members was Canon C. W. Foster, a country parson whose list of abandoned Lincolnshire villages, published in 1924, has been noted as a pioneer work on the subject.[30]

Across the Humber in Hull another local history initiative was launched in 1931, its work reinforced when Hull University appointed Maurice Barley (yet another east midlander and Reading graduate) as organizing tutor. Amateur archaeologists were drawn in. One of them was Ted Wright, the son of an East Riding businessman. In 1937, while searching the Humber foreshore near Ferriby, Wright and his brother found an ancient boat made of oak planks sewn together with yew withies. Wright thought it might be Viking. The following August Barley was one of those enlisted to try to extract it. By then they had found another. The boats were accessible for only a few hours between tides, and even then the clay was 'like stiff butter' so that if you stood in one place for long it became difficult to move. In 1946 the Wrights enlisted the help of C. W. Phillips, the excavator of Sutton Hoo, to retrieve the vessels. Their discovery later turned out to be more significant than anyone expected. Calibrated radiocarbon measurements put the age of one boat at between 3,730 and 3,930 years. Wright subsequently found another craft that was even older.[31] With crews of up to eighteen oarsmen, bearing cargoes of amber, metalwork, furs, animals and people, craft of the Ferriby type had journeyed the North Sea and the rivers that ran out of central Europe and far into England. Thus could muddy local finds illuminate transcontinental travel in the Bronze Age.

Pre-war local history tutors were rather like itinerant Methodist preachers a century before. Covering thirty or forty miles a night to take the word to remote villages, they were also explorers. Nowadays the search for regional and local sources begins in a library or an archive. In the 1920s there were few public archives, most local documents were unpublished, and their very existence or whereabouts was usually unknown. Original records still awaited discovery in town-hall cellars, among dead pigeons in the muniment rooms of country houses or in church vestries where 'sometimes a Tudor register had to be peeled away from the damp side of the cast-iron box which parishes had been obliged to provide in 1812'. From enthusiasm for local records it was but a step to the recording of ancient customs, songs, Plough Monday plays, vernacular architecture, dialect, place and field names, even plants and fruit, for the particularity of a place could be as well expressed through its land-races of weeds or plums as by its church-wardens' accounts. After the war, it was often from departments of adult education (Hoskins and Beresford were both committed extra-mural teachers) and the Workers' Educational Association that such effort was taken forward.[32]

For a time, England became again what it had been in the sixteenth century – a realm 'waiting to be explored and described'.[33] A sense of expectancy hums behind some of the descriptions, like Nikolaus Pevsner's *The Leaves of Southwell* (Nottinghamshire, again), which appeared in

1945, or Jacquetta Hawkes's *A Land* (1951). Illustrated by Henry Moore, *A Land* was a study in consciousness that traced Britain's cultural personality from the rocks, clays and gravels of her pre-human foundations into history.[34] As we saw in the Prologue, Pevsner's *Buildings of England* was launched in the same year. Like John Betjeman's evocations of suburbia and one-service-a-month churches at lane ends,[35] 'Pevsner' (the name of the man and the series soon became interchangeable) was savoured not just for its accounts of buildings but also for portraits of the regions in which they stood. Another series, *The Face of Britain*, had been begun before the Second World War by the publisher Harry Batsford,[36] who recruited Hoskins to write one of its volumes. *Midland England* appeared in 1949. It completed a trio of books – Chambers's *Nottinghamshire* and the Orwins' *Open Fields* were the others – which propelled locality and landscape into mainstream historical thinking. It was around this time that Hoskins reflected 'there is not one book which deals with the historical evolution of the landscape as we know it'.[37] So he set about writing it.

The Making of the English Landscape appeared in 1955, the year after *Lost Villages*, which contained ideas that *Midland England* had in turn helped to inspire. Hoskins's book marked an epoch, or so it is often said. In fact, as we have already begun to see he was less of a solitary mould-breaker than one of a like-minded company who at least from the 1930s had realized that in landscape lay a record that had not previously been much considered. It was not that no one had previously grasped this,[38] but rather that no one had yet set it out so systematically or in such an accessible way. Hoskins's gift as a communicator made landscape history approachable, and thereby helped to define it. He also widened it. Hitherto field evidence had been viewed as a disjointed scatter of places, buildings and monuments which glimmered on distribution maps like the lights of a continent seen from a satellite at night. What lay between them was so much dark space, as if all history had been enacted within listed buildings or ancient monuments. The paramount achievement of Hoskins and his colleagues was to show that meaning lay everywhere. Important, too, was their enthusiasm for 'all those delicate peculiarities in human habits … differences in the way that people make their cakes and pies, build their haystacks or fasten their gates',[39] or come to that, the mystery of why some things hundreds of miles apart should look the same. 'Provincial', hitherto a kind of slur, was for Hoskins an accolade. His hungriness for history written upwards from the mingled complexities of different localities, the individualism of myriad unknown lives, rather than downwards from superimposed and often ill-fitting national generalizations, gave a new outlook towards place, people and history itself.

Thus did the pioneers open a new front. Yet at first, in some respects, they were marching away from it. Hoskins and Beresford were hampered by the inherited master narrative which said that fields and villages had been mostly laid out by Anglo-Saxon settlers in surroundings which either were uncleared or had reverted to wildwood following post-Roman collapse. Since Anglo-Saxon homesteaders were imagined to have taken land into cultivation a little at a time, furlongs were initially visualized as units of clearance, which in turn would explain why peasant holdings were scattered through the open fields rather than parcelled together, for reasons of equity, following each new co-operative intake. Everything seemed to fit. Yet evidence collected since the 1950s tells the opposite: that open fields were laid out as entities, typically on terrain already cleared, and that in some areas at least furlongs were later subdivisions.[40]

Anglo-Saxon villages were once supposed to have arrived in the early Middle Ages rather like container-grown plants, as physical and institutional entities in which house types, street plans, customs, common law and the open-field system were all introduced together. As time passed and population grew, opinion stated, primary settlements grew while secondary settlements were formed by descendants who moved on to land hitherto unoccupied. When population rose further, new houses were added to existing villages and more arable was taken at the expense of woodland or marginal areas. If population fell, the process went into reverse. Places grew, places shrank. Like breathing in and out, it all seemed very natural.

Even by the mid-1950s, however, *Lost Villages* and *The Making of the English Landscape* were flagging enigmas. One of them was the demography of village desertion. It looked capricious. Why should so many villages have been deserted in Yorkshire and Norfolk, for instance, yet so few in Lancashire or Essex? What subtle variations lay behind this? A related question was what a 'village' was. The sociable cluster of crofts and houses which Beresford at first took as standard was in fact but one of many settlement types, most of which tended to melt in the face of classification; and 'village' itself was no single thing.[41] Beresford saw that to describe any lost village as typical was hazardous, because failed villages were as varied as living ones.[42] And aback of all this are different kinds of England.

On the one hand, as in Essex or Herefordshire, we have the England of hamlets, medieval farms in hollows of the hills, lonely moats and great barns in the clay-lands, pollards and ancient trees, cavernous holloways and many footpaths, fords, irregularly shaped groves with thick hedges colourful with maple, dogwood, and spindle – an intricate land of mystery and surprise. On the other hand there is the Cambridgeshire type of landscape, the England of big villages, few, busy roads, thin hawthorn hedges, windswept brick farms, and ivied clumps of trees in corners of fields; a predictable land of wide views, sweeping sameness, and straight lines.[43]

The contrasts have been noted for centuries. Sixteenth-century topographers had called the intricate land 'woodland' or the 'several', while the land of sameness was 'champion' or 'champaign' (from the Latin *campus*, 'a field', via the French *champagne*). 'Here was in sight little wodde, as yn a country of chaumpaine,' wrote the antiquary John Leland on his way between Rockingham and Staunton in the late 1530s. King Lear uses the same language when he divides his kingdom in Goneril's favour, 'even from this line to this, With shadowy forests and with champains rich'd'.[44] Another word for 'champaign' was 'feldon', from feld – a tract of open land.

What lay behind such differences? Nineteenth- and earlier twentieth-century writers on regional personality had explained it either as an effect of interactions between terrain, environment and geology, or by landholding contrasts conjectured between Celt and Saxon.[45] In neither case did they grasp the intricate relationships between Nature and human decision witnessed in the landscape itself. Between degrees of nucleation and dispersion, entanglement and regularity lay areas where different elements mingled.[46] If it was true that England had been made by the English, which England was it?

In the first years after *Lost Villages* appeared there was a tendency to view desertion as a kind of syndrome to which certain places were prone and others immune. Scholars became settlement epidemiologists, seeking meaning in which places had ailed and which had thrived. The malady had gradations. Villages which declined, for instance, did not always disappear. Some shrank to hamlets; others dwindled to a farm or two, a manor house, a lonely church. When mapped, the most vulnerable sites appeared to lie in a belt running from south-west to north-east. West of the Pennines, in the western midlands and south-west there was less sign of them. In the east, the distributions looked perplexing.

Lincolnshire's Wolds, for instance, were strewn with casualties whereas only a few miles away in Cambridgeshire, or in Lincolnshire's Fenland, there seemed to be hardly any. Essex, too, was almost devoid of them, and so – aside from a sprinkling along the coastline of Kent and Sussex – was most of the south-east.

In seeking to explain such contrasts it was natural that scholars should have looked first at the conditions that prevailed when places waned. From Beresford's work the losses seemed heaviest during the fifteenth and earlier sixteenth centuries. In all but a handful of cases this ruled out the prime suspect, the Black Death, and while it seemed likely that desertion was related to the continuing fall in population that apparently followed,[47] the nature of the link was not clear. In a number of cases, as Tudor complainants said at the time, settlements were depopulated by landlords who wished to switch from arable to pastoral farming. However, there was often more to it than this. Some economic historians wondered if the failed settlements were latecomers, very likely established in the twelfth or thirteenth century when rising population was supposed to have forced the intake of new arable either from marginal soils hitherto avoided, or at the expense of other valuable resources like woodland. In this 'last in, first out' model it was supposed that such land would soon have become over-burdened, or that new-sprung settlements would have been more vulnerable to failure when population and land values slumped. Yet fieldwork revealed no such pattern. Many of the villages that would be lost were on good soils, or at least on land no worse than places which survived, and their histories usually ran back just as far.

A more promising line was indicated by Beresford's discovery from fourteenth-century tax quotas that before the Black Death many of the villages that would later be lost had been smaller than the run of their neighbours. The issue here, presumably, was that smaller villages had less social or economic critical mass with which to withstand forces which influenced desertion. But why were they smaller? It was not because of the fourteenth-century plagues and famines, which had tended to cull across the board and accentuated disparities that were already there. Some places showed signs of depopulation up to half a century before the Black Death. They lay in areas where later desertions were also numerous, which suggested that the underlying influences were older, and that different sources might be illuminating different stages of long-term processes.[48] Was it then possible that certain villages had been predisposed to failure, as if by weight at birth or some genetic flaw? Could it be that human choices and environmental factors had predestined desertion centuries before it came to pass?

Concepts like 'desertion' and 'shrinkage', or indeed 'growth', begged the question of what 'normality' would look like. Such terms were problematic, for they implied a standard condition for the country-side against which change could be measured. Desertion-as-failure and failure-as-destiny also highlighted local crises and events, thereby foregrounding the fate of particular places and individuals. A different viewpoint might look beyond such specifics in search of longer-term slowly evolving processes. To use an analogy, by focusing too closely upon a crumb on a table one might miss the shape of the table.

At any rate, by the late 1970s it was clear that to view a depopulated village as some sort of miscarriage was to define a narrow kind of normality. Archaeology now showed that in their beginnings, layout, fabric and material life the histories of to-be-lost villages were similar to those which were to survive. The label 'deserted medieval village', DMV (archaeologists love initials), was thus no more useful in defining the subject of village than a crashed car might assist the general characterization of transport.

By now, too, it was understood, villages were but one of many settlement types, all of which had been co-evolving in different ways and at different speeds. Clustered and dispersed settlements, villages and hamlets, were not opposites but degrees in a continuum, while the places where people lived could not be usefully studied apart from the fields they cultivated or the other rural resources upon which they relied. Landscape itself was the theme, and by the 1980s a number of scholars were exploring it. One of them was the historical ecologist Oliver Rackham, whose *The History of the Countryside* (1986) traced the making of landscape through the interaction of human activities and the natural world.[49] The evocations of provincial contrast quoted above are his. Another was Christopher Taylor, the landscape archaeologist first met in Chapter 6, who three years before the appearance of Rackham's book had broken away from study by period to approach settlement as a continuum from prehistory to recent times.[50] Taylor's book was called *Village and Farmstead*. The two books together seemed to give binocular vision.

Taylor explored three ideas. One, that the history of settlement had been shaped less by geographical determinism than by human choices. Two, that the story of settlement in a given area is likely to be intricate rather than simple. And three, that settlement is typically protean.

Hence, the settlements we see today will not usually be the result of outward growth from ancient nuclei, but the result of a succession of reconfigurations. Such transformation can occur in many ways – by relocation, slow drift, coalescence, fission, fusion – and at differing tempos in which beats of different measure may run in counterpoint. At some periods stability is long held; in others, change is rapid or spasmodic.

Taylor drew attention to one process which seemed to offer a key to other questions. Many settlements, he said, had been deliberately planned. In itself, this was not controversial. Purposely laid-out settlements were well known from the eighteenth and nineteenth centuries, from Roman days and later prehistory, and it had long been realized that systematic planning must lie behind the medieval villages which consist of rows of house garths that face each other across a street or green. Such settlements occur widely in certain parts of England, and this consistency had already caused historical geographers to ask if they might all belong to one period, or be the result of one cause, such as widespread reconstruction after William the Conqueror's wasting of the north in 1069–70 (an example of putting event and individual before long-term process).

Taylor showed how widespread planning had been. By examination in the field he showed that places which looked amorphous were in fact often made up of planned elements which had, so to speak, gone out of shape as time passed – for instance through piecemeal addition or the loss, subdivision or amalgamation of holdings. Many places displayed several stages of planning. Others that lacked planned features could nevertheless be seen as the result of deliberate development.[51]

The significance of these discoveries was magnified by another, namely that formal planning was not confined to areas where its signs are clearest. There was evidence for masterminding wherever in southern Britain there were nucleated villages. And to the obvious questions of when and how these regroupings took form, there were also 'why?' and 'on whose say-so?' Methodical nucleation often appeared to go hand in hand with the creation of the classic open-field systems, which could have been achieved only by the redistribution of land on a large scale.[52]

Of the four questions, answers to 'when' came soonest. In the central province the laying out of open fields in association with compact settlements typically began in the ninth or tenth century and continued to the end of the twelfth.[53] However, there were exceptions; in some areas the process began sooner.

How? There is continuing debate about whether the transition was usually made in one step or several. In some areas restructuring seems to have been sudden and comprehensive, in others it was apparently gradual and incremental, with no simple relationship between the creation of open fields and planning of settlements.[54] Associated with both are 'long lands': individual master strips that run continuously for long distances, sometimes right across a township.[55] Like a buried cable, long lands can run 'through and underneath what can be deduced to be later sub-divisions of the arable land into furlongs', and hence appear to have acted as baselines for later developments.[56] In some areas the inscription of long lands was a first step in a radical redrawing countryside; in others, they were inherited from earlier ages – as in western Cambridgeshire, where traces of prehistoric field layouts seem to have been embodied within common field furlongs.[57]

Why? This radical redrawing has been described as one of the great finds of British archaeology in the later twentieth century.[58] The changes were so far reaching that a powerful cause seems called for. Yet simple explanations fail because of the abundance of exceptions and sub-regional differences. One point at issue is whether from the start open fields functioned as *common fields* – that is, as communally worked fields governed by complex and seasonally varied access rights. Arrangements of this kind are known from the later Middle Ages, and can be inferred from the organization of common fields on the eve of parliamentary enclosure. Communal regulation was needed to govern processes that were of concern to all members of the community – such as fallowing. Did such collective, customary behaviour accompany the laying out of open fields or emerge later?[59] A related point is that open/common-field villages were being created and augmented for over four centuries – a period equivalent to that between Elizabeth I and now – and it seems unlikely that the driving influences behind the process remained the same throughout. The subject might better be approached in terms of a spectrum of influences which worked at different strengths and at different times, sometimes in conjunction, sometimes alone.

One possible factor is that in a countryside increasingly cluttered with boundaries, customary rights and inherited practices, there was a lot to be said for sweeping most of it away and starting again.[60] Another may have been a switch from a landscape hitherto composed of federal manors covering sizeable areas embracing different units of specialized production to the more largely self-sufficient and varied economies of the local manor, parish or vill.[61] A desire to integrate the use of rural resources, to put access to grazing, woodland, waste and arable, and decisions on the balance between them, on a more systematic and equitable footing across a wider area, would indeed be understandable, although in the common-field heartlands we often see the opposite – arable areas so extensive as to be more specialized than the landscapes they replaced.

A linked factor may have been the break-up from the ninth century of federal manors which had previously been held by or through the favour of the king. This would have had several effects. One was the decoupling or regrouping of places of specialized production that hitherto had existed within a larger network whose varied resources had been collectively exploited by kings and magnates. Another was an increase in the number of lords who lived locally and sought ways to make more efficient use of the lands on which they lived.[62] The manorial populations over which these lesser aristocrats presided were not socially uniform, but made up of different grades of peasant, ranging from estate workers over whom the lord had close control to free tenants who were smallholder farmers. The marshalling of the lord's workers in estate villages assisted their housing and self-sufficiency, while bringing them and their obligations under the eye of the lord or his officers. With that could go other kinds of intensification, such as the building of a local church which could improve upon, and eventually supplant, the ability of a more distant mother minster to collect tithes and dues, supervise burial or be a focus for feasts and community recreation. Significantly, it is from the tenth century that the survival of carved stones commemorating the founders of local dynasties becomes common.[63]

In films and novels the relationship between local lord and peasants is often simplified, a stark contrast between those who took and those who gave. In practice it may have been mutually reinforcing.[64] A lord wishing to maximize rents would need tenants, which could lead him to provide smallholdings to attract them, or for the occupancy of his *servi*, on jointly advantageous terms. In the Danelaw – the part of England where Scandinavian influences were strongest between the ninth and eleventh centuries – renders and tribute were no longer removed to the tables of faraway magnates, while the collapse of monastic landlords under the pressure of Danish land-taking likewise meant that more produce was left in local hands. This enabled investment in local infrastructure, like mills and houses. A church took tithes and dues, but if the lord or neighbours who owned it lived locally then part of what was taken stayed in local circulation, while the church, its saint and graveyard became a focus for community and family memories. The process of making a new village is hardly ever glimpsed in contemporary records, but when it is the operation looks collaborative, with boundaries and customs validated by peasant elders under the lord's charge.

If reorganization assisted the state and the proto-gentry, one of its side-effects was to provide new ways in which peasants could earn cash. Thanks not least to the already noted gross mapping of single coin losses enabled by metal-detector finds, it is clear that the volume of coin circulating through villages was increasing from the late ninth century to the twelfth. This had both a local and a wider context. Locally it reflected an intensification of markets whereat manorial surpluses could be negotiated for goods like ironwork or pottery, visible in the finds trays of village excavations, which a rural population just a few generations before might either have made for itself or have foregone.[65] It also reflected the changing external environment brought about by the growth of towns and cities, and the appetite of such places for provisions, raw materials and people. For administrators, the new on-the-ground arrangements simplified the gathering and calculation of land-based levies that in addition to tithe included rents, the assignment of public burdens and, later, *heregeld* – 'army tax' to buy off threatening Vikings. The newly divided landscape was in effect a diagram of who owed what to whom.

An underestimated factor is the extent to which local history has a continental context. The open-field villages sketched above have counterparts as far away as Poland, and in trying to make sense of pottery scatters as possible proxies for the pattern of late Anglo-Saxon manure-spreading we need to be aware of the influence of demand for English produce in far-away places. The finding of those Ferriby boats in the sticky inter-tidal Humber mud reminds us that trading journeys across the North Sea and Channel had been going on at least since the early Bronze Age. Trade seems to have intensified from the late tenth century, and its stimulant lay some six hundred miles to the east of England's midlands, in the Harz Mountains of Germany, where late in the 960s a large new source of silver was discovered, augmenting an earlier silver supply from central Europe which had been fuelling the expansion of coinage at least since the early eighth century.[66] The silver enabled Germans to import 'cloth and other goods on a much larger scale than previously, and contributed to the rapid growth of various industries in the towns of the Rhineland, Lorraine and Flanders. These in their turn needed food and raw materials that England was well placed to supply.'[67] The result was an inflow of silver which enabled late Saxon kings to mint good-quality coins in huge numbers, and to continue

30. Hurdle pen with sheep, from the Luttrell Psalter, f.163v (c.1325 × 1350). Wool may have been economically important centuries before the documented wool trade in the later Middle Ages. Ewes' milk could be converted to cheese – a versatile food that could be stored for long periods.

doing so despite Viking pressure. The scale of that pressure can be gauged from the fact that from the 990s to the 1040s most of the coins minted in England which are available for study come from Swedish hoards. Over fifty thousand pennies have been found on the island of Gotland alone. Other bulk finds have been recorded from Finland, Russia, Poland and the Baltic Republics. These transfers of Anglo-Saxon pennies to Scandinavia were a consequence of Scandinavian attacks or threats. Tribute of £10,000 was paid to the Danes in 991, for instance, and £48,000 in 1012. Other sensational payments, of gold, plate, jewellery and church ornaments, are recorded on Scandinavian runestones. Or as a chronicler put it in the 1140s: 'although little silver was mined in England, much was brought from Germany by the Rhine on account of England's wonderful fertility in fish and meat, in most precious wool, and in cattle without number. As a result, a larger supply of silver is found in England than in Germany.'[68] By this time the English coinage had become standardized, the fixed type changing every few years in a fiscally efficient system whereby the worn coin was called in for reminting, the exchanging being by count not weight, so that on each occasion the crown took a percentage for itself.

Continental demand cannot have lessened the incentives to intensify the production of lowland England, and may have added to them. This is reinforced by finds of the coins themselves. Casual losses give a rough measure of economic activity. The map of lost silver shows a striking affinity with the provinces of settlement we are considering, and gradations of wealth. The fact that at the beginning of the eleventh century Æthelred had to gather money to pay tribute to Vikings shows that coin was dispersed through society, which in turn indicates the presence of active markets in which peasants could buy and sell. The ability of the English to replenish large withdrawals of Viking protection money reminds us, too, that England's wealth in the century before the Norman Conquest, if not much sooner, was based at least in part on the same resource that powered the economy in the fifteenth century: sheep and wool.[69]

Almost without realizing it, we have linked an age of village-making with the age of village-unmaking where we began. In so doing we see that these were aspects of a process of transformation that ran for centuries. That is, the abandonments which become locally common after the fourteenth century can be seen not as sudden crises which rocked an immemorial pattern, but as the result of yet another set of influences on a great landscape revolution that had only recently been concluded.

All places have their own stories, but there are things about which generalization is worth the risk. The demographic slump in the later fourteenth and fifteenth centuries both aggravated and created discords. Demand for agricultural produce fell, while calls for skills rose. As village populations shrank, or at least did not rise, old loyalties and obligations became weakened. Tenancies became harder to fill, customary services could no longer be relied upon. Rents fell. Hiatuses of occupancy increased, unless countered by leases on more favourable terms. Wealthier peasants acquired extra land, but in putting it to use may have been challenged by the shortage and cost of labour. Conversion of arable to pasture could be a practical and profitable way round that, but could also cause stress by posing a threat to common grazing, while tempting entrepreneurs to turn bundles of strips into enclosed pastures.

One of the main reasons why larger villages shrank and intermediate hamlets disappeared may simply have been that their inhabitants went elsewhere. Many headed for towns, some of which by the later sixteenth century were expanding fast. Labour and skill shortages meant that work in towns and larger villages was easy to find. Rural emigration reinforced the enclosures, intensifying their causes while reducing resistance to their consequences.[70] Peasants thus emerge not simply as victims of village desertion but also as beneficiaries, and as co-agents behind the processes we are trying to explain.

It is not long since historians pictured peasants as a uniform mass of soil-bound serfs whose brief lives when not labouring for their lord or raising food for their families were lived in frail hovels.[71] Since the 1970s historians disposed of this fiction,[72] though not before an earlier generation of medieval archaeologists had deferred to it. As recently as 1983 the traces of peasant houses being excavated under the leadership of Maurice Beresford and John Hurst at Wharram Percy were thought to represent buildings so rickety as to require incessant rebuilding, lived in by people whose poverty and insecurity provided neither the means nor the incentive to build better.[73] Yet within five years a fresh look at the same evidence led to the opposite conclusion, that the houses had been well made and were long lasting.[74]

Alter an assumption, and you get a new answer to an old question. When archaeologists began to study peasant housing, conventional wisdom assured them that as late as the days of Chaucer most people lived in houses 'built of logs or planks, or of uprights and beams supporting rubble and clay'.[75] Vernacular architecture was accordingly a story of gradual advance from frailty to durability. Houses built to last, it was said, did not appear until the end of the Middle Ages, and there was no general sense of permanence until the later sixteenth century, whereafter Hoskins claimed to see 'abundant and inescapable' evidence for a universal rebuilding.[76] For as long as this was accepted, medieval peasant houses remained invisible because nobody expected to see them. The assumption of rural architectural inferiority thus became self-sustaining, and for years excavated evidence was held to confirm it.[77]

Yet there were pointers in other directions. During the 1960s several dissident academics drew attention to sources which showed that peasant houses had often been larger and more substantially built than social historians and vernacular architecture experts had been willing to allow.[78] Out in the field, moreover, the excavators of deserted villages were finding hinges, locks, keys, strapwork, hinge staples – things which meant doors, chests and caskets. A lockable door is of no use in a building that will fall down if it is slammed too hard, or where robbers seeking a strong-box can bypass the door simply by barging in through a flimsy wall. And what would be in the strong-box? Chests, caskets and locks reflect private property. Excavated villages have yielded a welter of personal possessions and specialized items: needles, scissors, thimbles, nails, buckets, spade-sheaths, cauldrons, glass and pottery vessels, most of them made by specialized manufactories and bought at market. They contradict the idea that the sole object of each farmer aside from serving his lord was to grow food to feed his family. Later medieval peasants were neither subsistence farmers nor members of one undifferentiated class. The better-off or more entrepreneurial were selling surplus produce, generating cash which was used to buy goods, pay others to work their holdings and hire craftsmen to build and repair the houses in which they lived.

Tree-ring dating shows that sturdy peasant houses were being built at least as early as the thirteenth century; archaeological evidence points to their existence a millennium sooner. Examples from the thirteenth century are few, however, whereas several thousand houses built after the Black Death are still standing, their diversity of size and construction a further witness to the social range of those who first lived in them.[79] Whether this reflects an actual increase in peasant house-building after the Black Death, or simply an increase in the availability of evidence (which could be explained by other factors), is still debated.[80] It certainly looks as though aristocratic house-building waned for some decades. As just noted, the later fourteenth century was a time of falling demand for produce, deflationary strain on rents and inflationary pressure on wages. Such conditions favoured peasants over landlords, at the same time as it created a material legacy of contrary trends in which new and better peasant houses were built while others were left to fall down. Acquitted from the charge of destroying villages, the Black Death reappears as an agent of progress and permanence. After the Black Death, risen wages 'and the letting of land on longer and more secure leases, seem to have brought a wave of rural housebuilding in more substantial materials than had been possible before'.[81]

The distribution of extant timber-framed buildings shows a marked contrast between the 'champion' areas, where they are now scarce, and adjoining regions where they are comparatively abundant. While we should not rule out the possibility that this distribution has been influenced by events since the houses were built, the underlying factor looks like the difference between a relatively treeless central zone and the regions to either side in which timber was more plentiful. Timber was used universally in medieval housebuilding; hence, the contrast is not between areas which built in wood and others which did not, but between areas in which timber was used generously and those in which it was in short supply.[82] This seems to be what the Tudor scholar William Harrison had in mind in the 1580s when he made a distinction:

between the plain and woody soils; for as in these, our houses are commonly strong and well-timbered (so that in many places there are not above four, six or nine inches between stud and stud), so in the open champaign countries they are forced, for want of stuff, to use no studs at all, but only frankposts, raisins, beams, prickposts, groundsels, summers (or dormants), transomes, and such principals, with here and there a girding, whereunto they fasten their splints or raddles, and then cast it over with thick clay to keep out the wind.[83]

By this time the last of the tall oaks, straight-grown from acorns that had germinated before the Norman Conquest, had been felled.[84]

A few medieval houses still bear layers of their original thatch. Such stems provide a botanical diary of what was going on in particular summers in surrounding medieval fields. What emerges is biodiversity accumulated since the Neolithic, and the evolution of plant races indigenous to particular districts or even villages, where crops sown from the previous season's seed were grown year in, year out, in locally different conditions. (One late Saxon charm for the improvement of land directs that 'seed from elsewhere be taken from beggars in exchange for twice as much' – genetically, a good strategy.) In result,

every plant in a land race is slightly different from its neighbour, and medieval cereals were consequently very uneven in straw height, ripening time, grain yield and other agronomic traits. This diversity ensured that a portion of the crop almost always set seed irrespective of the many environmental stresses that can destroy a crop such as drought, waterlogging, frost or crop disease.[85]

Amid threshing waste are traces of crop weeds which stippled medieval fields with colour – charlock, mayweed, corncockle, cornflower.[86] Bracken, nowadays exiled to acidic or wilder terrain, was once common in furrows between ridges and along field edges, from which it was cut for use as fuel, livestock litter, compost, mulch and thatch.[87]

In such and more ways have archaeology, economic history and historical ecology helped to change long-held assumptions. Land and people differ from those once pictured: the land more intricate, locally varied, longer settled and more efficiently managed; the people better housed, more socially and economically diverse, bearing more responsibility for events and change. This throws down a gauntlet to early modern historians, for whom a shift from long-term social equilibrium to rapid change is one of the defining characteristics of the industrial revolution. Of course, it is important not to swing from one over-simple generalization to another. Skeletal remains of villagers from places like Wharram Percy show that poverty, malnutrition, hunger, infant mortality and infection took their toll at least as much in the countryside as in urban slums.[88] But medieval centuries have no monopoly on transience or tragedy. And if the artistic variety of cathedrals, ten thousand parish churches and literature did not already do so, the archaeology of ordinary places and people argues the later Middle Ages to have been a time of innovation and mental and practical curiosity, as well as poverty and hardship.

While it was intriguing, even thrilling, to find that the classical landscape of the open-field village was the result of an intricate metamorphosis, and at last to solve the mystery of what became of villages that had disappeared, by the late 1980s it was coming to seem that traditional readings of the landscape at large had been too simple.[89] By concentrating on villages other settlement forms and regional differences had been neglected.[90] In southern Britain, the village has never been the predominant settlement form. Outside central and north-eastern England we see a kaleidoscope of forms – farms, hamlets, irregular strings of houses along lanes and green sides, houses and single farms encompassed by moats – which were smaller, more freely held, and more diverse than those of villages.[91] Moats were the result of a twelfth-to-thirteenth-century vogue among gentry and upper-echelon peasants for improving the security and status of their homes by surrounding them with water. A map of them looks familiar: it is almost a negative of the map of lost villages, which was itself a proxy for village country.

This realization incidentally amended an impression that settlement abandonment had mostly occurred in the central province. In fact, late medieval depopulation was widespread, its apparent degree in the village region simply reflecting the prevalence of villages themselves. Losses also occurred in areas of dispersed settlement, but farms or hamlets which fell vacant or shrank are less archaeologically salient than entire villages, and the framework of settlement in these regions was better able to withstand piecemeal losses without collapse of the whole.[92] In parts of the south-west there are tiny settlements, typically just two or three farms standing together, which in times of decline have lessened to a single occupancy or none, the empty buildings falling into ruin, only to rise again generations later when new users came forward.

Such contrasts bring us back to Oliver Rackham's lands of mystery and uniformity. He titled them Ancient and Planned Countryside respectively, and in a seminal chapter of *The History of the Countryside* he mapped them.[93] Planned Countryside, the central province of expansive fields and organized villages, extends south-westward from the Tees, broadens through the midlands and then narrows to a frontage on the south coast. Ancient Countryside lies to the north and west, and in the south-east. The case for acknowledging these provinces has since been reinforced by other means, their boundaries sharpened, and local regions and sub-provinces defined.[94]

What do the provinces represent? Not the least intriguing thing about them is their disregard for cultural boundaries. Shires, counties, dioceses, kingdoms and boundaries of Roman government all ignore them. So do building types. For example, over three thousand buildings survive in which pairs of naturally curved timbers form the main structural skeleton. Such timbers are known as crucks, and the tradition of using them was well established by the later Middle Ages. Cruck distribution corresponds with no geographically recognizable province, nor with settlement regions. A theoretical distribution of portable objects (like, say, late Saxon silver pennies) will normally thin towards its edges. Distributions of immobile objects, like houses, behave differently. 'Initially they should spread out from a focus, but in due course alternative ways of achieving the desired result will be encountered, and the diffusion will stop. Thereafter, the original type may dominate the structures of one area, while quite nearby the alternative is preferred.'[95] This may be why the personalities of settlement regions have as much to do with human decision as with decrees of Nature. In one respect, however, the map of crucks, like Rackham's map of contrasting countrysides, points to a characteristic of regionality in the British Isles: its underlying trend runs from south to north, its banding from east to west.

For reasons already discussed, these contrasts must go back at least to the ninth century, when the open-field revolution had begun. Could they be older? What are we to make of the presence of Ancient Countryside on opposite sides of the country? A journey from, say, Colchester to the Welsh border was once imagined as a kind of ethnic transition, from an Anglicized east to a Celtic west. But as Rackham points out, parts of Essex have more in common with Herefordshire than do either counties with most of the land between.[96] Could it then be that Ancient Countryside once prevailed throughout lowland England, and that Planned Countryside overwrote it, like a swash of spilled paint? Again, probably not. The idea that lands to either side of the central province are necessarily older, or have themselves escaped the kind of totalizing

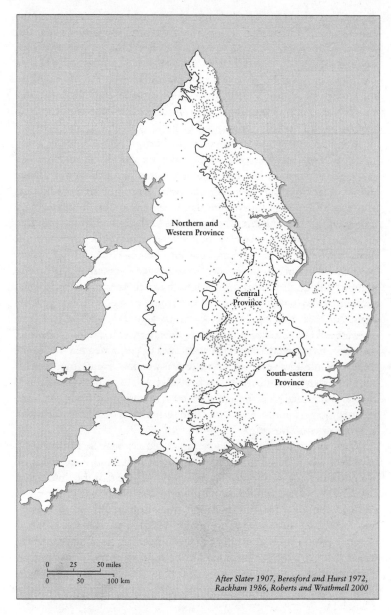

0   25   50 miles
0   50   100 km

*After Slater 1907, Beresford and Hurst 1972,
Rackham 1986, Roberts and Wrathmell 2000*

*31. Pre-modern settlement provinces of England (after Oliver Rackham,
1986; Brian Roberts and Stuart Wrathmell, 2000)*

change that produced village England, is at odds with evidence from those areas.[97] Moreover, in trying to put dates on the period when the provinces emerged, we need to beware of fastening on one aspect of regional identity in isolation from any other. It is a question whether landscape can ever be an artefact of particular date. As Major Allen knew when he scanned the lands of the Evenlode, the Windrush and the Ock on summer evenings in the 1930s, countryside is not a fixed pattern but an evolving condition. Clearly, particular kinds of settlement and agriculture do go together. The balance between arable, grazing, woodland and waste has implications for the shapes and sizes of fields, the whereabouts of homes, the positioning of droveways, lanes and stock enclosures, types of barn, even spacing between buildings. Moreover, the parts of a working landscape are mutually influencing, and change in one will alter the dynamics of the rest. All this is so. But the countryside is a place where individual features routinely outlast the agricultural systems that bring them into being. Most of what makes up the countenance of the modern countryside is inherited. At base is geomorphology, governing things like drainage, the make-up of soils, or features like rivers or scarps that determine where we live or how we move. Next, the inhabited landscape: in parts of Cornwall or Yorkshire there are field boundaries in use today which were laid out four thousand years ago. Even today's 'modern' landscapes of parliamentary enclosure are several hundred years old. Landscape is a sum of events, modified by pulses of change yet inherently conservative. What is recent sometimes ghosts something older, which may now be disjoined from whatever originally gave it purpose, and which in turn had its own history, shaped by processes now obscure.

All of which gives pause about some old certainties. Hitherto we have been accustomed to classify settlement by period – we speak of 'Roman villas' and 'medieval villages' – yet it may be that the underlying characteristics have as much or more to do with place as with time. For example, the idea that the transition from Roman Britain to Anglo-Saxon England was a time of economic breakdown and hiatus is one of history's givens, yet if agriculture carried on largely undisturbed, where would that leave the supposition of external intervention or calamitous discontinuity?

8

BECOMING ENGLISH

Coiled entrenched England: brickwork and paintwork
stalwart above hacked marl. The clashing primary
colours – 'Ethandune', 'Catraeth', 'Maldon', 'Peng-
wern'. Steel against yew and privet. Fresh
Dynasties of smiths.

Geoffrey Hill, *Mercian Hymns*, XX, 1971

'The natural vice of historians', writes James Campbell, 'is to claim to know about the past. Nowhere is this claim more dangerous than when it is staked in Britain between AD 400 and 600.'[1] This is wise, although in 1972, as a callow member of that team readying itself for a new campaign of excavations around the headquarters of the Roman legionary fortress at York, I really did expect that we would discover what had happened during those mysterious centuries when Roman Britannia was transformed into early England. To explain that, of course, you would first of all need to believe in 'Roman Britain'.

Nineteen-seventy-two was the year in which a letter arrived from a young man in the spring, asking if he could join us. We often received such requests, but there were odd things about this one. It was written on an air-letter form (which for a message posted in Colchester seemed unnecessary) and the writer pulled no punches about how good an archaeologist he was. At that time such frankness was looked upon as a kind of character defect, and since the author was still a sixth-former we declined. A few weeks later he turned up anyway, but as a member of another team which was being formed to excavate in York. Tall, pencil-thin, crowned by a cloud of curly hair, given to wearing stripy pullovers, there was no mistaking the silhouette of Dominic Powlesland, nor the trail of smoke from his roll-ups as he loped down Deangate on summer evenings. Occasionally I had a sense that some inner storm was whirling inside Dominic, but in those days our paths seldom crossed. I had no idea that here was a field archaeologist whose influence might eventually be as considerable in the twenty-first century as that of Pitt Rivers had been at the start of the twentieth.

In autumn 1977 Powlesland was asked to examine some early sixth-to seventh-century Anglo-Saxon burials that had turned up during the widening of the A64 trunk road in the Vale of Pickering in eastern Yorkshire. Such grave fields are not unusual, and maps of them are held to indicate the geography of early Anglo-Saxon settlement. However, this was the first trace of early Anglo-Saxons in that area – as far as the early Middle Ages went, the Vale of Pickering was at that time a blank. Moreover, while plenty of cemeteries containing the remains of some thousands of supposed Anglo-Saxons have been excavated down the years, not many have been closely and independently dated.[2]

By a fluke that no novelist could invent, the cemetery Powlesland went to explore lay in probably the only parish in England where archaeology had been a mainstay in the local primary school in the 1950s and 60s. The headteacher was Tony Brewster, whose life included service in the Spanish Civil War, some years as an officer in the Red Army and a rumoured Cold War career as a consultant for who knows whose intelligence. Leaving aside the politics, the result was a local community which valued archaeology. 'We may have had long hair,' recalls Powlesland, 'we may have been students, but everyone understood why we were there and encouraged and supported us from the very first day.'[3] This context was important in what followed.

Powlesland and his colleagues worked for nine seasons. In that time they explored the entire cemetery apart from the half-acre or so that was inaccessible beneath the A64 York–Scarborough road. The evidence indicated that burials had taken place between about AD 450 and 650, and that the cemetery had been co-located with a group of prehistoric graves and ritual monuments, one of which was a timber circle.[4] This sort of association is now known to have been widespread. It is sometimes explained as Anglo-Saxon immigrants seeking to associate themselves with the ancestors who presided over the places they took over. If so, a corollary must be that the ancient burials and ritual monuments to which Anglo-Saxon settlers gravitated were still identifiable for what they were.

As time passed, the name of the site cropped up in conversation with increasing frequency. It was, is, in a parish called West Heslerton (*hæsel* in later medieval records is 'hazel'), and there was more to Powlesland's work than the unearthing of 201 graves and a dead horse. Between 1986 and 1995 he and his team found where the people had lived, and began to examine their homes, workplaces and fields. The excavation of an entire community, the realms of the living and the dead together, enabled the re-asking of basic questions which had long baffled historians. Who were these people? Where were they from? When did they come, and what did they do? And what could be said about the structure and development of their community, and the society of which it formed a part?

Never one to think small, in 1980 Powlesland embarked on the Heslerton Parish Project: a campaign using all available means to explore six square miles of landscape which straddle the boundary between the Vale of Pickering and the Yorkshire Wolds. Here we had best pause, and return to set the scene.

Yorkshire's Wolds are the last of the chalk downs that curve north-eastwards across England from Dorset to Yorkshire, until they are cut by the North Sea at Flamborough Head. Seldom rising above 650 feet, in places scarcely hills at all, their undulating spaces and dry valleys are pervaded by a bleak softness. Haunted by barrows and engraved by ancient earthworks, reordered by eighteenth- and nineteenth-century landowning families whose houses and churches mark great estates, the Wolds are among the most archaeologically rich and long-studied land-scapes anywhere in Europe.[5] Like their counterparts in Lincolnshire and East Anglia, the Wolds are also places where fifteen centuries ago recently arrived Anglo-Saxon settlers cremated and buried their dead. Or so the books said.

Near by is the Vale of Pickering, the floor of a lake that formed after the last glacial period. Today the Vale is a low-lying plain enclosed to the south by the Wolds, to the north by foothills of the North York Moors, by the North Sea on the east and the Howardian Hills to the west. The Vale of Pickering is forty miles long, and the lake it once held was the largest body of water in southern Britain. Although the lake has gone, deposits of clay, gravel and peat mark its shrinking, and its edge seven or eight thousand years ago can still be traced by a tidemark of post-glacial plant and animal remains and prehistoric tools. In places, even now if you dig a hole you will soon come to peat or water.

Through the middle of the Vale flows the River Derwent (more on the name later), which rises close to the sea yet initially flows inland, setting forth on an eighty-mile journey that runs out of the Vale through the Kirkham Gorge and into the Humber basin.

The Vale and its margins have been occupied for close on eleven thousand years.[6] Towards the Vale's east end is Star Carr, where the former boundary between lake and land is one of the Europe's best-known and most closely studied scenes of early post-glacial human activity. There are hints of both residence and ritual here,[7] and it is intriguing that over nine thousand years later the same inland coast should be marked by one of the greatest concentrations of early medieval religious houses anywhere in Britain.[8] In the Roman period the Vale had formed part of the hinterland of the legionary fortress at York, and the nearby fort and town at Malton. Later villages which dot the Vale's floor coincide with former islands (the remains of moraines dumped by retreating glaciers), while along the lake's old coastline are villages and market towns. The Heslerton Parish Project took in a section of this landscape across boundaries between different zones, from the damp Vale by the Derwent up to the Wold top. Within the Vale their different soils can be mapped to within a few feet.

As Powlesland became acclimatized to these intricacies, he began to see fluctuating patterns of survival and loss. For instance, drifts of hillwash and sand at the Wold foot were found to be shielding Anglo-Saxon and earlier remains. This meant that the places where settlement traces were best preserved beneath the sand were invisible to the usual methods of prospection like fieldwalking or airborne survey. Certain kinds of geophysical survey, on the other hand, could detect them.

A little further into the Vale lay low dunes of windblown sand. Barely perceptible today behind the mask of modern agriculture, the dunes had shifted sideways at different times in history, and sheltered older structural remains and strata. In places the sand was too deep for geophysics to penetrate, so survey results in this zone were discontinuous, like land seen through broken cloud. A little further towards the Derwent and the picture changed yet again, as crop marks burgeoned, and geophysics could compensate when the aerial camera drew a blank. An extension of airborne imaging to wavelengths in the near infra-red and thermal parts of the spectrum filled gaps and refined detail. Millennia ago, when the Vale was wetter than now, more creeks and streams ran into it. Used for fishing, to water livestock and (later) drive mills, under geophysical imaging the ancient water-courses reappeared like veins seen through the translucent skin of an elderly hand.[9] Many of them had been diverted, by people, in antiquity.

After twenty years of applying and comparing different methods of survey to contrasting soils, refining imagery, then testing what was being seen with meticulous excavation, Powlesland built up a mosaic of complementary records. This has since developed into a synthesis in which different kinds of remote sensing – especially magnetometry – have been combined across more than eight square miles of countryside. The cumulative results (in the course of which the magnetometer operators walked a distance equivalent to a quarter of the circumference of the Earth) are a fulfilment of the work pioneered by Crawford and Allen three-quarters of a century before. The implications give pause. We already knew that crop and soil marks picked up by the aerial camera are usually a ghostly side-effect of destruction by modern agriculture. Unsupported faith in the corollary, that the areas in which you see nothing may be those where survival is most complete, is harder to sustain. Yet in the southern half of the Vale, at least, absence usually does signify presence, and when all the presences are mapped together nothing anywhere else can be see in the same way again.

To take some obvious things first: the landscape has been open for five or six thousand years; Neolithic and Bronze Age land divisions run for miles; henge-like enclosures occur every few thousand yards; barrows which traditionally have been associated with particular kinds of terrain occur more widely. Here, the dead and ritual places mingled with daily life and the living; entirely new kinds of ritual construction are found, among them a galaxy of tiny earthen structures that contained the ashes of local farmers and their families in late prehistory. For each one of these last picked up by the magnetometer, excavation detects ten more.

Chastening, too, are the implications for landscape archaeology. Over the last fifty years landscape study has come to rely on complementary methods that include map regression (the systematic dismantling of a landscape, removing its man-made features in reverse order of their creation, what is left being the earliest elements), aerial reconnaissance, fieldwalking (the systematic collection, plotting and analysis of cultural material), historical research and the study of place names. Such methods are used to build up a model of land-use history which is then tested in the field through targeted excavation, localized geophysics and scientific sampling. The application of this approach in the Vale, however, did not produce the picture (or anything like it) that has actually been revealed by large-scale geophysics.

There is also the question of the scale upon which landscape study is carried out: many (not all) landscape projects dwell on a particular locality or parish, whereas the work in the Vale now borders the sub-regional, running across a number of parishes and so enabling clearer perception of what patterns recur and what are unusual.

What patterns recur? One of the most striking is a near-continuous chain of paddocks, yards and buildings which cohered along a trackway that follows the boundary between the wet and dry zones of the Vale. Similar ladders of settlement, usually in shorter or discontinuous lengths, were already known from airborne reconnaissance over the Wolds, where they were tentatively considered to belong to the Iron Age or Romano-British period, and to reflect an economy in which livestock and transhumance had been important.

As first encountered, this ladder of settlement was blurred and disjointed. After twenty years, however, Powlesland and his geophysics team were beginning to gain its measure. What they saw was a continuous string of farmsteads, each about 250 yards from the next, each with structures, corrals, fence-lines and ditches which were periodically redefined as buildings wore out and patches of ground became rank. Centuries of such overwriting produced multiple boundaries, as if the system was shuddering from side to side. As Powlesland used different methods of remote sensing, teasing new information from land hitherto blank, it became clear that the ladder ran right across the area under study – over six miles. More than this, conventional and multi-spectral imaging in nearby parishes showed that the system continues far beyond, to Hovingham over twenty miles to the west. At intervals, however, there were real breaks, allowing access into the carr and marsh of the wet Vale, while to the south tracks and droveways led up on to the Wold tops. Short lengths of such settlement are well known and widely found. However, there is every sign that this one extended the length of the Vale – a new kind of settlement, neither nucleated nor dispersed, but a filament of farms, a linear agricultural commune one building wide and tens of miles long. Taking shape around 500 BC, it was occupied for more than a thousand years. In existence long before the Romans arrived, still existing after their army left, it was in near association with the ladder that the first buildings and finds that are conventionally regarded as 'Anglo-Saxon' begin to appear.[10]

Historians have yet to acclimatize to these discoveries,[11] which do not readily correspond with conventional thinking about the making of England. To see why, it will help to outline what that conventional thinking is. There are different tellings, but migration is at the heart of most of them. One reason for that is the account written in the eighth century by the Northumbrian scholar-monk Bede, who in turn drew upon an earlier British writer, Gildas,[12] both later rebroadcast by the *Anglo-Saxon Chronicle*. As retold in mid-twentieth-century textbooks it went something like this.

After the departure of the regular Roman army at the beginning of the fifth century, the provinces of Britain became detached from the Roman empire. Bereft of direction, the indigenous Britons drifted into lassitude, incapable or unwilling to stoke hypocausts, throw pots on a wheel, mint coins, make bricks or maintain walls. Their buildings and economy fell to pieces. Raiders broke in. Picts plundered down the coast from the north, Scotti (Irish) from the west. Angles, Saxons and Jutes began to nose across the North Sea from homelands in Schleswig, the Elbe–Weser area, Jutland and the Frisian coast to settle in what is now eastern and southern England. At first they came by invitation, hired by a British leader to oppose the Picts. But the relationship between hirer and hired turned sour, the mercenaries sent home for reinforcements, and thus began the take-over of Roman Britain. Teutonic people 'poured' into a land where there was 'room to spare'. There was no army to keep them out, and the Britons – save when rallied by inspirational leaders – were no match for the newcomers, who by AD 600 had advanced deep into lowland Britain.

Early versions of the story had the Britons being slaughtered or fleeing into western hills. In later accounts some of the Britons became refugees while others were overrun and assimilated. Later still, historians began to question the scale of immigration. The 'new archaeology' of the 1960s and 1970s, suspicious of mono-causal explanations, took against mass migration, while others asked if Englishing might have been achieved by a relatively small number of powerful leaders with whom indigenous Britons aligned themselves. As is the cyclical way of things, migration has now been restored to fashion, albeit in a more discriminating way. More recently still we have been offered models which view ethnic identity not as a biological or merely territorial or linguistic phenomenon, but as a matter of social practice.[13] This is promising. Yet wherever the argument stands, it tends to split southern Britain into a Celtic west and an English east, and it marches to a drumbeat of new beginnings. The Anglo-Saxons are presented as pagan not Christian, they replace whatever might have been left of the Roman political system with an ethnic polity, they introduce new kinds of dress, weapon, funeral and building, and they speak a new language.

We saw in Chapter 5 that in the earlier twentieth century the

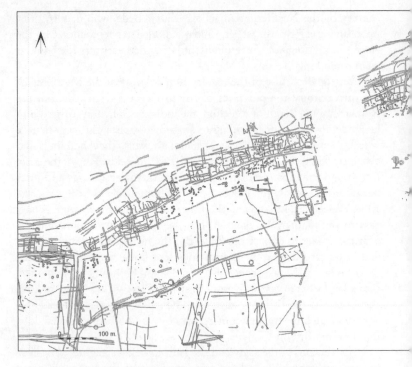

32. *Linear settlement revealed by large-scale geophysics at Sherburn in the Vale of Pickering. Trackways up to c.4,000 years old run across the lower part of the image. To the north, a chain of superimposed paddocks, yards and farmsteads follows the contour between the 'dry Vale' and the 'wet Vale'. The ladder took shape from about 500 BC and was elaborated until the fifth century AD, when clusters of cavity-floor buildings (seen as small oval features) begin to appear near by to the south. The blank area at the centre is the ghost of the modern village of Sherburn where underlying deposits are inaccessible to geophysics.*

The pronounced feature running more or less south–north just to the east of the village is the trace of an extinct watercourse, canalized to run a mill. Recent trial excavation amid the dense tangle of features hereabouts reveals this to have been a place where huge quantities of grain were being processed in the seventh century.

landscape was read as a metaphor for this contrast – that England
before the English was largely unsettled. Looking further back it seems
that this forest-emptiness was actually desired by constitutional historians and romantics in the nineteenth century who visualized it as a
space wherein Germanic settlers were able to reproduce ancient institutions of their homeland without hindrance. Forest and national identity
thus went together, and since most English historians saw Britain as an
extension of England, the forest became part of Britain's story as well.
The English credited themselves with making their own land, succeed-
ing where others had failed or had not tried. With this achievement
went an idea that native English law and institutions, even the monar-
chy, could be traced to the first settlers, and thence directly to a Teutonic
forest past. A sparsely settled prehistoric landscape was thus indispensable to a particular view of English selfhood: the isolationist legend
of an English nation that was self-assured and self-sufficient, capable
from birth of organization within its own conventions and means, displaying a different history from the rest of Europe.[14] The Old Wood

enabled William Stubbs to declare: 'From the Briton and the Roman
… we have received nothing.'[15] Or, as Professor Henry Darby, doyen of
historical geographers, put it more discerningly fifty years later, while
Rome's legacy to the geography of England was 'no mean one', 'even
so, as far as there ever is a new beginning in history, the coming of the
Angles, Saxons and Jutes was such a beginning'.[16]

By the end of the nineteenth century the idea that England's landscape had been made by the English hinted at another formation:
America, the big country, pioneered by egalitarian descendants of settlers who themselves had once crossed a sea to escape oppressors.[17]
Native Americans, hitherto sidelined by historians, were by the 1890s
akin to Ancient Britons, visible mostly in pageants or anthropologists'
textbooks. The influence of contemporary culture and politics on history, less reacting to evidence than deciding what the evidence is, is
visible in the idea of backward peoples who progressed in technological ability, even grew in physical stature, under the serial influences of
superior cultures. Iberians, Beaker people, Hellenes,[18] Celts, Romans,
Saxons: all found analogy in Britain's self-image as a colonial power.
There were resemblances between Britain's ancient hunter-gatherer
population and 'wild tribes' on far colonial frontiers being administered
by the Imperial Civil Service. As recently as the 1960s some historians
used words like 'cowering' and 'furtive' to describe the normal behaviour
of hunter-gatherers, and the 'hostile tribesmen' who long ago haunted
Britain's Old Wood were not unlike the Mau Mau or insurgents in the
Malayan jungle (communists to boot) with whom National Servicemen
had recently had difficult dealings. In a nation still held spellbound by
ideas of class, horses and good breeding, there were some born early in
the century for whom the thought of descent from 'aborigines sleeping
like beasts in caves and pits' was disquieting. A national story in which
hunter-gatherers had been largely replaced by more advanced peoples
was easier to accept, just as it gave a context for the inflow of a succession of skills and traits (like farming, improvisatory flair, seafaring and
pioneering) which just happened to foreshadow those with which mid-
twentieth-century Britons credited themselves. Other ideas like 'migration streams' and 'transit camps' were redolent of the 1930s and 1940s.
Above all, the expansionist model made space for belief that the early
Bronze Age of central and northern Europe had been sunned by the
brilliant world of Mycenaean Greece.[19] Public school classics masters
found wistful attraction in the idea that 'The wars of the early Greeks,
fought in Aegean sunlight and sung by Homer, were matched by wars

fought under the misty skies and dripping hills of western Britain by men of the same remote ancestry.'[20] The alumni of such schools went on to be cabinet ministers, university teachers, bishops and chiefs of staff. And so it went on.

Deference to the foundation myth of a people finding its destiny in an unclaimed land persisted well after the Second World War. Jacquetta Hawkes wrote that the Anglo-Saxons 'settled at first along the open river sides where they left their boats, and on the light soils already cleared', but then 'began an assault on the forests which was to alter the whole character of the occupation of the land'.[21] Professor Henry Loyn summed up the story of Anglo-Saxon settlement as 'more of the saga of man against forest than of Saxon against Celt'.[22] The geographer Darby said: 'In spite of four centuries of Roman civilisation, Britain was very largely a wooded land when the Anglo-Saxons arrived. Perhaps the greatest single physical characteristic of most of the Anglo-Saxon countryside was its wooded aspect.' Or again: 'The frontiers of expansion came to lie not to the west and north against the Welsh, but everywhere against the woods.'[23] In *The Country and the City* (1973) Raymond Williams summed up the villages of the Roman period as 'cultivating just two or three per cent of today's land', and settlement of the first millennium AD as in large measure 'a direct struggle with nature, the clearing of wild land'.[24] Sir Frank Stenton, greatest of the mid-twentieth-century Anglo-Saxonists, was less categorical than some of his colleagues, but his picture was nevertheless broadly consistent with theirs, or theirs a more extreme version of his. Stenton considered the forests recorded in later Saxon charters and Domesday Book to be 'attenuated survivals of vast stretches of wooded or scrub-covered ground, within which patches of cultivation had slowly been brought into permanent existence'.[25] He suspected that the heavy midland clays had been 'deliberately avoided' by the earliest colonists. 'These clays have produced remarkably little evidence of occupation in the Roman period.' It was, he agreed, probable that 'large stretches of them were heavily timbered when the Anglo-Saxon invasions began'.[26]

Popularizing historians embellished the story. In his book *The Medieval Foundation*, published in 1966 (and described in *The Listener* by a former Regius Professor of History as resting upon 'a close acquaintance with the latest scholarship'), Sir Arthur Bryant asked his readers to picture the 'great farmers' who drove their ploughs 'through mysterious forest and dark earth to make the land we love'. The first settlements were, as usual, on the lighter soils, 'but presently, with their iron axes and deep four- or eight-ox ploughs', they embarked on the stupendous task of clearing the forests and heavier clays of the eastern midlands: 'rich land that Neolithic and Bronze Age men, Celts and Romans alike had left untouched'. The 'sturdy colonists' who created new villages left intervening areas for later expansion, witnessed in place-name elements like *lēah* which are 'reliable' indicators of 'ancient woodland' and hence the progressive clearance of 'ancient forests'.

Looking back we can see the circle: early settlement was sparse because the forest was impenetrable; the forest remained unmastered because early settlement was sparse. Eventually, as if in a story by Angela Carter, Saxons broke the spell by cutting 'the rich kingdom of Mercia from land which had long been hidden under a dense covering of oak forest and tangled undergrowth'.[27]

Evidence for a more complicated picture comes from the patterning of coins – the gold tremissis produced on the continent in the later sixth and seventh centuries, shillings produced in England from about 600, but above all the silver pennies which were minted in different places from about 675. Often astonishingly intricate, such coins are also tiny. Individual coins are hard to see in the ground, and hence to recover, which is why until recently most discussion of coinage in early England turned on the evidence of finds from graves and hoards. Hoards certainly have a Gothic drama of their own. Likened by Mark Blackburn to 'flashes of lightning by which we can read (or guess at) momentous events', they also touch us, for behind each one is the mystery of an owner who never came back. However, these stroboscopic moments do not do much to illuminate the day-to-day circulation of coin. Accidental losses, on the other hand, do offer such a picture, although for reasons just given until recently single finds from this period were too few to cohere into convincing patterns. This is now changing. Since the early 1980s the metal detectorists (New Labour's 'unsung heroes' of historical understanding) and the computer have revolutionized our ability to map the distributions of single finds. The results contradict the older view of the seventh and eighth centuries as a time of economic standstill.[28] What they show, on the contrary, is that from the middle of this period small silver coins were being minted by the million, possibly on a scale greater than at any time until the later Middle Ages. We have already seen that the use of these pennies across southern Britain was not uniform, and that they were most frequently lost in the south and east, hardly ever so in the west. Where they occur in quantity, the tempo of economic activity they imply is brisk. High-volume trade in basic and

33 a–e. Examples of tiny silver coins minted in large numbers in eighth-century England, Jutland and the Low Countries (a–d). Such coins are characterized by exuberant imagery and images of rulers who profiles recollect those of Imperial Rome. Images on coins issued in the tenth and eleventh centuries, like the penny of William I (e) are more standardized, reflecting the trend towards centralized monetary control (cf. pp. 198).

bulk commodities is reciprocally reflected by the many Anglo-Saxon coins found on the continent, and by items such as querns and hone stones from the Rhineland, imported pottery and glass[29] which routinely occur at West Heslerton and places like it.

Production and demand on such a scale could hardly have sprung out of a solitude. Yet notions of emptiness linger. Regardless of the extent of the Old Wood, historians and many archaeologists turned instead to the idea that the 'lost centuries' were a time when population fell and the area under cultivation shrank, all encapsulated in the idea of 'post-Roman collapse'. 'In the early Saxon period,' writes Christopher Taylor, 'perhaps for the first time in 2000 years, there was a retreat of settlement, abandonment of land and presumably a marked drop in the total population of the country.'[30] J. N. L. Myres pictured barbarian chieftains 'carving up derelict estates'. There is 'plenty of evidence', he wrote, without producing much, 'to show that wide areas of lowland Britain which had been cleared of forest and brought into cultivation in the later Roman centuries reverted at this time to wilderness, waste and scrub. This fact by itself is enough to show how very sharply the British population must have declined during these years.'[31] Helena Hamerow:

'A phenomenon apparent in most of the former western provinces of the Roman Empire is a marked reduction in the density of early medieval settlement in comparison to the Roman period.'[32]

There are some who would link this 'marked reduction' with an environmental catastrophe. Professor Mike Baillie points to worldwide tree-ring evidence for an otherwise unrecorded abrupt climatic downturn in AD 540.[33] The tree-ring signal might have been caused by the screening out of sunlight by cometary debris or a large volcanic eruption. The immediate effect could have been several summerless years, whence famine and epidemic. This could give a context for localized reversion to woodland of some once-cultivated areas, but it is a question whether such an episode would have been solely responsible for the long-term demographic effects that have been claimed, especially as by the mid-sixth century many of the things attributed to such a crisis had already taken place.

There is no sign of post-Roman collapse in the Vale of Pickering geophysics. A more basic approach would be to ask if the 'marked reduction' in settlement took place at all. The notion of such a fall looks all the more strained when it is set alongside the ever rising levels to which archaeologists and historical demographers have hoisted the citizenry of Roman Britain, from Wheeler's estimate in 1930 of 1,500,000 to the three, four, even five million people being entertained by the early 1990s.[34] Since plausible limits for the population of Domesday England have settled between 1,500,000 and 2,500,000, acceptance of both orders of magnitude would mean that Roman Britain contained more people than at any time until the early fourteenth century, if not the sixteenth – a conclusion which in itself demands a demographic crash or decline somewhere along the line to reconcile the two. Unless one of the estimates is wrong.

To demonstrate a collapse one would look to the environmental record. If collapse was abrupt, then as J. N. L. Myres claimed above, trees and scrub would retake land that had recently been farmed. A walk through derelict land will show how swiftly this happens: if left alone, railway sidings abandoned only five years ago will already be woodland. We saw in Chapter 5 that some medieval woodlands do indeed overlie Roman and prehistoric settlement. But does this reflect general retreat or crisis?

If trees did repossess arable or grazing, then this ought to be reflected in the pollen record, whereas on the whole it is not. The cumulative palaeo-botanical picture is that, while woodland regeneration does occur in some areas, arable was generally sustained, and in some areas clearance of remaining woodland actually continued.[35] Elsewhere, it is far from clear that any retreat from tillage was the result of a post-Roman slump, and before this idea is fed into any larger model there are questions to be answered about degree and staging.[36] Even the idea of 'retreat' (with its unspoken implication of miscarriage) may be tendentious.

Lavishly fitted-out Roman villas are prominent in some areas, like the Cotswolds and parts of the south-west, and their abandonment has often been held to reflect a general collapse. Yet such households (not all of which were in use at one time), some in the hands of absentee owners (p.117), can never have employed more than a handful of the local population. In the longer flow of things their demise might stand comparison with the widespread abandonment of country houses in later twentieth-century Britain – losses to be regretted, a cause of upset in local landholding, symptomatic of change in the circumstances of a powerful yet highly restricted social class, but not a sign of general crisis. Romano-British farming at its zenith probably exploited more land than at any time for another thousand years, and as the demands of Roman authority were removed, what followed might be seen less as depression than as a post-colonial rebalancing of rural resources. While the disappearance of market goods like commercially made pottery may give an impression of fewer people or economic failure, because there is a fall-off in the visibility of material to be picked up, there was no diminution of agricultural activity at Heslerton, or indeed of pot-making.[37] Sieving of the sands shows that pottery remained plentiful, although such was the continuity between prehistoric and early medieval fabrics that when they are seen out of context it is easy to mix them up.

Rather than assume a demographic crash where no compelling evidence for it exists, or exaggerate it where it does, it is simpler to postulate stability. Stability, at any rate, is what we see in the Vale of Pickering, where rural resources were as fully exploited in the two centuries after the Roman withdrawal as they had been beforehand. Elsewhere, however, a thinly populated land with room to spare is still the starting point for most academic discussion. Descriptions of the earliest known Anglo-Saxon settlements stress their dispersal,[38] their unconfined, rather haphazard layouts, a lack of boundaries 'or other signs of delineation', and see in them the periodic replacement of hamlets or single farms.[39] 'The normal pattern of rural settlement in the Migration period was dispersed.' In this sparsely settled land, when a building became

dilapidated or the fertility of a plot declined, the inhabitants moved and
began again.

Such a story of reincarnation is told of the Thameside gravels at
Mucking in Essex, where some fifty early medieval timber buildings
and over 200 sunken-featured buildings were excavated in the 1960s and
1970s. The numbers are explained as cumulative: that is, it is argued that
not all of the buildings stood at once, and that the focus of settlement
shifted over a large area in the course of 250–300 years, as buildings were
abandoned and replaced. On this view it seems likely that, on average,
only around ten household units stood at any one time.[40] This sort of
reading has become the standard view. Reflecting on the area bordering
the confluence of the Thames and the Evenlode in Oxfordshire, John
Blair describes a near-continuous scatter of settlements and cemeteries
which 'hugs the terrace-edge around the fringe of the alluvial floodplain' – circumstances reminiscent of the dry Vale and the Wold foot in
east Yorkshire. No run-of-the-mill excavation could do justice to one of
these complexes, Blair mused: 'a total view needs a trench a mile wide!'[41]

Which is broadly what Dominic Powlesland had in mind when,
having found the Anglo-Saxon settlement at Heslerton, he launched
one of the largest excavations in the world to examine it. The dig began
in 1986, worked across thirty-two acres and took ten years. By its end,
all of the settlement had been laid open and half its features excavated.
Until then, no early Anglo-Saxon settlement and its cemetery had been
so fully examined, entire and together. So here, if anywhere, archaeology should be able to verify the conventional view of the fifth and sixth
centuries as a time when the economy contracted, and newcomers bearing a new material culture settled in a landscape where there was little
to tie them down.

What he found was the opposite: a large and spaciously planned settlement, occupied between the fifth and ninth centuries, within which
functions of residence, craft and industry, storage, devotion and burial
had been grouped in different areas. Metalworking, malting and butch-
ery were pursued in one zone, crop processing in another. Land was
fully used. This was not a hamlet in a depopulated landscape but a
stable, cohesive community which had been systematically laid out and
was co-operatively worked. Nor was it an anomalous enclave: to either
side, the large-scale geophysics have detected a run of similar communities, some smaller, some larger. Seen from the opposite side of the Vale
on a still day, their twists of smoke would have risen at intervals closer
than those of the villages which are there now.

A key aspect of these settlements is the way they embraced a cross-section of rural resources between the Vale floor and the Wold top: river frontage, marshland, arable, water, upland grazing. This sort of arrangement implies some degree of self-sufficiency, and local transhumance, which is also hinted in the elongated parishes hereabouts in the later Middle Ages and in the economy of the linear settlement which the early medieval villages superseded. While it is not yet clear how far this picture might hold good in similar surroundings elsewhere, it is easy to see how the canonical view of small clusters of farmsteads drifting haphazardly in space and time could have arisen. Conditioned by notions of collapse and shrinkage, and perhaps a desire to align findings in England with what has been found on the continent, archaeologists may have missed contrary signs of stability; few had previously worked on a big enough scale to see that the 'farmsteads' (which at sites hundreds of miles apart show a high degree of structural uniformity) might be parts of larger, coherent patterns rather than disembodied elements of small ones.

A contributory factor here is how early Anglo-Saxon settlements have been dated. Heslerton's dates are anchored by a framework of radiocarbon determinations. In some ways the framework is almost too supposable: burial in the Anglo-Saxon burial ground (that overlies a prehistoric cemetery) begins in the fifth century and ceases in the later seventh century – that is, at just the time when kings and noblemen were beginning to attach churches to their estate centres, to which controls over burial were subsequently reserved. The nearest candidate for such a foundation is the neighbouring village of Sherburn, where sure enough there is early medieval sculpture, and the large-scale geophysics shows an enormous spread of early medieval buildings and structures spilling out to either side of the gardens of the modern village.

Earlier Anglo-Saxon Heslerton was occupied until the ninth century, when it looks as though fields and homes suddenly changed places. Towards AD 900 the remnants of the early settlement were dismantled, the present village of West Heslerton was presumably formed a short distance to the west, and the site of the former community was ploughed into ridge and furrow – the open fields considered in the previous chapter. Again, the large-scale geophysics shows this process repeating all down the Vale, and incidentally detects open fields that were laid out at the same time but are today invisible to the eye. Again, walk-over survey alone would not have found these fields. Systematic collection of potsherds can sometimes enable the reconstruction of manuring patterns, and hence of the fields themselves, but here even that would have been misleading. In controlled experiments fieldwalking produced no more than a few grams of early medieval and prehistoric pottery (the yield of such work is in any case as much a result of recent ploughing as what there actually is in the ground) whereas sieving of all the ploughsoil from metre-square samples produced as much as 1.5 kilograms of pottery from a single square.

To summarize so far, the story of settlement in the Vale looks like a series of steps, in each of which one kind of entity morphs into another, some things being retained and others discarded at each step. A first step, taken five or six millennia ago, was the dividing up of land with long-distance boundaries. There follows a florescence of pastoralism and ritual, where the living and their ancestors mingle at every turn, their ritual enclosures, barrows, posts and rings running in broad parallel strips between the Wold foot and the Derwent. From the large-scale geophysics we can see many more prehistoric mausolea than are visible from surface evidence alone. Among them are earthen barrows, monuments of the founding farmers, akin to those discussed at the end of Chapter 6. Far from being typically sited on prominent landmarks or on slopes to create 'false crest' effects, they are everywhere. By the middle of the first millennium BC, the linear commune comes into being, although its droveways are retained from an older age. This thread of farms, we recall, was occupied for a thousand years, until the first settlements we describe as Anglo-Saxon begin to take shape beside it.

In the traditional story, these would be communities of settlers out of Angeln, a region of what today is southern Denmark. The Anglians, conspicuous by their own kinds of pottery, weapon, metalwork and building and by a completely different language, would have either displaced the indigenous peasantry or taken over unused or abandoned land. One thing which makes them salient is their architecture. Like the farmers who occupied the linear commune they live in a wooden world, but they introduce a new kind of structure, often with a post at each end (hitherto usually interpreted as having carried a ridge-pole) which in reconstruction looks a bit like a wooden tent pitched over a hollowed-out space. Buildings of this kind are known as *Grubenhäuser* ('dug-out houses' – the Teutonic associations sound more emphatic in German), or more neutrally as 'sunken-featured buildings'.

Sunken-featured buildings are found all over Europe; their uses varied and what holds good in one region is not necessarily true for another. They were first excavated in England at Sutton Courtenay in Berkshire in the early 1920s.[42] At that time it was assumed that they were houses, and the accumulations of rubbish, dead dogs, even remains of infants which were found in their hollows did much to enhance the Anglo-Saxons' reputation as barbarians who lived in squalid scrapes and hovels. This in turn reinforced the idea of the Middle Ages as a slow ascent from barbarism to civility. As recently as c.1970 the houses of Anglo-Saxon peasants were described as 'little better than holes in the ground'. The apparent simplicity of these structures also led to an assumption of transience – Grubenhäuser were surely for people (like immigrants) who were on the move, or were shelters for seasonal workers like shepherds.

Subsequently it has become clear that the shadowy, artefact-laden fills of Grubenhäuser are more easily recognized than the traces of other types of building. Both from the air and through geophysics the signals of Grubenhäuser show up well – more than 1,300 of them can be seen on Powlesland's large-scale geophysics. This means that larger post-built farmhouses and halls could be easily be missed by remote sensing survey while smaller Grubenhäuser stood out. In terms of survival, too, the traces left by post-built houses were often more evanescent than those of Grubenhäuser, the fills of which were deeper and less at risk from disturbance by the plough. Hence, the early view of early Saxon settlements as being dominated by a preponderance of temporary sunken huts was misleading, although where such structures were recognized they could often be taken as proxies for the likely presence of other buildings. It also came to be realized that Grubenhäuser were usually functional or occupational rather than domestic. Some claimed them as weaving sheds, partly on the strength of lines of loom weights found in their fills. In places there was evidence to explain the original purpose of the hollows as cavities beneath planked floors.[43]

The scale and innovative methods of Powlesland's excavations and geophysical survey revealed more. First, in the Vale of Pickering, Grubenhäuser are indeed surrogates for substantial early medieval settlements made up of a variety of building types. While some continue to see them as annual bivouacs for seasonal pastoralists (the great constellations witnessed by the geophysics presumably accumulating in ones and twos over centuries)[44] evidence from the fully excavated settlement at West Heslerton, where Grubenhäuser formed a zone differentiated from the great carpentered buildings, shows that this is not what was happening there. Heslerton was a well-organized village, and from the evidence of the large-scale geophysics there were others like it all along the Vale. Whatever was going on elsewhere in England,[45] settlement in the Vale of Pickering was extensive and life was busy.

If we are trying to measure Heslerton's economy the rubbish in the hollows can only be a fraction of what the community threw away. Powlesland's recording methods made it possible to trace discarded material across the site, to the point of being able to show that shards from a single shattered pot might fetch up many hundreds of yards apart. This reveals that such material did not simply lie where it fell, but was redistributed, mixed and remixed with other material, to be spread and respread around the site at large. This means that finds from *Grubenhäuser* have little or nothing to say about what such structures were for, since they derive from rubbish used to backfill them after they went out of use. (This incidentally scotches the weaving-shed idea: hereabouts, at least, the lines of loom weights can be explained as sets of unfired clay rings, stored on sticks and discarded if they dried out.) Moreover, since the objects found in *Grubenhäuser* are residual they tell us nothing about when a given *Grubenhaus* was built or for how long it was used.[46] The best one could hope for would be a radiocarbon determination on something like an articulated limb from a dead animal thrown into the fill, since while this would not date the birth of a *Grubenhaus*, it would date its infilling.

Do these findings in one place have consequences for interpretation of early medieval settlement elsewhere? We have seen that the contemporary timber buildings, often interpreted as farmhouses, do not always produce any datable artefacts. This being so, the houses at several sites have been dated by association with nearby *Grubenhäuser*. However, if the *Grubenhäuser* themselves are undated, then the moorings for such settlement sequences – and with them assumptions about settlement size or patterning – are no longer secure.[47]

One interesting aspect of the cavity-floor buildings is that, while they tend towards sameness in construction, they vary in scale. This may suggest that they had no single function – a view that might also be applied to the larger post buildings. An analogue might be the versatile yet stereotyped wartime Nissen hut, which was prefabricated in spans based on multiples of six or twelve feet and could be anything from a storage hut to a cinema or mess hall. Liberated from preconceptions, many of the Heslerton cavity-floor buildings emerge from several kinds of evidence as grain stores, the under-floor airspace being a means to insulate seed corn from damp. 'In other cases they appear to have formed general-purpose storage buildings associated with small-scale craft and industrial processes.'[48]

The ubiquity of cavity-floor buildings on settlements we call Anglo-Saxon has led to their routine equation with Germanic settlers: *Grubenhäuser* mean colonists. Yet Heslerton shows that the first sunken-featured buildings were erected beside the ladder settlement and sometimes in its interstices, probably from around the early fifth century. In other words, the 'early Saxon' settlement did not originate in contrast to the thousand-year-old ladder but rather was condensed out of it. The trigger for that change may have been environmental – an increasingly wet Vale (for which there is evidence) which caused the linear city to step back and rearrange itself in open-order settlements closer to the Wold foot. At any rate, the wealth and resources of the linear settlement – based on cattle, goats, sheep, mixed arable, orchards – did not change greatly during its life. The Roman age looks more affluent, but for reasons already broached this may be illusory. Certainly, when coinage and the mass-produced pottery it purchased both disappeared in the fifth century, Heslerton's lifeways remained much as they had been for a thousand years. Pottery fired on the spot using local clays differed little from prehistoric wares; weaving continued in a regional tradition which had existed since the Iron Age;[49] sheep and cattle still trekked up and down the great droveways between the wetland and the Wold top, a journey that had been made at least since the later Bronze Age. Similarities between the economies of the ribbon of farms and the 'Anglian settlers' were greater than the differences. In the Vale of Pickering, an historical framework defined by how people lived, rather than how they were governed, would see the period from 500 BC (or sooner) to AD 500 (or later) as an entity. Seen thus, the birth of early medieval England occurs not in the aftermath of a post-Roman collapse, but as an evolution from late prehistoric society that Rome had ruled and exploited but not significantly altered.[50]

At Heslerton this proposition is vividly illustrated in a dry valley running from a spring to the Wold foot. Several enclosures and structures built during the fourth century were found around the springhead. Among them, 'a large structure constructed on rammed stone rafts appears to have blocked off the entrance to a dry valley which, beyond this building, had been terraced by the deliberate dumping of large quantities of material'. Other structures cut into the valley slopes overlooking the terraces:

included a complex of bread ovens, a large, unusual and finely built
structure, with flattened apses at each end cut back into the valley side
and apparently deliberately removed to re-establish the valley profile,
a large well and fragments of other structures again cut back into the
side of the valley. The bread ovens and extensive spreads of oyster
and mussel shells associated with the structure built across the valley
might be interpreted as food bars we find at pilgrimage sites today.[51]

Here is a shrine. Environmental evidence shows it to have been much
visited in March – the old new year. Significantly, the area remained a
place apart after the linear commune had metamorphosed into the line
of 'Anglian' villages. Of course, just as the 'Anglian villagers' chose to
bury their dead in areas co-located with funerary and ritual monuments
two thousand years older, this could be taken as an instance of newcomers seeking to associate themselves with old ancestors of the place.[52]
But a simpler explanation would be that the focus of devotion was frequented throughout. We now know of other shrines in side valleys of
the Vale. Some of them had votive histories going back into prehistory,
and in the early Middle Ages at least one of them was selected as the
site of a religious community.

Here we come up against another of those things that 'everyone
knows' – that the Anglo-Saxons introduced a Germanic pantheon led
by Wodan and Thor. Before looking at that it is useful to note that
pre-existing religion was no single thing. We distinguish native cults,
often ancient and deeply rooted in local terrain; cults introduced from
the Graeco-Roman world; and latterly mystery religions from the
Levant, like those of Mithras and Serapis. The different categories were
not independent but mutually influencing, so that features of one cult
could be copied into others and identities merged or parted. Native
cults embraced an immense plurality, ranging from deities of Europe-
wide status to 'the certainty of hundreds of lesser beings, Shakespeare's
"Elves of hills, brooks, standing lakes and groves", perhaps (rather like
the Roman *lares familiares*) also domestic hobgoblins'.[53] The 'standing
lakes' in their turn recollect places where offerings of special things,
weapons, sometimes animals and people, had been made for at least
thirteen centuries before the arrival of the Romans, and in some places
(as we shall see) for many centuries afterwards. The roll call of divine
powers was always changing, while the Roman practice of recruiting
military forces from different provinces led to the posting into Britain
of units from overseas, whose members brought affections for deities

from afar.[54] Among them was the cult of the Hebrew god Yahweh and
his son Jesus, which by the early fourth century had been adopted as the
official religion of the Roman Empire.

The effect of Anglo-Saxon heathenism, the story often goes, was to
supersede indigenous local cults and late-Roman Christianity in the
eastern part of Britain, and to confine Christianity to a Celtic fringe,
where in the absence of regular contact with the outside world it
became increasingly idiosyncratic. In this telling the Roman missionary
Augustine arrives on a clear stage at the end of the sixth century as the
agent of a new beginning.

This story of perfect contrasts will no longer do. To go into detail
would take us out of our way, but it is worth itemizing some of the
issues. One of them is the absence of evidence for the kind of paganism
most often ascribed to the Anglo-Saxons in the homelands from which
it is assumed they came. The cults of Thor and Wodan, for instance,
were not conspicuous in the areas associated with the Angles, Saxons
and Jutes.[55] Moreover, there is little archaeological evidence on either
side of the North Sea for the kind of ritual infrastructure – temples,
idols, a priesthood – which Bede, writing in the earlier eighth century,
attributed to the Anglo-Saxons at the end of the sixth. Despite much
searching and interpretative ingenuity,[56] not one certain instance of an
idol which can be credited to the Anglo-Saxons has been found. Yet
Bede's references cannot all be dismissed as invention, because some of
them were drawn from original correspondence between Augustine and
Gregory: letters which survive independently, in which contemporary
realities were under discussion.

The least fanciful explanation is that the elaborated heathenism
described to Bede was neither general nor imported, but locally and
variably made up from materials, practices and ideas already available
on the spot – that it was part of the Anglo-Saxons' construction of
themselves. Idols, for instance, would be drawn from Romano-British
religious statuary, temples from former Roman shrines or churches, or
both, and the idea of priests and priesthood from Christianity. Other
cult sites were contributed from prehistory, as at Yeavering, where the
seventh-century royal centre has markedly British (and Roman) features and an underlay of Neolithic and Bronze Age ceremony.[57] The
obvious period for such eclecticism would be the later sixth century, as
part of an invention of rites and customs to define and vindicate the
polities and dynasties of rulers which were taking shape in different
parts of the country. Genealogies which the Anglo-Saxons compiled in

the late seventh and eighth centuries tend to trace the descent of royal
dynasties from Wodan. Interestingly, these lists appear to be 'reasonably
accurate once they record kings who existed after a particular horizon.
This horizon essentially falls in the third quarter of the sixth century,
that is, in the generation before the arrival of Augustine's mission to
Kent.'[58] This would help to explain why funeral customs, which vary
regionally and indeed intra-regionally, become curiously inventive in
the later sixth century. Walter Pohl reminds us that an important area in
ethnic practice is that of 'symbolic strategies and the preservation and
propagation of ethnic traditions. As in the field of politics, their implicit
goal is to construct stability and meaning beyond the span of individual
lives.'[59] This gives a context for the small number of fabulously impressive (whence assumedly 'royal') burials which have been found under
great mounds at places like Sutton Hoo, Caenby in Lincolnshire, Asthall
in Oxfordshire, Taplow in Buckinghamshire, maybe Woodnesborough
('Wodan's barrow') in Kent, and now Prittlewell in Essex.

The singularity of these funerals is striking. Dating from the late sixth
or earlier seventh century, they occur in some parts of the country but
not others, and like the great long barrows in southern England 4,300
years before their heyday was brief: just two or three generations. It is
unlucky that so many of the few about which we know were dug in
the nineteenth century, and doubtless there were others which, being
conspicuous, were lost to earlier robbing. Yet even allowing for the
possibility that new finds might change our view, all the great barrow
burials really seem to typify is themselves – they come from nowhere,
briefly light up the scene like fitful starbursts (casting all kinds of distorting shadows in the process) and then fade. Sutton Hoo, the greatest
of them, 'appears without precedent or successor'.[60] The sources of the
objects in the ship at Sutton Hoo are instructive: they form a kind of
artefactual cosmology, their range embracing most of the world of late
antiquity, from pagan Scandinavia to India and Africa to the Arctic.
Cosmopolitan in improvising rituals, regalia and institutions, English
kingship in the early seventh century was in some sense a function of
its horizons. This realization of span is replicated on a lesser scale by the
Sutton Hoo purse of Frankish gold, wherein each Merovingian mint is
represented by a different coin.

Some see the outbreak of ostentatious barrow burial as a pagan reaction to Christianity's intrusion, and the Merovingian predominance
which might come with it. Augustine reached Kent in 597, and it is
tempting to ascribe changes in burial to the influence of his mission.

Yet for several reasons this is doubtful. We have just seen that the idea of Anglo-Saxon paganism's coherence (as distinct from an ability to improvise with eclecticism and native cultus) is a modern assumption. Nor is there any reason to think that pagan Anglo-Saxons were unfamiliar with Christianity. Apart from the continuing British Church and contacts through trade, Kent's king at the time of Augustine's arrival had been married to a Frankish Christian princess for several decades, and a number of the continental peoples who are said to have contributed to Anglo-Saxon immigration had previously had contact with Rome. Further, the notion of political overtones has to be taken in the light of evidence that the papacy launched its mission to Kent by invitation, following earlier Frankish unresponsiveness to Kentish requests for bishops.[61] The leadership of late sixth-century Kent, in other words, wanted to contract *in* to the one late Roman institution which remained intact, and turned to Rome only when the nearer-to-hand Merovingians (with whom Anglo-Saxons had constant dealings) were unable to oblige. More generally, the reason that Christianity and synthesized 'Anglo-Saxon paganism' occur side by side is surely not that they were in opposition but that they were alternative expressions of the same thing: the invention and anointing of tradition in newborn kingdoms. This is more or less what Bede says when he tells us that the seventh-century East Anglian king Redwald worshipped in a temple in which there was one altar for Christian sacrifice and another for demons.[62]

Even nearer to hand than the Merovingian Franks in the late sixth century were the Christian British, and it may be asked, first, how much Anglo-Saxon pagan practice imitated Christianity, and second, why the king of Kent did not turn to the neighbours on his doorstep for Christian instruction. The answer to the first question may be linked to the second. Bede criticized the British for what he alleged to be their sin in failing to evangelize the Anglo-Saxons. On the other hand, it would not have suited Bede's purpose for the people he called English to have been converted by the British. In his *Ecclesiastical History*, completed early in the 730s, he depicts the Anglo-Saxon settlements with an almost biblical fervour: southern Britain is a Canaan which passes to the Anglo-Saxons because the British have grown unfit to hold it for themselves, and the title deeds for this promised land come from Rome. It is therefore necessary for the British role to be downplayed. Small wonder, then, that by the late seventh century there are signs of a stand-off. The depth of antipathy on the part of British churchmen towards their Roman counterparts is illustrated in a letter written about

705 by Aldhelm, Bishop of Sherborne, which describes how the British not only refused to eat with him and his colleagues, but threw food they had touched to pigs and dogs.[63] For their part, the Anglo-Saxons' use of *wealh*, their word for 'a Briton', gradually takes on secondary meanings of 'slave' and 'foreigner', which in turn tinged the name the English gave to their neighbours, the *wealas* or Welsh, as distinct from names like Cymru and Cumberland which the British derived from 'Combrogi', their own word for themselves.[64]

By the eighth century, then, the idea of an Anglo-Saxon nobleman being converted by a Briton, or an Anglo-Saxon bishop consecrated by one, might have been unpalatable. This is not to say that it did not happen (in the latter case, it did), only that later English sources might have concealed it. A case where this may have happened concerns King Edwin, ruler of the Deirans, the dynasty of the Derwent, Heslerton's overlord early in the seventh century. According to some later Welsh sources Edwin was baptized by the son of a British king. If this is so then Bede either did not know about it or did not say, stressing instead Edwin's conversion and baptism some years later at the hands of a Roman missionary. Like the reported survival of later Roman Christian cults such as those of Alban, Aaron and Sixtus,[65] such episodes have never fitted readily into the traditional framework of early Anglo-Saxon history.

More fundamental is the realization that the 'primary, defining features of Roman culture were not, after all, money but the Latin language coupled with Christianity'.[66] This might in any case have been deduced from the work of Gildas,[67] a British Latin author writing in the sixth century, whose account of British degeneracy bears the stamp of a first-class late Roman education which he presumably received somewhere in late fifth-century Britain. This accords with other evidence for access to Jerome's Vulgate Bible and biblical-style composition, some of it from inscriptions carved on several hundred stones found in south-west England, Wales and south-west Scotland.[68]

Was it Latin that lay at the heart of the Britons' preclusivity? 'Throughout the West, untouched beyond centuries of barbarian turmoil and national scene-shifting, Christianity was first and foremost a faith whose induction, practice, sacraments and manuals were *only* in Latin.'[69] In sixth-century Britain, the British were Latin's custodians, and thus the authentic link with Britain's Christian history. The effect of the Augustinian mission may have been to exacerbate Anglo-British relations, for by bringing *Latinitas* and Christianity to the Anglo-Saxons the missioners deprived the British of something that

had hitherto defined them, and set up a contest for what it meant to
be the true heirs to Rome which the Anglo-Saxons went on to win.
Culturally outflanked, the British retreated into the aloofness in which
Aldhelm found them – the background against which Bede wrote his
Ecclesiastical History of the English People.

This may help to explain Bede's simplified and self-contradicting
account of the migration of Germanic peoples to Britain in the fifth and
sixth centuries, which was written both from the standpoint of conditions in the eighth century and to explain how that state of affairs had
come about. Bede appears to give two different stories of English ethnic
origins. In Book One of the *Ecclesiastical History* he tells us that the
English came from 'the strongest peoples of Germania – that is, from
the Saxons, the Angles, and the Jutes'.[70] In Book Five, by contrast, he
implies that the ancestors of the Anglo-Saxons were 'the Frisians, the
Rugini,* the Danes, the Huns, the Old Saxons and the Boructuari'.†
This is more like it – yet we cannot be sure that even this list is complete, or that its definitions were stable either in Bede's day or two centuries before. One of the most striking things to emerge from studies
of the north Germanic peoples was their comparatively recent origins
at the time when migration is supposed to have begun. Far from being
immemorial entities their geography in the fourth and fifth centuries
was fluid, and their structures varied. Some had forms of kingship and
others not; several, but not all, were used to Roman influence. Their
names were protean abstractions,[71] sometimes acquiring passing meanings or subsuming one another, and changing in weight and definition
as time elapsed. The Saxons, for instance, are not easily differentiated
from Franks in the fourth century, whereas by Bede's day these names
stood for distinct continental groupings with very different political
systems.[72]

While Bede's second list cannot be relied upon as complete or solid,
it does give an idea of the degree of the social and political diversity
which lay behind the creation of the idea of England. This was not a
systematic migration in which three ethnic entities transferred from
one land to another, but a bundle of sporadic episodes involving groupings of different size and varying composition (Bede himself describes
the Angles as a plurality of peoples), some peaceful, some violent, some

---

* Tacitus called them the Rugi, and placed them in southern Denmark.
† Gregory of Tours called them the Bricteri, a group variously described as Frankish
and Saxon.

small and some large, some fleeting, some possibly long drawn out, and all mapped on to an indigenous population which for the most part continued to live where it was in local ways that had changed little since the Iron Age. While the concept of a *gens Anglorum* is found in the letters of Pope Gregory I, only in hindsight was Englishing depicted as a coherent enterprise. Whoever the immigrants actually were, and whatever part they played within the larger story, the Anglo-Saxons as we know them historically derive from an idea created several centuries later. As Nicholas Brooks has said, 'Gentes ("races" or "peoples") were not, as a rule, the products of large-scale tribal invasions by communities of ethnically and linguistically pure warriors whose descendants inherited an ethnically cleansed landscape.[73] Early medieval peoples should rather be seen as artificial creations …'[74]

Many of the contributing peoples were seafarers, who to a large extent 'can be seen as nations of pirates'.[75] In the fifth century their raiding extended to Aquitaine and the Loire, and Anglian settlements were launched on the continent from Britain.[76] The evacuation of some settlements in the face of rising sea levels along what is now the coast of Holland and north-west Germany is well attested archaeologically and may have been a spur to the recirculation of migrants and opportunists around Europe's coasts. The fourth and fifth centuries were a time when people were on the move. Just as a wrinkle on one side of a carpet will have an effect on the other, so population movements which in themselves may have been quite modest may have had large cumulative repercussions. In the seventh and eighth centuries, this long experience of sea travel and the links with Frisia stood Anglo-Saxon trade in good stead. The opening of Bede's *Ecclesiastical History* is a lyrical meditation on the sea, coasts, rivers, tides, whales and shellfish, and a map of the places mentioned by him (in turn, an indication of the spread of his sources) has the east coast not as its edge but at its heart. This was part of a continuum: we recall from earlier chapters that people had been journeying back and forth across the North Sea for thousands of years. Given this history of coming and going, Stephen Oppenheimer's suggestion that Germanic dialects may have been spoken in some communities in eastern England *before* the Anglo-Saxon period is less radical than its critics have made it seem. The proposal has clear attraction.[77]

By the eighth century many important figures and events had become stylized in legendary form, without clear distinction between myth and history, or between old or current matters.[78] Hengest and Horsa, the mythic first leaders of the Angles, are said to be descendants of

Uecta, described by Bede as the son of Wodan, although more plausibly derived from the Roman name for the Isle of Wight – Vecta. Hengist means 'stallion', which sounds like a nickname or a Roman *signum*, just as Artos (Arthur, not mentioned by Bede) means 'bear', and 'Vortigern' – allegedly the British king who takes the fateful step of bringing in German mercenaries – is perhaps the name of an office rather than a person, 'the chief'.[79] (Nearly a millennium later, the Plantagenets were rumoured to be descendants of a demon. A tradition circulating in the twelfth century stated that the Northumbrian earl Siward was a descendant of Ursus, who was the son of a noblewoman and a white bear.[80] Such claims might associate great leaders with *mirabilia* – marvels rooted in the idea of a world that was an 'inverted mirror of the real world'.)[81] And as Robert Bartlett points out, another form of association between 'animal symbol and human dynasty' was heraldry.[82]

Past insistence on the completeness of the transition to an Anglo-Saxon England of self-governing local communities has 'concealed the antiquity of many features of early English government and society',[83] while simultaneously ignoring the implications of two leading characteristics of early medieval nation-making: the acceptance for all of a common history or myth of origin, and 'a collective amnesia concerning awkward facts, especially the traditions of rival, older or subject peoples'.[84] Yet despite Bede's desire to downplay British presence and influence, he could not bleach out every detail. Anglo-Saxon princes on the run are glimpsed in exile as guests of British, Irish and Frankish kings. German princes marry British princesses, Anglo-Saxon princes marry Irish women. In this jumbled age where key figures are remembered by their sobriquets, the stallion, the bear and the chief, it is not surprising to find that some kings or ancestors of Anglo-Saxon dynasties bore names like Cerdic and Cædwalla which were British. These may be figures of German origin who chose to identify themselves as British, or individuals who were British by birth but chose to identify themselves as English. The very idea of kings may have come from the British, either directly (kings are mentioned in inscriptions surviving from the fifth and sixth centuries, and rulers described as *Rex* or *Ricon*, 'king', are earlier mentioned on coins) or as another of those makings-up in the later sixth century which selectively drew from continental and insular example. Either way, it was very likely reinforced by Christianity, for did not the Bible speak of Christ as the king of kings and lord of lords? And while it is a question where the sources of the idea of kingship lay, it is the case that some of the kingdoms ruled by Anglo-Saxon kings bore

names of British origin – like Kent, which had been a Celtic principal-
ity and then a Romano-British *civitas* with its capital at Durovernum
Cantiacorum, Canterbury. Kent's survival as a distinct unit is paralleled
by the continued existence of its name.

> ... *Cantium* and *Cantia* are the learned forms known to Ptolemy,
> Caesar and Bede respectively, but they probably all represent a mono-
> syllabic *C(h)ant* or *Cænt* in the vernacular, whether British or Old
> English. The survival of the name, perhaps paralleled in the north-
> ern English kingdoms of Deira and Bernicia, may suggest that the
> Anglo-Saxon kingdom had been formed not simply by the coalescing
> of groups of English settlers, but that it had inherited something of
> its structure from the Celtic and Roman past.[85]

The Roman fort and town of Derventio and the River Derwent which
flows past Heslerton are among a bundle of names (Dere Street is
another) with a pre-Roman root that lie behind the *prouincia* or kingdom of the Deiran people that is mentioned many times by Bede and
several other early medieval writers. Etymologically, 'Derwent' and
'Deira' have usually been derived from a conjectured British word *deruā*,
'oak', Deira thus being 'the land of the oaks'.[86] A simpler explanation
is that the 'Der' of Derwent derives from an ancestor to the modern
Welsh *dwr*, 'water'. If so, Deira becomes 'the land of the waters', and
the Derwent is its muse.[87] Either way, the least assertive way for us to
identify Heslerton's people in the sixth and seventh centuries might be
the one in which available sources suggest they ascertained themselves
– as Deirans.

The kingdoms of Wessex, Mercia and Northumbria were among those
which early medieval sources tell us contained large British populations.
The speed with which leaders annexed northern England and southern
Scotland in the seventh century shows how topography could assist take-
over: poorer soils and hill land supported fewer magnates, who relied
on larger areas for their renders and tribute. Killing a few or persuad-
ing them to switch sides led to rapid territorial gains.[88] Northumbria's
position as a kingdom of largely British population under emergent
English leadership (not to say the birthplace of Bede) illustrates the fallacy of supposing that the triumph of the English language was simply
a result of mass immigration. Language is an uncertain guide to ethnic
origin; rather it is a status symbol, something adopted in the course of
the creation of identity.[89] We recall Ernest Gellner's example of early
nineteenth-century Tunisia, where 'the ruling stratum considered itself

to be Turkish, though quite unable to speak that language, and in fact of very mixed ancestry and reinforced by recruits from below'.[90] In the later seventh century, to judge from images on their first mass-produced coins, if Deiran leaders identified with anyone it was with Rome.

Which brings us to another supposition of the 'clean sweep' school of Germanist historians, namely that being Anglo-Saxon precluded being anything else. Our own experience argues the opposite – that many-sidedness is our norm. It is not clear how Bede's predecessors saw them-selves – whether as Northumbrians, Angli, Garmani (which, along with Eingl, is apparently what the British were calling them in the eighth century) or indeed Romans, like whom Anglo-Saxon kings contrived to look. Nor is it clear what any of those terms might then have meant. But there is no reason why they should have limited themselves to a single identity; their self-image may have been complicated. This is one reason why we need to beware the later use of terms which ascribe a sense of individuality which was not necessarily shared at the time.[91] Meanings latent in the words 'Anglo-Saxon' have reached us through a body of concepts which have been actively evolving at least since the sixteenth century. Bede's very act of writing the *Ecclesiastical History* codified memories which up to that point had been fluid. His written-down ethnic model no longer leaves any room for interplay or complexity:

> people can come and go, or even be destroyed, but they do not mix or change. Thus, after almost 400 years of Roman rule, the Romans can simply leave or be killed, and leave the Britons they have once conquered to themselves. Bede also disregards – or rather denies – the possibility that many Britons might have become Angles or Saxons.[92]

Both the Anglo-Saxons and the eighteenth- and nineteenth-century historians who wrote about them fashioned a past for their own pur-poses. Bede saw the origins of their insular kingdoms 'in terms of a simplified pattern of migration and conquest – one which, by 731, emphasised Angles, Saxons and Jutes, and which would come later to settle on the single name "English"'.

> Like all rewritings of history it was a rewriting which ignored the true complexity of the formation of a people – neglecting the diversity of Continental origins, the influence of indigenous peoples and the continuing influence of the outside world.[93]

Here is another reason to be wary about the conclusions which can be drawn from archaeological sites and objects. The traditional – yet specious – tendency to define artefacts (and by extension the people who made, carried or wore them) by ethnic shorthand (as in 'Anglian spearhead' or 'Jutish brooch') becomes yet more risky when our definitions of 'Anglian' or 'Jutish' are themselves anachronistic. When we remember that objects are defined at least as much by how they are culturally deployed as by their physical or artistic properties, it becomes historically lethal. An example comes from the study of Kentish graves, which do contain objects strongly indicative of links between Kent and Jutland. The old way to explain these things would be to see them as the possessions of immigrants who had arrived in Kent from a Danish homeland. But the artefacts in the Kentish graves give contextual signals that differ from those of their continental prototypes.[94] Such placing may convey messages more subtle than the equivalent of a manufacturer's mark on a manhole cover – relationships with age, standing within a community, gender. It is less likely that they will tell us where people came from.[95] Artistic and symbolic ideas took on lives of their own in different places, and if individual styles cannot be mapped on to identities, then in logic we should be just as cautious about what we make of the many instances in which 'Anglo-Saxon' art assimilates motifs and traditions from Roman and Celtic craftsmanship.

Let us take stock. Since the sixteenth century the English have regarded themselves as the sons and daughters of an incoming people who displaced an existing population. By the early twentieth century everything in this story pivoted on a theory of difference: the newcomers lived in new kinds of building, bore new objects, worshipped new gods, made a new landscape and spoke a new language. One by one these simplicities have dissolved. Yet for all its weaknesses the old account did integrate different kinds of evidence into a coherent story. Modern approaches have laboured under a corresponding drawback, for while being academically up to date and theoretically respectable, they offer no similarly integrating narrative and leave much unresolved. If early medieval ethnicity was not clear-cut, perhaps contradictions are what we should expect. How much of a new story can be told?

As we have seen, continuity of land use from late antiquity into the early Middle Ages in the Vale of Pickering was complete. On this view some aspects of the provincial contrasts noted in the previous chapter were already present in the land which the Anglo-Saxons entered. This would account for large disparities in the distribution of rural resources only a few generations later – why, for instance, some parts of early Middle Saxon England had much woodland while others had next to none. It would also explain signs that by c.700, at least, some districts were concentrating on different things – the growing of grain, pastoral farming, the management of woodland. Such contrasting resources could be co-ordinated through federal manors,[96] for which – coincidentally – there is noteworthy evidence around the Vale of Pickering. If such institutions originated in prehistory, before the days of Roman colonial exploitation – and it is difficult to avoid the conclusion that they did – the interesting question becomes not why Ancient Countryside might have changed after the exploiters departed, but why the Central Province stayed open. From there it is but a step to the thought that many Anglo-Saxon place names which describe landscape refer not to a land that the Anglo-Saxons made, but to the countryside they found.

But – who were 'they'? As a pattern for what happened elsewhere, Heslerton is a realm of ambiguities. On one level, the reconfiguration in the fifth century, and the adoption of new burial practices and dress, look like a break with the past. On another, the adoption of new dress and living fashions is part of the practice of ethnogenesis, and just as powerful are signs of change from within. The first sunken-featured buildings appear in the ladder settlement early in the fifth century, the shrine in the dry valley is not forgotten, the underlying economy continues, and rising groundwater meant that the ladder settlement was due to move anyway. And some assumptions are double edged. Where, for instance, does the idea of inhumation in a bounded area come from? When the Heslerton excavators say that the lack of 'similarly associated Romano-British burials makes it clear that this marks a break with Romano-British burial tradition',[97] it is precisely the absence of such a tradition in the immediate vicinity which makes late Roman Christianity entertainable as an influence on the widespread adoption of inhumation.

Not far hence, science – for instance, through stable isotope analysis, which maps childhood upbringing on to geochemistry, and high-precision radiocarbon dating – will tell us whether strangers arrived in the Vale, when, in what numbers and from which directions. One thing this may do is to remind us again that people have always been coming and going, and that historians regularly underestimate the extent to which they do so, striving instead to cram population movements into singular episodes that give us the 'pivotal moments' and 'watersheds' upon which history likes to rely.

The first stable isotope results from Heslerton may be a bellwether: of twenty-four burials sampled, just four – one in six – seem to be from the continent. All four, apparently from Scandinavia, are female, and

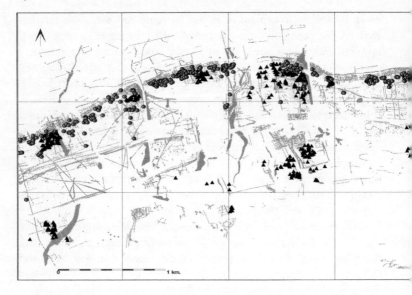

34. Linear settlement, boundaries of different ages and former watercourses revealed by large-scale geophysics across five miles (about eight kilometres) in the Vale of Pickering. Circular symbols represent cremation burials made from the line of farms in the later first millennium BC and earlier first millennium AD. Triangular symbols indicate cavity-floor buildings which in turn point to the whereabouts of early medieval settlements. Forthcoming study of the buildings in these places may suggest that they were more robust and long-lasting than their reputation for transience has hitherto made them seem.

the graves of three were unfurnished – the kind that historians have hitherto been tempted to imagine as local girls who made wives for incoming Anglo-Saxons. Of the rest, a substantial proportion of those furnished with 'Anglo-Saxon' objects seem to have come from the west, perhaps across the Pennines. This tentative picture, therefore, shows perpetuation tempered by incomers from elsewhere in Britain as well as the continent.[98]

Does this mean that we should abandon the idea of colonists? And, if not, into what picture do they now fit?[99] Undoubtedly, there were pulses of migration within the continuum. About twenty miles south of Heslerton is Sancton Wold – the site of a cemetery containing possibly four, five or even six thousand cremations. Sancton is the

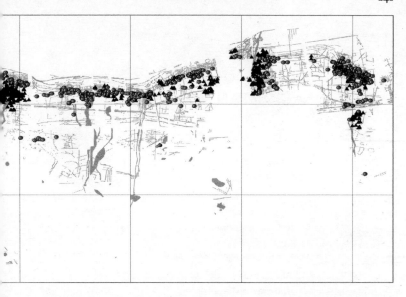

northernmost of a small group of necropolises containing dead who were burned rather than buried, and in big numbers. These crematoria had outliers. The mapping of their populations gives a different impression from a simple plot of cemeteries; unlike Heslerton some of them imply close links with specific continental places. Loveden Hill in Lincolnshire and Spong Hill in Norfolk are examples. Spong has been carefully excavated.[100] Like a deck of cards riffled in a stream from one hand to another, some groups of burials are so similar to others from the Danish–German border that it is difficult not to assume that for a few decades, years or even months there was a direct link between two particular places on opposite sides of the North Sea.[101] From the evidence of the great crematoria, the scale was of the order of tens of thousands – no more. Here and at Sancton the calcined bones of people were commonly mixed with those of sheep, horses, pigs, dogs, foxes, beavers, hares, birds, fish, antlers – a pantheon of Nature. One went to the grave with the tooth of an extinct mammoth. One or two were burned with the skins of bears.[102]

If we want a generalization pending a fuller telling, it is that England's story begins from within as well as being a result of external influences. The story differs according to where you are, and it begins not in the fifth century AD after Roman colonialists departed, but in prehistory, before they arrived.

9

A COMPANY OF SAINTS

V. Sancte Michael.
　　R. Ora pro nobis.
V. Sancte Gabriel.
　　R. Ora pro nobis.
V. Sancte Raphael.
　　R. Ora pro nobis.
V. Omnes sancti Angeli et Archangeli.
　　R. Orate pro nobis.
V. Omnes sancti beatorum Spirituum ordines.
　　R. Orate pro nobis.
V. Sancte Joannes Baptista.
　　R. Ora pro nobis.

From The Litany of the Saints

Some time in 1955 Francesca Wilson sent the proofs of a book she had edited to Nikolaus Pevsner. Wilson was the teacher and humanitarian activist who had been Pevsner's landlady in Edgbaston back in 1933–5.* Her book was an anthology of visitors' impressions of Britain. She called it *Strange Island* and Pevsner quoted from it in his first Reith Lecture on 'The Englishness of English Art'.

> That the 'gloomy fogs', the 'foul smoke … with which the city is covered eighteen hours of the twenty-four' appear prominently in such an anthology goes without saying. What is remarkable is that they do not come into the book at all before the middle of the eighteenth century. A moist climate may be natural, but fog is moisture plus

* See p. 2.

soot, and so what one complains of as climate is the combination of climate with such things as the exploitation of coal, a development of industry that calls for vast masses of coal, and in the house a system of heating evolved for wood fires and not yet universally adjusted to the use of coal. Perhaps this staunch conservatism in the teeth of the greatest discomforts is English? Perhaps the early and ruthless development of mining and industry is English? That we shall see later. What I wanted to show you already now is that even climatic conditions are not entirely permanent in the way they affect us.[1]

Few today would find anything untoward in Pevsner's challenge to the then prevalent view of climate as a fixed influence on national character. This is not only because climate's unfixed nature is all too apparent in the legacy of burning those 'vast masses of coal', but also because Britain's 'gloomy fogs' have mostly been dispersed by measures to control air pollution. There are still foggy days, of course, but nothing like the smog of December 1952 when walkers lost sight of their own feet and farm animals were asphyxiated. The Great Smog lasted for five days and some 12,000 people are now thought to have died in result of it.[2] Clean-air legislation was passed in 1956, but of course it took time to have an effect and in the meantime there were more smogs. One of them began on Wednesday 4 December 1957.

You may remember from Chapter 1 that in the early 1950s there was no parish of Longbridge. To be baptized, married or buried, therefore, Longbridge Anglicans needed to go either to the old parish church at King's Norton, which was two miles away, or to a wooden hut on Oak Walk known as the Church of the Epiphany. The Epiphany had originated as a mission of King's Norton in 1918. That was about to change. A new church had been built, and earlier in the year the Privy Council had approved an Order providing for a new parish of Longbridge to be formed out of part of the parish of King's Norton. The Order's delineation of the new parish reads like the boundary clause of a medieval charter:

> All that part of the parish of King's Norton ... which lies to the west of an imaginary line which commences at a point on the boundary which divides the parish of Northfield from the parish of King's Norton in the middle of Fairfax Road and proceeding thence southwestwards along the middle of Fairfax Road to a point opposite the middle of the footpath which leads from Fairfax Road to Cofton Common and continuing thence southwards to and along the said

footpath to the boundary which divides the parish of King's Norton from the parish of Cofton Hackett.[3]

For two years I had watched the church being built, and – in those less health-and-safety-fixated days – swung on its scaffolding and played amid its walls after the builders went home. Now it was finished, the last service in the wooden mission church had been held, and the moment for the first service in the new church had arrived. This was good because it meant brief release from boarding school. I was supposed to return afterwards, but by late afternoon there was a yellow-green thickening of the air which grew so dense that motorists became disorientated, pedestrians lost their sense of direction, and buses inched along kerbs in first gear until their drivers gave up. I would have to spend the night at home. Reunited with the dog, back in my own bed, end of term fore-seeable and Christmas not far off, things were looking up. The church was being dedicated to St John the Baptist, and as the congregation launched into the great Advent hymn 'On Jordan's bank the Baptist's cry / Announces that the Lord is nigh' it seemed to me that John had become the patron saint of homecoming.

While we gathered, the crowded and delayed 4.56 train from Cannon Street to Ramsgate overran a signal in the fog and collided with a sta-tionary train near St John's railway station in Lewisham. The collision brought down a bridge that added to casualties by flattening several coaches. By the time the service began ninety had died. Honoured in Birmingham that evening, maybe St John had taken his eye off other things.

Why St John? Not far from the centre of Birmingham (not far indeed from Francesca Wilson's house) is the district of Deritend. The antiquary John Leland passed through its 'pretty Street' on his way into 'Bermingham Towne' in the 1530s.*

In it dwell Smithes and Cutlers, and there is a Brooke that divi-deth this Street from Bermingham and is an Hamlett or Member belonginge to the Parish therebye. There is at the End of Dirtey a propper Chappell and Mansion House of Tymber hard on the Ripe as the Brooke runneth downe ...[4]

That 'propper chapel' was dedicated to St John the Baptist. Rebuilt

---

* Leland heard the first syllable as 'der': 'This Street as I remember is called Dirtey.' It is a question whether this is the same root as the *der-* behind 'Derwent' that we met in the last chapter (p. 236).

in 1736, it became a parish church in 1890, only to close in 1938 when the parish was merged with next-door St Basil. Bombed in 1940, the church was demolished in 1947. Proceeds from the sale of its site were put towards the new church in Longbridge. To mark this, the dedication passed from Deritend to Longbridge. And there we were, hushed, expectant, at twenty-five minutes past seven on that foggy Wednesday evening.

35. St John, Deritend, Birmingham, c.1944

The ceremony opened with the entrance out of the fog of a procession that included the bishop, and the vicar and churchwardens of King's Norton.

'The Bishop shall knock on the door three times with his Pastoral Staff. The door being opened, the Bishop shall enter the Church, and the Vicar of King's Norton shall say:

"Right Reverend Father in God, we pray you to consecrate this church."'[5]

The vicar of King's Norton was volunteering to give up part of his own parish. The bishop received the keys of the church from the architect. Then with the foot of his pastoral staff he traced on the pavement the first and last letters of the Greek alphabet: alpha and omega, the beginning and the end of all things. Afterwards a mason incised the marks. The ritual was followed by others that culminated in the newly admitted churchwardens of the just-inaugurated parish of St John the Baptist leading the new incumbent to the porch under the tower where he 'shall toll the bell to signify his taking possession'.[6] One Saturday back in the summer my father had taken me up the tower. At the top we had looked out over the Austin towards the Lickeys and the Clent Hills. On the way down I knocked the bell gently and heard it hum a C sharp in reply. Around the mouth ran an inscription: PREPARE YE THE WAY OF THE LORD. Now it spoke for the first time. Ancient bells sometimes bore the names of saints, their voices calling across field and town to proclaim the Sabbath, hurry the unpunctual, quell lightning, lament the dead, calm the enraged and disperse the winds.[7]

Fourteen years later to the month I was fifteen feet down a hole at the foot of the north-west tower of York Minster, listening to Great Peter (all 10.8 tons of him) tell the hour while excavating the remains of a Roman centurion's billet.* I was there because in 1966 engineers had discovered that parts of the building were sinking, twisting and tilting. All buildings move, but this one was threatening to break up in a kind of slow-motion shudder. To save it, said the engineers, parts of the substructure would have to be strengthened and extended. Doing this would mean digging enormous holes.

Holes through what? York Minster stands across the centre of the

---

*Around that bell runs the inscription SANCTI PETRI APOSTOLI CAMPANA MAGNA VOCOR – 'I am called the great bell of St Peter the Apostle'.

Roman fortress of Eburacum. During the later years of Roman government Eburacum was capital of Britain's northern province, and it was from this building that Britannia Secunda was administered. In the seventh century York, like Canterbury, was connected with the conversion of the Anglo-Saxons. Writing early in the eighth century, the scholar-monk Bede tells us that an oratory made of wood was put here in AD 627 for the baptism of the Northumbrian king Edwin. Soon afterwards a larger stone church was built around the site of the wooden one.[8] When finished it housed the *cathedra*, the throne, of the bishop of York.

As places go, then, this was somewhere special. On the other hand, the cathedral that replaced the Anglo-Saxon church was one of the most studied and well-visited buildings in the world; was there really that much more to be known about it? This simplifies, but on the eve of the great cutting open that seems to have been the gist of the discussion. In some quarters it may have been tinged by rationalization, for it was realized that the involvement of archaeologists would lengthen the repairs and add to their costs. Even so, in 1966 it really was widely believed that churches had been so well studied that the duty of modern scholarship, aside from solving an occasional puzzle, was the largely formal one of validating what was already known. Behind this lay a feeling in some quarters that churches were *architecture* – which was *art* and so for people of refined sensibility, which did not normally include archaeologists – a last twitch of the social tension we met in Chapter 3. Churches, moreover, were living places of worship and *not ancient monuments*. This was repeated like a chant, as if the success of Anglican bishops in 1913 in exempting churches from the Ancient Monuments Amendment Act had had some transubstantiating effect on the nature of archaeological evidence which exonerated deans and chapters from looking after it. However that may be, the exemption of archaeology from secular ancient monuments legislation half a century before had not encouraged thought about what historical questions the archaeological study of churches might usefully tackle. Some saw little use for it at all, supposing that excavation's usefulness must decrease as time passes and written records become increasingly full.[9]

Thus it was that when, in 1967, engineers calculated that York Minster was too close to collapse for comfort, and that drastic excavation would be needed to provide it with a new understructure, there were many who hoped that archaeology would not be too bothersome. Among them was the advisory committee which had been set up by the Dean and Chapter – the cathedral's governing body – to guide them on archaeological matters during the coming repairs. Chaired by Sir Mortimer Wheeler and composed of some of the most eminent architectural historians and archaeologists of the day (one of them was C. A. Ralegh Radford, the director of Ditchley met earlier in his career in Chapter 4), this committee decided that in view of the emergency and shortage of funds only the lower levels below the central tower – deposits which were believed to contain the remains of Roman buildings and the Anglo-Saxon cathedral – merited recording. The rest could be shovelled away under the eyes of an observer with a notebook. This was a throwback to the days when excavation had been the mere exposure of structures, as if all that was needed was the vacuuming away of some neutral material. Although the cathedral's archaeological team was later enlarged, and gained more time, this early impression of minimal needs continued to dominate official thinking for the rest of the project's five-year life.[10]

At Canterbury a quarter of a century later the issue was different. In the twelfth century one of the cathedral's monks had described the church as it had stood at the end of the Anglo-Saxon era, on the eve of reconstruction by the Normans. Architectural historians had long pored over this text in an effort to picture the lost church, and had arrived at different readings. In 1993 works to replace worn paving in the nave provided a chance to bring speculation to an end.

In doing so, archaeology could also settle an argument about Anglo-Saxon architecture in general. So far-reaching had been the rebuilding of cathedrals, abbeys and castles after the Norman Conquest that no prime building of the earlier age was left standing. This meant that the greatest Anglo-Saxon architectural achievements were unknown. Moreover, there were some who doubted whether there had ever been any great achievements. Among them was John Harvey, one of postwar Europe's leading architectural historians. When Harvey revised his *Cathedrals of England and Wales* in 1974, he reflected on the recently completed excavation of the Anglo-Saxon cathedral at Winchester. All that was left of this structure were the outlines of its foundations, but these were enough to indicate what a Saxon royal church and cathedral might have looked like. Harvey was not impressed. True, in its final form just before AD 1000, the church had been quite large – nearly 250 feet long. This scale, however, was deceiving, since it was the cumulative result of joining several smaller, older structures together. Harvey declared this to be a 'relatively un- or even anti-architectural' way of proceeding. Until then, he reflected, it had been possible to give the benefit of the doubt to literary remarks about the beauty and grandeur of later Saxon buildings. Now, he reasoned, since no other Saxon cathedral was likely to have exceeded Winchester, any chance that Anglo-Saxon churches had been in the mainstream of European architectural development must be remote. Since architecture is the mistress of art, it followed that pre-Norman England had been a cultural backwater, and that after the Norman Conquest art started afresh.[11] Canterbury would test this.

Or would it? While the excavations at York and Canterbury were only a few years apart, the attitudinal climates in which they took place were different. As we have just seen, the work at York began against a background of structural crisis and academic apathy. At Canterbury, by contrast, the Dean and Chapter took responsibility for the archaeological consequences of the new floor. The issue here was what the consequences should be. The laying of the floor did not in itself require much disturbance, and new heating called only for shallow ducts. However, there was more to it than this: the lifting of the old floor was a rare opportunity for a full-scale excavation to answer long-standing questions. Just how long-standing was indicated by the date of the pavement that was being replaced: 1787. By that measure, the next chance to ascertain Canterbury's pre-Norman development might not come round until the twenty-third century. Three hundred years was a long time to wait for answers to questions with large implications for architecture elsewhere in England, and for England's relations with Europe.

The alternative was to record what lay immediately beneath the old floor, and leave the rest for posterity. Such restraint was now official policy. Until the 1980s the costs of rescue archaeology ahead of commercial development had been largely borne by the government. This often went by the name of 'preservation by record', a phrase which implied to some that an excavation's archive could be a sufficient proxy for a site destroyed. By the late 1980s the result of this approach was a lot of records and not much preservation. In 1991, in circumstances to be described more fully in the chapter that follows, the government told developers that in future they themselves should bear the expense of the archaeological consequences of their schemes. This was an extension of the 'polluter pays' principle. Along with it ran something more contentious. The government's archaeological advisers figured that much of the material which had been rescued at public expense would be better off if it were still in the ground, and so available for interrogation with improved resources in the future. There were several motives for this.

One was based in a morality of safekeeping, in part borrowed from Charles Rothschild's* dictum of Nature conservation, that 'the only effective method of protecting nature is to interfere with it as little as possible'. Archaeologists had no more right to go about annihilating archaeological deposits than zoologists were licensed to destroy wildlife. Another took its cue from a widened sense of community, wherein archaeology should be something for everyone to use, in their own ways. Hence, the fact that one group had an academic interest in archaeological evidence (that is, one sort of understanding, out of many possible kinds) should not confer pre-eminence in decisions about what should happen to it. If academics wished to destroy sites by digging them up, they now had to take the public with them. A third argument said that abstinence today would enable communities in the future to ask questions arising from their own historical agendas rather than on the basis of collecting strategies in the late twentieth century. In the United States this was called 'conservation archaeology'. What it meant was that the main aim of public archaeology became the safekeeping rather than the immediate understanding of archaeological evidence. Seen by some as ethically responsible and by others as a kind of over-regulated austerity, it was this recently adopted policy which was applied at Canterbury.

Thus did the two projects take different shape. At York, six feet of archaeological deposits were hacked out while the great and the good shrugged and looked on. At Canterbury, most of the archaeology was left where it was because the great and the good (with exceptions) did not wish it disturbed.

The proposed depth of excavation in Canterbury's nave was not to be greater than seventeen inches. Yet even this produced an astonishing succession of cathedrals, the plans nested one inside the other like Russian dolls. Without further excavation, however, little could be said about their dates. In result,

> the dating of the sequence of Anglo-Saxon cathedrals can only be established on the basis of perceived parallels with structures elsewhere. A consequence of this is that the English structures will always be dated later than their continental counterparts, begging the question of the direction in which architectural influences flowed at any one particular period.[12]

---

* Rothschild was an amateur naturalist who founded the Society for the Promotion of Nature Reserves (now the Royal Society for Nature Conservation) in 1912.

36. Excavation inside Canterbury Cathedral (1993) reveals the western apse (curving foundation, left) of an Anglo-Saxon predecessor flanked by a stair turret (lower centre). Mortar ridges between piers of the existing nave show the impress of late eleventh-century paving. Rectangular shafts are graves and brick burial vaults.

But at least one issue was settled. The last Anglo-Saxon rebuilding had been in the European mainstream. Confirmation that there were after all great buildings in pre-Conquest England had repercussions elsewhere. In seeking to account for the additive way in which the pre-Conquest cathedral in Winchester was built, for instance, simple ideas about Anglo-Saxon insularity would no longer do. We shall come back to this.

A common fallacy about medieval cathedrals is that they took centuries to build. Clergy preach about the pious tenacity of craftsmen who laboured in the knowledge that they would never see the end of the work upon which they were engaged. This misses the point about what was actually happening. In fact, medieval builders could work fast. The cathedral begun in Canterbury by Archbishop Lanfranc in 1070 took only seven years from start to finish – faster even than the planning decision for London Heathrow airport's fifth terminal. The main hindrances to fast work were political disruption that distracted or killed patrons, and irregular funding – the latter condition illustrated today in the time being taken to complete Antoni Gaudí's Church of the Holy

Family in Barcelona. The difficulty of guaranteeing sustained cashflow is one reason why after the great renewal that followed the Norman Conquest so few English cathedrals and parish churches were ever again rebuilt in one go. More usually, a church was transformed a bit at a time. At York four centuries did indeed pass between the building of the Norman cathedral and the final consecration in July 1472, but this was not because the original church was four hundred years in the making – it was because at least ten subsequent campaigns were made to extend and modernize its different parts. For only one-tenth of those four hundred years was there not some new work in hand or in prospect.[13]

Most English cathedrals show a similar story – total Norman rebuilding followed by incremental renewal. In this they differ from some continental churches, where one rebuilding could be husbanded for centuries. What it was that fed England's rejuvenating impulse is a question to be considered later; here we note simply that one of its effects was the overwriting of earlier stages of building by later ones. The explorer in heating ducts and dusty underfloor chambers beneath the eastern arm of York Minster will see hundreds of carved architectural fragments recycled in later foundations. These pieces are from an eastern arm built during the third quarter of the twelfth century when the Romanesque style was transforming into Gothic.[14] That eastern arm was at least the second on the site, and was in its turn replaced two centuries later.

As an architectural reality, the initial, eleventh-century York Minster has vanished. Yet its former presence tarries, visible in shreds of early fabric left in places where later works joined, and by proxy in the way later developments were often placed on earlier foundations.

Renewal introduces a second fallacy about medieval cathedrals, and indeed concerning technical innovation generally, namely that expertise improves as time passes. At York, in some respects it was rather the opposite. While the extensions of the later Middle Ages were better finished than those they replaced, they were not always so well founded. Bearing in mind that construction had been more or less continuous between the eleventh century and the fourteenth, it is a question how that forgetting occurred.[15] The fact that it did was a large part of the reason for the crisis discovered at the end of 1966: later builders had used the unmodified substructure and lower walls of the original eleventh-century church to bear the weight of their massive additions.[16]

In 1966, no one was quite sure what that first substructure actually represented. Parts of it had been seen before. In 1829, clearance after a damaging fire had exposed remains of a twelfth-century crypt, beneath and around which ran walls and foundations of coarser appearance. The study of these earlier remains and of the Minster's fabric became the devotion of John Browne, a local artist and amateur antiquary whose *Architectural History of York Cathedral* was issued in thirty-nine parts between 1838 and 1847. Browne's finely illustrated account of his discoveries and work on the Minster's medieval building records was indispensable to following scholars, who between them over the next century published at least twelve variant interpretations of what he had found. These accounts, augmented by results from further excavations, fell into two broad groups in their conclusions: those which took the early remains under the choir to be traces of an Anglo-Saxon church, and those which saw them as the remains of an early Norman building, presumably the cathedral mentioned in a near-contemporary source as having been built by Thomas of Bayeux, the first Norman Archbishop of York (1070–1100).

Within the foundations ran a network of channels, some of which were void while others contained lengths of oak. Browne reasoned, correctly, that the entire system had originated as a unified scheme of reinforcement and that the timbers had since decayed. Some of the channels were waterlogged. By floating rods along several of them Browne was able to probe their length as far as the west side of the central crossing. In 1930 another excavation took place, this time under the supervision of England's Chief Inspector of Ancient Monuments, Sir Charles Peers. Peers found similar channels further east, where there were remains of an eastern apse. He repeated Browne's observations and found that the foundations continued for at least 197 feet beyond the central crossing. By conflating these records made at different times it was possible to produce a composite picture of the channels. On the strength of this, Peers concluded that the timber-laced foundations had supported an Anglo-Saxon basilica.

This interpretation differed from the one which had been put forward eighty-four years before by Robert Willis, Cambridge's Jacksonian Professor of Applied and Experimental Philosophy – a title that disguised his real work as a teacher of mechanical engineering.[17] Willis had been a protégé of the engineer Thomas Telford, and his lectures were renowned for their virtuoso flair and use of working models to illustrate subjects as diverse as sound, gears, voice production and the mechanization of mining. His hobbies were just as vigorously pursued. An accomplished violinist, Willis invented a chromatic harp, while his enthusiasm for historic buildings was practised to an extent that in anyone else's life would have amounted to a career in itself. His analytical eye, draughtsmanship and careful use of original documents made him the foremost architectural historian of his day. Willis's studies included twelve English cathedrals, the entire University of Cambridge, work in Italy on the history of vaulting, in Greece on Orthodox churches and in Jerusalem on the Church of the Holy Sepulchre. Willis also published a facsimile edition of the sketchbook of the thirteenth-century mason Villard de Honnecourt and an account of the ninth-century plan of the monastery of St Gall in Switzerland.

Willis set a pattern. Just as, a few years later, Pitt Rivers sought to divide 'facts' from 'interpretation' in his archaeological reports,* so Willis insisted upon an initial separation between the history of a building derived from written sources and the evidence of the fabric itself. He saw, correctly, that the inferences to be drawn from one would not automatically be reflected in the other. For instance, a well-documented phase in the history of a building might not now be visible (let us say, because it was removed a hundred years later), while the present fabric may show phases of work for which no documents survive. Only when conclusions from the two kinds of source had been independently drawn could they be compared and maybe married. More fundamentally, Willis 'created a kind of developmental archaeology in which a structure is seen to be the end-result of a long process of accretion, demolition and replacement, in response to changes in need and fashion'. Such staging need not be confined to a building; it could be extended to the site, and so became 'a way of looking at both buildings and the ground on which they stand'.[18] It was Willis who devised the phase plan in which different episodes of building are defined by various shadings or colours, or through a series of plans that illustrate successive changes. This affected archaeology's practice, and the way in which monuments are presented. As we saw in Chapter 2, the search for changes in construction became an aim of architectural history, while the task of excavation beside a ruin was to follow the succession of periods underground and extend coloured phases on the dated plan. Periodization spread into other branches of archaeology, and in this respect it has been suggested that archaeology owes more to Willis than to Pitt Rivers.[19]

York Minster was one of the buildings Willis studied. In 1846 he presented his results to the Archaeological Institute, and published

* See p. 69.

them two years later.[20] Willis realized that the Norman crypt uncovered by Browne belonged not to the generation after the Conquest but to the later twelfth century. This meant that an earlier Norman church, the one recorded as having been built by Thomas of Bayeux towards the end of the eleventh century, must await recognition. Just north of the entrance to the choir he noticed a few feet of curving masonry. He correctly identified this as the springing of an apse – a small semi-circular chapel – which bulged eastwards from the eleventh-century transept. The apse adjoined the north-east pier of the tower, which showed that the transept had had no eastern aisle, which in turn made it a safe bet that there was no western aisle either, because there was no known case of a Norman transept embodying the latter without the former. And since it could be assumed that the two arms of the transept would be symmetrical, Willis had reconstructed a third of the plan of Thomas's church on the basis of a few yards of masonry. Willis was similarly percipient about the nave, where evidence in the roof showed that the main span of the eleventh-century nave had been only inches narrower than its late thirteenth-century successor, and that the four piers of the central tower stood upon the prints of their Norman predecessors.

In two respects, however, Willis was led astray. In 1840, following another fire, Browne had been given permission to dig a small hole in search of the south wall of the Norman nave. A wall obligingly appeared, and both Browne and Willis duly extrapolated from it a wide nave with narrow aisles. Aisles were expected – all known Norman cathedrals had them. However, the wall seen by Browne belonged to another building. Browne later compounded the misunderstanding when, in 1863, in a trench being dug through the nave to lay pipes to supply the cathedral with gas, he mistook the portion of an external buttress for part of a nave pier. His published drawing combined what he had actually seen with its presumed mirror image, making no distinction between the two, to the confusion of architectural historians for the next 150 years.[21]

Secondly, Willis (like Browne) misunderstood the significance of the walls under the choir. He thought that the space they enclosed was too narrow for the walls to have had anything to do with the church built by Thomas, and their workmanship did not seem to resemble the parts of Thomas's fabric he could see elsewhere. The walls under the choir looked cruder, and were thus presumably older. Willis considered it 'pretty certain' that they had belonged to the Anglo-Saxon cathedral which either had been temporarily retained in the 1080s pending its replacement or else was overwritten by Thomas's eastern arm which in its turn was swept away by later rebuilding.[22]

Not everyone agreed. Over the next century a number of architectural historians pointed out that the workmanship of the walls under
the choir was typical of the late eleventh century, and that both the
walls and the timber-stiffened foundation which carried them should
be ascribed to Archbishop Thomas.[23] Nevertheless, a strong body of
opinion continued to contend that the walls, the foundation and the
apse discovered in 1930 were all parts of a great Anglo-Saxon church.
This was the prevailing view just before the repairs began, when in
1965 Harold and Joan Taylor, authors of the newly published *Anglo-
Saxon Architecture*, declared the remains to be pre-Conquest. (Harold
Taylor, like Robert Willis, was a former Cambridge mathematics don.)
However, whereas Willis had seen the foundations as belonging to a
seventh-century cathedral, the Taylors sided with Peers and Browne in
attributing them to a church described in luminous language by the
eighth-century scholar Alcuin, consecrated in 780.[24]

Small wonder, then, that when the great breaking open began in 1967
scholars were on tenterhooks. Many of them expected to see part of a
typical Norman cathedral under the western half of York Minster, and
an Anglo-Saxon church (for which there were several candidates) to the
east. What actually emerged was quite different – a Norman cathedral
of a kind that no one had anticipated.

One reason for this surprise was the notion that contrasts of workmanship should indicate work of different date. This is the general belief,
and we have met it before – with flint tools, pots, styles of window. Yet
by altering the scale of study, local variations in finish turned out to
typify a highly unified building. The lessons: by concentrating on one
apparent set of differences, we may miss another group of semblances;
what you think depends upon what you see, and what you see depends
upon what you anticipate as well as where you stand.

Another reason: the focus on walls (drawn and photographed) at the
expense of intervening deposits (shovelled out) had caused everyone to
miss evidence for the fact that the pavement of Thomas's cathedral had
been raised above the ground. This meant that the lowest courses of
the inner faces of walls had been buried from the start, and that strictly
speaking they were not walls at all, but footings. Antiquaries who had
imagined themselves to be looking at the building from the side, were
in reality seeing it from below.

A third factor was hazy, yet vital – a likelihood that Thomas's cathedral marked a deliberate break with tradition. Beneath it ran remains of

the former Roman legionary fortress of Eburacum, military buildings
and streets, all on a gridiron plan. While it is a question how strong this
sense of vector was by the eleventh century, it is certain that parts of
Roman York were then still visible (as indeed some of them are today),
and that the evolving topography of the Anglo-Saxon city had been
influenced by the axis of the Roman fortress. The Norman cathedral-
builders, on the other hand, had pointedly ignored it. This made it likely
that the Anglo-Saxon cathedral was not directly beneath the cathedral
but near by, on the older, Roman alignment.

And last, it had long been an axiom that great Anglo-Norman
churches begun in the generation after the Conquest had been planned
according to one of two schools of design.[25] Since York's cathedral resembled neither of them, art-historical theory did not provide for it until
it was found. Some scholars actively wanted an Anglo-Saxon church
to be there: even in the presence of the new discoveries, some members of the Dean and Chapter's Archaeological Advisory Committee
projected their own wishes on to the visible fabric. In 1968 it was pub-
licly announced that the Norman cathedral rested on the walls of a
seventh-to-eighth-century cathedral, with a red floor. In fact, the walls
were Norman, the floor Roman.[26]

As historians came to terms with the facts, attention shifted to what
they meant. At the broadest level they meant that no great building
could ever again be regarded as 'understood' in the absence of adequate
study. A lot of assumptions about other cathedrals would have to be
rechecked.

Then there were revelations to ponder. It became clear, for instance,
that the rather drab masonry of Thomas's building belied its original
appearance. When new, the entire cathedral had been jacketed in white
plaster, outside as well as in, and then painted with red lines to simu-
late the joints of masonry. Whether seen from across the city in winter
twilight, or as a distant gleaming shape from the Pennine flank thirty
miles away, this had been a building of surpassing presence. Presumably
other great buildings of the twelfth and thirteenth centuries had been
similarly finished. Place names like Whitchurch could now be taken
literally.

Or again: the fifty-foot timbers required for tie beams in the roof
implied access to exceptionally tall, straight oaks. Trees of such size
must have been at least two to three hundred years old, and must have
grown in high, dark woodland, growing side by side with interlocking
canopies. Whereabouts was this wood? Shorter oaks had been used as

reinforcing timbers in the foundation channels rodded by Peers and Browne. When Derek Phillips came to add up the total length of oaks in the substructure, the answer came out at over two miles. Whatever other problems Thomas's builders may have faced, timber supply was evidently not one of them.

There were new puzzles: what was the source and significance of Thomas's aisleless plan, and if the Anglo-Saxon church was not underneath the present building, where was it? The lack of any obvious source for Thomas's church in Normandy at first caused searchers to look in Anjou and Poitou, where naves without aisles were fashionable, in the Rhineland, in Spain, even in the past.[27] Other possibilities have since been put forward. Small communities of nuns and canons often worshipped in unaisled buildings, and it was asked if Thomas's architect took a lesser church as a model and scaled it up. But why had Normandy been ruled out? In other respects, artistically and technically, Thomas of Bayeux's cathedral was in the mainstream of Anglo-Norman Romanesque. The fact that there was no known instance of a similar layout in mid-eleventh-century Normandy did not necessarily mean that none existed. The earlier misreading of York itself showed how piecemeal records linked by supposition could lead historians astray. The eleventh-century phases of several important Norman churches (including Thomas's home town of Bayeux itself) are no better known today than York was forty years ago.[28]

Whether or not Norman York Minster was as unusual as it first seemed, its design draws attention to the context in which it was built. Eleventh-century York was a great city, but the cathedral and archbishopric were poor, and made poorer by invasions and insurrections in the five years before Thomas's election in 1070. Unrest continued during Thomas's pontificate – the old cathedral was plundered by raiders in 1075 – and alongside the tasks of securing the cathedral's economy and modernizing its governance, there was work to restore a devastated diocese. With all this and the need for stopgap repairs to the old Minster and its buildings, the skills and funds available for a new cathedral must have been limited. In a newly mastered country, on the other hand, labour was less of a problem. A cathedral that was imposing yet did not call for too many craftsmen would suit those conditions, which were intensified from the later 1070s when the escalation of new schemes elsewhere may have exceeded the craft resources needed to build them. With no columns or piers, well engineered but austere, Thomas's cathedral was a logistical rather than an artistic tour de force for which basic ingredients – timber, ready-cut stone from Roman buildings, rubble and mortar – were available close to hand.[29]

This matching of means to circumstance had a larger context. In the year of his appointment Thomas was in dispute with Lanfranc over whether the holder of the northern archbishopric should be required to make a written profession of obedience to Canterbury, and over a claim that the dioceses of Lichfield, Worcester and Dorchester belonged in the province of York. When both disputes were settled in Canterbury's favour in April 1072, the decision deepened York's poverty, and may have fostered a determination that York's forthcoming cathedral should be as unlike Canterbury's as possible. York duly made Lanfranc's church look modest and old fashioned. But this was temporary.[30] By the mid-1090s Canterbury was being remodelled, while from the late 1070s a new generation of Benedictine churches like Winchester, Ely and Bury were in progress on a triumphalist scale that rivalled the greatest churches anywhere in Europe.[31]

The new generation of monumental churches was built to honour and house Anglo-Saxon saints, from whose tombs power flowed, and with whom the new rulers wished to be on good terms. At Ely, Durham and Bury, the conquerors in their turn submitted to the resident saints, building churches in honour of Etheldreda, Cuthbert and Edmund that reflected not only England's affluence but also her royal, sacred past.

The foundation-raft of Thomas's church thus expresses more than a vanished building. It belongs to the opening of an age when nowhere else in Latin Christendom would so much be built in so short a time, 'nor in so many imaginatively designed ways'.[32] Within that time it was both a moment of repose and a step from the first efforts of the 1070s to the more expansive and sophisticated schemes of the generation that followed. And as the unfolding of architectural ideas accelerated at a rate not far from that of modern avionics, it went out of date. To keep up, one had to spend, yet York's poverty and lack of a saint were problems. While other churches were modernized several times over during the first quarter of the twelfth century, Thomas's church may have stood substantially unaltered into the days of Henry II. By now, however, and not coincidentally, it did have a candidate for sainthood: William Fitzherbert, an archbishop whose death in mysterious circumstances on 8 June 1154 had been followed by his interral in a retouched Roman coffin ostentatiously placed at the east end of the nave.

'Saint' is rooted in Latin sanctus, 'holy'. As a concept evolved in Catholic thought, sainthood denotes a person who through the merits of martyrdom or virtue has bypassed purgatory, the place of waiting for the General Judgement, and gone straight to heaven. Nearness to God enabled saints to intercede on behalf of the living. Since it was believed that saints lived simultaneously in heaven and in the tomb,[33] their graves were simultaneously sources of power and doorways between worlds where prayers crossed the borders of time.*[34]

Places like this were suitable for churches, which became the saints' earthly homes. St Peter's in Rome was built in a former cemetery, upon what was remembered as Peter's grave. The ultimate model was the presumed tomb of Christ himself, over which the Church of the Holy Sepulchre had afterwards been raised by Helen, the mother of Constantine, and reputedly of British birth.[35] Moreover, since a Christian's death (like Christ's) was also a birth into eternal life, the anniversary of a saint's death was a birthday upon which to celebrate mass beside the saint's tomb – an idea which grew from the older custom of commemorating a dead relative by going to the grave to eat a meal with friends on the person's birthday.

Saints enriched the calendar. They also made it uneven, some days being more promising or prominent than others,[36] while their presence both in the temporal world and in the divine homeland simultaneously located them within and outside earthly time. The ecclesiastical arithmetic required for the reckoning of Easter drew on menology, the measurement of time by the moon (from Greek *menologion*, 'account of the months'), which in medieval usage became a calendar with biographies of the saints. Beyond this,

> by the fourth century at least, the Christian Fathers had shifted the Church's preoccupation away from … consideration of the ending of the world and last things … towards concern for history, as testimony of the providential plans of God. Particularly, they were interested in the incarnate life of Christ as historically recorded in the gospels. Pilgrimages had begun to the sacred places recorded in the gospels, where Christ was born, died, rose again, and ascended into heaven. By walking in the footsteps of the historical Christ, the faithful entered into deeper spiritual oneness with the living Christ. The liturgy of the Church had also begun to consolidate the principle of daily commemorating the whole great sequence of salvation history. In the liturgical offices and seasons of the Church, running in tandem with

* See pp. 266–7 and 379–81.

the natural cycle and the astronomical calendar of the year, Christians perceived Time itself to be sanctified.[37]

Saints, through their stories and the places they frequented, increased the network of pilgrimages, invested landscape and journey with new meanings and stirred thought about the past. Pilgrimage was not limited to holy places – the idea was everywhere, written into the environment by the Creator's intent. The waxing and the waning of the moon signified the journey from birth to death.[38] Life was perceived as a pilgrimage through time, a day as representing the world's term, the term as a kind of lineal temporal space through which the world moves towards its end, beyond which lay eternity. That voyage was in turn a metaphor for the *impulse* to wayfaring, as were the rolling seasons and the path of the sun. And because 'man is the world in miniature' (*homo mundus minor est*, as the precept ran), and a day a microcosm of time, 'humankind registers all this as a yearning within'.[39] The longing stemmed from the belief that the world is not our home but a place of exile for the soul – that we are strangers here, and that the pilgrim is homeward bound.

All of this, and more, was linked to the cult of saints. Which is why, from the seventh century to the sixteenth, the giving of land and offerings to saints was the greatest single economic movement. Saints became proprietors of the churches that housed them or took their names. They befriended those who gave to them, and became enemies to any who disturbed their repose. A map of their resting places is a diagram of power.[40] Like some vast gravitational force, a saint's grave could attract people and trade, or pull a city out of shape.

Saints' power was transmissible. If holy remains were moved, their potency went with them. Sometimes this led to the distribution of a saint's bones, so that a number of churches could possess a relic of one man or woman. A reflex of that was the power of *virtus* to irradiate anything else with which it came into contact. So a saint's grave remained powerful even when it was empty. It also explains the phenomenon of secondary relics – the distribution of things like pieces of cloth which had been placed in proximity to saints' remains.[41] Like the lighting of many candles from a single flame, the cult and power of a saint could be spread.

While everyone knew what a saint was, until the twelfth century there was no fixed route to becoming one.[42] Saints had hitherto been made in a variety of ways, and with varying degrees of formality. There were also variations of degree. Bishops, for example, were sometimes seen as lesser saints, because they were a little closer to God than people who were not bishops.[43] Wulfstan, York's archbishop at the beginning of the eleventh century, was informally venerated after his death in 1023.[44] What such an informal cult might involve is visible at Wells, where, at the end of the twelfth century, the remains of Anglo-Saxon bishops were transferred into a new cathedral. By the end of the Middle Ages, several of their skulls had been limewashed for display, 'two had had discs of bone cut from the back of the cranium (presumably for use as amulets), and some were worn to a polished state in places where hands had been repeatedly laid upon them in acts of veneration'. The placing of a special cloth over a tomb was a way of declaring sanctity. In a further sign that the dead bishops were regarded as wonder-workers, some of their bones had been wrapped in red silk.[45]

37. *Medieval skulls from Wells Cathedral showing (above) whitening and the polish of many hands, and, in reverse view (below), cuts to provide amulets*

Archbishop Wulfstan was buried at Ely. In late Saxon York, archbish-ops were the king's agents – mostly southerners, and six of the last seven of them asked to be buried in other places.[46] Only Ealdred, Thomas's predecessor, was buried in the old Minster. When Thomas's church was finished his remains were transferred into it. Perhaps, like his colleague Giso at Wells, he was buried with a cross-shaped plaque to say who he was, maybe bearing a thin lead foil inscribed with lines from the Latin mass for the dead. Such crosses were common accessories at magnate funerals in the eleventh and early twelfth centuries. In 1063 Wulfmaeg, sister of the abbot of St Augustine's abbey, 'journeyed out of this life' with such a cross which is itself speaking: *By this Alpha and Omega of Christ I mark all resting places.*[*47]

Ealdred's translation into the Norman cathedral caught the attention of contemporaries, who wrote about it. So did the funeral of Thomas, who was buried beside him. If there were hopes for them as borderline saints, their skulls to be polished by the touch of a million hands, that would explain why these events were recorded. It would also give a con-text for William Fitzherbert's burial at the east end of York's nave in 1154, and for the vast rebuilding of the transept which followed during the thirteenth-century pontificate of his successor but three, Walter de Grey. When de Grey himself was buried he went to the grave in his robes, beneath a full-length colour portrait of himself on a sheet of plaster. And what a grave: de Grey's tomb was built in the likeness of a full-size shrine. His neighbour, Godfrey de Ludham, was embalmed, perhaps so that if his tomb were opened a few years later he would appear incorrupt.[48] That is speculation, but to the south of de Grey lay the tomb of his immediate successor, Sewal de Boville, who did become the focus of a local cult. Even more remarkable was the nearby tomb of William de Langton, York's dean from 1260 until his death in 1279 (a kinsman of de Grey, his election to archbishop was vetoed by the pope), who was buried under an avant-garde bronze effigy of a type more usu-ally associated with kings. Prominent in the splendid new transept, the tombs of York's thirteenth-century archbishops and deans suggest that they were grooming themselves, or each other, as future saints. And however that might be, was it by coincidence that beneath them lay another, older elite?

Directly beneath de Grey, de Ludham and the rest was an old grave-yard. The axis of the graves ran diagonally below the Minster's transept,

---

* *Alpha Christi ex hoc Omega signa cunabula cuncta.*

and the graveyard was in an area probably coextensive with the demolished basilica of the headquarters (*principia*) of the former Roman
fortress. This cemetery, bordered by the basilica's cut-down walls, had
come into use in the ninth century or sooner, and remained so until it
was engulfed by Thomas's east–west church in the later 1070s. Material
dumped upon this landscape then sealed it for the next 890 years, until
the Minster's hard-pressed archaeological team (now expanded to three)
came upon it in 1969.

What they saw was like the contents of some long-walled-up room.
Here was the necropolis of York's late Saxon patricians, their graves
aligned in close-packed rows, marked by richly carved slabs and end-
stones cut from Roman building blocks. Some of the slabs had been
reused, so that their designs of undulating animals and dragons were
older than the individuals they commemorated. When new, the stones
had been painted. Most were products of a commercial workshop, but
there were variants, and other ways of marking graves.[49] One monument was an inscribed Roman memorial that had been fetched from
an ancient cemetery at the city's edge. Another funeral had taken place
inside what may have been a low, wooden-railed enclosure. Children had
been buried in an area edged by stones.[50] These are glimpses. Below the
slabs lay a plethora of ways in which individuals were actually interred:
in oak coffins, on biers, on mattresses of charcoal, in sarcophagi, within
tile- or stone-lined pits, in iron-bound trunks with elaborate locks, even
in part of a boat.[51] The people had been buried in their clothes, and
with them were rings of silver and copper, earrings, coins, keys and gold
thread from fine garments.

Rated as the most important sculpture discovery in Britain since the
beginning of the twentieth century, the gravestones mostly belonged
to the early tenth century – the middle of the period between the 860s
and 950s, when most of Northumbria was under Scandinavian power.
Standing in what must have been the burial ground of the Anglo-Saxon
cathedral (which must surely therefore have stood near by), these stones
became the metropolitan models for monuments marking the graves of
local lords beside their newly founded village churches all over Yorkshire.

Who decided to use the fallen *principia* in this way? And why? Was it
a site that York's Anglo-Scandinavian high society marked out for itself,
or was it a graveyard that already existed? And what of the rubble, the
Roman rubble, that was strewn across the site – was this a factor? In the
emergency conditions of 1969 it was not possible to be sure. But there
were clues. Several graves contained objects which predated the Danish

take-over, while others yielded radiocarbon dates that allow the possibility of older funerals. More telling may be the amount of loose human bone that lay in the soil. Such charnel is usually a sign that the diggers of later graves had churned up earlier ones. They would not have had to delve far to do so – the depth available for graves within the debris of the Roman basilica was so little that skeletons were found nuzzling the bases and drums of Roman columns. For the most part it was only the latest or deepest burials that survived intact.[52] All of which suggests that the decision to use the area was something more than opportunism. What did the fallen *principia* and recut Roman stones signify other than an iconic reuse, a continuity of touch from Constantine, Rome and Peter?

Only one of the tenth-century monuments found under York Minster bore writing. Curiously, this was the already inscribed stone taken from a Roman cemetery, to which was added a line beseeching prayer for the soul of Costan. Costan (the name suggests a Hiberno-Norse fashion) died in his twenties, apparently as a result of a sword-blow to the back of his neck.

The taste of York's Anglo-Scandinavian leaders was for images rather than text. Alongside Christian motifs there were scenes from Scandinavian myths, like the stories of Sigurd (for whom the York carvings predate any written source) and Volundr – in English, Wayland – the metalworker who made a robe of feathers to fly away from the king who had maimed him to retain his services. Other scenes from north European mythology feature on gravestones in parts of the Danelaw at this time. It may be that they point to some sort of hybridization between the Scandinavian pantheon and Christianity in the Viking Kingdom of York in the early tenth century. Such a compromise would explain why the Archbishop of York retained his office after the Viking take-over, and why southern English chroniclers denigrated the compromise as 'paganism'. A further strand here is the reputation of Sigurd and Volundr as heroes. Heroes had special meaning for Christians, and it has been wondered if there is a comparison to be made between these Norse figures and the Graeco-Roman cult of heroes that had involved the public veneration of their tombs and treasuring of associated objects.

Lying in and around the graveyard were fragments of older monuments. Dating from the seventh and eighth centuries, finely cut from creamy limestone, smooth rubbed, often inscribed, these stones belonged to the age of scholars and saints – the days of Wilfrid, Bede and Alcuin. Most of them turned out to belong to a type of monument that had not been previously recognized – the inscribed stele or obelisk, a four-sided tapering monolith with a flat top. Such stelae seem originally to have stood against walls inside the Anglo-Saxon cathedral, where they honoured a departed ecclesiastical elite.[53] In their Grecian classicity, clean geometries, cross- and letter-forms evoking models from southern France to Constantinople, these stones were as redolent of a literary, Mediterranean world as the later boisterous, dragon- and myth-bearing stones were of the Volsungs. A few had been reused several times, journeying down a time-path from high culture to rubble.

One such lump bore an incised drawing of a long face with lentoid eyes. When it was brought into the finds hut on a cold evening in November 1971, the face stared with confrontational directness. Late at night when the contractor's men had gone home, it was easy to imagine the murmur of names, words and phrases inscribed on the things we were finding. *The ninth cohort made this ... Here beneath this turf rests Wulfhere ... To the spirits of the departed and of Antonius Gargilianus ... Pray for the soul ... Legio IX Hispana ... Pray, Pray, Pray for the soul of Costan.*

'Pray for the soul of ...' Until the 1540s, we recall, purgatory was the place of souls between death and the General Judgement – a realm where the soul is purified.[54] Here, wrote Augustine, the mildest pains of cleansing were worse than the worst pains on earth. The intensity and duration of chastisement could be lessened by acts of charity performed in life, and by prayers and masses offered by the living for the souls of the dead. Awareness of the alleviating power of prayers and masses is sometimes said to have emerged towards the end of the Middle Ages; in truth it was there early on. Bede, writing around 730, within a few years of the time when the York stelae were being cut, told of otherworldly visions which pointed to a place beyond the space and time of this world. One of Bede's stories is about a man reported dead in battle. The warrior's brother is a priest who offers masses for the absolution of his kinsman's soul. In fact, the kinsman still lives. He is a prisoner. The effect of the masses is to loosen his fetters each time his captors try to bind him.[55] By the fifteenth century purgatory's main features had been elaborated by scholars, sculptures and poets, and purgatory rather than hell had become the main source of Christian fear. The underlying idea, however, was at least a thousand years old.

Prayers for the dead were outlawed at the English Reformation. Reformers considered purgatory to be at best speculative, at worst mumbo-jumbo. For traditionalists, the forbidding of prayers for the dead put souls beyond help, just as it put the living beyond the help of saints. In traditional religion, community embraced the living and the dead, each supporting the other in a fellowship that extended across history. When Reform snuffed out that coloured world of saints, lights, signs, gestures and seasons it shrank the boundaries of community, dimmed collective memory and diminished time. Before, in the old religion, all had prayed for all. After, there was no all: you were on your own. This attack on the cult of the dead was 'an act of exorcism, to limit the claims of the past, and the people of the past, on the people of the present'.[56] And as the exorcism took effect, the study of time through antiquities and historical topography began to accelerate.

Reform's process and tempo varied. In some parishes the outward signs of tradition were seized and destroyed. In others, they were hidden or dispersed.[57] Archaeology sometimes finds them – slabs of stone with tiny plugs of lead containing relics, strange-shaped vessels, fragments of coloured images, bells, pyxes, spoons, gatherings of bones. What we see in such cases are devotional materials that were hidden in the hope of recovery, or in perplexity. Such finds modify the old notion that medieval saints were ailing and that Protestantism was an inevitable sweeping out of decadent customs. The objects and the manner of their concealment or reuse are rather consonant with the view that traditional religion exerted a 'strong, diverse, and vigorous hold over the imagination and the loyalty of the people up to the very moment of Reformation'. They remind us, too, of the depth of field behind tradition.

> Not every religious custom in the fifteenth century, however apparently well-established, was immemorial. The greatest feast of the late medieval church, Corpus Christi, was of comparatively recent institution, and the Corpus Christi play cycles, which absorbed the energies of a large proportion of the citizens of towns like York for months on end every year, were new in the fourteenth century. New feasts emerged as optional pious practices, and were eventually imposed as universal observances. New saints were venerated and the old, if not forgotten, at least gracefully retired. New devotional fads were enthusiastically explored by a laity eager for religious variety, increasingly literate, and keenly if conventionally devout.[58]

St William is a case in point. Back in the thirteenth century the bones of York's now canonized archbishop had been translated from the Roman sarcophagus in the Minster's nave to a shrine behind the high altar. A century later, when the cathedral's east end was enlarged in the saint's honour, they were moved again, to a shrine built in 1471–2 by Robert Spillesby, a master mason.[59] When the shrine was destroyed at some time before 1541, William's bones, partly wrapped in two pieces of woven silk, were gathered in a lead box and eventually returned to the stone coffin in the nave which had been his first resting place. Its location had not been forgotten.[60] William had not been alone. On the eve of the Reformation York Minster contained sixty altars, 'dedicated to a bewildering variety of saints', and at least two more shrine-tombs of former archbishops.[61]

Medieval contemplation of saints' tombs and shrines took place in mental surroundings that are gone, and evoked responses we cannot re-feel. But we do know that in medieval thought there was a theory of wonder (*admiratio*), which was a delicious sensation of *not* knowing, a state of awestruck enchantment in the presence of mystery beyond reason.[62] It is this which illuminates the final state of the Anglo-Saxon cathedral at Winchester – a mosaic of buildings, we recall, which John Harvey mistook for a kind of architectural defeatism. The point, we now see, is that reluctance to sweep away the seventh-century nucleus and start again stemmed not from narrowness of horizon, but from vitality. The first church had itself become a shrine, a place soaked in the power of the saints and bishops who had walked its floors. Such buildings (of which there were many in Anglo-Saxon England) were more marvellous than mere modern architecture. Being so, they were places to treasure, and treasuring was achieved by incorporating them into later structures rather than knocking them down. At pre-Conquest Winchester, the grave of its bishop St Swithun (who died in 862) became a new focus. Originally sited in the open outside the west door of the old cathedral, where people would come and go, in due course the church was extended across the grave to make the entire building his shrine.

Five hundred years later wonder was undimmed, and had spread.[63] Many factors had influenced the changing geography of devotion – chance, rumour, an individual's enthusiasm, fervency kindled by the circulation of versified biographies, 'news of striking cures or other favours'.[64] And whereas early medieval devotion to saints was focused on their relics, by the fifteenth and sixteenth centuries popular piety had become fixated by statues and paintings. As often as not these were local cults, like the one surrounding Sewal de Bovill. Late medieval wills commonly refer to sub-regional and parochial shrines – the world (whence time) in an image.[65]

Lifelike images were thus at the top of the iconoclasts' hit-list. The

modern visitor to almost any British medieval church will see that it
was particularly towards statues' heads that the hammers were swung.
In the early medieval Byzantine world, a sacred image was a kind of
two-way lens, its main purpose being to channel 'prayers to God, and
God's goodwill back to the individual or community'.[66] This explains
the attack on faces, for the beheading or disfeaturing of an image cut off
power by breaking the eye contact which was its source. Such action also
stilled forces which might otherwise be at the disposal of images that
had become proxies for saints. For just as a saint was a living presence
in the tomb or reliquary, so could a statue become 'the saint's new body,
which, like a living body, could also be set in motion in a procession'.[67]

> Statues that were dressed and carried in procession, carvings that
> were painted with vivid likeness to living persons, saints who gazed
> at worshippers with a frontal directness that invited communication
> through the meeting of eyes: these were the most dangerous forms
> of religious imagery ... [A religious statue] was as real as any masked
> player who conceals the living reality behind the painted visage.[68]

The merging of image and actor took this further. By the fifteenth century, popular drama used a rich stock of body language, movement and
sounds.[69] Plays based on legends about local saints were performed in
villages.[70] As we shall see, churchyards were places for all kinds of fun
and show business. Suspense and climax had long been a part of what
went on inside churches, where the mass itself was one kind of drama,
and the procession another. Ceremonies at Candlemas and Easter
involved re-enactment. In Anglo-Saxon days some churches had been
laid out to assist the flinging of dialogue and music back and forth
between spatially separated speakers and choirs. Something of this kind
very likely lies behind the bipolar plan revealed by the lifting of the
cathedral pavement at Canterbury. At Easter, entire church interiors
became incorporated in the geography of events at the sepulchre – the
journey of the Marys, angels at the tomb, astonishment, Peter and John
running, public rejoicing. Side chapels or crypts could represent the sepulchre. In a few places (examples survive at Gernrode, Magdeburg and
Constance) a scaled-down setpiece replica of the Holy Sepulchre in
Jerusalem was built inside a church to assist the staging of the *Visitatio
Sepulchri*. In the twelfth century, a chapel dedicated to St Mary and the
Holy Angels, popularly known as St Sepulchre's, was added on the north
side of the nave of Archbishop Thomas's cathedral at York. Enactments
could be accompanied by special effects. In the Christmas ceremony at

Besançon, for instance, the Magi journeyed from the east for the entire length of the darkened church following a star.[71]

Some effects were climactic. In the thickness of the west front of Wells Cathedral, behind a sculptured portrayal of the Coronation of the Virgin, there is a singers' gallery with sound holes, so that on special occasions the building itself could appear to sing. We can imagine choristers stationed here on Palm Sunday,

> their faces pressed into the openings, listening and watching for their cue to begin the singing of the 'Gloria laus', which would be answered antiphonally from the ground. Below, looking up, the procession and the lay congregation would have seen only the brilliantly painted angels flanking the Coronation group as the source of the sound of the clear, high voices drifting down.[72]

There are similar galleries at Salisbury and Lichfield. Cathedral west fronts were places for the imagery of Revelation, and hence cosmological boundaries. Above the high vaults of Wells's nave there are sound holes for trumpeters to herald the arising of the dead in the twinkling of an eye, and the end of time.

Reform silenced the trumpets, and finished the cycles of religious plays put on in provincial towns by trade guilds. Protestants gunned for popular religious drama partly because of its theology, but more particularly because its calendar was tied to traditional feasts and festivals, many of which were in their turn governed by the cycles of the moon. ('From Septuagesima Sunday nine weeks before Easter, through Lent, onwards to Ascension Day, Whit Sunday and Trinity Sunday eight weeks after Easter – about one third of the ecclesiastical calendar proves to be dependent upon the lunar system of dating Easter.')[73] Nor had anyone forgotten that the original and underlying intention of the guilds was the support of departed as well as living members. Guild fellowship ran across time, and at base was a part of the cult of the dead.

At first the Reformers demanded that the plays be cut and changed, and at first the guilds and corporations acquiesced.[74] By the late 1560s, however, the scope for bowdlerization was fast reducing. York's Creed plays were dropped in 1568, and the city's last performance of the Corpus Christi cycle took place in 1569.[75] The Paternoster plays were performed for the last time (provocatively, on the feast of Corpus Christi) in 1572. When the Coventry cycle ceased in 1581, William Shakespeare was seventeen years old.

10

WHITSUN GAMES

Can this cockpit hold
The vasty fields of France?

William Shakespeare, Prologue,
Henry V, c.1599

No one is quite sure how William Shakespeare was occupied between 1582, when he turned eighteen and married Anne Hathaway, and 1592, when he appears in London's theatre world.[1] Unknown, too, is the date of *Richard III*, although most scholars agree it was one of his earlier plays. First mentioned around 1593–4, it could have been written sooner. Its portrait of an amoral charismatic who could 'set the murd'rous Machiavel to school' was in a genre anticipated by Christopher Marlowe in *Tamburlaine*. But it also kept a foot in the traditional, consoling world of Robert Spillesby, the master mason who made the shrine of St William in York.*

Robert Spillesby's great-grandson, or even a grandson if he had lived long enough, could have been in the audience of the first performance of *Richard III*, watching as the king falls into an unquiet sleep on the eve of Bosworth Field. One by one, ghosts of his victims rise. In their procession are Clarence ('Let me sit heavy on thy soul tomorrow'), Rivers, Hastings, the two young princes, Buckingham and Lady Anne, his wife that 'never slept a quiet hour with thee'. Richard wakes in a flash of precognition.

> Give me another horse! Bind up my wounds!
> Have mercy, Jesu!

* See p. 268.

Gradually, he collects himself.

> There is no creature loves me;
> And if I die, no soul shall pity me:
> Nay, wherefore should they, since that I myself
> Find in myself no pity to myself?[2]

Behind Richard's contempt for the solace of traditional religion lay a late Elizabethan audience's awareness of what such belief had involved. The dream itself is telling; the medieval Church believed that the dream was one of the main contexts in which God and Satan vied for the possession of a man's soul.[3]

The repetition of 'pity' is another clue. Before the final general throwing out of images thirty years before, all parish churches had contained a screen between the nave and the chancel upon which stood the Rood – an image of the crucifixion – flanked on one hand by an image of Mary and on the other by John, her supporter when all others had deserted. Mary stood for pity, the striving of one soul to feel the suffering of another. During the fifteenth and earlier sixteenth centuries the image of Our Lady of Pity – Mary with her Son's corpse on her lap – became increasingly common as a devotional focus in local churches.[4] Alongside Our Lady of Pity ran another cult, the Image of Pity. All the sacraments drew their meaning from the blood of Christ. The mass, the sacrament of Christ's blood, was the ultimate source of their vitality. From the later fifteenth century imagery which linked the consecration of the bread and wine during the mass with the appearance of Christ displaying his wounds spread into books, painting, sculpture and windows of painted glass. Christ's blood also found its way into drama, as in the Croxton Play wherein a group of Jews recrucified Christ by stabbing a consecrated Host and nailing it to a post. The Host oozes blood, and later resolves into Christ himself, bleeding from unbound wounds. By the 1530s, attachment to the Image of Pity and other aspects of Christocentric devotion was widespread.[5] Shakespeare's portrayal of Richard as an image of pitilessness thus hints at a blasphemous counter-image, just as his inability to feel pity for himself puts him beyond pity's consolation. What must really have shocked the audience was what followed the awakening Richard's 'Have mercy, Jesu!'; as he gathers his wits, he repudiates his own plea.

We do not know how long or how widely such associations survived in the memories of Tudor and Jacobean playgoers, but we do know that prayers for the dead were still being said in some places when *Richard*

III was new. About a decade later, the ghost of Hamlet's father is:

> Doomed for a certain term to walk the night,
> And for the day confined to fast in fires,
> Till the foul crimes done in my days of nature
> Are burnt and purged away.

Old Hamlet is in purgatory. The slightest word about what this is like will 'harrow up' his son's soul.[6] Claudio's meditation on death in *Measure for Measure* similarly assumes that purgatory's 'worse than worst' is still in people's minds,[7] just as young Hamlet's allusion to an actor who 'out-Herods Herod' supposes audiences who still remember a histrionic performance tradition in mystery plays. In the playmaking of the 1590s and 1600s, then, some ideas were defined by memories of the pre-Reformation past. And just as blood had been the source of all the sacraments when Shakespeare's father was young, there is a lot of blood in Elizabethan drama.

Hamlet and *Measure for Measure* were performed in the Globe, a playhouse put up in Southwark in 1599 and rebuilt in 1614. The Globe's frame came from an earlier north London playhouse known as the Theater which had been dismantled and its parts sent south of the river for reassembly. Mystique surrounds it, partly because of its connection with Shakespeare, who held a share in the playhouse and wrote for its resident company, but also because of the Globe's place in the history of English drama. The Globe was an open-air playhouse consisting of tiers of galleries around a central space. Up to a dozen such playhouses were built in London (and apparently nowhere else – the nearest analogues seem to be the *corrales* theatres in Spain) between the mid-1560s and the early seventeenth century. Under names like the Red Lion, the Rose, Swan, Hope,[8] Fortune and Curtain, they provided bases for companies of hitherto itinerant actors who had earlier worked on makeshift stages in inn-yards, market-places, houses and halls.

The influence of these newly resident companies was large. Most of them played six days a week, to audiences which by the early 1600s, from the combined estimated daily capacity of the playhouses, could number up to ten thousand. Even in the mid-1590s, when licensing restrictions capped the number of officially permitted companies at two, the weekly total of London playgoers has been estimated at fifteen thousand – the population of a late Saxon city. The number of plays, too, was prodigious. One company, the Admiral's Men, offered thirty-eight different plays in the 1594–5 season, 'of which twenty-one were new to the repertory, added at more or less fortnightly intervals. Two of the new plays were performed only once, and only eight survived through to the following season.[9] Between 1567 (when the Red Lion opened in Stepney) and the Civil War (when playgoing was curtailed) an estimated fifty million plus visits were made to hear plays.[10]

In late sixteenth-century London, churches and theatres were the main places in which people congregated. Fifty years before, churches had been painted, thronged with images, aglow with candles, the mass a weekly drama enacted by clergy in embroidered vestments, while plays were performed in do-it-yourself surroundings. By the century's end this had been reversed – the playhouses were coloured and actors costumed, while churches were whitewashed and vestments plain. However, whereas churches survive today by the thousand, not one playhouse of that seventy-year climacteric has come down to us, nor even lasted long enough for anyone to describe it in unambiguous detail. Until recently, therefore, no one knew for sure what the first purpose-built playhouses looked like or how they were used – a hiatus all the more frustrating for their seminal place in the history of stagecraft. The finding of the Rose playhouse in February 1989 was thus one of those rare, once-in-a-lifetime events which divide a subject into before and after. For other reasons, it had a similar effect on British archaeology itself.[11]

The Rose stood in Bankside, a neighbourhood of Southwark between London Bridge and Paris Gardens. Tudor Bankside specialized in leisure. Long before the Rose was begun in 1587 the area was famous for its bars, brothels and bears; by the sixteenth century's end there were more playhouses here than in any other part of London. The Rose was abandoned probably between 1603 and 1606, but its sometime presence was never quite forgotten. Visible on near-contemporary maps and panoramas, mentioned in passing references by citizens and visitors, until the 1980s it was known chiefly through the accounts kept by its owner, the impresario Philip Henslowe.[12] Theatre historians had long sifted these papers, which made the archaeological find doubly notable, for the opportunity to interrelate the day-to-day records of an individual's life and work with archaeological remains comes rarely. Excavation began just before Christmas in 1988. The extent of the Rose's survival was a new year's surprise. The superstructure, of course, was gone (long gone – the playhouse was pulled down early in 1606), but despite a succession of later buildings and perforation caused by piling for post-war offices, much of the ground plan were still there.

Even as a muddy shape the Rose retained its power to attract and

38. Bankside, Southwark: detail from panorama of London by Braun and Hogenburg, c.1572, showing arenas for bull- and bear-baiting

rouse. Actors, academics, local people, tourists and the merely curious mustered at the site, the diversity of the new audience recalling that of the old. The excavation itself became a piece of theatre. It was soon clear that the two months which had been allowed for it were arbitrary in relation to what was actually needed. The developers offered an extension. When that, too, turned out to be insufficient, an impassioned public demanded further postponement.

By now, early summer 1989, a philosophical controversy had broken out. In fact, two. One was the appropriation of the Rose as a symbol of values beyond the measure of accountancy. A site which had been touched by figures like Marlowe and possibly Shakespeare stood for things which many felt to be the antithesis of Thatcherism. The other was a collision of archaeological values. In an ideal world, what *should* have happened to the Rose? In an ideal world the nation would have valued the site simply for what it was, and it would not have been earmarked for an office block. But national priorities were not so attuned, and in any case by May 1989 that option was no longer seen as realistic. Many thought that the next best thing would be full scientific

39. Rose playhouse under excavation

investigation. Historians of Elizabethan theatre were at the limit of what they could derive from reworking a static database, and a chance to gain new knowledge about an early playhouse seemed too good to be true. Such knowledge, however, would call for complete and closely recorded excavation – in effect, the slow-motion demolition of everything that was there. Yet in parallel came emotional calls for *preservation* of the remains as a tangible link with figures like Marlowe and Shakespeare. The price of knowledge was destruction, and the price of feeling was ignorance. What was it to be?

The answer, another metaphor, was neither. While the government bought time, English Heritage brokered a revised design to stand the new development on a piled substructure of lesser footprint which would leave the greater part of the remains undisturbed. This meant that excavation need only continue in those places where the foundations would actually pierce the site – the rest could be lagged by sand and left beneath the new building, to be investigated in time ahead under more beneficial conditions, and at someone else's expense. The result was a half-dug theatre entombed in a basement. Hailed as a conservation victory by some and condemned as cryonics by others, the idea of husbanding evidence rather than trying to understand it became a bellwether for the state's approach to archaeology and development generally. One reason why Canterbury Cathedral's nave was left largely undisturbed three years later was the philosophy of the Rose.

The halting of the Rose excavation left potentially knowable things obscure while condemning most of what had been found to provisionality. Even so, some questions were answered. Some scholars had speculated that Henslowe had put his playhouse on the site of a former bear-baiting ring. We now know that he did not. It had also been conjectured that the Rose began not purely as a playhouse but as a multi-purpose gamehouse. Again, it did not. Pictorial evidence for the shapes of playhouses was equivocal – had the Rose been polygonal or circular? The 1587 Rose was polygonal – a roughly ring-shaped figure of fourteen not-quite-equal sides. Thatched or tiled? Thatched. With or without stair-towers? Without. There were other answers like this, not the least interesting of them being an indication of the time-honoured design system which had been used to lay the building out.[13]

Rather as in a quadratic equation, where the solving for one value helps the finding of others, the Rose discoveries assisted comparison with playhouses elsewhere. With an overall diameter of about seventy-two feet, the original Rose turned out to have been smaller than the later Fortune (Henslowe's next enterprise, its dimensions known from his contract with the builder).[14] Sureness about size also enabled the first likely estimate of capacity: with standing room for about 530 in the yard, and depending on the extent of the galleries, a full house for *Tamburlaine* in the 1580s could have been about 1,600. The yard had a slight rake down towards the stage. What kind of stage? The Fortune contract specified a rectangular platform, and a 1596 sketch of the Swan likewise showed a large quadrangular stage thrusting well into the yard, with a pavilion-like tiring-house behind. The Rose was different. Here, the first stage was quite small, thirty-six feet at its widest, with canted sides, no cover and a tiring-house that was absorbed into the main plan. The dramaturgical implications are stirring. No one in the audience

would have been more than forty-five feet from the centre of the stage.
Most would have been closer. In this kind of nearness, an actor playing
Richard III could shriek to the sky at one moment –

> Give me another horse! Bind up my wounds!

– and then whisper to 1,600 people,

> Have mercy, Jesu!

Towards the end of 1591 Henslowe closed the Rose and began to refur-
bish it. His diary for February 1592 records large outlay, which some
scholars had taken to concern repairs. Excavation showed that Henslowe
was not maintaining the building but remodelling it. By changing the
plan, extending the yard (now surfaced with cinders and cracked hazel-
nut shells), giving greater thrust to the stage, introducing a stage-cover
and enlarging the tiring-house, he created what was practically a new
building. One of the first plays to be put on when it reopened was *Titus
Andronicus*, a new work by the up-and-coming actor-writer William
Shakespeare.

Eight years later Henslowe built another playhouse in Islington, 'near
unto the fields' on the far side of the city. He called it the Fortune. It was
his answer to the Globe, which had opened within shouting distance of
the Rose on Bankside in 1599. The Fortune was now his main venture,
so when negotiations to renew the lease of the Rose's site fell through,
the old playhouse was first mothballed, then demolished. By May 1606
the Rose was a 'late playhouse'.

To sum up so far, not only do all the playhouses about which we know
anything differ from each other, but the 1592 Rose is now seen to have
differed from its earlier self, just as Henslowe's Fortune of 1600 departed
from the layout of the 1592 Rose that it superseded, and both differed
from the Globe. In the autumn of 1989, after the crisis at the Rose had
subsided, and again in 1991, exploratory excavations were mounted to
locate the Globe and see if anything of it had survived. Sensationally,
part of Shakespeare's playhouse was found. Not much can yet be said
about it, but it seems to have been larger than the Rose, and embodied
features that the Rose lacked. In its contrasts and transience the Rose
suggests that in place of some stereotyped 'Elizabethan playhouse' we
should think of eleven or twelve different buildings with overlapping
histories, co-evolving at different tempos and in different ways, between
them presenting hundreds of plays.[15]

It was a theatrical age. Some livery companies and the court commissioned indoor theatres, modelled on the banqueting halls of palaces and great houses, where plays could be provided for guests.[16] The prodigy houses visited by the Elizabethan court on summer progresses were often akin to film sets, glorious yet thinly built for the moment. The houses stood amid landscapes adapted to the enactment of open-air horse ballets, disguisings and water-pageants.[17] In such gardens and buildings lay encoded all kinds of allusions. Sir Thomas Tresham's banqueting house at Lyveden bore emblems of traditional religion, just as the heart-shaped pond at the centre of the gardens at Shifnal Manor in Shropshire signalled the owner's Catholic sympathies.*[18] (Curiously, the relationship of the heart to the circulation of blood was just then on the verge of discovery: William Harvey's *De motu cordis et sanguinis in animalibus* ('On the motion of the heart and blood in animals') was published in 1628.)

Towns, too, took pleasure in extravaganzas. London's annual mayor-making was accompanied by elaborate scenic effects and texts commissioned from poets. State funerals, entry pageants and processions were adorned by heraldry, banners and images which expressed ideas about historical identity that ran back through late Saxon rulers into a fictitious cavernful of British kings and eventually to Thebes and Troy.[19] Londoners rejoiced in their legends, believing Westminster to have been founded by a Roman King Lucius and the City to have been Lud's Town, so named after a king of Britain whose grave lay outside Ludgate.[20] The Welsh *Mabinogion* related how the head of Bran, a great mythological figure, had been carried about by his companions for a term of years and then taken to London. Another legend claimed the embalmed body of Cædwallon, a seventh-century king of Gwynedd, to have been encased by a bronze statue above the city's west gate. While drawing heavily from the imagination of Geoffrey of Monmouth, such stories may sometimes have contained faint memories of real encounters with rich graves in former Roman cemeteries outside the city walls.

It was to this half-mythic world of Cymbeline and Lear, looking back to traditions of Wales and Rome as well as England, of Celtic names still reverberant on the coins that turned up in Warwickshire fields and Bankside mud, that Shakespeare turned for a number of his stories. Legendary British history was dominated by Arthur, the ruler of Britain's golden age, whose reputation had waxed in literature and art

* The importance of blood in traditional religion has been discussed above, p. 272.

since the twelfth century. At least in retrospect, the Plantagenets traced themselves to British ancestors. Coincidentally, Sir Thomas Malory's Arthurian cycle *Le Morte d'Arthur* was printed in 1485, the year that Henry Tudor slew Richard III and took the throne. The Welsh Tudors presided over a cosmopolitan court where playmaking emerged from a swirling milieu of inherited stories, the rhetorical dramatic tradition and Renaissance literature. Henry VII named his eldest son Arthur, and under his encouragement the Tudor court was frequented by scholars and artists from across Europe. Among them was Polydore Vergil, an Italian cleric whose *Twenty-Six Books of English History* traced Henry VIII's descent back to the Christianizing Roman emperor Constantine (who had been proclaimed Caesar at York) and his reputedly British mother Helen, via Arthur.

Artos, as we saw in Chapter 7, was possibly the byname of a leader remembered as 'The Bear'. Bears signified a special kind of indefatigable courage – we recall the significance of bearskins, and those calcined fragments of bear paws mingled with cremated human remains in fifth-to-sixth-century Norfolk. Although wild bears had not been seen in Britain since the earliest Middle Ages, the baiting of imported captured animals was popular at all social levels.[21] There had been a royal office of Master of the Bears at least since the days of Richard III,[22] and baitings were sometimes held in the halls at court. The office of 'bearward' is recorded in account books of medieval noblemen.[23] Out in the country bearwards 'wacked' and toured their bears from township to township, holding baitings at accustomed times. *Venatio*, the display and baiting of wild animals, had been a spectator sport in the Roman world. For roistering London prentices, hammer-men and apple-wives, however, the place for baitings was Bankside. From John Alleyn's papers[24] comes a handbill that gives the flavour.

> Tomorrowe bein ae Thursday shal be seen at the Beargardin on the bankside a great Mach plaid by the gamsters of Essex who hath chalenged all comers what soever to plaie v dogges at the single beare for v pounds and also to wearie a bull dead at the stake and for your better content shall have plasant sport with the horse and ape and whiping of the blind bear.
>
> *Vivat Rex*[25]

Lupold von Wedel, a visitor to London in 1584, described a baiting:

> There is a round building three storeys high, in which are kept about

40. *Bear baiting, Luttrell Psalter, f.161r. The last indigenous brown bears indicated by archaeology in Britain date from the 5th–6th century AD – the 'Age of Arthur'. Later zoo-archaeological evidence for bears points to imports, either as pelts or for baiting.*

a hundred large English dogs, with separate wooden kennels for each of them. These dogs were made to fight singly with three bears, the second bear being larger than the first and the third larger than the second. After this a horse was brought in and chased by the dogs, and at last a bull, who defended himself bravely.[26]

The ring was also a place of magic. 'Right over the middle of the place,' wrote von Wedel, 'a rose was fixed, this rose being set on fire by a rocket: suddenly lots of apples and pears fell out of it down upon the people standing below.'[27]

Galleried baiting rings had stood in Bankside at least from the 1540s.[28] They are depicted on sixteenth- and seventeenth-century panoramas, heard of in occasional crises (as when a blind bear broke loose and killed a man), and seen as a pattern for the amphitheatre playhouses a few decades later.[29] A complementary model was the inn-yard enclosed by galleries. Coaching inns had been common venues for plays before the advent of permanent playhouses, and at least two public playhouses, the Boar's Head (1602) and Red Bull (1604), were inn conversions. However, these were later than the custom-built amphitheatres, where factors which shaped the purpose-built playhouse were the need for an effective pay perimeter, accommodation for players, and storage for wardrobe and props.

Images of beset or blinded bears were part of a wave of allusions, phrases and new words which spread into the language from plays in the 1590s and early 1600s. They remind us not only that Banksiders knew their animals but also that plays belonged to a wider genre of public boisterous entertainment that embraced things like fence play, dancing, wrestling, carousing, drama and fireworks. Some buildings actually functioned as multi-purpose gamehouses. The Bel Savage, an inn-yard used for fencing displays and baitings, was also used for plays, while the multi-purpose Hope of 1613–14 was provided with a demountable stage which enabled its use for playing one day and baiting the next. The confederacy of playgoing with whoring and boozing, and a tendency for plays to trigger 'tumults', in turn explain Bankside's Macao-like reputation, and the distribution of playhouses outside the jurisdiction of the City's government.

Eight centuries before Philip Henslowe built his all-in-one play- and gamehouse, the Old English words *pleg* and *gamen* were already a twosome, the one implying exercise, delight and risk-taking, the other fun, athletic contests and the hunting of animals – whence big game, game birds, gamecock. The most strenuous kind of contest was war.

> The game's afoot.
> Follow your spirit, and upon this charge
> Cry 'God for Harry, England and Saint George!'

A kin-word *gamel*, 'to sport', is ancestor to 'gamble'. In 'game', there is an element of risk, of thrill. Pastimes like dancing, baiting and hearing plays were joined in practice as well as underlying sense: all of these things together could be 'a game'. The extent to which this was so becomes clear as we turn to consider two cardinal issues: where plays were played before playhouses, and what was going on outside London.[30]

Globe audiences were familiar with the kind of travelling troupe that turns up at Elsinore during *Hamlet*. Such groups played for hire in private halls, guild halls and the market-places of provincial towns. At Norwich, for instance, the chamberlain's accounts for 1546/7 detail costs of timber for 'making of the scaffold' and drink for the Queen's Players who 'played an interlude at the common Hall' the week after Michaelmas, and again on St Katherine's Day. In Bewdley, Worcestershire, the accounts of St Andrew's Chapel and the bridge-wardens record 'the quenes plaiers in

the church' in 1571–2. Bewdley liked its theatre. The Lord of Leicester's
Players visited in 1573; in 1593 the Lord President and his Players were in
town; in 1598 came the Earl of Pembroke's Players; in 1608 they 'payd for
the beare at my lordes cumming'.[31] Touring players were in demand in
aristocratic households, especially around Christmas. So were minstrels,
who at this date were typically instrumental performers who *played*
their instruments.

There was a distinction between touring companies and the biblical
or mystery plays put on by guilds. Visiting players were profession-
als, whereas plays like the Corpus Christi cycles were mounted by the
community, which put big effort into them and linked the traditional
ritual calendar with civic conviviality. King's Lynn's accounts for 1447/8
give a sociable glimpse of players retiring after their performance in
the market-place to Corpus Christi hall for drink and cooked chicken
with the mayor and town dignitaries. In some towns there were civic
pageants organized by craft guilds. This was so in fifteenth-century
Hereford and Worcester, for instance, and at Worcester there were two
pageant houses.[32]

Another breed of player is represented by Peter Quince and his
friends in *A Midsummer Night's Dream*. 'This green plot shall be our
stage, this hawthorn-brake our tiring-house':[33] the transience of aspir-
ing amateurs who wrote their own material and could rehearse anywhere
makes them easy to underrate, or indeed to disregard archaeologically
on the grounds that they cannot have left any mark. Yet such groups
are central to our quest, and they are fugitive only if we demand some
typical site (like a playhouse) to represent them. Their traces are there,
for us to seek and bring together. To begin, let us look at some written
records.

In 1542, twenty-five years before the building of London's first known
playhouse, Edmund Bonner, Bishop of London, ordered that:

> no parsons, vicars, no curates permit or suffer any manner of common
> plays, games or interludes, to be played, set for, declared, within their
> churches or chapels, where the blessed Sacrament of the altar is, or
> any other sacrament administered, or Divine service said or sung.[34]

In May 1551 John Hooper, Bishop of Gloucester, for whom the Catholic
mass was sorcery, enquired whether his ministers were disturbed during
divine service by 'any noise, brute Cryes, clamours, Playes, Games,
Sports, Dancing or Suchlike'.[35] In 1577 the newly appointed Bishop
of Worcester, John Whitgift, asked whether 'any lords of misrule or

players do dance … any unseemly parts in the church or churchyard; or
whether there are any plays or common drinking kept in the church or
churchyard'.[36]

Forbiddances against dancing, playing and carolling were made
on either side of the Reformation, but intensified during the reign of
Edward VI, were in some respects relaxed under Mary, and reappeared,
now to stay, with Elizabeth. They were aimed at several things which had
become enmeshed. One of them was devotional drama. Churchwardens'
accounts and other sources show that by the later Middle Ages plays
on biblical subjects, the lives of saints and miracles of the Virgin were
commonly performed in parish churches.[37] Another was dancing. The
word 'carol' means a round dance to music provided by the dancers' own
singing. Dancing circles were led by a solo singer (whence 'ring-leader')
and dancing in churchyards went back at least to the twelfth century.[38]
The author of the *History of the Kings of Britain*, finished in the 1130s,
knew Stonehenge as *chorea gigantum*, 'the giants' dance'.[39] The allusion
is not simply to the idea of great stones as petrified giants, but to the
resemblance of the ring and the lintel stones to carolling dancers, the
arms of each upon the shoulders of the next. Is there a clue here to what
Stonehenge was originally for – a place for special dancing at turning
points of the year?

Customs like dancing on the dedication day of a church had long been
of concern to sterner members of the Church, who saw them – rightly
– as remnants of pagan custom, ever poised to topple into libidinous
spontaneity. In the spring of 1308, for instance, the Bishop of London
reprimanded the people of Barking for dancing, wrestling and holding athletic contests in their churchyard, and in the parish and abbey
churches.[40] Where there were contests there was gambling. Enthusiasm
for betting explains the underlying popularity of bear baiting and cock
fighting, just as it accounts for official nervousness towards events that
drew 'idle, licentious, and dissolute persons' together, with associated
risks of disorder or spread of epidemic. Since fear of infection ran with
fear of strangers who might bring it, itinerant bearwards and players
were looked upon with mixed feelings, as figures associated at once with
pleasure and anxiety.

A plethora of customs shadowed the Church calendar but did not officially belong to it. Examples are the upside-down rules of Hocktide (the
second Monday and Tuesday after Easter), when women caught men,
and then men caught women, and demanded ransoms for their release
(whence 'in hock'),[41] or the kind of play organized in fifteenth-century

Bristol by the guild of St Katherine,* where 'play' meant the saint and her followers going from door to door to exact ritual submission and a fee from householders.[42] Such customs blurred into the plays or games which were held at particular times of the year, commonly at Whitsuntide or midsummer. Games have no modern analogy, although their joining of drinking to mumming and morris dancing,† maypoles, bowers of flowers and greenery, the presence of Robin Hood and his followers and the staging of plays (starring figures like Peter Quince, Tom Snout and the tailor Robin Starveling) suggests a mood combining elements of parish fête, agricultural show, beer festival and race meeting. Games were presided over by summer kings and queens who were chosen for the purpose. Robin Hood represented wilderness and all that it stood for in medieval imagination. Games had their own kinds of furniture, which included bowers formed of green branches to shelter the revellers. There was also a special drama, involving a ritual battle between two halves of the year.[43] Presumably this is what is happening at the end of *Love's Labour's Lost* when Don Armado calls members of the cast forward in two groups:

> This side is *Hiems*, Winter; this *Ver*, the Spring; the one maintained by the owl, the other by the cuckoo. *Ver*, begin.

Spring performs 'When daisies pied and violets blue'. Winter replies with its evocation of the Little Ice Age.

> When all aloud the wind doth blow,
> And coughing drowns the parson's saw,
> And birds sit brooding in the snow ...

The contest recollects Persephone and Hades, Persephone's abduction and annual return to the world and bringing of spring.

Summer games drew crowds. The celebrations held over Whitsuntide at Kingston upon Thames early in the sixteenth century attracted around two thousand people.[44] A central purpose of such events was to raise money for the church of the parish in which they were held, so a summoner was sent out to advertise in surrounding towns and villages.

---

* Patron saint of young women and weaving crafts.

† A heavily stylized dance performed in fancy costume representing a particular set of characters, often linked to the Robin Hood legend – typically, Maid Marian, the fool, the friar and piper. A hobby-horse and moriscoes – dancers in a supposed Moorish style – are also often involved.

Kingston's summer lord went on a progress through other parishes. A century later, the Maygames at Longdon in Worcestershire were still attracting 'rude ruffians and drunken companions' who came in from neighbouring townships for 'Morrices, and dancings'.

While games often took place in churchyards, they could also be held at a traditional Game Place. Parish accounts which refer to them only begin to become available in the period when games were being phased out, but as far as one can tell Game Places were customary, tending to keep their use even when the land itself changed hands. They may also have been more common than we think, since Game Places that made use of natural features may have been overlooked in the field. (It will not be a surprise if some of them coincide with the 'productive sites' of the early Middle Ages.) Some Game Places were certainly man-made. The one at Walsham-le-Willows, Suffolk, for instance, was 'an open-air circular theatre with a central stage and an outer bank on which the audience sat'.[45] It sounds a bit like a Neolithic henge.

More can be learned about games and entertainments from attempts to suppress them. Biblical plays and parish entertainments involving hobby-horses, the bearing of lights in processions and summer lords and ladies were being curbed by the end of the reign of Henry VIII, and were diminished in the days of Edward VI when the dissolution of religious guilds put an end to most parish customs and institutions. During the swing back to traditional religion under Mary, churchwardens' accounts sometimes show the refurbishing of costumes, garters of 'Morres belles', drumming and shoes, or the bringing out of costumes and props from storage.[46] Another case is Lincoln, where the city's Minute Books show that when the pageants associated with Corpus Christi were wound up their costumes and props were stored in a disused chapel. During the reign of Mary, the play-gear was retrieved when performances resumed.

In most areas the revival was brief: Elizabeth's bishops reversed it. However, although this was the final break, it was not a clean one. Games tended to be abolished soonest and most completely in areas where senior clergy were keen, and to persist or resurface where control was weak. The incentive to keep games going sprang as much from practicality as from sentiment: churchwardens relied on the income of games and ales for church upkeep. That is to say, parishioners had been accustomed to pay for the upkeep and enhancement of their churches by having fun. Saints, maintenance and conviviality went together. The painted images which stared out in the last chapter were partly funded by the profits of games and plays. The alternative, a parish rate, was unpopular; to enjoy games and the pleasure of drinking with friends was preferable to yet another tax 'that had the potential to exacerbate community relations rather than enhance them'.[47]

Here and there, resistance to the reformers can be sensed in parish records which document the efforts of officialdom to close games down. At Wantage in Berkshire, for instance, Whitsun games were held in 1582/3. The accounts show a pause of nine years. Then the games resume. Officials of the Dean of Windsor warn the churchwardens to look for other ways of raising money. The games stop again. The wardens struggle to make ends meet, until 1597 when once more they chance it.

The diocese of Oxford is rich in such episodes, perhaps because for most of Elizabeth's reign the see was vacant and parishes escaped close supervision. In villages under the Berkshire Downs, places like Aston Tirrold, Longcot and Blewbury, places through which the teenage Osbert Crawford cycled three hundred summers later, there were citations against dancing during service time. Some of them involved the churchwardens themselves, who innocently protested that they had been trying to keep order. In 1584 we hear of a play being performed inside the church of Duns Tew. At Great Marlow an infraction results from travelling players using the church loft. Across at Tewkesbury, the midsummer play was performed until the early 1600s. The play- and morris-gear were made available to surrounding parishes. For the rest of the year they were kept in the church.[48]

In the diocese of Worcester – the diocese in which Shakespeare was born, grew up and married – games, plays, Sunday dancing and boozing continued well into the seventeenth century. In 1609, Archdeacon John Johnson's list of frowned-upon activities included not only dancing and drinkings but also the selling of victuals 'and other merchandise' in church and churchyard.[49] In 1616 Johnson's successor noted fighting, brawling, chiding and gaming in churchyards, and 'dancing the morris upon the Lordes day'. In the same period Worcester's consistory court admonished Richard Chandler for 'playing his fiddle on Low Sunday last', Thomas Dugard 'for playing to dancers' and George Barber for playing his drum 'in service time to draw the youth from the church' at Great Malvern.[50] In 1611, Edward Bartlemewe was fined 'for playing an interlude with divers others at the time of divine service', and Ralph Lyddiat was accused of 'playing in a stage play upon the Sabbath days and upon St Peter's day in time of divine service'. The illegitimate staging of plays in churches was noted at Tenbury and Rock.[51] In December 1617 a parishioner at Martin Hussingtree was reported for causing a puppet play to be performed in the chancel of the parish church.[52] The autobiography of the minister Richard Baxter records that in 1642 enormous painted giants were manipulated by parishioners holding poles as they walked the streets of Kidderminster, surrounded by what he called a 'beggarly drunken rowt in a very tumultulating disposition'. The rowt's ringleaders were supporters of the king, while citizens 'who were accounted religious, were called Roundheads and openly reviled and threatened as the king's enemies'.[53]

By cutting the link between games and God, the Reformation outlawed things which had previously been at the heart of community. Many townships dealt with this by acquiescing in the new norm. But in some townships parishioners divided between those who conformed and went to worship in newly limewashed churches with the Book of Common Prayer and those who stayed outside to bang drums, dance or drink – and by so doing harked back to the old days. In such places, Sunday became a day of contest between old and new ways. The finishing stroke to old ways was given by the Civil War.

The link between churches and games extended to the keeping of things. At Abbots Bromley in Staffordshire the reindeer antlers worn for the annual ten-mile dance around the parish are kept in the church to this day. Since reindeer had been long extinct in Britain, the antlers must have been imported, presumably from Scandinavia or a Baltic country. The extent to which things like head-dresses and special objects were kept in churches is difficult to know, since the items concerned were nearly always sold or destroyed at the Reformation, while as just noted the records that might document them start to become generally available only in the period when the customs were being discontinued. All we can say is that there were ties between storage and church practice. Most obvious is the link we have already seen – a general affection for the parish church, and a view of the parish as a community that included past as well as living members:[54] when there was dancing in a churchyard, the dancers' forebears were with them. It was thus natural for play- and dance-gear to be kept in the church of a particular parish, and loaned or hired to parishioners of surroundings places.[55]

Urban as well as rural playgoers knew about such traditions, which had survived in villages around London like Battersea and Wandsworth at least until the 1570s. It was only a few years since that there had been midsummer fires in the capital's streets. A song in *As You Like It* assumes that a London audience will know customs of the forest, such as the award of a deer's antlers and skin to its hunter.

> What shall he have that kill'd the deer?
> His leather skin and horns to wear.
> Then sing him home.

The song goes on to suggest that, as at Abbots Bromley, deer men will belong to particular families, their roles passing like a thread between generations:

> It was a crest ere thou wast born:
> Thy father's father wore it …[56]

How far back did such customs run? There has been a tendency to view them either as immeasurably ancient or as fads which originated towards the end of the Middle Ages.[57] The morris dance, for instance, is not heard of until the 1450s, whereafter its near-simultaneous appearance in different parts of Europe has caused historians to think that it spread as a court fashion. Proponents of a late chronology for other customs see them as manifestations of a growing taste for physical and ceremonial display among groupings with the wealth to indulge them.[58] We are also warned against the influence of romantics whose obsessions with pagan origins have coloured subsequent discussion. 'Flushing out the constructed nature of institutions' that have been claimed as ancient has 'become a favourite sport of historians'.[59]

All of which is fair. Yet we must also beware the extent to which the apparent popularity and elaboration of games after 1450 may reflect the increasing survival of sources which describe them. We have seen incidental references to games and dances much earlier than this. The fact that such episodes cannot be classified as 'morris' or 'games' in a sixteenth-century sense is arguably less interesting than the volume of prohibitionist warnings about churchyard dancing, and dressing up as animals, which in parts of Europe go back at least to the fifth century.

One custom which on accepted definitions does fall into the family of morris is the dance of the Abbots Bromley deer men described above. A radiocarbon date from one of the six antler sets centres in the eleventh century.[60] If all the sets are of the same age then we have here the gear for a customary dance, performed at least since the end of the Anglo-Saxon age, which became, if it was not always, a morris dance. Later records link the horn dance with the feast of the martyr Bartholomew. Whether by coincidence or connection, the cult of St Bartholomew became prominent in England early in the eleventh century when Queen Ælfgifu Emma,* an avid relic collector, brought Bartholomew's arm to Canterbury. Bartholomew was said to have been flayed alive before being beheaded, and was thus a patron saint of those who work with animal skins. As for the recent construction of institutions, where have we met deer head-dresses before? At Star Carr, in the Vale of Pickering – where the red deer antler head-dresses are about 9,500 years old.

Another case: riots, saints, games and miracles were things that went together, and when John Leland visited Droitwich in the sixteenth century he was told about Bishop Richard de la Wich who had miraculously caused a brine spring to revive in time of drought. In memory of this event, the Wich-men were accustomed to 'hang about' the spring on the anniversary of the miracle, and there have 'drinking games and revels'. The Wich-men had long memories: Richard de la Wich died in 1253.[61]

The date of the Abbots Bromley antler or the Droitwich miracle does not of course prove that the mimetic customs which appear so popular in the sixteenth century all went back for hundreds of years. Many of them may indeed have been recent introductions. What it does show is that such customs *could* go back so far, and that the genre in which they stood actually did do so. It further reminds us that tradition does not mean indefinite repetition or sameness. Just as traditional religion gained and lost devotional enthusiasms as time passed, so did folk customs acquire new features and shed old ones. Hence, while features of the 'Moresdaunce' may have been newly fashionable in the mid-fifteenth century, it is the evolving *idea* of such dancing that is the thread to follow.

The issue of date, and with it the debate about whether particular customs are traceable to ancient pagan or recent Christian sources, may thus have been oversimplified. The point is that they were both. The early Church's compromise with paganism was never a secret. Early in the seventh century Pope Gregory I wrote to Mellitus, a member of the mission he had recently sent to the Anglo-Saxons. In the letter Gregory advised Mellitus not to confront the Archbishop of Canterbury, to convert pagan shrines to churches and to assimilate popular customs.

---

* Daughter of Richard, Count of Normandy, from 1002 wife of Æthelred (King of England 979–1016), afterwards married to Cnut (King of England 1016–35), latterly queen mother.

So on the day of the dedication or the festivals of the holy martyrs, whose relics are deposited there, let them make themselves huts from the branches of trees around the churches which have been converted out of shrines, and let them celebrate the solemnity with religious feasts … Thus while some outward rejoicings are preserved, they will be able more easily to share in inward rejoicings.[62]

The huts sound like the bowers in which revellers sheltered during Whitsun games.

Puritans attacked customary activity not simply because they saw it as superstitious, but because it continued the calendar of traditional belief. Games stood for the cult of saints (whence 'holiday') and the unevenness of time. Games were even accused of reflecting the structure of the Church itself, for instance in the idea that a dance could be an epitome of a Catholic ceremony. And beyond these, there is a correlation between places renowned for their games at the time of the Reformation and mother parishes which had taken shape eight centuries before.

We saw in earlier chapters that by the ninth century some parts of southern Britain were dotted with churches which had been founded by kings and magnates during the preceding two hundred years. Archaeology reveals many of them to have been substantially built, often in ample enclosures which contained additional chapels and ancillary and economic buildings. It was from such 'old minsters' (as tenth-century clerks knew them) that pastoral care was exercised, until their responsibilities for Christian initiation and burial were decentralized to the local, manorial or community churches which appeared on the scene in large numbers during the tenth and eleventh centuries.[63]

Old minsters also housed district saints, typically aristocrats or royalty of the seventh and eighth centuries. Evidence for such cults survives especially well in the south midlands, where they have been correspondingly well studied. Dorchester housed Birinus. Beornwald lay at Bampton.[64] Charlbury fostered the cult of Diuma. Eadburh was at Bicester, Frideswide at Oxford, Osyth at Aylesbury. 'Recent research has emphasised the tenuous, sometimes accidental nature of the surviving evidence for local cults: it is quite possible that many more have been forgotten.'[65] It may even be that every old minster had a saint:[66] an idea which archaeology encourages to the extent that there are many more surviving fragments of Anglo-Saxon shrines than we have known saints to occupy them or written records to explain. To give examples, at Hovingham in North Yorkshire, Wirksworth in Derbyshire and South Kyme in Lincolnshire there are pieces of shrines that indicate former cults revolving around lost saints. The spacious, near-complete Anglo-Saxon churches at Brixworth in Northamptonshire and Wing in Buckinghamshire were provided with elaborate circulatory crypts for the display of relics to visitors, yet in neither case do we know who the saint was. While it is possible that these costly structures were built to hold secondary relics, it is simpler to see them as the lodgings of sub-regional saints whose identities were later forgotten, transposed or downplayed outside their immediate localities to avoid attracting papal attention.

This likelihood increases when we approach the same places through sixteenth- and early seventeenth-century sources. Wing and South Kyme were leading centres of Whitsun games, holding out beyond 1600 for their continuance with the support of local Catholic gentry families who felt themselves to be guarding powerful traditions. The Dormer family at Wing were neighbours of Sir Henry Lee, courtier, poet, warrior, holder of a number of Crown preferments, and another whose family shows 'considerable evidence for Catholic sentiment'. Lee owned several residences in Oxfordshire and Buckinghamshire; the formal gardens and designed landscape around his house at Quarrendon may show Catholic allusions akin to those on recusant estates elsewhere.[67] To continue the tour: Bampton and Charlbury were centres of games and morris dancing. A list of other south midland places with active morris traditions by the sixteenth century reads like a roll call of Anglo-Saxon minsters – Adderbury, Thatcham, Eynsham, Shipton under Wychwood, St Helen's in Abingdon.[68] Kingston upon Thames, site of possibly the greatest Whitsun games in the Thames valley, situated at the river's tidal limit, had been a scene of coronations.

Former mother churches sometimes retained an honorary identity late into the Middle Ages, typically through token payments from churches which had been built within their ancient parishes, or gestures like the token surrender of the keys of daughter churches on patronal days, or the attendance of their clergy at the mother church for particular feasts. Other things now drop into place. For instance, the keeping of play- and dance-gear by ex-minsters, and the loan or hire of such gear to surrounding communities, mirrors the ancient relationship between the church of a mother parish and its dependencies. Fairs and mother churches went together because old minsters attracted people on special days – and when people come together, they buy, sell and drink.[69]

The curvilinear churchyards of some old minsters are reminiscent of the Game Places considered earlier in the chapter. Some of them were larger than they now appear, as archaeology attests at Aylesbury where graves dating from the eighth century and later run out under the modern town. Such size may reflect the function of minster cemeteries not only as sub-regional gatherings of the dead, but also as places for convening the living on special days. At any rate, the days for dances, plays, fairs and games read across into the calendar of the Church. Just as the ecclesiastical sequence of principal feasts ran from Christmas at midwinter through to the Nativity of St John the Baptist at midsummer, so did the year of folk customs divide into ritual and non-ritual halves which are battling it out at the end of *Love's Labour's Lost*.[70]

More speculatively, there may be links between church towers and Rogationtide customs like dancing along the boundaries of townships and open fields. We have seen how between the later ninth and twelfth centuries parts of England were reorganized into open fields worked from communal settlements. Such modern landscapes called for new customs and dances to define them. As their communities took shape they also needed places in which to store things which belonged to the community – in later centuries these included parish records, and the props and gear which went with plays and dancing. In the later cases about which we know the keeping place was the church tower, which was typically added at the west end of the building. Enough churches have now been archaeologically excavated for us to be sure that the fashion for building such towers began around 1000 – the time when manorial churches were breaking loose from the monopoly of minsters, creating centralities of their own. A west tower was the part of the church furthest from the chancel, the domain of the priest balanced by the domain of the people. It was a place which parishioners felt to be theirs. Certainly, in later centuries it was they who paid for it: when towers were added or rebuilt, it was chiefly with money from their bequests and funds raised in ways for which morris- and play-gear were accessories. Such towers came to be called belfry towers, and a strong case has recently been made to explain at least some of them as being originally built to house a particular stage in the office of the dead.[71] In late eleventh-century Lincolnshire, and probably also in Yorkshire, it was in the unlit lower stage of such towers that the dead parishioner rested overnight before the funeral, when the bells above in the highest point of the tower – the domain of St Michael – were meant to catch the ear of God. The going forth of a soul was another kind of communal event, reflected also in the food and drink that would be consumed after the funeral, and another kind of drama. In parts of eastern England after the Norman Conquest, this is what such towers seem to have been 'about'. It was only by assonance and 'common sense' that the word 'belfry' came to be associated with bells. Belfry's root-words seem to have meant something like 'safe place' or 'high protected place'.

The main arguments of this chapter have been three. First, that religion and recreation, the spiritual and the carnal, life and death, things which nowadays are normally considered separately or as opposites, were until the Reformation aspects of each other. In old religion, neither dancing on a grave nor drinking beside it was profane. The fact that religion and games are now seen as antithetical is a measure of the Puritans' success in destroying that synthesis. If the synthesis is remembered there are no contradictions between sacred and profane in the fantastic carvings which adorned some church walls.

Second, the Church's year, its cults and ceremonies, was paralleled by customs and images in the surroundings in which churches stood. By connecting types of evidence which are usually considered apart, something of that mirroring can be reinstated. What it suggests is that Pope Gregory I's advice about assimilating pagan customs and sites can be read literally, and that in following centuries pastoral care, customary rituals and landscape evolved together. Perhaps this is why English-speakers know Christianity's greatest festival – held on days decided by the movements of the moon – by a pagan name, Eostre.

Third, games and traditional religion formed a nursery for plays and players like Rob Starveling, who plays Moonshine before the Athenian court.[72] Traditional religion at the end of the Middle Ages displayed a 'remarkable degree of religious and imaginative homogeneity across the social spectrum, a shared repertoire of symbols, prayers, and beliefs which crossed and bridged even the gulf between the literate and the illiterate'[73] – words which could equally be applied to playgoing during the 1590s and early 1600s, when in reply to the question 'Who might go to hear a play?' the answer seems to be, 'Almost anyone.'[74]

The fall of Catholicism created silences which drama filled. Plays and poetry, like the words of the traditional liturgy, were meant to be heard, not read. Some of playmaking's roots grew from a tilth of the old religion. Playhouses supplanted Game Places. Churches were now transient, like human lives. 'I do love these ancient ruins,' says Antonio in Webster's *The Duchess of Malfi*:

We never tread upon them, but we set
Our foot upon some reverent history,
And, questionless, here in this open court,
Which now lies naked to the injuries
Of stormy weather, some men lie interr'd
Lov'd the church so well, and gave so largely to't,
They thought it should have canopi'd their bones
Till doomsday. But all things have their end;
Churches and cities, which have diseases like to men
Must have like death that we have.[75]

In place of Catholicism's uneven time, when some days were better than others, were the distorted times of dramatic storytelling – the kind of times met in *The Winter's Tale* where years are skipped in an instant, or the 'small time' into which epic events are condensed in *Henry V*.[76] Painted actors followed painted images. Elizabethan drama was the vibrant unreality beyond the paint, and thick with memory of what Reformation had stifled. Peter Quince and his friends stepped from one world to the other. You, that way; we, this way.[77] This was the ground on which Shakespeare stood, and why in 1989 the finding of the Rose struck such a shattering chord.

PART FOUR
VOICES FROM THE GROUND

41. (Previous page) *Poster by Frank Newbould, 1942*

11

FIELDS AFTER BATTLE

Now entertain conjecture of a time
When creeping murmur and the poring dark
Fills the wide vessel of the universe.
From camp to camp, through the foul womb of night,
The hum of either army stilly sounds,
That the fix'd sentinels almost receive
The secret whispers of each other's watch;
Fire answers fire, and through their paly flames
Each battle sees the other's umber'd face;
Steed threatens steed, in high and boastful neighs
Piercing the night's dull ear; and from the tents
The armourers; accomplishing the knights,
With busy hammers closing rivets up,
Give dreadful note of preparation.

William Shakespeare, *Henry V*,
c.1599 Act IV, Prologue

A field
After battle utters its own sound
Which is like nothing on earth, but is earth.

Geoffrey Hill, 'Funeral Music', *King Log*, 1968

On the morning of 25 June 1876, a 250-strong detachment of the United States 7th Cavalry perished to a man under Indian fire beside the Little Bighorn River in Montana. Some have seen their deaths as noble, others as a useless slaughter reflecting poorly on their commander, General George Armstrong Custer. An official inquiry was inconclusive. In the 1980s, archaeology testified. Battles leave bits, and survey with metal detectors across the entire battlefield, systematically plotting and identifying every scrap, showed the extent of the engagement. Each spent cartridge case was matched to the weapon whence it came, and by extension to the position of the individual who fired it. Successive plots enabled the movements of the troopers to be traced. The result suggested that there had been no valiant knot of troopers being circled ever closer by Sioux and Cheyenne horsemen. In the last minutes, Custer's unit had become a fragmented straggle.[1]

42. Musket accoutrements depicted in seventeenth-century memorial window, church of St Chad, Farndon, Cheshire. Powder boxes dangle from the bandolier (centre). A priming flask hangs from the centre of the bandolier by a longer cord; next to it is a small round bullet bag, with an oil bottle just to the right. A hank of match is looped around the bandolier on the left side. On the right is a scourer for cleaning the barrel; at bottom right is a cover to shield match for use at night or in wet weather.

Nothing like this fine-grained fieldwork had then been seen in Britain. This might seem odd, for Britain has been a much fought-over place. Actions like Hastings or Bannockburn, Maldon or Culloden, are remembered the world over – and Britain's parliamentary democracy emerged from a civil war. Strangely, perhaps the only British battle which until then had been studied with the kind of close precision used at the Little Bighorn was an assault on a hilltop enclosure which took place over four thousand years ago. This was at Crickley Hill, on the edge of the Cotswolds, overlooking the Vale of Severn, where excavation of the enclosure had chanced upon its traces. From the plotting of more than a thousand arrow-heads recovered during excavation,

Crickley was found to have undergone a co-ordinated onslaught. But who was fighting whom, whether their action stood alone or was part of some long-running prehistoric war, we do not know.[2]

In 1980s Britain there were several reasons for unresponsiveness to the battlefield archaeology emerging across the Atlantic. One was that in most minds battlefields were still spaces where things had happened in the past, a kind of historically tinged greenbelt rather than ground with archaeological potential. Another was the confidence with which military historians had dealt with historic battles, often in such detail as to suggest that they had taken part in them. 'Boudicca then moved her forces to this hill, and looked back at the Roman legion encamped on the far side of the valley ...' With that kind of knowledge, who needed archaeology? The same applied to battlefield sites. Those crossed swords on Ordnance Survey maps surely left no room for doubt as to where the battles had been fought. A third factor was continuing antipathy towards metal detecting. This was significant because battle archaeology consists very largely of scatters of metal objects – things like bullets, the tops of priming flasks, arrowheads, buckles, pieces of horse harness – and the only practical way to pinpoint them is to use a metal detector. Since few archaeologists in the 1980s were either using these machines themselves or co-operating with those who did, scope for progress was small. To many, the three factors together meant that there was no need for battlefield archaeology because there was little new to learn. And because nothing was being learned there was no way to discover what battlefield archaeology could teach.

Archaeologists were nonetheless aware that some metal-detector users were active on battlefields and that they were finding things. Here lay another set of problems. Individual finds do not reveal much. To be useful, each find must be identified and mapped, the resultant pattern assessed and its potential exploited. This is big work. It can take years. Hence, when people unknown to each other metal-detect on a battle-field no composite distribution plan of what they find can be created. Further, their removals will deplete the evidence that is left and so skew the results of any subsequent archaeological study. Around five thousand bullets were fired in the first volley of the Battle of Naseby (1645). If a representative sample of them is recovered and plotted, the result is new knowledge about the battle's opening minutes. If the same musket balls go on to a dozen different mantelpieces, the result is dispersed souvenirs.

Naseby was one of the battlefields where detectorists were at work.

The site is in Northamptonshire, where the then county archaeologist was a man called Glenn Foard. Foard's interests included landscape history and aerial reconnaissance. He was also an authority on the Civil War and early in the 1990s became aware of the detectorists' activity. They met, and the detectorists agreed to make available information they had recovered. They drew a map of their finds, and Foard then worked with them to try to define the areas they had examined and to clarify detail. Although the metal detecting had been unsystematic the picture which emerged was interesting: the area across which fighting had taken place turned out to be much larger than historians had previously supposed. The action seemed to have been a series of encounters in different places. It had begun where tradition and contemporary sources said it did, on the level ground of a hilltop about a mile outside the village. However, analysis showed that the fighting moved on, that the armies had regrouped, and that there had been a denouement of unsuspected scale and significance several miles from where battle had first been joined.[3]

Foard's experience of Naseby raised methodological questions. Analysis of a battle, he realized, first of all called for a backdrop against which to map the archaeology. In practice this meant reconstructing the terrain across which the action had been fought. Hedges, woodland, ditches, marshes, rivers, heath, slope – all set limits upon where cavalry could or could not go, provided cover or offered protection to flanks. Understanding of contemporary landscape was further important because eyewitnesses often referred to its features, and knowing where they were would help to trace different stages of the action. Beyond this, the land-use history of the battlefield will have introduced biases in what survives or what is likely to be found or missed. Lead ball, for instance, is less easily detected under permanent pasture than from ploughsoil. Since land-use has nearly always changed since a battle was fought, its reconstruction is a considerable project.[4]

Next, documents. The Great Civil War is rich in contemporary sources. Letters, diaries and reports are especially valuable if they were written when the experience was fresh, but must be cross-checked: one person's view of an action involving more than twenty thousand people spread across a large area is inevitably selective. Financial accounts and inventories, while more impersonal, may throw light on numbers taking part or strength in weaponry. Knowledge of what weapons could do or how they would have been used is important, as too is familiarity with manuals like Cruso's *Military Instructions for the Cavallrie* or Elton's

Compleat Body of the Art Military, published in 1632 and 1650 respectively, which recommended dimensions for regimental formations and the spacing for men and horses. Plans or engravings prepared with the aid of 'headquarters plans' are all invaluable, yet need to be used critically: were they drawn to scale? Are they copies? Or copies of copies? Are perspectives accurate?

By comparing and conflating information from different sources, Foard reasoned, a scheme for the battle's unfolding can be constructed, which archaeology can then test. Testing is itself conditioned by influences. Finds of bullets, for instance, do not reflect the totality of the battle, only the kinds of situation in which bullets were deposited – typically during distribution, loading or in flight. The numbers that were accidentally dropped were small in comparison with those which were fired, which are usually found where they came to rest after passing beyond their targets, unless they impacted short, for instance because of rising ground. Survey will not recover all that was lost or fired. The variables which govern what survives are still not fully understood, but alongside subsequent land-use and modern souvenir hunting we must also reckon the effects of clearance and scavenging by locals after a battle. While this could have had only a marginal effect on the distribution of shot, it could have influenced other patterns – arrows, for instance, which were reusable if recovered intact. What is retrieved will also be affected by the skills of detectorists, the extent to which other detectorists have worked the area – even the weather when fieldwork takes place. Musket shot is recovered more often than pistol or carbine rounds, in part because the latter were smaller and hence harder to find, but also because it was the muskets which generally laid down a higher proportion of fire. Since muskets were used by infantry while pistols were cavalry weapons, infantry formations are more evident in the archaeological record. However, the matching of shot to a specific type of weapon is not always hard and fast. While written records and the weapons themselves testify to a fair degree of standardization in bore by the mid-seventeenth century, analysis of large numbers of archaeologically recovered munitions shows that bullets are a lot like other artefacts – normal distributions come into play.

Bullet scatters reflect an action's cast and speed. The discharge of five thousand muskets in a single salvo may leave a concentrated pattern, whereas firing spread over minutes might be more dispersed. However, not all troops used firearms, and not all fighting led to the fall of shot. Formations of pikemen (in the 1640s, ideally these would make up about one-third of an infantry regiment) will leave few tokens in the ground beyond the occasional buckle or strap end. In theory such formations might show as gaps between the bodies of musketeers which flanked them, but this would require survey at a level of detail which has yet to be seen in Britain. Mounted troops typically carried a pair of pistols, sometimes a carbine (a firearm intermediate between pistol and musket). In either case the weapons would be used sparingly, usually just before the two bodies met, when if the horse were in close formation only the front ranks would be able to fire. Some cavalry commanders preferred to hold their fire until they were among their opponents, but once at close quarters, cavalry actions were fought mainly with the sword. 'Hence the quantity of pistol and carbine bullets compared to musket shot should be far less than the relative proportions of horse to foot on the field. Hand to hand fighting leaves little shot other than that which was dropped.'[5]

Such are considerations to weigh. Then we must ask if a given scatter is the result of one episode of fighting, or the superimposition of several clashes at different times – as during a siege.

> In contrast to battles, which were short and where the action often moved decisively across the landscape, sieges frequently took place over many weeks or months and some garrisons were besieged on several separate occasions. Except for brief sieges … there will probably be a complex superimposition of patterns of shot and hence the problems of interpretation are likely to be very different … from those encountered on battlefields.[6]

Sieges can leave evocative finds. During the investigation of 119 High Street in Oxford in 1999 a printed passport, signed by the Parliamentary commander Sir Thomas Fairfax, permitting a Royalist soldier to leave the city after the siege of 1645, was found tucked behind a chimney.[7] Excavators at Pontefract Castle discovered a listening shaft – a deep pit with a bulbous space at its base in which a defender would have been stationed to listen for the tap and thud of enemy miners as they hacked through the rock to undermine the defences and blow them up. In this space were fragments of clay pipe – the cigarette butts of the 1640s.[8] Occasionally it is possible to separate out material from an overall distribution to show fine detail deriving from the events of a particular episode. At Hayes Barton, near Exeter, evidence for the direction of an attack supports its identification with an assault to drive Royalists from a 'very strong house' which they were using as an advanced position beyond the main defences.[9] At Grafton Regis, with its Tudor house, hedged closes and deer park, Sir John Digby and other Royalists manned makeshift fortifications during Advent 1643.

Eager to improve on the casual and improvised methods that had been used at Naseby, Foard enlisted the help of a team led by an archaeologically minded metal-detector user called Bob Kings. With Kings's help, Foard designed a survey strategy for Grafton Regis in which Kings did the detecting while Foard concentrated on digital mapping, written sources and reconstruction of terrain. In hindsight, Foard considered the survey design to have been too complex, so yielding results that were slow to acquire and difficult to use. Distributions of shot to either side of a road on the western side of the village did seem to reveal a particular hedge which was initially held by the defenders but then abandoned when they were driven back.[10] Other records combined with this figuration give us another of those moments when an episode is lit up for a few minutes. We can visualize Digby's men sheltering behind the hedge in the mud and rain of atrocious December weather. Then the picture dissolves, and we are back to the impersonality of the general account, which ends with Digby's surrender on Christmas Eve and the burning of the house.

Foard was now seized by battlefield archaeology. Determined to develop its method and to overcome the difficulties encountered at Grafton Regis, in 2003 he began a survey of Edgehill (1642).

> I took the lesson of the Little Bighorn survey – using transects – but applied my fieldwalking experience to this and developed the systematic method we now use, including GPS* for tracking and find locations. We chose 10m survey as the intensity through a calculation of what was achievable and what I thought might work. We tested it in the field for a few months and decided it was OK. But we decided that re-survey would be needed and played around in 2005 with the options if I recall correctly and then implemented 2.5m transects for intensive survey in 2006. The measured laying out of transects with poles and tapes etc came in January 2005 as we refined the method (originally it had been paced and this proved very inaccurate).[11]

There are two growing preoccupations – with realism, and with precision. The ten-metre transects are not to study the detail of the battle

---

* Global Positioning System – a hand-held receiver that takes navigational bearings from satellites to locate the carrier to within a few square yards (or less).

but to recover a sample of material sufficient to define its extent. With that done, the transect interval is narrowed, the focus is tightened and a fuller range of material recovered. The use of a portable GPS by each detectorist meant that each find could be rapidly located, the position data being digitally transferred to an overall database at the end of each day. It also meant that the survey path traced by each detectorist could be reconstructed. After four years of work recording thousands of artefacts, the result was the first archaeological record for a large English battle to modern standards.

Foard embarked on a doctoral thesis to examine evidence provided by the bullets themselves. By a mixture of observation and experiment – live firing and the recovery of the munitions to see what had happened to them – he learned to tell a bullet that had been fired from one that had not, whether it had hit something, and what had happened to it in the ground. Edgehill also brought another development.

> [The] survey started on the 1st August 2004 and by 8th August I was trying my hand at detecting. From the 10th October I was a regular member of the detecting team. Only from that point onwards did I really start to understand battlefield survey – unless one detects … then one cannot fully understand the nature of the resource or the methods of survey and their limitations. I genuinely believe all battlefield archaeologists need to master the practical detecting if they are to do their job effectively.[12]

At first sight this does not seem controversial. Yet for reasons discussed in Chapter 2, following the hostility between archaeologists and treasure hunters most British archaeologists still declined to handle metal detectors themselves. If such machines were needed, then detectorists could be enlisted to use them. One effect of this was that very few archaeologists discovered the subtleties of detecting for themselves, and hence what the limitations or possibilities of a given survey might be. An analogy lies in music: while it is perfectly feasible for a non-piano-playing composer to write a good piano concerto, the really idiomatic concertos tend to be written by composers who know the instrument as performers. The same applies to metal detecting. The machines work variably under different conditions, and different operators working over the same ground may produce different results. In looking for significance in a pattern of musket balls or pieces of case shot, Foard realized, one needed to know whether the pattern was representative of the action, or a phantom created by the variables of modern retrieval.

On some battlefields, detectorists had taken the lead themselves. One of them was Simon Richardson, who from 1980 had been detecting systematically across the field of Towton. In 1996 interest was stepped up by the chance discovery near by of a pit containing the remains of forty men. The grave dated from the 1460, and some of those in it had perished in brutal ways.[13] In due course Richardson was joined by archaeologists, and an integrated survey project has ensued.[14]

Towton has a grim reputation. Fought on Palm Sunday 1461 amid blustery snow showers, if later sources are to be believed its casualties were on a colossal scale, and it was the largest and longest battle of the Wars of the Roses. While the first contention is probably an exaggeration, and the second an oversimplification,[15] few medieval battle sites are so accessible to modern imagination. Standing amid the open undulating farmland between the villages of Towton and Saxton, looking east across the Vale of York it is not difficult to imagine the sunny gleams that lit up distant York Minster between squalls. Looking west from the bluff above the Cock Beck one can refeel the desperation of Lancastrian soldiers who struggled to cross its floodwaters after their ranks had collapsed. Richardson's detecting along the bluff has found a poignant trail of copper-alloy objects – badges, heraldic details, good-luck charms, scraps of horse gear – which may signify the Lancastrian fall-back.[16]

Towton is further remembered above all for its arrow-storms, and for the tradition that advantage lay with the Yorkists because their archers were firing downwind. The Yorkists thus enjoyed extra range, whereas Lancastrian salvoes fell short.

Here we meet a key issue, namely that objects deposited during battles in some periods survive for longer than those laid down in others. Lead, for instance, resists decay, and bullets accordingly survive well, their evidence being all the better for the very large numbers in which they were fired. However, as we look back from gunpowder weapons in the seventeenth century to hand-held weapons like bows in the fourteenth and fifteenth, the predominant finds turn from lead (which lasts) to iron points and blades (which rust). In result, the signal from medieval battles may have faded, or be fading. Some hundreds of ferrous arrowheads have been recovered from Towton, but aside from a few at Tewkesbury no other survey of a fifteenth-century battlefield has yet produced them. Moreover, those from Towton were found not spread across the site but in a cluster. To the archaeological team this appeared to indicate not the arrow-storm itself but some special circumstance of deposition or preservation.[17]

Foard took increasing interest in actions where bows and firearms had been used side by side. If lead survived where iron usually did not, he reasoned, then the patterns left by lead munitions might provide clues to the character and size of late medieval formations. By working backwards from the now well-understood patterns created by gunpowder weapons, might it be possible to find a route into the as yet unknown archaeology of medieval conflict? It was with this question in mind that in 2005 he embarked upon a further project – a search for the Battle of Bosworth.

> Give me another horse! Bind up my wounds!
> Have mercy, Jesu!

Despite Bosworth's prominence in English cultural memory, knowledge of its actual place had been forgotten. This was partly because in the immediate aftermath it had no steady name (early references variously called it Brown Heath, Redemore, Bosworth Heath), and the 'Bosworth' from nearby Market Bosworth was simply a handy way in which to denote the general area. Early map-makers like Saxton and Speed had included the battle in their atlases, but the scale of their maps was quite small, and without knowledge of the exact site successive map-engravers nudged the typography back and forth for aesthetic reasons, until by the later eighteenth century it had become identified with Ambion Hill in Leicestershire.[18] Legends about Ambion Hill duly arose – a classic case of 'history' being conjured up to give warrant to supposition, complete with a King Richard's Well (first recorded in 1788) from which – according to the plaque accompanying a nearby cairn erected in 1813 – Richard drank during the battle. This was good enough for the Ordnance Survey, which recorded the well as an antiquity, and for Leicestershire County Council, which in 1974 bought Ambion Farm and later renamed it as the Bosworth Battlefield Heritage Centre.

In 1985 the historian Colin Richmond wrote an article in *History Today* which pointed out that the earliest accounts of the battle – such as they were – did not correspond with Ambion Hill.[19] While they all pointed to the action as having taken place in the vicinity of the townships of Shenton, Sutton, Dadlington and Stoke,[20] the early sixteenth-century historian Polydore Vergil had written of Henry's force using a marsh as protection for a flank. A hilltop is an unusual place for a marsh. There were other discrepancies.

Interest in Richard III is global, his reputation contested. For some he remains the 'black legend' of Shakespeare's portrayal, for others a king who in his own lifetime was as well regarded as many medieval monarchs, and more than some.[21] But few are neutral and new theories accordingly came thick and fast. One relocated the action to the western slopes of Ambion Hill.[22] Another argued that it took place close to Atherstone, nearly four miles away.[23] In 1990, re-reading of the sources and study of local field and place names led Peter Foss to propose a site somewhere along Fen Lane, successor to the Roman road that runs north-eastward past Ambion Hill towards Leicester, whence Richard had marched to confront Henry Tudor.[24] In 2005 Leicestershire County Council commissioned the Battlefields Trust to settle the matter through an interdisciplinary study to be undertaken over three seasons.

By now Foard had refined the methodological steps. He knew what to do. First, use contemporary written records to narrow down the locality in which the battle took place. Next, use historical maps, air photographs, fieldwork, environmental science, place-name analysis and documents to reconstruct the landscape as it was at the time when the battle was fought. Third, with knowledge of military practice of the time and inherent military probability, populate the reconstructed landscape with hypothetical forces and positions. Fourth, go out into the landscape with an archaeological metal-detecting team, lay out the initial transects and test the hypothesis. If battle archaeology is found, narrow the transects and intensify the search. With a team of experts in different fields, this is what he did.

Three years later and with £154,000 from the Heritage Lottery Fund nearly spent, Foard was a worried man. In a tour de force of historical reconstruction, the fifteenth-century landscape of five townships had been digitally mapped. Pasture, open fields, furlongs and meadow had been located down to the last ditch and strip. 'Find the marsh', said Foard, 'and one had probably located the battlefield.'[25] He and his colleagues had accordingly checked for former wetlands in areas where they could have lain. Soils mapping identified those soils which had developed in waterlogged conditions, and they tested for the survival of peat by augering at regular intervals. Areas of ancient wetland were duly located, and in one place there were traces of a substantial former marsh in an area promisingly known as Fen Meadow that corresponded with Foss's argument. However, when samples of peat were sent for radiocarbon dating the results showed that the marsh had gone centuries before the Wars of the Roses.

Metal detecting is time-consuming – thousands of man-hours were spent in the search for Bosworth. Foss's argument seemed so persuasive that for three seasons the team concentrated on the area he had proposed on Fen Lane. However, this was still large, and the ten-metre intervals between the sampling transects meant that less than 20 per cent of the surface was being scanned. Sampling of other potential areas had produced a few potentially battle-related finds, but in no convincing concentration. Foard agonized: if they worked more intensively or started to look for ferrous objects the survey would slow down, and they were running out of time.

Meanwhile, a small peat deposit had been identified about a thousand yards further west in an area called Fen Hole. It was so small that the augering survey had missed it – a further and salutary reminder that if the sampling intervals were too wide, they might be within the battlefield yet not recognize it. The project was granted a six-month extension:

> with a medieval marsh in Fen Meadow disproved and that in Fen Hole confirmed, we shifted the focus of survey. In the final week, as we started to close the last gap between previously surveyed areas on the western periphery, we recovered a single 30 mm lead ball. Such larger lead munitions have such a specialised function that we knew immediately that we had found the main action.[26]

The discovery of the area of action meant that survey could now switch to narrower transects, so increasing coverage from less than 20 to close to 80 per cent. More lead munitions were recovered, together with a scatter of related material. One of these other items was a silver-gilt boar.

The boar was the personal device of Richard III. Base-metal boar badges were widely distributed among his supporters; those in silver-gilt were worn by those of knightly status or above in his own retinue. It was with a small group of such close companions that Richard rode in a do-or-die attempt to reach and kill Henry Tudor, and so halt the battle and end the rebellion. They came close, but were held, then driven back. Richard's horse became mired. Unable to move away, he was dragged from his saddle and done to death. The silver-gilt boar was found within a hundred yards of Fen Hole. It is difficult not to believe that the badge was worn by one of those who were with him, and that it takes us close to where he died. And if the boar had been found and taken home by a treasure hunter, we would never have known.

Bosworth has so far produced thirty-four roundshot – more than have been recovered from all other European fifteenth- and sixteenth-century battlefields together. In size the munitions range up to nearly 100 mm, indicating that Richard's artillery train included weapons as large as a saker. In form some of them are decidedly curious, consisting of flint nodules or chunks of iron cast about with lead. Firepower was to become a key instrument of Western imperialism and is a leading feature of the modern world. We tend to think of its evolution as a linear process of increasing technical efficiency, but to think thus is to think backwards, whereas here we are near the start in a period of innovation and experiment. Intrigued, Foard had already been co-operating with a weapons scientist in experiments of their own, using live firing and ballistic analysis to see how such munitions would behave. The results were startling: medieval roundshot would travel for over a kilometre, were transonic, and certain types of artillery will leave an individual signature on the ball.

One hundred and sixty years separated Bosworth from the battle at Naseby that had first drawn Foard into the subject. Important at Bosworth, firepower had been even more critical at Naseby. It is strange that no one has made a film of events on that day when the New Model Army first saw action, and Charles I lost his veteran infantry and, in due course, his kingdom. It has a filmic shape – rising tension in preceding days as the armies manoeuvred, suspenseful twists during the action itself, an extended climax and an outcome which influences many parts of the world to this day. In the eyes of film-makers perhaps the story seems too parochial, too entangled with the background of ridge and furrow, furze heaths and early enclosures against which it was fought to merit their attention. They should look again. The metal-detector plots, each dot laboriously attained and in itself tedious, are cumulatively eloquent. So are the surroundings.

By 1645 Parliament controlled much of England's wealth, and had reorganized to raise and train the New Model Army – a force which the King's seasoned infantry and cavalry derided as being composed of low-born clodpoles, and taunted as cuckolds. In May the New Model arrived under the generalship of Sir Thomas Fairfax to invest the city of Oxford. The Royalists countered by seizing Leicester, thereby drawing Fairfax away from Oxford. In following days the New Model tried to shadow the King's army, the patrols and scouts of each side reporting back to the generals of the main forces. The armies drew closer. So close that on the evening of 13 June it became clear from skirmishes and surprise encounters between patrols that battle was inevitable. Next morning, after several shifts of position the armies faced each other across a shallow valley a mile north of Naseby village.

The Parliamentarians had taken up position on a low flat-topped hill. The Royalist force was experienced, but smaller – fewer than twelve thousand men against maybe fifteen thousand in the New Model Army's ranks. Some time after ten o'clock, trumpets calling and drums throbbing, the Royalists began to advance across the eight hundred or so yards of open ground which lay between the armies. The drum calls were specific to infantry, each call a particular command. The custom in some New Model regiments of singing psalms as they advanced added to the sinfonia. In the Royalist formation, commanded musketeers were interlined with horse, flanked by cavalry to left and right. Prince Rupert, commander of horse on the Royalist right, squared up to the cavalry led by Henry Ireton on Parliament's left wing. At the same time, the experienced Royalist infantry were gaining ground, pushing at the Parliamentary front line.

Rupert's aim was to do what he always did: strike the enemy cavalry head-on. What this involved bears thinking about. Rupert led two thousand cavalry divided into troops, each troop tight packed, 'every left man's right knee ... close locked under his right hand man's left ham', three ranks deep, three feet between each rank. The riders were lightly armoured, each man wearing a helmet and, ideally (but not always), a back and breast plate. Keeping in close order, swords drawn, each phalanx approached the other at 'a good round trot'. The effect was rather like riding into a wall, and the aim was to break the other side's intactness by the impact of doing so. The mere sight of a disciplined body of horse intent on this could intimidate inexperienced troopers.[27] On this occasion both forces knew what they were doing. Ireton's cavalry withstood the first shock and turned to attack the Royalist infantry. Ireton himself was injured, however, and shortly afterwards he was captured. Rupert's cavalry bore down again, this time breaking through. Parliament's left horse began to scatter. The Royalist horse pursued some of them out into the surrounding countryside, while back on the main battlefield the Royalists continued to advance. The Parliamentarians were hard pressed, the centre of the infantry folding back. But there was no general collapse. Elements of Ireton's cavalry were still on the field, and Major General Skippon, commander of the left wing regiment which had withstood the Royalist assault, brought up reserves. Bullets along the ridge show where the counter-action took effect, and incidentally show how far the New Model Army had been pressed. It is possible that

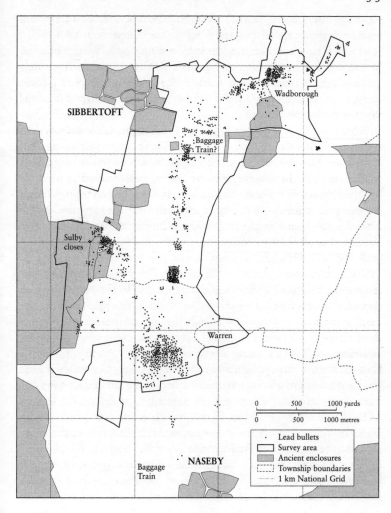

43. Naseby bullet distribution

for a time the two bodies stood back from each other, perhaps firing by rank. In these minutes the war's outcome and Britain's future governance teetered in the balance. Skippon was hit, but like the regiment he was commanding he stayed on his feet.

Thirty, maybe forty minutes had passed. On the Parliamentary right, New Model regiments of cavalry commanded by Whalley and Pye moved forward, pushing back their Royalist counterparts. Cromwell sent cavalry reserves against the King's infantry and the main Royalist reserve. Having been at the brink of triumph only twenty minutes before, the Royalists began to retreat. The New Model, derided only an hour ago, hoisted up some colours captured from a troop of horse, along with the pair of cuckold's horns with which Royalist soldiers had taunted them, and charged.

Accounts vary about what followed. Some suggest that the Royalists collapsed, beaten 'quite out of the Field' under the weight of 'one hot charge'; others imply an inexorable Parliamentarian advance in textbook formation. Either way, historians have tended to use few words to sum it up: the Royalist foot left the field, and that was that. But when all finds are mapped, it is clear that neither the battle nor the battlefield ended here. Archaeological evidence now comes to the fore and demands re-reading of sources for what happened during the battle's final hour.[28]

A trail of bullets runs for over a mile along the road from Naseby into the neighbouring parish of Sibbertoft. This could point to a fighting retreat, and corroborates an account, hitherto largely ignored, which speaks of 'about three hundred' who 'lay slaine' in 'two mile space', as distinct from the hundred or so who had fallen on the ground initially held by Parliament. Clusters of bullets might hint at companies of Royalist infantry successively pausing to give covering fire to their comrades as they fell back – or they could be a function of where the detectorists did or did not search. The bullets thicken beside the Sibbertoft–Clipston road, as if there were efforts here to hold a line or defend the wagons of the Royalist baggage train. To judge from the density of bullet finds here, the fighting was grim. The withdrawal resumed, now in the direction of a small hill called Wadborough, two miles from the original field, where the King's standard was raised and the massing of shot suggests that the King's 'old infantry' and some of the remaining horse made a last stand. Surrounded, outnumbered and under constant fire, by one o'clock most of the survivors had surrendered. A few set off to escape, and there were further outbreaks of fighting in surrounding valleys and woods.

Still it was not over. Rupert's cavalry rejoined the battle, having spent the previous hour first chasing many of Ireton's scattered horse towards Northampton, and then in an attack on the Parliamentarian train. Elements of Royalist cavalry regrouped further north. Their journey might be glimpsed in a scatter of bullets, sparser now and including as many pistol as musket rounds, which seems to stretch even further, from Wadborough almost to Farndon village. But the nature and extent of this pattern has not been surveyed, and we are entering a kind of archaeological twilight: it is very difficult to understand how the horse acted in this later phase of the action, or who for practical purposes was in control of it. But whoever it was seems to have been oblivious to the need for a rearguard action to extricate what was left of the Royalist army, and organize a new stand. Fairfax responded by placing his cavalry in battle formation and awaiting the New Model infantry, which duly marched up. The Parliamentarian force was near intact and ominously well ordered. The King demanded a charge. Unnerved, seeing the New Model's 'horse and foot in good order', and 'mightily discourag'd', the remaining Royalists 'immediately made to run'. Hours later, New Model cavalry were still 'upon the chase knocking them down'. Remnants of fleeing Royalist horse were being hunted miles away after nightfall. As the distributions of shot thin and distances increase, the archaeological picture fades.

Even in this original, not yet specialized way, the metal detector had altered understanding of Naseby's dynamics, and dilated the battlefield far beyond its traditional core. The new picture was not at odds with original records, but rather furnished a fuller context in which to read them. On-the-day accounts of the distribution of the dead, and other sources, corroborate archaeological indications that Naseby was not a compact event, but a series of articulated actions fought over some square miles. Behind this lies promise of the metal detector's ability to pinpoint thousands of tiny objects which collectively delineate fine-grained patterns. At Naseby the broad patterns denote the swirl of events across four parishes in half a day. Those events would in their turn determine the evolution of parliamentary democracy. 'In the last throes of the Naseby fight the King was trying to do the impossible. He should have recognised that all was lost and that his and Rupert's duty was to organise a rearguard action to cover their retreat to enable as many as possible of his cavalry to escape.'[29] But he did not, and during that last hour Charles's pleas for 'one charge more' ensured the completeness not only of his defeat, but also of the neutering of royal power that followed.

12

COVER HIM GENTLY

Tall nettles cover up, as they have done
These many springs, the rusty harrow, the plough
Long worn out, and the roller made of stone:
Only the elm butt tops the nettles now.

The corner of the farmyard I like most:
As well as any bloom upon a flower
I like the dust on the nettles, never lost
Except to prove the sweetness of a shower.

Edward Thomas, 'Tall Nettles', *Poems*, 1917

Thomas dated his draft of 'Tall Nettles': 24 April 1916. That day was a Monday, and that Monday fell exactly fifty-four weeks before his death in action on the first day of the second Battle of Arras.

Eighty-four years later, Alain Jacques, the chief archaeologist of Arras, began a precautionary excavation on the site of a proposed car factory about three miles north-east of the town. Jacques was expecting Romano-Gallic remains. What he actually found were the remains of twenty British soldiers slain during the open stages of the battle, probably on the same day as Edward Thomas. Whoever buried them had arranged them arm in arm.

It was another of archaeology's moments, and when the story broke in June 2001 newspapers flocked to it. A photograph published in the *Daily Mail* was described as the 'week's most haunting picture'. What it showed was pitiable, yet tinged by a kind of absurdity. With their linked elbows, spindly, bird-like legs and Minnie Mouse boots, these lads could pass for some grotesque swaying chorus line, liable at any moment to launch into a high-kicking routine, as if dancing to the world's end.

Who were they? No identity discs were found, but shoulder flashes

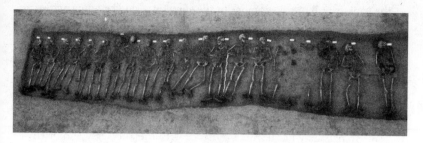

44. Remains of British soldiers, buried near Arras April 1917, excavated June 2001

indicated that three, at least, had been members of the 10th Battalion of the Royal Lincolnshire Regiment. The 10th Lincolnshires were one of those units which back in 1914 had been made up of men from one town or city who had enlisted together. Their town was Grimsby, and they called themselves the Grimsby Chums. By 1917 hardly any original Chums were left. But the name stuck. This may have been reflected in the way the men were buried. Some of them were incomplete. Where this was so, fragments had been placed carefully, almost reverently, where they would have been if the entire frame had survived. Like the linked arms, these were acts of special care.

The Battle of Arras was around the time my grandfather, Jack, was injured. Looking at the newspaper photograph I suddenly recalled climbing about on his lap as a child, and him asking if I could reach the crown of his head and feel the lumps of shrapnel that were embedded in it. Years later I was told that my grandmother's twin sister Kitty began to nurse a man who had been retrieved from a shell-hole with his identity disc blown off and injuries so bad that for more than a year he had lain paralysed, unable to speak, so that nobody knew who he was. His parents thought he was dead. Eventually he recovered enough for Kitty to marry him, although he so abounded in shrapnel that most of the rest of his life was passed in a wheelchair, lest sudden movement should cause a shifting splinter to kill him. How, I wondered, did they make love? Was it like Russian roulette?

Landscape is thick with war's leavings. There can hardly be a field in Britain which does not contain some martial debris – a button, a badge, shrapnel that rained from heavy anti-aircraft fire during the Second World War and was collected and bartered by children. In the 1950s, W. G. Hoskins railed against Cold War paraphernalia, and likened the vapour trail of a V-bomber to the slime of a slug crawling across a sky painted by Gainsborough. Today the paraphernalia are studied by English Heritage, and the last airworthy V-bomber – a shape described by Hoskins as 'obscene' – has been returned to the sky with the aid of a grant from the Heritage Lottery Fund.

On both sides of the Atlantic the twentieth century's wars have become archaeological projects. Amid a slew of publications,[1] heritage agencies seek military installations of all kinds for protection and display. Archaeology has begun a romance with the once ugly and briefly commonplace – hutting, sheds, ablutions blocks, benches upon which servicemen sat to watch nuclear tests in the 1950s, hard-standings from which to fire missiles, the rubbish dropped at camp sites of anti-nuclear protesters. An attempt to preserve one of Britain's few remaining Second World War bomb sites failed only because the government doubted that a bomb site would meet the legal test of a monument. No one had built it.

Why do we study such remains? And why is the public so interested in them? Amid academic talk of 'contemporary archaeology' and 'a present past',[2] another possible reply is one to which archaeologists seldom own, that we are again in the realm of Gothic archaeology. If Gothic fiction is the art of disquiet, what could be more exquisitely disturbing than to stand in the place where a missile might have risen on its way to Armageddon? We do not need archaeology to tell us that the Battle of Arras was a slaughter; but why were those men buried together arm in arm? The same principle extends to structures which were stereotyped, mass produced or esoteric – like hutting, or the strange experimental concrete acoustic mirrors that stand near Dungeness, their concrete ears forever straining to catch the sound of aircraft that do not come. Evidentially, they have little to supply. The archive contains their designs, tells us who built them, when, and contextualizes their purpose. For a discipline that prides itself on chronology, documents date their construction with a precision that archaeology will seldom approach, nor needs to try. In Gothic archaeology, however, none of that matters. Standing outside the empty pillbox beside the canal, the dragonflies darting on a still afternoon, or among huts dangling over a cliff on the eroding east coast, it is the thought of who was there, or what happened to them, imagined contact with the time itself, that makes us pause, exciting the imagination without allowing it to be gratified.

This view is rather reinforced by English Heritage's declaration that Cold War sites 'differ from those of other wars in that they are often not the scenes of conflict and death; their importance and value lies in what they represent and what might have been'.[3] This is a little parochial. While lucky Westerners may remember the Cold War as a time of tension – an impossible peace, but 'all mischief short of war' – there were real casualties, millions of them, in wars around the world that the superpowers fought by proxy. If we really want to get to grips with the archaeology of the Cold War, we are in the wrong place, and smug heritage belittles it. Moreover, some of the most vital aspects of the subject either lie beyond archaeology, or else – like intelligence[4] – have been ignored by archaeologists in favour of a continued fixation with machines, concrete and menacing installations.

Having suggested one answer to the question why we pay attention to such remains, let us ask another: *should* we study them? There is a suspicion that conflict archaeology is not morally neutral. Some who have qualms suppose interest in military remains to reflect a deep-down, sickly (and implicitly male) devotion to militar*ism*. Others object lest nostalgic enthusiasm for wartime structures should fan militant insularity (although no one ever claims that the demolition of wartime fabric would cause xenophobia or jingoism to abate). Yet others are wary of the relation between material remains of twentieth-century war and the structures of authority that led to the very wars being studied.

Let us go back to the first question. Are there academic reasons for this kind of work? Are there things about a 1917 practice trench or a 1944 asbestos hut that only archaeology can tell us? And even if there are, given all those other areas for which archaeology is our only source – like 700,000 years of prehistory – how pressing is our need to know?

Part of one possible answer is that wars, and especially the twentieth-century wars, were accompanied by rapid technological change. Some features of Second World War airfields, for instance, changed several times within five years, and radar evolved significantly even during 1940.[5] The ability to point to such things, at least to have examples, seems to matter. So does the keeping of selected waypoints in the history of technology – things like the sound mirrors which preceded radar and stand as correctives to history's tendency to favour a simplified linear narrative in which the logic of improvement is emphasized at the expense of things that turned out to be dead ends.

A second, complementary, reply would dwell on the idea introduced near the end of Chapter 3, that man-made things are not simply sources of information about the past but working influences in history's processes.[6] A further reason is that there is more to war than fighting: the study of concrete is not a stand-alone movement but part of the wider span of social archaeology, the everyday lives of ordinary people, and hence themes like the family, bereavement or dissent. Whether archaeology can add much to them is a different question. It may be that in studies of protest, graffiti, occupation or detention all we sometimes see is the attraction of novelty – but if insights flow, then all well and good.[7]

Recent wars arguably provide a reality check on some of the postmodern counter-readings of earlier periods in which violence has fallen from fashion. In such revisionism things like ditches and ramparts become symbolic rather than merely defensive. Granted that ancient material evidence cannot automatically be decoded on the basis of contemporary experience, war is generally regarded as a male domain, 'male' not in a biological sense so much as a set of martial values, in turn symbolized by weapons like the Tomahawk Cruise which in the 1980s came to be repudiated by all-female protests. Yet while a flying bomb might be the descendant of a spear, it turns out that not all ancient people buried with spears were men. DNA evidence now shows that some of them, at least, were women. How are we to think of them? As Calamity Jane-like figures, a hero slung under each arm? As warriors' widows, taking weapons to the grave rather as the sons of modern war veterans might bear their fathers' medals? Or is this a showing of the contention met in Chapter 2, that past reality cannot be inferred from simple observation of its inert traces – that knowledge is created, not found, and that context and standpoint are everything?

While the tilt of this book is patently towards context and standpoint, the argument of this chapter is that, nevertheless, some historical truths are found, not created, and that the study of conflict, and especially prehistory, is necessary for history's safekeeping. The argument follows a path that runs through landscape, culture, ecology and prehistory. It begins at the gas chambers.

There are some who say that gas chambers never existed. According to them, evidence for systematic extermination of the Jews was concocted by the Allies, initially as an alibi for their refusal to compromise with Germany and to fight through to an unconditional surrender, and subsequently to bolster the emerging state of Israel. Jews did die, they agree, but mainly from epidemic and ill-treatment, and not in millions. The order of magnitude was less – there may indeed have been gassings, but not 'factories of death': there was no industrialized murder.

Like worshippers of the Antichrist parodying the mass, those who say these things impersonate historical scholarship while inverting its values. Deniers in the United States established an Institute for Historical Review which published what resembled an academic journal, and portrayed its disagreement with accepted opinion as part of history's normal debate. By presenting dissent as less than absolute, an attempt was made to give an impression of reasonableness. The IHR professed to fight distortion with objectivity, prejudice with honesty, falsehood with fact, and to stand up for 'real history'. Its efforts continue through a website.

The means and motives of Holocaust denial have been compassed elsewhere.[8] For present purposes it is enough to recall that towards the end of 1944, as Germany's military position deteriorated, the SS began to hide evidence for the mass killings they had overseen. In late November, Heinrich Himmler ordered the demolition of the Auschwitz-Birkenau crematoria and the gas chambers attached to them. Crematorium 1 was already superseded. Crematoria 2 and 3 were gutted of their installations and later blown up. Crematorium 4 had been disabled in the course of a prisoner revolt in October 1944; what was left of it was dismantled. Crematorium 5 was dynamited in January 1945, just before the arrival of the Red Army. Hence, none of the buildings used for mass killing at Auschwitz now survives intact, and not all aspects of their construction and use are fully documented by original records.

The gas chambers and their working are nonetheless well attested. Eyewitness testimony given after the war established that in Crematoria 2 and 3 (similar buildings) hydrogen cyanide was introduced into the killing chambers in pellets, downward from the roof, through four wire-mesh columns. The columns passed up through the roof to the outside, where they resembled small chimneys which were plugged with wooden lids. The introduction vents appear in wartime photographs taken both from the air and on the ground.[9]

Deniers mistrust the witnesses and dispute the photographs. Some say that the pictures have been doctored, or that the marks on the roof have been misinterpreted. Only archaeological proof will do. As the wounds of Christ were to Thomas's faith in the resurrection, so the holes became to those who contested the Holocaust. Show us the holes, they said, and we will believe.

When David Irving sued Professor Deborah Lipstadt and her publisher for stating that he was a mouthpiece for Holocaust denial who distorted historical evidence, he put this to Professor Robert Jan van Pelt, an architectural and cultural historian who testified on Lipstadt's behalf.

> IRVING [...] You have not seen any holes in the roof, have you [...]
> when you went there? You have not found any holes?
>
> PROFESSOR VAN PELT I have not seen the holes for the columns, no.
>
> IRVING Not for the introduction of the cyanide?
>
> PROFESSOR VAN PELT No.
>
> IRVING May I say that if the Auschwitz authorities were now to agree
> to clean off that rubble off the top of that concrete slab and find the
> holes I would tomorrow halt this case and abandon my action.[10]

Some half-million lives had been taken in this building. If that were
so, said Irving, it would put the building at 'the geocentre of the atlas
of atrocities'.[11] There again, he said, if it could be shown that it had not
after all functioned as a gas chamber, then the case for Auschwitz as an
extermination camp would be uncorroborated. And that, Irving reasoned, would cancel the Holocaust.

> IRVING [...] So we have narrowed it down to this building which has
> collapsed. The roof, as we see it in the air photographs, is in a mess.
> Beneath that roof we would have found all the equipment, bits and
> pieces, that would have been incriminating, but the Russians ...
> somebody blew up the building and it pancaked downwards, this
> roof, and for some reason the archaeologists have never gone in
> there to find out what is still there, have they?
>
> PROFESSOR VAN PELT No [...][12]

Again:

> IRVING [...] There are many archaeological sites around the Auschwitz
> camp, I would have thought, which would have helped to solve
> a lot of questions. For example, mass graves, burning pits, which
> could have been investigated with modern archaeological means
> like proton magnetometers, something which would detect the
> pattern of burning, things like this. Has any investigation like that
> been conducted by the Polish or any other authorities?
>
> PROFESSOR VAN PELT As far as I know, not.[13]

Again:

> IRVING Have you never felt the urge to go and start scraping just
> where you know those holes would have been because you know
> approximately where, like a two or three foot patch of gravel to
> scrape away?
>
> PROFESSOR VAN PELT I have authored the report already in 1993 for

the Poles in which I actually argued that they needed very, very strict preservation standards; and the last thing I would ever have done is start scraping away at the roof without any general plan of archaeological investigations.

IRVING But now that these serious doubts have been raised as to the integrity of the gas chamber notion, and now that neo-Nazis around the world are benefiting from these doubts, would it not be in everybody's interests if this last element of uncertainty should be so easily removed, that the gravel there should be scraped off the virgin concrete slab beneath to see if those holes were there?[14]

And again:

IRVING And you do accept, do you not, that if you were to go to Auschwitz the day after tomorrow with a trowel and clean away the gravel and find a reinforced concrete hole where we anticipate it would be from your drawings, this would make an open and shut case and I would happily abandon my action immediately?

PROFESSOR VAN PELT I think I cannot comment on this. I am an expert on Auschwitz and not on the way you want to run your case.[15]

Irving asked why the Defence had not done more 'to establish the rights and wrongs of this particular allegation about the factory of death'. The judge intervened.

MR JUSTICE GRAY What do you mean by 'this particular allegation'? The roof?

IRVING Well, if they could have proved that I was wrong on this particular matter, this would really knock the pillars from beneath my case.[16]

But there again, would it? Mr Justice Gray was not trying a case about whether the buildings had been gas chambers. The case he was trying turned on whether Irving had approached the Holocaust in an historically scrupulous way. And at its end Mr Justice Gray concluded that he had not.

While the judgement was widely welcomed as a triumph for historical reasoning, not everyone saw it like that. Some voiced concern lest the trial's result should inhibit honest revisionism. Was it not the proper business of historians to rattle the doors of orthodoxy? Did not history's establishment have room for a few mavericks who could ask awkward questions and bring colour to a pallid scene? Had not the war in question been fought to defend the liberty to be wrong?

Those who asked such questions seemed not always to realize that this had not been a judgement in which one historical interpretation had prevailed over another. As Professor Richard Evans, the main expert witness against Irving, later put it, 'the judgment had had nothing to do with the interpretation of a body of knowledge at all. What it dealt with, on the contrary, was the *creation* of a body of "knowledge" that was not really knowledge but invention, manipulation and falsification of source material.'[17] Irving had not lost because of his views, but because – as Mr Justice Gray had put it – his treatment of historical evidence fell short of what was to be expected of a conscientious historian.

The post-trial debate seemed to dodge the archaeological point which Irving had worked hard to raise. What would the presence or absence of holes in the concrete slab have shown? As it happens, the holes have since been found.[18] Archaeological evidence for them was there all along, but in the absence of appropriate survey methods it had not entered the record – another instance of the influence of how we look affecting what we see. But this aside, was Irving's attempt to extrapolate a vast reinterpretation from a particle of detail, regardless of context and the bounds set by other sources, reasonable?

We have seen that much of the meaning we derive from objects is neither stable nor self-communicating: the ways in which we obtain meaning rest on lessons learned, from knowledge accumulated and reworked along the way, and from context. The lessons are easily accessible, although that is not popularly known. On one level this does not matter. We live in a mutual society, dependent on one another's skills, and the fact that most people are unfamiliar with the theory of archaeological knowledge is no more problematic than is most people's unfamiliarity with neuroscience, or the working of their mobile phone. We live in an age of growing specialization, and we delegate. But the debate over the holes shows what can happen when one constituency loses faith in the skills or motives of another. Ignorance of archaeology's foundations must be some kind of drawback, because without it illusions can gain ground, and a common basis of understanding for the human family is postponed. If archaeologists are the only guardians of their subject's epistemology, who is to know if or when they have been overpowered by falsifiers?

In the same month that Mr Justice Gray adjudged Irving an historical falsifier, the editor of the magazine *British Archaeology* reflected on the disquiet that had attended the recent removal of a prehistoric timber circle from the beach at Holme-next-the-Sea on north Norfolk's coast. Like the Rose playhouse, but for different reasons, the circle detonated an extraordinary reaction. It began on 19 January 1999, when a national newspaper published a photograph showing a ring of timbers encircling an upturned oak, all under a blue-grey winter sky. It was a scene that Constable might have painted, and it flashed round the world. Few at the time realized how much of the force of this image was entirely ser-endipitous. Forty centuries back the circle had stood inland. The posts were thus remnants of timbers that had once stood taller; their lower-most parts had originally been buried, just as the roots of the tree had probably once been flush with the ground. In other words, what was now visible more or less corresponded with what would not have been seen when the circle was new. Yet however the image had been formed, it was compelling. The upside-down tree was still entwined by a honey-suckle rope.[19]

These are stormy shores, and the timbers were fragile. Sooner or later, probably sooner, they would be destroyed by the sea. English Heritage, the government's archaeological adviser, decided to fund the removal of the timbers and the central oak, to enable continued study, better under-standing and in due course, if others wished it, preservation and display.

The decision excited an outcry. Local people, Druids, eco-Druids, pagans, New Agers and not a few archaeologists all laid emotional claim to different aspects of the site and criticized the planned removal. Pagans and Druids formed a protest movement. New theories about prehistoric Britain appeared as fact. The movements of two Druid protesters were restricted by court injunctions. One Traveller-Druid described the surge of spiritual energy that had passed through him on contact with the circle. Feelings ran high when eco-warriors occupied the circle between tides in an attempt to foil the excavation. The Council of British Druid Orders sent a representative Druid ritually to reclaim the site. A reader of *British Archaeology* described the chainsawing out of a wedge of wood from the central oak for tree-ring dating as 'the worst case of environ-mental rape' she had ever seen.[20] Millions watched on television, some weeping at the spectacle of the great oak bole being yanked from the sand. No honeysuckle rope now; just chains. Animists said the timbers and the tree had been spiritually alive, and accused English Heritage of murdering the spirit. To Simon Denison, *British Archaeology*'s editor, the circle's forcible removal seemed 'inexpressibly sad and misguided'.

Denison certainly caught the mood, and there was romantic grace in the counter-proposal to leave the circle where it was and let it subside into the elements whence it had emerged. Yet look again at the words. *Forcible*, for instance. Had the timbers resisted? 'Environmental rape': who was the victim? The response, said Denison, was heartfelt. The presence of this structure in this place, hidden in the sand and peat for forty centuries, transcended modern desire to understand it. The attempt to do so, indeed, infringed Scott's axiom that in the art of 'exciting surprise' it is the state of *not* knowing that so deliciously intensifies our responses.

While the eco-Druids were a handful, popular anger backed them. Together they demonstrated the point made earlier about the diminution of archaeology's standing, from English Heritage as a branch of the state with more or less definitive things to say – rather like the Meteorological Office or the government's Chief Veterinary Officer – to reactionary imperialism over the past. This was evident at a public meeting held in March 2000, when Druids, local people, pagans and busloads of postgraduates from various courses on heritage management howled the English Heritage representative down for interfering 'in local perceptions of cultural identity' and negating 'pagan perceptions of place'. At one point in that meeting, its chairman, the late Professor Peter Ucko, director of the Institute of Archaeology at University College London, declared: 'Archaeologists have to recognize that, when the public sees something as a pagan site, then it is one, whether or not there is evidence for it being sacred in the past.'

In the following month, Simon Denison wrote in *British Archaeology*: 'Knowledge for its own sake is among the most trivial of substances. Dates, dimensions, construction techniques – in the final reckoning, who cares?'[21] In the next issue of *British Archaeology* a reader replied by pointing out that a problem with putting feeling before knowledge is that both individually and as a public we can be as much affected by fiction as by fact. It is knowledge that enables us to tell them apart.[22] But in that same issue, another reader said: 'If we are to have a multivocal archaeology that fully engages with the public at large then we cannot dictate whose views are to be listened to and whose should be ignored.'[23] If we substitute the Auschwitz-Birkenau crematoria for Seahenge, where does that leave us?

The Seahenge controversy and the Irving trial were roughly concurrent. Each stirred a debate about historical reality. Of course, if someone wishes to claim that a dead tree in Norfolk is inhabited by a spirit, there should be liberty for them to do so. The idea is hardly stranger than the Nordic Atlantis with which National Socialist ideologists flirted in the

1930s, or Hans Hörbiger's *Welteislehre* embroidery of the theory that the Earth had successively captured and discarded a number of moons, on each occasion causing tidal fluctuations, polar shifts and ice ages which in turn had been responsible for the rise and disappearance of 'root-races'.[24] Along with other products of Nazi mythopoeia that have since fertilized a subculture of arcane theories, such a cultural phenomenon is interesting in its own right; but does 'multi-vocal history' require scholars, broadcasters or anyone else to give even-handed attention to unfounded ideas simply because some people happen to believe them? The question cannot be parried with discussion about intention or context, for it is about the foundations of knowledge, not the circumstances in which knowledge is used.

In a detail unnoticed at the time, the Irving trial and Seahenge were also linked by imagery. Eco-Druids saw removal of the upturned oak as an assault on Nature. Some of those who ran Auschwitz sported oak leaves on their uniforms. Thinking about Nature ran deep in German culture. Wilhelm Heinrich Riehl's *Natural History of the German People as the Basis of a German Social Policy* (1851–5) amounted to 'an attempt to prove that the essence of the German *Volk*, and its regional variations, could be explained by reference to the landscape and climate of Germany'.[25] By affecting landscape and air quality, industrialization 'affected Germanness itself'.[26] The garden-city movement, state-sponsored nature conservation[27] and modern ecology all had roots in German thought.[28] As for the oak leaves, under National Socialism trees and woodland gained meaning that went beyond the romantic anti-industrialism of Riehl or Alexander von Humboldt's conception of the *Naturdenkmal*, 'natural monument'.[29] Forests and the animals within them evoked hunting; with hunting went liberty, and woodland yields charcoal – whence smiths, whence transformation, steel, heroes and chivalry. No surprise, then, that Germany's National Socialist government was among the first in Europe to designate state nature reserves.

With the cult of Nature ran farms and farming, and with them concepts that underlie twentieth-century green thought. 'The idea of being rooted in a particular *Gemeinschaft* (community) and landscape by shared language, history traditions and ancestry is fundamental to recognition of *Umweltschutz* (protecting the environment) being synonymous with *Lebensschutz* (protecting life), *Heimatschutz* (protecting the homeland) and *Volksschutz* (protecting the people/nation).'[30]

Organicism prized land and farm. For all its architectural dreams and fondness for advanced technology, National Socialism's underlying

mood was rural, its values epitomized by the 'blood and soil' rallying call
of Richard Walther Darré,[31] Reich Minister for Food and Agriculture
between 1933 and 1942. Darré was also head of the Race & Settlement
Office, and, with Heinrich Himmler, the co-founder of the Ahnenerbe
Forschungs-und-Lehrgemeinschaft – the Society for Research and
Teaching of Ancestral Heritage.[32] Born out of the earlier Herman
Wirth Society, and subsequently assimilated to the SS, the Ahnernerbe
housed 'institutes' for subjects as diverse as folk music, linguistics (it was
thought that languages corresponded to racial hierarchy), the Eddas,
anthropology, racial biology and archaeology. Its products included the
Ahnenpass (a document carried by citizens which defined them ances-
trally) and the '*Ausgrabungswesen-SS* (Excavating SS), which had the
job of providing archaeological underpinning for Nazism'.[33]

Reich sponsorship of archaeology went down a number of paths,
not all of which led in the same direction. In this it mirrored National
Socialism itself, which was Janus-faced in its simultaneous eyeing of
the anciently rooted and the futuristic. When the Nazis took power
there were calls for the replacement of the internationally progressive
Römische-Germanische Kommission by a Reichsinstitut für Deutsche
Vorgeschicht (National Institute for German Prehistory). This did
not happen, partly because war supervened, partly because of Hitler's
personal admiration for Graeco-Roman culture (privately, he thought
early German artefacts rather tedious), and perhaps too because of the
ebbing prestige of the idea's champion, Alfred Rosenberg, founder of
the Fighting League for German Culture (1929) and author of *The Myth
of the Twentieth Century* (1930), who saw history in terms of 'culture-
bearing' and 'culture-destroying' races.*[34] Even so, a trend of thought was
there, and led to the archaeological sifting of supposed Germanic type-
sites such as Detmold, Paderborn, Haithabu and rocky Externsteine –
places which represented a heartland that had held out against Romans
and Franks. It also led to an emphasis on German prehistory never
paralleled in Britain, and to public explanation through open-air recon-
structions and archaeological films.

Responsibilities for archaeology, Nature, ecology and German destiny

* Earlier exponents of this idea had included Arthur Joseph, comte de Gobineau (1816–
82), who claimed that human races are anatomically and psychologically unequal. The
Swiss-born American Louis Agassiz argued that 'races' of man were different species.
Rosenberg also looked to Houston Stewart Chamberlain (1855–1927), postulator of an
Aryan Jesus, whose writings had contrasted the positive influence of Germanic people
with the regressive forces exerted by organizations and systems of international span.

were gathered under the eye of Heinrich Himmler, who by the early 1940s held sway over functions that included the SS, the police, the consolidation of German national identity, and settlement of the East. The East was a kind of destiny, a space marked down for the German people, not to be conquered so much as regained.[35] Its medieval castles were warrant of the claim. 'One truth', wrote Himmler, 'stands at the beginning and the end of each historical epoch: stones will talk when the people have fallen silent. Great times already speak in stone to the present.'[36]

Plans for colonization of the East involved its reordering on the largest scale and attention to the smallest detail. Polish peasants would be displaced. Uneconomic smallholdings would be merged to make larger German farms. There would be new farmhouses, byres, stables and barns. At intervals there would be civilizing towns which once again would be radiant centres of German culture. One of the places so earmarked was Auschwitz. In history's hindward view Auschwitz is visible only as a place of human perversion. In 1940 its future was as a place of social progress – a model city.[37]

Himmler and his friend Hanns Johst toured Upper Silesia in 1940. On several occasions,

> the Reichsführer-SS stopped the car … walked into fields … took some dirt between his fingers, smelled it thoughtfully with his head bowed, crushed crumbs of the field between his fingers, and then looked over the vast, vast space which was full, full to the horizon, with this good fertile earth.[38]

Ecological change was part of the plan. Villages on poorer soils would be levelled. Woodland would return.

> The two men reflected on how the German settlers would soon change the appearance of the land. Trees and hedges would be planted. Shrubs would grow, and weasels and hedgehogs, buzzards and falcons would prevent the destruction of half the harvest by mice and vermin. All of this was a great work of culture undertaken in awe of nature. They speculated on how these changes would 'create protection from the wind, increase dew, and stimulate formation of clouds, force rain and thus push a more economically viable climate further toward the East'.[39]

Even the weather, it seemed, lay within Himmler's sway.

Let us leave them gazing eastward, and turn to another who loved buzzards, and ancient sunlight, Henry Williamson, author of *Tarka the*

Otter and *Salar the Salmon*, one of the great nature writers of the twentieth century, and a Holocaust denier.

Williamson came to empathize with National Socialism not through ideology but through the pity of inter-war Britain's derelict farms, urban squalor and unemployment. In Nazi Germany he found a government that reversed joblessness, fostered family farms and cherished Nature. After attending the Nuremberg Congress in 1935, Williamson returned to Devon with magic in his eyes. Even at the second war's end, he did not budge from his view that Hitler had been fundamentally a good man, and to his last day he attributed the Holocaust chiefly to disease and famine brought about by the collapse of public services under Allied bombing.

How should we locate Williamson? On one level his work belongs in a tradition of visionary mystical nature writing represented by figures like Richard Jefferies and W. H. Hudson. Jefferies's book *The Story of my Heart* (1883) had a profound effect on Williamson: 'The sun was stronger than science; the hills more than philosophy.' Jefferies was also a pioneer of eco-fiction, his *After London* (1885) depicting an environmental disaster which caused London's abandonment to waste and marsh. W. H. Hudson's evocations of rural life, crafts and Nature were paralleled by his ecologically instrumental *Green Mansions* (1904), a book about the South American rainforest, and in his work from 1894 as chairman of the new-founded Society for the Protection of Birds.

On another level, Williamson's writing embodied affection for landscape, native arts and crafts which had been welling up in poetry, music and art from the nineteenth century. As a movement ruralism has been oversimplified, its elegaic pensiveness equated with escapism, its pastoral written off as undemanding, its passions as immaterial. That is a debate we cannot get into, save to notice that ruralism's themes were taken from widely contrasting sources, and that they reflected something more complicated than nostalgic rusticity or the revival of morris dancing.[40] The Great War intensified its brooding poetics.

Ruralism had a campaigning edge. By the 1920s, several crusades begun by the Land Nationalization Society back in the 1880s were well advanced. Others campaigned for access to mountains and moors,[41] and against the blighting of countryside by crass development while good land was abandoned.[42] Reporting the formation of the Council for the Preservation of Rural England in 1926, the *Manchester Guardian* noted 'widespread alarm about the steady spoiling of rural England' and the unregulated chaos which resulted from a weak planning system. One reason that measures to establish national parks, protect buildings, wildlife and geology all found a place in the programme of the Attlee government in 1945 was that most of the preparatory work for their legislated protection had been done before the war, some of it as far back as the Great War. The determination to see this through was driven not only by the sense of crisis in the face of rural decline, but also by a parallel intensification of urbanism whereby one England blotted out another in a way that was 'not organic, but mechanical'.[43]

Britain's industrial cities – the places where so many who died in the Great War were born – stained the sky and blistered the land. London was an exorbitant polluter. Depending on the wind's quarter, the city's charred clouds could stain a garden in Dorset. Late in the nineteenth century it was a heavily laden wind, in one year depositing around 1,250 tons of soot and tarry hydrocarbon on one square mile of the city alone. Rich in sulphuric acid, London's air was lethal, poisoning those who trod the narrow lanes of its 'strange incongruous chaos of wealth and want'. Londoners who had not yet been 'entirely engulfed in the mass of iniquity by which they are daily surrounded', wrote Engels in 1845, 'are daily losing their power to resist the demoralising forces of poverty, dirt and low environment.'[44]

It was partly in reaction to such squalor and moral degradation that conservation in Britain originated. That is not only why conservation had its heart in the countryside – where despite a century of urbanism the heart of England's identity still lay – but why historically it was anti-urban.[45] The National Trust was founded to protect land 'against development and industrialization'. And as we saw near this book's beginning, one of the staunchest gladiators in the campaign to provide green spaces for public benefit was Darwin's co-evolutionist and scientific biographer, chairman of the Land Nationalization Society, Alfred Russel Wallace.

Towards the end of the 1890s Wallace and other reformers had denounced the landlords' monopoly which forbade the use of 'native soil on fair terms to the workers', believing that it was this that led to instability, unemployment, flight to the towns, social disorder, 'millions of acres of land going out of production', and the perversity whereby entire crops were left to rot while labourers starved.[46] The Depression saw new episodes of agricultural breakdown and, in some areas, the abandonment of farmland to waste.[47] After the Great War, stricken by declining incomes, rising taxes and the effects of the worldwide post-war fall in food prices,[48] some landowners broke up their estates, selling portions to former tenants whose lack of capital often led to unsustainable borrowing, followed by further break-up, piecemeal sell-off and development. In the eyes of one onlooker in the 1930s, all England was now suburban 'except for the slums at one extreme and the Pennine moors at the other'.[49] Or as E. M. Forster put it in 1937: 'In the last fifteen years we have gashed it to pieces with arterial roads, trimmed the roads with trash, and ruined several selected areas systematically.'[50] For some, the Second World War came almost as a relief, for it brought land back into use and restored the sense of worth of those who worked it. In 1943: 'England has become a well-kept land again.'[51]

Two years previously Rolf Gardiner, Viscount Lymington, H. J. Massingham and nine others had formed the Kinship in Husbandry, a group dedicated to the redemption of England through attachment to the earth.[52] The Kinsmen called for restoration of the independent, self-sufficient family farm, to be worked in balance with Nature, in a land of regional differentiation. Massingham emphasized that their aim was not to preserve old places or customs (he called preservation 'a losing game') but to encourage the rehabilitation of communities.[53] Rolf Gardiner was a trained forester, a poet, folk dancer and visionary.[54] On his estate at Springhead in Dorset he had founded the Springhead Ring, a network that aimed to renovate rural life in Wessex and reverse the damage done by unimaginative landowners.[55] Gardiner 'wanted to create a vibrant, productive rural England where quality was paramount and where men were taught to understand the basic reality of farming as a sacramental act whereby closeness to the earth and a holistic understanding would ensure long-term sustainability'.[56]

Organicists stood against automatism, unbridled markets, chemicals, industrialism and global finance. Especially finance. For it seemed to be money that drove the cycle of despoliation. 'The moneylender bled the producer; cheap foreign food downed the good English stuff. Big business swallowed little craftsmanship. The town invaded the country, the machine conquered man. Debt declared war on security, economics on life, finance on God.'[57] This is familiar subsoil. Give or take some trace elements, it is not unlike that of Richard Walther Darré. And it is the context for Henry Williamson's unwillingness to accept that between five and six million of his fellow humans had been systematically murdered.

In 1940 Williamson was interviewed by the Special Branch, and then released under caution to his newly acquired Norfolk farm. Also spared was the Anglocentric historian Arthur Bryant, another of the Kinsmen, whose pre-war cordiality towards the Nazis was softened by a post-war CBE, a knighthood and membership of the Companion of Honour.[58] Others who were seminal to organic farming and what has since evolved into Dark Green politics were detained under Defence Regulation 18B.[59] Among them were Lord Lymington (a colleague of William Joyce,* who in the 1930s had been much involved with the English Array, a freemasonry which was part gardening club and part a campaign for English racial purity)[60] and Captain George Henry Pitt Rivers, the great-grandson of British archaeology's mentor. Pitt Rivers had been an officer of the British Eugenics Society, a body with members who believed in 'racial hygiene' and the 'criminal type', recognizable from physiological characteristics.[61]

Anti-Semitism and racism were not, of course, components of organicism, but it is not surprising that they sometimes went together. Equally, there were plenty of occasions when they did not. For all the Kinship in Husbandry's apparent proximity to fascism, for instance, H. J. Massingham rejected the 'obsession with racial problems, culminating in the dangerous fallacies of the Nordic school, with its cant of racial superiority'.[62] Similarly, while Rolf Gardiner was acquainted with Darré and had promoted links between English and German youth,[63] his loyalties to German culture and history put him 'among the enemies of National Socialism'.[64]

There is also a question of context, the extent to which eugenics formed part of the mental furniture of the 1930s, when much of Britain was only just emerging from the rule of an elite for whom ideas of 'stock' and 'blood', obvious from the horses in their fields and spaniels visible through their country-house windows, were read across into theories of race and identity. As recently as the 1960s archaeologists routinely measured the skulls of people they excavated, calculating cranial indices and other dimensions in the belief that these were 'racially significant'.[65] 'Belief in dominant importance of heredity was progressive,' said E. H. Carr in notes for a projected second edition of *What is History?*, 'so long as you believe that acquired characteristics were inherited. When this was rejected, the belief in heredity became reactionary.'[66] This can be read the other way. Down to 1940 there was a degree of laissez-faire, even admiration, in the private attitudes of many Britons towards Hitler. Even in May 1945, when the requisitioned country houses stood haggard from five years' lack of maintenance, and cinema audiences watched the first newsreels of Belsen, the racial suppositions

* Later 'Lord Haw-Haw'.

held by many Britons and Americans were separated from those of the Nazis less by outright contrast than by degree.

In summary, conservation, organicism and ruralism are connected, and for more than a century have drawn on a body of green thought that in its beginnings was counter-industrial, fired by social concern and inspired by international experience. In the later 1880s, for instance, Alfred Russel Wallace toured the United States, where he passed time with John Muir, the man who in 1892 founded the Sierra Club, in the tradition of Thoreau, one of the first movements anywhere dedicated to the protection of Nature for the sake of Nature herself. In 1912, follow-ing Wallace's encouragement, a Society for the Promotion of Nature Reserves was founded in Britain. It, too, had at its heart the principle of interfering with Nature as little as possible. Archaeological sites fitted into this because they are a subset of the environment, and because by being instructive they assist the purpose of conservation to make possible self-renewal. And as we saw in Chapter 3, aback of this was a perception of the 'pre-industrial past as a place in time that paralleled wilderness in geographical space – a slower-paced realm of pure life-giving existence, as it was, before everything became sullied or began to fail. What was old was more ennobling than what was new, because it had its own organic, creatively true and coherent network – the result of deep-rooted tradition which set it beyond fashion or unthinking utilitarianism.' It was a militant splinter-group of the inheritors of this tradition who just over a century later sought to barricade Seahenge against science.

It may seem that we have strayed from the subject. In fact, like a procession which folds back on itself while winding through the twist-ing streets of an old city, the head and tail are inter-visible down side streets. The fact that there may be no all-inclusive 'truth' in history does not lessen the crisis that arises when one version of history is accepted as being as valid as another. The issue is whether in writing history we are faithful to its sources. Reasoned history is under attack from within by those who say that what you believe is what it was, and from with-out by marchers under a rainbow of banners who put instinct or self-indulgent conjecture before source criticism. An example is the idea of ley lines, which archaeologists more or less gave up trying to dispute years ago, and in which thousands, possibly millions (including prac-titioners in the hard sciences), now believe. New Age mystics act 'as though knowledge does not have to be won but can be scavenged'.[67] Like the activity of some wood-boring insect in furniture that looks sound, unreason gnaws from within, leaving non-historians bewildered. The invention of a fact-free explanation for Seahenge causes no obvious harm, but when one of the world's leading prehistorians says that 'when the public sees something as a pagan site, then it is one, whether or not there is evidence for it being sacred in the past', it becomes a question how we should answer those engaged in, say, the 'struggle for an English Bioregion'. And whether we take the English Heathen Front seriously or see it as a joke, Henry Williamson and H. J. Massingham (for all his detestation of racism) are now in the pantheon of the ultra-right.

More subtle, yet just as enfeebling, is the tendency for legends about sources to gain lives of their own which bear no relation to evidence actually available. One of the reasons why archaeology engaged with the study of Britain's Second World War defences in the 1990s was the widespread assumption that they had been largely improvised, and so for the most part undocumented. If this was true, then it meant that the evidence for what and where they were could be found only in the field. This was encouraged by the perfunctory treatment given by the official historian, and by the fact that much of what had originally been a UK-wide system had long since either faded from view or been dismantled. In result, those bits that did remain often did so in isolation, their presence making no sense to the onlooker in the absence of the rest.

This narrative was given out by all Britain's heritage agencies at least until 1994. Its corollary was that any reconstruction of Britain's anti-invasion defences in 1940 had to be undertaken from the field. This was understandable save that no one had been to the archives to look. When they did, it was at once clear that these defences had been an integrated, sophisticated system, and that the record of where they were and how they were meant to work was detailed and copious.[68]

The discovery did not mean that archaeology no longer had business with remains of the period. There are good reasons for study, two of them being public explanation of a remarkable system hitherto largely unknown, and the need for analysis of what it was meant to do. Both are illustrated by recent gross mapping of its components – a mixture of rapid new-build and enhanced natural obstacles.[69] Yet despite the correcting knowledge, the legend of unrecorded amateurism continues to be repeated. It is as if there are some who wish it to have been so. Is that because of a wish to rationalize licence for fieldwork to feed Gothic sensation? Whatever it is, by indulging fiction about sources, history is bruised. An early task for all tyrannies is to take control of history. Historians alone do not overpower tyrants, but tyrants cannot rule for long in the glare of scrupulous history. Unwillingness to defend source criticism is a key that turns in the locks of gas chambers.

If the flight from history extends to events of recent years, how much more does it affect prehistory? In 1943, the Holocaust in progress a thousand miles or so to the east, its basis warranted by Nazi archaeology, the prehistorian Grahame Clark – then working as an air-photo interpreter – wrote an essay called 'Education and the Study of Man'. Part of it was quoted at the end of Chapter 2. This is how it continued:

> Anthropology, like the idea of evolution itself, was older than Darwin, but it was the publication of *The Origin of Species* that made it a subject of widespread interest and concern. In the same way Prehistory achieved a new meaning in the light of the extended vistas of human existence opened up by acceptance of the new doctrines. Together they have unfolded in the last eighty years a story of human development and achievement which ought to rank high in the heritage of every human being capable of receiving education. Yet it is a fact that, up to the present, educationists as a body have ignored the story of men as completely as did the scientists of the pre-Evolutionary era.[70]

They still do.

These are more than esoteric niceties. If, as the writer and scholar George Steiner says, war's embers are worth sifting 'to discover the relations between those done to death and those alive then, and the relations of both to us',[71] then archaeology's impressionability in the presence of shifting fashions becomes an unavoidable issue.[72] Nowhere is this more obvious than at the places which stand for collective pain that have been set aside and commemorated. The husk of St Michael's Cathedral in Coventry now stands for reconciliation. Auschwitz, designated a museum by Poland's parliament in 1947, was inscribed on UNESCO's World Heritage List in 1979. Even under the eye of guardians, however, historical interpretation is at risk, posing new technical and philosophical challenges. The public display of fabric requires its upkeep, yet flimsy huts, corrugated iron or temporary brickwork were for the moment, not posterity. When William Morris and his friends wrote their manifesto for the care of old buildings in 1877, saying it was for buildings 'of all times and styles', they did not have before them the Curved Asbestos Hut, or the phoney clock on the dummy station at Treblinka, where the hands always pointed to one time because they were painted.[73] What should the curators do with rusting tin sheds, or the forest scene painted on the wall of a mess hut in County Durham by

45. Painting in mess hut of prisoner-of-war camp, Low Harperley, Co. Durham. Built in 1942, the camp came to house nine hundred German prisoners who wrote their own newspaper, Der Quell *('The Gen') and produced shows in a theatre with raked seating and space for an eleven-piece band. Some still awaited repatriation in 1948. A few remained in Britain. There were about 1,500 such camps. Most have gone.*

a homesick German prisoner of war? Should they be conserved, or left to decay? How much should be left undisturbed for posterity to ask its own questions? Remember the holes. Collapse and the triumph of time make a dignified pall but do not easily translate into public understanding. Rebuild in facsimile? Unless that is carefully explained, it will elicit – in some places, already has elicited – the deniers' jeer that the monuments are fakes. In *What Happened in History*, Gordon Childe wrote: 'Progress is real if discontinuous. The upward curve resolves itself into a series of troughs and crests. But in those domains that archaeology as well as history can survey, no trough ever declines to the level of the preceding one, each crest out-tops its last precursor.' Those words were published in 1942. One wonders if Childe would have written so in 1945.

And the Grimsby Chums?

Easter Monday 1917 dawned cold and sleety. At 05.30 whistles shrieked, and men of the 34th Division went forward from the suburbs

TIME'S ANVIL

338

of Arras. Among them were the 10th Lincolnshires. Further north, the Canadian Corps advanced on Vimy Ridge. The assault moved well: advancing behind a creeping barrage, the Allies overran the first German line in less than three-quarters of an hour, and forty-five minutes later they were across the second. Watching them was the poet Edward Thomas, laureate of the English countryside, stationed in a forward observation post.

By evening the Lincolnshires had covered nearly two miles, and had taken up position on a line of low hills. The assault was losing momentum. Allied tanks – George Allen with them – were lagging, and artillery pieces could not be moved forward. As dusk fell, snowflakes glittered in the candescent light of arcing flares. Wounded men lying in the open froze. A hundred Lincolnshires were unaccounted for, twenty in one place. Among the twenty were the Grimsby Chums found by Alain Jacques. We do not know whether they died in ones and twos, or together from the splintery gust of a single shell. We can only guess how they were gathered and buried under fire, or over what length of time. Their grave was a length of trench from the German second line.

And the linked arms, the swaying chorus line about to swing into a high-kicking routine? The archive answers the archaeology. A photograph of the Grimsby Chums under training shows linked arms as a battalion tradition. This means that the men who oversaw the burials were very likely Chums themselves. All soldiers realized, 'usually with a touch of terror and guilt, their capacity to be hardened about the death of others'; the careful positioning of limbs and part-bodies in an anatomically correct relationship, under fire, typifies combatant communities who 'often took great risks and expended considerable energy to honour, under horrific circumstances, their own dead' and 'were themselves communities in mourning and communities of mourning'.[74] Or as Alain Jacques the excavator put it: 'These people were friends.'[75]

The composer-poet Ivor Gurney of the 2/5 Glosters had been working near by until Good Friday, three days before, when he was shot through the arm and sent back from the line to hospital. *Severn and Somme* – the binary of countryside and conflict runs through many of his poems. I have wondered when he heard about the death of Edward Thomas, or who told him. Thomas had been dead for most of the day, killed by a shell just after half-past seven that morning. 'Cover him, cover him soon!'[76] In life Thomas had been a great walker. The closing verses of one of his last poems, 'Roads', anticipated that incipient, swaying dance of the Chums who died on the same day as he.

46. Grimsby Chums at Strensall, 1915. The linking of hands was a battalion tradition (p. 317). The man seated in a deckchair third from right holds a rabbit on his lap – a mascot?

Now all roads lead to France
And heavy is the tread
Of the living; but the dead
Returning lightly dance:

Whatever the road may bring
To me or take from me,
They keep me company
With their pattering,

Crowding the solitude
Of the loops over the downs,
Hushing the roar of towns
And their brief multitude.

PART FIVE
BACK TO BIRMINGHAM

47. (Previous page) *Daisy Bank marl pit, Edensor, Stoke-on-Trent, Staffordshire*

13

'NICKEL PLATE AND BRUMMAGEM'

> One has not great hopes from Birmingham. I always say there is
> something direful in the sound ...
>
> Jane Austen, *Emma*, 1815

Direful it may have been, but if Jane Austen's Emma Woodhouse and George Knightley had gone on to raise a family, much in their household would have come from Birmingham. As the children grew, Birmingham buttons would fasten their clothes, the city's buckles would hold up their breeches, its pins the girls' hair, and mirrors would reflect their beauty. If Emma's son joined the army, his men would bear Birmingham firearms, very likely with Birmingham bayonets on the ends of them, and very likely encountering enemies who were likewise armed. Across the world wars would be fought and revolutions launched with Birmingham-made guns and swords, and since the pen is mightier than the sword, when young Captain Knightley wrote to his mother he did so with a Birmingham-made pen. Ulysses S. Grant reflected that a million American schoolchildren were as familiar with the pens of the Birmingham nib-maker Joseph Gillott as with Noah Webster's dictionary. The city was then turning out twenty million nibs a week. When Emma sleeps, the knobs on her bed, probably the bed itself, come from Birmingham. When she awakes, as like as not the ticking clock will bear the name of a Birmingham maker. The books she reads are printed in typefaces designed by Birmingham's resourceful John Baskerville, whose black gloss lacquer covers her jewellery box and the doors of the coach in which she rides. Her piano is strung on a frame from Birmingham, and when her daughter marries the wedding ring is made by a Birmingham goldsmith. Toys for Emma's grandchildren will be Birmingham-made, as indeed are the coins with which she buys them – just as they would be if she bought them in Chile, or the hundred other countries which use coinages minted in Hockley. And when Grandmother Emma dies, full of years, the grips on her coffin come from Birmingham. 'One might even say', mused Johanna Schopenhauer in 1803, 'that there is not a village in civilized Europe, perhaps not a house, where there cannot be found some industrial product made in that city, if only a button, a needle, or a pencil.'[1]

Since a few years before Schopenhauer's remark, some of Birmingham's manufacturers, scientists and professional men had taken to meeting in each other's homes to exchange ideas. Among them were the physician and poet Erasmus Darwin, the chemist Joseph Priestley, the steam pioneers Matthew Boulton and James Watt, and Josiah Wedgwood. From their habit of gathering on the evening of the Monday closest to the full moon, they called themselves the Lunar Society.[2] The Lunaticks understood the complexity of global links that had come to lie behind the humblest things. Like buttons – which archaeology often finds. Alongside buttons of metal, jet or horn Birmingham also made the mother-of-pearl type, for which shells were imported:[3] rainbow-coloured Macassars from the East Indies, lustrous Bombays and Alexandras from the Persian Gulf and the Red Sea, yellow-lipped oysters from Australian coasts, or the Panamas which offered little useful fabric but came very, very cheap.[4]

Or nails. When visitors described Birmingham to their friends it was often the knocking and banging that went on for miles and continued all day that they recalled. A lot of it was nailing: by 1875 the city was making over ten thousand billion nails a year, in hundreds of different sizes and varieties. By 1900 it is a question whether two pieces of wood anywhere in the world were unjoined by a Brummy nail. Long before that, around 1538, John Leland noted the 'great many Naylors' in the town.[5] A visitor in 1776 was drop-jawed at the sight of a 'continued village of nailers' that ran for three miles along the road between Birmingham and West Bromwich. This 'region of Vulcans' was just then entering hard times, for a sizeable part of its market had been cut off by the American Revolution. Revolution was in the air: in music, in art and in France, which partly in revenge for its recent humiliation in the Seven Years War (when both sides fought with Birmingham-made weapons) took the American rebels' part, inhaled their principles and crackled into a revolution of its own.

What can archaeology bring to understanding of what it was that predisposed Britain to become the first heavily industrialized society in the world? Like the Cold War, industrial capitalism affected every-one and changed everything, yet precisely because of that pervasive-ness neither its causes nor its effects are easily individualized. And as history fashions come and go, different determinants are emphasized or relegated accordingly.[6] Was it, as once thought, a combination of conveniently adjoining natural assets and a native gift for technological innovation? Or was it a complex of causes that worked in co-varying and sometimes inadvertent ways – factors like the influence of legis-lation upon particular industries, the protected colonial markets that stimulated imports and resale of goods overseas, the effect of institu-tional structures and taxation regimes, a new ideology of improvement or the consequences of wars?[7] Could it have been intellectual – the way to analysis of the world and its materials opened, say, by David Hume's *Treatise* of 1739–40, which put experience and observation in place of metaphysical speculation about ultimate 'original principles'?[8] Whatever it was, why did industrialization begin?

Arnold Toynbee, following J. L. and Barbara Hammond,[9] saw the intensification of industrial production as a revolution.[10] This idea, that industrial progress was something that 'broke out', like fighting in the street, is still with us. It is another result of the lumpish way in which we cut up time – a tendency which previous chapters have shown can encourage fixation with difference at the expense of affinity, put change before flow and predispose us to simple determinism. History does have its thunderclaps (the onset of the Neolithic, we have seen, appears to have been one of them), but an effect of declaring a revolution (and locating its 'birthplace' somewhere like Coalbrookdale) is to exaggerate contrasts with what went before, and to simplify explanations.

One contribution archaeology can make is to show the timing and tempo of individual advances.[11] Sarah Tarlow has demonstrated that before the middle of the eighteenth century little was published about the idea of 'improvement', whereas from c.1750 (a decade after Hume's *Treatise*) there was a sharp increase in such discussion, and use of the term in book titles.[12] On the basis of what people were saying to each other at the time, then, we might suppose the period 1750–1850 to have been giddy with the idea of improvement. In some senses it was, but if we single out some of the things that were being improved, the pic-ture changes. For instance, the agricultural enhancement that is often mentioned as having sustained urban industrialization and workforce growth was more long drawn out than the notion of 'revolution' has made it seem.[13] Medieval agriculture was not a slack, unfruitful enterprise awaiting the arrival of bustling figures like Jethro Tull to set the world straight. Sheep and cattle bones excavated from later medieval contexts show that increases in size resulting from selective breeding and changing strategies were occurring at least two centuries before the appearance of acknowledged improvers.[14] Likewise, in metallurgy, excavation shows that water power was harnessed to operate bellows and trip hammers before 1200, and that blast furnaces were being used to smelt iron by the end of the fifteenth century.[15] Cast-metal toys were being mass-produced by the reign of Edward III.[16] Coal was being mined on a substantial scale at least from the later Middle Ages. Stationary steam engines went back to the early 1700s. Britain's first canals were Roman. Wooden-railed tramways for horse-drawn coal or mineral wagons were laid as far back as Norman times.

In Reformed parts of Europe, one strong influence upon industrial development was the changed position of the Church. We have seen how traditional religion encouraged the giving of land to saints, and gifts of all kinds to fund the cult of the dead. These gifts built up; by the early sixteenth century something like a third of southern Britain was in ecclesiastical hands. Collectively, as owners of assets and as potential investors, religious communities and parishes wielded huge economic power. As corporate bodies capable of looking beyond the individual lifetime they could afford to take slow-maturing entrepreneurial decisions – witnessed, for instance, in the many years that might be required to patch together the land holdings needed to release landlocked mineral wealth. Trans-European orders like the Cistercians and Cluniacs were akin to international corporations, motivated to store, share or withhold knowledge independently of the social surroundings or political borders within which individual houses stood. In those parts of Europe where it took hold the Reformation broke this monopoly and redistributed the resources. The finding of ores, coal, fireclay or glass-suitable sands beneath infertile land altered the map of wealth. Some poor farmers became millionaires.

Reformation changed perceptions of time as well as access to resources. In the early seventeenth century 'modern' simply meant 'now'. Later, the idea of rolling change, of things of the latest kind as distinct from 'old-fashioned', takes hold. For some, indeed, the onset of the industrial revolution is defined by the point at which an individual would expect radical change in technology, fashion and landscape within their own lifetime. The pulse of medieval time, where clocks in towers called hours and the calendar was a perpetual re-enactment of history (p. 261),[17] was less hectic than the pace of industry in which time was measured in minutes and minutes were money. Of course, the Middle Ages were not changeless; parish churches built in the fourteenth century did not look like those built in the twelfth, and the effigies inside them remind us that hairstyles and fashion were always changing. Even so, it can be hazarded that a time traveller from the days of, say, Henry III to those of Henry VII would have been able to find his way about, whereas a Mancunian from the time of Charles II would be lost in his city by the end of the reign of George III.

Possibly the largest class of material recovered from early modern sites is ceramics.[18] Excavations among the six towns which make up Stoke-on-Trent show that Staffordshire's distinctive lead-glazed earthenwares were emerging from a semi-rural and technically mature milieu at least by the fifteenth century.[19] By the mid-seventeenth century, a full century before Toynbee declared 'the revolution', Staffordshire's posset pots, fuddling cups, tygs and dishes were being shipped to America and the Caribbean. Stoke's products in following decades reflect a world in change. The growth of intercontinental trade in the sixteenth century introduced exotic drinks like coffee, tea and choco-late. Initially, these drinks were so precious that they were consumed in elfin quantities. Around them, new social habits formed, which ceramics reflect. Delicate, elegant forms and wares, thinner walled and more finely glazed, were added to the existing repertoire of earthen-wares, and experiments began to produce a fabric which resembled Chinese porcelain. In the variety of these products and the places where they are found lie clues to the new kinds of social consensus and aspi-ration. Sarah Tarlow has asked why there was a shift from the natu-ral earth-toned colours of seventeenth-century ceramics and textiles towards whiteness. In bone china, the bleaching of cloth, white candles, white bread and sugar rather than brown she suggests we see a univer-sal shift in public expectation. Did this reflect a desire for purity in the presence of pollution, politeness in contrast to crudity, greater social dif-ferentiation reflected in what the visitor saw and what was used in the kitchen and back room?[20] The introduction of bone china in the later eighteenth century provided surfaces on which transfer printing could depict sophisticated images. The images chosen, commonly scenes of British landscape, or episodes from established novels, bear upon themes such as national and cultural identity.[21] 'Membership of polite society in the nineteenth century was no longer based primarily on birth and blood, but on subscription to a set of shared values and tastes which could be demonstrated in daily material practice.'[22]

To gather up so far: the industrial revolution in its arousal was not a sudden outbreak of invention but a nexus of interdependencies which from the seventeenth century began to surge both qualitatively and in scale, and in which artefacts acquired new meanings and offered new opportunities. The physical upwelling was remarkable. By the 1850s, wire was reeling out of Birmingham so fast that just one week's output was enough to run a fence across Australia. Yet for as long as history was dominated by high culture, many aspects of that story seemed prosaic, even distasteful, and perhaps because of that it is only lately that historians have begun to notice them. An example is the use of cast iron in the mills and factories which were put up from the 1770s. This is familiar enough, although so accustomed are we to factories and industrial units it is easy to forget that in the eighteenth century the idea of bringing hundreds of workers together to concentrate production under one roof was itself novel. Up to then, production had mostly been from home. Indeed, if the industrial revolution had a defining moment it was the point at which large sections of the workforce switched from selling things they made to selling their labour. Cluster working called for new kinds of organization, time-discipline,[23] building and place. The only structures previously built to shelter large indoor gatherings were great churches, barns and the halls of magnates and guilds. Factory design thus had to be worked out from scratch.[24] This was not straightforward: wood-floored mills were susceptible to fire, while it took time to get to know the engineering properties of cast iron beams within larger structures. Some early iron-framed mills fell down. Examples of the first generation, like the flax mill at Ditherington, built 1796-97 on the outskirts of Shrewsbury, are correspondingly rare.

The building of stable, fire-resistant multi-storey factories called for reliable iron beams. A beam is a kind of dispute between two kinds of stress, the upper part being squeezed by the load it carries, the lower being stretched. In the early 1800s, the physicist Eaton Hodgkinson (from 1847, Professor of Mechanical Engineering at University College London) tested iron beams in the foundry of an iron-master called William Fairbairn at Ancoats. Fairbairn was a friend of George Stephenson, with whom he had served a wheelwright's apprenticeship in South Shields. He was besotted by iron.[25] By trying beams of different shape, Hodgkinson and Fairbairn found that a beam with a cross-section in the shape of a capital letter I, with elliptical flanges, was not only more efficient than other types but also lighter and cheaper. Such beams were timely, for they suited the bridges* and wide-span train sheds of the railways begun in the 1820s. The first mills known to use them were put up in the mid-1820s.[26] Within fifteen years this form of construction was itself being overtaken by regional and simplified variants.[27]

The success of the factory system, and from that the expansion of cities and national economies, can in several senses be said to rest on types of girder like the humble Hodgkinson beam. Beams of derived type also provided the wherewithal for the 'gospel of height' which was preached in American cities from the 1870s. Fairbairn was still alive when R. M. Hunt's Tribune Building was begun in New York in 1873, and other early high-rise structures like Chicago's Home Insurance Building (1885) relied on technology which had been tested by Hodgkinson and Fairbairn back in the days of Jane Austen. By the century's end, such buildings were having a reflex influence on the design of structures like theatres and hotels back in Europe. Even the Black Horse, that great Tudor pastiche in Northfield, was built around an armature of steel girders.

Technology and commerce were sustained by venture capital, insurance, shipping administration and a framework of company law. Such functions required accommodation and government, often in new kinds of building. The buildings tended to clump together because of the interdependence of what went on inside them, and to use materials symbolically, like stone for banks, to impart a sense of permanence. Architectural references to the classical world and the national past brought city centre squares and temple-like town halls into connection with Grecian culture, democracy and fine achievements. With them went slums. In 1844–5, Friedrich Engels described them.

> Every great city has one or more slums, where the working-class is crowded together. True, poverty often dwells in hidden alleys close to the palaces of the rich; but, in general, a separate territory has been assigned to it, where, removed from the sight of the happier classes, it may struggle along as it can. These slums are pretty equally arranged in all the great towns of England, the worst houses in the worst quarters of the towns; usually one- or two-storied cottages in long rows, perhaps with cellars used as dwellings, almost always irregularly built.

---

* In 1846, Fairbairn and Hodgkinson collaborated in the revolutionary design of the bridge over the Menai Strait, in which the bridge derives strength from the form of a hollow tube.

These houses of three or four rooms and a kitchen form, throughout England, some parts of London excepted, the general dwellings
of the working-class. The streets are generally unpaved, rough, dirty,
filled with vegetable and animal refuse, without sewers or gutters,
but supplied with foul, stagnant pools instead. Moreover, ventilation
is impeded by the bad, confused method of building of the whole
quarter, and since many human beings here live crowded into a small
space, the atmosphere that prevails in these working-men's quarters
may readily be imagined. Further, the streets serve as drying grounds
in fine weather; lines are stretched across from house to house, and
hung with wet clothing.[28]

The human consequences of the slums, like the enormous yet evanescent temporary camps that housed those who built railways, have thus
far received little archaeological attention. Given that the massing of
workers in small spaces was arguably the greatest single physical change
wrought by industrialization, this is strange. Slums in which industrial-
ists treated individuals as dehumanized particles ran hand in hand with
a big idea, propounded in 1832, that information or numbers or cotton,
like factory workers, can be processed in ways governed by universal
principles. A contemporary of Robert Willis at Cambridge designed
what he called a Difference Engine – a device to make calculations,
which in its breaking down of big tasks into sub-sequences of small
ones foreshadowed the modern computer.[29]

From the sixteenth century, it becomes less and less possible to study
the past 'as if it happened in only one place'.[30] Crafts were transplanted
around the world. The printing and dyeing skills behind the vivid cotton
fabrics we know as chintz, for instance, were learned from India in the
seventeenth century and mechanized in Britain. Manchester-designed
mills were erected in Russia. Lamps in London houses burned oil from
whales hunted near Greenland. Mountains in Wales were hollowed out
for slates to roof American factories. Travellers in Argentina boarded
trains at English country railway stations. A bowl thrown on a wheel in
Buckley might be broken in Cairo. Cornish engine houses were built in
Mexico. Ceramics made in British kilns in Britain now help to anchor
chronologies in Australia.[31] And in Australia, too, indigenous people
turned shards of European glass and porcelain back into Mesolithic
tools.

Merchant fleets became the circulatory system of a planet-wide economy, taking goods to overseas markets, returning with supplies of raw

materials for reworking and selling on. The ships themselves could alter land. So many colliers worked in and out of the rivers of north-east England that the dumping of ballast taken from south-east England changed the shorelines of the Tyne and Wear. People, as well as ballast, were shipped about. During the sixteenth century alone some 370,000 now unnameable men, women and children were taken against their will from Africa to the Caribbean and America.[32] In the eighteenth century the figure rose to six million – more than the entire population of medieval Britain. This trade, with its triangular voyages from Europe to west Africa, the notorious middle passage and return from the Caribbean, is a subject for eternal reproach. It explains why, for some today, conventional 'heritage' does not merely have an elitist tinge, its country houses and monuments of power seeming to exclude where most people live, but bears the stain of association with colonialism and slavery.[33] Some great houses were indeed built with profits from slaving, just as others were built before European navigators ever reached west Africa, and many since were funded by other enterprises – although how one might disentangle 'dirty' capital from other areas of the economy in which it was reinvested is a question. More problematic, however, is the implication that blame for slavery is historically localized. It is true that the Atlantic slave trade, like the Holocaust, has an infernal immensity and organizational coherence which demands to be seen as an entity. But that in turn has a context. Long before Portuguese, French or British traders began to plunder Africa, Europe's peoples were selling each other. Iron Age metalwork recovered from the former lake of Llyn Cerrig Bach on Anglesey included several sets of slave chains. According to Strabo, probably writing in the first century AD, slaves were one of later prehistoric Britain's main exports. Raiders from both sides of the North Sea took slaves. So did the Irish – which is (we are told) how Patrick, a citizen of Roman Britain, became apostle to Ireland. The story about Pope Gregory the Great being stirred to thought about a mission to England by the sight of English boys for sale in a Roman market is almost certainly a legend.[34] However, in 595 Gregory did write to his agent in Gaul telling him to use income from papal estates to buy Anglo-Saxon boys, who were to be placed in monasteries.[35] Four hundred years later, the last Anglo-Saxon Bishop of Worcester* confronted ship-masters at Bristol to protest against the export of boys and girls to Ireland.[36] The possibility dawns that much of the wealth which

---

* Wulfstan, 1062–95.

has been noticed across southern Britain in earlier chapters was derived not only from agricultural surpluses but also from the export of surplus people.[37] After the Battle of Worcester in 1651 hundreds of Scottish prisoners were transported to Virginia and sold as slaves.[38] History is honeycombed with exclusions, and it is right that they should be made good. However, just as the twentieth century's vast killings have left some uneasy lest their suffering has been less than others, an indefinite dividing of the past will lead to vying between victims until nothing is held in common.[39] The singling out of the country house as a symbol for the oppression of one category of victim arguably narrows a theme – slavery – which might actually be a cause for cultural adherence.

Although Britain's industrialization has attracted the close attention of economic historians, its material legacy is still under-valued. Of course, there are plenty of exceptions, but aside from nostalgia and the earmarking of token monuments much of the *general* archaeology of recent times – the gasworks, the back-to-back houses, the saltworks – is still looked upon as something to be academically indulged while environmentally abjured. In England, only one deep-mine colliery complex survives; the rest were intentionally obliterated within five years of the run-down of the coal industry in the 1980s. While waste tips of vanished industries are greened, archaeology buries itself in technical detail, and by lending its name to single-interest enthusiasms – for railways, for crashed aircraft, for canals. Such narrowing is reflected in a continuing tendency for the archaeology of recent times to be considered as *industrial* archaeology, as distinct from the archaeology of the age and society in which industry burgeoned. This in turn sets up an antagonism between archaeology and the counter-industrial eco-ruralism we met in the last chapter.

Nowhere is this more obvious than in the popular supposition that public amenity must wear green, or that green and brown are mutually exclusive. Coketown conurbations are taken as the norm to repudiate, yet, as we have seen, most of the activities that we think of as 'industrial' have historically taken place in rural surroundings. Runcorn's landscape of chemical manufacturing and flaring stacks lies where it does because of proximity to the rock-salt strata of Cheshire that have been exploited at least from later prehistory. Leeds in 1800 was neither uninterrupted buildings nor unbroken countryside, but an interleaving of mills, houses and fields. Out-working was still practised in the 1940s, when the Mosquito in which Jack and Bess's son went to war was built from sub-assemblies contributed by local workshops. When he came back, there were nailers' cottages still standing in Northfield, where many of the nailers had been girls. The National Parks which cover 10 per cent of England and 20 per cent of Wales were established to 'preserve and enhance natural beauty', yet they are criss-crossed with lead rakes, pierced by mines and pocked by waste that most people do not notice because they are now covered by grasses, bracken and heather. Around the coast, many places now thought of as unspoiled were once smoky little ports, each with its own lime kilns, warehouse and quay for the shipping out of slate, minerals, bricks and roadstone. Roadstone: the coming of the motor car called for smooth surfaces upon which vehicles could run. The laying and relaying of motor roads came at a double cost: of tracts of landscape dug up to supply the materials, and other tracts buried. Something like 1.5 per cent of the UK's surface now lies under roads.

Farming became industrialized. From the 1840s rising prices and the advance of agricultural science encouraged efforts to push up yields from hitherto unproductive land. After the repeal of the corn laws there was investment in the bringing of cattle into covered yards where they could be fed on compounds, steam power for threshing and haulage, railways to carry fodder, even lighting fuelled by methane from the ordure of animals. Here is the progressive world of Donald Farfrae in Hardy's *The Mayor of Casterbridge*. Something of Farfrae's spirit is seen in a farm created during the 1850s at Leighton, near Welshpool in Powys, by a Liverpool banker. Leighton was a temple to interdependency, where manure from the stock house was mixed with bone meal ground on the site, and then pumped up to a slurry tank whence it was distributed to fields. Hayricks were borne by a broad-gauge railway into a cavernous barn. There was a funicular railway, water turbines, a saw mill, rotunda piggeries, a root house and gasworks, all built with bricks fired in the farm's own brickworks.[40]

How much of this worked? Some historians dismiss places like Leighton as quirky monuments to an uncritical faith in technological novelty. To leave it at that, however, would be to yield to the tendency to trivialize or glamorize token aspects of recent times while ignoring the rest. Such selectivity might be seen as a kind of displacement, a backing away from the delineation of fields of study in the face of the vastness of what there is to explore. At any rate, our two main inherited images of industrialization, those of stinking hardship and of headway led by brilliant scientists and entrepreneurs, seem equally unsatisfactory. Moreover, as we have seen in earlier chapters the history of technology is usually simplified to the history of what worked, which puts stress on the inevitability of success rather than all the varying forces and processes that may actually have been in play.

There is, too, a question of how much we really want to know, and what role the heritage industry has in trying to explain. Museums which claim to bring industrial history back to life are often sentimentalized substitutes for truths which are hard to endure. At some industrial museums you will meet friendly, well-fed and well-intended volunteers in period costume who tell you 'what it was like' to work in a place a hundred years ago. This cobbled past is not the gasping world in which everyone's lungs in parts of the Potteries were scoured by the inhalation of powdered calcined flint, where child prostitution and incest were rife, where poor women and children went barefoot, where thousands in the lead industry died young, where copper miners daily climbed into and out of 2,000-foot-deep mines by ladder. Nor is it the past where the last act of saltworkers fleeing from a flooding mine gallery was to shoot the horses that had served them for years, because the exit was too narrow to get them out in time, or where entire cities stood on the brink of insurrection. A map of the cavalry barracks around many northern cities is telling. It must be a map, for in most cases the barracks have gone. No museum or carefully restored specimen of workers' housing can either reproduce or do justice to the scale of the human tragedy witnessed by Engels – the filth, ruin, stink, degradation, despair and putrefying animal and vegetable materials.[41] Perhaps it should not try.

In seeking archaeology's forefront in the historical period it is instructive to look abroad. In Australia and New Zealand, the Caribbean and America, the buildings, landscapes and artefacts from pre-colonial contact to the present day are treated in one sweep.[42] In Australia one can watch the contest between imported and locally developed technology, or the clearance of land, and subtle graduations of servitude.[43] In America, the relations between native and European, woman and man, slave and planter, are illuminated by details of ordinary life revealed by material culture and, later, by town planning, architecture and houses. In Chapter 1 we met an example of such – what shall we call it? – domestic archaeology: that estate of kit houses imported to Longbridge from Bay City, Michigan, by Herbert Austin in 1917.

Bay City began as a lumber town, served by tributaries of the Saginaw River down which were floated millions of logs cut from primordial woodland. The years 1850 to 1880 were a boom period, when Saginaw mills converted cypress, cedar, oak, maple, yellow pine and Oregon fir

48. Advertisement for mail-order city in Aladdin Homes' 1917 catalogue, which advertised homes built of timber brought 'Direct from the Forest to the Home'.

into practically anything, and sent it around the world. When the trees began to dwindle, Bay City diversified. In 1895 one enterprising firm began to sell house plans along with building materials. Soon afterwards the Aladdin Company of Bay City extended the idea of kit boats to buildings. (In the story of Aladdin, you remember, Aladdin's slave built a castle in one night.) Initially, the kits were for simple things like sheds or hog houses, but as time passed the idea was extended to entire dwellings, supplied as pre-cut, numbered parts, accompanied by full instructions and every screw, hinge and blob of putty needed to put them together. Aladdin became dream-makers, their economies of scale, mechanization and finance packages putting home-ownership within the reach of ordinary people. Aladdin enlisted the friendship of customers, and so confident were they over the quality of their wild-wood timber that they promised to pay one dollar for every knot which could be found in the Red Cedar boards with which their houses were sheathed.

By 1916 Aladdin's catalogue illustrated seventy-five different types of house, from the impressive 'Villa' which cost $3,420 to the tiny 'Erie' at less than $290. How or when one of these catalogues came into Herbert Austin's hands we don't know, but by 1916 his Motor Company needed to accommodate a workforce that had expanded tenfold in eighteen months and was spending a large part of each day travelling. In that year the Austin Company purchased 120 acres from Thomas Middlemore of Hawkesley Farm, and placed an order for 200 Readi-cut bungalows. The scheme was set back when the ship bringing the first consignment of kits was torpedoed. However, the lost parts were replaced, and in 1917 the bungalows were built. At intervals were larger brick houses, inter-spersed at the insistence of the city council as firebreaks.[44]

The idea of model housing provided by altruistic employers had precedents, for instance at Saltaire in the West Riding of Yorkshire.[45] More recently, altruistic thinkers like Ebenezer Howard had argued for new kinds of places in which the best of urban and rural life could be combined.[46] This idea was launched by Howard at Letchworth from 1903, later at Welwyn, and by others abroad, but most locally it had been pioneered just up the Bristol Road in the garden village of Bournville, begun through the formation of a trust by the cocoa and chocolate tycoon George Cadbury.[47] Bournville was begun in reaction to the abjection of Birmingham's slums, its aim being to restore Nature to everyday surroundings. Something similar was in mind at New Earswick, begun by Joseph Rowntree on the outskirts of York in 1904, after his son published a book about York's poverty.[48] As at Longbridge, New Earswick's roads were edged by grass and named after the species of tree with which they were lined. Perhaps some of this got back to Bay City, for over the next few years the Aladdin Company tried out the idea of a mail-order city which came complete with its own schools, sidewalks, churches and fire-station. This never caught on, but an American's description of the 'Chester' as a 'rich man's house in reach of every working man' was exactly the point. The Austin Village houses were based on the 'Chester', and by the standards of Birmingham working-class housing, they were luxurious.

Whereas New Earswick's bricks were fired from local clay, so that in true organicist spirit the place rose from the ground on which it stands, the Longbridge Estate took its materials from the primeval forest for which we searched in Chapter 6, and its architecture was invested with other kinds of meaning. High among them was modernity, explicitly reflected in Aladdin catalogues which described a complex of virtues as well as a system of construction. The company professed moral soundness in dealings with customers, and the efficiency of 'modern

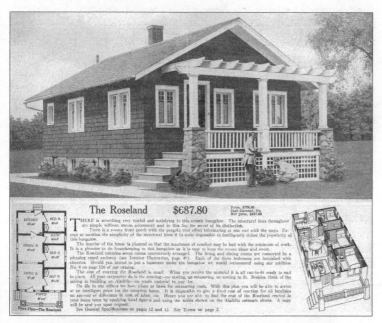

49. 'The Roseland', Aladdin catalogue, 1917

power-driven machines' which reduced waste and costs.[49] Here was no Ruskinian threnody for a golden age of lost crafts: Aladdin's pitch was the opposite, that machines performed many tasks better than people, and that economies of scale put top designers at the service of ordinary folk. In American thought, newness was not a threat but a virtue: readers of Aladdin's 1917 catalogue were reminded that whereas the steel system used to build skyscrapers was twenty-five years old, the Aladdin system was a mere twelve years old.

The houses themselves epitomized what were imagined to be American values. Thus the 'Lamberton' was described in the 1917 catalogue as 'straight, simple and massive', while the double doors at the centre of the 'Kentucky's' verandah 'seem to open wide a hospitality of true American spirit'. The 'Sunshine' was distinctively American because its simplicity implied 'character, quality and taste … cheerfulness, happiness and light'.[50] The ideals of family life were stressed in points of convenience about the 'New Eden', illustrated by photographs arranged in the style of a family album. Technical modernity was balanced by the reassuring appearance of tradition. 'New England' characteristics (defined as 'severe, simple and quiet') were combined with those of the colonial South. Names like 'Dresden' and 'Old English', or a roof line borrowed from Japan, reflect cosmopolitan influences which played upon American culture. Even poverty was given a wholesome tinge, being represented as simplicity and thrift. Catalogue readers were assured that 'many good families' were living cosily in the four rooms of the 'Rodney' ($340.10, with discount), while for those of even more moderate means who would dearly like to own their 'own little home' there was the tiny four-roomed 'Selwyn', at just $294.50.

As well as being soundly made and progressively equipped, a Readi-cut home was a subscription to an identity – a selfhood which was at once progressive yet recollected the resourcefulness and fellowship associated with pioneering during the century just gone. Aladdin emphasized individual decision (buyers were encouraged to specify their own variations of layout and finish) and devotion to family. What could be more American than building your own house with your own hands, with the help of your friends?[51]

The Longbridge houses are still there. Few now retain their original fittings, although a handful are said to have kept their radiators and pipes, and one or two doors may still wear the knobs and locks with which they were first supplied. (Future archaeologists will need to be on their mettle lest some of the original fittings have since been reused in other buildings.) Each house will have a corona of shards, fragments and things discarded – items like gas brackets, ornaments, toys, food remains, the debris of hobbies. A comparison of Aladdin properties on the Longbridge estate and in the United States would be instructive, for the different milieux in which they were occupied will have left contrasting kinds and mixtures of material, which collectively bear on aspects of life such as childhood, pastimes, differences and changes in living standards, and the growing influence of the new world's popular culture.

A dollar a knot. Many who browsed Aladdin catalogues in the 1920s would have had grandparents who lived through the American Civil War, and a contrasting example of social archaeology is found about 160 miles south of Bay City, in the site of the Confederate Officers' Prison on Johnson's Island, in Lake Erie, close to Sandusky, Ohio. About four hundred thousand prisoners were taken during that war, of whom nine thousand were interned on Johnson's Island. The experiences of these men and their captors are documented in diaries, letters, military records, and in the amnesty register which prisoners signed to regain their freedom when the war ended in 1865. There are photographs, too, for this war was one of the first to be fought under the camera's stare.

In other ways the place is its own record. The sixteen acres enclosed by Johnson's Island's stockade contained a dozen wooden accommodation blocks, outdoor privies, a hospital, mess halls, wells and a sutler's shop to meet small wants like sewing sets, combs and ink. Beyond the enclosure stood the guards' barracks and married quarters, stables and stores. Begun late in 1861, the huts were complete by February 1862 and housing prisoners by April. The green timber shrank. In the humid Ohio summer, prisoners poked out knot holes for extra ventilation. In winter, they shivered as the scant warmth given out by their oak- and hickory-burning stoves leaked away. If the Aladdin Company's dollar-a-knot guarantee had applied on Johnson's Island, the prisoners would have left as millionaires.

Archaeology pencils shadows on this picture. Most artefacts, excavation tells us, derived from one of two directions, prisoners' families or the Union, and many of them have to do with eating. One has an impression that food was an aching, all-day, everyday fixation. Games and gaming pieces betoken dragging time. Objects whittled from wood or made from bits of scrap were produced for sale, to raise a few cents which probably take us back to food. Although the first inmates were a mix of all ranks and political prisoners, the camp later came to hold

officers only, its pre-eminence as a centre of the Southern elite being
reflected in the quality and character of objects sent from home. Some
of the prisoners had access to china and crystal, even when they were
eating scraps. Particularly emotive are the nibs of pens through which
passed tens of thousands of words in letters to loved ones, and the
perimeter ditch dug down to bedrock as a precaution against tunnels
through which attempts were made to rejoin them.[52] At one point the
Confederate Secret Service tried to organize a mass breakout, and each
winter when Lake Erie froze there were officers who chanced the walk
across the ice to Canada. Lake Erie is a small sea, one side invisible from
the other, and to succeed an escaper had to trek for thirty-five miles
in sub-zero weather. A few of the men who attempted this were still
living when Tom and Emily Wearne settled on the far side of Lake Erie
in 1925. Like millions of others, the Wearnes were economic migrants.
They came from England. They are my other grandparents.

50. *Emily Smith, c.1904*   51. *Tom Wearne, c.1904*

14

COUSIN JACK

Blow the Stars home, Wind, blow the Stars home
Ere Morning drowns them in golden foam.

Eleanor Farjeon, 'Blow the Stars Home',
Silver-sand and Snow, 1951

Orb and Sceptre, William Walton's march for the coronation of Elizabeth II, brings it all back: sitting on the floor that Tuesday, while my parents listened to the broadcast from London. It seemed to go on for a long time. We had no television, so I did not see the archbishop place the orb in the Queen's right hand, or place the rod of equity and mercy in her left. The bitter-sweet counter-melodies around the last statement of the 'sweeping tune in C major, reminiscent of Parry and Elgar' (as *The Times* put it)[1] made the march seem half regretful as well as the opening of a new Elizabethan age. It was a strange day; something was in the air.

Next morning we were up at six, and there was a taxi at the door. Taxis were rare – a curate's stipend was then about five pounds a week. But our luggage included a trunk, and we couldn't carry that to the station. We were going away for three months. We were going to Canada.

Two memories remain of our journey to Southampton. One centres on a small hedged field just down the road. In this field was a mare called Blackie. As the taxi pulled away under the clear sky and warming sun, there in the glittering dew was her new-born foal. When we returned in September they had gone. The other is Southampton itself. As we sat in a wooden café eating egg and chips late in the afternoon, there was immense open space between us and liners moored in the docks. My parents explained that this was the result of bombing twelve years before. One of the liners we were looking at was the SS *Atlantic*, the vessel that would take us to Quebec. She was painted white. Records of ships tell us that she was built in Philadelphia in 1926 and refurbished in 1937. We boarded late in the afternoon, and by evening we were at sea.

My mother had not seen her mother, nor indeed most of her relatives, since her return to England in 1946. The relatives had clubbed together to pay our fares. Five days later I stood on deck, marvelling at icebergs and watching a distant dolphin launch itself vertically out of the water. To the west was a line of cloud. Next morning when I looked out there were pine trees on a lofty steep slope: we were on the St Lawrence River. On the dockside were railway tracks, and big locomotives with cow-catchers and swinging bells that clanged as they moved to and fro. By the end of the day we were at Point Pelee in Nana Wearne's wooden house. She was small and a little frail, but bright and decisive, and pleased to see her daughter and her grandson. For the grandson it was a good place to be – the back door led straight on to the beach, and Lake Erie was like the sea.

Nana Wearne had been born Emily Smith in 1880 in Tansor, Northamptonshire. She was the second in a family of nine, most of whom were born not in Northamptonshire but in Yorkshire, at Skinningrove on the North Riding coast. Here her father, originally a farm labourer, found work at the Iron and Steel Works, where blast furnaces gasped rhythmically, *puff*, *puff*, with alternately strong and weak exhalations, and after dark the undersides of clouds were bronzed by the glow from tipped slag.

Emily's schooling ended at thirteen. She went into domestic service with two sisters in Ilkley. In due course she fell in love with a young man, and he with her. Unluckily, the man belonged to one of Ilkley's wealthy families. His parents stepped in with warnings about marrying out of class. He was sent away. When Emily did marry, in 1906, it was to Tom Wearne.

Tom was born around 1875, at Carnkie, near Redruth in Cornwall. Like Emily, he was one of a family of nine. There was a tin mine at either end of the hamlet. The family were miners, but they also leased a smallholding, kept a cow and made clotted cream over a kitchen fire. The cream was so thick that it would support a four-pound weight. The older boys worked in tin and copper mines, and one by one left to work abroad – in Australia, Cuba, Pennsylvania, Indiana – and then come home to die of drink or pneumoconiosis.

The Wearnes are a microcosm of the society that sustained the industrial revolution elsewhere in Britain, and the transfer of mining and steam technology to the rest of the world.[2] Cornish tin was used to make pewter, solder and tin plate for the canning industry. Alloyed with copper, it made bronze for machine bearings and marine propellers. Copper went into the boilers, vats and piping used for dyeing and the processing of sugar. Copper was also the main constituent of brass, and hence the making of parts for steam engines, brass goods and cartridges for fighting wars. Birmingham's brass industry relied on Cornish copper. Arsenic went into dyes and pigments for the Lancashire textile industry, and was exported as an early insecticide.[3]

The rocks that produced tin and copper had been exploited since prehistory. From the early 1800s, rising demand stimulated innovations in processing, expanded transport and deep-shaft mining that in turn prompted the development of high-pressure steam pumps. This know-how travelled.

> As a leader in mining expertise [Cornwall's] miners were in demand in other, new mining regions. By the 1820s Cornish miners were being recruited for mines in Latin America. Within a generation a flourishing culture of emigration had been created and links with North America and Australia forged. During the fall in world copper prices in the late 1860s and the crisis decade of the 1870s, when tin prices were also in recession, the Cornish had a ready-made option. They left.[4]

From the 1830s, Cornwall was one of Europe's leading regions of emigration, passing traditions, expertise, culture and stories around the world. This is why the Adelaide Hills are full of Cornish place names, why Australia's Yorke Peninsula is known as 'Little Cornwall', and why the townships of Moonta, Wallaroo and Kadina are 'the largest Cornish communities beyond Land's End'.[5] And if there was a job to be done a Cornish migrant worker would always have a cousin called Jack who could be invited to join them to do it.

Young Tom was a frustrated musician. Self-taught, in his small spare time he would climb Carn Brae to dream among its giant stones and study the *Smallwood Pianoforte Tutor*. Eventually he read that there were jobs in Yorkshire at the Iron and Steel Works at Skinningrove, and a few days after his twenty-first birthday left home and went to Yorkshire. The four-roomed house in New Company Row in which he lodged with six or seven other Cornish migrants is still there. It was overlooked by Emily's family house, at the top of the hill behind the blast furnaces. Tom got a job as a blast-furnace keeper. He and Emily raised five children, first in Skinningrove, then in nearby Redcar, then from 1914 at Cadishead near Manchester, where Tom had a supervisor's job at the ironworks.

Strangeness lay around Cadishead. To the north lay the peaty print of another long-vanished lake. The district supplied vegetables to nearby Manchester and Liverpool but while the area was cultivated it also felt remote. Just to the south ran the Manchester Ship Canal, along which ships whirred to or from the Atlantic. From a distance, a ship gliding through the fields was an incongruity. Closer to it was an approaching drama, its bows sucking the water down, exposing oily rocks, junk and sludge. As the vessel passed, deckhands sometimes threw oranges to watching children on the path below.

At the end of August 1925 the Wearnes themselves boarded a ship and went to Canada. Immigration records catch their arrival on 4 September: Edna, fifteen; Emily, forty-five; Helena May, twelve; Arthur, nineteen. Tom had gone ahead, finding work with an engineering company (metal again), while his eldest daughter Elsie stayed behind to complete her School Certificate. In the following year, a few days after her last exam, the seventeen-year-old set out to rejoin her family. She took the train to Liverpool and boarded the SS *Montcalm*. Next day, early, the *Montcalm* anchored a mile or so off Cork and waited for a tender to bring out Irish passengers. Cork looked near in the sharp light. There were splashes of green on the cliff tops. As the approaching tender ploughed between the glittering tops of breaking waves, Elsie heard the sound of a trumpet. Someone was playing 'I'll take you home again, Kathleen'.[6] Later that day, looking down the foamy highway of the *Montcalm*'s wake that led back towards England, she wept. Years later, now a teacher in Ontario, she sometimes saw vessels passing through the Great Lakes, crewed by men who threw apples and oranges to children. Among them were ships that had passed through Cadishead.

Tom and Emily's descendants have spread across North America, their heartlands of Cornish tin and copper and Skinningrove steel mostly unremembered. Only Elsie went back, twenty years later, to that cold, unfurnished nineteenth-century house wedged between a pen works and cardboard-box factory in inner Birmingham, where this book began.

Around 1980 I came upon this house. I found it by chance, after taking a wrong turning when leaving the city after a lecture. I nearly missed it, for there was little else still standing from when we lived there. Yet beside a desolate plain where plastic bags blew, there it was. I stopped

52. The Clergy House, New John Street West, Birmingham, 1950

the car. Near by, the cardboard-box factory was still there, and so too the Brandauer pen works. The gate into the asphalt yard was open. Through the letterbox I could see the light-green rubbery lino on the stairs down which I fell in 1950, and the alcove in which my father set a great fir tree one Christmas. That tree was a vast excitement, bought cheap as the market was closing on Christmas Eve 1951, dragged home at the head of a cheering procession of small boys, and decorated with exotic ornaments from Canada. Above, the freezing bedroom which had had nothing in it apart from my cot, the room in which my mother had danced to cheer me when I had measles.

A year or two later I went to look again, but the house had gone.

Birmingham. A kind of poetry blooms out of the names of its inhabitants' occupations, revealed by the census of 1891. Building and transport trades are prominent (*slater, bricklayer, steam train inspector, boatman*); so too glass working, even more so clothiers (*fur cutter, button dipper, linen machinist, straw bonnet maker, staymaker, milliner*) and footwear (*clog maker, boot finisher, shoe finisher*). Horse-drawn transport remains important long into the twentieth century (*horse collar maker, bridle stitcher, leather stitcher*). As late as the 1920s the Austin car makers used shire horses to haul cartloads of components around their factory. But of course it is the metal trades which loom largest. *Revolver, spring maker, gunbarrel fitter, gun finisher* – over a hundred different aptitudes went into the making of a single gun. Such specialization, led by independent craftsmen, and the absence of dominant mass employers, enabled religious diversity to thrive. This is partly why the religious geography of Birmingham differs from that of, say, Manchester or Bradford. Aside from the Anglicans and a strong Catholic community, here flourished dissenters of all kinds – Particular Baptists, Swedenborgians, Arminian Baptists, Calvinists, Welsh Calvinistic Methodists, Primitive Methodists, Methodist New Connection, Countess of Huntingdon's Connection, the Plymouth Brethren, Unitarians – each with their own chapels and meeting-houses, most of which have risen and fallen in the space of two hundred years.[7]

A list of residents' occupations in the street where we lived gives a conspectus of the city's work and history: *japanner, bicycle fitter, brass finisher, steam engine maker, brass knob turner, street lamp maker, metal roller, pen slitter, nail caster, steel pen temperer, bicycle spoke screwer, brass founder, pearl button carder, jewel case finisher, pen worker, pen grinder, lacquerer, gun maker, hair pin maker, metal annealer, clock maker, tube caster, bedstead tube worker, gilt chain maker, gun engraver …*

What stories are here? What became of Leah Zissman, twenty-three and out of Russia, with her son Myer, three, and daughter Zetta, one? For Joseph and Annie Maginski, what lay between Russia and Irving Street? When did Marks and Esther Freedman leave Poland? What had happened to bring Sarah Shineberg, Hifman Asher or Cairy Weinstein to Birmingham? Within a generation, maybe two, many of their names will have been anglicized, their birthplaces merged with those of other Warwickshire families. Archaeologically, this coalescence is part of a continuum which embraces the gold-adorned man from central Europe who was buried near Stonehenge around forty-three centuries ago, the travellers from north Germany who came to Sancton Wold in the sixth century, and the Wearnes fanning across America and Australia in the twentieth. We underestimate movement in the past, preferring invasion to continuum – it is easier to explain things that way. Yet just as striking a thing about the birthplaces listed in the 1891 census is how many of them were local. Birmingham was cosmopolitan, yes, but most of its citizens had grown up amid its smoke and hammering, just as contemporary photographs of its back streets reveal how many outbuildings and inns were skeletoned by the timber frames of an older Warwickshire.

Gilder, wire weaver, brass polisher, iron filer, nail cutter, fork polisher, spoon filer, screwmaker, wire drawer, kettle maker, solderer, chandelier brass filer, *watch bluestoner*, *silver burnisher*, *gold cutter* ... All these trades dealt in artefacts, the very stuff of archaeology, but it does not seem likely that excavation would reflect some of the intricacy or subtlety of craft differentiation that is revealed by written records. *Gold cutter*, for instance. Despite Birmingham's prowess in gold working, future excavators will not find much gold. By the mid-eighteenth century the fine sweepings from goldsmiths' and silversmiths' workshops were being collected and chemically refined for reuse; by the late nineteenth, some jewellers had even installed iron gratings on their floors to prevent valuable filings being taken out on the soles of their workers' shoes.[8] Yet in the first century BC, we recall from Chapter 2, gold and electrum neck-rings were carefully left in a Norfolk field. What goes on?

15

UNSETTLED REMAINS

By walking men's reversèd feet
I chanced another world to meet;
Though it did not to view exceed
A phantom, 'tis a world indeed;
    Where skies beneath us shine,
    And earth by art divine
Another face presents below,
Where people's feet against ours go.

Thomas Traherne, 'Shadows in the Water',
The Poetical Works of Thomas Traherne, 1636?–1674:
from the original manuscripts, 1906

The 1950s slum where we started borders Birmingham's Jewellery Quarter. Described in 2000 as a 'national treasure', the Jewellery Quarter has become the subject of much scholarship.[1] Birmingham itself is now archaeologically studied.[2] The trams have their museum. The block of flats which demanded the demolition of medieval Hawkesley Farm has in turn been condemned. The tract of rough pasture where I lay one summer's evening looking up at butterflies has become a close-mown recreation ground. The stream where newts swam runs underground in a concrete culvert. The starlings have gone. From Google Earth I can see that the rowan tree planted by Bess and Jack in 1947 has gone too, although a copper beech in which I loved to climb still flourishes. The Austin Motor works, latterly known as MG Rover, went into administration in 2005. Most of the factory has been pulled down; what is left now belongs to the Nanjing Automobile Group of China. The Black Horse, steel-framed and half-timbered, where Jack and my father would go for their Christmas halves of bitter, is now a listed building.

The horses dragging Time's car tread on history's heels, and we have come a distance. Like characters flitting between different plays, some subjects have been met over and over again – metal, forest, special times and places, saints, journeys. And there has been a tendency for places of special meaning in one era to re-emerge as important in another. That complex of cursūs and rings photographed by Major Allen at Dorchester-on-Thames adjoined the site selected in AD 635 for the mother church of an Anglo-Saxon diocese. Over four thousand years separated the creation of the cursūs and the cathedral; as in the space-time conventions of Noh theatre, where two characters standing side by side may not be in each other's presence, could it be that a medieval religious house and a Neolithic monument belong to the same drama?

Back in the 1950s, when newts flourished in the brook, this seemed unlikely. That was partly to do with the climate of the time. Although by now much influenced by the evolutionary science of man, Anglo-British history was still seen through the lens of Christian society, the corollary of its 'truth' being a break with older false religions. Almost by definition, then, a cathedral of the Church of England could not connect with prehistory. Archaeology seemed to confirm this, showing that monuments like cursūs and henges had fallen from use millennia before the onset of Christianization.

Period compartmentalization was abetted by academics themselves. The Middle Ages were the business of medievalists. Romanists did Roman Britain, and anything earlier was for prehistorians who were themselves much subdivided. So discussion of common themes was there little. What common themes were there? Places like Knowlton (Dorset) where a church stands inside a henge were but quirky exceptions.

No system of periods is adequate because any age combines things and ideas that began and flourished at different times and speeds. We have seen how often what seem to be the defining traits of particular epochs – like the industrial revolution – were launched in earlier ages. Like objects bowling through space which gradually enlarge as they approach and then flick past, so do fresh characteristics come into view before those in the foreground have departed. In other words, our cultural periods do not lie end to end, but telescoped, cupped together, earlier impacting into later. In the Fulham home of Bess's parents in the 1890s, the women engaged in a monthly ritual of covering all objects of glass with cloths to prevent the light of the full moon shining through them. Lunar ceremonies were still being practised in industrial England.

Periodization on the basis of things people built and made brings

53. Ruined medieval church within Neolithic henge, Knowlton, Dorset

back to mind Einstein saying to Werner Heisenberg: 'It is the theory which decides what can be observed' (p. 71). The study of prehistoric stone axes, for instance, is older than archaeology itself. For four hundred years they have been collected, drawn and classified. Entire careers have been devoted to their petrology, sources, typology, distributions and methods of their making.[3] For over a century it has been known that some types of axe occur far from the rock outcrops from which they were derived, and must thus represent either the opportunistic working of glacial erratics or some form of long-distance exchange. Change the theory, however, and you see new things. In 2007 the prehistorian Richard Bradley pointed out that in some parts of Britain the movement of portable stone artefacts was paralleled by exceptional monuments beside the routes along which they were carried.

> [Stone axes] were made in the Cumbrian mountains throughout the Neolithic period and were brought down to the surrounding lowlands, where they were ground and polished. There are a number of major monuments in this area, each one of them located on one of the routes leading to one of the quarries.[4]

One such monument is a henge at Mayburgh in Cumbria, an embanked enclosure which lies beside a principal route across the Pennines. On the far side of the Pennines, at Catterick, is another henge built in the same way: 'the two sites seem to be paired'. More than this, 'A ground stone axe was deposited in the entrance of Mayburgh, whilst the lowlands between the Pennines and the North Sea contain an unusual concentration of artefacts from Cumbria.'[5]

Catterick and Mayburgh lie close to the entrances of a trans-Pennine route. Three and a half thousand years later, these same places resurface in Bede's *Ecclesiastical History*. Writing in the early 730s, Bede tells us that Dacre (1.6 miles from Mayburgh) is the site of a seventh-century religious house, otherwise unexplained,[6] while in the seventh century the Roman missionary Paulinus baptized Deiran converts in the River Swale 'which flows past the town of Catterick'.[7] We do not know for certain where these baptisms took place, but Paulinus stayed in a place 'near' Catterick. A likely candidate is Easby, on the banks of the Swale between Richmond and Catterick. From Easby comes a sculptured orthostat of c.800 – presumably the shaft of a free-standing cross – which bears Christ in majesty and apostles on one face and stylized forest with wild animals and birds on another.[8] Such a work could hardly have originated anywhere other than in the context of a religious house or place of high patronage in existence by the eighth century. Such places often attracted religious communities at later dates – which would help to explain why in c.1151 Easby was selected by the constable of nearby Richmond Castle to be the home for a community of White Canons – the Order of Canons Regular of Prémontré.

There are other juxtapositions in north-east England between trans-Pennine routes, Neolithic henge complexes, rivers and early medieval religious houses. A kindred instance has been traced out north-east of Lincoln. In the area between the city and Barlings Abbey is an entity characterized by a variety of resources (cf. the federal manors discussed in Chapters 7 and 8), and a scale somewhere between a county or small polity and township. In a number of respects (successive significance from prehistory to early modern, a medieval religious house, a sub-regional name) this resembles the kinds of locale just noticed along the eastern Pennine flank. The Barlings authors identify the land-block in which the abbey held a stake for four hundred years as 'a more ancient entity, which was understood to "belong to" Lincoln itself'. They argue that this perception of landscape 'both pre-dated and outlived the monastic episode. The abbey's tenure was a way, appropriate for its age, through which the perception of an ancient identity … was sustained and passed on.'[9] Just as religious houses could operate in ways outside the interests of a single lifetime, so might such communities in their turn be one in a succession of keepers of keys to some underlying sense of locality.

Although we should probably not make too much of the fact that Barlings, like Easby, was a Premonstratensian house, there are things about Premonstratensians that in this connection are worth notice. They were among a number of European religious orders that emerged in the later eleventh and twelfth centuries in a drive towards simplicity, abstinence and adherence to the letter and spirit of an original Rule. The founder-leader here was Norbert, a man of noble birth from the Rhineland town of Xanten. Coming to a strict form of canonical life in his later career, around 1120 Norbert was led by a vision to practise it in the out-of-the-way uncultivated and marshy valley of Prémontré, in the forest of Coucy between Laon and Coucy-le-Château, in what is now the department of Aise. According to a fourteenth-century biography, Norbert shared the place with itinerant charcoal-burners, for whom at some time in the past a chapel to St John the Baptist had been built. Norbert and his companions also shared the place with creatures of the forest; a wolf befriended one of the canons. In due course they looked for a site upon which to begin to build. At first nowhere seemed suitable. Then a vision revealed a crucifixion radiating seven rays of light, and files of pilgrims approaching from four different directions. Here they began to build.[10] The likeness of the name Prémontré to the word *praemonstratus* ('shown beforehand') lent itself to a legend that the sites of Premonstratensian houses were divinely foreshown. As custodians of place, therefore, they had repute.

The case for taking a longitudinal, prehistoric to early modern view of some localities grows stronger when we look at places used for sequestering votive material. Those Snettisham neck-rings spun from filaments of electrum were not lost, nor hidden in panic, but carefully set apart. They formed part of a larger, longer tradition in which swords, shields, daggers, ornaments, war trumpets and, on occasion, people were in certain periods deliberately deposited in particular places all over a large part of the western hemisphere. An example is Flag Fen, near Peterborough, now well inland but three thousand years ago an inlet of the sea, in which was built a vast artificial island, linked to land by files of posts. In the peat alongside this prehistoric pier were spears, rings, daggers, helmets and swords, together with ceramics and the bones of animals. Weapons were released into the water on one side, bones on the other.[11]

Hundreds, possibly thousands, of leaving-places have been identified. While some, like Flag Fen, were large,[12] they could also be local and intimate – and dry. The great 'congregational' wet sites may stand out in the record because their concentrations of finds are more readily recognized than, say, a small spring into which people placed (say) tufts of wool. As we become accustomed to the idea of the leaving-place, as to the level of light in a darkened room, so do more kinds of place emerge: the phenomenon is now known to include peat-mosses, meres, particular reaches of rivers, and stretches of water between the ends of specially built opposing jetties which gave passage across braided rivers, floodplains and fens. Even this is not the full picture. For reasons explained in Chapter 3, the preservation of metal and organic objects is usually better in water than on land, and for that reason we have probably underestimated the extent of dry leaving-places that included pits, shafts, natural crevices and artificial mounds.

Pools, springs, holes and crannies appear to have been regarded as points of interchange with another existence. In their diversity they are mirrored by the objects themselves.[13] Archaeology shows that the

54. *Crickley Hill, Gloucestershire, the site of an early Neolithic causewayed enclosure and a long mound that functioned as an offering place from prehistory into the early modern period. On the horizon are the Malvern Hills (left) and Clent Hills (centre). The Clents form part of the Longbridge skyline.*

deposition of metalwork was persistent in some periods and rare in others. It is not clear whether the practice reflects one phenomenon or several, for example, whether some finds reflect weapons that were removed from circulation when their owners died while others were purely votive, or whether each of these actions was an aspect of the other. Some objects were perfect, others had seen use, yet others were deliberately damaged. In the later Bronze Age, the blades of weapons show that they had often seen action, their vanishing from terrestrial graves apparently being complemented by their appearance in rivers, often in a condition suggesting that they had been put beyond use.[14] At other times it looks as though deposited objects had been made for the purpose. A significant part of later Iron Age precious metal coinage may have been more or less created for votive deposition. A thousand years earlier (this is an example) a comely shield was hammered out of a sheet of bronze into which were punched over nine thousand bosses, painstakingly arranged in concentric rings. This was big work, yet the shield would have been no use in a fight – its metal was flimsy, unbacked and easily pierced. It seems to have been made for display, and after it had been repeatedly poked with a blade and pointed pole it was placed in a peat-moss near Beith in what is now Ayrshire.[15] Did the jabbing reflect a custom involving stylized battle – something foreshadowing the mock fights held at parish festivals 2,500 years later? Did the shield, like many swords later on, have a name?

Some deposited objects were base-metal copies of finer things, apparently made to be discarded, reminiscent in their imitation of the wax models of body parts which were hung around the shrines of medieval saints to betoken successful cures. Yet others hint at consciousness of time. A remarkable hoard of some six hundred pieces deposited near Salisbury around 200 BC included objects up to 2,200 years older.[16] While we do not know whether the inclusion occurred by chance (one hoard, say, incorporating the discovery of another), and there is no reason to think that the people who buried the ancient objects knew how very old they were, an idea of 'past' is implied.

Late prehistoric shields are not often found; most of the great examples have come from wet places, like the spectacular shields found in the Thames at Chertsey and Battersea.[17] Spectacular, too, was the bronze shield dating to maybe 400–300 BC that was recovered from the River Witham in 1826. Mediterranean red coral glows in its central boss, and the ghost of a wild boar – denizen of the wilderness – appears on its front. The boar's silhouette is the shadow of a leather outline that was applied to the surface of the shield and has been lost.[18] The find-site seems to have been at Stamp End, in the parish of Canwick, on the eastern side of Lincoln, looking towards Barlings.[19]

Archaeological study of the River Witham between Lincoln and Tattershall gives this shield a fuller context. At least from the Bronze Age onwards communal rituals took place at special places along the river. Lincoln itself may have been one of them.[20] The locations were regularly spaced, and at each the initial focus seems to have been a group of burial mounds. However, as time passed the barrow groups were flooded by rising water levels and the rituals were shifted to particular pools and meres along the river's course.[21] These watery places coincided with causeways that crossed the valley floor to enable people and animals to pass across the river's washlands. Ten such causeways have been identified, of which nine have so far yielded prehistoric finds. One, at Fiskerton near Lincoln, has been excavated. At Fiskerton objects were released into the River Witham during the Iron Age. The causeway's timbers yield tree-ring dates which show that it was being repaired or augmented at intervals of sixteen to eighteen years. This implies that oak trees were being felled and prepared for incorporation in the causeway at times that coincided with 'observable and unusually spectacular astronomical events, namely total eclipses of the Moon'.[22] Here is a hint that the meaning of deposited objects may have as much to do with ceremonies and times as with the objects themselves. The faces of those who slipped objects into water at places like Fiskerton would have been silvered under a moon. Mirror-making becomes sophisticated in later prehistory; aback of words like 'mirror', 'marvellous' and 'miracle' lie Latin terms like *miror* and *mirus* to do with wonder and awe – the same concepts met in the context of saints in Chapter 9.

Deposition did not stop in prehistory. At least six causeways have produced sequences of material which continued into the Middle Ages.[23] Further, a medieval monastery or parish church was established at every causeway's end. In itself this is not unusual: chapels and churches were often built beside medieval bridges or causeways, not least because such sites were profitable (what is more natural than to give thanks for a journey completed, or to pray for one beginning?) and their income could be applied to upkeep of public crossing places. In the Witham cases, however, the prehistoric finds enable us to see that the ecclesiastical foundations were co-located not only with causeways, but also with ancient offering places – and that the practice of putting things into the river carried on after the churches were built. Indeed, more metalwork was deposited in the Witham between the eleventh and fourteenth centuries AD than during the Roman centuries or early Middle Ages. And when the practice ceases around 1400, funerary swords and armour begin to appear in local churches – armour of the kind on the wall in Sir Walter Vivian's private museum.[24] Barlings and its land-block was part of this landscape.

Swords began in the Bronze Age as a kind of magic, metal being miraculously drawn from stone with fire. Perhaps this is why the link between minerals and mythology is so strong.[25] A sword without an owner was magic on the loose. *Sequester* – 'seclude, isolate, set apart' – comes from Late Latin *sequestrare*, 'to commit for safe keeping'. The return of an ownerless sword to the other world from which it came completes a circle – as Thomas Malory knew when he described the dying King Arthur ordering Sir Bedivere to throw Excalibur into the lake.[26]

Of course, by focusing on things like swords we may be missing part – maybe a large, even the greater part – of the picture. There may have been periods when the things being deposited were made of materials that have left no trace. Deposition may thus have been as or more frequent in the times when we see it least, and because of that we could underestimate the extent to which ritual behaviour formed part of everyday life. Travel across water itself may have involved special conventions.[27] And it may be that what was sequestered depended on who you were, or what kind of journey you were making. On this view, the distinction between 'votive' and 'funeral' offerings may be over-fussy, for what is dying but an incomparable journey? When John Bunyan's pilgrim reaches the end of his journey and beholds the city of gold on a hill, he hesitates. He is on the border between earthly time and infinity. The boundary is a river: 'but there was no bridge to go over: the river was very deep'.

There are so many religious houses in the Witham valley that it seems as if it was landscape itself which early bishops and missionaries set out to convert.[28] The river finds suggest that they saw their task less to cancel old powers or significances than to act as a kind of lens through which to refocus them. Conversion-period religious houses are found next to causeways and crossing points on many other rivers, and while in most cases the existence of earlier contexts has yet to be tested the phenomenon invites thought about influences behind the location of religious houses generally. Some of them, at least, emerge as guardians of older identities.

The war on paganism and draining of the Fens were largely monastic undertakings, while as types of desert, fens and levels were appropriate places for religious houses to be, within which to construct new causeways which led the faithful across formerly sacred pools and reaches of river.[29] East Anglian Fenland was rich in religious communities. Peterborough Cathedral is intervisible with Flag Fen. The eighth-century *Life of St Guthlac* tells how Guthlac chose to live at Crowland, which was an isle of the dead. The elongated naves of Benedictine churches at Ely, Norwich and Bury St Edmunds, the angel-thronged roofs of fifteenth-century Fenland churches – are these continuations of ancient wealth-holding and oblation, once measured, stored and offered in metal? Among the Norfolk churches was the shrine of Our Lady of Walsingham.[30] Centred on a Holy House built in supposed imitation of the home of Mary in which the Annunciation took place, Walsingham became England's Nazareth. Begun, it was said, following a vision during the reign of Edward the Confessor, by the end of the Middle Ages it was one of the most visited places of pilgrimage in Britain. North Norfolk is an out-of-the-way corner of England, though well connected to London and the midlands by an ancient road network that included the Icknield Way and the Roman Peddar's Way, both of which stop at the Wash coast, their continuation on the far shore implying a ferry.[31] And virtually the last thing the roads pass before reaching the water, and just a few miles from Walsingham, is the leaving-place for the two hundred plus torcs and hundred bracelet and ring ingots at Snettisham.[32]

The Annunciation and Nature meet in the word 'nature' itself. In *The Reckoning of Time*, written by Bede at Jarrow (which was then a waterside monastery at the end of a causeway) in the 720s, Bede let slip the name of the goddess who his predecessors believed had set the stars in the heavens as the signs of the seasons, days and years. She was called Natura.[33] The idea of Nature *as opposed to* Man is the paradox of humanity and the dilemma of environmentalism. Behind it stands the Latin *natura* ('birth, constitution, the course of things') which has the same root-stock as nativity – *naturans*, 'being born'. In its underlying meaning, then, Nature is creative action. She is thus distinct from the idea of a supreme being. Indeed, although much of the ritual behaviour we have noticed – the drowning of swords, the making of great earthen circles – is today attributed to the worship of ancient gods, there is no clear sign of such divinities before the later third and second millennium BC.[34] Myths dealing with first and last things, like those in Genesis and

Revelation that require a creator and judge external to the mortal world, seem to have taken shape later than those in which time was conceived in other ways. Identifiable gods and goddesses become prominent in the first millennium BC. Before this, the structures or landscapes we think of as 'ritual' are more in the nature of meeting-places, localities for particular kinds of behaviour, or the culmination of cosmological observances. In recent literature much has been made of early devotion to ancestors – the idea of first occupiers of land who become identified with its locality and fertility and so loom large in collective memory. We have seen that the Bayesian revolution places their coming around 4,000 BC, their monuments of memory a few generations later (p. 172). The subsequent arrival of pushy Graeco-Roman gods reflects growing complexity and layering in society, framed by ceremony, wherein leaders positioned themselves, and buried and remembered each other, within a loftier power structure with supernatural figures at its head. From this comes an idea that gods, like people, must have special places in which to dwell, wherein mortals may do them honour or pray favours.

Stages in our passage might thus be seen as a struggle for harmony in a Nature whose nature is always to change, the ceding of Nature to deities who mirror the affairs of men, and latterly the overthrow of deities and a fallacious faith in our self-importance as a species and supremacy over Nature. From the fourteenth century, the division of time by mechanical clocks spreads to the regulation of communities, and thence to an idea that control over time's measure assures our sovereignty. In fact, as we have seen at every step, it is the other way about: history is part of natural history, and archaeology is not a lens through which the past is examined, but part of the story it seeks to tell. Archaeology itself, indeed, might be seen as but a late ripple in the cult of ancestors.

The argument of this book is that we have underestimated connections between periods, things, institutions and ideas that are normally studied apart and assumed to be unrelated. Great churches, like ritual monuments which preceded them by three thousand years, were carefully oriented, served the cult of ancestors and were made of stone. They housed processions, chants, dances and stylized journeys, and were implicated in drama and the conventions of space and time. Yet only by coincidence, we are urged to suppose, did the name of the chief apostle Peter mean 'stone', or did the drama of the *Visitatio Sepulchri* take place on the eve of a season called Eastertide, at a time determined by the moon. If nothing else, they show Man to be an animal characterized by propensity for ritual as well as curiosity. It is proposed that a significant number of medieval religious houses acted as upholders of deeper memories.

From this – and from the many kinds of landscape and evidence we have met in previous chapters – a kind of counter-periodization can be proposed. In England, at the level of locality, village and family, there was more solidarity in perception and imagined genealogical closeness across the forty-five or so centuries from the later Neolithic to the mid-nineteenth century, than between 1850 and now, or between the end of the last glacial period and the arrival of the innovators just before 4,000 BC. During the last century and a half that long-lasting age of – what shall we call it? – affinity has been overtaken by changes in thought, information flow and global population dispersion. Prior to the Neolithic arrival, there was the time of Dark Wood and, before that, the ice. But from 3000–2000 BC 'place' and 'land' take on the kind of meaning that Shakespeare knew, and there is continuity of local aware-ness, even if it is expressed in a succession of contrasting ways. In terms of identity someone living in Longbridge around 1800, or Bess's family with their full-moon sheets and towels in late Victorian Fulham, had more in common with people who let slip bronze weapons into watery places than we with them.

If we look beyond compartmentalization, familiar things can be seen in new ways – like purgatory (p. 266). An intermediate time and place in another world,[35] purgatory is sometimes depicted as a creation of the later Middle Ages. Yet comparison of evidence for the deposition of material from the second millennium BC to the Reformation offers a point of departure for investigating concepts of space and time related to the geography of the other world.[36] In the later Middle Ages it was suspected that time on earth and time in the other-life were not in accord. 'Souls being punished in Purgatory felt that they had been there for a long time, but when they appeared to the living they discovered that they died only a short while ago.'[37] John Henry Newman's poem *The Dream of Gerontius*, written in 1865 (six years after Darwin's *On the Origin of Species*), deals with a man's dying minutes and after-death encounters of his soul. The soul pleads with the Angel to see God. As the moment of 'the glance of God' nears, the soul hears familiar sounds. The Angel tells him:

> It is the voice of friends around thy bed,
> Who say the 'Subvenite' with the priest.

The friends began this prayer while Gerontius was dying. For them, his death was a minute or two ago. From the poem, it is clear that the interval was longer; in Elgar's oratorio (and Elgar omitted much of the text) thirty-seven minutes have passed. The Angel explains:

> For scarcely art thou disembodied yet.
> Divide a moment, as men measure time,
> Into its million-million-millionth part,
> Yet even less than that the interval
> Since thou didst leave the body;

Newman's Angel meditates on Time:

> For spirits and men by different standards mete
> The less and greater in the flow of time.
> By sun and moon, primeval ordinances –
> By stars which rise and set harmoniously –
> By the recurring seasons, and the swing,
> This way and that, of the suspended rod
> Precise and punctual, men divide the hours,
> Equal, continuous, for their common use.
> Not so with us in the immaterial world;
> But intervals in their succession
> Are measured by the living thought alone,
> And grow or wane with its intensity.
> And time is not a common property;
> But what is long is short, and swift is slow,
> And near is distant, as received and grasped
> By this mind and by that, and every one
> Is standard of his own chronology.
> And memory lacks its natural resting-points
> Of years, and centuries, and periods.
> It is thy very energy of thought
> Which keeps thee from thy God.

Purgatory in *The Dream of Gerontius* is not the place of excruciating physical torture that was depicted on medieval church walls, but a state of exquisite desire, 'a golden prison'. Having glimpsed God,

> The longing for Him, when thou seest Him not;
> The shame of self at thought of seeing Him, –
> Will be thy veriest, sharpest purgatory.

Newman explained purgatory as one among a number of accretions that had evolved from the idea of Christianity, which had been given from heaven.[38] But as we have suggested it belongs within a larger family of stories which could have been told – with variation – since the third millennium BC. Comparatively recent legends describe travellers who believed that they had made a brief visit to the other world, but crumbled to nothing upon their return because their stay had outlasted their allotted lifetime.[39] Such gearing between different times is caught in folklore traditions of knights who lie asleep under a hill, awaiting their call. The long barrows of the thirty-eighth century BC are artificial hills in which original guardians sleep. They are models for successive ages of guardian – warrior elites, religious houses, saints, knights. Knights evoke shields, buckles, swords, spear tips. The finest metalwork in Iron Age Britain was to do with feasting, horse-riding, ornaments and fighting. What is this, asks Richard Bradley, but a pre-echo of the trappings of chivalry?[40]

Immensely strong, metal also symbolizes transformation. Ores are changed into copper, lead, tin and iron, as at death are men and women into souls. Woodlands (reminding us of charcoal-burning and Norbert) were the places for doing this, and thus places for marvels.[41]

Alteration by turn invokes journeys. Down to the later Middle Ages the extraction and initial working of raw materials and final manufacture were often widely separated – sometimes thousands of miles apart. Until the eighth century AD, for instance, most of Europe's glass came from Palestine and Egypt in bulk ingots that were then cut up and reworked into vessels, window glass or jewellery. Conversely, the manufacture of bronze objects in late antique Egypt 'presupposes either the importation of tin' (a constituent of bronze, which was not mined in Egypt) 'or the recycling of bronze on a significant scale'.[42] A continuing supply of tin from outside Egypt is supposed. Indeed, around the eastern Mediterranean, tin was known as 'the British metal'.[43] Within Britain herself:

> The production of bronze artefacts involved a combination of copper and tin, both of which had restricted distributions in prehistoric Europe. One problem lay in bringing these materials together, and another concerned the circulation of the finished products. Some of the densest concentrations of Late Bronze Age metalwork were in areas which lacked metal sources of their own.[44]

Almost by definition, then, raw materials were an aspect of the exotic, of stories from over the hills and far away. The fact that extraction and production were in different places not only gave reason to travel, but lent power to those who could regulate it.

The Iron Age, for long viewed as a step along the road of linear technological progress, has recently been argued to have begun because from around 1100 BC the supply of accessible continental copper began to dwindle, thus stepping up the search for other kinds of ores closer to hand.[45] If copper was a metal of journeys and mysteries, then, iron eventually became a metal of localities. Its stories differ from those of copper and gold.

Within the British Isles, copper was extracted first from south-west Ireland about four and a half thousand years ago, then from sites in mid- and north Wales, and Alderley Edge in Cheshire.[46] Archaeologists have only recently learned how to detect these places, and have yet to adjust to the light they shed. The greatest of them in Britain, possibly anywhere in the world, is on the Great Orme, a headland near Llandudno, yet it is a new find, known only since the 1980s. The mines are a three-dimensional labyrinth, of which the four miles of tunnels that have so far been explored are but a part. Some of them are so cramped that only children could have worked them. Tens of thousands of beach cobbles, once used as mauls to pound out rock, witness copper extraction on a scale previously unimagined. And as embalmers repack a body voided of its organs, so caches of mauls were sometimes left in the spaces they had been used to create.[47]

Seventy or so miles to the east is Alderley Edge, a chip of the world continent of Pangaea, its sandstones laid down in oceans and deserts between 206 and 250 million years ago, later tilted and infused with minerals. Malachite and galena colour its earths; sulphur and cobalt lace the waters of its springs. Recent centuries have seen the mining of a cornucopia of metals – cobalt, nickel, zinc, molybdenum. The element vanadium was discovered here, in the midst of another tangle of ancient tunnels. If a giant were to tap the Edge it might crumble, so many are the miles of passages with which it has been riddled. When Roman engineers drilled deep shafts on reconnaissance for lead and copper they broke into tunnels and crawlways that were already old. Some of the earliest Bronze Age workings are still visible as bulb-shaped hollows, mauled out from surface exposures four thousand years ago.[48] Alderley is almost as rich in stories and strangeness as it is in minerals. When voiced by wind, some of the tunnels produce unearthly sounds, like bass flutes. Faces and glyphs have been carved on rock exposures. Legends tell of a wizard, and a leader, asleep in a different time, under the hill.[49]

Thus it is that imaginative geographies lie behind the landscapes in which we live and archaeology studies. Open-field agriculture, settlements where people lived in groups, and the idea of the town, were things that went together. Their contrary was wilderness – the source of prophetic powers and the holy, a place of exile, penitence, refuge and renewal, and the proper place of the amazing.[50] Each contained its own kinds of people. When Imogen flees Cymbeline's court in Shakespeare's play, she goes to the Preseli Hills (whence come parts of Stonehenge,

55. Alderley Edge, Cheshire: the Devil's Grave at Stormy Point. Concavities where malachite was mauled out in prehistory are visible at intervals along the fissure.

56. Carn Menyn, Pembrokeshire, one of the outcrops on the Preseli Mountains from which some stones used to build Stonehenge were derived. Debate continues about whether the stones were carried from west Wales to Wiltshire by people or by ice.

whether borne by ice or people) and meets coarse woodmen, who in fact are princes in disguise. Wilderness was powerful and fecund. Images of wolves and boars appear on our earliest coins. Desert did not have to be, in the modern sense, natural. Ambiguity is everywhere; myths are seldom directly representational; often they work through a dialogue with the opposite of what they explore. Pigs, for instance, were allies in clearance, yet denizens of forest. Woodlands, in their turn, were seldom primordially wild. Forests in the later Middle Ages were often areas of wood pasture or heath set apart for deer (creatures at once noble yet untamed, outriders of light and dark), or simply ordinary farmland under special jurisdiction. That is, while forests were delineated by kings (*foris* simply meant 'outside', in this context 'outside ordinary law'), literature and legend merged them with wilderness. Forests became idealized deserts, regions for monasteries and (later) for dissent. As Jacques Le Goff reminds us, wilderness is a kind of wisdom, mediated by hunters, hermits and charcoal-burners who are at home in both forest and town. Desert could also be internal, a mental condition of displacement. As we saw in Chapter 9, a lifetime wandering through strange lands was a homeward journey.

The significance of mental associations is no less real for their confinement in imagination. In a comparison between Robin Hood and open-field agriculture in popular awareness, Robin Hood would win hands down. This may help us to understand why, in the later Middle Ages, the consequences of settlement desertion seemed so distressing, for the things a village stood for – civilized values, a higher realm of space – were nullified by depopulation. Culture's root – *coulter*, the blade of a ploughshare that turns the sod – goes with clearance, well-worked farmland, enclosed gardens and open fields. It is the opposite of *wald*.

Elaborations of the relationship between culture and wilderness in monastic geography and courtly literature have fed a supposition that the imaginative continuum originated in the Middle Ages – that the history of 'desert' in the West began somewhere around 400, in succession to desert holiness in the East. We have seen, however, that the concept was older.[51] The example of stone is telling. The ideas that quarries and raw materials generally belong to the 'wild' side of the landscape, that stone sources (whence also those of metal – and *metallum* is the Latin word for quarry) are hallowed, and that stone eventually defines what is sacral, all point to the likelihood that developed symbolism relating to different kinds of landscape emerged somewhere between four and five thousand years ago. Since then, much of what archaeologists have been trying to explain in material or functional terms has enjoyed a more vivid reality in human hearts and stories. A boundary, civilization to one side, wilderness, bears and charcoal-burners to the other, slants across every parish. In Britain at large, Shakespeare, Arthur the bear and Birmingham lie more or less along its line.

So does John Henry Cardinal Newman, who died on Monday 11 August 1890 and was buried eight days later at Longbridge. Well, not quite *in* Longbridge – at Rednal, next door, not far from the tram terminus, where the Birmingham Oratory had a retreat house at the foot of the Lickey Hills, towards whose wavy skyline I looked when out with the dog, and the site of William Buckland's geological fieldwork in the early 1820s. In the later 1950s I was unaware of Newman's grave, but was conscious of Elgar's setting of Newman's poem. Vinyl long-playing records that rotated at 33 rpm were invented the year after I was born, and Malcolm Sargent's 1955 recording was one of the first to reach our household. I listened to it incessantly, stirred by the heroic upwellings in the Prelude, and by the going forth of the soul on its journey.

The Dream of Gerontius was first performed at the Birmingham Festival in 1900. When Elgar travelled up to Birmingham for rehearsals, his train passed within half a mile of Newman's grave. I have wondered if Elgar knew this. Completed in 1840, the Birmingham–Gloucester railway was one of the first mainline railways in the world. It was famous for the challenging gradient of the Lickey Bank, to which on days when there was nothing else to do we would walk or cycle to watch steam locomotives gasp their way up from Bromsgrove. From the top of Lickey Bank the railway then runs along the edge of Cofton Park, where Pope Benedict XVI beatified Newman on 19 September 2010.

Two years before, on the Feast of the Guardian Angels 2008, an attempt was made to exhume Newman's remains. The plan was to translate his bones to a shrine in the Birmingham Oratory. However, nothing of Newman himself was found. The Fathers of the Birmingham Oratory released a statement:

> During the excavation the brass inscription plate which had been on the wooden coffin in which Cardinal Newman had rested was recovered from his grave.
>
> Brass, wooden and cloth artefacts were found. However there were no remains of the body of John Henry Newman. An expectation that Cardinal Newman had been buried in a lead lined coffin proved to be unfounded.
>
> In the view of the medical and health professionals in attendance, burial in a wooden coffin in a very damp site makes this kind of total decomposition of the body unsurprising.

The Fathers drew attention to a possible reason for the disappearance of Newman's bones. A contemporary press report of the burial that took place a little after 3.30 in the afternoon mentioned the covering of his coffin with 'a quantity of black earth' taken from the grounds.[52] The grave had been dug through gravel; the introduction of humic material was perhaps to accelerate decay.

> When the rites had been achieved, the crowd without the gates was suffered to enter by batches and see the grave; and then the coffin was covered with mould of a softer texture than the marly stratum in which the grave is cut.
>
> This was done in studious and affectionate fulfilment of a desire of Dr Newman's which some may deem fanciful, but which sprang

from his reverence for the letter of the Divine Word; which, as he conceived, enjoins us to facilitate rather than impede the operation of the law 'Dust thou art, and unto dust shalt thou return'.[53]

In his will, Newman had insisted that he be buried in the same grave as that of his friend, Father Ambrose St John, who had died in 1878. Of St John, Newman afterwards wrote: 'I have ever thought no bereavement was equal to that of a husband's or a wife's, but I feel it difficult to believe that any can be greater, or anyone's sorrow greater, than mine.' Was Newman a reluctant saint, unwilling to be parted from the friend with whom he had hoped to be reunited for the rest of time?

The relics recovered from the attempted exhumation were a modest collection: the brass inscription that had been screwed to the coffin, some pieces of cloth and bits of coffin wood. Newman might have had them in mind when he wrote for the jeering demons who threaten the soul of Gerontius as the Angel leads him towards the judgement-court:

> What's a saint?
> One whose breath
> Doth the air taint
> Before his death;
>
> A bundle of bones,
> Which fools adore,
> Ha! ha!
> When life is o'er,
> Which rattle and stink,
> E'en in the flesh.

Press accounts of Newman's funeral contrast the colour, throng and brilliance of his requiem in the Hagley Road Oratory with the quiet and simplicity of the committal in the burying ground at Rednal retreat.[54] Between the two the cortège passed through Longbridge. A writer for the *Birmingham Daily Mail* was struck by the seclusion and quiet of the private graveyard under the Lickeys: 'from the heather and bracken-mantled slope of the hill above, where hundreds of excursionists from this great city but a few days back pleasured themselves with gazing on the wide stretch of golden cornfields and winding lanes' there came 'no sound … louder than the song of birds'.

Why did so many writers begin in the few square miles around this place? Geoffrey Hill's boyhood was passed just over the skyline to the west. A. E. Housman grew up on the other side of the bracken-mantled hill; blue remembered hills were his horizon. At eighteen miles to the south-east Shakespeare was further afield, but Tolkien was on the spot, as a twelve-year-old staying in a cottage in the grounds of the Oratory Retreat and wandering the Lickey Hills. (Later, he called one of his Hobbits Gerontius.) Auden was only a cycle ride away, passing much of his later childhood a few streets from Francesca Wilson. In succession to religious houses, saints, warrior elites and founding farmers, poets have become the wardens of locality. Who will follow them?

EPILOGUE

The Lickey skyline beyond the now vanished Austin Motor works where metal was beaten day and night is made of some of the oldest rocks in the world. The Bytham River, beside which Old Ones trekked westward half a million years ago, rose hereabouts. What seems to be one of the earliest written references to a medieval open field, written about a thousand years ago, refers to Cofton Hackett, where Pope Benedict XVI came in 2010.[1] Is this area unusual, a concentration of special things – or is everywhere like here, and all that denotes this place is my memory? Look at the 1948 aerial photograph of Longbridge. There are the Aladdin bungalows from Bay City in the Saginaw Valley, and the LMS railway, upon which travel two goods trains trailing feathers of steam. Even if official records did not tell us that this photograph was taken on 8 December, the shadows cast by trees and industrial chimneys would enable us to work it out. One of the Austin smokestacks is acting like the gnomon of a giant sundial, showing that the photograph was taken close to midwinter, in the morning. (The trains and shadows remind us that until the mid-nineteenth century different places ran by their own times. And since such local times were ascertained from the sun, cathedral clocks in places of different longitude – Exeter and Norwich, let us say – would strike as much as ten minutes apart. The railways' need for consistency led to 'Railway Time', a uniformity which prevailed at places along the routes of different companies, and eventually to the Definition of Time Act, which in 1880 established Greenwich Mean Time as Britain's legal standard. Thus did time pass from the sacral to the merely bureaucratic.)

The 8th of December 1948 was a Wednesday. That morning, we see from the photograph, was quiet and clear, with a gentle southerly breeze. From written records we know that the airmen who took the photograph were stationed near Dorchester in Oxfordshire, just six miles from the place whence Major Allen had been making his reconnaissance flights

57. Longbridge, 1948. The Austin estate of Aladdin houses (upper centre) has been augmented (to the right) by wartime prefabs. Hawkesley Farm and its moat lie just beyond the esate's right-hand corner.

ten years before. Ridge and furrow shows up well. Indeed, I see that the new vicarage into which we moved in 1956 was built atop ridge and furrow. Near by, etched by the low sun, is the River Rea – more of a large brook really – which wriggles beside the railway and flowed through my childhood on its way to top up the Stratford-upon-Avon Canal. Rea is another of those names from prehistory, like Humber, Don or Ouse, some of which (like Don) occur continent-wide, which we might now assign to the period of great transformation that began about forty-two centuries ago.

Stratford. At some point between 1604 and 1612 Shakespeare had returned to New Place, his house in Stratford, and based himself there until his death in April 1616. *The Tempest* was probably his last complete play. It was extant by the autumn of 1611, when it was performed before the court on Hallowmas night, although the notion that he then went

into retirement is contradicted by his involvement in collaborative work
at least until the end of 1613.[2] There are threads in *The Tempest* that run
through earlier chapters. The building of the Rose, for instance, coincided with Walter Raleigh's attempt to establish a colony at Roanoke,
Virginia, and seeds of New World vegetables were recovered from the
playhouse site. Roanoke's governor was John White, an artist and surveyor who may once have worked for the Office of the Revels as a set
designer for masques, and had since sailed with Raleigh, mapping the
Virginian coast up to Chesapeake Bay. Abram Ortel's *Theatrum orbis
terrarum*, the first atlas to depict the world as a whole and to co-locate
its 'extraordinary varieties', had been in print only since 1570.[3]

Publication of White's drawings in 1590 caused the kind of sensation now associated with pictures of Mars or Jupiter's moons – they
gave Europeans their first clear view of neighbours on a strange continent, and their first comparative view of that continent and their own.[4]
The Inuit and Algonquin peoples wore clothes, lived sociably and had
access to considerable technology. They did not look like the children of
wild nature, 'new-made by the hands of gods',[5] who peopled Michel de
Montaigne's essays. Ten years later a sub-plot of *The Tempest* touched on
the money to be made from a public famished for news of life on other
continents. Passers-by who wouldn't give one low-denomination coin to
relieve a lame beggar, mused Trinculo, would 'lay out ten to see a dead
Indian'.[6] Many in Shakespeare's audience would have classified natives
of other continents as domesticated or wild animals, in line with a view
of the world as a realm of ascendant humans and dominated biota. Is
Caliban a New One or an Old One? 'Caliban is neither a mere animal
nor a simple colonial rebel.'[7]

In the month before Shakespeare's death, on 25 March – Lady Day,
the first day of the new year in the old style – Shakespeare called for
his attorney to change his will. As he did so, Jesuit missionaries were
working their way up the Saginaw Valley, preaching to hitherto pacific
Chippewas. Thus did saints expelled from Britain a century before arrive
in a place whence three centuries later trees of the wildwood would be
felled to make kit houses for export to Longbridge.

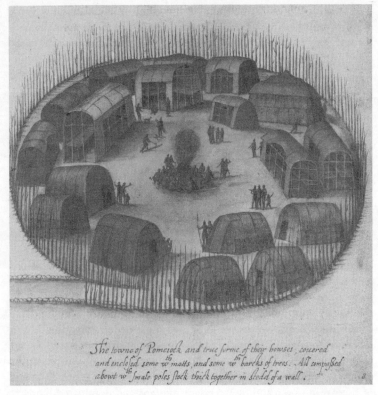

The towne of Pomeiock and true forme of their howses, couered
and encloſed ſome wᵗʰ matts, and ſome wᵗʰ barcks of trees. All compaſſed
abowt wᵗʰ ſmale poles ſtock thick together in ſtedd of a wall.

58. Pomeiooc, Virginia, by John White, 1585–6

But leave it now, leave it; as you left
a washed-out day at Stourport or the Lickey,
improvised rainhats mulch for papier-mâché,
and the chips floating.
Leave it now, leave it; give it over
to that all-gathering general English light,
in which each separate bead
of drizzle at its own thorn-tip stands
as revelation.[8]

ACKNOWLEDGEMENTS

All authors owe unrepayable debts – to colleagues, to friends, critics, family, all of whom (often without knowing it) give information, ideas, theories, leads, references, cautions, encouragement, or just time and space. For their generosity and help in such ways and more I thank Tony Abramson, Allen Anderson, David Baker, Paul Barnwell, Bob Bewley, Martin Biddle, Chris Brooke, Paul Buckland, Dave Bush, John and Bryony Coles, Neil Cossons, Rosemary Cramp, Anthony Crawshaw, John Crook, Barry Cunliffe, Paul Daniel, Simon Denison, Philip Dixon, Colin Dobinson, Karen Dorn, Anna Eavis, the late Geoff Egan, Angela Evans, David Morgan Evans, Paul Everson, Margaret Faull, Georgina Ferry, Glenn Foard, David Fraser, Jane Grenville, the late Richard Hall, Fred Hartley, Mike Heyworth, Emilia Jamroziak, Philip de Jersey, Bill Klemperer, Hilary Lade, George Lambrick, Keith Laybourn, Rob Light, Andrew Lawson, Keith Miller, Jean Mitchell, Steve Moorhouse, Axel Müller, Alan Murray, Taryn Nixon, Robert van de Noort, Kate Owen, Sebastian Payne, Matt Pope, Dominic Powlesland, Francis Pryor, the late Philip Rahtz, Colin Renfrew, Simon Richardson, Brian Roberts, Mark Roberts, Warwick Rodwell, Peter Sawyer, John Schofield (London), Chris Scull, Jae Shannon, Mick Sharp, Laura Sole, Paul Stamper, Brian Sytch, Christopher Taylor, Simon Thurley, Steve Trow, Geoffrey Wainwright, Tosh Warwick, Lorna Watts, Leslie Webster, Nicki Whitehouse, Jean Williamson, Ian Wood and Stuart Wrathmell.

For help and advice in archives I thank colleagues in the Ashmolean Museum, the British Library, British Museum, Clarke Historical Library of the University of Central Michigan, National Monuments Record, Royal Commissions on the Ancient and Historical Monuments of Wales and Scotland, and Special Collections at the University of Leeds.

For their care in reading and criticizing parts of the book in draft I thank Julian Bowsher, Bob Cywinski, Glenn Foard, Sam Lucy, Dominic Powlesland, David Stocker and Ian Wood, none of whom should be held responsible for anything that I have said. Special thanks go to my wife Jane for proof-reading the manuscript.

For permission to quote from the work of others I thank Eamon Duffy for the extract from *The Stripping of the Altars*; Sid Bradley for a passage from *Orm Gamalson's Sundial: the Lily's Blossom and the Roses's Fragrance* (the 1997 Kirkdale Lecture); the Literary Trustees of Walter de la Mare and Society of Authors for lines from Walter de la Mare's poem 'The Traveller'; Mrs Rosemary Vellender for Edward Thomas's poem 'Tall Nettles' and the extract from 'Roads'; David Higham Associates Ltd for lines from *Silver-sand and Snow* by Eleanor Farjeon, published by Michael Joseph; Penguin Books for lines from Geoffrey Hill's *The Triumph of Love*, *Mercian Hymns* and 'Funeral Music'; Desmond Graham and Faber & Faber for the extract from Keith Douglas's poem 'Simplify me when I am dead' from *Keith Douglas: The Complete Poems* (2000), and the Estate of W. H. Auden / Curtis Brown Ltd for W. H. Auden's poems 'Progress?', 'The Old Ones', 'Archaeology' and extracts from 'Consider' and 'Domesday Song'. Extracts from the verbatim record of the libel case brought by David Irving against Deborah Lipstadt and Penguin Books are used with the consent of Ubiqus UK (formerly Harry Counsell & Company) of Cliffords Inn, Fetter Lane, London EC4A 1LD. The caption of Illustration 42 uses information provided by the Battlefields Trust.

Time's Anvil was begun in 2000, and for extraneous reasons was put to one side and worked on intermittently. One of the penalties of doing that is that others begin to publish parts of the book you are writing. Keeping up to date can itself bring drawbacks. The appearance of new, sometimes conflicting data while the book was being written meant that several chapters had to be repeatedly revised and even now may not reflect the thrust or range of current thinking. Meanwhile, correction in one place can alter sense in another, and repeated tinkering may turn writing stale. Concern about both has led me to live precariously by avoiding some new books altogether. An example is Steven Mithen's *The Singing Neanderthals* (2005), which appeared after the drafting of 'Swan Music', and which publication of *Time's Anvil* now allows me to read.

We have seen that evidence from the past is profuse, and that archaeologists and historians necessarily tend to concentrate on periods, themes, areas, types of material. Going outside such limits inevitably runs the risk of inexpert incursion into others' fields. Taking a long view is thus a perilous venture. Arbitrary selectivity, neglect of complexity, maybe even getting things wrong: here at the end I am conscious that these and more have been costs of trying to reach beyond the particular or connect things usually seen apart. It is for others to judge whether the price of doing so has been worth paying.

Richard Morris
New Year's Eve 2011

NOTES

PROLOGUE

1. Nikolaus Pevsner, Reith Lectures 1955: *The Englishness of English Art*, 1: 'The Geography of Art', BBC Home Service, 16 October 1955, 6; Susie Harries, *Nikolaus Pevsner: The Life*, Chatto & Windus, 2011.

2. Brian Harrison, 'Pevsner, Sir Nikolaus Bernhard Leon (1902–1983)', *Oxford Dictionary of National Biography*, Oxford University Press, 2004 [http://0-www.oxforddnb.com.wam.leeds.ac.uk/view/article/31543, accessed 20 December 2011].

3. Nikolaus Pevsner, *Leipziger Barock. Die Baukunst die Barockzeit in Leipzig*, Dresden: Wolfgang Jess, 1928.

4. Ute Engel, 'The Formation of Pevsner's Art History: Nikolaus Pevsner in Germany 1902–1935', in Peter Draper, ed., *Reassessing Nikolaus Pevsner*, Ashgate, 2004, 29–56, at 29, 34–7.

5. Nikolaus Pevsner, Reith Lectures 1955: *The Englishness of English Art*, 1: 'The Geography of Art', BBC Home Service, 16 October 1955.

6. Harries, *Nikolaus Pevsner*, 129.

7. Quoted in ibid., 152.

8. Harrison, 'Pevsner', *Oxford Dictionary of National Biography*.

9. Siân Lliwen Roberts, 'Place, Life Histories and the Politics of Relief: Episodes in the Life of Francesca Wilson, Humanitarian Educator Activist', unpublished PhD thesis, University of Birmingham, 2010, 113–14.

10. Quoted in Harries, *Nikolaus Pevsner*, 152.

11. Nikolaus Pevsner, *Pioneers of the Modern Movement from William Morris to Walter Gropius*, Faber & Faber, 1936; *An Enquiry into Industrial Art in England*, Cambridge University Press, 1937; Engel, 'The Formation of Pevsner's Art History', 29.

12. Harries, *Nikolaus Pevsner*, 381–2.

13. Ibid., 384–8.

14. Matthew Bell, 'From the Outside Looking In: The Man Who Opened a Window on Englishness', review of Susie Harries, *Nikolaus Pevsner: The Life*, *Independent*, 28 August 2011.

15. Harries, *Nikolaus Pevsner*, 396–403.

16. Nikolaus Pevsner, Reith Lectures 1955: *The Englishness of English Art*, 7: 'Architecture and Planning: the functional approach', BBC Home Service, 27 November 1955.

17. L. P. Hartley, *The Go-Between*, Hamish Hamilton, 1953, 1.

18. David Verey, *Gloucestershire 1: The Cotswolds*, The Buildings of England, Penguin, 1970, 15.

19. Michael Williams, *Deforesting the Earth: From Prehistory to Global Crisis*, University of Chicago Press,

2003, 102; cf. Charles Higounet, 'Les Forêts de l'Europe occidentale du Ve au XIe Siècle', in *Agricoltura e mondo rurale in Occidente nell'alto medioevo*, Settimane di Studio del Centro Italiano di Studi sull' Alto Medioevo, Spoleto, 1966, xiii, 343–97; and see Chapter 6.

20. Paul B. Sturtevant, 'Based on a True History?: The Impact of Popular "Medieval Film" on the Public Understanding of the Middle Ages', unpublished PhD thesis, University of Leeds, 2010.

21. Anthony Pollard, *Imagining Robin Hood: The Late-Medieval Stories in Historical Context*, Taylor & Francis, 2004; Jeffrey Richards, *Swordsmen of the Screen: From Douglas Fairbanks to Michael York*, Routledge & Kegan Paul, 1988.

22. David Verey and Alan Brooks, *Gloucestershire 1: The Cotswolds*, The Buildings of England, Yale University Press, corrected edn, 2002, 21–47.

23. See for example Odd Arne Westad, *The Global Cold War: Third World Interventions and the Making of our Times*, Cambridge University Press, 2006.

24. P. R. Kitson, 'British and European River-Names', *Transactions of the Philological Society*, 94:2, 1996, 73–118, at 74.

INTRODUCTION:
ON TIME AND ARCHAEOLOGY

1. *Tempus edax rerum*: Ovid, *Metamorphoses*, 15, 234. Cf. William Shakespeare, Sonnet 19.1; Shakespeare and George Wilkins, *Pericles*, Act 2, sc. 3.45–8.

2. Isaac Newton, *Philosophiae naturalis principia mathematica*, 1687.

3. Lewis Mumford, *Technics and Civilization*, Harcourt, Brace, 1934, 15; cf. E. P. Thompson, 'Time, Work-discipline and Industrial Capitalism', *Past and Present*, 38:1, 1967, 56–97.

4. Bede, *The Reckoning of Time*, ed. and trans. Faith Wallis, Liverpool University Press, 2004, 2: 'Three ways of reckoning time', at 13.

5. Ibid.: 'Three ways of reckoning time', at 14.

6. Ibid., 14.

7. Ibid., 36: 'Natural Years', at 103.

8. Jonathan Bate, *The Song of the Earth*, Picador, 2000, 109.

9. Hyam Maccoby, 'Crescas's Concept of Time', in Gerhard Jaritz and Gerson Moreno-Riaño, eds, *Time and Eternity: The Medieval Discourse*, Brepols, 2003, 163–70, at 164; C. F. Arden-Close, 'Time and Memory', in W. F. Grimes, ed., *Aspects of Archaeology in Britain and Beyond: Essays Presented to O. G. S. Crawford*, H. W. Edwards, 1951, 18.

10. Maccoby, 'Crescas's Concept of Time', 164; Aristotle, *Physics*, IV, 217–18; *Metaphysics*, XI.

11. Augustine, *Confessions*, XI, 12.

12. Ibid., 20, 26; Wesley Stevens, 'A Present Sense of Things Past', in Jaritz and Moreno-Riaño, eds, *Time and Eternity*, 13.

13. Bede, *The Reckoning of Time*, 3: 'The smallest intervals of time', at 15–16.

14. R. J. Mercer, *Causewayed Enclosures*, Shire, 1990, 51; cf. *Hambledon Hill – A Neolithic Landscape*, Edinburgh University Press, 1980.

15. Alan Bowman and David Thomas, *The Vindolanda Writing Tablets (Tabulae Vindolandensis II)*, British Museum Press, 1994, TVII Tablets 156, 190, 154, 164, 291, 343.

16. Flecker, 'To a Poet a Thousand Years Hence', in *The Collected Poems*

of James Elroy Flecker, ed. Sir John Squire, Martin Secker, 1935.

17. Olaf Swarbrick, letter, *British Archaeology*, 74, January 2004, 28.

18. For caution about the 'long chronology' and the scientific challenges of dating posed by the Chauvet images, see Paul Pettit, 'Art and the Middle-to-Upper Paleolithic Transition in Europe: Comments on the Archaeological Arguments for an Early Upper Paleolithic Antiquity of the Grotte Chauvet Art', *Journal of Human Evolution*, 55:5, 2008, 908–17.

19. For the 'practical purposes' see David Cannadine, Jenny Keating and Nicola Sheldon, *The Right Kind of History: Teaching the Past in Twentieth Century England*, Palgrave Macmillan, 2011.

20. Hélène Valladas and Jean Clottes, 'Style, Chauvet and Radiocarbon', *Antiquity*, 77:296, 2003, 142–5.

21. William Shakespeare, *Henry VIII*, 4.2.

22. Alasdair Whittle and Alex Bayliss, '"The Times of their Lives": From Chronological Precision to Kinds of History and Change', *Cambridge Archaeological Journal*, 17:1, 2007, 21–8.

23. N. J. Higham, *Bede as an Oral Historian*, Jarrow Lecture 2011, 19.

24. Philip Grierson, 'Commerce in the Dark Ages: A Critique of the Evidence', *Transactions of the Royal Historical Society*, 9, 1959, 123–40.

25. Clare A. Simmons, *Reversing the Conquest: History and Myth in 19th-century British Literature*, Rutgers University Press, 1990, 6.

26. Bede, *The Reckoning of Time*, Wallis, commentary 356–9.

27. Ibid., 10: 'The week of world-ages', 39–41, and 66: 'The six ages of the world', 156–7; Wallis, commentary, 354.

28. Ibid., 67: 'The remainder of the sixth age', 240.

29. Ibid., 70: 'The day of judgement', 248.

30. Seneca, *Epistles*, 56, 57, 78, 90.

31. Keith Thomas, *Religion and the Decline of Magic*, Penguin, 1988, 511.

32. David S. Landes, *Revolution in Time: Clocks and the Making of the Modern World*, Harvard University Press, 2000.

33. Thomas, *Religion and the Decline of Magic*, 511.

34. Jacques Le Goff, *The Medieval Imagination*, trans. Arthur Goldhammer, Chicago University Press, 1988, 13.

35. Ovid, *Metamorphoses*, 15.66 ff. For discussion and references, Katherine Duncan Jones, ed., *Shakespeare's Sonnets*, Arden Shakespeare, 1997, 228.

36. Thomas, *Religion and the Decline of Magic*, 509–13.

37. André Burguière, *The Annales School: An Intellectual History*, trans. Jane Marie Todd, Cornell University Press, 2009, 2–3.

CHAPTER 1: HEARTLAND

1. The Rev. W. Awdry's first railway stories combining landscape, talking locomotives and rebellious trucks were written in the house in King's Norton in which we temporarily lived before moving into a new-built vicarage at Longbridge. Awdry and his family were the previous occupants.

2. Alexis de Tocqueville, *Journeys to England and Ireland*, Transaction Publishers, 2003, 94.

3. Raymond Williams, *The Country and the City*, Chatto & Windus, 1973.

4. Geoffrey Hill, *The Triumph of Love*, Penguin, 1999, LII.

5. Katherine S. Albert, 'Forged from the Fire Within', *Anvil Magazine*, August–September 2002.

6. Elihu Burritt, *Walks in the Black Country and its Green Border-Land*, Sampson, Low, Son, & Marston, 1868, 330–1.

7. Rev. William Buckland, *Reliquiæ Diluvianæ, or, Observations on the organic remains contained in caves, fissures, and diluvial gravel, and on other geological phenomena, attesting the action of a universal deluge*, John Murray, 1823; Stephen Aldhouse-Green, ed., *Paviland Cave and the 'Red Lady': A Definitive Report*, Western Academic and Specialist Press, 2000.

8. J. B. Priestley, *Daylight on Saturday*, William Heinemann, 1943, 1.

9. T. D. Kendrick, *The Archaeology of the Channel Islands*, vol. 1: *The Bailiwick of Guernsey*, Methuen, 1928, 131–54.

10. V. C. C. Collum, 'The Re-excavation of the Déhus Chambered Mound at Paradis, Vale, Guernsey', *Transactions of La Société Guernesiaise*, 1933, 1–105.

11. F. C. Lukis, 'On the Primeval Antiquities of the Channel Islands', *Archaeological Journal*, 1, 1844, 222–32; 'Observations on the Celtic Megaliths, and the Contents of Celtic Tombs, Chiefly as They Remain in the Channel Islands', *Archaeologia*, 35, 1853, 232–58; Heather Sebire, *From Antiquary to Archaeologist: Frederick Corbin Lukis of Guernsey*, Cambridge Scholars Publishing, 2007.

12. Rick Schulting, Heather Sebire and John E. Robb, 'On the Road to Paradis: New Insights from AMS Dates and Stable Isotopes at Le Dehus, Guernsey, and the Channel Islands Middle Neolithic', *Oxford Journal of Archaeology*, 29:2, 2010, 149–73.

13. Vicent Gaffney, Simon Fitch and David Smith, *Europe's Lost World: The Rediscovery of Doggerland*, Council for British Archaeology, 2009; cf. B. J. Coles, 'Doggerland: A Speculative Survey', *Proceedings of the Prehistoric Society*, 64, 1998, 45–82.

14. Brian Funnell, 'Global Sea-level and the (Pen-)insularity of the Late Cenozoic Britain', in R. C. Preece, ed., *Island Britain: A Quaternary Perspective*, Geological Society, 1995, 3–13; I. Shennan and K. Lambeck, 'Holocene Isostasy and Relative Sea Level Changes on the East Coast of England', in I. Shennan and J. Andrews, eds, *Holocene Land–Ocean Interaction and Environmental Change around the North Sea*, Geological Society, 2000, 275–98.

15. David Russell, 'A Radical View from the Countryside', in Kate Clark, ed., *Conservation Plans in Action*, English Heritage, 1999, 133.

16. Bernard Campbell, *Human Evolution*, Aldine de Gruyter, 1998, 408.

17. Simon Schama, *Landscape and Memory*, Fontana, 1996, 12.

18. Lynn White Jnr, 'The Historical Roots of our Ecological Crisis', *Science*, 155:3767, March 1967, 1203–7.

19. John Frere, 'Account of Flint Weapons Discovered at Hoxne in Suffolk, in a Letter to the Rev. John Brand, Secretary', *Archaeologia*, 13, 1800, 204–5.

20. Jack Repcheck, *The Man Who Found Time: James Hutton and the Discovery of Earth's Antiquity*, Simon & Schuster, 2003.

21. Arthur McCalla, *The Creationist Debate: The Counter between the Bible*

and the Historical Mind, Continuum, 2006, 124–7.

22. William Buckland, Geology and Mineralogy with Reference to Natural Theology, Pickering, 1836.

23. William Buckland, Description of the Quartz Rock of the Lickey Hill in Worcestershire ..., Transactions of the Geological Society, London, 1821, 39.

24. William Coleman, Georges Cuvier, Zoologist: A Study in the History of Evolutionary Theory, Oxford University Press, 1964.

25. Georges Cuvier, Essay on the Theory of the Earth, William Blackwood / T. Cadell, 1822.

26. Glyn Daniel, A Short History of Archaeology, Thames & Hudson, 1981, 50. For the context, Martin J. S. Rudwick, Bursting the Limits of Time: The Reconstruction of Geohistory in the Age of Revolutions, Chicago University Press, 2005.

27. 'Cave at Kirkdale', Caledonian Mercury, 27 May 1822.

28. Rev. William Buckland, Reliquiae Diluvianae, John Murray, 1823.

29. Rudwick, Bursting the Limits of Time, 573.

30. Louis Agassiz, Études sur les glaciers, Jent & Gassmann, 1840, repr. 1966, for Dawson of Pall Mall; Edward Lurie, Louis Agassiz: A Life in Science, Chicago University Press, 1966.

31. Boucher de Perthes dealt with this allegation in a letter to Charles Darwin: letters, 23 June 1863.

32. Jacques Boucher de Crèvecoeur de Perthes, De le création: essai sur l'origine et la progression des êtres, Treuttel et Wurtz, 1839–41; Antiquités celtiques et antédiluviennes: mémoire sur l'industrie primitive et les arts à leur origine, Treuttel et Wurtz, 3 vols, 1847–64; De l'homme antédiluvien et de ses oeuvres, Jung-Treuttel, 1864.

33. Charles Lyell, Geological Evidences of the Antiquity of Man, J. M. Dent, 1914 (first pub. 1863), 75–6.

34. The supervising committee included Sir Charles Lyell, Hugh Falconer, Joseph Prestwich, Andrew Ramsay and Richard Owen.

35. Anne Born, 'William Pengelly and his Circle', Devonshire Association for the Advancement of Science, Literature, and the Arts: Report and Transactions, 126, 1994, 41–55.

36. Donald A. McFarlane and Joyce Lundberg, 'The 19th Century Excavation of Kent's Cavern, England', Journal of Cave and Karst Studies, 67:1, 2005, 39–47.

37. William Pengelly, Presidential Address to the Geological Section of the British Association, Reports of the British Association, 47:2, 1877, 54–66.

38. Birmingham Daily Post, 20 September 1859.

39. W. Boyd Dawkins, Early Man in Britain and his Place in the Tertiary Period, Macmillan, 1880.

40. Anne O'Connor, 'Brixham Cave and the Antiquity of Man: Reassessing the Archaeological and Historical Significance of a British Cave Site', Lithic, 21, 2000, 20–8.

41. 'The British Association for the Advancement of Science', Morning Post, 19 September 1859, 2.

42. Rudwick, Bursting the Limits of Time.

43. Eric S. Wood, Collins Field Guide to Archaeology, Collins, 1963, 102.

44. Albrecht Penck and Eduard Bruckner, Die Alpen im Eiszeitalter, Trauchnitz, 1909.

45. Thomas Hardy, Jude the Obscure, Harper & Brothers, 1895.

46. David Brown, Tradition and Imagination, Oxford University Press, 1999, 6.

47. Alan Garner, 'Oral History and Applied Archaeology in East Cheshire', in *The Voice that Thunders*, Harvill Press, 1997, 71.

48. Andrew Lawson, Edward Martin and Deborah Priddy, *The Barrows of East Anglia*, East Anglian Archaeology Report No. 12, 1981, 8–9.

49. See for example Hans Krahe, *Die Struktur der alteuropäischen Hydronomie*, Akademie der Wissenschaften und der Literatur, 1963; W. F. L. Nicolaisen, 'The "Old European" Names in Britain', *Nomina*, 6, 1982, 37–42; T. Vennemann, 'Linguistic Reconstruction in the Context of European Pre-history', *Transactions of the Philological Society*, 92:2, 1994, 215–84.

50. P. R. Kitson, 'British and European River-Names', *Transactions of the Philological Society*, 94:2, 1996, 73–118; Richard Coates, 'Four Pre-English River Names in and around Fenland', *Transactions of the Philological Society*, 103:3, 2005, 303–22.

51. R. M. Jacobi and T. F. G. Higham, 'The "Red Lady" Ages Gracefully: New Ultrafiltration AMS Determinations from Paviland', *Journal of Human Evolution*, 55.5, 2008, 898–907.

52. S. Aldhouse-Green, 'Artefacts of Ivory, Bone and Shell from Paviland', in S. Aldhouse-Green, ed., *Paviland Cave and the 'Red Lady': A Definitive Report*, 2000, 115–32.

53. Jacobi and Higham, 'The "Red Lady" Ages Gracefully', 905.

54. D. H. Lawrence, 'Things Men Have Made', in *The Complete Poems of D. H. Lawrence*, ed. Vivian de Sola Pinto and Warren Roberts, Penguin, 1977.

55. Richard Bradley, 'Bridging the Two Cultures', *Antiquaries Journal*, 86, 2006, 11.

56. L. Du Garde Peach, *Stone Age Man in Britain*, Wills & Hepworth, 1961, 6.

57. L. Du Garde Peach, *William the Conqueror*, Wills & Hepworth, 1956, 50.

58. Thomas Carlyle to John A. Carlyle, *The Carlyle Letters Online*, 2007, http://carlyleletters.org, Vol. 3, 120-4, accessed 12 May 2012.

CHAPTER 2: 'THAT SECRET AND RESERVED FEELING'

1. R. Rainbird Clarke, 'The Snettisham Treasure', *East Anglian Magazine*, February 1949, 282–90; R. Rainbird Clarke, 'The Early Iron Age Treasure from Snettisham, Norfolk', *Proceedings of the Prehistoric Society*, 20, 1954, 27–86.

2. C. M. Johns, *The Snettisham Roman Jeweller's Hoard*, British Museum Publications, 1997.

3. Andrew Selkirk, 'The Snettisham Treasure', *Current Archaeology*, 11:6, 1991, 260–2.

4. I. M. Stead, 'The Snettisham Treasure: Excavations in 1990', *Antiquity*, 65, 1991, 447–64.

5. Roger Bland and Catherine Johns, *The Hoxne Hoard*, British Museum Publications, 1993; Tim Potter and Catherine Johns, *Roman Britain*, British Museum Publications, 2nd edn, 2002.

6. Department for Education, *History: Programme of Study*, 2011, 2.

7. Marc Bloch, *The Historian's Craft*, Manchester University Press, 1954.

8. http://www.education.gov.uk/schools/teachingandlearning/curriculum/primary/b00199012/

history [accessed 28 January 2012]; *History: Programme of Study for Key Stage Three and Attainment Target*, QCA, 2007; *A Journey to Citizenship*, Home Office Life in the UK Advisory Group, 2nd edn, 2007.

9. Walter Scott, 'Introduction', *The Castle of Otranto*, James Ballantyne, 1811, iii–xxxvi, at xvii.

10. David Mallett, *Excursion*, 1726.

11. John Keats, *Hyperion*, 2.34–7.

12. Walter Scott, 'On the Supernatural in Fictitious Composition; and Particularly on the Works of Ernest Theodore William Hoffmann', *Foreign Quarterly Review*, 1:1, 1827, 60–98.

13. Stuart Piggott, 'Prehistory and the Romantic Movement', *Antiquity*, 11:41, 1937, 31–8.

14. Poem by William Bowles, *Gentleman's Magazine*, August 1912, 121.

15. Adrienne Mayor, *The First Fossil Hunters: Paleontology in Greek and Roman Times*, Princeton University Press, 2000.

16. Lizabeth Paravisini-Gebert, 'Colonial and Postcolonial Gothic: The Caribbean', in J. E. Hogle, ed., *The Cambridge Companion to Gothic Fiction*, Cambridge University Press, 2002, 229–58.

17. For reflection on the STOP ('Stop Taking Our Past') campaign of 1981, see Patrick Wright, *A Journey through Ruins: The Last Days of London*, Oxford University Press, 2009, 160–9.

18. N. J. Brodie, J. Doole and P. Watson, *Stealing History: The Illicit Trade in Cultural Material*, McDonald Institute for Archaeological Research, 2000; N. J. Brodie, J. Doole and C. Renfrew, eds, *Trade in Illicit Antiquities: The Destruction of the World's Archaeological Heritage*, McDonald Institute for Archaeological Research, 2001; R. Atwood, *Stealing History: Tomb Raiders, Smugglers, and the Looting of the Ancient World*, St Martin's Press, 2004.

19. Kevin Leahy and Roger Bland, *The Staffordshire Hoard*, British Museum, 2010. Other rich finds have included the fourth-century Roman Christian silver from Water Newton (Kenneth Painter, 'The Water Newton Silver: Votive or Liturgical?', *Journal of the British Archaeological Association*, 152, 1999, 1–23), and the treasures from Mildenhall (K. S. Painter, *The Mildenhall Treasure: Roman Silver from East Anglia*, British Museum Press, 1977) and Hoxne (see note 5).

20. Mark Blackburn, '"Productive" Sites and the Pattern of Coin Loss in England, 600–1180', in Tim Pestell and Katharina Ulmschneider, eds, *Markets in Early Medieval Europe: Trading and 'Productive' Sites, 650–850*, Windgather Press, 2003, pp. 20–36.

21. Colin Dobinson and Simon Denison, *Metal Detecting and Archaeology in England*, English Heritage and Council for British Archaeology, 1995.

22. The Portable Antiquities Scheme: for the record of what is being reported see www.finds.org.uk; Richard Hobbs, *Treasure: Finding our Past*, British Museum Press, 2003.

23. Rosemary Sweet, 'Antiquaries and Antiquities in Eighteenth-Century England', *Eighteenth-Century Studies*, 4:2, 2001, 181–206, at 188; Thomas Pownall, *Treatise on the Study of Antiquities*, 1782.

24. Richard Gough, *Archaeologia*, 1, 1770, ii.

25. Sweet, 'Antiquaries and Antiquities', 186–7.

26. Alfred Tennyson, *The Princess: A Medley*, Prologue, Edward Moxon, 14th edn, 1866, ll.14–25.

27. Sweet, 'Antiquaries and Antiquities', 187.

28. Rosemary Sweet, *Antiquaries:. The Discovery of the Past in Eighteenth-Century Britain*, Hambledon & London, 2004; Glyn Daniel, *A Short History of Archaeology*, Thames & Hudson, 1981; Paul G. Bahn, ed., *The Cambridge Illustrated History of Archaeology*, Cambridge University Press, 1999.

29. John Collis, *Digging Up the Past: An Introduction to Archaeological Excavation*, Sutton, 2001, 2–3.

30. Richard Bradley, 'Seeing Things: Perception, Experience and the Constraints of Excavation', *Journal of Social Archaeology*, 3:2, 2003, 151–68.

31. Luke Howard, *Essay on the Modification of Clouds*, John Churchill & Sons, 3rd edn, 1865; Richard Hamblyn, *The Invention of Clouds*, Picador, 2001.

32. Hamblyn, *The Invention of Clouds*, 124.

33. John Aubrey, *Chronologia Architectonica*, in John Fowles, ed., *Monumenta Britannica*, Dorset Publishing, 1980.

34. Conrad Rudolph, 'A Sense of Loss: An Overview of the Historiography of Romanesque and Gothic Art', in C. Rudolph, ed., *A Companion to Medieval Art: Romanesque and Gothic in Northern Europe*, Blackwell, 2006, 1–43, at 10.

35. For example: John Carter, *The Ancient Architecture of England*, 2 vols, 1795, 1807; *Views of Ancient Buildings in England*, 6 vols, 1786–93.

36. Thomas Miller Rickman, *Notes on the Life and on the Several Imprints of the Work of Thomas Rickman*, G. J. W. Pitman, 1901.

37. H. M. Taylor, 'The Foundations of Architectural History', in P. V. Addyman and R. K. Morris, eds, *The Archaeological Study of Churches*, CBA Research Report 13, 1976, 3–9.

38. Review of Simpson's *Ancient Baptismal Fonts*, *Gentleman's Magazine*, August 1830, 151.

39. Hamblyn, *The Invention of Clouds*, 124.

40. Richard Colt Hoare, *The History of Ancient Wiltshire*, 2 vols, W. Miller, 1810–21.

41. Stuart Piggott, *Ruins in a Landscape: Essays in Antiquarianism*, Edinburgh University Press, 1976, 127.

42. James Douglas, *Nenia Britannica: or, a sepulchral history of Great Britain, from the earliest period to its general conversion to Christianity*, George Nichol, 1793; Ronald Jessup, *Man of Many Talents: An Informal Biography of James Douglas, 1753–1819*, Phillimore, 1975.

43. Simon Winchester, *The Map that Changed the World*, Viking, 2001, 41.

44. Francis Bond, *Gothic Architecture in England*, Batsford, 1905, xx.

45. Megan Aldrich, 'Gothic Architecture Illustrated: The Drawings of Thomas Rickman in New York', *Antiquaries Journal*, 65, 1985, 427–33.

46. James Hutton, *The Theory of the Earth*, 1785; cf. Charles Lyell, *Principles of Geology*, John Murray, 1833.

47. Colin Renfrew and Paul Bahn, *Archaeology: Theories, Methods and Practice*, Thames & Hudson, 2nd edn, 1996, 24.

48. Jonathan Crary, *Techniques of the Observer: On Vision and Modernity in the Nineteenth Century*, MIT Press, 1990.

49. Charles Darwin, *On the Origin of Species by Means of Natural Selection, or the Preservation of Favoured Races in the Struggle for Life*, John Murray, 1859.

50. Grahame Clark, 'Education and the Study of Man', *Antiquity*, 17:67, 1943, 113–21.

CHAPTER 3: LET US SEE

1. Clare Simmons, *Reversing the Conquest: History and Myth in Nineteenth-Century British Literature*, Rutgers University Press, 1990, 6; Michael W. Thompson, *General Pitt-Rivers: Evolution and Archaeology in the Nineteenth Century*, Moonraker Press, 1977.

2. J. Evans, 'The Coinage of the Ancient Britons and Natural Selection', *Proceedings of the Royal Institution of Great Britain*, 7, 1875, 476–87.

3. Within the decade were published Charles Lyell's *Antiquity of Man*; George St Clair's *Darwinism and Design, or Creation by Evolution*; St George Myvart's *Man and Apes*; the American anthropologist Lewis Henry Morgan's *Ancient Society*; Alfred Russel Wallace's *Comparative Antiquity of Continents* and – at the decade's end – his *How to Nationalize the Land*.

4. Simmons, *Reversing the Conquest*, 6; John Acton, *A Lecture on the Study of History, Delivered at Cambridge June 11 1895*, Macmillan, 1895.

5. William Wordsworth, *Guide to the Lakes with a new preface by Stephen Gill*, Frances Lincoln, 2004.

6. Ralph Waldo Emerson, 'Nature' (1844), in Brooks Atkinson, ed., *The Selected Works of Ralph Waldo Emerson*, Modern Library, 1950, 409.

7. George Catlin, *Letters and Notes on the Manners, Customs, and Conditions of the North American Indians*, vol. 1, Wiley & Putman, 1842, 262; Henry D. Thoreau, 'Walking' (1862), in *Essays, English and American*, Harvard Classics 28, P. F. Collier & Son, 1910, 407.

8. Henry D. Thoreau, *The Maine Woods*, Ticknor & Fields, 1864, 82.

9. Ibid., 173.

10. The Select Committee on National Monuments and Works of Art: see A. D. Saunders, 'A Century of Ancient Monuments Legislation', *Antiquaries Journal*, 63, 1983, 11.

11. William Morris, 'Gothic Architecture', lecture given to the Arts and Crafts Exhibition Society, 1889, published by the Kelmscott Press, 1893.

12. Alfred Russel Wallace, *Land Nationalization: its necessity and its aims: being a comparison of the system of landlord and tenant with that of occupying ownership in their influence on the well-being of the people*, W. Reeves, 1882, 129–30.

13. Horace Hutchinson, *Life of Sir John Lubbock, Lord Avebury*, Macmillan, 1914.

14. Mark Bowden, *Pitt Rivers: The Life and Archaeological Work of Lieutenant-General Augustus Henry Lane Fox Pitt Rivers, DCL, FRS, FSA*, Cambridge University Press, 1991; Thompson, *Pitt-Rivers*.

15. C. N. Warren and S. Rose, *William Pengelly's Techniques of Archaeological Excavation*, Torquay Natural History Society Publication No. 5, 1994; Donald A. McFarlane and Joyce Lundberg, 'The 19th Century Excavation of Kent's Cavern, England', *Journal of Cave and Karst Studies*, 67:1, 2005, 39–47, at 43.

16. Bowden, *Pitt Rivers*, 49.

17. Letter, Pitt Rivers to George Payne, 20 December 1895, published in T. B. Barry, 'Two Letters from the General', *Antiquity*, 45:179, 1971, 217–20.

18. R. E. M. Wheeler, *Still Digging*, Dutton, 1955, 66–7.

19. R. E. M. Wheeler, *Archaeology from the Earth*, Clarendon Press, 1954, 182.

20. Ibid., 188.

21. R. J. C. Atkinson, *Field Archaeology*, Methuen, 1946, 180.

22. John Barrett, 'Stonehenge, Land, Sky and the Seasons', *British Archaeology*, 29, November 1997, 8–9.

23. 'Archaeology', in W. H. Auden, *Collected Poems*, ed. E. Mendelson, Faber & Faber, 1994, 895.

24. Letter, Charles Darwin to Henry Fawcett, 18 September 1861.

25. Recalled by Heisenberg as having been said during a lecture by Heisenberg in 1926.

26. A. A. Manten, 'Lennart von Post and the Foundation of Modern Palynology', *Review of Palaeobotany and Palynology*, 1, 1967, 11–22.

27. O. G. S. Crawford, 'Woodbury. Two Marvellous Air Photographs', *Antiquity*, 3:12, 1929, 452–5; cf. Martyn Barber, *A History of Aerial Photography and Archaeology*, English Heritage, 2011, 172–5.

28. J. D. Hill, 'Great Sites: Little Woodbury', *British Archaeology*, 54, August 2000, 14–17.

29. G. Bersu, 'Excavations at Woodbury, near Salisbury, Wiltshire' (1938), *Proceedings of the Prehistoric Society*, 4, 1938, 308–13; 'Excavations at Little Woodbury, Wiltshire', *Proceedings of the Prehistoric Society*, 6, 1940, 30–111; J. Brailsford and J. W. Jackson, 'Excavations at Little Woodbury, Wiltshire (1938–39)', *Proceedings of the Prehistoric Society*, 14, 1948, 1–23.

30. For example: Sarah M. Colley, 'The Analysis and Interpretation of Archaeological Fish Remains', *Archaeological Method & Theory*, 2, 207–53; A. K. G. Jones, 'Experiments with Fish Bones and Otoliths: Implications for the Reconstruction of Past Diet and Economy', in David Robinson, ed., *Experimentation and Reconstruction in Environmental Archaeology*, Oxbow Books, 1990, 143–6.

31. The National Parks Committee and its advisory Wild Life Conservation Special Committee were established on 21 July 1945. John Dower's report *National Parks in England and Wales* (HMSO, 1945) had been published two months before. Cf. John Sheail, 'John Dower, National Parks, and Town and Country Planning in Britain', *Planning Perspectives*, 10:1, 1995, 1–16; 'The Concept of National Parks in Great Britain 1900–1950', *Transactions of the Institute of British Geographers*, 66, 1975, 41–56.

32. J. Sheail, *Nature in Trust: The History of Nature Conservation in Britain*, Blackie, 1976, 119; Karl Ditt and Jane Rafferty, 'Nature Conservation in England and Germany 1900–70: Forerunner of Environmental Protection?', *Contemporary European History*, 5, 1996, 1–28.

33. J. G. Evans, *Land Snails in Archaeology: With Special Reference to the British Isles*, Seminar Press, 1972; Paul Davies, *Snails: Archaeology and Landscape Change*, Oxbow Books, 2008.

34. Terry O'Connor, *The Archaeology of Animal Bones*, Sutton, 2000; cf. J. M. Bond and T. P. O'Connor, *Bones from Medieval Deposits at 16–22 Coppergate and Other Sites in York*, Archaeology of York, 15/5, 1991; Terry O'Connor, *The Analysis of Urban Animal Bone Assemblages:*

A Handbook for Archaeologists, Archaeology of York, 19/2, 2003.

35. P. Tomlinson, *Environmental Archaeology Bibliography: A Guide*, Reports from the Environmental Archaeology Unit, York, 95/27, 1995.

36. V. H. Galbraith, *Historical Research in Medieval England*, Athlone Press, 1951, 42.

37. R. G. Collingwood, *The Idea of History*, Oxford University Press, 1946, 12.

38. Julian Thomas, *Archaeology and Modernity*, Routledge, 2004.

39. Lars Lönroth, 'The Vikings in History and Legend', in Peter Sawyer, ed., *The Oxford Illustrated History of the Vikings*, Oxford University Press, 1997, 225–49.

40. David Brown, *Tradition and Imagination*, Oxford University Press, 1999, 19.

41. For surveys of theory, Bruce G. Trigger, *A History of Archaeological Thought*, 2nd edn, 2006; Ian Hodder, ed., *Archaeological Theory Today*, Polity Press, 2001; Julian Thomas, *Archaeology and Modernity*, Routledge, 2004.

42. H. J. Massingham, *Downland Man*, Jonathan Cape, 1926, 41.

43. Ibid., 41.

44. Lewis Henry Morgan, *Ancient Society*, H. Holt, 1878.

45. T. Earle, ed., *Chiefdoms: Power, Economy, and Ideology*, Cambridge University Press, 1991.

46. V. Gordon Childe, 'The Urban Revolution', *Town Planning Review*, 21, 1950, 3–17.

47. Jim Allen, 'Aspects of V. Gordon Childe', *Labour History*, 12, May 1967, 52–9, at 52.

48. Stuart Piggott, 'Vere Gordon Childe', *Proceedings of the British Academy*, 44, 1958, 810.

49. Kent Flannery, 'Childe the Evolutionist: A Perspective from Nuclear America', in David R. Harris, ed., *The Archaeology of V. Gordon Childe*, University College Press, 1994, 109–10.

50. Michael E. Smith, 'V. Gordon Childe and the Urban Revolution: A Historical Perspective on a Revolution in Urban Studies', *Town Planning Review*, 80:1, 2009, 3029; Andrew Sherratt, 'V. Gordon Childe: Archaeology and Intellectual History', *Past and Present*, 125, 1989, 151–85.

51. V. Gordon Childe, *The Dawn of European Civilization*, K. Paul, Trench, Trubner, 1925; *The Danube in Prehistory*, Clarendon Press, 1929.

52. O. G. S. Crawford, 'Human Progress: A Review', *Antiquity*, 10:40, 1936, 391–404, at 391; V. Gordon Childe, *Man Makes Himself*, Watts, 1936.

53. Bruce Trigger, 'Childe's Relevance to the 1990s', in Harris, ed., *The Archaeology of V. Gordon Childe*, 9–34, at 20.

54. Ibid., 11–12.

55. Ibid., 12–13; Childe, *The Danube in Prehistory*, 248.

56. Crawford, 'Human Progress', 392.

57. Trigger, 'Childe's Relevance', 21; V. Gordon Childe, *Prehistoric Communities of the British Isles*, 3rd edn, W. & R. Chambers, 1949; *Piecing Together the Past: The Interpretation of Archaeological Data*, Routledge & Kegan Paul, 1956.

58. Childe, *Prehistoric Communities*, 91.

59. V. Gordon Childe, *What Happened in History*, Penguin, 1942, 42.

60. For which now: Chris Stringer, *The Origin of our Species*, Allen Lane, 2011, 167–200.

61. Linda Colley, *Britons: Forging the Nation 1707–1837*, 2nd edn, Yale University Press, 2005.

62. Axel Steensberg and J. L. Østergaard Christensen, *Store Valby. Historisk-arkaeologisk undersøgelse af en nedlagt landsby pø Sjaelland*, Det Kongelige Danske Videnskabernes Selskab, 3 vols, Munksgaard, 1974; Emma Bentz, 'The Danish Connection: Axel Steensberg and Wharram Percy' in *Wharram: A Study of Settlement on the Yorkshire Wolds, XIII. A History of Wharram and its Neighbours*, ed. Stuart Wrathmell, York University Archaeological Publications 15, 2012, 10–23, esp.13–17.

63. John Collis, *Digging Up the Past: an Introduction to Archaeological Excavation*, Sutton, 2001, 12.

64. Colin Renfrew and Paul Bahn, *Archaeology: Theories, Methods and Practice*, Thames & Hudson, 2nd edn, 1996, 35.

65. Sheridan Bowman, *Radiocarbon Dating*, British Museum Publications, 1990; M. J. Aitken, *Science-based Dating in Archaeology*, Longman, 1990.

66. http://c14.arch.ox.ac.uk/embed.php?File=calibration.html#conventions [accessed 1 February 2012].

67. Martin Bailey, 'Discovery of Earliest Illuminated Manuscript', *Art Newspaper*, 214, June 2010, 46.

68. Colin Renfrew, *Before Civilization: The Radiocarbon Revolution and Prehistoric Europe*, Jonathan Cape, 1973.

69. Richard Bradley, 'Bridging the Two Cultures', *Antiquaries Journal*, 86, 2006, 1–13, at 11; Alasdair Whittle and Alex Bayliss, 'The Times of their Lives: From Chronological Precision to Kinds of History and Change', *Cambridge Archaeological Journal*, 17:1, 2007, 21–8.

70. Thomas Bayes, 'An essay towards solving a problem in the doctrine of chances', *Philosophical Transactions*, 53, 1763, 370–418; reprinted in E. S. Pearson and M. G. Kendall, eds, *Studies in the History of Statistics and Probability: A Series of Papers*, Griffin, 1970.

71. D. R. Bellhouse, 'The Reverend Thomas Bayes FRS: A Biography to Celebrate the Tercentenary of his Birth', *Statistical Science*, 19:1, 2004, 3–43, at 18.

72. Cited in ibid., 20.

73. Alex Bayliss and Christopher Bronk Ramsey, 'Pragmatic Bayesians: A Decade Integrating Radiocarbon Dates into Chronological Models', in C. E. Buck and A. R. Millard, eds, *Tools for Constructing Chronologies: Tools for Crossing Disciplinary Boundaries*, Springer, 2004, 25–41; Alex Bayliss, Christopher Bronk Ramsey, Johannes van der Plicht and Alasdair Whittle, 'Bradshaw and Bayes: Towards a Timetable for the Neolithic', *Cambridge Archaeological Journal*, 17, 2007, 1–28.

74. Alasdair Whittle, Frances Healy and Alex Bayliss, 'The Domestication of Britain', *British Archaeology*, July–August 2011, 14–21, at 15; cf. Alasdair Whittle, Frances Healy and Alex Bayliss, *Gathering Time: Dating the Early Neolithic Enclosures of Southern Britain and Ireland*, Oxbow Books, 2011.

75. Tom Higham, Tim Compton, Chris Stringer, Roger Jacobi, Beth Shapiro, Erik Trinkhaus, Barry Chandler, Flora Gröning, Chris Collins, Simon Hillson, Paul O'Higgins, Charles FitzGerald and Michael Fagan, 'The Earliest Evidence for Anatomically Modern Humans in North-western Europe', *Nature*, 479, November 2011, 521–4; Stringer, *The Origin of our Species*, 39–40.

76. M. G. L. Baillie, *Tree-ring*

Dating and Archaeology, Croom Helm, 1982; *A Slice Through Time: Dendrochronology and Precision Dating*, Routledge, 1995; Jennifer Hillam, *Dendrochronology: Guidelines on Producing and Interpreting Dendrochronological Dates*, English Heritage, n.d.; Daniel Miles, 'Interpretation of Tree-Ring Dates', *Vernacular Architecture*, 28, 1997, 40-56.

77. A. E. Douglass, 'The Search of the Southwest Solved by Talkative Tree Rings', *National Geographic*, 56:6, 1929, 736-70.

78. D. W. H. Miles, *The Tree-ring Dating of the Roof Carpentry of the Eastern Chapels, North Nave Triforium, and North Porch, Salisbury Cathedral, Wiltshire*, Centre for Archaeology Report 94, 2002; Oxford Dendrochronology Laboratory, Major Projects, Salisbury, www.dendrochronology. com [accessed 29 June 2007].

79. Jacqueline A. Stedall, 'Of our own Nation: John Wallis's Account of Mathematical Learning in Medieval England', *Historia Mathematica*, 28, 2001, 73-112, at 88, 91-2, 98-9 (for Grosseteste). Stedall views the earliest arrival of Arabic numerals in northern Europe as 'slow and uneven'; they were known to a few scholars, and probably some travellers and traders from the tenth century. Later, in part possibly as a result of Crusade contacts, and certainly with 'the flood of new translations in the 12th century', the numerals began 'to appear more commonly in written texts, particularly astronomical tables. After 1200 the numerals were brought to England by Grosseteste and others, and together with the associated algorithms, were

disseminated and popularized through the widely copied texts of Jordanus, Sacrobosco, and Ville Dieu': 109-10.

80. Gustav Milne and Brian Hobley, eds, *Waterfront Archaeology in Britain and Northern Europe*, Council for British Archaeology Research Report 41, 1981; Gustav Milne, 'London's Medieval Waterfront', *British Archaeology*, 68, December 2002, 20-3.

81. Gwyn Jones, *A History of the Vikings*, Oxford University Press, 1968, 99.

82. Peter Sawyer, ed., *The Oxford Illustrated History of the Vikings*, Oxford University Press, 1997, 5, 160-1.

83. 'The Oldest European: Boxgrove Man throws new light on man's place in the world', *The Times*, 18 May 1994, 17.

84. Nikolaus Pevsner, quoted in Susie Harries, *Nikolaus Pevsner: The Life*, Chatto & Windus, 2011, 87.

85. Stuart Piggott, 'The Origins of the English County Archaeological Societies', in *Ruins in a Landscape: Essays in Antiquarianism*, Edinburgh University Press, 1976, 1889.

86. Cited in J. Kenyon, *The History Men: The Historical Profession in England since the Renaissance*, Weidenfeld & Nicolson, 2nd edn, 1993, 155.

87. Lecture delivered in the Ashmolean Museum, 2 November 1870.

88. Glyn Daniel, *Some Small Harvest*, Thames & Hudson, 1986, 424.

89. 'Oh, whistle, and I'll come to you my lad', *The Collected Ghost Stories of M. R. James*, Edward Arnold, 1931, 121.

90. Wheeler was born in Glasgow in 1890. The family moved to Bradford in 1894. Jacquetta Hawkes, *Mortimer Wheeler: Adventurer in Archaeology*, Weidenfeld & Nicolson, 1982.

91. Martin Carver, *Sutton Hoo: Burial Ground of Kings?*, British Museum Press, 1998, chapter 1, 'Mrs Pretty digs up a ship', 2–24.

92. Richard Dumbreck, quoted in ibid., 5.

93. Ibid., 5.

94. Ibid., 18, 28–9.

95. Sue Hirst, *The Prittlewell Prince: The Discovery of a Rich Anglo-Saxon Burial in Essex*, Museum of London Archaeology Service, 2004.

96. Tom Williamson, *Sutton Hoo and its Landscape: The Context of Monuments*, Windgather Press, 2008.

97. Terry O'Connor, ed., *Biosphere to Lithosphere: New Studies in Vertebrate Taphonomy*, Oxbow Books, 2005.

98. André Burguière, *The Annales School: An Intellectual History*, trans. Jane Marie Todd, Cornell University Press, 2009, 188.

99. Ibid.

100. Gordon Willey and Philip Phillips, *Method and Theory in American Archaeology*, Chicago University Press, 1958; S. R. Binford and L. R. Binford, eds, *New Perspectives in Archaeology*, Aldine Press, 1968; David L. Clarke, *Analytical Archaeology*, Methuen, 1968; Bruce Trigger, *A History of Archaeological Thought*, Cambridge University Press, 2nd edn, 2006.

101. Ernest Gellner, *Nations and Nationalism*, Cornell University Press, 1983, 8–14, at 11; for critique, Roderick J. McIntosh, *Ancient Middle Niger: Urbanism and the Self-organizing Landscape*, Cambridge University Press, 2005, 21.

102. Renfrew and Bahn, *Archaeology*, 39.

103. Burguière, *The Annales School*, 188.

104. Timothy K. Earle and Robert W. Preucel, 'Processual Archaeology and the Radical Critique', *Current Anthropology*, 28:4, 1987, 501–38.

105. Mark Bowden, *Unravelling the Landscape*, Tempus, 1999.

106. Matthew Johnson, *Ideas of Landscape*, Blackwell, 2007, 148, 162.

107. Jonathan Bate, *The Song of the Earth*, Picador, 2000, 110–11.

108. Bradley, 'Bridging the Two Cultures', 9–10.

109. Martyn Barber, *A History of Aerial Photography and Archaeology*, English Heritage, 2011.

110. J. C. Capper, 'Photographs of Stonehenge as Seen from a War Balloon', *Archaeologia*, 60, 1907, 571–2.

111. Robert de Marolles, *Aviation, école de l'homme*, Plon et Nourrit, 1938.

112. Robert Wohl, *The Spectacle of Flight: Aviation and the Western Imagination, 1920–1950*, Yale University Press, 2005, 277–322, at 294.

113. Le Corbusier, *Aircraft*, Albada Editores, 2003 (first pub. 1935), 96.

114. Ibid., Introduction,13; Marolles, *Aviation*, 64.

115. Le Corbusier, *Aircraft*, 10.

CHAPTER 4: ALBION FROM ABOVE

1. 'Major Allen killed near Burcote', *Oxford Mail*, 25 November 1940; 'Tragic death of Major G. W. G. Allen', *Oxford Times*, 29 November 1940; 'Obituary: Major G. W. G. Allen MC', *Implement and Machinery Review*, 1 January 1941, 788;

2. The account of Major Allen's family background is derived from two main sources – an MS note by Allen W. Anderson, and the MS Memoirs of Phebe Elizabeth Jane Anderson née Allen (1894–1985).

3. *Allen's Activities* (company magazine), 10:37 & 38, 1958.

4. George Allen service record, TNA WO 372/1.
5. References to flights are taken from a photocopy of Allen's flying log book, kindly made available by Allen W. Anderson. The original is held by the Ashmolean Museum in Oxford.
6. G. W. G. Allen, 'Discovery from the Air', *Aerial Archaeology*, 10, 1984, 39.
7. John L. Myres, 'The Man and his Past', in W. F. Grimes, ed., *Aspects of Archaeology in Britain and Beyond: Essays Presented to O. G. S. Crawford*, H. W. Edwards, 1951, 3; O. G. S. Crawford, *Said and Done: The Autobiography of an Archaeologist*, Weidenfield & Nicolson, 1955, 14–17.
8. Kitty Hauser, *Bloody Old Britain*, Granta, 2008, 10.
9. Ibid., 14.
10. Myres, 'The Man and his Past', 6.
11. Hugh Driver, *The Birth of Military Aviation: Britain, 1903-1914*, Royal Historical Society Studies in History/Boydell & Brewer, 1997, 107–11, 116, 120.
12. Nicholas C. Watkis, *The Western Front from the Air*, Wrens Park Publishing, 2000, 7–13.
13. Hugh Durnford, *The Tunnellers of Holzminden*, Cambridge University Press, 1920.
14. Myres, 'The Man and his Past'.
15. C. W. Phillips, *Archaeology in the Ordnance Survey 1791–1965*, CBA Occasional Paper, 1980, 27–8.
16. 'Air Survey and Archaeology', read at a meeting of the Royal Geographical Society, 12 March 1923, published in *Geographical Journal*, 61, 342–60, reissued as Ordnance Survey Professional Paper, New Series, No. 7, HMSO, 1924.
17. L. Murray, *A Zest for Life: The Story of Alexander Keiller*, Morven Books, 1999.
18. Martyn Barber, *A History of Aerial Photography and Archaeology*, English Heritage, 2011, 114–24.
19. O. G. S. Crawford, *Air Photography for Archaeologists*, Ordnance Survey Professional Papers, New Series, No. 12, 1929; O. G. S. Crawford and A. Keiller, *Wessex from the Air*, Oxford University Press, 1928.
20. Alasdair Whittle, Joshua Pollard and Caroline Grigson, *Harmony of Symbols*, Oxbow Books, 1999; Rosamund Cleal, 'Windmill Hill', *British Archaeology*, 67, October 2002, 21–5.
21. D. L. Kennedy and D. N. Riley, *Rome's Desert Frontier from the Air*, Batsford, 1990.
22. O. G. S. Crawford, 'Air Photographs of the Middle East', *Geographical Journal*, 73, 1929, 497–512; G. A. Beazley, 'Air Photography in Archaeology', *Geographical Journal*, 53, 1919, 330–5; W. H. C. Frend, *The Archaeology of Early Christianity: A History*, Geoffrey Chapman, 1997, 182; David Kennedy, 'Aerial Archaeology in the Middle East: The Role of the Military – Past, Present … and Future?', in R. H. Bewley and W. Raczkowski, eds, *Aerial Archaeology: Developing Future Practice*, NATO Science Series, IOS Press, 2002, 33–48.
23. O. G. S. Crawford, 'The Stonehenge Avenue', *Antiquaries Journal*, 4, 1924, 57–9.
24. G. S. M. Insall, 'The Aeroplane in Archaeology', *Journal of the Royal Air Force College*, 9:2, 1929, 174–5.
25. For the find, excavation, context and references, Barber, *History of Aerial Photography and Archaeology*, 154–61; cf. Mike Pitts, *Hengeworld*, Century, 2000, 31–9.
26. Crawford, *Air Photography for Archaeologists*.
27. J. K. St Joseph, 'A Survey of

Pioneering in Air-photography', in Grimes, ed., *Aspects of Archaeology*, 303–15.

28. 'The palimpsest of Britain', *The Times*, 16 August 1924, 11.

29. Cited in Barber, *History of Aerial Photography and Archaeology*, 175–6; Stuart Piggott, 'Archaeological Retrospect 5', *Antiquity*, 57:219, 1983, 28–37, at 32.

30. Sam Smiles, 'What Lies Beneath', *Oxford Art Journal*, 31:3, 2008, 454–7; Kitty Hauser, *Shadow Sites: Photography, Archaeology, and the British Landscape 1927–1955*, Oxford University Press, 2007, 32.

31. C. W. Phillips, *My Life in Archaeology*, Alan Sutton, 1987, 38.

32. C. W. Phillips, 'The Fenland Research Committee, its Past Achievements and Future Prospects', in Grimes, ed., *Aspects of Archaeology*, 258–71; C. W. Phillips, ed., *The Fenland in Roman Times*, Royal Geographical Society Research Series 5, 1970. For a more recent picture, see D. Hall and J. M. Coles, *Fenland Survey: An Essay in Landscape and Persistence*, English Heritage Archaeological Report 1, 1994; cf. Francis Pryor, *Farmers in Prehistoric Britain*, Tempus, 1998, and *Seahenge: New Discoveries in Prehistoric Britain*, HarperCollins, 2001.

33. Hall and Coles, *Fenland Survey*.

34. Charles Thomas, *Exploration of a Drowned Landscape: Archaeology and History of the Isles of Scilly*, Batsford, 1985.

35. Martin Millet and Sean McGrail, 'The Archaeology of the Hasholme Logboat', *Archaeological Journal*, 144, 1987, 69–155.

36. Letter to A. D. Passmore, Ashmolean Museum, 14 July 1933.

37. E. T. Leeds, 'The Late G. W. G.

Allen MA FSA', *Oxoniensia*, 5, 1940, 172.

38. J. S. P. Bradford, Foreword to Allen, 'Discovery from the Air', 23; cf. A. Barclay and J. Harding, eds, *Pathways and Ceremonies: The Cursus Monuments of Britain and Ireland*, Oxbow Books, 1999.

39. For the book itself and a conspectus on Allen's work see Allen, 'Discovery from the Air', ed. Derek A. Edwards, with contributions by J. S. P. Bradford, O. G. S. Crawford and D. N. Riley.

40. S. W. Wooldridge and D. L. Linton, 'The Low Terrains of South-Eastern England and their Relation to its Early History', *Antiquity*, 7:27, 1933, 297–310.

41. Cyril Fox, *The Personality of Britain: Its Influence on Inhabitant and Invader in Prehistoric and Early Historic Times*, National Museum of Wales and University of Wales, 2nd edn, 1933 (first pub. 1932), 82.

42. Ditchley Villa, Harden Archive 160–341, Ashmolean Museum.

43. C. A. Ralegh Radford, *Tintagel Castle, Cornwall*, His Majesty's Stationery Office, 1939. Radford's 'monastic' interpretation held sway until the 1980s, when fresh fieldwork followed by new excavation revealed something more complicated: a larger, denser, elite settlement in contact with southern Europe and the Mediterraean: C. Barrowman, C. E. Batey and C. D. Morris, *Excavations at Tintagel Castle, Cornwall, 1990–1999*, Society of Antiquaries of London, 2007

44. C. A. R. Radford, 'The Roman Villa at Ditchley, Oxon.', *Oxoniensia*, 1, 1936, 24-58, at 25.

45. Paul Booth, 'Ralegh Radford and the Roman Villa at Ditchley: a

Review', *Oxoniensia*, 64, 1999, 39–49, at 40.

46. Radford, 'The Roman Villa at Ditchley', 27.

47. Radford, 'The Roman Villa at Ditchley', 58.

48. Martin Wood, *Nancy Lancaster: English Country House Style*, Frances Lincoln, 2005; Robert Becker, *Nancy Lancaster: Her Life, Her World, Her Art*, Knopf, 1998.

49. Deborah Devonshire, *The DailyTelegraph*, 20 August 1994.

50. Bentz, 'The Danish Connection', 16; C. Evans, 'Archaeology and modern times: Bersu's Woodbury 1938 and 1939', *Antiquity*, 63:240, 1989, 436-50.

51. Hauser, *Bloody Old Britain*, 108–9.

52. O. G. S. Crawford, 'Air Photography, Past and Future: Presidential Address for 1938', *Proceedings of the Prehistoric Society*, 4, 233–8.

53. 'Archaeology in Britain. Five years' finds', *The Times*, 22 March 1938, 13.

54. Crawford, *Said and Done*, 248–50.

55. O. G. S. Crawford, 'A Century of Air Photography', *Antiquity*, 28:112, 1954, 206–10.

56. Barber, *History of Aerial Photography and Archaeology*, 181–214.

57. Christopher C. Taylor, 'Aerial Photography and the Field Archaeologist', in D. R. Wilson, ed., *Aerial Reconnaissance for Archaeology*, CBA Research Report 12, 1975, 136; Don Benson and David Miles, *The Upper Thames Valley: An Archaeological Survey of the River Gravels*, Oxford Archaeological Unit Survey 2, 1974; T. Gates, *The Middle Thames Valley: An Archaeological Survey of the River Gravels*, Berkshire Archaeological Committee Publication 1, 1975; Roger Leech, *The Upper Thames Valley in Gloucestershire and Wiltshire: An Archaeological Survey of the River Gravels*, Committee for Rescue Archaeology in Avon, Gloucestershire and Somerset, 1977; D. T. Yates, 'Bronze Age Field Systems in the Thames Valley', *Oxford Journal of Archaeology*, 18:2, 1999, 157–70.

58. D. N. Riley, 'Archaeology from the Air in the Upper Thames Valley', *Oxoniensia*, 7/8, 1943/4, 64–101; 'The Technique of Air Archaeology', *Archaeological Journal*, 101, 1946, 1–16.

59. D. N. Riley, *Early Landscape from the Air: Studies of Crop Marks in South Yorkshire and North Nottinghamshire*, University of Sheffield, 1980.

60. W. S. Hanson, 'Go East Young Man: A New Reconnaissance Programme in Romania', *Aerial Archaeology Research Group News*, 18, 1999, 15–17, at 16.

61. R. Bewley, Otto Braasch and Rog Palmer, 'An Archaeological Training Week, 15–22 June 1996, held near Siófok, Lake Balaton, Hungary', *Antiquity*, 70:270, 1996, 745–50; Otto Braasch, 'Goodbye Cold War! Goodbye Bureaucracy? Opening the Skies to Aerial Archaeology in Europe', in R. H. Bewley and Włodzimierz Rączkowski, eds, *Aerial Archaeology: Developing Future Practice*, NATO Series 1, 337, 2002, 19–22; cf. Dimitra Papagianni, 'Palaeolithic Archaeology in a United Europe', *Antiquity*, 77:298, 2003, 842–7; Lech Czerniak, Włodzimierz Rączkowski and Wojciech Sosnowski, 'New Prospects for the Study of Early Neolithic Longhouses in the Polish Lowlands', *Antiquity*, 77:297, 2003.

62. Hauser, *Bloody Old Britain*, 110.

63. Ibid., 252–3.

64. Royal Commission on Historical Monuments, England, *A Matter of Time: An Archaeological Survey*,

HMSO, 1960; Marion Shoard, *The Theft of the Countryside*, Temple Smith, 1980, 9.

65. Glyn Daniel, *Some Small Harvest*, Thames & Hudson, 1986, 233.

66. O. G. S. Crawford, foreword to 'Discovery from the Air', written 3 September 1949, published in *Aerial Archaeology*, 10, 1984, 17.

CHAPTER 5: THE OLD ONES

1. John Wymer, *The Lower Palaeolithic Occupation of Britain*, Wessex Archaeology/English Heritage, 1999; Clive Gamble, *The Palaeolithic Societies of Europe*, Cambridge University Press, 1999; Mark Roberts and Simon Parfitt, *Boxgrove: A Middle Pleistocene Hominid Site at Eartham Quarry, Boxgrove, West Sussex*, English Heritage, 1999; S. A. Parfitt et al., 'The Earliest Record of Human Activity in Northern Europe', *Nature*, 438, 2005, 1008–12; C. Stringer, *Homo Britannicus: The Incredible Story of Human Life in Britain*, Allen Lane, 2006; S. A. Parfitt et al., 'Early Pleistocene Human Occupation at the Edge of the Boreal Zone in Northwest Europe', *Nature*, 466, 2010, 229–33.

2. Vincent Gaffney, Simon Fitch and David Smith, *The Rediscovery of Doggerland*, Council for British Archaeology, 2009.

3. Sanjeev Gupta, Jenny S. Collier, Andy Palmer-Felgate and Graeme Potter, 'Catastrophic Flooding Origin of Shelf Valley Systems in the English Channel', *Nature*, 448, 2007, 342–5.

4. F. Wenban-Smith and R. Hosfield, ed., *Palaeolithic Archaeology of the Solent River*, Lithic Studies Society Occasional Papers, 7, 2001.

5. Stringer, *Homo Britannicus*, 223.

6. Paul Buckland, 'Conservation and the Holocene Record: An Invertebrate View from Yorkshire', *Recording and Monitoring Yorkshire's Natural Environment Conference Proceedings, 2002*, 'Yorkshire Naturalists' Union', 24.

7. Roberts and Parfitt, *Boxgrove*, 414.

8. Geoffrey Hill, *Mercian Hymns*, André Deutsch, 1971, XXVIII.

9. W. Boismier et al., 'A Middle Palaeolithic Site at Lynford Quarry, Mundford, Norfolk: Interim Statement', *Proceedings of the Prehistoric Society*, 69, 2003, 315–24.

10. S. A. Parfitt et al., 'The Earliest Record of Human Activity in Northern Europe'.

11. Parfitt, S. A. et al., 'Early Pleistocene Human Occupation at the Edge of the Boreal Zone in Northwest Europe'.

12. Theodosius Dobzhansky, *Mankind Evolving*, Yale University Press, 1962.

13. Ernst Mayr, 'Taxonomic Categories in Fossil Hominids', in *Evolution and the Diversity of Life: Selected Essays*, Harvard University Press, 1997 (first pub. 1976), 530–45

14. P. Brown et al., 'A New Small-bodied Hominin from the Late Pleistocene of Flores, Indonesia', *Nature*, 431, 2004, 1055–61; J. Krause et al., 'The Complete Mitochondrial DNA Genome of an Unknown Hominin from Southern Siberia', *Nature*, 464, 2010, 894–7.

15. Simon Parfitt, Mike Pitts, Tony Stuart and Chris Stringer, '700,000 Years Old: Found in Suffolk', *British Archaeology*, 86, 2006; for qualification on the chronological context of the Happisburgh/Pakefield exposures, Stringer, *Homo Britannicus*, 64.

16. Stringer, *Homo Britannicus*, 61–2.

17. Ian Tattersall, *Becoming Human: Evolution and Human Uniqueness*, Oxford University Press, 1998, 145; Stringer, *Homo Britannicus*, 44–5; B. Wood and N. Lonergan, 'The Hominin Fossil Record: Taxa, Grades and Clades', *Journal of Anatomy*, 212:4, 2008, 354–76.

18. Roberts and Parfitt, *Boxgrove*, 425.

19. C. Stringer and C. Gamble, *In Search of the Neanderthals: Solving the Puzzle of Human Origins*, Thames & Hudson, 1993; Stringer, *Homo Britannicus*.

20. Tjeerd H. van Andel and William Davies, ed., *Neanderthals and Modern Humans in the European Landscape during the Last Glaciation*, McDonald Institute for Archaeological Research, 2003; C. Stringer, *The Origin of our Species*, Allen Lane, 2011, 51–4, 220–1.

21. C. Stringer and R. McKie, *African Exodus*, Jonathan Cape, 1996; for more recent discussion of the chronology and geography of colonization of the world, see P. A. Underhill et al., 'The Phylogeography of Y Chromosome Binary Haplotypes and the Origins of Modern Human Populations', *Annals of Human Genetics*, 65, 2001, 43–62.

22. Stringer, *Homo Britannicus*, 185–99, at 190.

23. J. Hahn and S. Munzel, 'Knochenflöten aus dem Aurignacien des Geissenklösterle bei Blaubeuren, Alb-Donau-Kreis', *Fundberichte aus Baden-Württemberg*, 20, 1995, 1–12.

24. But see N. J. Conard, P. M. Grootes and F. H. Smith, 'Unexpectedly Late Dates for Human Remains from Vogelherd', *Nature*, 430, 2004, 198–201.

25. Gamble, *Palaeolithic Societies*, 337–8.

26. Ernst Mayr, *Systematics and the Origin of Species*, Harvard University Press, 1942.

27. Stringer, *Origin of our Species*, 27–8, 32–3.

28. Ibid., 33.

29. R. E. Green et al., 'A Draft Sequence of the Neanderthal Genome', *Science*, 328:5979, May 2010, 710–22.

30. Stringer, *Origin of our Species*, 192.

31. Ibid.

32. Ibid., 41–4.

33. Ibid., 192–5.

34. W. F. Bodner and L. L. Cavalli-Sforza, *Genetics, Evolution and Man*, Freeman, 1976, 584.

35. Niles Eldredge and Stephen Jay Gould, 'Punctuated Equilibria: An Alternative to Phyletic Gradualism', in T. J. M. Schopf, ed., *Models in Paleobiology*, Freeman Cooper, 1972, 82–115, at 84.

36. Clifford Jolly, cited in Stringer, *Origin of our Species*, 193; Charles Darwin, 'On the Imperfection of the Geological Record', in *On the Origin of Species by Means of Natural Selection*, John Murray, 1859.

37. Francisco J. Ayala and Mario Coluzzi, 'Humans, Drosophila, and Mosquitoes', *Proceedings of the National Academy of Sciences of the United States of America*, 102, suppl. 1, 3 May 2005, 6535–42.

38. Marc Ereshefsky, 'Philosophy of Biological Classification', in Keith Roberts, ed., *Handbook of Plant Science*, Wiley, 2007, 8–10.

39. Eldredge and Gould, 'Punctuated Equilibria: An Alternative to Phyletic Gradualism', 92.

40. Richard Dawkins, *Climbing Mount Improbable*, Penguin, 1997, 96–7.

41. Tattersall, *Becoming Human*, 81.

42. Ibid., 91.

43. Ernst Mayr, *Animal Species and*

Evolution, Belknap Press, 1963; *Populations, Species, and Evolution: An Abridgment of Animal Species and Evolution*, Belknap Press, 1970; Tattersall, *Becoming Human*, 92.

44. Ernst Mayr, 'Change of Genetic Environment and Evolution', in J. S. Huxley, A. C. Hardy and E. B. Ford, eds, *Evolution as a Process*, Allen & Unwin, 1954, 157–80; Niles Eldredge and S. J. Gould, 'Punctuated Equilibria: The Tempo and Mode of Evolution Reconsidered', *Paleobiology*, 3:2, 1977, 115–51; cf. S. J. Gould and Niles Eldridge, 'Punctuated Equlibirum Comes of Age', *Nature*, 366, 1993, 223–7.

45. Ian Tattersall, 'The Case for Saltational Events in Human Evolution', in Tim J. Crow, ed., *The Speciation of Modern* Homo Sapiens, *Proceedings of the British Academy* 106, Oxford University Press, 2002.

46. Krause et al., 'The Complete Mitochondrial DNA Genome of an Unknown Hominin from Southern Siberia'.

47. Stringer, *Origin of our Species*, 195.

48. Alan Garner, *The Voice that Thunders*, Harvill Press, 1997.

49. David Blackbourn, *Conquest of Nature: Water, Landscape, and the Making of Modern Germany*, W. W. Norton, 2006.

50. Jonathan Bate, *The Song of the Earth*, Picador, 2000, 177.

51. Reinhold Niebuhr, *The Nature and Destiny of Man*, Nisbet, 1941, 1.

52. Tjeerd H. van Andel and William Davies, eds, *Neanderthals and Modern Humans in the European Landscape during the Last Glaciation*, McDonald Institute for Archaeological Research, 2003.

53. Stringer, *Origin of our Species*, 192–3.

54. J. Clottes, ed., *Return to Chauvet Cave: Excavating the Birthplace of Art: The First Full Report*, Thames & Hudson, 2003.

55. Frederick Charles Bartlett, *Remembering: A Study in Experimental and Social Psychology*, Cambridge University Press, 1932, introduction by Walter Kintsch, 1995; Michael C. Corballis and Stephen E. G. Lea, *The Descent of Mind: Psychological Perspectives on Hominid Evolution*, Oxford University Press, 1999.

56. S. Aldhouse-Green, ed., *Paviland Cave and the 'Red Lady'*, Western Academic and Specialist Press, 2000; R. M. Jacobi and T. F. G. Higham, 'The "Red Lady" Ages Gracefully: New Ultrafiltration AMS Determinations from Paviland', *Journal of Human Evolution*, 55:5, 2008, 898–907.

57. Keri A. Brown and Mark Pluciennik, 'Archaeology and Human Genetics: Lessons for Both', *Antiquity*, 75:287, 2001, 101–6.

58. Lounès Chikhi et al., 'Y Genetic Data Support the Neolithic Demic Diffusion Model', *Proceedings of the National Academy of Sciences*, 99:17, 2002, 11008–13, argued that indigenous hunter-gatherers contributed less than 30 per cent, whereas Martin Richards considers that 'both mitochondrial DNA and Y-chromosome analyses have indicated a contribution of … Near Eastern lineages to the gene pool of modern Europeans of around a quarter or less'. Cf. Ornella Semino, Giuseppe Passarino et al., 'The Genetic Legacy of Paleolithic *Homo sapiens sapiens* in Extant Europeans: A Y Chromosome Perspective', *Science*, 290, 2000, 1155–9; Cristian Capelli et al., 'A Y Chromosome Census in the British Isles', *Current Biology*, 13:11, 27 May 2003, 979–84.

59. Stephen Oppenheimer, *The Origins of the British: A Genetic Detective Story*, Constable, 2006.

60. Eilert Ekwall, *English River-Names*, Clarendon Press, 1928; for recent discussion of Old European examples, P. R. Kitson, 'British and European River-names', *Transactions of the Philological Society*, 94:2, 1996, 73–118; 'Four Pre-English River-names in and around Fenland: *Chater, Granta, Nene* and *Welland*', *Transactions of the Philological Society*, 103:3, 2005, 303–22.

61. H. Krahe, *Unsere ältesten Flussnamen*, Harrassowitz, 1964; W. F. H. Nicolaisen, '"Old European" Names in Britain', *Nomina*, 6, 1982, 37–42; Kitson, 'British and European River-names'.

62. Richard Coates, 'Stour and Blyth as English River-names', *English Language and Linguistics*, 10:1, 2006, 23–9, at 23.

63. Alasdair Whittle, 'The Neolithic Period', in J. Hunter and I. Ralston, eds, *The Archaeology of Britain*, Routledge, 1999, 58–76.

CHAPTER 6: NOTES FROM A DARK WOOD

1. Tacitus, *Germania*, trans. J. B. Rives, Clarendon Press, 1999, chapter 9.

2. Harold Fox, 'The Wolds before *c.*1500', in Joan Thirsk, ed., *The English Rural Landscape*, Oxford University Press, 2000, 50–3.

3. Oliver Rackham, *Trees and Woodland in the British Landscape*, Dent, 1976; *Ancient Woodland: Its history, Vegetation and Uses in England*, Edward Arnold, 1980; and *The History of the Countryside*, Phoenix, 1997; Harry Godwin, *History of the British Flora*, Cambridge University Press, 2nd edn, 1975.

4. *The Dream of the Rood*, ed. Michael Swanton, University of Exeter Press, 1987.

5. For *wuduwasa* and the cult of Nature see H. D. Ellis, 'The Wodewose in East Anglian Churches', *Proceedings of the Suffolk Institute of Archaeology*, 14, 912, 282–93; William Anderson, *The Green Man: The Archetype of our Oneness with the Earth*, London, 1990; Hayden White, 'The Forms of Wildness', in Edward Dudley and Maximilian Novak, eds, *The Wild Man Within*, Pittsburgh, 1972, 2–38; Ronald Sheridan and Anne Ross, *Grotesques and Gargoyles: Paganism in the Medieval Church*, David & Charles, 1975.

6. Jacques Le Goff, 'The Wilderness in the Medieval West', in *The Medieval Imagination*, trans. Arthur Goldhammer, Chicago University Press, 1988, 47–59, esp. 58.

7. H. C. Darby, 'The Clearing of the English Woodlands', *Geography*, 36, 1951, 71–83.

8. D. Goodburn, 'The Death of the Wildwood and Birth of Woodmanship in South-east England', in Kathryn Bernick, ed., *Hidden Dimensions: The Cultural Significance of Wetland Archaeology*, University of British Columbia Press, 1998, 130–8.

9. G. M. Trevelyan, *History of England*, Longmans, 3rd edn, 1945, 1962 impression, Map I, 8.

10. Ibid., 9. The notion of extensive woodland in the later Middle Ages recurs: Michael Williams, *Deforesting the Earth: From Prehistory to Global Crisis*, University of Chicago Press, 2003, 102. Cf. Charles Higounet, 'Les Forêts de l'Europe occidentale du Ve au XIe Siècle', in *Agricoltura e*

mondo rurale in Occidente nell'alto medioevo, Settimane di Studio del Centro Italiano di Studi sull'Alto Medioevo, Spoleto, 1966, xiii, 343–97.

11. H. C. Darby, ed., *A New Historical Geography of England before 1600*, Cambridge University Press, 1973, 1.

12. C. W. Phillips, *My Life in Archaeology*, Alan Sutton, 1987, 30–1.

13. H. J. Massingham, *Downland Man*, Jonathan Cape, 1926; *The Golden Age: The Story of Human Nature*, G. Howe, 1927.

14. Trevelyan, *History of England*, 9.

15. R. Hippisley Cox, *The Green Roads of England*, Methuen, 1914; A. Watkins, *The Old Straight Track*, Methuen, 1925.

16. V. Gordon Childe, *Prehistoric Communities of the British Isles*, 3rd edn, W. & R. Chambers, 1949, 33. See also O. G. S. Crawford, 'The Distribution of Early Bronze Age Settlements in Britain', *Geographical Journal*, 40, 1912, 184–97, 304–17; E. G. Bowen, 'Prehistoric Southern Britain', in H. C. Darby, ed., *An Historical Geography of England before A.D. 1800*, Cambridge University Press, 1936.

17. Eilert Ekwall, 'The Scandinavian Element', in Darby, ed., *An Historical Geography of England before A.D. 1800*, 133–64; F. M. Stenton, 'The Historical Bearing of Place-name Studies: The Danish Settlement of Eastern England', *Transactions of the Royal Historical Society*, 4th series, 24, 1943, 1–24.

18. Darby, ed., *A New Historical Geography of England*, 35.

19. W. G. Hoskins, *English Landscapes*, BBC Books, 1973, 23.

20. Walter Rose, *Good Neighbours: Some Recollections of an English village and its People*, Cambridge University Press, 1942.

21. Christopher Taylor, *Village and Farmstead*, George Philip, 1983, 20.

22. Peter Sawyer, *From Roman Britain to Norman England*, Methuen, 1978, 145.

23. Margaret Gelling, *Signposts to the Past: Place-names and the History of England*, J. M. Dent, 1978, 15.

24. P. J. Fowler, 'Archaeology and the M4 and M5 Motorways, 1965–1978', *Archaeological Journal*, 136, 1979, 12–26; E. Fowler, ed., *Field Survey in British Archaeology*, CBA, 1972; H. C. Bowen and P. J. Fowler, eds, *Early Land Allotment in the British Isles: A Survey of Recent Work*, British Archaeological Reports (British series) 48, 1978.

25. Francis Pryor et al., *Archaeology and Environment in the Lower Welland Valley: The Fenland Project 1*, East Anglian Archaeology 27, 1985; A. Clark, *Excavations at Mucking*, vol. 1: *The Site Atlas: Excavations by M. U. & T. W. Jones*, English Heritage Archaeological Report 20, 1993; D. N. Hall and N. Nickerson, 'Sites on the North Bedfordshire and South Northamptonshire Border', *Bedfordshire Archaeological Journal*, 3, 1966, 1–6; D. N. Hall and J. B. Hutchins, 'The Distribution of Archaeological Sites between the Nene and the Ouse Valleys', *Bedfordshire Archaeological Journal*, 7, 1972, 1–16; Gill Hey, 'Neolithic Settlement at Yarnton, Oxfordshire', in P. Topping, ed., *Neolithic Landscapes*, Oxbow Books, 1997, 99–112; Christopher Evans and Mark Knight, 'A Fenland Delta: Later Prehistoric Land-use in the Lower Ouse Reaches', in M. Dawson, ed., *Prehistoric, Roman and Post-Roman Landscapes of the Great Ouse Valley*, CBA Research Report 119, 2001, 89–106; Frances Healy and Jan Harding, 'Raunds,

Northamptonshire Pre-Iron Age
Project: Research on a Prehistoric
Ritual Landscape', *Centre for
Archaeology News*, 5, 2003, 4–7.

26. B. Schumer, *The Evolution of
Wychwood to 1400: Pioneers, Frontiers
and Forests*, Department of English
Local History Occasional Paper,
University of Leicester, 3rd series, 6,
1984.

27. M. Gardiner, 'The Archaeology of
the Weald: A Survey and Review',
Sussex Archaeological Collections, 128,
1990, 33–53.

28. Christopher Dyer, 'Woodlands and
Wood Pasture in Western England',
in Thirsk, ed., *The English Rural
Landscape*, 100.

29. Examples included Whiteparish
in Wiltshire (see p. 193);
Chalton, Hampshire; Wootton,
Northamptonshire; West Penwith,
Cornwall; and Witton, Norfolk.
Christopher Taylor, 'Whiteparish',
*Wiltshire Archaeological & Natural
History Magazine*, 62, 1967, 79–102;
Barry Cunliffe, 'Chalton, Hants:
The Evolution of a Landscape',
Antiquaries Journal, 53, 1973, 173–90;
D. N. Hall, 'Wootton Parish
Survey, 1973', *Northamptonshire
Archaeology*, 11, 1976, 151–8; V.
Russell, *West Penwith Survey*,
Cornwall Archaeological Society,
1971; Andrew Lawson et al., *The
Archaeology of Witton*, East Anglian
Archaeological Report 18, 1983.

30. James Campbell, ed., *The Anglo-
Saxons*, Penguin, 1991, 9.

31. L. V. Grinsell identified 600 to
640 burial cairns: 'Dartmoor
Barrows', *Proceedings of the Devon
Archaeological Association*, 36,
1978, 85–180; Catherine Linehan,
'Deserted Sites and Rabbit-Warrens
on Dartmoor, Devon', *Medieval
Archaeology*, 10, 1966, 113–44.

32. Andrew Fleming, 'Dartmoor
Reaves: A 19th Century Fiasco',
Antiquity, 52:204, 1978, 16–20.

33. Elizabeth Gawne and J. V.
Somers Cocks, 'Parallel Reaves
on Dartmoor', *Transactions of
the Devon Association*, 100, 1968,
277–91; Andrew Fleming and John
Collis, 'A Late Prehistoric Reave
System near Cholwich Town,
Dartmoor', *Proceedings of the Devon
Archaeological Association*, 31, 1973,
1–21.

34. Andrew Fleming, 'The Prehistoric
Landscape of Dartmoor: Part 1,
South Dartmoor', *Proceedings of the
Prehistoric Society*, 44, 1978, 102.

35. D. J. Maguire and C. J. Caseldine,
'The Former Distribution of Forest
and Moorland on Dartmoor', *Area*,
17, 1985, 193–203; Phil Newman,
The Field Archaeology of Dartmoor,
English Heritage, 2011, 24–6, with
further references.

36. Newman, *Field Archaeology of
Dartmoor*, 60.

37. Fleming, 'The Prehistoric Landscape
of Dartmoor', 107; *The Dartmoor
Reaves: Investigating Prehistoric Land
Divisions*, Batsford, 1988.

38. Fleming, 'The Prehistoric Landscape
of Dartmoor', 97.

39. Francis Pryor, *Farmers in Prehistoric
Britain*, Tempus, 1998, 150.

40. Newman, *Field Archaeology of
Dartmoor*, 60–82, esp. 77, 81–2.

41. Fleming, 'The Prehistoric Landscape
of Dartmoor', 112; cf. Bowen and
Fowler, eds, *Early Land Allotment
in the British Isles*; Francis Pryor,
'Fen-edge Land Management in the
Bronze Age', in C. Burgess and R.
Miket, eds, *Settlement and Economy
in the Third and Second Millennia
BC*, British Archaeological Reports
(British series) 33, 29–50; D. N. Riley,
Early Landscape from the Air: Studies

of Crop Marks in South Yorkshire and North Nottinghamshire, University of Sheffield, 1980; Pryor, Farmers in Prehistoric Britain.

42. D. T. Yates, 'Bronze Age Field Systems in the Thames Valley', Oxford Journal of Archaeology, 18:2, 1999, 157–70; 'Bronze Age Agricultural Intensification in the Thames Valley and Estuary', in J. Brück, ed., Bronze Age Landscapes: Tradition and Transformation, Oxbow Books, 2001, 65–82; D. T. Yates, Land, Power and Prestige: Bronze Age Field Systems in Southern England, Oxbow Books, 2006; A. Fleming, The Dartmoor Reaves, Oxbow Books, 2nd edn, 2008.

43. Taylor, Village and Farmstead, 15.

44. Andrew Lawson, Edward Martin and Deborah Priddy, The Barrows of East Anglia, East Anglian Archaeology Report 12, 1981, 49.

45. Timothy Champion, 'The Later Bronze Age', in J. Hunter and I. Ralston, eds, The Archaeology of Britain, Routledge, 1999, 100.

46. I. G. Simmons, M. A. Atherden, E. W. Cloutman, P. R. Cundall, J. B. Innes and R. L. Jones, 'Prehistoric Environments', in D. A. Spratt, ed., Prehistoric and Roman Archaeology of North-East Yorkshire, CBA Research Report 87, 1993, 15–50, at 40.

47. Rackham, The History of the Countryside, 306–7; Brian Huntley, M. Baillie, J. M. Grove et al., 'Holocene Palaeoenvironmental Changes in North-west Europe: Climatic Implications and the Human Dimension', in G. Wefer, W. H. Berger, K.-E. Behre and E. Jansen, eds, Climate Development and History of the North Atlantic Realm, Springer-Verlag, 2002, 259–98.

48. The Thorne–Hatfield area was mapped in c.1407, when it was known as Inclesmoor (TNA DL 42/12, fos. 29v–30r), and again in the mid-fifteenth century (TNA MPC 56): see M. W. Beresford, 'Inclesmoor, West Riding of Yorkshire', in R. A. Skelton and P. D. A. Harvey, Local Maps and Plans from Medieval England, Oxford University Press, 1986, 147–61.

49. G. D. Gaunt, Geology of the County around Goole, Doncaster, and the Isle of Axholme, British Geological Survey, HMSO, 1994.

50. Rackham, The History of the Countryside, 68.

51. H. J. B. Birks, 'Holocene Isochrone Maps and Patterns of Tree-spreading in the British Isles', Journal of Biogeography, 16, 1989, 503–40.

52. Rackham, The History of the Countryside, 68.

53. P. C. Buckland and M. H. Dinnin, 'The Rise and Fall of a Wetland Habitat: Recent Palaeoecological Research on Thorne and Hatfield Moors', Thorne & Hatfield Moors Papers, 4, 1997, 13.

54. K. D. Bennett, 'A Provisional Map of Forest Types for the British Isles 5,000 Years Ago', Journal of Quaternary Science, 4, 1988, 141–4.

55. Peter Marren, Woodland Heritage: Britain's Ancient Woodland, David & Charles, 1990, 43; Rackham, The History of the Countryside, 69.

56. Nicola J. Whitehouse, 'Insect Faunas Associated with Pinus sylvestris L. from the Mid-Holocene of the Humberhead Levels, Yorkshire, UK', Studies in Quaternary Entomology – An Inordinate Fondness for Insects, Quaternary Proceedings No. 5, 1997, 293–303.

57. P. T. Harding and F. Rose, Pasture-woodlands in Lowland Britain, Abbots Ripton, Institute of

Terrestrial Ecology, NERC, Monks Wood, 1986; cf. Paul Davies, John G. Robb and Dave Ladbrook, 'Woodland Clearance in the Mesolithic: The Social Aspects', *Antiquity*, 79:304, 2005, 280–8; T. Brown, 'Clearances and Clearings: Deforestation in Mesolithic/Neolithic Britain', *Oxford Journal of Archaeology*, 16:2, 1997, 133–46; Paul A. Mellars, 'Fire Ecology, Animal Populations and Man: A Study of Some Ecological Relationships in Prehistory', *Proceedings of the Prehistoric Society*, 42, 1976, 15–45.

58. Paul Buckland, *Thorne Moors: A Palaeoecological Study of a Bronze Age Site: A Contribution to the History of the British Insect Fauna*, University of Birmingham Department of Geography, Occasional Publication 8, Birmingham, 1979.

59. J. Coles and B. Coles, *Sweet Track to Glastonbury*, Thames & Hudson, 1986.

60. M. Robinson and G. Lambrick, 'Holocene Alluviation and Hydrology in the Upper Thames Basin', *Nature*, 308, 1984, 811; S. Limbrey, in S. Limbrey and J. G. Evans, eds, *The Effect of Man on the Landscape: The Lowland Zone*, CBA Research Report 21, 1978, 21–7.

61. Gretel Boswijk and Nicola J. Whitehouse, '*Pinus* and *Prostomis*: A Dendrochronological and Palaeoentomological Study of a Mid-Holocene Woodland in Eastern England', *Holocene*, 12:5, July 2002, 585–96.

62. K. D. Bennett, 'The Post-glacial History of *Pinus sylvestris* in the British Isles', *Quaternary Science Reviews*, 14, 1984, 133–55.

63. Buckland and Dinnin, 'The Rise and Fall of a Wetland Habitat', 13.

64. Nicola J. Whitehouse, 'Forest Fires and Insects: Palaeoentomological Research from a Subfossil Burnt Forest', *Palaeo*, 164, 2000, 247–62; 'Silent Witnesses: An *Urwald* Fossil Insect Assemblage from Thorne Moors', *Thorne & Hatfield Moors Papers*, 4, 1997, 39; cf. Paul Mellars, 'Fire Ecology, Animal Populations and Man: A Study of Some Ecological Relationships in Prehistory', *Proceedings of the Prehistoric Society*, 42, 1976, 15–46.

65. Oliver Rackham, 'Ecologists against the Triumph of Unreason', Electronic TEG, British Ecological Society, Summer 1996.

66. Whitehouse, 'Silent Witnesses'; cf. N. J. Whitehouse, P. C. Buckland and M. H. Dinnin, 'Holocene Woodlands: The Fossil Insect Evidence', in K. J. Kirby and C. M. Drake, eds, *Dead Wood Matters: The Ecology and Conservation of Saproxylic Invertebrates in Britain*, English Nature Science No. 7, English Nature, Peterborough, 1993.

67. For example: R. W. Smith, 'The Ecology of Neolithic Farming Systems as Exemplified by the Avebury Region of Wiltshire', *Proceedings of the Prehistoric Society*, 50, 1984, 99–120; Yates, 'Bronze Age Field Systems in the Thames Valley'; Pryor, *Farmers in Prehistoric Britain*; Susan Oosthuizen, 'The Roots of the Common Fields: Linking Prehistoric and Medieval Field Systems in West Cambridgeshire', *Landscapes*, 4:1, 2003, 40–64; Richard Bradley, *The Prehistory of Britain and Ireland*, Cambridge University Press, 2007, 188.

68. J. M. Coles, S. V. E. Heal and B. J. Orme, 'The Use and Character of Wood in Prehistoric Britain and Ireland', *Proceedings of the Prehistoric Society*, 44, 1978, 1–45.

69. Taylor, *Village and Farmstead*, 192.

70. Christopher Taylor, 'Polyfocal Settlement and the English Village', *Medieval Archaeology*, 21, 1977, 189–93.

71. V. H. Galbraith, 'The Making of Domesday Book', *English Historical Review*, 57, 1942, 161–77; Reginald Lennard, *Rural England 1086–1135: A Study of Social and Agrarian Conditions*, Clarendon Press, 1959; H. C. Darby, *Domesday England*, Cambridge University Press, 1977; D. R. Roffe, 'Domesday Book and Northern Society', *English Historical Review*, 100, 1990, 310–40; J. C. Holt, ed., *Domesday Studies*, Boydell Press, 1987; Peter Sawyer, ed., *Domesday Book: A Reassessment*, Edward Arnold, 1985; David Roffe, *Decoding Domesday*, Boydell Press, 2007.

72. Sawyer, *From Roman Britain to Norman England*, 136–7; H. C. Darby and E. M. J. Campbell, eds, *The Domesday Geography of South-East England*, Cambridge University Press, 1962, 496–7.

73. Dyer, 'Woodlands and Wood Pasture in Western England', 112.

74. M. J. Dobson, 'Malaria in England: A Geographical and Historical Perspective', *Parassitologia*, 36:1–2, August 1994, 35–60.

75. O. Oelschaeger, *The Idea of Wilderness*, Yale University Press, 1991, 24.

76. Davies, Robb and Ladbrook, 'Woodland Clearance in the Mesolithic'.

77. Rackham, *The History of the Countryside*, 87, 92.

78. Ibid., 12–16. In 1995 the figure was just under 8 per cent.

79. Ibid., 26. Goodburn, 'The Death of the Wildwood and Birth of Woodmanship in South-east England'.

80. T. Darvill, *Prehistoric Britain*, Batsford, 1987, 43.

81. Alex Bayliss et al., 'The World Recreated: Redating Silbury Hill in its Monumental Landscape', *Antiquity*, 81:311, 2007, 26–53.

82. C. Evans, J. Pollard and M. Knight, 'Life in Woods: Tree-throws, "Settlement" and Forest Cognition', *Oxford Journal of Archaeology*, 18:3, 1999, 241–54.

83. Martin Carver, *Sutton Hoo: Burial Ground of Kings?*, British Museum Press, 1998, 94.

84. Richard J. Bradley, *Altering the Earth: The Origins of Monuments in Britain and Continental Europe: The Rhind Lectures 1991–2*, Society of Antiquaries of Scotland Monograph Series, 8, 1993; *The Significance of Monuments*, Routledge & Kegan Paul, 1998; Alasdair Whittle, 'The Neolithic Period', in J. Hunter and I. Ralston, eds, *The Archaeology of Britain*, Routledge, 1999, 58–76, at 60.

85. M. Girling and J. Grieg, 'A First Fossil Record for *Scolytus scolytus*: Its Occurrence in Elm Decline Deposits from London and its Implications for the Neolithic Elm Decline in the British Isles', *Journal of Archaeological Science*, 12, 1985, 247–351; A. Parker et al., 'A Review of the Mid-Holocene Elm Decline', *Progress in Physical Geography*, 26, 2002, 1–45.

86. Whittle, 'The Neolithic Period', 62.

87. Bradley, *The Prehistory of Britain and Ireland*, 35.

88. A. J. Ammerman and L. L. Cavalli-Sforza, 'The Rate of Spread of Early Farming in Europe', *Man*, New Series, 6:4, 1971, 674–88; 'A Population Model for the Diffusion of Early Farming in Europe', in C. Renfrew, ed., *The Explanation of*

Culture Change: Models in Prehistory, Duckworth, 1973, 343–58; 'The Wave of Advance Model for the Spread of Agriculture in Europe', in C. Renfrew and K. L. Cooke, eds, Transformations: Mathematical Approaches to Culture Change, Academic Press, 1979, 275–94.

89. Colin Renfrew, Archaeology and Language: The Puzzle of Indo-European Origins, Penguin, 1989 (first pub. Jonathan Cape, 1987), 129.

90. A. J. Ammerman and L. L. Cavalli-Sforza, The Neolithic Transition and the Genetics of Populations in Europe, Princeton University Press, 1984; L. L. Cavalli-Sforza and F. Cavalli-Sforza, The Great Human Diasporas: The History of Diversity and Evolution, Addison-Wesley, 1995.

91. Renfrew, Archaeology and Language, 1989.

92. For example: Martin Richards, 'The Neolithic Invasion of Europe', Annual Review of Anthropology, 32, 2003, 135–62; Lounès Chikhi et al., 'Y Genetic Data Support the Neolithic Demic Diffusion Model', Proceedings of the National Academy of Sciences.

93. Mariana Gkiasta, Thembi Russell, Stephen Shennan and James Steele, 'Neolithic Transition in Europe: The Radiocarbon Record Revisited', Antiquity, 77:295, 2003, 45–62.

94. Whittle, 'The Neolithic Period', 63.

95. Mark Collard, Kevin Edinborough, Stephen Shennan and Mark H. Thomas, 'Radiocarbon Evidence Indicates that Migrants Introduced Farming to Britain', Journal of Archaeological Science, 37, 2010, 866–70, at 855.

96. Alasdair Whittle, Frances Healy and Alex Bayliss, Gathering Time: Dating the Early Neolithic Enclosures of Southern Britain and Ireland, Oxbow Books, 2011.

97. Bradley, Altering the Earth; Alasdair Whittle, Europe in the Neolithic: The Creation of New Worlds, Cambridge University Press, 1996.

98. R. J. Mercer, Causewayed Enclosures, Shire, 1990, 8.

99. Alastair Oswald, Carolyn Dyer and Martyn Barber, The Creation of Monuments: Neolithic Causewayed Enclosures in the British Isles, English Heritage, 2001; Frances Healy, Causewayed Enclosures and the Early Neolithic: The Chronology and Character of Monument Building and Settlement in Kent, Surrey and Sussex in the Early to Mid-4th Millennium cal BC, South East Research Framework resource assessment seminar, https://shareweb.kent.gov.uk/Documents/Leisure-and-culture/heritage/serf-seminar-papers-neolithic-and-early-bronze-age/frances-healy.pdf [accessed 14 February 2012].

100. Alasdair Whittle, Frances Healy and Alex Bayliss, Gathering Time: Dating the Early Neolithic Enclosures of Southern Britain and Ireland, Oxbow Books, 2011.

101. Oswald, Dyer and Barber, The Creation of Monuments, 4–5.

102. A. Whittle, J. Pollard and C. Grigson, The Harmony of Symbols: The Windmill Hill Causewayed Enclosure, Wiltshire, Oxbow Books, 1999.

103. Richard Bradley, The Significance of Monuments, Routledge, 1998.

104. Bradley, The Prehistory of Britain and Ireland, 72.

105. Whittle, 'The Neolithic Period', 65.

106. Mark Edmonds, Ancestral Geographies of the Neolithic: Landscapes, Monuments and Memory, Routledge & Kegan Paul, 1999; Julian Thomas, Time, Culture and Identity, Routledge, 1996.

107. One of them, albeit later, is Stonehenge, where excavations on the site of the 1960s car park produced evidence for a number of large pinewood orthostats dating 7500–6700 cal BC. It is not clear whether these uprights stood together to form one monument in one period, or successively over a longer period of time.

108. For summary of discussion and references, see Oswald, Dyer and Barber, *The Creation of Monuments*, esp. 104–6.

109. A. Barclay, G. Lambrick, J. Moore and M. Robinson, *Lines in the Landscape: Cursūs Monuments in the Upper Thames Valley: Excavations at the Drayton and Lechlade Cursūses*, Thames Valley Landscapes Monograph 15, Oxford Archaeology, 2003; T. Malim, 'Cursūses and Related Monuments of the Cambridgeshire Ouse', in A. Barclay and J. Harding, eds, *Pathways and Ceremonies: The Cursūs Monuments of Britain and Ireland*, Oxbow Books, 2003, 77–85.

110. Francis Pryor, *Seahenge: New Discoveries in Prehistoric Britain*, HarperCollins, 2001, 76.

111. The Neolithic palisade at Hindwell, Powys, for instance, enclosed eighty-four acres: Alex Gibson, 'Hindwell and the Neolithic Palisaded Sites of Britain and Ireland', in A. Gibson and D. Simpson, eds, *Prehistoric Ritual and Religion*, Sutton, 1998, 68–79; A. Gibson, 'Round in Circles: Some Possible Relationships and Transformations', in R. Cleal and J. Pollard, eds, *Monuments and Material Culture*, Hobnob Press, 2004; A. Gibson, *Stonehenge and Timber Circles*, 2nd edn, Tempus, 2005.

112. K. D. Thomas, 'Neolithic Enclosures and Woodland Habitats on the South Downs in Sussex, England', in M. Bell and S. Limbrey, eds, *Archaeological Aspects of Woodland Ecology*, British Archaeological Reports (International series) 146, 1982, 147–70.

113. Whittle, 'The Neolithic Period', 74.

114. Alex Bayliss and Alasdair Whittle, eds, *Histories of the Dead: Building Chronologies for Five Southern British Long Barrows*, Cambridge Archaeological Journal 17:1, Supplement, 2007.

115. Alex Bayliss, Don Benson, Dawn Galer, Louise Humphrey, Lesley McFadyen and Alasdair Whittle, 'One Thing after Another: The Date of the Ascott-under-Wychwood Long Barrow', in ibid., 29–44.

116. Alasdair Whittle, Alex Bayliss and Michael Wysocki, 'Once in a Lifetime: The Date of the Wayland's Smithy Long Barrow', in ibid., 103–21.

117. John Meadows, Alistair Barclay and Alex Bayliss, 'A Short Passage of Time: The Dating of the Hazleton Long Cairn Revisited', in ibid., 46–64.

118. Alex Bayliss, Alasdair Whittle and Michael Wysocki, 'Talking about my Generation: The Date of the West Kennet Long Barrow', in ibid., 85–101.

119. Alasdair Whittle, Alistair Barclay, Alex Bayliss, Lesley McFadyen, Rick Schulting and Michael Wysocki, 'Building for the Dead: Events, Processes and Changing Worldviews from the Thirty-eighth to the Thirty-fourth Centuries cal. BC in Southern Britain', in ibid., 123–47.

120. David A. Hetherington, Tom C. Lord and Roger M. Jacobi, 'New Evidence for the Occurrence

of Eurasian Lynx (*Lynx lynx*) in Medieval Britain', *Journal of Quaternary Science*, 21, 2006, 3–8.

121. 'The etymology of the name has not been found': Eilert Ekwall, *The Concise Oxford Dictionary of English Place-Names*, 4th edn, Clarendon Press, 1960, 261; but cf. A. Mawer, *The Place-names of Bedfordshire and Huntingdonshire, Cambridgeshire*, Cambridge University Press, 1925, 405.

122. *British Archaeology*, 31, February 1998, 4; cf. Mike Pitts, *Hengeworld*, Century, 2000, 368, n. 466.

123. Andrew Sherratt, 'Why Wessex? The Avon River Route and River Transport in Later British Pre-history', *Oxford Journal of Archaeology*, 15:2, 1996, 211–34. For the Thames as a prehistoric highway, John Steane, *Oxfordshire*, Pimlico, 1996, 112.

124. John Mitchell Kemble, *The Saxons in England: A History of the English Commonwealth till the Period of the Norman Conquest*, Longman, Brown, Green & Longmans, 1849; Gelling, *Signposts to the Past*, 106.

125. A. H. Smith, 'Place-names and the Anglo-Saxon Settlement', *Proceedings of the British Academy*, 42, 1956, 67–88.

126. The revolt was less than complete; while it retreated from the old interpretation, it attempted to substitute another whereby names ending in -*ham* were indicative of the immigration phase of the English conquest, while the -*ingas* names were reinterpreted as indicators of a later phase.

127. Dyer, 'Woodlands and Wood Pasture in Western England', 104.

128. Darby, *New Historical Geography*, 29.

129. H. W. C. Davies, 'East Anglia and the Danelaw', *Transactions of the Royal Historical Society*, 5th series,

5, 1955, 23–9; Peter Sawyer, 'The Density of the Danish Settlement in England', *University of Birmingham Historical Journal*, 6, 1958, 1–17; *The Age of the Vikings*, London, 1962, 145–67.

130. Gelling, *Signposts to the Past*, 220.

131. Peter Sawyer, *Anglo-Saxon Lincolnshire*, History of Lincolnshire, vol. 3, 1998, 113.

132. Simon Schama, *Landscape and Memory*, Fontana, 1996, 225.

133. *The Tempest*, 2.2.

CHAPTER 7: TALL NETTLES

1. M. W. Beresford, *The Lost Villages of England*, Lutterworth Press, 1954, 1.

2. Christopher Gerrard, 'The Society for Medieval Archaeology: The Early Years (1956–1962)', in R. Gilchrist and A. Reynolds, eds, *Reflections: Fifty Years of Medieval Archaeology*, Society for Medieval Archaeology, 2009, 23–46.

3. Stuart Piggott, *Ruins in a Landscape: Essays in Antiquarianism*, Edinburgh University Press, 1976, 171–95.

4. Interview with the late John G. Hurst FSA, recorded at Cambridge University Museum of Archaeology and Anthropology, by Pamela Jane Smith, on 20 July 2000, Society of Antiquaries of London.

5. O. G. S. Crawford, 'Air Photograph of Gainstrop, Lincs', *Antiquaries Journal*, 5, 1925, 432–4.

6. C. W. Foster and T. Longley, eds, *The Lincolnshire Domesday and the Lindsey Survey*, Lincoln Record Society, vol. 19 (1921), 1924.

7. E. M. Jope and R. I. Threlfall, 'Excavation of a Medieval Settlement at Beere, North Tawton, Devon', *Medieval Archaeology*, 2, 1958, 112–40.

8. R. L. S. Bruce Mitford and E. M. Jope, 'The Excavations at Seacourt, Berks, 1939: An Interim Report', *Oxoniensia*, 5, 1940, 31–41.

9. Ibid.

10. M. W. Beresford, 'The Lost Villages of Medieval England', *Geographical Journal*, 117:2, 1951, 129–47; M. W. Beresford, 'The Deserted Villages of Warwickshire', *Transactions of the Birmingham and Midland Archaeological Society*, 66, 1950, 49–106.

11. Nicholas Orme, 'Rous, John (c.1420–1492)', *Oxford Dictionary of National Biography*, Oxford University Press, 2004, http://o-www.oxforddnb.com.wam.leeds.ac.uk/view/article/24173 [accessed 10 February 2012].

12. *Historia Regum Angliae*, British Museum Cotton Vespasian MS A xii.

13. W. G. Hoskins, *Transactions of the Leicestershire Archaeological Society*, 22, 1948.

14. Christopher Dyer, 'The Lost Villages of England, 1954–1998', introductory essay to Beresford, *The Lost Villages of England*, Sutton, 1998 edn (first pub. 1954).

15. E. Benz, 'The Danish Connection: Axel Steensberg and Wharram Percy', in *Wharram: A Study of Settlement on the Yorkshire Wolds, XIII. A History of Wharram Percy and its Neighbours*, York University Archaeological Publications 15, 2012, 10–22, at 12–13.

16. Edwin F. Gay, 'Inclosures in England in the Sixteenth Century', *Quarterly Journal of Economics*, 17, 1903, 576–97, at 594–5.

17. G. M. Trevelyan, *English Social History*, Longmans, 1944, 117.

18. John Clapham, *A Concise Economic History of Great Britain*, Cambridge University Press, 1949, 197 (cf. note on p. 80).

19. M. W. Beresford, 'Author's Preface 1998', *The Lost Villages of England*, 1998 edn, x–xi; 79.

20. C. S. and C. S. Orwin, *The Open Fields*, Clarendon Press, 1938.

21. Eric Kerridge, 'Ridge and Furrow and Agrarian History', *Economic History Review*, 4:1, 1951, 14–36.

22. M. W. Beresford and J. K. S. St Joseph, *Medieval England: An Aerial Survey*, Cambridge University Press, 1979, 37.

23. Beresford, *The Lost Villages of England*, 53.

24. David Hall, *Turning the Plough: Midland Open Fields: Landscape Character and Proposals for Management*, English Heritage & Northamptonshire County Council, 2001.

25. Beresford, *The Lost Villages of England*, 53.

26. Antonia Gransden, 'Antiquarian Studies in Fifteenth-century England', *Antiquaries Journal*, 60, 1980, 74–97.

27. W. G. Hoskins, *Local History in England*, Longman, 3rd edn, 1984, 30.

28. Ibid., 25–6.

29. Erwin Nasse, *On the Agricultural Community of the Middle Ages, and Inclosures of the Sixteenth Century*, 1869, translated from the German by H. A. Ouvery, 1877; Frederic Seebohm, *The English Village Community Examined in its Relations to the Manorial and Tribal Systems and to the Common or Open-Field System of Husbandry: An Essay in Economic History*, Longmans, Green, 1883.

30. Beresford, *The Lost Villages of England*, 95; C. W. Foster, Appendix, *Lincolnshire Domesday*, Lincolnshire Record Society, 1924.

31. Ferriby 1 has been dated by AMS

radiocarbon to 1880–1680 cal BC. Ferriby 3, the oldest of the trio, found in 1963, is dated 2030–1780 cal BC: Edward V. Wright, Robert E. M. Hedges, Alex Bayliss and Robert Van der Noort, 'New AMS Radiocarbon Dates for the North Ferriby Boats: A Contribution to Dating Prehistoric Seafaring in Northwestern Europe', *Antiquity*, 75, 1990, 726–34.

32. Sarah Speight, 'Localising History 1940–1965: The Extra-mural Contribution', *Journal of Educational Administration and History*, 35:1, 2003, 51–64.

33. W. G. Hoskins, radio talk, 1955, printed in *Provincial England: Essays in Social and Economic History*, Macmillan, 1963, 209–29.

34. An earlier essay in much the same genre: Jacquetta Hawkes and Christopher Hawkes, 'Land and People', in Ernest Barker, ed., *The Character of England*, Oxford University Press, 1947, 1–28.

35. John Betjeman, ed., *Collins Guide to English Parish Churches*, Collins, 1958, 18.

36. Catherine Brace, 'Publishing and Publishers: Towards an Historical Geography of Countryside Writing, c.1930–1950', *Area*, 33, 2001, 287–96.

37. W. H. Hoskins, *The Making of the English Landscape*, Hodder & Stoughton, 1955 (rev. edn 1988), 13.

38. For example, H. J. Randall, 'History in the Open Air', *Antiquity*, 8:29, 1934, 5–23; P. Abercrombie, 'The Preservation of Rural England', *Town Planning Review*, 12, 1926, 5–56. The substantial earlier literature, developed through several disciplinary traditions since the nineteenth century, is reviewed by John Chandler, 'The Discovery of Landscape', in Della Hooke, ed.,

Landscape: The Richest Historical Record, Society for Landscape Studies supplementary series 1, 2000, 133–42. See also Brian K. Roberts and Stuart Wrathmell, *An Atlas of Rural Settlement in England*, English Heritage, 2000, 4–6.

39. Hawkes and Hawkes, 'Land and People', 28.

40. David Hall, *The Open Fields of Northamptonshire*, Northamptonshire Record Society, 38, 1995.

41. William Page classified only four types of rural settlement in 'Notes on the Types of English Villages and their Distribution', *Antiquity*, 1, 1927, 447–68; cf. Brian K. Roberts, *Village Plans*, Shire, 1982; *The Making of the English Village: A Study in Historical Geography*, Longman, 1987; *Rural Settlement*, Macmillan, 1987.

42. Beresford, *The Lost Villages of England*, 29.

43. Oliver Rackham, *The History of the Countryside*, J. M. Dent, 1986, 4–5.

44. William Shakespeare, *King Lear*, I.I l.63.

45. F. W. Maitland, *Domesday Book and Beyond*, Cambridge University Press, 1897; Cyril Fox, *The Personality of Britain: Its Influence on Inhabitant and Invader in Prehistoric and Early Historic Times*, National Museum of Wales/University of Wales, 1932; cf. Charles Scott-Fox, *Cyril Fox: Archaeologist Extraordinary*, Oxbow Books, 2002.

46. Rackham, *The History of the Countryside*, 1.

47. John Hatcher, *Plague, Population and the English Economy, 1348–1530*, Macmillan, 1977, 27.

48. Christopher Dyer, 'Deserted Villages in the West Midlands', *Everyday Life in Medieval England*, Hambledon & London, 2000, 31.

49. Rackham, *The History of the Countryside*, 1986, xiii.

50. Christopher Taylor, *Village and Farmstead*, George Philip, 1983; cf. Brian K. Roberts, *The Making of the English Village*, Longman, 1987.

51. Taylor, *Village and Farmstead*, 146–7.

52. For caution, Susan Oosthuizen, 'Medieval Field Systems and Settlement Nucleation: Common or Separate Origins?', in N. Higham, ed., *The Landscapes of Anglo-Saxon England*, Boydell & Brewer, 2010, 108–31.

53. Della Hooke, 'Overview: Rural Production', in Helena Hamerow, David A. Hinton and Sally Crawford, eds, *The Oxford Handbook of Anglo-Saxon Archaeology*, Oxford University Press, 2011, 315–26, at 321–2.

54. David Hall, 'The Late Saxon Countryside: Villages and their Fields', in Della Hooke, ed., *Anglo-Saxon Settlements*, Blackwell, 1988; *The Open Fields of Northamptonshire*; Richard Jones, Christopher Dyer and Mark Page, 'Changing Settlements and Landscapes: Medieval Whittlewood, its Predecessors and Successors', *Internet Archaeology*, 19, 2006, 5.2.2; for more complicated and longer-term processes, Susan Oosthuizen, *Landscapes Decoded: The Origins and Development of Cambridgeshire's Medieval Fields*, University of Hertfordshire Press, 2006, 147–8.

55. Paul Stamper, 'Landscapes of the Middle Ages: Rural Settlement and Manors', in J. Hunter and I. Ralston, eds, *The Archaeology of Britain*, Routledge, 1999, 258; Hall, *The Open Fields of Northamptonshire*.

56. Stamper, 'Landscapes of the Middle Ages', 258.

57. Susan Oosthuizen, 'Prehistoric Fields in Medieval Furlongs? Evidence from Caxton, Cambridgeshire', *Proceedings of the Cambridgeshire Antiquarian Society*, 86, 1997, 145–52; 'The Roots of the Common Fields: Linking Prehistoric and Medieval Field Systems in West Cambridgeshire', *Landscapes*, 4:1, 2003, 40–64; 'New Light on the Origins of Open-field Farming?', *Medieval Archaeology*, 49, 2005, 165–94.

58. Stamper, 'Landscapes of the Middle Ages', 260.

59. Susan Oosthuizen summarizes evidence for open fields subdivided into strips 'in, if not before, the mid Saxon period', and suggests continuities between infield–outfield and open-field practices that predate communal regulation. She also contends that it was not until after c.1100 that demand for grazing passed the point at which it could be satisfied by pasture outside open fields, and thus called for communal regulation of fallowing: 'Anglo-Saxon Fields', in Helena Hamerow, David A. Hinton and Sally Crawford, eds, *The Oxford Handbook of Anglo-Saxon Archaeology*, Oxford University Press, 2011, 377–401, at 392–4.

60. Carenza Lewis, Patrick Mitchell-Fox and Christopher Dyer, *Village, Hamlet and Field: Changing Medieval Settlements in Central England*, Manchester University Press, 1996.

61. Jones et al., 'Changing Settlements and Landscapes: Medieval Whittlewood, its Predecessors and Successors'.

62. Pauline Stafford, *The East Midlands in the Early Middle Ages*, Leicester University Press, 1985, 61–2.

63. David Stocker, 'Monuments and

Merchants: Irregularities in the Distribution of Stone Sculpture in Lincolnshire and Yorkshire in the Tenth Century', in D. Hadley and J. Richards, eds, *Cultures in Contact: Scandinavian Settlement in England in the Ninth and Tenth Centuries*, Brepols, 2000, 179–212.

64. John Blair, *Anglo-Saxon Oxfordshire*, Sutton, 1998, 141.

65. Peter Sawyer, 'Early Fairs and Markets in England and Scandinavia', in B. L. Anderson and A. J. H. Latham, eds, *The Market in History*, Croom Helm, 1986, 185–99.

66. Mark Blackburn, '"Productive" Sites and the Pattern of Coin Loss', in Tim Pestell and Katharina Ulmschneider, eds, *Markets in Early Medieval Europe*, Windgather Press, 2003, 20–36.

67. Peter Sawyer, *Anglo-Saxon Lincolnshire*, History of Lincolnshire, vol. 3, 1998, 180–1.

68. Henry of Huntingdon, *Historia Anglorum*, ed. T. Arnold, Longman, 1879, 5–6.

69. Peter Sawyer, 'The Wealth of England in the Eleventh Century', *Transactions of the Royal Historical Society*, 5th series, 15, 1965, 145–64; *From Roman Britain to Norman England*, Methuen, 1978, 232–3.

70. Christopher Dyer, David Hey and Joan Thirsk, 'Lowland Vales', in Joan Thirsk, ed., *The English Rural Landscape*, Oxford University Press, 2000, 84–5.

71. Trevelyan, *English Social History*, 6.

72. R. H. Hilton, *The English Peasantry in the Later Middle Ages*, Oxford University Press, 1975; Christopher Dyer, *Lords and Peasants in a Changing Society*, Cambridge University Press, 1980; P. D. A. Harvey, ed., *The Peasant Land Market in Medieval England*,

Clarendon Press, 1974; Christopher Dyer, 'English Peasant Buildings in the Later Middle Ages', *Medieval Archaeology*, 30, 1986, 19–45; G. G. Astill and A. Grant, eds, *The Countryside of Medieval England*, Blackwell, 1988; Christopher Dyer, *Standards of Living in the Later Middle Ages: Social Change in England c.1200–1520*, Cambridge University Press, 1989.

73. J. G. Hurst, 'The Wharram Research Project: Results to 1983', *Medieval Archaeology*, 27, 1984, 77–111.

74. Stuart Wrathmell, *Wharram: A Study of Settlement on the Yorkshire Wolds*, vol. 6: *Domestic Settlement 2: Medieval Peasant Farmsteads*, York University Archaeological Publications 8, 1989.

75. Trevelyan, *English Social History*, 21.

76. W. G. Hoskins, 'The Rebuilding of Rural England 1570–1640', *Past and Present*, 4, 1953, 44–59.

77. E. Mercer, *English Vernacular Houses*, HMSO, 1975.

78. R. K. Field, 'Worcestershire Peasant Buildings, Household Goods and Farming Equipment in the Later Middle Ages', *Medieval Archaeology*, 9, 105–45, was an early challenge to the orthodoxy that pre-fifteenth-century peasant housing was ephemeral.

79. For a summary and review of the debate on peasant housing see Jane Grenville, *Medieval Housing*, Leicester University Press, 1997, 121–56.

80. E. B. Fryde, *Peasants and Landlords in Later Medieval England, c.1385–c.1585*, Sutton, 1996; Sarah Pearson, 'Tree-ring Dating: A Review', *Vernacular Architecture*, 28, 1997, 25–39; Edward Roberts, 'The Potential of Tree-ring Dating', in S. Pearson and R. Meeson, eds,

Vernacular Buildings in a Changing World: Understanding, Recording and Conservation, Council for British Archaeology, 2001, 111–21.

81. Tom Beaumont James, 'Years of Pestilence', *British Archaeology*, 61, October 2001, 9–13.

82. Brian K. Roberts and Stuart Wrathmell, *Region and Place: A Study of English Rural Settlement*, English Heritage, 2002, 24–6.

83. Raphael Holinshed, William Harrison et al., *The description and history of England*, 1587, 1; cited in L. Withington, *Elizabethan England*, W. Scott, 1902 (first pub. 1876), 113.

84. Damian Goodburn, 'The Death of the Wildwood and Birth of Woodmanship in South-east England', in Kathryn Bernick, ed., *Hidden Dimensions: The Cultural Significance of Wetland Archaeology*, University of British Columbia Press, 1998, 130–8.

85. John Letts, 'Living under a Medieval Field', *British Archaeology*, 58, April 2001, 12.

86. John B. Letts, *Smoke-blackened Thatch: A Unique Source of Medieval Plant Remains from Southern England*, English Heritage/ University of Reading, 2000.

87. L. Rymer, 'The History and Ethnobotany of Bracken', *Journal of the Linnaean Society (Botany)*, 73, 1976, 151–76.

88. S. Mays, C. Harding and C. Heighway, *Wharram: A Study of Settlement on the Yorkshire Wolds, XI. The Churchyard*, York University Archaeological Publications 13, 2007; cf. Simon Mays, 'Human Osteology at Wharram Percy: Life and Death in a Medieval Village', *Conservation Bulletin*, 45, 2004, 22–3.

89. Michael Aston, David Austin and Christopher Dyer, *The Rural Settlements of Medieval England: Studies Dedicated to Maurice Beresford and John Hurst*, Blackwell, 1989.

90. This was a rediscovery. Maitland had declared, 'We are not entitled to make for ourselves any one typical picture of the English vill': Maitland, *Domesday Book and Beyond*; cf. Jones et al., 'Changing Settlements and Landscapes: Medieval Whittlewood, its Predecessors and Successors', 1.1.

91. Christopher Dyer, 'Dispersed Settlements in Medieval England: A Case Study of Pendock, Worcestershire', *Medieval Archaeology*, 34, 1990, 97–121.

92. Dyer, introductory essay to Beresford, *The Lost Villages of England*, 1998 edn, xviii.

93. Rackham, *The History of the Countryside*, 3–5.

94. Roberts and Wrathmell, *Atlas of Rural Settlement in England*.

95. N. W. Alcock, *Cruck Construction: An Introduction and Catalogue*, CBA Research Report 42, 1981, 57.

96. Rackham, *The History of the Countryside*, 1.

97. Stephen Rippon, *Beyond the Medieval Village: The Diversification of Landscape Character in Southern Britain*, Oxford University Press, 2008.

CHAPTER 8: BECOMING ENGLISH

1. James Campbell, ed., *The Anglo-Saxons*, Penguin, 1991, 20.

2. Sam Lucy, *The Anglo-Saxon Way of Death*, Sutton, 2000, 16–64; Christopher Scull and Alex Bayliss, 'Radiocarbon Dating and Anglo-Saxon Graves', in U. von Freeden, U. Kock and A. Wierczorek, eds, *Wölker*

an Nord- und Ostsee und die Franken, Bonn, 1999, 39–50.

3. Dominic Powlesland, *Twenty-five Years of Archaeological Research on the Sands and Gravels of Heslerton*, Landscape Research Centre, 2003.

4. Christine Haughton and Dominic Powlesland, *West Heslerton: The Anglian Cemetery*, 2 vols, Landscape Research Centre, 1999.

5. Catherine Stoertz, *Ancient Landscapes of the Yorkshire Wolds*, Royal Commission on the Historical Monuments of England, 1997, 6–7, with further references.

6. J. G. D. Clark, *Excavations at Star Carr, an Early Mesolithic Site at Seamer near Scarborough, Yorkshire*, Cambridge University Press, 1954; Paul Mellars and Petra Dark, *Star Carr in Context: New Archaeological and Palaeoecological Investigations at the Early Mesolithic Site of Star Carr, North Yorkshire*, McDonald Institute for Archaeological Research, 1998.

7. C. Conneller, 'Becoming Deer: Corporeal Transformation at Star Carr', *Archaeological Dialogues*, 11, 2004, 37–56.

8. Richard Morris, '"Calami et iunci": Lastingham in the Seventh and Eighth Centuries', *Bulletin of International Medieval Research*, 11, 2005, 3–21; I. N. Wood, 'Monasteries and the Geography of Power in the Age of Bede', *Northern History*, 45, 2008, 11–25.

9. Dominic Powlesland, 'The Heslerton Parish Project: An Integrated Multi-sensor Approach to the Archaeological Study of Eastern Yorkshire, England', in Stefano Campana and Maurizio Forte, eds, *Remote Sensing in Archaeology*, All'Insegna del Giglio, 2001, 233–55.

10. Dominic Powlesland, 'West Heslerton', in John Schofield, ed.,

Great Excavations: Shaping the Archaeological Profession, Oxbow Books, 2011, 247–69; 'Identifying the Unimaginable – Managing the Unmanageable', in D. Cowley, ed., *Remote Sensing for Archaeological Heritage Management in the 21st Century*, EAC Occasional Paper 5, 2011, 17–32; 'Why Bother? Large Scale Geomagnetic Survey and the Quest for Real Archaeology', in S. Campana and S. Piro, eds, *Seeing the Unseen: Geophysics and Landscape Archaeology*, Taylor & Francis, 2009, 167–82; 'The Heslerton Parish Project: 20 Years of Archaeological Research in the Vale of Pickering', in T. Manby, S. Moorhouse and P. Ottaway, eds, *The Archaeology of Yorkshire: An Assessment at the Beginning of the 21st Century*, Yorkshire Archaeological Society, 2003, 275–92; 'The Heslerton Parish Project: An Integrated Multi-sensor Approach to the Archaeological Study of Eastern Yorkshire, England'.

11. In *Framing the Early Middle Ages* (Oxford University Press, 2005, 501, n. 159) Christopher Wickham says 'this site seems atypical in many ways'. The project is mentioned several times but not discussed in detail in Helena Hamerow, David A. Hinton and Sally Crawford, eds, *The Oxford Handbook of Anglo-Saxon Archaeology*, Oxford University Press, 2011.

12. Bede, *Ecclesiastical History of the English People*, i.15; cf. v.9.

13. Walter Pohl, 'Ethnic Names and Identities in the British Isles: A Comparative Perspective', in J. Hines, ed., *The Anglo-Saxons from the Migration Period to the Eighth Century: An Ethnographic Perspective*, Boydell Press, 1997, 7–32;

Patrick Geary, *The Myth of Nations: The Medieval Origins of Nations*, Princeton University Press, 2002.

14. Edwin Jones, *The English Nation: The Great Myth*, Sutton, 1998.

15. William Stubbs, *Select Charters and Other Illustrations of English Constitutional History*, 9th edn, Oxford University Press, 1921, 3.

16. H. C. Darby, ed., *A New Historical Geography of England before 1600*, Cambridge University Press, 1973, 3.

17. Reginald Horsman, *Race and Manifest Destiny: The Origins of American Racial Anglo-Saxonism*, Harvard University Press, 1981.

18. Stuart Piggott, 'The Early Bronze Age in Wessex', *Proceedings of the Prehistoric Society*, 4, 1938, 52–106.

19. Colin Renfrew, *Before Civilization: The Radiocarbon Revolution and Prehistoric Europe*, Jonathan Cape, 1973, 236.

20. Arthur Bryant, *The Medieval Foundation*, Collins, 1966, 28.

21. Jacquetta Hawkes, *A Land*, Cresset Press, 1951, 153.

22. H. R. Loyn, *Anglo-Saxon England and the Norman Conquest*, Longman, 1962, 36.

23. Darby, ed., *A New Historical Geography of England*, 29.

24. Raymond Williams, *The Country and the City*, Hogarth Press, 1993 (first pub. 1973), 38.

25. Frank Stenton, *Anglo-Saxon England*, Oxford University Press, 3rd edn, 1971 (first pub. 1943), 284. Work on the third edition was incomplete at Stenton's death in 1967.

26. Ibid., 285.

27. Hawkes, *A Land*, 153.

28. Mark Blackburn, '"Productive Sites" and the Pattern of Coin Loss in England, 600–1180', in Tim Pestell and Katharine Ulmschneider, eds, *Markets in Early Medieval Europe: Trading and 'Productive' Sites, 650–850*, Windgather Press, 2003, 20–36.

29. David Whitehouse, '"Things that Travelled": The Surprising Case of Raw Glass', *Early Medieval Europe*, 12:3, 2003, 301–5.

30. Christopher Taylor, *Village and Farmstead*, George Philip, 1983, 121.

31. J. N. L. Myres, *The English Settlements*, Oxford University Press, 1989, 214.

32. Helena Hamerow, *Early Medieval Settlements: The Archaeology of Rural Communities in Northwest Europe, 400–900*, Oxford University Press, 2002, 106.

33. M. G. L. Baillie, *Putting Abrupt Environmental Change Back into Human History*, Linacre Lectures 1997–8, Oxford University Press, 2000; *Exodus to Arthur: Catastrophic Encounters with Comets*, Batsford, 1999.

34. M. E. Jones, 'Climate, Nutrition and Disease: An Hypothesis of Romano-British Population', in P. J. Casey, ed., *The End of Roman Britain*, Tempus Reparatum, 1979, 231–51; Nicholas Higham, *Rome, Britain and the Anglo-Saxons*, Seaby, 1992.

35. S. P. Dark, 'Palaeoecological Evidence for Landscape Continuity and Change in Britain *c.*AD 400–800', in K. R. Dark, ed., *External Contacts and the Economy of Late and Post-Roman Britain*, Boydell Press, 1996; Martin Bell, 'Environmental Archaeology as an Index to Continuity and Change in the Medieval Landscape', in Mick Aston, David Austin and C. C. Dyer, eds, *The Rural Settlements of Medieval England: Studies Dedicated to Maurice Beresford and John Hurst*,

Blackwell, 1989, 269–86; J. Turner, 'The Vegetation', in Martin Jones and Geoffrey Dimbleby, eds, *The Environment of Early Man: The Iron Age to the Anglo-Saxon Period*, British Archaeological Reports (British series) 87, 1981, 67–73; J. P. Huntley and S. Stallibrass, *Plant and Vertebrate Remains from Archaeological Sites in Northern England: Data Reviews and Future Directions*, Architectural & Archaeological Society of Durham and Northumberland Research Paper 4, 1995.

36. Simon Esmonde Cleary, 'Changing Constraints on the Landscape AD 400–600', in Della Hooke and Simon Burnell, eds, *Landscape and Settlement in Britain*, University of Exeter Press, 1995, 11–25.

37. For a similar view in the upper Thames valley see Gill Hey, *Yarnton: Saxon and Medieval Settlement and Landscape: Results of Excavations 1990–96*, Oxford Archaeology, 2004, 85.

38. Hamerow, *Early Medieval Settlements*, 104.

39. Ibid., 93–4.

40. Ibid., 94; *Excavations at Mucking 2: The Anglo-Saxon Settlement*, English Heritage Research Report 21, 1993; cf. the interpretation for sixty-six timber buildings excavated on a terrace overlooking the River Trent at Catholme, Staffordshire, which reduce to five or six farms being rebuilt over several centuries: Stuart Losco-Bradley and Gavin Kinsley, *Catholme: An Anglo-Saxon Settlement on the Trent Gravels in Staffordshire*, Trent & Peak Archaeological Unit, 2002.

41. John Blair, *Anglo-Saxon Oxfordshire*, Sutton, 1998, 18, 20.

42. E. T. Leeds, 'A Saxon Village near Sutton Courtenay, Berkshire', *Archaeologia*, 72, 1923, 147–92.

43. S. E. West, 'The Anglo-Saxon Village of West Stow: An Interim Report of the Excavations, 1965–68', *Medieval Archaeology*, 13, 1969, 1–20; J. Tipper, 'Grubenhäuser: Pit Fills and Pit Falls', unpublished PhD thesis, University of Cambridge, 2000.

44. David Stocker and Paul Everson have made a case for equating *Grubenhäuser* with temporary seasonal shelters at nearby Wharram Percy: 'Wharram before the village moment', in Wharram: *A Study of Settlement on the Yorkshire Wolds, XIII. A History of Wharram and its Neighbours*, ed. Stuart Wrathmell, York University Archaeological Publications 15, 2012, 164–72.

45. Helena Hamerow, 'Overview: Rural Settlement', in Hamerow, Hinton and Crawford, eds, *The Oxford Handbook of Anglo-Saxon Archaeology*, 119–27, at 121.

46. Jess Tipper, *The Grubenhaus in Anglo-Saxon England*, Landscape Research Centre, 2004.

47. For a recent survey, Hamerow, 'Overview: Rural Settlement'.

48. Dominic Powlesland, 'The Anglo-Saxon Settlement at West Heslerton, North Yorkshire', in Jane Hawkes and Susan Mills, eds, *Northumbria's Golden Age*, Sutton, 1999, 55–65.

49. Ibid., 62.

50. See for instance David Mattingly, *An Imperial Possession: Britain in the Roman Empire, 54 BC–AD 409*, Penguin, 2006.

51. Powlesland, 'The Anglo-Saxon Settlement at West Heslerton', 58.

52. Richard Bradley, 'Time Regained: The Creation of Continuity', *Journal of the British Archaeological*

Association, 140, 1987, 1–17.

53. Charles Thomas, *Christianity in Roman Britain to AD 500*, Batsford, 1981, 27.

54. Ibid.

55. Philip Shaw, 'Uses of Wodan: The Development of his Cult and of the Medieval Literary Responses to It', unpublished PhD thesis, University of Leeds, 2002.

56. John Blair, 'Anglo-Saxon Pagan Shrines and their Prototypes', *Anglo-Saxon Studies in Archaeology and History*, 8, 1995, 1–28.

57. Ian Wood, 'Before and After the Migration to Britain', in Hines, ed., *The Anglo-Saxons from the Migration Period to the Eighth Century*, 46; Brian Hope-Taylor, *Yeavering: An Anglo-British Centre of early Northumbria*, HMSO, 1997; Paul Frodsham and Colm O'Brien, eds, *Yeavering: People, Power and Place*, Tempus, 2005.

58. Wood, 'Before and After the Migration to Britain', 40; D. N. Dumville, 'The Anglian Collection of Royal Genealogies and Regnal Lists', *Anglo-Saxon England*, 6, 1976, 23–50; 'Kingship, Genealogies and Regnal Lists', in P. H. Sawyer and I. N. Wood, eds, *Early Medieval Kingship*, University of Leeds, 1977, 72–104.

59. Pohl, 'Ethnic Names and Identities'; N. P. Brooks, *Anglo-Saxon Myths: State and Church, 400–1066*, Hambledon Press, 2000.

60. Catherine Hills, 'Economic and Settlement Background to Sutton Hoo in Eastern England', in J. P. Lamm and H. A. Nordström, eds, *Vendel Period Studies: Transactions of the Boat-Grave Symposium in Stockholm, February 2–3 1981*, Museum of National Antiquities, Stockholm, 1983, 99–104.

61. Ian Wood, 'The Mission of Augustine of Canterbury to the English', *Speculum*, 69:1, 1994, 1–17.

62. Bede, *Ecclesiastical History*, ii.15.

63. *Aldhelm: The Prose Works*, ed. and trans. Michael Lapidge and Michael Herren, D. S. Brewer, 1979.

64. Margaret Lindsay Faull, 'The Semantic Development of Old English *Wealh*', *Leeds Studies in English*, 8, 1975, 20–44.

65. David Rollason, *Saints and Relics in Anglo-Saxon England*, Blackwell, 1989, 13–18; Margaret Deanesly and Pierre Grosjean, 'The Canterbury Edition of the Answers of Pope Gregory I to Augustine', *Journal of Ecclesiastical History*, 10, 1959, 28–9.

66. Martin Henig, 'Roman Britons after 410', *British Archaeology*, 68, December 2002, 9; *The Heirs of King Verica*, Tempus, 2002.

67. *Gildas: The Ruin of Britain and Other Works*, ed. and trans. Michael Winterbottom, Phillimore, 1978.

68. D. R. Howlett, *The Celtic Latin Tradition of Biblical Style*, Four Courts Press, 1995; *British Books in Biblical Style*, Four Courts Press, 1997; Charles Thomas, *Christian Celts: Messages and Images*, Tempus, 1998.

69. Thomas, *Christian Celts*, 37.

70. Bede, *Ecclesiastical History*, i.15.

71. Pohl, 'Ethnic Names and Identities', 12.

72. Wood, 'Before and After the Migration', 42–4.

73. Walter Pohl, 'Ethnic Names and Identities', 7–40; John Moreland, 'Ethnicity, Power and the English', in William O. Frazer and Andrew Tyrell, eds, *Social Identity in Early Medieval Britain*, Leicester University Press, 2000; Hines, ed., *The Anglo-Saxons from the Migration Period to the Eighth Century*.

74. Nicholas Brooks, *Bede and the English*, Jarrow Lecture 1999.

75. Wood, 'Before and After the Migration', 45; 'The Channel from the 4th to the 7th Centuries AD', in Seán McGrail, ed., *Maritime Celts, Frisians and Saxons*, CBA Research Report 71, 1990, 93–7; John Heywood, *Dark Age Naval Power*, Routledge, 1991, 54–62.

76. Edward James, *The Franks*, Blackwell, 1988, 101–4, 114; Heywood, *Dark Age Naval Power*, 59.

77. Stephen Oppenheimer, *The Origins of the British: A Genetic Detective Story*, Constable, 2006. Bede (*HE* i.1) wrote that 'at the present time [c.734] there are five languages in Britain ... these are the languages of the English (*Anglorum*), British, Irish (*Scottorum*), and Latin'.

78. Pohl, 'Ethnic Names and Identities', 9.

79. Eric John, *Reassessing Anglo-Saxon England*, Manchester University Press, 1996, 4–5.

80. Robert Bartlett, *England Under the Norman and Angevin Kings, 1075–1225*, Oxford University Press, 2000, 245.

81. Jacques Le Goff, *The Medieval Imagination*, trans. Arthur Goldhammer, Chicago University Press, 1988, 32.

82. Bartlett, *England Under the Norman and Angevin Kings*, 683.

83. Peter Sawyer, *From Roman Britain to Norman England*, Methuen, 1978, 89.

84. Brooks, *Bede and the English*, 5.

85. Nicholas Brooks, 'The Creation and Early Structure of the Kingdom of Kent', in Steven Bassett, ed., *The Origins of Anglo-Saxon Kingdoms*, Leicester University Press, 1989, 57.

86. Eilert Ekwall, *English River Names*, Clarendon Press, 1928, 121–3; J. G. F. Hind, 'Elmet and Deira – Forest-names in Yorkshire?', *Bulletin of the Board of Celtic Studies*, 28, 1978–80, 541–52.

87. I. N. Wood, 'Monasteries and the Geography of Power in the Age of Bede', *Northern History*, 45, 2008, 11–25.

88. F. M. Stenton, *Anglo-Saxon England*, 3rd edn, Clarendon Press, 1971, 91; John, *Reassessing Anglo-Saxon England*, ix–x.

89. Oppenheimer, *The Origins of the British*.

90. Ernest Gellner, *Nations and Nationalism*, Cornell University Press, 1983, 11.

91. Pohl, 'Ethnic Names and Identities', 25.

92. Ibid., 24; D. N. Dumville, *Bretons and Anglo-Saxons in the Early Middle Ages*, Variorum, 1993.

93. Wood, 'Before and After the Migration', 51.

94. B. Brugmann, 'The Role of Continental Artefact Types in Sixth-century Kentish Chronology', in J. Hines, K. Høilund Neilsen and F. Siegmund, eds, *The Pace of Change: Studies in Early Medieval Chronology*, Oxbow Books, 1999, 37–64.

95. Lucy, *The Anglo-Saxon Way of Death*, 183–5.

96. G. W. S. Barrow, *The Kingdom of the Scots*, Edinburgh University Press, 2003, 2nd edn, 1–68; G. R. J. Jones, 'Multiple Estates and Early Settlement', in Peter Sawyer, ed., *English Medieval Settlement*, Edward Arnold, 1979; John, *Reassessing Anglo-Saxon England*, 12–13.

97. Haughton and Powlesland, *West Heslerton: The Anglian Cemetery*, 3.

98. P. Budd, A. Millard, C. Chenery, S. Lucy and C. Roberts, 'Investigating Population Movement by Stable Isotopes: A Report from Britain', *Antiquity*, 78:299, 2004, 127–41.

99. Catherine Hills, *Origins of the English*, Duckworth, 2003.

100. Catherine Hills, *The Anglo-Saxon Cemetery at Spong Hill, North Elmham*, Part 1 (Catalogue of Cremations), East Anglian Archaeology (EAA) Report 6, 1977; Catherine Hills, Kenneth Penn and Robert Rickett, Part 3 (Catalogue of Inhumations), EAA Report 21, 1984; Parts 4 & 5 (Catalogues of Cremations), EAA Reports 34 and 67, 1987, 1994; Frances Healy, Part 6, *Occupation during the Seventh to Second Millennia BC*, EAA Report 39, 1988; Robert Rickett, Part 7, *The Iron Age, Roman and Early Saxon Settlement*, EAA Report 73, 1995; Jacqueline McInley, Part 8, *The Cremations*, EAA Report 69, 1994.

101. Catherine Hills, 'Did the People at Spong Hill Come from Schleswig-Holstein?', *Studien zur Sachsenforschung*, 11, 1999, 145–54.

102. Lucy, *The Anglo-Saxon Way of Death*, 112, with references.

CHAPTER 9: A COMPANY OF SAINTS

1. Nikolaus Pevsner, 'The Geography of Art', 16 October 1955, BBC Home Service.

2. Virginia Berridge, ed., *The Big Smoke: Fifty Years after the 1952 London Smog*, Institute of Historical Research, 2005; Peter Brimblecombe, *The Big Smoke: A History of Air Pollution in London since Medieval Times*, Routledge & Kegan Paul, 1987.

3. *London Gazette*, 29 March 1957, 1955.

4. *The Itinerary of John Leland the Antiquary*, Vol. the Third, published in the Bodleian Library by Thomas Hearne, 3rd edn, 1771, 114.

5. *The Form and Order of the Consecration of the Church of St John Baptist, Longbridge with the Institution of the Reverend John Richard Morris, M.A. and the Inauguration of the Parish of Longbridge*, 1957, Birmingham City Archives, EP109/7/4/1, 2.

6. Ibid., 14.

7. *Funera plango – Fulgura frango – Sabbato pango – Excito lentos – Dissipo ventos – Paero cruentos*: inscription on bell, cited in Charles Carroll Bombaugh, *Gleanings from the Harvest-fields of Literature: A Mélange of Excerpta, Curious, Humorous, and Instructive*, T. N. Kurtz, 1860, 133.

8. Bede, *Ecclesiastical History of the English People*, ii.14.

9. Moses Finley, *The Use and Abuse of History*, Hogarth Press, 1976, 93.

10. Derek Phillips, *Excavations at York Minster*: vol. 2: *The Cathedral of Archbishop Thomas of Bayeux*, HMSO, 1985, 42–3.

11. John Harvey, *Cathedrals of England and Wales*, Batsford, 1974, 5–6, 91–2.

12. Martin Biddle, 'Introduction', in Kevin Blockley, Margaret Sparks and Tim Tatton-Brown, *Canterbury Cathedral Nave Archaeology, History and Architecture*, Dean & Chapter of Canterbury Cathedral and Canterbury Archaeological Trust, 1997, xvii.

13. Phillips, *Excavations at York Minster*, 2.176.

14. David Stocker, *The College of the Vicars Choral of York Minster at Bedern: Architectural Fragments*, The Archaeology of York 10/4, York Archaeological Trust & Council for British Archaeology, 1999.

15. Phillips, *Excavations at York Minster*, 2.173–6.

16. Ibid., 2.29, 176.

17. Michael Thompson, 'Robert Willis and the Study of Medieval Architecture', in Tim Tatton-Brown and Julian Munby, eds, *The Archaeology of Cathedrals*, Oxford University Committee for Archaeology Monograph 42, 1996, 153–64.

18. Ibid., 162–3.

19. Ibid.

20. R. Willis, *The Architectural History of York Cathedral*, Archaeological Institute, 1848.

21. Phillips, *Excavations at York Minster*, 2.111–12.

22. Willis, *The Architectural History of York Cathedral*, 12–14.

23. A. Hamilton Thompson, 'The Building of York Minster', *York Minster Historical Tracts*, No. 2, SPCK, 1927; *The Cathedral Churches of England*, SPCK, 1927, 25; J. S. Miller, 'The Norman Staircase Turrets', *The Friends of York Minster 38th Annual Report*, 1966, 15–19; G. Baldwin Browne, *The Arts in Early England*, vol. 2: *Anglo-Saxon Architecture*, John Murray, 1925; K. Harrison, 'The Saxon Cathedral at York', *Yorkshire Archaeological Journal*, 39, 1956–8, 436–44.

24. Alcuin, *Versus de patribus regibus et sanctis Euboriensis ecclesiae*, ed. and trans. Peter Godman, Oxford University Press, 1982; H. M. Taylor and J. Taylor, *Anglo-Saxon Architecture*, vol. 2, Cambridge University Press, 1965, 709.

25. Alfred Clapham, *English Romanesque Architecture after the Conquest*, Oxford University Press, 1934, 11, 19–20.

26. David M. Wilson and Gillian Hurst, 'Medieval Britain in 1967: 1 Pre-Conquest', *Medieval Archaeology*, 12, 1968, 162.

27. Eric Fernie, *The Architecture of Norman England*, Oxford University Press, 2000, 122, 124.

28. Christopher Norton, *Archbishop Thomas of Bayeux and the Norman Cathedral at York*, University of York, Borthwick Paper 100, 2001, 32.

29. Phillips, *Excavations at York Minster*, 2.7.

30. Norton, *Archbishop Thomas of Bayeux*, 28.

31. Fernie, *The Architecture of Norman England*, 32.

32. Ibid., 299.

33. David Rollason, *Saints and Relics in Anglo-Saxon England*, Blackwell, 1989, 7.

34. Wim Berbaal, 'Timeless Time', in Gerhard Jaritz and Gerson Moreno-Riaño, eds, *Time and Eternity: The Medieval Discourse*, Brepols, 2003, 240.

35. Martin Biddle, *The Tomb of Christ*, Sutton, 1999.

36. Keith Thomas, *Religion and the Decline of Magic*, Penguin, 1988, 740.

37. S. A. J. Bradley, *Orm Gamalson's Sundial: The Lily's Blossom and the Roses' Fragrance*, 1997 Kirkdale Lecture, Friends of St Gregory's Minster, 2002, 10–11.

38. Ælfric, *De temporibus anni,* ed. Heinrich Henel, Early English Text Society, 213, 1942, 14.

39. Bradley, *Orm Gamalson's Sundial*, 12, and passim.

40. Rollason, *Saints and Relics*, 1–20.

41. Ibid., 10–11.

42. The process was finalized by Pope Gregory IX in 1234: E. W. Kemp, *Canonization and Authority in the Western Church*, Oxford University Press, 1948; for the early stages see Peter Brown, *The Cult of the Saints: Its Rise and Function in Latin Christianity*, University of Chicago Press, 1981.

43. Rollason, *Saints and Relics*, 3–4.

44. Janet Cooper, *The Last Four Anglo-Saxon Archbishops of York*, University of York, Borthwick Paper 38, 1970, 3.

45. Warwick Rodwell, 'Archaeology in Wells Cathedral', in Tatton-Brown and Munby, eds, *The Archaeology of Cathedrals*, 122–3.

46. Frank Barlow, *The English Church 1000–1066*, Longman, 1979, 228–9.

47. Warwick Rodwell and C. A. Ralegh Radford, 'Lead Plaques from the Tombs of the Saxon Bishops of Wells', *Antiquaries Journal*, 59, 1979, 407–10.

48. H. G. Ram et al., 'The Tombs of Archbishop Walter de Gray (1216–55) and Godfrey de Ludham (1258–65) in York Minster, and their Contents', *Archaeologia*, 103, 1977, 101–47. For discussion of all the tombs in their architectural and clerical context, see Sarah Brown, *'Our Magnificent Fabricke': York Minster: An Architectural History c.1220–1500*, English Heritage, 2003, 37–43.

49. Jim Lang, *Corpus of Anglo-Saxon Stone Sculpture*, vol. 3: *York and Eastern Yorkshire*, British Academy, 1991, 39.

50. Derek Phillips and Brenda Heywood, ed. M. O. H. Carver, 'The Pre-Norman Cemetery', *Excavations at York Minster*, vol. 1, part 1: *The Site*, HMSO, 1995, 75–92.

51. Birthe Kjølbye-Biddle, 'Iron-bound Coffins and Coffin-fittings from the Pre-Norman Cemetery', in Derek Phillips and Brenda Heywood, ed. M. O. H. Carver, *Excavations at York Minster*, vol. 1, part 2: *The Finds*, HMSO, 1995, 489–521.

52. Phillips and Heywood, *Excavations at York Minster*, 1.1.80.

53. J. Lang, 'Pre-Conquest Sculpture', in Phillips and Heywood, *Excavations at York Minster*, 1.2, 433–67.

54. *Penitential of Theodore*, book 1, v. 13. For discussion of purgatory's origins and evolution see Jacques Le Goff, *The Birth of Purgatory*, trans. Arthur Goldhammer, Scolar Press, 1991.

55. Bede, *Ecclesiastical History*, iv.22.

56. Eamon Duffy, *The Stripping of the Altars: Traditional Religion in England 1400–1580*, Yale University Press, 1992, 8.

57. J. J. Scarisbrick, *The Reformation and the English People*, Oxford University Press, 1984; Eamon Duffy, *The Voices of Morebath: Reformation and Rebellion in an English Village*, Yale University Press, 2001.

58. Duffy, *The Stripping of the Altars*, 3.

59. Christopher Wilson, *The Shrines of St William of York*, Yorkshire Museum, York, 1977.

60. Phillips, *Excavations at York Minster*, 2.125–7.

61. Eric Gee, 'The Topography of Altars, Chantries and Shrines in York Minster', *Antiquaries Journal*, 64, 1984, 337–50.

62. Caroline Bynum, *Metamorphosis and Identity*, New York, 2001, 50.

63. Stacy Boldrick, David Park and Paul Williamson, *Wonder: Painted Sculpture from Medieval England*, Henry Moore Institute, 2002.

64. Duffy, *The Stripping of the Altars*, 165.

65. Ibid., 167.

66. Lesley Brubaker, 'The Sacred Image', in R. Ousterhout and L. Brubaker, eds, *The Sacred Image, East and West*, Illinois Byzantine Studies 4, 1995, 11.

67. Hans Belting, *Likeness and Presence: A History of the Image before the Era of Art*, trans. E. Jephcott, 1994, 299.

68. Margaret Aston, *England's Iconoclasts*, vol. 1: *Laws against Images*, Oxford University Press, 1988, 401.

69. Duffy, *The Stripping of the Altars*, 579; Dunbar H. Ogden, *The Staging*

of Drama in the Medieval Church, University of Delaware Press, 2002.

70. D. L. Jeffray, 'English Saints' Plays', in N. Denny, ed., *Medieval Drama*, Stratford upon Avon Studies 16, 1973, 68–89.

71. Ogden, *The Staging of Drama in the Medieval Church*, 39–99.

72. Jerry Sampson and Peter Lasko, *Wells Cathedral West Front: Construction, Sculpture and Conservation*, Sutton, 1998, 170.

73. Bradley, *Orm Gamalson's Sundial*, 18.

74. Duffy, *The Stripping of the Altars*, 580.

75. H. C. Gardiner, *Mysteries' End: An Investigation of the Last Days of the Medieval Religious Stage*, Yale University Press, 1946, 72 ff.; A. F. Johnston, 'The Plays of the Religious Guilds of York', *Speculum*, 50, 1975, 55–90.

CHAPTER 10: WHITSUN GAMES

1. Jonathan Bate, *Soul of the Age: The Life, Mind and World of William Shakespeare*, Viking, 2008, 161–6, 314–23.

2. *Richard III*, 5.3.178–9, 201–4.

3. Jacques Le Goff, *The Medieval Imagination*, trans. Arthur Goldhammer, Chicago University Press, 1988, part 5, 193–242.

4. Eamon Duffy, *The Stripping of the Altars: Traditional Religion in England 1400–1580*, Yale University Press, 1992, 260–1.

5. Ibid., 107–9; Elizabeth New, 'Christological Personal Seals and Christocentric Devotion in Later Medieval England and Wales', *Antiquaries Journal*, 82, 2002, 47–68.

6. *Hamlet*, 1.5.10–13, 15–16.

7. *Measure for Measure*, 3.1.

8. Excavation in 2001 at Bear Wharf and Riverside House may have glimpsed the Hope: *Museum of London Archaeology Service 2002: Annual Review for 2001*.

9. From *Henslowe's Diary, Edited with Supplementary Material, Introduction and Notes*, ed. R. A. Foakes and R. T. Rickert, Cambridge University Press, 1961; cf. Andrew Gurr, *The Shakespearean Stage, 1574–1642*, Cambridge University Press, 1980, 102.

10. Andrew Gurr, *Playgoing in Shakespeare's London*, Cambridge University Press, 1988, 4.

11. Details of the Rose that follow rest on the account by Julian Bowsher and Pat Miller, *The Rose and the Globe – Playhouses of Shakespeare's Bankside, Southwark. Excavations 1988–90*, Museum of London Archaeology Monograph 48, 2009.

12. For instance, *The Diary of Philip Henslowe, from 1591 to 1609*, ed. J. Payne Collier, Shakespeare Society, 1845; *Henslowe's Diary*, ed. Foakes and Rickert.

13. Bowsher and Miller, *The Rose and the Globe*.

14. John Orrell, 'Spanning the Globe', in S. Blatherwick and A. Gurr, 'Shakespeare's Factory: Archaeological Evaluations on the Site of the Globe Theatre at 1/15 Anchor Terrace, Southwark Bridge, Southwark', *Antiquity*, 66:251, 1992, 329–33.

15. C. Walter Hodges, *Enter the Whole Army: A Pictorial Study of Shakespearean Staging 1576–1616*, Cambridge University Press, 1999, 16–27.

16. Gurr, *Playgoing in Shakespeare's London*, 12.

17. Jean Wilson, *Entertainments for Elizabeth I*, Brewer, 1980; 'The Harefield Entertainment and the Cult of Elizabeth I', *Antiquaries Journal*, 66, 1986, 315–29.

18. Paul Everson and Tom Williamson, 'Gardens and Designed Landscapes', in *The Archaeology of Landscape: Studies Presented to Christopher Taylor*, Manchester University Press, 1998, 147.

19. John A. Goodall, 'Some Aspects of Heraldry and the Role of Heralds in Relation to the Ceremonies of the Late Medieval and Early Tudor Court', *Antiquaries Journal*, 82, 2002, 69–91.

20. J. S. P. Tatlock, *The Legendary History of Britain: Geoffrey of Monmouth's Historia Regum Britanniae and its Early Vernacular Versions*, University of California Press, 1950.

21. Andy Hammon, 'The brown bear', in T. P. O'Connor and Naomi Sykes, eds, *Extinctions and Invasions: A Social History of British Fauna*, Windgather Press, 2010, 95–103.

22. Susan Cerasano, 'The Master of the Bears in Art and Enterprise', *Medieval and Renaissance Drama in England*, 5, 1991, 195–209.

23. 'Bear baiting patent', http://www. henslowe-alleyn.org.uk/essays/ bearsandbulls.html [accessed 15 February 2012].

24. The Henslowe and Alleyn papers are now available digitally: http://www. henslowe-alleyn.org.uk/index.html.

25. http://www.henslowe-alleyn.org.uk/ images/MSS-2/Article-041/01r.html [accessed 9 May 2012].

26. Ibid., 'Journey through England and Scotland made by Lupold von Wedel in the years 1584 and 1585', trans. G. von Bülow, *Transactions of the Royal Historical Society*, 9, 1895, 223–70, at 230.

27. Ibid.

28. G. E. Dawson, 'London's Bull-baiting and Bear-baiting Arena in 1562', *Shakespeare Quarterly*, 15, 1964, 97–101.

29. Anthony Mackinder and Simon Blatherwick, *Bankside: Excavations at Benbow House, Southwark, London SE1*, Museum of London Archaeology Service, Archaeology Studies Series 3, 2000.

30. Lloyd Kermode and Jason Scott-Warren, eds, *Tudor Drama before Shakespeare, 1485–1590*, Palgrave Macmillan, 2004.

31. David N. Klausner, ed., *Records of Early English Drama: Herefordshire Worcestershire*, University of Toronto Press, 1990, 361–2.

32. Ibid., 309, 324, 331, 412, 451.

33. *A Midsummer Night's Dream*, 3.1.2–4.

34. W. H. Frere and W. M. Kennedy, eds, *Visitation Articles and Injunctions of the Period of the Reformation*, Alcuin Club, 1910, vol. 2, 88.

35. Klausner, *Records*, 350.

36. Ibid.

37. Alexandra F. Johnston and Sally-Beth MacLean, 'Reformation and Resistance in Thames/Severn Parishes: The Dramatic Witness', in K. French, G. Gibbs and B. Kümin, eds, *The Parish in English Life 1400–1600*, Manchester University Press, 1997, 178–200; Sally-Beth MacLean, 'Festive Liturgy and the Dramatic Connection: A Study of Thames Valley Parish Ceremonial', *Medieval and Renaissance Drama in England*, 8, 1996, 49–62.

38. Richard Leighton Greene (ed.), *A Selection of English Carols*, Oxford University Press, 1962, 2.

39. Geoffrey of Monmouth, *The History of the Kings of Britain*, 8.18–13.

40. *Registrum Radulphi Baldock*, Canterbury & York Society 7, 1911, 73–4.

41. Sally-Beth MacLean, 'Hocktide: A Reassessment of a Popular Pre-Reformation Festival', in Meg Twycross, ed., *Festive Drama*, D. S. Brewer, 1996, 233–41.

42. Johnston and MacLean, 'Reformation and Resistance'.

43. Alexandra Johnston, 'Summer Festivals in the Thames Valley Counties', in T. Pettit and L. Sondergaard, eds, *Custom, Culture and Community*, Proceedings of the 17th International Symposium of the Centre for the Study of Vernacular Languages, Odense, 1994, 37–56.

44. Johnston and MacLean, 'Reformation and Resistance', 182.

45. David Dymond and Clive Paine, *The Spoil of Melford Church: The Reformation in a Suffolk Parish*, Salient Press, 1992, 59.

46. Johnston and MacLean, 'Reformation and Resistance', 188.

47. Ibid., 192.

48. Ibid., 193–5.

49. Klausner, *Records*, 351.

50. Ibid., 378–9.

51. Ibid., 390–2.

52. Ibid., 383–4.

53. Ibid., 379–80.

54. Clive Burgess and Eamon Duffy, eds, *The Parish in Late Medieval England: Proceedings of the 2002 Harlaxton Symposium*, Shaun Tyas, 2006.

55. Michael Heaney, 'Kingston to Kenilworth: Early Plebeian Morris', *Folklore*, 100:1, 1989, 88–104.

56. *As You Like It*, 4.2.

57. For the view that games enjoyed 'a short-lived popularity' in the late sixteenth and early seventeenth centuries, see Norman Pounds, *A History of the English Parish*, Cambridge University Press, 2000, 261.

58. Ronald Hutton, *The Rise and Fall of Merry England: The Ritual Year 1400–1700*, Oxford University Press, 1994, 62–3.

59. André Burguière, *The Annales School: An Intellectual History*, trans. Jane Marie Todd, Cornell University Press, 2009, 187–8.

60. Teresa Buckland, 'The Reindeer Antlers of the Abbots Bromley Horn Dance: A Re-examination', *Lore and Language*, 3.2, Part A, 1980, 1–8.

61. Cited in Klausner, *Records*, 351

62. Bede, *Ecclesiastical History of the English People*, i.30.

63. John Blair, *The Church in Anglo-Saxon Society*, Oxford University Press, 2005, 79–121, 182–245, 291–498.

64. John Blair, 'St Beornwald of Bampton', *Oxoniensia*, 49, 1984, 47–55.

65. John Blair, *Anglo-Saxon Oxfordshire*, Sutton, 1998, 73–7.

66. John Blair, 'A Saint for Every Minster? Local Cults in Anglo-Saxon England', in R. Sharpe and A. Thacker, eds, *Local Saints and Local Churches in the Early Medieval West*, Oxford University Press, 2002, 455–94.

67. Paul Everson, 'Peasants, Peers and Graziers: The Landscape of Quarrendon, Buckinghamshire, Interpreted', *Records of Buckinghamshire*, 41, 2001, 41–2; D. Stocker and M. Stocker, 'Sacred Profanity: The Theology of Rabbit Breeding and the Symbolic Landscape of the Warren', *World Archaeology*, 28:2, 1996, 265–72.

68. Blair, *Anglo-Saxon Oxfordshire*.

69. Peter Sawyer, 'Early Fairs and Markets in England and Scandinavia', in B. L. Anderson and A. J. H. Latham, eds, *The Market in History*, Croom Helm, 1986, 59–77.

70. Charles Phythian-Adams, *Local History and Folklore: A New Framework*, Standing Conference on Local History, 1975.

71. David Stocker and Paul Everson, *Summoning St Michael: Early Romanesque Towers in Lincolnshire*, Oxbow Books, 2006.

72. *A Midsummer Night's Dream*, 1.2, 5.1.

73. Duffy, *The Stripping of the Altars*, 3.

74. Gurr, *Playgoing in Shakespeare's London*, 49–79.

75. Webster, *The Duchess of Malfi*, 5.3.

76. *Henry V*, 5.2.

77. *Love's Labour's Lost*, 5.2.

CHAPTER 11: FIELDS AFTER BATTLE

1. D. D. Scott, R. A. Fox, Melissa A. Connor and Dick Hermon, *Archaeological Perspectives on the Battle of the Little Bighorn*, University of Oklahoma Press, 2000; W. Raymond Wood and R. A. Fox, *Archaeology, History, and Custer's Last Battle: The Little Bighorn Re-examined*, University of Oklahoma Press, 2003.

2. Philip Dixon, *Crickley Hill*, vol. 1: *The Hillfort Defences*, Crickley Hill Trust and Department of Archaeology, University of Nottingham, 1994; Jonas Christensen, 'Warfare in the European Neolithic', *Acta Archaeologica*, 76:2, 2004, 29–156; Ian Armit, Chris Knüsel, John Robb and Rick Schulting, 'Warfare and Violence in Prehistoric Europe: An Introduction', *Journal of Conflict Archaeology*, 2:1, 2006, 1–11.

3. Glenn Foard, *Naseby: The Decisive Campaign*, Pryor Publications, 1995.

4. Glenn Foard and Richard Morris, *The Archaeology of English Battlefields*, Council for British Archaeology, 2012.

5. Foard, *Naseby*, 58–64; Glenn Foard, 'The Investigation of Early Modern Battlefields', in *Tagungen Des Landesmuseums für Vorgeschichte Halle*, 2, 2009, 1–9.

6. Glenn Foard, 'The Archaeology of Attack: Battles and Sieges of the English Civil War', in P. W. M. Freeman and A. Pollard, eds, *Fields of Conflict: Progress and Prospects in Battlefield Archaeology*, British Archaeological Reports (International series) 958, 2001.

7. Julian Munby, 'A Note on Building Investigations at 113–119 High Street, Oxford', *Oxoniensia*, 65, 2000, 441–2.

8. Ian Roberts, *Pontefract Castle: Archaeological Excavations 1982–86*, Yorkshire Archaeology 8, Oxbow Books, 2002.

9. C. G. Henderson, 'Excavations at Hayes Barton, St Thomas', *Exeter Archaeology*, Exeter Museums Archaeological Field Unit, 1987, 53–4; M. Stoyle, 'St Thomas during the Civil War', *Exeter Archaeology*, Exeter Museums Archaeological Field Unit, 1987, 54–7.

10. Glenn Foard, 'The Civil War Siege of Grafton Regis', in C. Fitzroy and K. Harry, *Grafton Regis – The History of a Village*, Merton Priory Press, Cardiff, 2000.

11. Glenn Foard, letter to author, 7 April 2011.

12. Ibid.

13. Christopher Knüsel, Anthea Boylston and Veronica Fiorato, eds, *Blood Red Roses: The Archaeology of a Mass Grave from the Battle of Towton AD 1461*, Oxbow Books, 2000.

14. Tim Sutherland and Armin Schmidt, 'Towton, 1461: An Integrated Approach to Battlefield Archaeology', *Landscapes*, 4:2, 2003, 15–25.

15. Tim Sutherland, 'Killing Time: Challenging the Common Perceptions of Three Medieval Conflicts – Ferrybridge, Dintingdale and Towton – "The Largest Battle on British Soil"', *Journal of Conflict Archaeology*, 5:1, 2009, 1–25.

16. Simon Richardson, conversation

with author, at Towton, 20 October 2009.

17. T. L. Sutherland and S. Richardson, 'Arrows Point to Mass Graves: The Location of the Dead from the Battle of Towton AD 1461', in D. Scott, L. Babits and C. Haecker, eds, *Fields of Conflict: Battlefield Archaeology from the Roman Empire to the Korean War*, Praeger, 2006, 160–73.

18. Glenn Foard and Ann Curry, *Bosworth 1485: A Battlefield Rediscovered*, Oxbow Books, forthcoming.

19. Colin Richmond, 'The Battle of Bosworth', *History Today*, 35:8, August 1985, 17–22.

20. William Burton, *The Description of Leicestershire*, John White, 1622, 47.

21. Paul Kendall, *Richard the Third*, Allen & Unwin, 1955.

22. Daniel Williams, '"A Place Mete for Twoo Battayles to Encountre": The Siting of the Battle of Bosworth, 1485', *Ricardian*, 90:7, September 1985; cf. Christopher Gravett, *Bosworth 1485: Last Charge of the Plantagenets*, Osprey, 1999.

23. Michael K. Jones, *Bosworth 1485: Psychology of a Battle*, Tempus, 2002.

24. Peter J. Foss, *The Field of Redemore: The Battle of Bosworth, 1485*, 2nd edn, Kairos Press, 1998.

25. Glenn Foard, 'Discovering Bosworth', *British Archaeology*, 112, May/June 2010.

26. Ibid.

27. Foard, *Naseby*, 251.

28. Ibid., 275.

29. Ibid., 284.

CHAPTER 12: COVER HIM GENTLY

1. For example: Yves Desfosses,

Alain Jacques and Gilles Prilaux, *L'Archéologie de la Grand Guerre*, Editions Ouest-France, 2009; Nicholas J. Saunders, *Killing Time: Archaeology and the First World War*, 2nd edn, History Press, 2010; Nicholas Saunders, 'Excavating Memories: Archaeology and the Great War, 1914–2001', *Antiquity*, 76:291, 2002, 101–8; Martin Brown and Richard Osgood, *Digging up Plugstreet: The Archaeology of a Great War Battlefield*, Haynes, 2009; Paul Virilio, *Bunker Archaeology*, Les Editions du Semi-Circle, 1994; W. Cocroft and R. J. C. Thomas, *Cold War: Building for Nuclear Confrontation, 1946–89*, English Heritage, 2003; J. Schofield, A. Klausmeier and L. Purbrick, eds, *Re-mapping the Field: New Approaches in Conflict Archaeology*, Westkreuz-Verlag, 2006; John Schofield, *Aftermath: Readings in the Archaeology of Recent Conflict*, Springer Verlag, 2009; John Schofield, *Combat Archaeology: Material Culture and Modern Conflict*, Duckworth, 2005; Douglas Scott, Lawrence Babits and Charles Haecker, eds, *Fields of Conflict: Battlefield Archaeology from the Roman Empire to the Korean War*, Praeger, 2006; John Schofield, William Gray Johnson and Colleen M. Beck, eds, *Matériel Culture: The Archaeology of Twentieth-century Conflict*, One World Archaeology 44, Routledge, 2002; Neil Forbes, Robin Page and Guillermo Pérez, eds, *Europe's Deadly Century: Perspectives on 20th Century Conflict Heritage*, English Heritage, 2009.

2. Victor Buchli and Gavin Lucas, eds, *Archaeologies of the Contemporary Past*, Routledge, 2001; Robert W. Preucel and Stephen A. Mrozowski,

eds, *Contemporary Archaeology in Theory: The New Pragmatism*, Wiley-Blackwell, 2nd edn, 2010; Rodney Hamson and John Schofield, *After Modernity: Archaeological Approaches to the Contemporary Past*, Oxford University Press, 2010.

3. John Schofield and Mike Anderton, 'The Queer Archaeology of Green Gate: Interpreting Contested Space at Greenham Common Airbase', *World Archaeology*, 32:2, 2000, 236–51, at 237; D. Uzzel, 'The Hot Interpretation of the Cold War', in *Monuments of War: The Evaluation, Recording and Management of Twentieth-Century Military Sites*, English Heritage, 1998, 18–21.

4. Peter Hennessy, *The Secret State: Preparing for the Worst 1945–2010*, Penguin, 2010.

5. Colin Dobinson, *Building Radar: Forging Britain's Early-warning Chain, 1939-45*, Methuen, 2010.

6. For intellectual context: Paul Courtney, 'The Current State and Future Prospects of Theory in European Post-Medieval Archaeology', in T. Majewski and D. Gaimster, eds, *International Handbook of Historical Archaeology*, Springer, 2009, 169–89.

7. Gillian Carr, 'The Archaeology of Occupation, 1940–2009: A Case Study from the Channel Islands', *Antiquity*, 84:323, 2010, 161–74; J. K. Pringle, P. Doyle and L. E. Babits, 'Multidisciplinary Investigations at Stalag Luft III Allied Prisoner-of-war Camp: The Site of the 1944 "Great Escape", Zagen, Western Poland', *Geoarchaeology*, 22:7, 2007, 729–46; W. Cocroft, D. Devlin, J. Schofield and R. J. C Thomas, *War Art: Murals and Graffiti – Military Life, Power and Subversion*, Council for British Archaeology

Research Report 147, 2006; N. J. Saunders, *Trench Art: Materialities and Memories of War*, Berg, 2003; Nicholas J. Saunders and Mark Dennis, *Craft and Conflict: Masonic Trench Art and Military Memorabilia*, Savannah, 2003; Vince Holyoak, 'Out of the Blue: Assessing Military Aircraft Crash Sites in England, 1912–45', *Antiquity*, 76:293, 2002, 657–63; Vince Holyoak, 'Airfields as Battlefields, Aircraft as an Archaeological Resource', in P. W. M. Freeman and A. Pollard, eds, *Fields of Conflict: Progress and Prospect in Battlefield Archaeology*, Archaeopress, 2001; Colin Dobinson, Jeremy Lake and John Schofield, 'Monuments of War: Defining England's 20th-century Defence Heritage', *Antiquity*, 71:272, 1997, 288–99.

8. Deborah Lipstadt, *Denying the Holocaust: The Growing Assault on Truth and Memory*, Penguin, 1994; Richard J. Evans, *Telling Lies about Hitler: The Holocaust, History and the David Irving Trial*, Verso, 2002, 250; Robert Jan van Pelt, *The Case for Auschwitz: Evidence from the Irving Trial*, Indiana University Press, 2002.

9. Yisrael Gutman and Michael Berenbaum, eds, *Anatomy of the Auschwitz Death Camp*, Indiana University Press, 1994.

10. High Court of Justice 1996 I. No. 113, Queen's Bench Division, Transcript, day 11, 130–1.

11. Ibid., day 11, 141, at l.20.

12. Ibid., day 9, 82.

13. Ibid., day 9, 83.

14. Ibid., day 11, 133–4.

15. Ibid., day 11, 151.

16. Ibid., day 11, 135.

17. Evans, *Telling Lies about Hitler*, 250.

18. Daniel Keren, Jamie McCarthy and Harry W. Mazal, 'The Ruins

of the Gas Chambers: A Forensic Investigation of Crematoriums at Auschwitz I and Auschwitz-Birkenau', in *Holocaust and Genocide Studies*, 18:1, 2004, 68–103.

19. Francis Pryor, *Seahenge: New Discoveries in Prehistoric Britain*, HarperCollins, 2001, chapters 12 and 13; Charlie Watson, *Seahenge: An Archaeological Conundrum*, English Heritage, 2005.

20. Letter from Polly Bolton, *British Archaeology*, June 2000, 25.

21. Simon Denison, 'One Step to the Left, Two Steps Back', *British Archaeology*, April 2000, 28.

22. Letter from Peter Pickering, *British Archaeology*, 53, June 2000, 25.

23. Letter from Mike Williams, *British Archaeology*, 53, June 2000, 25.

24. Robert Bowen, *Universal Ice: Science and Ideology in the Nazi State*, Bellhaven Press, 1993; Heather Pringle, *The Master Plan: Himmler's Scholars and the Holocaust*, Fourth Estate, 2006, 179–80.

25. Colin Riordan, 'Green Ideas in Germany: A Historical Survey', in Colin Riordan, ed., *Green Thought in German Culture: Historical and Contemporary Perspectives*, University of Wales Press, 1997, 3–41, at 9–10; Wilhelm Heinrich Riehl, *Die Naturgeschichte des Volkes als Grundlage einer deutschen Sozial-Politik*, I, *Land und Leute*, J. G. Cotta, 1855, 44.

26. Riordan, 'Green Ideas in Germany', 10.

27. Andreas Knaut, 'Die Anfänge des staatlichen Naturschutzes. Die frühe regierungsamliche Organisation des Natur- und Landschaftsschutzes in Preussen, Bayern und Württemberg', in Werner Abelshauser, ed., *Umweltgeschichte. Umweltverträgliches Wirtschaften in*

historische Perspektive, Vandenhoeck & Ruprecht, 1994, 143–62.

28. Aspects of ecological thought had been present in German intellectual life for at least a century before Ernst Haeckel, Professor of Zoology at the University of Jena, actually coined the term 'ecology' in 1866: Riordan, 'Green Ideas in Germany', 7, 11.

29. Alexander von Humboldt, *Ansichten der Natur: mit wissenschaftlichen Erläuterungen*, Cotta'scher Verlag, 1859; Joachim Radkau, 'Wood and Forestry in German History', *Environment and History*, 2:1, 1996, 63–76; Robert A. Pois, *National Socialism and the Religion of Nature*, Croom Helm, 1986.

30. Alison Statham, 'Ecology and the German Right', in Riordan, ed., *Green Thought in German Culture: Historical and Contemporary Perspectives*, 125–38, at 126–7. For another strand: Gregory A. Barton, *Empire Forestry and the Origins of Environmentalism*, Cambridge University Press, 2002.

31. Anna Bramwell, *Blood and Soil: Richard Walther Darré and 'Hitler's Green Party'*, Kensal Press, 1985; cf. Piers H. G. Stephens, 'Blood, Not Soil: Anna Bramwell and the Myth of Hitler's Green Party', *Organization and Environment*, 14:2, 2001, 173–87.

32. Michael H. Kater, *Das 'Ahnenerbe' der SS, 1933–1945: Ein Beitrag zur Kulturpolitik des Dritten Reiches*, Deutsche Verlags-Anstalt, 1974; Pringle, *The Master Plan: Himmler's Scholars and the Holocaust*.

33. B. Arnold, 'The Past as Propaganda: Totalitarian Archaeology in Nazi Germany', *Antiquity*, 64:244, 1990, 464–78.

34. Klaus Junker, 'Research under Dictatorship: The German

Archaeological Institute 1929–1945',
Antiquity, 72:276, 1998, 282–92.

35. SS-Hauptamt-Schulungsamt
beim Reichsführers der SS, *Der
Kampf um die deutsche Ostgrenze
(Ein Längsschnitt von der früh
germanischen Zeit bis zur Jetztzeit)*,
Berlin, 1941, 41ff, cited in Robert
Jan van Pelt, 'A Site in Search of a
Mission', in Yisrael Gutman and
Michael Berenbaum, eds, *Anatomy of
the Auschwitz Death Camp*, Indiana
University Press, 1994, 93–156, at
100–101.

36. Cited van Pelt, 'A Site in Search of a
Mission', 100.

37. Ibid.; Deborah Dwork and Robert
Jan van Pelt, *Auschwitz*, W. W.
Norton, 2002.

38. Hanns Johst, *Ruf des Reiches – Echo
des Volkes: Eine Ostfahrt*, Munich,
1940, 86; cited and trans. in van Pelt,
'A Site in Search of a Mission', 103.

39. Van Pelt, 'A Site in Search of a
Mission', 103.

40. Georgina Boyes, *The Imagined
Village: Culture, Ideology and the
English Folk Revival*, Manchester
University Press, 1993; Catherine
Brace, 'Finding England
Everywhere: Regional Identity
and the Construction of National
Identity, 1890–1940', *Ecumene*,
6, 1999, 90–109; 'Publishing and
Publishers: Towards an Historical
Geography of Countryside Writing,
c. 1930–1950', *Area*, 33, 2001 287–96.

41. E. Baker, *A Forbidden Land: A
Plea for Public Access to Mountains,
Moors and Other Wastelands in Great
Britain*, Witherby, 1924.

42. P. Abercrombie, 'The Preservation
of Rural England', *Town Planning
Review*, 12, 1926, 5–56; Clough
Williams-Ellis, *England and
the Octopus*, Bles, 1928; Clough
Williams-Ellis, ed., *Britain and

the Beast*, J. M. Dent, 1937; Richard
Morris, 'Breathing the Future: The
Antiquaries and Conservation of
the Countryside', in Susan Pearce,
ed., *Visions of Antiquity: The Society
of Antiquaries of London 1707–2007*,
Archaeologia 111, 2007; J. Sheail, *Rural
Conservation in Inter-War Britain*,
Oxford University Press, 1981.

43. D. H. Lawrence, *Lady Chatterley's
Lover*, Viking, 1972 (first pub. 1928),
86–7, 193, 207.

44. Friedrich Engels, *The Condition of
the Working Class in England* (1845),
trans. W. O. Henderson and W. H.
Chaloner, Blackwell, 1958.

45. R. J. Moore-Colyer, 'From Great
Wen to Road Hall: Aspects of the
Urban–Rural Divide in Inter-war
Britain', *Rural History*, 10, 1999, 105–7.

46. Alfred Russel Wallace,
'Reoccupation of the Land', in
Forecasts of the Coming Century, The
Labour Press, 1897.

47. Malcolm Chase, 'Heartbreak Hill:
Environment, Unemployment and
"Back to the Land" in Inter-war
Cleveland', *Oral History*, 28, 2000,
30–42.

48. R. J. Moore-Colyer, 'Rolf Gardiner,
English Patriot and the Council
for the Church and Countryside',
Agricultural History Review, 49:2,
2001, 187–209, at 189; Edith H.
Whetham, 'The Agriculture Act 1920
and its Repeal – The "Great Betrayal"',
Agricultural History Review, 22:1, 1974,
36–49. For a more nuanced and, in
some respects, contrary view, see
Paul Brassley, Jeremy Burchardt and
Lynne Thompson, *The English
Countryside Between the Wars:
Regeneration or Decline?*, Boydell,
2006; and Alun Howkins, *The Death
of Rural England: A Social History of
the Countryside Since 1900*, Routledge,
2003.

49. A. J. P. Taylor, *English History 1914–1945*, 1965, Oxford University Press, 167–8.

50. E. M. Forster, 'Havoc', in Williams-Ellis, ed., *Britain and the Beast*, 44–5.

51. Richard Harman, ed., *Countryside Mood*, Blandford Press, 1943, 6.

52. R. J. Moore-Colyer, 'Back to Basics: Rolf Gardiner, H. J. Massingham and "A Kinship in Husbandry"', *Rural History*, 12:1, 2001, 85–108; R. J. Moore-Colyer and Philip Cornford, 'A "Secret Society"? The Internal and External Relations of the Kinship in Husbandry, 1941–52', *Rural History*, 15, 2004, 189–206.

53. H. J. Massingham, *The Wisdom of the Fields*, Collins, 1945.

54. Moore-Colyer, 'Rolf Gardiner, English patriot and the Council for the Church and Countryside', 187.

55. Patrick Wright, *The Village that Died for England*, Faber & Faber, rev. edn 2001, esp.180–93.

56. Moore-Colyer, 'Rolf Gardiner, English Patriot and the Council for the Church and Countryside', 189; Rolf Gardiner, *England Herself: Ventures in Rural Restoration*, Faber & Faber, 1943.

57. H. J. Massingham, *Remembrance: An Autobiography*, Batsford, 1942, 40.

58. Julia Stapleton's biography finds that while Bryant did show sympathies towards National Socialism he was essentially Tory, vehemently monarchist and above all committed to national cohesion: *Sir Arthur Bryant and National History in Twentieth-Century Britain*, Rowman & Littlefield, 2006.

59. Richard Griffiths, *Fellow Travellers of the Right: British Enthusiasts for Nazi Germany: 1933–1939*, Constable, 1980.

60. Wright, *The Village that Died for England*, 204–10.

61. Mrs C. B. S. Hodson, *Eugenics Review*, 1934, p. 164; Bishop Edward Barnes, Address, Liverpool Cathedral, 1933.

62. H. J. Massingham, *Downland Man*, Jonathan Cape, 1926, 313.

63. Moore-Colyer, 'Rolf Gardiner, English Patriot and the Council for the Church and Countryside', 190–1; Walter Laqueur, *Young Germany: A History of the German Youth Movement*, Routledge & Kegan Paul, 1962.

64. Wright, *The Village that Died For England*, 187–8; Moore-Colyer, 'Rolf Gardiner: English Patriot and the Council for the Church and Countryside', 187–209.

65. Sonia Cole, *Races of Man*, British Museum (Natural History), 1965, esp. chapter 2; cf. Julien Parsons, 'Belas Knap', *British Archaeology*, 63, 2002, 18–23.

66. R. W. Davies, *From E. H. Carr's Files: Notes towards a Second Edition of What is History?*, Palgrave, repr. 2001, lxiii.

67. Alan Garner, 'The Voice in the Shadow', in *The Voice That Thunders*, Harvill Press, 1997, 154–5.

68. Dobinson, Lake and Schofield, 'Monuments of War: Defining England's 20th-century Defence Heritage'.

69. William Foot, *Beaches, Fields, Streets, and Hills … The Anti-invasion Landscapes of England, 1940*, Council for British Archaeology, 2006.

70. Grahame Clark, 'Education and the Study of Man', *Antiquity*, 17:67, 1943, 113–21.

71. George Steiner, *Language and Silence*, Pelican, 1969, 193.

72. Henry Rousso, *La Hantise du passé: entretien avec Philippe Petit*, Paris, Textuel, 1998, 89; trans. Catherine Temerson in Stéphane Audoin-

Rouzeay and Annette Becker, *14–18: Understanding the Great War*, Hill & Wang, 2002, 2.

73. Steiner, *Language and Silence*, 192.

74. Audoin-Rouzeay and Becker, *14–18*, 204, cf. 2–3.

75. Alain Jacques, quoted in the *Independent*, 20 June 2001.

76. Ivor Gurney, 'To his Love', *Collected Poems*, P. J. Kavanagh, ed., Carcanet, 2004, 21 (first published in *War's Embers*, Sidgwick & Jackson, 1919).

CHAPTER 13: 'NICKEL PLATE AND BRUMMAGEM'

1. Ruth Michaelis-Jena and Willy Merson, *A Lady Travels: The Diaries of Johanna Schopenhauer*, Routledge, 1988, 16.

2. R. E. Schofield, *The Lunar Society at Birmingham: A Social History of Provincial Science and Industry in Eighteenth-century England*, Oxford University Press, 1963; Jenny Uglow, *The Lunar Men: The Friends Who Made the Future, 1730–1810*, Faber & Faber, 2002.

3. Bennet Bronson, 'Pearls without Price: The Rise and Fall of a Sometimes Precious Gem', paper delivered to the Chicago Literary Club, 10 April 2000.

4. John Pemberton Turner, 'The Birmingham Button Trade', in Samuel Timmins, ed., *The Resources, Products, and Industrial History of Birmingham and the Midland Hardware District*, Robert Hardwick, 1866, 432–51; http://hammond-turner.com/index.php?option=com_content&view=article&id=17&Itemid=49 [accessed 16 February 2012].

5. John Leland, *The Itinerary of John Leland the Antiquary*, 3 vols, Oxford, Thomas Hearne, 1719, 114.

6. Richard H. Trainor, *Black Country Élites: The Exercise of Authority in an Industrialised Area 1830–1900*, Clarendon Press, 1993.

7. R. M. Hartwell, *The Industrial Revolution and Economic Growth*, Methuen, 1971; Pat Hudson, *The Industrial Revolution*, Edward Arnold, 1992; Pat Hudson, *Regions and Industries: A Perspective on the Industrial Revolution in Britain*, Cambridge University Press, 1989; Joseph E. Inikori, *Africans and the Industrial Revolution in England: A Study in International Trade and Development*, Cambridge University Press, 2002; Gregory Clark, 'The Political Foundations of Modern Economic Growth: England 1540-1800', *Journal of Interdisciplinary History*, 26, 1996, 563–88; Ralph Davis, 'The Rise of Protection in England, 1689–1786', *Economic History Review*, 19:2, 1966, 306–17; Douglass C. North and Barry R. Weingast, 'Constitutions and Commitment: The Evolution of Institutions Governing Public Choice in Seventeenth-century England', *Journal of Economic History*, 49:4, 1989, 803–32; John Brewer, *The Sinews of Power: War, Money and the English State, 1688–1783*, Unwin Hyman, 1989; William Ashworth, *Customs and Excise: Trade, Production and Consumption in England, 1640–1845*, Oxford University Press, 2003; Sarah Tarlow, *The Archaeology of Improvement in Britain, 1750–1850*, Cambridge University Press, 2007.

8. David Hume, *A Treatise of Human Nature*, ed. David Fate Norton and Mary J. Norton, Oxford University Press, 2000.

9. Stewart A. Weaver, *The Hammonds: A Marriage in History*, Stanford University Press, 1997.

10. Arnold Toynbee, *A Study of History*, vol. 1, Oxford University Press, 1934, 17–21; J. L. and Barbara Hammond, *The Rise of Modern Industry*, Methuen, 1925.

11. Geoff Egan, 'Material Culture in London in an Age of Transition: Tudor and Stuart Period Finds c. 1450–c. 1700', from *Excavations at Riverside Sites in Southwark*, Museum of London Archaeology Service, 2005.

12. Tarlow, *The Archaeology of Improvement in Britain*, 13–18.

13. G. Clark, 'Too Much Revolution: Agriculture and the Industrial Revolution 1700–1860', in J. Mokyr, ed., *The British Industrial Revolution: An Economic Assessment*, Westview Press, 1999, 206–40.

14. Richard M. Thomas, 'Zooarchaeology, Improvement and the British Agricultural Revolution', *Journal of Historical Archaeology*, 19:2, 2005, 71–88; Simon J. M. Davis and John V. Beckett, 'Animal Husbandry and Agricultural Improvement: The Archaeological Evidence from Animal Bones and Teeth', *Rural History*, 10, 1999, 1–17; Umberto Albarella, 'Size, Power, Wool and Veal: Zoological Evidence for Late Medieval Innovations', in Guy de Bow and Frans Verhaeghe, eds, *Environment and Subsistence in Medieval Europe*, Instituut voor het Archeologisch Patrimonium, 1997, 19–30; cf. E. Kerridge, *The Agricultural Revolution*, Allen & Unwin, 1967; C. Dyer, *Standards of Living in the Later Middle Ages: Social Change in England c.1200–1520*, Cambridge Medieval Textbooks, 1989; J. Langdon, *Horses, Oxen and Technological Innovation*, Cambridge University Press, 1986.

15. G. G. Astill, *A Medieval Industrial Complex and its Landscape: The Metalworking Watermills and Workshops of Bordesley Abbey*, Council for British Archaeology Research Report 92, 1993.

16. Geoff Egan, *Playthings from the Past*, Jonathan Horne, 1996; Hazel Forsyth with Geoff Egan, *Toys, Trifles and Trinkets: Base-metal Miniatures from London 1200 to 1800*, Unicorn Press, 2005.

17. S. A. J. Bradley, *Orm Gamalson's Sundial: The Lily's Blossom and the Roses' Fragrance*, 1997 Kirkdale Lecture, Friends of St Gregory's Minster, 2002, 9.

18. Jo Draper, *Post Medieval Pottery 1650–1800*, Shire, 1986.

19. John Harold Kelly, *Post-Medieval Pottery*, City of Stoke on Trent Museum Archaeological Society Report No. 8, 1975; *Post Medieval Pottery from Duchess China Works, Longton, Stoke-on-Trent … Post Medieval Pottery from Newcastle Street, Burslem*, City Museum & Art Gallery, Stoke-on-Trent, 1975.

20. Tarlow, *The Archaeology of Improvement in Britain*, 163–89, esp. 178–83.

21. A. Brooks, 'Building Jerusalem: Transfer-printed Finewares and the Creation of British Identity', in S. Tarlow and S. West, eds, *The Familiar Past? Archaeologies of Later Historical Britain*, Routledge, 1999, 51–65; G. Lucas, 'Reading Pottery: Literature and Transfer-printed Pottery in the Early Nineteenth Century', *International Journal of Historical Archaeology*, 7:2, 2003, 127–43.

22. Tarlow, *The Archaeology of Improvement in Britain*, 181.

23. E. P. Thompson, 'Time, Work-discipline, and Industrial Capitalism', *Past and Present*, 38:1, 1967, 56–97.

24. Gillian Darley, *Factory*, Reaktion, 2003.

25. *The Life of Sir William Fairbairn, bart.*, partly written by himself, edited and completed by William Pole, 1877, repr. David & Charles, 1970; William Fairbairn, *On the Application of Cast and Wrought Iron to Building Purposes*, John Weale, 2nd edn, 1857–8; *Treatise on Mills and Millwork*, Longmans, 3rd edn, 1871–4.

26. Ron Fitzgerald, 'The Development of the Cast Iron Frame in the Textile Mills to 1850', *Industrial Archaeology Review*, 10, 1987–8, 127–45.

27. Colum Giles and Ian Goodall, *Yorkshire Textile Mills 1770–1930*, Royal Commission on Historical Monuments and West Yorkshire Archaeological Service, HMSO, 1992, 63–5.

28. Friedrich Engels, *The Condition of the Working Class in England*, English edn 1891 (first pub. 1845), 'The Great Towns'.

29. Charles Babbage, *On the Economy of Machinery and Manufactures*, C. Knight, 1832; Georgina Ferry, *A Computer Called Leo*, Fourth Estate, 2003, 49–52.

30. Charles Orser, *A Historical Archaeology of the Modern World*, Plenum, 1996, vii.

31. *An Archaeological Guide to British Ceramics in Australia, 1788–1901*, Australian Society for Historical Archaeology, 2005.

32. Anne C. Bailey, *African Voices of the Atlantic Slave Trade: Beyond the Silence and the Shame*, Beacon Press, 2005.

33. Hugh Thomas, *The Slave Trade: The History of the Atlantic Slave Trade,*

1440–1870, Picador, 1997; Elizabeth Kowaleski Wallace, *The British Slave Trade and Public Memory*, Columbia University Press, 2006.

34. Bede, *Ecclesiastical History of the English People*, ii.1.

35. Gregory I, *Register* 6.10, ed. Paul Ewald and Ludo Hartmann, MGH Epistolae 1 and 2, Berlin, 1887–99; cf. Ian Wood, 'The Mission of Augustine', *Speculum*, 69, 1994 1–17.

36. R. R. Darlington, ed., *The Vital Wulfstani of William of Malmesbury*, Royal Historical Society, Camden 3rd series, 1928, 43.

37. David Pelteret, 'Slave Raiding and Slave Trading in Early England', *Anglo-Saxon England*, 9, 1981, 99–114; *Slavery in Early Medieval England: From the Reign of Alfred to the Twelfth Century*, Boydell & Brewer, 1995.

38. *The Diary of the Rev. Henry Newcome from Sept. 30 1661 to Sept. 29 1663*, ed. Thomas Haywood, Chetham Society, Old Series, 1849, xiv–xv.

39. Jean-Michel Chaumont, *La Concurrence des victimes: génocides, identité et reconnaissance*, Paris, La Découverte, 1997; Stéphane Audoin-Rouzeay and Annette Becker, *14–18*, *Understanding the Great War*, Hill & Wang, 2002, 2.

40. Kate Clark, 'The Industrial Revolution', in J. Hunter and I. Ralston, eds, *The Archaeology of Britain*, Routledge, 1999, 293; Susannah Wade-Martins, *Historic Farm Buildings*, Batsford, 1991.

41. See for example the National Trust's 'atmospheric glimpse into the lives of ordinary people' at the Birmingham Back to Backs: www.nationaltrust.org.uk/main/w-birmingham_backtobacks [accessed 24 April 2011]; Chris Upton, *Living Back to Back*, Phillimore, 2010.

42. Clark, 'The Industrial Revolution', 295.
43. Alasdair Brooks and Graham Connah, 'A Hierarchy of Servitude: Ceramics at Lake Innes Estate, New South Wales', *Antiquity*, 81:31, 2007, 133–47.
44. Douglas Adams et al., *The Austin Village*, Austin Village Preservation Society, 2002.
45. Jack Reynolds, *Saltaire: An Introduction to the Village of Sir Titus Salt*, City of Bradford Metropolitan Council Art Galleries and Museums, 1976.
46. Ebenezer Howard, *Garden Cities of To-morrow: (being a second edition of 'To-morrow: a peaceful path to real reform')*, S. Sonnenschein, 1902; Robert Beevers, *The Garden City Utopia: A Critical Biography of Ebenezer Howard*, Macmillan, 1988.
47. *The Bournville Village Trust, 1900–1955*, Bournville Village Trust, 1955.
48. B. Seebohm Rowntree, *Poverty: A Study of Town Life*, Macmillan, 1901.
49. Aladdin sales catalogue 1917, 3, Clarke Historical Library, Central Michigan University.
50. Ibid., 54.
51. Robert Schweitzer and Michael W. R. Davis, *America's Favorite Homes: Mail Order Catalogues as a Guide to Popular Early 20th-century Houses*, Wayne State University Press, 1990.
52. Phillip Shriver, *Ohio's Military Prisons in the Civil War*, Ohio State University Press, 1964; Dave Bush, 'Doing Time', *Archaeology*, 52:4, 1999, 46–51; Christopher Britten, 'Cooped Up and Powerless When my Home is Invaded: Southern Prisoners at Johnson's Island in their own Words', *Ohio Valley History*, 10:1, 2010, 53–72.

CHAPTER 14: COUSIN JACK

1. 'Eighth Coronation Concert', *The Times*, 8 June 1953, 3.
2. Philip Payton, *The Cornish Overseas*, Alexander Associates, 1999.
3. *Nomination of the Cornwall and West Devon Mining Landscape for Inclusion on the World Heritage List*, 2004, Statement of Significance, 18–20.
4. Ibid., 21.
5. A. C. Todd, 'Foreword', in Payton, *The Cornish Overseas*, vi, 'Introduction', ix.
6. Elsie Morris, MS memoir, 1973.
7. Asa Briggs, *Victorian Cities*, Penguin, 1968.
8. John Cattell, Sheila Ely and Barry Jones, *The Birmingham Jewellery Quarter: An Architectural Survey of the Manufactories*, English Heritage, 2002, 28.

CHAPTER 15: UNSETTLED REMAINS

1. John Cattell, Sheila Ely and Barry Jones, *The Birmingham Jewellery Quarter: An Architectural Survey of the Manufactories*, English Heritage, 2002; J. Cattell and R. Hawkins, with photographs by P. Williams, J. Davies and M. Hesketh Roberts, *The Birmingham Jewellery Quarter: An Introduction and Guide*, English Heritage/Birmingham City Council, 2000.
2. Mike Hodder, *Birmingham: The Hidden History*, Tempus, 2004.
3. T. H. McK. Clough and W. A. Cummins, *Stone Axe Studies*, CBA Research Report 23, 1979; Vin Davies and Mark Edmonds, *Stone Axe Studies III*, Oxbow Books, 2011.
4. Richard Bradley, *Prehistory of Britain and Ireland*, Cambridge University

Press, 2007, 134.

5. Ibid.

6. Bede, *Ecclesiastical History of the English People*, iv.31.

7. Ibid., ii.14, 20.

8. James Lang, *Corpus of Anglo-Saxon Stone Sculpture*, vol. 6: *Northern Yorkshire*, British Academy, 2002.

9. Paul Everson and David Stocker, *Custodians of Continuity? The Premonstratensian Abbey at Barlings and the Landscape of Ritual*, Lincolnshire Archaeology and Heritage Report No. 11, 2011, xx.

10. *Vita Norberti*, ed. Roger Wilmans, *Monumenta Germaniae Historica Scriptores*, 12, 1856, 670–703; Theodore J. Antry and Carol Neel, *Norbert and Early Norbertine Spirituality*, Paulist Press, 2007.

11. Francis Pryor, *The Flag Fen Basin: Archaeology and Environment of a Fenland Landscape*, English Heritage, 2001, 421–7; *Flag Fen: Life and Death of a Prehistoric Landscape*, Tempus, 2005.

12. N. Falkner, 'Testwood Bridge', *Current Archaeology*, 190, 2004, 428–9; J. Siddell, J. Cotton, L. Rayner and L. Wheeler, *The Prehistory and Topography of Southwark and Lambeth*, Museum of London, 2002; T. Allen, 'Eton College Rowing Course at Dorney', *Current Archaeology*, 181, 2002, 20–5; Bradley, *Prehistory of Britain and Ireland*, 203.

13. Anthony Harding, *European Societies in the Bronze Age*, Cambridge University Press, 2000, 352–68.

14. Bradley, *Prehistory of Britain and Ireland*, 202–3, 206, 236.

15. John Coles, 'The Great Bronze Shield from Beith', *Antiquary*, 7, 2003, 6.

16. Ian Stead, *The Salisbury Hoard*, Tempus, 1998.

17. I. M. Stead, *The Battersea Shield*, British Museum Press, 1985; 'Many More Iron Age Shields from Britain', *Antiquaries Journal*, 71, 1991, 1–35.

18. A. J. White, *Antiquities from the River Witham*, part 1: *Prehistoric and Roman*, Lincolnshire Museums Information Sheet, Archaeology Series No. 12, 1979.

19. Michael J. Jones, David Stocker and Alan Vince, *The City by the Pool*: *Assessing the Archaeology of the City of Lincoln*, City of Lincoln Council/ English Heritage, Oxbow Books, 2003, 25.

20. Ibid., 19–33.

21. David Stocker and Paul Everson, 'The Conversion of the Landscape in the Witham Valley', in Martin Carver, ed., *The Cross Goes North: Processes of Conversion in Northern Europe, AD 300–1300*, Boydell Press, 2006, 271–88; *Custodians of Continuity*, 393–404.

22. A. T. Chamberlain, 'Lunar Eclipses, Saros Cycles and the Construction of the Causeway', in Mike Parker Pearson and Naomi Field, *Fiskerton: An Iron Age Timber Causeway with Iron Age and Roman Votive Offerings*, Oxbow Books, 2003, 136–43, at 136.

23. Stocker and Everson, 'Conversion of the Landscape', 284.

24. Tennyson, *The Princess*, Prologue, 125.

25. Paul Budd and Timothy Taylor, 'The Faerie Smith Meets the Bronze Industry: Magic versus Science in the Interpretation of Prehistoric Metal Making', *World Archaeology*, 27, 1995, 133–43.

26. Thomas Malory, *Le Morte d'Arthur*, 21.5; Richard Bradley, *The Passage of Arms: An Archaeological Analysis of Prehistoric Hoards and Votive Deposits*, Cambridge University Press, 1990; Hilda Ellis Davidson,

The Sword in Anglo-Saxon England,
Boydell Press, 1998 (first pub. 1962).

27. C. Evans, 'Metalwork and the
"Cold Clay-lands": Pre-Iron Age
Occupation on the Isle of Ely', in
T. Lane and J. Coles, eds, *Through
Wet and Dry*, Heritage Trust of
Lincolnshire, 2002, 33–53.

28. Stocker and Everson, 'Conversion of
the Landscape'.

29. Ibid., 284–5.

30. J. C. Dickinson, *The Shrine of Our
Lady of Walsingham*, Cambridge
University Press, 1956.

31. The Lincolnshire road is Margary
27: Ivan Margary, *Roman Roads in
Britain*, John Baker, 3rd edn, 1973.

32. R. Rainbird Clarke, 'The Early Iron
Age Treasure from Snettisham,
Norfolk', *Proceedings of the
Prehistoric Society*, 20, 1954, 27–86;
A. P. Fitzpatrick, 'The Snettisham,
Norfolk, hoards of Iron Age
torques: Sacred or profane?',
Antiquity, 66, 1992, 395-8; D. Garrow,
Chris Gosden and J. D. Hill, eds,
Rethinking Celtic Art, Oxbow Books,
2008.

33. Bede, *The Reckoning of Time*, ed.
and trans. Faith Wallis, Liverpool
University Press, 2004, 14.

34. Mike Parker Pearson, 'From
Ancestor Cult to Divine Religion',
British Archaeology, 45, 1999.

35. Jacques Le Goff, *Medieval
Imagination*, trans. Arthur
Goldhammer, Chicago University
Press, 1988, 67.

36. Jacques Le Goff, *The Birth
of Purgatory*, trans. Arthur
Goldhammer, Scolar Press, 1984, 229.

37. Le Goff, *Medieval Imagination*, 73.

38. John Henry Newman, *An Essay
on the Development of Christian
Doctrine*, James Toovey, 1845, chapter
2, section 3, paragraph 2, 92–8.

39. Le Goff, *Medieval Imagination*, 73–4.

40. Bradley, *Prehistory of Britain and
Ireland*, 268–9.

41. Budd and Taylor, 'The Faerie Smith
Meets the Bronze Industry', 133–43.

42. David Whitehouse, '"Things that
Travelled": The Surprising Case of
Raw Glass', *Early Medieval Europe*,
12:3, 2003, 301–5, at 301.

43. Roger D. Penhallurick, *Tin in
Antiquity: Its Mining and Trade
throughout the Ancient World with
Particular Reference to Cornwall*,
Institute of Metals, 1986, 212,
234, 237; cf. Ewan Campbell,
'The Archaeological Evidence
for Contacts, Imports, Trade and
Economy in Celtic Britain AD
400–800', 88–9, n. 15.

44. Bradley, *Prehistory of Britain and
Ireland*, 230.

45. Ibid., 226–7; L. Sperber, 'Crises in
Western European Metal Supply
during the Late Bronze Age: From
Bronze to Iron', in K. Demakapoulou,
C. Eluère, J. Jensen, A. Jockenhövel
and J. P. Mohen, eds, *Gods and Heroes
of the European Bronze Age*, Thames
& Hudson, 1999, 48–51.

46. Simon Timberlake and A. J. N. W.
Prag, *The Archaeology of Alderley
Edge: Survey, Excavation and
Experiment in an Ancient Mining
Landscape*, John and Erica Hedges,
2005.

47. A. Dutton and P. J. Fasham,
'Prehistoric Copper Mining on the
Great Orme, Llandudno, Gwynedd',
Proceedings of the Prehistoric Society,
60, 1994, 145–286.

48. D. Gale, 'Prehistoric Mining at
Alderley Edge', *Cheshire Past*, 2,
Cheshire County Council, 1993.

49. Alan Garner, *By Seven Firs and
Goldenstone: An Account of the Legend
of Alderley*, Temenos Academy, 2010.

50. Le Goff, *Medieval Imagination*,
47–59.

51. Brian K. Roberts and Stuart Wrathmell, 'Peoples of Wood and Plain: An Exploration of National and Local Contrasts', in Della Hooke, ed., *Landscape: The Richest Historical Record*, Society for Landscape Studies supplementary series 1, 2000, 85–95.

52. *Birmingham Daily Mail*, quoted in *Liverpool Mercury*, 20 August 1890.

53. *Birmingham Daily Post*, 20 August 1890.

54. 'The funeral of Cardinal Newman', *Daily News*, 20 August 1890.

EPILOGUE

1. Peter Sawyer, *Anglo-Saxon Charters: An Annotated List and Bibliography*, Royal Historical Society, 1968, No. 1272; cf. No. 117.

2. Jonathan Bate, *Soul of the Age*, Penguin, 352–363.

3. Paul Binding, *Imagined Corners: Exploring the World's First Atlas*, Review, 2003, 3.

4. Paul Hutton, *America 1585: The Complete Drawings of John White*, University of North Carolina Press, 1984.

5. Seneca, *Epistles*, 90.

6. *The Tempest*, 2.2.

7. Jacques, Le Goff, *The Medieval Imagination*, trans. Arthur Goldhammer, Chicago University Press, 1988, 117.

8. Geoffrey Hill, *The Triumph of Love*, Penguin, 1999, LIII.

INDEX

Page numbers in italics refer to illustration captions.